FOOD from your GARDEN & ALLOTMENT

All you need to know to grow, coo
your own fruit and vegetables

FOOD from your GARDEN & ALLOTMENT

Published by The Reader's Digest Association Ltd
London • New York • Sydney • Montreal

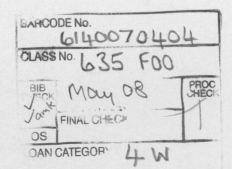

Foreword

More and more gardeners are rediscovering the tradition of growing their own fruit and vegetables. Not only do you reap satisfaction along with your harvest, but you can be sure of exactly what has gone into your fresh produce and practically eliminate the 'food miles' it travels.

Whether you take on an allotment, set aside a corner of the garden or dedicate raised beds or containers to your crops, you can easily produce a bumper yield of potatoes, tomatoes, beans, salad leaves, soft fruits and more. If you have room for a greenhouse – even a miniature lean-to one – you can also include chillis, peppers, aubergines and other Mediterranean crops. In fact, much of the joy of growing your own is the chance to raise unusual varieties, that you can't find in the shops, or little-grown crops that are expensive to buy.

In this complete A–Z grow-it, cook-it guide you'll find all you need to know about more than 100 different crops – from all the kitchen staples to more exotic ingredients, such as artichokes and kohlrabi – together with expert advice on planning your plot, sowing, planting, pruning and more.

You'll also find dozens of delicious recipe ideas for using your crops or preserving them as jams, chutneys, pickles and other preserves, so get growing – and cooking – and begin to enjoy the fruits of your labours.

A basic guide to the KITCHEN GARDEN

Replanning your garden

With good planning, you'll be able to grow crops of fruit and vegetables, even in a small garden. The best plans incorporate food-producing areas with the rest of the garden, so that they harmonise with children's play areas and ornamental beds.

You can achieve this happy balance in several different ways, as shown in the following pages.

Every garden has a unique set of challenges – whether these are to do with its shape, size or aspect. It's up to you to make the best choice of what to grow – not only taking your own garden's idiosyncrasies into account, but also thinking about what vegetables and fruit you and your family really enjoy. Here are some ideas to get you started.

Drawing up a plan

When planning a new garden, or redesigning one that is already established, first measure the plot and draw it to scale.

If you are replanning an old garden, mark features such as paths and trees that might be incorporated in the new design.

Before sketching your design, make a list of what you want to fit into the plan. For example, you may want a greenhouse, coldframes, a shed and a compost bin. Perhaps you want a herb garden. How many

SITING FRUIT TREES AND BUSHES

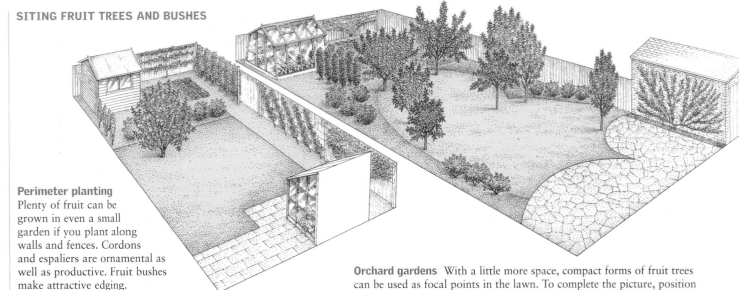

Perimeter planting
Plenty of fruit can be grown in even a small garden if you plant along walls and fences. Cordons and espaliers are ornamental as well as productive. Fruit bushes make attractive edging.

Orchard gardens With a little more space, compact forms of fruit trees can be used as focal points in the lawn. To complete the picture, position fruit bushes to act as a foil to the trees.

and what types of fruit trees and bushes are you hoping for?

Next, decide on how much space you want to give to vegetables. If you plan to grow only salad crops, then a 3m x 3m (10ft x 10ft) plot will be enough to provide regular supplies throughout summer.

If, however, you want to be able to gather foods from the garden all year round, you must allow for a vegetable plot measuring at least 9m x 6m (30ft x 20ft) – even bigger if you intend to grow main-crop as well as early potatoes.

Finding the right sites

Having listed the main items to be included in the garden, the next job is to fit them into the most suitable positions. You will probably have to keep amending your original rough sketch plan as you go along.

Vegetables Reserve an open site with plenty of sun and, if possible,

sheltering walls or fences along at least one side. Vegetables won't thrive within the rooting area of trees, or on a site that gets shade for much of the day (see page 30).

Paths In the vegetable garden, lay paths to points such as the tool shed, greenhouse, compost heap and coldframe. You will be pleased you did after heavy rain and when using the wheelbarrow.

Fruit When marking fruit trees and bushes on the plan, check planting distances (see page 46). Make the most of garden space by siting fan-trained trees, cordons and espaliers on walls or fences.

Lawn and patio These are the most flexible areas of your plan, as you can change their sizes to suit the area needed for fruit and vegetables. In a small garden you may even decide to do without a lawn altogether and use a patio as your main relaxing area.

Herb garden Ideally, plant herbs as near the kitchen as possible. You can grow most of the useful ones in a bed measuring about 1m x 2m (3ft x 6ft).

Flowers In a predominately food-producing garden, flowers will work best in bold beds rather than dotted about in narrow strips.

Greenhouse Site the greenhouse where the light is best all the year round. Placing it near the house makes it more accessible in bad weather – and cheaper for laying on a water and electricity supply, if you choose to do this – but take care to avoid the house's shadow.

Coldframes Put these next to the greenhouse to save work when transferring seedlings.

Compost bin Tuck the bin in a corner, but lay an approach path.

Shed If possible, site the shed within handy reach of both the house and the greenhouse.

Getting the balance right

Having decided on what you want in your garden, draw a rough sketch on your scale plan. You could start with the lawn, making bold curves until the shape pleases you. This will give you an accurate idea of how much land is left for growing fruit and vegetables.

If you have not left enough, draw curves inside the original line to reduce the size of the lawn and make a larger food-growing area.

In a formal garden with a rectangular lawn, work out the proportions on the plan in the same way. These methods can also be used for planning paved areas instead of a lawn.

Where to grow fruit

If you plan to grow a free-standing fruit tree in the lawn – a bush, perhaps, or even a half-standard, do not place it in the centre.

Instead, position it a little to one side. The same principle applies to groups of soft-fruit bushes.

Try different positions on your plan so that the tree will be placed happily in the shape of the lawn and provide a focal point. It may also help to mask a compost bin or shed, or even a building next door.

When planting several trees in a border with other plants, think about what they will look like when they mature into different-sized trees. The garden centre will be able to tell you what height and spread to expect (see page 46).

Screening the plot
Even the most enthusiastic gardener may not wish to contemplate rows of vegetables while relaxing in a deckchair. If you decide to form a screen, this should blend in with the general shape of the lawn or patio, rather than form an obvious barrier. Tall, flowering perennials or a rosemary hedge can make a summer screen. Soft-fruit bushes or trained fruit trees, make

permanent screens. Curve the path into the vegetable garden. This creates interest in what is on the other side but out of sight.

Vegetables on show
In a small garden, one way to increase food production is to make a virtue of attractive vegetables – such as sweetcorn, tomatoes, herbs and salad vegetables.

Cut beds of suitable size in a lawn near a path. Grow only one or two types of vegetables in each bed, so that the visual effect is stronger and the growing conditions can be varied to suit.

You can leave spaces in paved areas to create similar beds, though on a patio a raised bed is more practical.

In large gardens of the past, there were distinct frontiers between lawns and flower borders and the kitchen garden. Today, these barriers have been largely abandoned, and herbs, fruit trees and bushes not only provide worthwhile crops but also enhance

the beauty of the garden.

If, for example, you wanted a spring-flowering tree, you could plant a Morello cherry. Then you'll get spring blossom, and later, excellent fruit for jam making.

Grow fruit – such as apples, pears, peaches, apricots, red currants and gooseberries – on walls and fences, not only to save space, but also to make an attractive frame to the garden.

Some herbs and vegetables planted among flowers can add distinctive touches to a border as well as food and flavourings.

Putting the plan into action
Having drawn your scale plan, it's time to begin work. You'll find you make the best progress if you do jobs one at a time – allowing as much time as you need to fully complete one task before moving on to the next. Remember, you are creating a new, working garden, not conducting a speedy cosmetic makeover. Some jobs will take a day or so; others could take a week or more.

Don't try to tackle heavy jobs unless you are fit and strong enough to do so. Where necessary, enlist help – whether this is free of charge from relatives or friends, or involves paying someone to come.

Start with the structure Clear out all unwanted growth and old paths or paved areas that don't fit your new scheme first. If it's a new plot, dig it over and level it.

Now you have your blank canvas, the first constructive task is to lay the paths. To do this take measurements from the plan and drive in wooden pegs about 30cm (12in) apart to mark the edges of the paths. Make paths at least

SUITABLE TREES, BUSHES AND PLANTS FOR YOUR SITE

Walls Fan-trained peaches, nectarines and apricots are best grown on a south-facing wall. Fan-trained plums grow well on south, east or west-facing walls, as do blackberry and loganberry bushes.

Fruit trees Instead of growing purely ornamental trees in the lawn, plant a dwarf pyramid pear (if a cross-pollinating tree is nearby), a self-fertile pyramid plum or a pretty Morello cherry.

Patio Grow shrubby herbs, such as bay and rosemary, in tubs and sage and marjoram in pots. Plant tomatoes if the patio faces south.

80cm (30in) wide. The choice of material is up to you.

Concrete laid on a hardcore base is long-lasting and efficient, but looks pretty dull; paving stones and bricks are attractive but expensive; gravel is quick to spread and looks nice but gets carried on to the lawn and into the house and must be treated against weeds.

Whichever path material you choose, make the patio at the same time, pegging out the shape first.

Once you've laid your paths and patio, tackle the lawn. Dig the ground over, level, roll and rake it. Next, peg out the shape according to the plan. If sowing grass seed –

preferably in spring or autumn – follow the curves of the pegs, but allow a little seed to fall outside so that once growth is vigorous you can shape the edge neatly.

If turfing, lay the turfs over the pegs. Remove the pegs and replace them over the identical spot on top. Cut the turf against the line of the pegs. Roll the lawn and fill in small gaps between turfs with sifted soil.

Next plant fruit trees and bushes, site the greenhouse or shed, and dig over the vegetable garden.

Your first growing season is already under way.

Productive screens There are several forms of 'edible screen' – whether a pergola used to support a vine, a hedge formed of rosemary plants or an espalier bearing a crop of apples or pears.

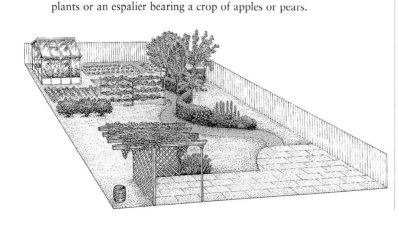

Making the most of limited space

With the help of pots and raised beds, any garden – even a balcony – can be used for growing a variety of crops. You will need a position that receives sun for most of the day to give you the widest selection, but even a spot in light shade can be used for growing blackberries and other hybrid berries, and a few herbs, such as mint and parsley.

Pots, troughs and tubs

Any container that will hold compost is capable of growing a crop of some sort. Fruit bushes on dwarfing rootstocks will grow happily in large tubs; most vegetables, including salads, turnips, carrots, beetroot and leaf vegetables can be cultivated in troughs, and lowbush blueberries, herbs and edible flowers are suitable for pot cultivation.

Potatoes can even be cropped in a black bin liner, while strawberries and herbs take up very little space when grown in strawberry pots and barrels. Frame your front door with a pair of bay trees, clipped into balls or pyramids – these will supply you with more bay leaves than you will ever need.

You may need to take weight into account when growing crops on a balcony, in which case plastic containers and a light, soil-less compost should be used.

Make sure your containers have plenty of drainage holes, and are raised above the surface of the ground on pot feet or bricks to prevent the holes from becoming blocked.

Thyme tower An urn-shaped pot (above left) with strategically placed holes makes a decorative home for thyme and marjoram.

Hanging herbs Instead of trailing lobelias, try planting a hanging basket with chives, sage, parsley, and perhaps some rosemary cuttings, too (above).

Hanging baskets and window boxes

A well-thought-out edible hanging basket or window box can look just as attractive as one planted with bedding plants and ornamental foliage plants. The best crops for this type of container are dwarf, bushy tomatoes, miniature peppers and perpetual strawberries, but salad leaves and beetroot can be just as productive and good to look at. Plant trailing nasturtiums or other edible flowering plants among the crops to brighten up an edible container. A semi-permanent basket or trough that will last several seasons can be created with perennial herbs such as thyme, sage, oregano, lavender and rosemary. For prettiest results, use variegated varieties and clip or pinch out regularly.

Raised beds

These are especially useful for growing crops where the existing soil is poor or waterlogged, but are also ideal for patio cultivation. You can buy plastic kits – all made from recycled plastic – with sides that clip together quickly and easily; these are ideal if you do not want the beds permanently, as they can be rapidly dismantled. The best kits have twin-walled sides, which help to prevent the compost from overheating or cooling excessively during very hot or very cold periods. Or you can build a more lasting structure from concrete, brick, stone or sleepers. Beds with timber sides are cheap and quick to construct, but the wood will rot after a few seasons.

To make life easier, no bed should be wider than you can reach from each side while standing on the ground. John Innes No. 2 is the best compost to use in a raised bed as it does not have to be replaced after every season. The optimum depth is 30cm (12in) for large-rooted crops like brassicas and 15cm (6in) for salads, leaf vegetables and dwarf beans.

Grow bags

These have become hugely popular over the past two decades and can now be bought from all kinds of retail outlets. Always buy thick, well-filled ones containing good-quality compost – this will be reflected in the price but the results will be worth the outlay.

Herbs, strawberries and most vegetables can be cultivated in grow bags, but taller ones need support. Garden centres sell a variety of supports; otherwise attach a trellis to a sunny wall or fence and tie large plants to this.

Compost

Soil-less composts are much cheaper and easier to handle than soil-based (John Innes-type) ones, but they are only suitable for temporary vegetable crops as they soon lose texture and quality. All permanent and semi-permanent plants, including herbs and fruit, should be grown in John Innes No. 2 Compost (choose John Innes No. 3 for fruit trees and bushes). These retain their structure indefinitely, and also hold water and nutrients better. Remember that semi-permanent hanging baskets and window boxes containing soil-based composts can be very heavy, so be sure to use suitably strong brackets and wall fixings.

Feeding and watering

Plants with a restricted root run need regular feeding. Quick-growing summer crops should be fed at least once a week with a proprietary liquid feed (tomato feed in the case of fruiting crops). Permanently planted containers, such as those containing fruit bushes, should have an annual top dressing of a slow-release, balanced fertiliser each spring, and supplementary liquid feeding once a week during the growing season.

Regular watering is vital for all edible crops, which must never dry out, even for a short period. Plants in soil-less composts will need watering daily during summer (twice a day in the case of hanging baskets and smaller containers).

The thinner the container wall, the quicker moisture will evaporate from the compost. The amount of regular watering needed for a raised bed will depend on its size, construction and depth of compost, with thin-walled, small beds needing about the same as pots and troughs. Permanent containers may also need watering in winter in long, dry spells.

Versatile raised beds Easier to reach and manage than a ground-level bed, you can make a permanent raised bed from stone, brick or railway sleepers that have not been treated with harmful preservatives.

Choosing and using garden tools

Only about half a dozen basic tools, and such essentials as a watering can and hose, are needed to grow vegetables and fruit for your family. Until you gain experience, avoid the more specialised gadgets displayed in garden centres.

Choose good-quality tools of a comfortable and convenient size and weight. Compare different makes by handling as wide a variety as possible before buying. Good tools can last for years – some, perhaps, for a lifetime – so it is false economy to buy cheap, poor-quality tools.

Tools you will need
The most useful tools and equipment for food growing are:

Spade At least one spade, with a blade measuring approximately 20cm x 30cm (7in x 11in), is needed for digging. A narrower

LIST OF ESSENTIAL TOOLS

- Spade
- Fork
- Rake
- Draw hoe
- Dutch hoe
- Short-handled hoe
- Trowel
- Dibber
- Garden line
- Secateurs
- Wheelbarrow
- Hose
- Watering can

border spade, with a blade about 15cm x 25cm. (6in x 9in), is a good alternative if you have heavy clay; it is also good for digging holes for planting and for posts.

Though relatively expensive, stainless-steel blades won't rust and the polished surface makes for easier digging on clay.

D-shaped handles made of polypropylene are stronger than those made of wood and are less likely to cause blisters. A flattened tread will be more comfortable for prolonged use and will help to prevent the blade from damaging shoes and boots.

A semi-automatic spade, such as the Terrex, is an effective alternative – especially for gardeners with weak backs. This works by leverage instead of lifting and enables the soil to be turned over with a minimum of effort.

The knack of using an ordinary spade lies in letting its weight do some of the work for you. A swinging, rhythmic movement when digging helps the blade to penetrate the soil.

Fork A four-tined fork is invaluable for breaking up lumpy soil, for turning over a plot between crops and for lifting deep-rooted plants. It is also useful for shifting compost and garden rubbish. The overall tine measurements should be about the same as those of a digging spade, or a little larger.

You can buy flat-tined forks designed for potato lifting, but the normal square-tined digging fork is adequate for lifting garden crops.

Do not use a fork for levering out obstinate stumps. Bent tines are difficult to straighten and the tool becomes awkward to use.

Rake For levelling soil and preparing seedbeds you will need a well-balanced rake with 10–14 teeth. Choose one with a light head and a slender ash handle. Test the rake's weight and balance, because to use a rake properly you should support at least part of it with your lower hand, rather than simply dragging the head through the soil. This ensures even penetration and makes it easier to level out ridges and hollows.

Hoe There are four main types of hoe to choose from:
Draw hoe With the blade turned over roughly at right-angles to the handle, this tool is excellent for chopping out weeds on heavily infested ground, for forming drills (shallow furrows) when sowing seeds, and for drawing soil around such plants as potatoes and leeks.
Dutch hoe The blade is almost in line with the handle and the tool is used with a pushing or prodding action. This hoe leaves the severed weeds uncovered by soil, making sure that they soon wilt and die.
Patent hoe Hoes such as the Swoe and Saynor are forms of the Dutch hoe. They are good for routine hoeing but less suitable for clearing heavy weed growth.
Short-handled hoe Also known as the onion hoe, this tool is like a miniature draw hoe and is ideal for working close to plants without damaging them. It is tiring to use unless you kneel.

Most gardeners develop their own technique for controlling weeds between rows of vegetable crops. It is best to hoe frequently – every week if possible, during the growing season – before weeds develop beyond the seedling stage. Row crops are easily hoed by first

A basic garden toolkit In spite of the many gadgets available, the small selection of tools shown above – and some good gardening gloves – will meet most needs in the vegetable garden and fruit garden.

weeding between the plants in each row – by hand, or by working forwards with an onion hoe or a draw hoe – and then working backwards between the rows with a Dutch hoe.

This allows close weeding between plants in the row but ensures that most of the severed weeds will be left uncovered and will not be pressed into the soil by your feet as you work.

Cultivation tools A draw hoe (above left) is used to chop out weeds and break up the soil, as well as for earthing up potatoes. A hand trowel (above right) has myriad uses, from digging weeds to planting.

Using a patent hoe, such as the Swoe, the two operations can be combined.

Trowel Choose a sturdy tool with a long, but not too broad blade. If you measure (and remember) the length of the blade, and of the whole tool, you will find these useful guides to spacing plants.

Dibber Though a trowel can be used instead, this tool is ideal for planting cabbages and other brassicas, leeks and lettuces. You can buy a steel-pointed dibber, or you can shape an old spade or fork handle to a point.

After placing the plant in the dibber hole, stab the tool into the ground a second time, just an inch or so away from the plant to firm the soil against the roots.

Garden line Though a length of string and two pegs will suffice for marking, a purpose-made reel and line save time and are easier to use. The line must be as long as your longest rows, and should preferably be of nylon, which will not retain moisture and grow soggy.

Secateurs These essential aids to fruit pruning are also handy in the vegetable garden. The basic choice lies between secateurs which have scissor-action blades, and those which have a single blade cutting against an anvil. Both are equally effective, provided they are kept rust-free and sharp.

Pruning tools Although secateurs can cope with cutting most vegetable plants and the young branches of soft-fruit bushes, you will need some sturdier tools (right) to prune established fruit trees. Invest in a strong pair of loppers, perhaps a long-armed lopper and a pruning saw.

Wheelbarrow You need a sturdy barrow, with as large a wheel as possible, for moving soil, rubble and paving materials while garden-making, and for carrying compost, garden rubbish and crops that have been harvested.

Flimsy barrows, and some with low-slung bodies on two small wheels, are less suitable for shifting heavy weights but fine for leaves.

Hose and watering can On all but the smallest plots, you will quickly realise the benefits of a hose. Watering with a can is slow and tedious, and you are unlikely to give plants the thorough soaking they need during prolonged dry weather.

Whether or not you have a reel, coil the hose neatly during winter. Plastic hoses become useless if they have been stored in a tangled heap. Before you attach tap connectors or extension pieces, dip the end of the hose in hot water to soften it.

A 9 litre (2 gallon) watering can – plastic or metal and with both a coarse and a fine rose – is essential for settling your plants into their beds, for applying liquid fertilisers and for occasional watering which does not call for a hose.

Caring for garden tools
Dry storage – first scraping damp soil from metal – ensures a long life for garden tools. Even better, oil or grease metal parts after removing the soil. Do this every time you put a tool away, not just before winter.

Keep hoe blades sharp by filing once or twice each season. Secure the head of the hoe in a vice, positioned so that you can sharpen the angled side. Use a broad file and make sweeping strokes in one direction only: away from your body. Remove burrs on the other side with a few light strokes.

Hiring a motor cultivator
It is not worth buying a motor cultivator for the average garden, but it may be worth hiring one for the day. There are two types:

Power-driven tines Cultivators with power drive to the tines only have tines mounted under or in front of the engine. The spinning tines draw the machine forward while digging the soil. The more robust ones are ideal for digging a new kitchen garden.

Power-driven wheels and tines
A cultivator with power drive to both wheels and tines has its tines mounted at the rear, under a hood. It minces the soil finely and is ideal for seedbed preparation, but small models are unsuitable for the initial breaking of heavy soil – especially as they don't dig very deep.

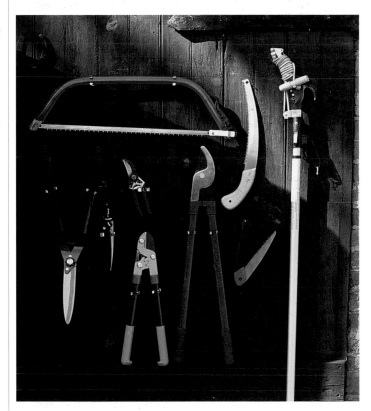

Keep pruning tools sharp Clean, sharpen and oil or grease all metal parts. Hang up sharp tools to minimise the risk of injury, or of damaging the blades.

Garden accessories

Along with a good set of hand tools and any machinery that helps to make growing your own food crops easier, you will find several other items either essential, or very helpful in the growing of vegetables and fruit. These items fall into six broad categories: kit for raising plants, weather protection, pest deterrents, wildlife attractors, compost makers and canes and ties.

Kit for raising plants
You can never have too many small pots – let friends know if you don't have enough – many gardeners have surplus. Plastic pots are hygienic and easy to clean. Terracotta ones are fragile, so need handling and storing with care.

Plastic seed trays can be bought cheaply from DIY chain stores. They come in various weights, and while the more solid ones should last a lifetime, even flimsier ones – supplied in multipacks – can last for years if properly looked after.

You can buy wooden seed trays, but while they may look lovely, they are expensive, do not last for ever and can be a source of infection if not sterilised after every use.

When you buy bedding and other young plants, keep the plastic modules. Always wash them out as soon as they are empty, so they are ready for immediate use.

Fibre pots are useful, as they allow you to plant out seedlings without touching the roots.

A large, plastic potting tray is handy for keeping the greenhouse bench (or even the garden table)

clean while you are working with compost.

A garden sieve is useful for sifting seed compost; a coarser riddle can be used to create a fine seedbed from stony soil or to break down garden compost.

Weather protection
Horticultural fleece provides shelter from wind and frost. In summer, you can replace the fleece with woven, plastic sheeting (known as Enviromesh). This allows better air circulation and more sunlight than fleece, while keeping birds off and acting as a barrier against pests and some diseases. A crop covered by fleece and mesh throughout its life will usually have few problems, and the sheeting also cuts down watering by reducing both soil evaporation and plant transpiration.

On a windy site, windbreak sheeting lessens crop damage and reduces water and heat loss, soil erosion and windborne diseases.

Pots and seed trays Plastic pots and seed trays are hygienic and easily cleaned, and even flimsy 'disposable' trays can last for several seasons. Vegetable seedlings grown in fibre pots can be planted out in their pots, so minimising root disturbance.

Pest deterrents
You can recycle household items as pest deterrents: cut brassica collars from offcuts of thin carpet, underlay or vinyl flooring. Hang CDs among the crops to scare birds. Pull old recording tape tightly between strong canes; this buzzes in the wind, a sound that some birds dislike. Other gardeners swear by flapping supermarket bags, tin foil or scarecrows. No one method will work for more than a short time – you need to ring the changes before the birds get wise.

Moles can sometimes be chased off if you half bury glass bottles near the runs. They don't like the noise of wind blowing across the open tops. The constant rattling of children's plastic windmills stuck in the ground has a similar effect.

Reduce greenhouse pests, such as whitefly, by hanging yellow sticky traps among the crops. They work like flypapers, but rely solely on glue to catch insects – they aren't treated with any insecticide so are completely organic. Buy from garden centres or online.

Use pheromone traps to control codling and plum moths without spraying your crops. The traps will last for many years if taken down after use and stored carefully; buy the lures from organic accessories suppliers.

Wildlife attractors
The more wildlife there is in the garden, the more productive it will be. Provide butterfly habitats, bee nests, ladybird and lacewing chambers, hedgehog and frog

shelters and so forth to achieve a balanced ecosystem – benefiting you and the environment around you. Wildlife organisations will show you the best ways to encourage wildlife, or get in touch with organic gardening suppliers.

Compost makers
No garden is complete without at least one compost bin. If you have two (or more) you can start a new one while a full bin is maturing. Most local authorities sell bins at discounted prices – just ask.

Plastic bins should be as large as possible and should have a well fitting lid and access at the bottom for digging out the compost.

Bins with double walls make compost more quickly and efficiently because of the insulation – wooden bins have insulation, too, but don't last forever.

A square bin takes up less floor area for the amount of compost it produces than a round one.

Ventilation is unnecessary as enough air is introduced each time material is added, and may, in fact, slow down rotting.

Wormeries A working wormery produces a soil that looks like sieved peat and a liquid that can be diluted and used as a fertiliser. Wormeries are excellent for breaking down kitchen waste. You can make your own or buy a kit. Be sure to follow the instructions closely or the worms will die and you will be left with a smelly mess.

Canes and ties
Keep a stock of canes of various lengths, a ball of soft twine and some plastic cable ties (readily available from electrical suppliers and much cheaper than plant ties).

Soil types

More than any other factor, the quality of your soil will determine how successful you are in growing fruit and vegetables.

Fortunately, practically every type of land can be made to yield good crops. But to make the most of your garden you should first understand the nature of the soil you are dealing with.

Getting to know your soil

Soils fall into five general groups – clay, loam, sand, chalk and peat – but only a minority of gardens can be classified so categorically. Most gardens have a mixture of soils, though often with one type predominating.

This guide will help you to identify your soil and cultivate it to the best advantage. Use it in conjunction with local knowledge gathered over the years by neighbours and garden societies.

To make your own classification, note first the reactions of the soil to extreme weather conditions, such as drought or prolonged heavy rain.

If puddles take hours, or even days, to disappear after heavy rain, and the soil bakes rock hard in a drought, you have a clay soil.

If water drains away fairly quickly after heavy rain but the ground stays unworkable for a day or two, you have a loam soil.

When water from even a heavy thunder shower drains away within minutes, your soil is probably light and sandy. In a drought, such soil must be constantly watered or heavily mulched. However, if speedy drainage is combined with a surface that appears dusty white or grey during a drought, you have a chalky soil.

As well as classifying the soil in your garden, you should learn when to cultivate it and when to leave it alone. Cultivation on clay soil, in particular, needs careful timing.

Where you have a choice, grow the crops best suited to your soil, and within any particular crop select the most suitable varieties. Grow long carrots, for example, on a light soil and stump-rooted varieties on heavy soil. Grow scab-resistant potatoes on chalk soil.

Bear in mind that whatever the type of soil in your garden, you will get out of it only as much as you put into it. To sustain and improve fertility, you need to feed it with manure and other fertilisers (see pages 18–19).

Heavy or clay soils Soils of this type are the hardest to work because they are difficult to dig at any time and impossible to cultivate during rainy spells. Their growing season is shortened because spring sowing and planting must be delayed until the wet soil becomes warmer and drier.

However, clays have the advantages in summer of not drying out as quickly as sandy soils and, when well cultivated, they yield heavy crops of good quality – particularly beans, brassicas, peas, potatoes (if you give them plenty of compost), salad crops, spinach, most soft fruits and many tree fruits.

On poorly cultivated land the exceedingly fine particles of clay – which are at least 1,000 times smaller than those of sand – clog together into a sticky mass when wet and set hard when dry.

TEST THE TEXTURE OF YOUR SOIL

The texture test
All soils are made up of a combination of components – sand, silt, clay and organic matter. The varying proportions of these will determine your garden's individual soil structure.

The easiest way to determine what sort of soil you will be dealing with is to pick up a handful and rub it. You'll quickly feel whether you've got gritty sand, sticky clay or crumbly loam – or a mixture.

Clay soils (above) have a smooth, soapy texture when moistened and rubbed between finger and thumb.

Sandy soils (above right) feel gritty when rubbed.

Peaty soils (right) are crumbly and fibrous when handled, due to their high level of organic matter.

Every third year, after digging is completed, spread carbonate of lime on the surface at the rate of 250g per square metre (8oz per square yard). Do not work it into the soil, but allow the rain to wash it in naturally.

If your soil drains so poorly that pools of water remain after rain, you may have to lay drainage pipes. This is expensive and it's better to see if the problem resolves after two or three years' cultivation.

Medium or loam soils A balance of clay and sand makes these soils highly fertile and easy to work. They are usually dark and contain plenty of humus. When moist, they feel neither gritty nor sticky. They break down to a good tilth when dry but they become lumpy if worked too soon after rain. All types of vegetables and fruits can be grown on loam.

Light or sandy soils These soils are easy to work and they warm up quickly in spring, so making them valuable for growing early crops.

They are so porous, however, that soluble plant foods are constantly leached, or washed out of them. This leaching can be reduced by digging in garden compost or well-rotted manure. The humus formed also acts as a sponge to retain moisture.

To reduce loss from leaching, add compost or manure in late winter or early spring rather than digging it in before the main winter rains or snow have fallen.

Many crops on light soils have to be watered in summer, but you can reduce the frequency of watering by spreading a mulch at least 8cm (3in) deep along the rows of plants. Suitable mulches include leaf-

mould, grass cuttings, straw and garden compost. You can even put down a sheet of black polythene, though it doesn't look very pretty.

Always soak the ground well before laying the mulch. If you plan to use bark chippings or straw, then first sprinkle on sulphate of ammonia at the rate of 60g per square metre (2oz per square yard) to counteract the acidity of the mulch.

Plants on sandy soils respond readily to general fertilisers. Give several small applications over the growing period rather than one heavy dressing.

Sandy soils are often deficient in potash, so supplement a general fertiliser by adding sulphate of potash at the rate of 30g per square metre (1oz per square yard), or use a tomato fertiliser, which has a high potash content.

Root crops, potatoes, onions, early cloche crops, outdoor tomatoes, asparagus and some of the less hardy tree fruits, such as peaches and apricots, can be grown successfully on well-cultivated light soils.

However, some vegetables vary in their success on light soils. French beans, for example, generally crop better than runner beans, and New Zealand spinach tends to be more productive than summer spinach.

Chalk soils A thin layer of topsoil usually lies on chalk or limestone subsoils, though lumps of rock may also be visible. Sometimes, as in parts of Kent and Sussex, the chalk is apparent in the greyish topsoil. The chalk will stick to your shoes in wet weather, but the surface seldom remains wet for more than a few hours.

Testing soil in water One of the clearest visual clues as to your garden's soil type is how it behaves in water. Stir a spoonful into a clear glass of water and leave it to settle. To the left is a mixture of clay with a little sand – the clay has sunk to the bottom and a layer of sand is sitting on top. In the middle, the soil is almost pure sand; and to the right is a humus-rich soil – the light organic material is floating on the surface.

In these conditions roots have difficulty in extracting the mineral nutrients on which plants feed. However, clay contains these minerals in abundance and you can make them available to plants by improving the soil texture. You can achieve this in two ways – by using

bulky manures, and by digging in autumn with the aim of breaking down the soil by frost action. If the clay is acid, dressings of carbonate of lime help to make the soil workable. Don't apply this to the type of alkaline soil known as chalky boulder clay.

Every autumn or early winter dig in all available organic material – garden compost, well-rotted manure and leaf-mould. As this continues to decay it opens up the texture of the soil and gives the roots a freer run. Weathered boiler ash and coarse sand also help.

When digging in autumn, leave large clods on the surface to be broken up by frost action. As the ground dries in spring – it should then look light brown – you should be able to break up the surface, eventually reaching the stage where you can rake it to produce a tilth fine enough for sowing seeds.

USE A KIT TO TEST YOUR SOIL'S ACIDITY LEVEL

Handle with care
Try not to touch your soil samples with your bare hands, because the pH value of your skin could affect the final reading.

Test several samples
Take soil samples from different areas of your garden for testing.

Soil-testing kits You can buy a simple kit to discover the pH value of your soil – whether it's acid, alkaline or neutral. Following the instructions, all you have to do is crush a sample of soil (top left) and add it to the test tube with the chemical supplied. Shake it vigorously and leave to settle. Then see which colour on the pH test card the liquid most closely matches. Greenish (above left) is alkaline; yellow (top right) is the acid end of neutral and ochre (above right) is neutral.

These soils are strongly alkaline – they have a high pH – and seldom need liming. Their main need is for organic matter.

Every autumn or early winter dig in all available garden compost or well-rotted manure. Peat substitute, reinforced with dried poultry manure or fertilisers, can be used as an effective, if expensive, substitute.

In spring give a dressing of sulphate of ammonia or nitrate of soda at the rate of 60g per square metre (2oz per square yard) to overwintered crops such as spring cabbages and sprouting broccoli. These crops often look pale and sickly after a wet winter on chalk soils, but a nitrogenous fertiliser will soon restore their colour and vigour.

Chalk soils dry out so quickly that in some seasons watering and mulching may be necessary as early as May, or even April. Even so, well-established plants will show drought symptoms later than on a sandy soil, and as long as you lay a mulch early enough, you should get continuing growth in all but the driest conditions.

To thrive, beds of blackcurrants, raspberries and strawberries need a permanent mulch of garden compost 5–8cm (2–3in) deep.

When well cultivated, a chalky soil suits most vegetables except potatoes, which tend to do better in slightly acid conditions. You could create more acidity artificially by covering each tuber with a couple of handfuls of ericaceous compost when planting.

Stone fruits, especially plums and gages, do well on chalk soils, but keep newly planted trees well watered during dry spells for the first year after planting.

Peat soils These are the least common garden soils. There are two completely different types: fen peats, which are probably the richest and most productive of all soils; and acid peats, which are sour, often waterlogged and difficult to make productive.

The acid peats are found on and around moorland where decaying vegetation has accumulated over wet or impervious subsoil, or rock. They are short of lime, and have a very low pH, and are low on essential nutrients.

Some form of drainage (see page 25) may be needed to bring them under cultivation. Every autumn, dress with carbonate of lime at the rate of 250g per square metre (8oz per square yard).

Use a general fertiliser at the rate of 60g per square metre (2oz per square yard) during the growing season. Until the land improves, concentrate on crops that you know will do well on acid or neutral soils, such as blueberries and potatoes.

Fen soils, on the other hand, are easy to work and almost any crop will thrive in them.

Taking on a new garden

Anybody who moves house must expect some surprises and a few problems when taking over the new garden. The biggest challenges are moving into a newly built house, where the builder may have left the garden strewn with rubble and subsoil, or into an old town house where the soil is exhausted.

When getting a house built, arrange with the builder as early as possible for topsoil removed from foundation trenches to be placed in a mound and subsoil to be removed. Later, when creating the garden, spread the topsoil on the vegetable plot.

If you take over a new house which has already been completed, you might want to make random trial diggings to determine the depth of topsoil and to see whether subsoil has been left on the surface.

If it is impossible to put things right by barrowing soil from one part of the garden to another, buy in a load of topsoil to provide an adequate depth for growing crops. A lawn may grow on a fairly shallow soil, but you will have little success with vegetables or fruit unless there is a minimum of 20–25cm (8–10in) of topsoil.

Feed neglected soil In the early years dig as much rotted manure as possible into the vegetable plot. In the first season turn a large part over to potatoes, which will help to clear the ground of weeds. Grow peas and beans, too, which add nitrogen to the soil, and quick-growing salad plants. Later you can adopt a rotational cropping plan (see page 29).

The soil in the neglected garden of an old town house is generally sour, with a high sulphur content. This is because 'acid rain' brought down large amounts of sulphur in the time of open coal fires and belching factory chimneys.

It is better to treat such ground as subsoil rather than try to put new life into it. If you can afford to, spread a deep layer of good topsoil over the surface – but since topsoil is expensive, treat a small part of the garden at a time rather than spreading a thin layer over a larger area. Alternatively, dig the garden over and add manure or compost, lime and fertiliser dressings to improve the soil's fertility.

Feeding vegetables and fruit

Plants, like people, thrive on a balanced diet. Just as a well-planned meal contains proteins, vitamins and carbohydrates, so a well-tended soil is rich in all the foods that plants need.

The three principal elements on which plant life depends – nitrogen, phosphorus and potassium – are dissolved in water and taken up as a 'drink' by hairs growing near the tips of the roots. Carbon, hydrogen and oxygen are absorbed from the atmosphere and the soil.

Principal nutrients Each major nutrient has a vital function. Nitrogen promotes the growth of leaves and stems. A nitrogen-rich soil is ideal for growing such plants as cabbages, celery, leeks, lettuces and onions. It soon gets washed out of the soil, however, and must be renewed every year.

Phosphates are needed for vigorous root development. They also play a part in the growth of plants and the production of flowers and seeds. Root crops, such as carrots, parsnips, swedes and turnips, do best in a soil with a good phosphate content. Phosphates remain in the soil as a plant food for two or three years after application.

Potassium, or potash, is vital for maintaining growth and for providing plants with resistance to disease and adverse conditions. It contributes to the building up of starches and sugars in vegetables, especially potatoes, carrots, parsnips, beetroot and sweetcorn.

Potash is also needed by all soft fruits. It stays in the soil for two or three years after application.

Trace elements As well as the three principal nutrients, plants need magnesium, sulphur, manganese, iron, boron, zinc, copper, chlorine and molybdenum. These are known as trace elements, because only minute quantities – or a trace – are taken up by plants. Finally, plants and soils require calcium, or lime.

With the exception of lime, all the needs of a plant can be met by enriching the soil with manure, which consists of animal droppings mixed with straw or other litter.

The highly productive Victorian kitchen gardens received huge quantities of stable manure, and the natural processes of the soil, aided by enough lime to keep it 'sweet', made it unnecessary for the gardener to worry about details of plant nutrition.

This simple solution is no longer practicable for most of us. Instead, we rely on whatever organic material is available, and boosting it with chemical fertilisers.

Organic manures are composed of decaying matter – plants that are decomposing or that have been digested by animals. In the soil they are converted into plant food by a teeming population of fungi and bacteria. Organic manures feed the soil and, through the soil's natural functions, the crop. They are slow-acting, and improve the structure of the soil and build up fertility from year to year.

Inorganic fertilisers feed crops more directly, supplying nutrients that a plant can absorb immediately. But they do nothing to improve the soil and may even deplete its reserves of organic material. Aim to strike a balance, adding as much organic manure as you can find, and using fertilisers to remedy known deficiencies.

Bulky organic manures

Two types of organic manures are used in the garden – for different reasons. Bulky farmyard manures are dug in during winter or used as mulches in summer. Not all are rich in plant foods, but they do all add to the soil's humus content and improve its condition.

The second type of organic manure consists of processed materials, such as bonemeal and dried blood. These concentrated foods are generally used as pre-sowing dressings or as top dressings for growing crops. They add very little humus to the soil. Bulky manures include:

Garden compost Town gardeners may find that the compost heap is their only source of bulky, organic material. However, well-made compost can be twice as valuable as farmyard manure in its content of plant foods.

Stable and farmyard manures

Horse manure is described as 'hot' – that is, it ferments rapidly – and for this reason was at one time widely used to form hotbeds for raising early crops. However, often that sold by riding stables contains mainly urine-soaked straw and a few droppings; it decays rapidly into a disappointingly small heap.

Pig manure is slow to ferment and, when fresh, tends to be caustic and to burn the roots of young plants. It is best composted with straw and left for at least three months before use.

Cattle manure containing straw from the yards is wetter, and lower in nutrients, than horse manure. But it decomposes slowly into the soil, and is ideal for sandy soils.

Spent mushroom compost Mushrooms are grown commercially on a compost based mainly on horse manure. It is carefully prepared to produce a controlled temperature over a period as the crop matures.

When all the mushrooms have been harvested the compost is sold either in bulk by the cubic metre, or, more expensively, at the garden centre in pre-packed bags that can be carried in a car boot. This is a good garden manure or mulch,

SUMMER FEEDING SOLUTIONS

Make your shaker For even distribution of granular fertiliser, make your own shaker by putting one plastic pot inside another. Offset the drainage holes to leave small gaps.

For large areas The easiest way to spread liquid fertiliser over a large area is via an applicator that fixes onto the end of a hose.

Mix a combination Stir a mixture of water-retaining granules and granular fertiliser into the compost when planting up pots and hanging baskets.

containing humus and plant foods. It also contains chalk, which makes it less suitable for soils that are already alkaline.

Deep litter poultry manure
Partly rotted litter from poultry houses may be bought by the load from poultry farmers, but it is unsuitable for gardeners living in built-up areas. The manure is usually dry and dusty and must be composted before use. When composted, it is rich in nitrogen but deficient in potash and phosphates.

It takes some weeks for the wood shavings or straw on which the manure is based to break down. During this time the heap may smell unpleasant; so even in a country garden it should be placed as far as possible from houses.

Leaf-mould Although leaves of all types can be composted, the best-quality leaf-mould is made from oak and beech leaves.

Place alternate layers of leaves and soil, each about 5cm (2in) deep. You can help decomposition by sprinkling general fertiliser on each layer of leaves. Do not make the heap more than 1m (3ft) high. Turn it every two or three months.

The compost will be ready in about a year. Apply at the rate of a bucketful per square metre (yard).

Spent hops Large breweries sell their hop waste to fertiliser firms, who improve its nutrient content before selling it in bags as hop manure. It is excellent, but pricey to use in large quantities.

Local specialities If you live near a small brewery, ask if they will sell you the spent hops. These untreated hops help to improve the

soil structure but don't add much in the way of nutrients, so always use them along with a general-purpose fertiliser.

Seaweed is rich in plant foods, especially nitrogen and potash, and breaks down quickly into humus. Stack for a month or two to allow rain to wash out most of the salt, then dig it in at the rate of about a bucketful per square metre (yard).

Wool shoddy – the waste from wool factories – is a traditional manure in parts of Yorkshire. Shoddy contains up to 14 per cent nitrogen, which it releases slowly over about three years. Dig the manure in, without first decomposing it, at the rate of about 500g per square metre (1lb per square yard).

Concentrated organic manures
Among concentrated organic manures that are rich in plant nutrients but which add little or no humus to the soil are:

Dried poultry manure Being extremely rich in nitrogen, this manure is best used sparingly. Also, use as a compost activator.

Bonemeal Animal bones, ground coarsely and sold as bonemeal, or ground more finely and sold as bone flour, provide phosphates.

Bonemeal releases phosphates slowly over at least two years, while bone flour acts more quickly but loses its effect within a year.

Work in coarse bonemeal at the rate of 120–180g per square metre (4–6oz per square yard) before planting fruit trees and bushes. Before sowing or planting vegetables, rake in bonemeal at the same rate.

Hoof and horn This is the main source of nitrogen in John Innes potting composts. It releases nitrogen slowly over a long period but its cost is about double that of sulphate of ammonia or nitrate of soda, the two main inorganic sources of nitrogen.

Dried blood A quick-acting nitrogenous manure that can be used as a substitute for sulphate of ammonia or nitrate of soda. Use along a row of vegetables as a top dressing at the rate of 30g per metre run (1oz per yard).

Fish meal Although an excellent plant food, fish meal is now scarce and expensive. It is now generally used in 'fish, blood and bone' mixtures. Before sowing, rake in fish meal at the rate of 90g per square metre (3oz per square yard).

Inorganic 'straight' fertilisers
Chemical or artificial fertilisers are divided into those classed as 'straight', each containing one or two of the three main nutrients, and 'compound', which provide a balance of plant foods.

Straight fertilisers include:

Sulphate of ammonia This nitrogenous fertiliser can be raked in before sowing at the rate of 30g per square metre (1oz per square yard) or used as a top dressing for growing crops, especially cabbages and related crops, and salads, at the same rate, or at 15g per metre run of the row (½oz per yard).

The effects of using sulphate of ammonia can usually be seen within 10–14 days. When used alone, sulphate of ammonia tends to make soils acid. It therefore

works better on chalky or well-limed soils. Best of all, use it with superphosphate and sulphate of potash to make up a compound fertiliser (see below).

Nitrate of soda This quick-acting nitrogenous fertiliser is often used as a stimulant for growing crops, especially where plants have been checked by bad weather. Apply 30g per square metre (1oz per square yard).

Nitro-chalk Another nitrogenous fertiliser, nitro-chalk is useful on acid soils because it does not make the ground sour. Use only as a top dressing, at 30g per square metre (1oz per square yard).

Superphospate The most popular fertiliser for supplying readily available phosphates, it is usually raked or forked into the soil at sowing and planting times at the rate of 60–120g per square metre (2–4oz per square yard). It is too slow-acting to be used as a top dressing but it remains in the soil as a plant food for some years.

Sulphate of potash This is the most popular fertiliser for supplying potash, because it can be used safely on all plants. Apply it as a top dressing at the rate of 30–60g per square metre (1–2oz per square yard) over the rooting area of fruit trees and bushes, and along rows of plants that will be in the ground for a long time. You can mix it with sulphate of ammonia and superphosphate to make a compound fertiliser.

Muriate of potash More concentrated than sulphate of potash, this fertiliser may damage

strawberries, red currants, gooseberries and tomatoes.

On other plants and bushes it can be applied as a top dressing at the rate of 30–60g per square metre (1–2oz per square yard).

Inorganic compound fertilisers
Plants need a balance of nutrients. Proprietary compound fertilisers contain the three main nutrients – nitrogen, phosphate and potash – plus traces of minerals such as magnesium and iron. The rate of application of compound fertilisers is generally given on the package.

To make your own balanced fertiliser, mix thoroughly 2kg (4lb) sulphate of ammonia, 2.5kg (5lb) superphosphate and 1kg (2lb) sulphate of potash. For most purposes apply at 60g per square metre (2oz per square yard).

Liquid fertilisers
Concentrated compound fertilisers, sold in both solid and liquid form, must be diluted before use. They are easy to apply as a top dressing and are quickly absorbed by plants.

Some liquid fertilisers are derived from seaweed and humus extracts; others are made solely from chemical elements.

They are mixed in various proportions to give a wide range of analyses to suit the needs of various plants and soils.

Foliar feeding
Plants take several days to make use of nutrients absorbed through their roots. However, you can speed up the process by spraying their leaves with diluted fertilisers.

You can buy fertilisers for foliar feeding at garden centres. Some are based on soluble, inorganic

PLANT FOODS IN ORGANIC MANURES AND FERTILISERS

This table shows the approximate percentages of nitrogen, phosphate and potash available to plants in each of the principal manures and fertilisers. Fertiliser manufacturers give the actual percentages of nitrogen, phosphate and potash – in that order – on each packet. The percentages are given either with the chemical formulae – N for nitrogen, P_2O_5 for phosphate and K_2O for potassium – or alone as a sort of code.

In this case, the chemical content of National Growmore would be stated as 7–7–7; the content of nitrate of potash as 13–0–44.

FERTILISER	NITROGEN	PHOSPHATE	POTASH
Farmyard manure	0.25	0.25	0.25
Sulphate of ammonia	21	0	0
Coarse bonemeal	3.30	29	0
Nitrate of soda	16	0	0
Fine bonemeal	1.30	29	0.2
Nitro-chalk	15.5	0	0
Dried blood	9.5	0.8	0
Superphosphate	0	20	0
Hoof and horn	13	2	0
Sulphate of potash	0	0	49
Fish meal	9.5	8	0
Muriate of potash	0	0	60
National Growmore	7	7	7
Nitrate of potash	13	0	44

fertilisers while other all-organic preparations have a seaweed base.

Foliar feeds should be regarded as a supplement to manures or fertilisers rather than as the sole means of feeding the crop. They are particularly useful, however, if the plants have a poor root system or during dry spells when the plants have difficulty in drawing nutrients from the soil.

Storing and using fertilisers

It is cheaper to buy fertilisers in bulk than in small quantities, but you need to store them properly.

Keep fertilisers in a dry place as they quickly absorb moisture from the atmosphere and set into a solid block or become a sticky mass. Do not store paper bags on concrete or against walls. It is best to keep fertilisers in plastic bags or tubs or in covered tins.

Do not apply more fertiliser than recommended. Measure roughly the area to be fed, then weigh the required amount of fertiliser on a kitchen scale. Use half the dose of fertiliser when farmyard manure or garden compost has been dug in.

A fortnight before sowing spread a general fertiliser evenly and hoe or rake it into the surface. Do not dig it in or it will soon wash down out of reach of the roots.

Do not scatter fertilisers along a seed drill as they may injure the germinating seedlings. Instead, apply top dressings along the sides of the rows and lightly hoe them in. Do not allow inorganic fertilisers – except the special foliar feeds – to touch the plant's foliage or it will be scorched.

In dry weather follow the application of fertilisers with a good watering because they cannot be absorbed by the plants until they are dissolved.

The condition of the soil and the weather also dictate the types of fertilisers to use. A light, sandy soil, for example, needs more potash than heavier soils, especially if you're growing soft fruits.

In districts with a heavy rainfall, nitrogenous fertilisers wash out quickly and should be replaced by regular top dressings of sulphate of ammonia or nitrate of soda.

Correcting soils that are too acid or too chalky

Acidity and alkalinity are measured by what is known as the pH scale, which runs from 0 to 14; neutral is 7. Readings higher than 7 mean that the soil is alkaline; readings below 7 show that it is acid.

Although most vegetables do best in a slightly acid soil with a pH level of about 6.5, some – including brassicas, beans, onions and asparagus – will still grow satisfactorily in fertile soils of pH7. This level would not be ideal for potatoes or strawberries, which require slightly acid soil.

Most fruits require a neutral or slightly acid soil, though figs and grapes will tolerate conditions that are slightly alkaline.

Most soils can be treated to lessen extreme acidity. Use a soil-testing kit to find out the condition of your soil (see page 17), and follow the instructions provided with it for the use of lime.

Adding lime If your vegetable plot is over-acid, but you are not sure to what degree, it's best to adopt a cautious approach so as to avoid the possibility of over-liming. Apply a dressing of hydrated or garden lime at the rate of 180g per square metre (6oz per square yard), or ground chalk or ground-limestone at 250g per square metre (8oz per square yard) after digging in autumn or early winter.

Spread the lime on the surface and leave it to be washed in by rain. Do not dig it in, otherwise surface soil will remain untreated. Clay soils are often, but not always, acid. A soil-testing kit will confirm if this is so.

Liming benefits an acid clay soil in two ways. It reduces the acidity and it also improves the soil structure by assisting the fine particles to collect into crumbs, which makes for quicker drainage and better rooting.

Over-liming, however, may reduce vegetable yields. Do not lime chalky soils; give only moderate dressings, where needed, to heavy soils overlaying a chalk or limestone subsoil.

Other heavy soils, as well as loams and acid sandy soils, are almost sure to need routine liming as part of a crop-rotation programme (see page 28). Add this before growing cabbages, cauliflowers and other members of the brassica family.

Neutralising lime Although acid soils can be corrected relatively easily, it is more difficult to make a limy soil neutral. A method worth trying, when digging in autumn, is to mix 250g (8oz) of flowers of sulphur with a bucket of peat – preferably moss peat, which is acidic. Fork in a bucketful to the square metre (square yard). Forking in peat even without the flowers of sulphur will also help.

A year after treating the soil, make another test. If there is an improvement, repeat the treatment. If not, don't waste any more money on the relatively expensive flowers of sulphur. Instead, build up the humus content of the soil with manure and peat. Use sulphate of ammonia when you need to add a nitrogenous fertiliser.

Symptoms of mineral deficiencies

Discoloration or blemishing of leaves, stems or fruits may indicate a deficiency of a particular element or an imbalance of the plant foods in your soil. But it is often difficult to diagnose which element is lacking as deficiency symptoms are similar for a number of elements.

Instead, try building up the soil's humus content by giving regular dressings of well-rotted manure or garden compost, and by applying the recommended amounts of fertiliser. A rotational cropping plan (page 28) is the best way to achieve a balance.

Although all plants require a balance of nutrients, the need for certain elements is greater in some plants than others. Choose crops and varieties that do well on your type of soil – brassicas on limy soil, for example, and potatoes on slightly acid soil. Before planting apple trees on a limy soil, ask a local supplier which varieties do best in your region.

Identifying the problem
Before jumping to the conclusion that mineral deficiency is causing the poor performance of your crops always check for an attack by a pest or disease (pages 238–47). This is the more likely cause if the soil has been properly fed with manure and balanced fertilisers. Never try to remedy a mineral deficiency by overdosing with fertiliser or lime as this upsets the balance of minerals in the soil.

SPOTTING THE SYMPTOMS OF MINERAL DEFICIENCY IN THE SOIL

ELEMENT	DEFICIENCY SYMPTOMS	SUSCEPTIBLE CROPS	TREATMENT
Nitrogen	Growth is poor; shoots are short; leaves are small and yellow brassicas turn pink then orange. Fruits or tubers are small.	Blackcurrants, brassicas and potatoes.	As a booster, top-dress with nitrate of soda, sulphate of ammonia or Nitro-chalk at the rate of 60g per square metre (2oz per square yard). As a more permanent cure, dig in all available garden compost or farmyard manure.
Phosphates	Root development and flower-bud formation are poor, and plants sometimes also show symptoms similar to that of nitrogen deficiency. Brown spots may appear on leaves, or edges may turn brown. Fruits have an acid flavour.	Beetroots, potatoes, swedes and turnips.	Before sowing or planting apply superphosphate at the rate of 25g per metre run (1oz per yard), hoeing it in so that the roots will reach it quickly – superphosphate is too slow-acting to use as a top dressing. Alternatively, work in bonemeal or bone flour at 120g per square metre (4oz per square yard) before sowing or planting.
Potassium	Growth becomes stunted, and leaves turn a dull blue-green, with browning at the tips or at leaf margins or showing as blotches. Leaves of broad-leaved plants curl downwards. Fruits may drop while still immature.	Apples, cauliflower, currants, peas, gooseberries, potatoes and tomatoes.	Before sowing or planting, hoe in sulphate of potash at 60g per square metre (2oz per square yard) as a top dressing. Apply at the same rate to the metre run. In January or February, give a top dressing over the rooting area of fruit bushes and trees at the rate of 30–60g per square metre (1–2oz per square yard).
Magnesium	Magnesium is a constituent of chlorophyll, the green colouring matter in leaves and stems. Any deficiency shows either as a loss of colour or as a mottling of red, orange, brown and purple tints. It may occur when a large amount of potash makes the magnesium inaccessible to the plants.	Apples, beetroots, brassicas, cherries and potatoes.	As soon as the deficiency is suspected, pray the leaves with a solution of magnesium sulphate (Epsom salts) at the rate of 250g to 12 litres of water (8oz to 3 gallons), plus a few drops of detergent.
Manganese	A lack of manganese is often found in sandy and alkaline soils, and frequently occurs with iron deficiency. Chlorosis, where leaves go pale or change colour, begins generally on older leaves. On green peas the deficiency shows on the leaves as brown patches, and the seeds are hollow. On beetroots, the leaves have red-brown speckling.	Apples, beetroots, cherries and peas.	Spray plants with a solution of manganese sulphate at 50g to 12 litres of water (2oz to 3 gallons), plus a few drops of detergent. Alternatively, water the soil with a solution of 275g manganese to 24 litres of water (10oz to 6 gallons).
Iron	Chlorosis (loss of colour) occurs at the tips of young shoots and through the leaves, in the early stages, while the veins remain green. Eventually shoots die-back. The condition usually occurs in limy soils, where the calcium carbonate prevents the plants or fruit trees from absorbing any iron that is naturally in the soil.	Apples and pears, particularly those on limy soils.	For a quick-acting, short-term measure, apply sequestered iron as a foliar spray. In January apply sequestered iron to the soil. Follow the manufacturer's instructions for the rate of application.
Boron	The roots of beetroots, swedes and turnips turn brown; brown cracks appear across the stalks of celery; apple cores become 'corky'; the growing points of plants die off.	Apples, beans, beetroots, brassicas, celery, grapes, pears, swedes and turnips.	Apply 30g of borax to every 17 square metres of soil (1oz per 20 square yards). Mix with light sand to ensure even distribution.
Molybdenum	Leaves, particularly of broccoli and cauliflowers, develop a disorder known as whiptail. Leaves become distorted and shrink back to the midrib, giving a tail-like appearance. On tomatoes, leaves become mottled and roll forward. Peas and beans show signs of nitrogen deficiency.	Beans, broccoli, cauliflowers, lettuce, peas and tomatoes.	Apply a solution of sodium molybdate at 30g to 8 litres (1oz to 2 gallons) to treat 8 square metres (10 square yards) of soil.

Making your own compost

When you make a compost heap, you are doing what nature does all the time – turning the remains of dead plants into food for yet more plants.

Many proprietary compost bins are available, including fast-acting closed bins, or you can easily build your own, see opposite page. Whichever you choose, position your heap on well-drained soil, so that any excess water can drain away.

A compost heap can be just that – a free-standing mound in an out-of-the-way corner of the garden, but for neatness and convenience it is often better to make it within a framework of wooden shutters or chicken wire netting. You can buy simple kits to construct or make your own (see opposite).

It is best to have a pair of bins, so that the contents of one are maturing while the other is being-filled. For a medium-sized garden, a bin 1m (3ft) square all round is ideal, but you can construct your bin to suit the material you have available if you are using offcuts or spare lengths of timber.

Alternatively, you can use a proprietary compost container. These are usually made out of black PVC and have a lid to keep out light and rain and to raise the temperature inside. They will turn your waste into compost much faster than a heap made in the open. Some models can be rotated on an axle, making the business of turning the heap quick and simple,

Autumn harvest to feed the garden Fallen leaves can be piled in a simple wire container and left to rot down into leaf-mould, which makes a rich mulch or soil conditioner. Leaves can also be added to a mixed compost heap with other garden waste.

and can make good compost in just a few weeks.

Most garden waste is suitable for composting: the tops of peas and beans, lettuces that have gone to seed, beetroot leaves, lawn mowings, dead flowers, leafy hedge clippings and annual weeds. Plus you can add straw from rabbit hutches, shredded paper and uncooked kitchen waste, such as tea leaves and tea bags, coffee

grounds, fruit and vegetable trimmings and egg shells.

Do not compost perennial weeds, such as docks and nettles; diseased plant material; woody material that will not decompose; or scraps of cooked food or meat that may attract vermin. Chop up hard roots and stems, such as those of cabbages, before adding them to the heap, and mix the material thoroughly.

Building the heap To start a compost heap, spread a layer of garden waste about 25–30cm (9–12in) deep, water the material if it is dry, then cover with a layer of animal manure 5cm (2in) deep.

If you can't get hold of manure – although you can buy it by the bag in most garden centres – use sulphate of ammonia as a compost accelerator, sprinkling it over the compost at the rate of 15g per square metre (½oz per square yard). Alternatively, use a proprietary compost activator.

Build a second layer of waste material the same thickness as the first and cover it with manure. If sulphate of ammonia was used on the first layer, sprinkle the second layer with garden lime at the rate of 120g per square metre (4oz per square yard).

Continue building the heap, sprinkling lime on alternate layers if you use sulphate of ammonia as an activator. Never mix the two together. If you have enough material, build the heap to a height

of about 1.2m (4ft), finishing with a layer of soil an inch or two deep.

In most gardens there is rarely enough waste to make a heap this big in one operation, so cover the top with polythene, sacking, a layer of straw, an old blanket or an offcut of carpet to keep in the heat until the next layer can be added. Check the heap periodically to make sure that it remains moist. A dry heap will not rot efficiently, so you may need to water it in hot weather. To keep the moisture levels up it is important to maintain a good mixture of soft green waste, such as grass cuttings, and woody, fibrous clippings.

Avoid adding large quantities of a single material all at once, such as a big pile of grass cuttings. Instead, mix them with other garden waste as you add it or fork the new material into the top layer of waste already in the heap.

Turning the heap Heat will build up rapidly at first but will die down after about a month, by which time the heap will have shrunk to one-third its original size. At this stage it is a good idea to turn the heap so that the outer material, which is slower to rot, can be moved to the hotter centre of the heap.

If you have a pair of compost bins, simply transfer the contents to the second bin. Mix the contents thoroughly as you do so, making sure that unrotted material is well buried within the heap.

While the material is rotting, and if the heap is to remain undisturbed for the winter, keep it covered.

Using a closed bin Compost made in a proprietary closed bin does not need turning. When ready, the compost should be moist, dark

Recycling waste In six to twelve months, raw kitchen and garden waste in a closed bin will rot into a dark, crumbly compost.

brown and of uniform consistency, with a smell resembling that of leaf-mould. In summer, composting may take only a month or two, but in winter it usually takes at least twice as long.

Wormeries The small amounts of kitchen waste that you generate when cooking can be used to make a rich compost in a 'wormery'. Kits are readily available and contain everything you need to get started – including the worms, which do the work of breaking down the waste. It is important to drain liquid from the bin from time to time to avoid drowning the worms, but most wormeries have a tap to make this easy. The liquid you collect can be diluted and used as a liquid plant feed. The compost is useful as a fertiliser for potting mixtures, as a lawn dressing or as a rich container compost.

Solving compost problems
A healthy, well-maintained compost heap should not smell unpleasant – and the finished compost should be crumbly and sweet. If your heap starts to smell, incorporate some fibrous material, such as shredded newspaper or straw, to reduce the moisture.

In cold weather the rate of decomposition will slow down, but you can help to keep your heap active by covering it with insulating material, such as an old blanket, square of carpet, sacking or even a layer of bubble plastic.

Flies are all part of the composting process and cannot be eliminated entirely from a compost heap, but if you find that they are becoming a problem, cover the heap or an open-topped bin with a sheet of blanket or a lid.

HOW TO BUILD A COMPOST BIN

You will need
- 4 x 1m (3ft) lengths of 5cm x 5cm (2in x 2in) wood for posts
- 10 x 1m (3ft) lengths of 9cm x 2cm (3½in x ¾in) timber for the side and back boards
- Hammer and galvanised nails
- 2 x 1m (3ft) lengths of scrap wood for temporary support
- 4 x 1m (3ft) lengths of 2.5cm x 2.5cm (1in x 1in) timber for front panel battens
- 10 x 1m (3ft) lengths of 15cm x 2.5cm (6in x 1in) timber for the front boards
- Timber preservative and paintbrush

Step 1 Make the first side by laying two posts on the ground, parallel to each other. Nail on the side boards, butting them up against each other. Make a second side in the same way.

Step 2 Stand the two sides upright and hold them in place by nailing a length of scrap wood across the tops of the back posts. Nail on the lowest back board then nail another piece of scrap wood across the tops of the front posts. This will keep the structure firm and square.

Step 3 Nail on the rest of the back boards, butting them up against each other.

Step 4 For the front, nail two battens vertically to one side of each post to form a channel for the boards. Slide in the first board and nail it in at an angle to the battens to stabilise the base. Add more boards as the compost level builds up, then slide them out as required to take out rotted compost.

Step 5 Paint the finished bin with one or two coats of timber preservative, wearing heavy-duty gloves. Pay particular attention to the bottom of the posts. Leave the preservative to dry thoroughly before starting to use the bin.

Digging and cultivating

Digging is the first stage of preparing soil for cropping. And in spite of lots of experiments to find alternatives, it has remained standard practice – thorough cultivation and good drainage are vital for providing the conditions in which crops will thrive.

Tackled in the right way, digging need not be as hard as many beginners believe.

Why dig?

Digging does a number of essential things effectively. It breaks up the top spit (spade depth) of soil, leaving the surface in a semi-rough condition to be broken down by frost and rain into finer crumbs suitable for sowing and planting. It improves drainage, yet makes it easier for moisture to be drawn upwards to the plants' roots.

Digging also aerates the soil, providing suitable conditions for the bacteria that make soil nutrients available to plants. It provides an opportunity for working manure into the soil, for burying annual weeds and for removing deep-rooted perennials.

The 'no-dig' alternative

Although some gardeners swear by them, methods of cultivation that avoid digging are still not generally accepted by the majority. If you are a beginner taking over a garden for the first time, 'no-dig' alternatives are impracticable; and, contrary to popular belief, they are not especially labour-saving.

The essential feature of a non-digging routine is that the soil, once cleared of perennial weeds, is kept covered with a layer of matured compost, adding at least 3cm (1in) a year. The action of bacteria and earthworms mixes this organic material with the soil, so that the upper 10–15cm (4–6in) becomes rich in humus and very fertile.

The surface remains well broken and easily worked, and the soil texture below is maintained by decaying vegetable matter and the presence of a large earthworm population.

Putting the theory into practice, however, may need more compost than the average garden can produce. In a new garden, where no compost will be available until a year after the first heap is started, it is out of the question.

To illustrate the scale of the problem, it is fair to assume that vegetable matter piled 30cm (12in) deep will, when rotted down, produce a 5–8cm (2–3in) layer of compost. Therefore, to estimate the amount of compost material you would have to collect for a full-scale 'no-dig' programme you must visualise your kitchen garden covered each year with, say, a 15cm (6in) layer of greenstuff, leaves and so forth. This may be difficult to provide.

A further obstacle to giving up deep cultivation is the likely regrowth of perennial weeds. When left undisturbed they establish themselves and spread rapidly. Farmers who practise direct drilling, which is a no-ploughing technique, control weeds with herbicides on a scale that most gardeners would be unwilling to contemplate.

If you wish to experiment with no-digging techniques, you are most likely to succeed on well-

Spadework There's a knack to inserting a spade. With the shaft vertical, place your left foot on the tread (if you are right-handed) and push the blade down.

drained, weed-free soil. Mark out a small trial plot and adopt a no-dig routine for several seasons – assuming that you have compost to spare for the experiment. This principle applies to most gardening innovations – try out new methods and varieties on a small scale, while relying on conventional methods and well-tried varieties until the new ones are shown to be better.

How to dig

If tackled sensibly, digging is neither as difficult nor as strenuous as many believe. Once you've got the knack, digging a vegetable plot

can be a satisfying and even relaxing occupation. However, beginners should not attempt too much at first, even when the work seems to be going well and easily. Don't try to do more than an hour at a time – until your spine and back muscles get used to the unaccustomed movements.

Types of digging

Normal digging consists of inverting the top spit of soil, and at the same time burying annual weeds, removing the roots of perennial weeds, and incorporating compost or manure if required.

This is known as single digging (see facing page), and is adequate for most purposes. The alternative, which involves turning the soil two spits deep and is known as double digging (page 26), takes longer but in certain conditions gives better results. Double digging is most worthwhile before growing deep-rooted crops, such as parsnips or

runner beans, on land where the subsoil is compacted. But as a rule it is something to try once you have mastered the basic technique of digging.

Whichever method you choose, avoid digging when the soil is soggy or frozen. Sandy, free-draining soils can be dug without difficulty at almost any time of year, except during a spell of freezing weather in winter, but late autumn is the best time to dig clay soils. They should not then be too wet, and winter frosts will help to crumble the soil into a fine tilth for sowing seeds in spring.

Single digging The method varies slightly, depending on whether you are digging bare soil or a plot covered with turf (shown on the facing page).

Before burying or stacking turfs, think about whether you could use some of them to renovate a worn area of the lawn.

Lifting and turning With your left hand near the base of the shaft, tilt the shaft backwards and lift the blade just clear of the soil.

If you're single-digging (see right) then tilt the blade to your right to tip and turn over the spadeful of soil.

Double digging Digging the soil two spits deep allows roots to penetrate more deeply, releases fresh reserves of nutrients and improves drainage.

Even so, not many gardeners find time for double digging. If you decide to try it, experiment on part of the plot to judge whether the effect is worthwhile (see page 26).

Spring cultivation

Final preparation of soil for sowing and planting will be straightforward if you managed to complete your digging and manuring by Christmas, or soon after. In the meantime it will have been crumbled, to some extent depending on how much clay is in your soil, by the action of frost, rain and drying winds.

Fortunately, suitable soil conditions generally coincide with the higher temperatures and longer days needed for germination of spring crops. However, the weather is not always in step with the calendar, so be guided by conditions in your garden, rather than the 'ideal' sowing dates suggested in this book or by seed packets and catalogues.

On clay soils, especially, you must wait until the soil is dry enough to be walked on without it sticking to your boots or shoes, or becoming compacted.

Preparing to sow Immediately before sowing or planting, rake the top few inches of the bed to break the remaining lumps into a crumb-like structure.

For small seeds, such as lettuce and carrots, this needs to be as fine as possible. Larger seeds, such as broad beans and peas, will grow in slightly rougher conditions.

If the surface has been compacted by heavy rain it will need loosening with the tips of the fork tines before it can be raked. Do not disturb more than the top inch or two, and walk backwards to avoid treading on your newly loosened surface. Allow it to dry before giving the final raking.

Start early If you were unable to dig during winter, make as early a start as possible in spring so that the soil has time to settle before you begin sowing or planting. A fork is better than a spade for this late digging as it will turn and break the soil in a single operation.

Although most spring cultivation concentrates on the top inch or two of soil, deeper forking is a help before planting potatoes. This crop does best in a loose, open soil, even if it is somewhat rough and lumpy.

For this reason, fork over the potato plot well in advance of planting, breaking up the soil thoroughly to a depth of one spit.

Cultivating between crops

Land cleared of one crop in the middle of the season, and then planted with another, must be cultivated in between. A garden fork is the best tool and the depth of cultivation will depend on the condition of the soil.

After lifting early potatoes, for instance, the soil will need little more than levelling and raking. Where spring cabbages or some other long-standing crop has been grown, you will need to loosen and break up several inches of the top spit. In both cases allow as long as possible for the soil to settle before sowing or planting another crop, and then firm it additionally with your feet.

SINGLE DIGGING TO CREATE A NEW PLOT FROM A TURFED AREA

Step 1 Dig a trench Having removed the turf from the area you want to cultivate, dig the first trench to one spade width and one spade depth.

Step 2 Put soil in a wheelbarrow The soil from the first trench will be used to fill the final one. Put it in a barrow and wheel it to the end of the plot.

Step 3 Dig a second trench As you dig, throw the soil into your first trench. Turn each spadeful upside down so the surface soil goes to the bottom.

Step 4 Continue digging Dig trenches across a long plot rather than along it. Once you've dug the final trench, fill it with the soil kept from the first.

Double digging

This methodical technique follows the same pattern as single digging, but once you've dug your trench, you fork over the soil below to break it up and remove any rubble before filling the trench again with soil from just behind. Keep the fertile topsoil and less fertile subsoil separate, so as not to dilute the fertility of your topsoil.

Most gardeners are daunted by the very notion of double digging, but the process is simple. The 'double' part involves a first dig with a spade, and a second 'dig, along the bottom of a trench, with a fork.

The best time to do the job is in autumn when your ground is damp but not sodden or frozen. Then, over winter, the ground will have time to settle and the frost can work its magic on heavy clods. If your soil is very heavy or poor, it will benefit from double digging every five years or so.

How to double dig

Dig your opening trench one spit deep and 60cm (2ft) wide from front to back. Using a fork, break up the base another spit deep. Work backwards from one end of the trench to the other.

If you have manure to add, put this over the loosened base of the trench. The nutrients it contains will leach down into the loosened subsoil and aid root development.

Then, dig a second trench behind the first, tipping the earth you dig out on to the loosened subsoil in the first trench, and repeat the pattern across the whole plot.

SIMPLE GUIDE TO DOUBLE DIGGING

Step 1 Define the plot Use a line to mark out the area you are going to dig. Dig the first trench one spit deep and 60cm (2ft) wide from front to back and take the soil to the far end for the last trench.

Step 3 Add organic matter Tip organic matter, such as garden compost or well-rotted manure, into the trench and lightly fork it in.

Step 5 Repeat the process When you reach the end of the plot, use the soil you dug out at the beginning to fill up the final trench. Give the soil a chance to settle before planting.

Step 2 Fork the subsoil Using the full length of the tines, fork over the base of the trench. This is where the term double-digging comes from, as you dig twice the normal depth.

Step 4 Dig the next trench Now measure about 60cm (2ft) along your line, and mark where to dig to with a cane. Dig out the soil, tipping it into your first trench on top of the organic matter.

Clean your spade If you keep your spade clean by scraping it frequently with a trowel, it will slice through the soil more easily.

Dealing with poor drainage

No vegetables or fruits will thrive in soil that remains wet for much of the year. Their roots will be starved of oxygen and it will be difficult to carry out necessary cultivation work at the correct time.

Signs of waterlogging include persistent puddles after rain, algae and moss growing on the surface, and overwintered plants – such as sprouting broccoli – going yellow and collapsing.

Often, a badly drained garden can be improved in the course of digging, particularly double-digging, which breaks up the hard sub-surface layer of impervious soil – known as an 'iron pan' – thus improving drainage. One or two trial holes will show whether such a layer exists. But while double digging (see facing page) is the ideal remedy, there is a slightly less laborious alternative.

Choose a time when the soil is fairly dry, and dig it over to a spade's depth. As you complete each row of digging, work along the bottom of the trench with a fork, driving it in to its full depth and levering it back so that the soil is lifted and fractures. A pickaxe or mattock may be needed to break the hardest type of iron pan.

Do not try to turn the layer of subsoil beneath the pan. Just push the fork in, move it until the soil begins to give, then pull it out.

In the worst cases, you may decide that you need to install underground drains before attempting to grow anything.

Pipe drains If waterlogging occurs on heavy or low-lying land and there's nowhere for the water to go, then pipe drains are probably the only answer. This is worth attempting only when the trouble is really serious and if there is a ditch into which the pipes can empty. If there isn't a ditch, you'll need to dig a soakaway – a large pit filled with stones or hardcore. Laying drains is heavy, specialist work, and you may want to hire someone to help you.

If you decide to lay pipe drains – also known as tiles – you can buy them from builders' merchants or agricultural merchants. For gardens, choose porous plastic or clay pipes with an interior diameter of 50 or 75mm (2 or 3in).

Land drain Whether leading to a ditch or a soakaway, a land drain involves laying porous clay pipes end to end, or a length of porous plastic pipe, on a porous ash or gravel base in a deep, gently sloping trench. The pipes are covered with more ash or gravel and then a 25–30cm (10–12in) layer of topsoil.

CREATING A RAISED BED

Making raised beds Make the bed 30–60cm (12–24in) high. You can make the frame from planks known as gravel boards, railway sleepers or a plastic kit that you simply clip together. Cover the base with stones, followed by gravel and a layer of turf; then fill with soil.

The best tool for digging deep, narrow trenches is a grafting spade with a narrow, slightly curved blade. You might be able to borrow one from a builder or fencing specialist; otherwise, use a narrow-bladed spade.

Lay the pipes with a slight fall towards the ditch or soakaway; a drop of not less than 30cm in 30m (12in in 30 yards) is sufficient. Set pipes with their ends about 2mm (1/16in) apart so that water can enter from the surrounding soil.

Before placing pipes in a trench, lay 3cm (1in) of gravel as a base. Place a further layer of gravel or small hardcore over them. You can cover this with inverted turfs before filling up with topsoil.

Raised beds Another solution to poorly drained soil, particularly for a small area, is to make raised beds, for growing a variety of crops, such as salads and tomatoes.

You can make a permanent bed with sides made from bricks, stone blocks or railway sleepers, or a less expensive and permanent structure using planks of wood or a proprietary plastic kit. Put a layer of rubble in the base to help drainage. The ideal size is 1.2m

Free draining Raised beds are ideal for heavy clay soils. Water drains from the raised bed allowing it to dry out ready for sowing or planting. The ideal size for a raised bed is about 1.2m (4ft) wide, as this allows you to cultivate the soil without walking on the bed. Once filled, allow the soil in a raised bed to settle for two weeks before planting.

(4ft) wide with a 45cm (18in) path in between raised beds for wheelbarrow access.

Raised beds are not merely a solution to poor drainage – they allow you to grow a wide range of plants when your garden has problem soil, because you can fill them with whatever soil mix you choose. Furthermore, the improved drainage means that the soil warms more rapidly in spring, allowing the vegetable growing season to start earlier. Once built, all you need do is to fork over beds each year, topping up with organic matter to maintain nutrient levels.

Planning the kitchen garden

Deciding where to grow your vegetables can make the difference between success and failure. But once you have chosen the site, you can use the same plot year after year.

Some of the kitchen garden's features – paths, a greenhouse or long-term crops like rhubarb – are permanent, but most of the cropping area will need replanning each season.

Crop rotation plays a key part in this annual allocation of space, as does the manuring programme that is linked with it.

Planning your plot

Vegetables grow best on land that gets plenty of sun and where the air moves freely. This is especially true of green crops, such as Brussels sprouts and cabbages, and also of swedes. So although shelter from north and north-east winds is an advantage, try to choose a part of the garden that is not hemmed in by trees or buildings.

However, all is not lost if the only available plot is in the shade for, say, half the day. The crops will not grow quite as well, but they can be helped by using cloches or a coldframe to provide a warmer start in spring.

You are unlikely to achieve worthwhile results if your site is in the shade for most of the day. It would be better to grow shade-tolerant plants, such as raspberries and blackberries, although even these benefit from some sunshine.

Paths A firm, all-weather path, such as one made of concrete, slabs or gravel, is an asset both when growing and gathering vegetables. For a gravel path, fix timber edgings to keep the material in place.

Do not plant fruit trees in the vegetable plot. They create shade and also take nourishment and moisture needed by other crops.

Deciding on a shape The need for sunshine and air may help to determine the size and shape of the vegetable garden. You may decide, for instance, to have more than one plot, or to grow vegetables in an existing flower border and choose shade-loving flowers and shrubs to grow in a part of the garden unsuitable for food crops.

A rectangle is the most manageable shape for a vegetable plot. In a small garden this will often be a single patch, with the crop rows running across the shorter dimension. In a larger garden, two or more beds, divided by paths, will work better than a large square plot.

Beds can be of any convenient width, but it is worth remembering that the contents of seed packets are often based on the amount needed for a 9m (30ft) row – sufficient to give worthwhile yields of a variety of crops.

In practice, most of us have to make the best of small or irregular shaped beds. Where a bed is much narrower at one end than the other, use the shorter rows for successional crops, such as lettuces and radishes, of which you will be making regular small sowings.

For most crops the direction of rows is not important, but east-west rows are better for crops overwintered under cloches. In winter, the sun traverses a short arc from south-east to south-west, and if the side of the cloche row is exposed to the south it will gather more warmth than if the sunlight falls obliquely along it. Plant rows from east to west if the garden is exposed to strong westerly winds.

As well as making plans for the main growing area, you should consider the following points.

Permanent crops Set aside space for long-term crops, such as asparagus, globe artichokes and rhubarb. Once established, they will remain undisturbed for years and should be put where they will not interfere with the planning and rotation of annual crops.

Herbs These are best grown near the house (see page 30), in a sunny but sheltered position. If you have to grow them in the kitchen garden, set aside a small permanent patch where they will not interfere with crop rotation.

Paths A path in the vegetable garden need be no wider than 80cm (30in), but it should provide a firm surface for walking on and for wheeling a barrow.

Grass paths are the least satisfactory. Gravel paths are better, though a board or other edging will be needed to keep the material in place; treat once a year with weedkiller. Best of all is concrete, either laid on site or in the form of paving slabs. Any weeds that appear between the slabs are easily dealt with.

Greenhouse and coldframe Ample light, a firm path and, if possible, a water supply, are the main considerations when deciding on a position. Do not site either under a tree (see pages 54–59).

Water supply A standpipe for a hose is not essential, but it saves the inconvenience of long hoses trailing down the garden.

Crop rotation and planning Even before digging the vegetable plot you should work out a rough cropping plan. This is because the vegetables will be grown in three groups, each requiring different soil treatment. Each of the groups is moved to different parts of the plot each year – a system known as crop rotation.

One reason for rotating crops is that different plants need differing quantities of the various soil foods. If the same type of crop is grown continuously in the same soil, it will need special feeding to make up for the depletion of these nutrients.

Even more importantly, while many crops suffer from soil-borne pests and diseases, infection is likely to become serious only when the host plant is grown on the same patch of land year after year.

A third advantage of crop rotation is that manures and fertilisers can be used to greatest effect, and not given to crops that may not benefit from them.

The three groups

Each of the following groups should occupy about a third of the plot.
Group 1 Hungry crops and salads – these include beans, celeriac, celery, leeks, lettuce, onions, peas, shallots, spinach, sweetcorn and tomatoes.
Group 2 Brassicas – crops in this group are broccoli, kale, Brussels sprouts, cabbages and cauliflowers.
Group 3 Root crops – these include beetroot, carrots, parsnips, potatoes, swedes and turnips.

Drawing a plan

Once the vegetable plot has been marked out and dug, you can make a fairly precise cropping plan for each of the three sections. Do this before ordering seeds. The easiest way is to make a plan on ruled paper, taking each square on the paper as, say, 30cm² (a square

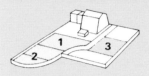

First year In an established rotation, group 1 ('hungry crops') is manured; group 2 (brassicas) is given lime and fertiliser; group 3 (roots) fertiliser only. On a new plot, plants in group 2 would also benefit from manure.

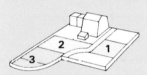

Second year Although they have been moved to fresh sites, each group of plants is given a similar application of manure or fertiliser to the previous year. To make full use of plant foods it is important to move crops in the order shown.

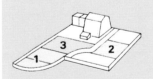

Third year A further change of position completes the rotation cycle. Each group of crops will now have occupied each of the three sections of the plot, in the order shown. Fertility will actually increase year by year.

foot) or any other workable dimension. For the correct crop spacings, refer to individual entries in the Growing and Cooking section, (pages 66–225).

When you plant crops requiring different row widths next to each other, leave a space equal to the difference between those widths. For instance, rows of lettuces are sown 30cm (12in) apart; rows of french beans are sown 45cm (18in) apart. So leave about 40cm (15in) between a row of lettuces and a row of french beans.

Remember that some crops, such as leeks, can be grown on land where another crop has been harvested. Others, such as lettuces, may be grown as a quick catch-crop between slow-growing plants.

Allow space for a seedbed where you can raise plants of Brussels sprouts, cabbages and other brassicas.

Making the most of your vegetable garden

The smaller your vegetable plot, the greater the challenge if you want to harvest crops throughout the year. The main task is not to allow any ground to lie idle. As soon as you've cleared one crop, follow it with another. This is known as successional cropping.

Catch crops Sometimes, there is a gap of a few weeks between the harvesting of one main crop and

Hungry crops and salads As part of your crop rotation, plant about a third of the plot each year with any of the following crops – beans, celeriac, celery, leeks, lettuce, onions, peas, spinach, sweetcorn and tomatoes.

the planting of another. Take advantage of this window by sowing a catch-crop – generally a quick-growing salad vegetable that you can pick before the ground is ready for another main crop.

After Brussels sprouts have finished, for example, sow 'Tom Thumb' lettuces in mid spring, to crop just before the bed is needed for tomatoes in early summer.

Inter-cropping Another form of intensive cultivation is inter-cropping – that is, growing quick-maturing vegetables, such as radishes, turnips or spring onions, between rows of slow-growing crops such as parsnips or sprouts.

Under certain conditions, some root crops may be sown closer together than is usually advised to produce a heavier crop. For instance, carrots may yield more heavily by being sown broadcast – that is, scattered thinly in drills 15cm (6in) wide and 1cm (½in) deep, instead of in traditional rows. When growing carrots like this, pull roots as they become large enough to eat, so that those remaining have more space to develop. In a few cases a slow-growing crop and quick-maturing salad crop may be sown together in the same ground.

Parsley is notoriously slow to germinate, and it is often difficult to find the seedlings among the weeds, so at sowing time mix the seeds with those of radishes. The radishes, which will appear in only a few days, mark the row to make it easier to hoe the weeds. In pulling radishes you will also be starting to thin the parsley.

You can also sow radishes in rows with slow-germinating parsnips and, again, in the potato bed immediately after planting.

Brassica bed A bed of kale and cabbage varieties from brassicas (group 2) adjoins a bed of beans and other group 1 crops.

Extend the cropping period of a row of lettuces by sowing a mixture of varieties that mature at different times – buy packets of ready-selected leaf seeds.

Successional crops
Some crops, such as sprouting broccoli, spring cabbage or early peas, are harvested at the height of the growing season. As soon as they are finished, prepare the ground for a successional crop, which may be quick-maturing for harvesting in autumn, or slower-growing for winter and spring use. Quick-maturing crops, such as lettuces, turnips, beetroot, peas and french beans, will not affect your rotation plan.

Those that are slower-growing – for instance, winter and spring cabbages, Brussels sprouts, sprouting broccoli and leeks – can be fitted into your rotation plan. Brassicas (group 2), will be followed next season by either root crops (from group 3) or by a summer crop of peas, beans, tomatoes and other 'hungry crops' (group 1). Here are some ideas for successional sowings:

Late spring – early summer To follow winter cauliflowers, winter lettuces, spring cabbages: lettuces, marrows, ridge cucumbers, spinach, sweetcorn or tomatoes.

Summer To follow early potatoes: early varieties of carrots and peas, leeks, celery, swedes, spinach beet or salad onions. To follow broad beans or early peas: turnips, globe beetroot, early varieties of carrots, calabrese, autumn or winter cauliflower or sprouting broccoli.

Late summer To follow second early potatoes, maincrop peas or dwarf beans: kale sown where it is to grow, spring cabbages (for transplanting, or to leave standing closely where sown for spring greens), lettuces, radishes and a final planting of leeks.

Successional crops are, by and large, sown or planted in summer, when the ground is generally dry. To prepare the bed, clear away the remains of the old crop and any weeds. Break up the top layer of soil with a fork or hoe, but do not dig deeply, or you will accelerate loss of moisture.

Dress the ground with a compound fertiliser at the rate of 60g per square metre (2oz per square yard), water drills before sowing and give a good soaking to the ground after planting.

Emergency sowings
If sowings of winter vegetables fail in the seedbed, make a direct sowing in the prepared bed just after midsummer. Sow a pinch of seeds, spaced at the distance the brassicas would normally be planted. When the plants are about 5cm (2in) high, carefully remove weak seedlings to leave only the strongest in each batch.

Growing herbs
Herbs are so useful in the kitchen that they merit a part of the garden to themselves – ideally, a sunny position near the kitchen door where they can be picked without bother.

This is not always possible, but herbs are so adaptable that they will thrive among flowers in a border, in pots on a patio, in a windowbox, even in pots on an indoor windowsill. They need free-draining, fertile soil or compost, but this should not be too rich.

Planning a herb bed Before planting an outside bed, draw up a plan. Put taller herbs, such as angelica, dill, fennel and rosemary at the back; and smaller ones, such as chives, marjoram, parsley and thyme, near the front.

There are all sorts of elaborate designs for herb gardens, including a chessboard design in which different herbs are planted in the 'black' squares, with paving or gravel filling the 'white' squares. If you enjoy growing herbs you could devise a pattern of your own. The principle can be followed in a small garden by using paving stones in the shape of a cross. Such designs have the merit of placing all the herbs within easy reach for picking.

Your choice of herbs depends on taste, but no herb garden can be complete without chives, mint, parsley, sage, marjoram and thyme. After these, the herbs most likely to occur in recipes are basil, bay, borage, dill, fennel, rosemary, savory and tarragon.

But part of the interest in growing herbs is to try something different, so a larger bed could include angelica, balm, burnet, chervil, coriander and lovage.

Growing herbs in a flower border Some herbs make an attractive addition to the flower border. Angelica, for example, can reach 3m (10ft) high in rich, moist soil, and makes an impressive backdrop for other flowers.

Other herbs worth growing in the border are fennel – of which there are bronze and purple forms – with its feathery foliage; borage, which has star-shaped, blue flowers; and sage, with its grey leaves – sometimes variegated – and spikes of blue or white flowers.

Parsley and chives make an interesting and productive edging.

A herb garden on a patio All herbs, except the tall angelica, can be grown successfully in tubs, boxes or flower pots on a patio or in a town garden.

In some ways this is a more practical way of growing herbs than in the open garden, since the roots of invasive plants such as mint are kept in check. Pots containing chives, parsley, bush basil and marjoram can be brought indoors for winter.

Ensure good drainage by drilling holes in the bottom of boxes, and put a layer of rubble at the bottom of all containers. You will get better results if you use a potting compost, such as John Innes No. 1, rather than a multipurpose, soil-less compost. Sow or plant as for herbs in the garden and keep the containers well watered, especially during dry periods.

Every spring remove 5–8cm (2–3in) of compost from the tops of tubs containing perennial herbs, such as bay, thyme or sage, and replace this with fresh potting compost, and apply a liquid feed once a fortnight between late spring and mid autumn.

Herbs in window boxes Low-growing herbs, such as chives, parsley, pot marjoram and winter savory, can be planted in window boxes in the same way as in containers on a patio.

If you want to grow tall herbs, such as tarragon or fennel, pinch out the growing points regularly to restrict the size of the plant. Plant mint in a separate box or it will soon smother the other herbs.

Growing herbs indoors The kitchen windowsill may seem the most obvious and also convenient place to grow herbs indoors, but often it is the least successful. A better place for indoor herbs is by a window or glass door in a cool room where there is plenty of light and also lower humidity.

Grow indoor herbs in John Innes No. 2 potting compost, which is richer than the soil they need outside. Even then, do not expect them to be of the same quality as herbs grown in outdoor beds during summer.

During late spring sow parsley, chervil and basil in separate pots. Let some of these plants grow on for early picking indoors, and plant out the remainder in the open in late spring or early summer.

During autumn start potting up some of the perennial herbs that have been growing in the open during summer. Sage, marjoram, chives and mint are among the most suitable.

Parsley can also be treated this way, but it is better to sow seed directly in a pot in summer and bring it indoors in autumn.

The size of the pot will depend on the size of the roots, but most herbs will do well in 13–15cm (5–6in) pots.

Propagating herbs Most herbs, both annual and perennial, can be raised from seeds. Instructions for sowing are given for each type in the Growing and Cooking section, (pages 66–225).

It is also possible to increase your stock of perennial herbs – or to replace old, straggly plants with new ones – by taking cuttings and setting them to root in pots containing equal parts (by volume) of multipurpose compost and sand. Alternatively, root them in a seed compost.

Dipping the base of the prepared cuttings in hormone powder encourages rapid rooting.

You do not need a greenhouse to root cuttings but a garden coldframe is a great help. This is not only for the warmth it provides but also for the still, humid conditions inside the closed frame.

If you do not have a coldframe, cover the pot of cuttings with a plastic bag and secure this with a rubber band to retain moisture. Place it on a windowsill.

The sort of cutting to take depends on the type of herb you are propagating.

Nodal cuttings Herbs propagated by this method include hyssop and marjoram in mid to late spring, and rosemary in late

NODAL CUTTINGS

1 After removing the shoot just below a leaf joint, pull away the lowest leaves.

2 Pinch off the soft tip, dip the base in hormone powder and insert in sandy compost.

summer. However, hyssop and rosemary can also be propagated as heeled cuttings in late summer.

Remove the top 8–10cm (3–4in) of a main stem just below a leaf joint, or node. Pull off or cut away the lowest pair of leaves and pinch off the soft tip. Plant the cuttings firmly in an 8cm (3in) pot of compost – several to a pot – water them and place in a coldframe.

The cuttings should begin to take root from four to six weeks. When rooted, pot them individually in 8cm (3in) pots of potting compost and grow them on in a ventilated frame.

HEELED CUTTINGS

1 Make an angled cut just below the shoot. Use a sharp knife or razor blade.

2 Make a second cut just above the shoot, which will then come away with the heel.

Heeled cuttings Take this sort of cutting when propagating thyme in late spring and early summer, and bay or sage in late summer.

Cut off semi-ripened shoots from the parent plant, complete with a heel, or sliver of wood, from the main stem.

To do this, make a slanting cut into the main stem just below the sideshoot joint, then make a similar cut above the joint to remove the shoot. A sharp knife is needed for this, so take care not to slip and cut yourself.

Rooting and aftercare is the same as for nodal cuttings.

Allotments

An allotment is a garden, no bigger than a quarter of an acre, rented from the local authority and used for growing food crops for the tenant's own use – but not for sale. If you want to find out about allotment growing in your area, get in touch with your local Parish, District or Borough Council, National Allotment Gardens Trust, or simply key the word 'allotment' into your favourite search engine.

The history of allotments

The word 'allotment' was first used in Britain in 1629 to describe a piece of land assigned to a person or for a special purpose. In 1819 an Act of Parliament was passed to allow parishes to acquire land to provide poor people with plots on which to grow vegetables. Further Acts were passed up to 1876 reinforcing this provision of land for 'field gardens' and recreational purposes for the 'labouring poor'.

Although technically this can mean an area of up to two – occasionally five – acres for use as a smallholding or garden, the term 'allotment' has come to describe a much smaller plot.

The 1908 Allotment Act made it an obligation of local councils to provide such parcels of land for use as gardens, if six ratepayers or parliamentary electors in their area applied for one. The 1950 Allotments Act endorsed this, providing suitable land was available. But during the 1960s and '70s demand for allotments declined in many parts of Britain, with

the result that much of the land was sold or built on. However, in recent years we have all become much more interested in growing our own food. This is partly due to the upsurge in television gardening and cookery programmes, but it's also in response to our growing

suspicion of chemical additives. On top of that, health experts are strongly advising us all to get our 'five a day' – and where better to get these than from our own plots? After all, you know exactly what's gone in so you know exactly what you're eating.

As many householders do not have the space for realistic fruit and vegetable cultivation, there is a strong demand for allotments once more, with many seed companies reporting that for the first time in years, vegetable seed sales are outstripping flower seeds.

This has meant that there is a shortage of allotments in most parts of the country. Many local authorities, which have to provide 15 allotments for every 1000 households by law – and must have no more than six people on the waiting list at any time – are having to divide allotments with standard dimensions of 9m by 6m (30ft by 20ft) into smaller plots to reduce their waiting lists.

However, although a smaller allotment may limit what you can grow, it will still give a good yield if you choose mini vegetable varieties and train fruit bushes and trees to occupy less space – cordons, for example. A smaller plot is also a far less daunting and more manageable prospect if you have many demands upon your time.

Getting started

One of the best ways to get started is to visit local allotments. You'll discover, when you visit, that there is a camaraderie about allotment growing that is unique. You can ask holders about the site – the rent, what facilities are provided, such as security and availability of water and electricity, whether there is a allotment association for the site, soil information, and what restrictions there are about the erection of sheds or greenhouses.

If you aren't happy about certain issues, then look at other sites until you are satisfied that, once you get your allotment, you will not be disappointed. Then find out who to approach about renting one. Some allotment sites belong to organisations other than the local authority – for example, a large landowner in the district or a local charity; again, the best way to find out how to apply for one of these is to talk to an existing holder.

A vital consideration is the proximity of the allotment to your home. Ideally, your plot will be within walking or cycling distance, as having to take the car every time you go there will eat into the savings you make on your crops, not to mention the impact on the environment.

Security is also an important issue. If you discover that the plots are regularly vandalised or stolen from, tools disappear or the sheds, greenhouses or similar structures are damaged as a matter of course, it is wise to look elsewhere.

It is unusual to find a neglected plot these days as most local authorities have waiting lists, but occasionally you might see an overgrown allotment, either for rent or next to the one that has been offered to you. Be aware that an untidy plot will take more work to get it into good heart than one that has been well maintained, and weeds in an adjoining one will spread into yours.

If you are offered an allotment which is larger than you think you can cope with, see if anyone else on the waiting list will share with you – but first check with the site owner that this is permitted.

What you will need

Once you obtain your allotment, you will need some kind of shed to keep your equipment in. Some allotment holders are allowed to

Apple pie order This established allotment has a greenhouse and shed, rainwater collecting cisterns, a paved area and even a boot scraper. An area has also been designated for colourful cut flowers.

construct their own buildings from recycled materials, and there can be quite a competitive spirit among holders regarding the ingenuity of these structures. Other landlords insist on buildings that come up to a certain standard in appearance, and these regulations may apply to other constructions like greenhouses and tunnels.

Whatever shed you have, it should be big enough to hold the tools you will need, as you will find it a bother to bring them from home every time. You'll also need space for pots, trays, string, fleece, canes and so forth. And don't forget home comforts – possibly a kettle and the means of warming it, mugs, teaspoons, tea, coffee and powdered milk.

Your shed must be lockable, and if the area is prone to vandalism or theft, it is best not to have a window. A greenhouse and coldframes are best glazed with shatterproof polycarbonate. Newer allotments on open sites may also need windbreak material, even if only temporary, while more permanent shelter grows up.

Once the allotment is up and running, you will regularly be bringing home the fruits of your labours. If it is within walking distance, a wheeled shopping trolley or an outgrown child's buggy will make transporting this much easier. If you cycle there, then consider buying a bike trailer.

Getting started

It may not be practical to cultivate the whole allotment at once. You could be better occupied working a part of it and keeping the rest weed free (using a weedkiller such as glyphosate, or sheeting it down with black polythene) until you are ready to expand.

It is a good idea to draw a plan of the site before you do anything else, allocating areas for vegetables, fruit, cut flowers, herbs and anything else you want to grow, and also where to position structures such as the shed, greenhouse, coldframes and compost bins.

If you take possession of your plot in autumn or winter, use the time before the weather warms up to get the ground properly prepared, then your first crops will get off to a flying start.

Don't be slapdash about tidiness on your allotment just because you can't see it from your house – a tidy kitchen garden is a healthy one, and it is as easy to keep the plot neat as it is to be disorganised. Your neighbours will appreciate a well-kept patch as much as they will dislike an unkempt one that spreads weeds into their own.

Sowing seeds in the open

Browsing through a colourful seed catalogue is one of the most satisfying pastimes for a gardener on a dull winter's day. It is also an essential job, because choosing the varieties to suit your garden and cropping plan will affect yields during the coming season.

Keep your cropping plan beside you when filling in the order form or making a list to take to a garden centre. You can then estimate the amounts you need and tick off each row as you order. This will also help you to avoid silly mistakes, such as ordering autumn-sown cabbages when your cropping plan calls for summer cabbages.

It's a good idea to order seeds as early as possible, otherwise you may find that some varieties are sold out.

Quantities and varieties

In many cases, a packet of seeds is sufficient for a row 9m (30ft) long. However, this is only a rough guide, as the amount of seeds in a packet varies and one gardener may sow with a heavier hand than another.

Often, a packet of a new variety contains fewer seeds than an established favourite. Even so, it will probably provide more plants than you need.

Choosing the varieties best suited to the soil and weather in your area is, to some extent, a matter of experience. Neighbours and local gardening clubs can suggest varieties that have proved reliable, though you may eventually find others that you think are of better quality.

Keep to the well-established varieties for the bulk of each crop, but every year try out a few that are different. In a small garden, try growing half a row of one variety and half a row of another, and compare results.

By all means experiment with varieties that are new on the market, but note that these seeds are generally more expensive. So also are F1 hybrids which are a cross of two distinct parent strains and produce plants of exceptional vigour – the 'F' standing for 'filial', and the '1' for first cross.

Pelleted seeds

Seeds sold in pellets look like small grey ball bearings. Each clay pellet contains one seed, so it is easy to space them evenly when sowing, making subsequent thinning much simpler.

Pelleted seeds are particularly worthwhile for crops such as carrots and lettuces, which are tedious to thin. For good results, the soil must contain the right amount of moisture (see opposite). This is not always easy to control.

Home-saved seeds

In only a few cases is it worth saving seeds from your own crops. Even where they could be saved, you might find it more useful immediately to sow or plant another type of vegetable to fit in with your cropping plan, rather than wait for the finished crop to go to seed.

Most small seeds are not worth harvesting. Do not, for example, save seeds of the cabbage family, because cross-fertilisation takes place readily between these and other brassicas and may result in worthless plants. The seeds from F1 hybrids do not reproduce true-to-type, and are not worth saving – you only get true-to-type seeds from a crossing of the original parent varieties.

Onion and leek seeds are worth saving – especially if you have a strain particularly suited to your area. But peas and beans are the crops from which you are most likely to achieve success with your own seeds. If you don't need the space for another crop, leave pods to ripen on the vine and shell the seeds when dry.

Spread out the seeds in a dry, airy place for a week before storing in paper envelopes (not polythene bags). Write the name of each variety on the envelope.

Keep even small seeds, provided they are well ripened, since they carry the genetic make-up of the parent plants and will still produce a normal crop. But do not save seeds from a crop with a large proportion of small or deformed pods, since this may indicate that the strain has deteriorated.

Sowing where plants are to grow

In order to germinate, a seed needs moisture, warmth and air. Therefore the soil must be damp, not too cold, and the seed must not be buried too deeply.

In spring, sow on land that has been dug in autumn or winter (see pages 24–26) and manured or dressed with fertiliser, if necessary, to suit the crop to be grown.

Sow when the soil is dry enough to be walked on without it sticking to your boots. This is the best test for judging the time to sow – do

SOWING SEEDS OUTDOORS

Create a drill Use pegs and a length of twine to mark straight lines the right distance apart. Create a shallow v-shaped groove or drill with the corner of a hoe.

Sow seeds thinly If the soil is dry, trickle water into the grooves before sowing. Sow seeds and cover them lightly with soil. Water gently through a fine rose.

not follow the calendar slavishly if conditions are unseasonably cold or wet. Plants sown a week or two later than the time suggested on the seed packet will still catch up and be ready to harvest on time.

If the ground is only slightly sticky, fork over the top 5cm (2in) so that the surface dries more quickly. When it is dry enough, firm the ground by treading, then rake to a fine, crumbly tilth.

Making a drill To make a straight drill (furrow) for sowing the seeds, use a garden line or push in pegs at each end of the row and tie string tightly between them. Straight rows make the most of the available space and are easier to thin and hoe between than rows sown haphazardly.

Make the drill along the line with a draw hoe. Use a corner of the blade to make a narrow, v-shaped drill for small seeds, such as carrots and spinach, and the full width of the blade to make a wide, flat drill for peas and beans.

In both cases form the drill with a succession of smooth, separate movements rather than pulling the hoe along without a break. Make the drills 0.5–1cm ($\frac{1}{4}$–$\frac{1}{2}$in) deep for the smallest seeds, such as carrots and lettuces; 1–2.5cm ($\frac{1}{2}$–1in) deep for slightly larger seeds, such as spinach and beetroot; and about 5cm (2in) deep for the largest seeds, such as peas and beans.

In each case, use the shallower depths specified for spring sowings when the soil is warmer near the surface, and the deeper drills in summer when the seeds need to be in damp ground below the surface.

If you are in any doubt about how deep to sow, then it is always better to err on the shallow side.

USEFUL FACTS ABOUT VEGETABLE SEEDS

VEGETABLE	AVERAGE LIFE OF SEEDS (YEARS) (OPEN GROUND)	AVERAGE DAYS TO GERMINATION FROM SOWING	AVERAGE TIME TO MATURE (WEEKS)
Beans, broad	2	21	20–26
Beans, french	2	14	9+
Beans, runner	2	14	13+
Beetroots	3	13	9–13
Broccoli	3	8	39–50
Brussels sprouts	3	8	26–31
Cabbages, early	3	8	17+
Cabbages, late	3	8	21+
Carrots	3	16	11–14
Cauliflowers	3	8	13–17
Celeriac	2	8 (indoors)	26–30
Celery	2	8 (indoors)	26–30
Chicory	3	9	17–21
Cucumbers	3	9	10–13
Kale	3	8	29+
Kohlrabi	3	7	11–14
Leeks	2	14	29–34
Lettuces	3	7	9–13
Marrows	3	7	9–13
Onions	2	14	21–30
Parsnips	2	17	21–30
Peas	3	10	11–17
Radishes	3	6	3–6
Salsify	2	12	19–24
Summer spinach	2	11	7–13
New Zealand spinach	2	11	10–13
Swedes	3	8	21+
Sweetcorn	3	9	17+
Tomatoes	3	7 (indoors)	14+
Turnips	3	8	7–12

Sowing too deep is a common cause of failure to germinate, especially on heavy soils.

In summer, water the ground thoroughly the day before sowing, or use a watering can without a rose to soak the bottom of the drill just before sowing.

Small seeds Sow small seeds as thinly and evenly as possible by shaking a few at a time into the palm of your hand and letting them dribble between thumb and forefinger into the drill. Do not try to shake them directly from the packet, or the row will be uneven.

Covering the seeds On light soils, cover the seeds by placing your feet on each side of the drill and shuffling the soil back. Or stand between the rows and pull the soil over the seeds with the back of the rake, then hold the rake vertical and tap the surface flat.

On heavy soils use only gentle pressure to firm the soil, otherwise it will become compacted and the seedlings may have difficulty in breaking through.

The best method of filling drills after sowing peas and beans is to stand between the rows, pulling the soil back with a draw hoe and then firming the surface with the blade of the hoe.

Before removing your marker line, insert a label identifying the vegetable and variety. Use a plastic plant label and write in pencil, wax crayon or indelible marker, as these will withstand rain and mud until the plants mature.

Where birds are a problem, cover the seedbed with fleece, or fasten wire or plastic netting to canes just above soil level.

Sowing pelleted seeds

The soil for sowing pelleted seeds, either in a seedbed or in their permanent positions, must be kept moist without becoming sticky. If the ground dries out after sowing, the protective covering will not break up to allow the seed to germinate. If the ground is too wet, the coating will become treacly and stifle the seed.

Although pelleted seeds reduce the work of thinning, it is not a good idea to risk sowing single seeds at final thinning distances. Instead, sow two pellets in each station and remove surplus seedlings later, if necessary.

Keep the soil moist by sprinkling every day until the seeds germinate, which will be about two days longer than the times given in the table (see left).

Sowing in a seedbed

Leeks and most brassicas are best raised in a seedbed and then transplanted. The plants tend to be 'leggy' if sown where they are to grow.

Relate the size of the bed to the size of your vegetable plot and the family taste for brassicas and/or leeks. As a rough guide, nine rows, each containing 30 plants, can be raised in a bed measuring 1.5m x 1.5m (5ft x 5ft).

The plants might comprise two rows of leeks, and one row each of summer cabbages, autumn cabbages, savoys, Brussels sprouts, cauliflowers, broccoli and either sprouting broccoli or kale. This selection would provide greenstuff for most of the year.

Preparing the ground Choose a piece of fertile ground and prepare the bed as for growing from seeds in the open – that is, digging during autumn or winter, treading the ground when the soil is suitably dry in spring, and raking to a fine tilth.

In such a small area there is no need to use a line and hoe to make the drills. Instead, form the drills on light soils by pressing a rake handle about 1cm (½in) into the surface. On heavy soils, use the rake handle as a guide and scratch the drill with a draw hoe.

Space the rows 15cm (6in) apart, labelling each row as you go. This is particularly important in a seedbed because, when young, the various brassicas look similar.

Birds may be troublesome, pecking out the brassica seedlings as they emerge, so cover the bed with netting stretched over pegs.

Sowing under cloches

Some crops can be harvested earlier if they are given a start under cloches. Sowing times can be advanced by two or three weeks for vegetables such as carrots, French beans and lettuces.

Prepare the ground as for sowing in the open and place the cloches in position two weeks before sowing to warm up the soil.

Distances between rows will be governed by the height and width of the cloches. As the seedlings grow they will need headroom, so do not sow too near the edges.

Surface soil dries out quickly under cloches, though usually there should be no problem if it was sufficiently moist at sowing time.

In hot weather you may need to water the soil before the seedlings appear. During damp weather, you will probably need to control slugs.

Causes of failure

The complete or partial failure of a sowing is rarely due to the quality of the seed. If the seeds do not come up, you probably have time to resow, but first make sure that the crop has failed. Check with the germination times shown (see left).

There are several common reasons for failure; you can identify the problem if the seeds are large enough to dig up and examine.

Soil too cold The seed will be soft and decaying, with no sign of a shoot. This occurs in hardy crops sown too early in spring, and in tender crops, such as marrows, also sown too early in spring.

Delay the first sowings of hardy crops until growth is evident in weeds and overwintered crops, and the soil feels warm to the touch after the sun has been on it. Take local advice and do not be misled by sowing dates based on latitude. Spring in parts of East Anglia, for example, is often colder than farther north.

Soil too dry The seed will be hard and appear much as it came out of the packet. In dry weather always soak the ground before sowing, and water at three-day intervals until seedlings emerge.

Fungus diseases Seeds are liable to attack by spores of a soil-borne fungus, and in this case will rot and may be hard to find. This is more common in heavy soils than in light ones. Peas and beans are particularly susceptible to these rotting-off troubles.

Slug damage Occasionally, slugs may clear seedlings as they emerge. You will need to treat the area against slugs and snails (page 241) immediately after sowing.

Mice Peas sown under cloches in autumn or early spring are the most likely target of mice. The only way to protect them is to set traps under the cloches.

Thinning seedlings It may seem a paradox of gardening that seeds must be sown thickly enough to ensure a full row, then thinned out to give the plants room to mature.

Thinning, however, is vital, otherwise seedlings become weak and spindly as they compete with each other for food and light. Pelleted seeds, sown in pairs at

THINNING OUT SEEDLINGS

Remove weak seedlings first
Lift unwanted seedlings out with one hand while holding down the soil around nearby seedlings with the other.

Thin the rest Remove seedlings to leave the remainder spaced at half the distance required. Don't leave the waste on the ground; they will attract pests.

their final spacings, only need thinning to a single seedling at each station. Plants in the seedbed need to be thinned only once before transplanting.

For all other seedlings, thin in three stages, starting as soon as the seedlings are large enough to handle, first to 2.5cm (1in) apart, then to 5cm (2in) and finally to the distance recommended for each vegetable (see pages 66–225).

Thin when the soil is damp to reduce root disturbance to the plants that are left. Put thinnings on the compost heap as they may attract pests if left between the rows – especially in the case of carrot thinnings. You can eat some early thinnings raw in salads.

Second and third thinnings At this stage, some of the plants removed – such as carrots, turnips and beet – can also be cooked and eaten. At the third thinning, check that only a single plant is left at each station. Sometimes a second plant may be missed, and this will be more difficult to remove later.

Germination times and age limits for seeds
To minimise risks at sowing time, use only fresh seeds. Every seed packet carries the year of packing and a guarantee of quality and compliance with legal standards.

It is particularly important to use fresh seeds if growing parsnips, as these seeds have a notoriously poor germination.

Other seeds may be sown safely a year after purchase if they have been stored in a dry, cool place. Some, indeed, have a much longer life, as the table (page 35) shows.

To avoid disappointment and the need to resow a second batch, test a sample of old seeds indoors a few weeks before you plan to sow them. Count ten seeds and sow them in a small tray of moist seed compost. Place the container in a plastic bag and leave in a warm place, such as an airing cupboard, for the number of days shown on the table in the column of germination times. If eight or nine seeds germinate, the rest will be worth sowing in the garden.

Sowing seeds indoors

Most vegetable seeds are sown directly into the ground, but there are two major groups that are sown in pots or trays – either in a coldframe or a greenhouse, or indoors.

One group comprises vegetables such as french and runner beans, which can be given an early start under glass and then planted outdoors when the danger of frost is past. These will mature several weeks earlier than crops sown outdoors.

In the other group are the seeds of more tender plants that need relatively high temperatures to germinate. These include aubergines, cucumbers, melons, peppers and tomatoes. The plants may then be grown in a greenhouse or, like beans, moved outside when all danger of frost is past.

All these plants are easy to grow if you have an electrically heated propagator (page 38) which produces the right temperature and humidity. You can use the propagator in a greenhouse to avoid heating the rest of the greenhouse, or you can stand it on a sunny windowsill.

If you have no greenhouse or propagator, you can still get seeds of hardy plants to germinate on a windowsill, but it is essential to pay attention to sowing times and to provide plenty of light to make sure that the seedlings are sturdy.

Seeds that need a fairly high temperature to germinate, such as cucumbers and melons, can be started in an airing cupboard, but again the timing must be right so that subsequent growth of the seedlings is not checked at any stage. (You will find the sowing times for each type of vegetable in the Growing and Cooking section, pages 66–225.)

Raising strong seedlings Risks of a check are minimised if you use a coldframe or cloches (pages 60–63) for hardening off, or acclimatising, plants before they are put in their positions in the garden. If you have neither, you will need to carry the plants outside on mild days and bring them in at night.

It is a waste of effort to sow seeds so early that seedlings either grow too spindly indoors to be of any use, or die in the cold outside. If sown too late they may not have time to mature, or for the fruits to ripen before autumn.

Always use fresh, sterilised compost, which can be bought from garden centres. Garden soil contains weed seeds and, possibly, fungal spores that could infect seedlings. Most garden soils have the wrong texture for use in pots and boxes, and will become caked and compacted after a short time.

Seed and potting composts
The composts used for sowing and potting are different from the compost made from decaying vegetable matter in the garden. Commercial composts are designed to give plants everything they need for growth. Many even contain water-retaining granules. They have been sterilised to kill weed seeds

and fungal spores, and are made of free-draining material that encourages root action and does not become waterlogged.

There are of two kinds of these composts – either loam based or peat or peat substitute based.

Loam-based composts The best known of these are the John Innes range, available in four grades: **Seed compost**, for sowing seeds; **No. 1** potting compost, for seedlings moved from seed compost; **No. 2**, for potting on the plants; and **No. 3**, for growing plants such as tomatoes and aubergines to maturity.

Sowing seeds in a greenhouse
Plants that cannot survive in the open during frosty weather are first sown in containers under cover in a greenhouse or indoors.

John Innes is not a brand name. The composts evolved after long experiments at the John Innes Horticultural Institute, and anybody can make them and sell them. The composts contain varying mixtures of sterilised loam, peat or peat substitute, sand and plant food to meet the needs of the plants at each stage of development.

Loam-based composts give a long-lasting supply of plant foods. Their disadvantage is that their principal ingredient is loam, and suitable types are now in short supply. To make sure you are buying the proper stuff, and not a poor imitation, look for the John Innes Manufacturers' Association (JIMA) seal of approval.

Soil-less composts These proprietary products are based on peat or a peat substitute to which plant foods have been added. In response to concerns about the destruction of peat moors, both here and abroad, manufacturers have replaced the peat element with a product made from various materials, including coir, wood waste and green household waste.

Soil-less composts are light and clean to handle, but plants left in them for more than about eight weeks need regular feeding with a general-purpose fertiliser. Soil-less composts are sold in plastic bags. They normally contain the right amount of moisture for sowing or planting, and will retain this moisture if the bag is resealed after only part of it is used.

When compost has dried out its surface is pale instead of dark brown. When this happens, tip out the compost and spread it thinly; water through a fine rose and mix well before using or re-bagging.

Soil-less composts have a finite shelf life that is greatly reduced if the bags are not stored under cover in a cool building or similar. Before buying, check that they have been stored correctly by the garden centre, and do not buy more than you can use in one season.

If the compost in a pot dries out, submerge the pot in water until air bubbles stop rising. Treat seedlings growing in a dried-out tray with repeated light waterings from a fine rose, rather than flooding them with a sudden heavy watering.

Seed trays and plant pots
Plastic pots and trays are all suitable for seed sowing. They can be washed easily after use and don't harbour disease spores, which is always a risk with wooden seed boxes. Indoors, any shape of container can be used, but in the greenhouse rectangular trays are the most practical as they do not waste space on the staging.

To save on compost, use the smallest container that will provide you with sufficient seedlings. Old yoghurt and margarine pots are useful, as long as you put drainage holes in the bottom. More than one variety can be sown in the same tray or pot, provided the divisions between them are clearly marked and each variety is labelled. The easiest way to do this is to write the names of the varieties on plastic labels and use these as the division markers.

Choosing pots Plant pots are available in sizes from 5cm (2in) to about 45cm (18in), the measurements referring to the inside rim diameters. The most useful sizes are 7.5–8cm (3in), for growing on seedlings, 10cm (4in)

for potting on when the roots fill the first pot and 20–25cm (8–10in) for mature plants.

Plastic pots are light, easy to clean and cheaper than clay pots. The rate of evaporation from the compost is slower, allowing less-frequent watering. However, clay pots give excellent results, so do not discard them in favour of plastic pots. Always soak new clay pots, or any that have been stored indoors for some time, in water for an hour before using. Without a soaking they will absorb too much moisture from the compost.

Fibre pots are used differently from those made of plastic or clay. At planting time the pot is put straight into the ground with the plant in it. The fibre disintegrates and the roots can grow through it and into the surrounding soil.

Fibre pots must be very damp when planted out and the soil must be well watered if it is at all dry, otherwise, the pot will form a hard case and the roots will not be able to break through.

Compost blocks You can omit pots altogether if you use compost blocks. These are made from compacted soil-less compost in which seeds can be sown or seedlings planted. They maintain their cohesion long enough for the plants to reach planting-out size.

Another type of block, the 'Jiffy 7', comprises a disc of highly compressed peat substitute which contains plant foods and may be enclosed in a fine-mesh net. When soaked in water it swells to a cylindrical block about 4cm (1½in) high on which a single seed is sown, or a seedling or cutting planted. These blocks are ideal for sowing large seeds, such as those

SOWING SEEDS IN A POT

Fill the pot with compost Firm it with the base of another pot.

Sow seeds thinly Sprinkle them onto the compost.

Cover the seeds Sprinkle on a thin layer of compost and label.

Water gently Use a fine rose so as not to flood the compost.

of cucumbers, and for raising seedlings on a windowsill.

Plastic modules, sold in all garden centres, are divided into cells of varying sizes and are designed to fit inside a more sturdy plastic seed tray. Most bedding, strawberry and young vegetable plants are also sold in them – so a good way to acquire a supply is to save and wash out those in which you have bought young plants.

Germination temperatures

Hardy vegetables, such as lettuces, need a minimum temperature of 5–7°C (41–45°F) to germinate. Tomatoes and marrows require 10–13°C (50–55°F), cucumbers 21°C (70°F) and aubergines 18°C (64°F). You can provide these temperatures in a propagator; or place a greenhouse heater under the staging and rig up a polythene tent over the seed trays, to provide a fairly steady warmth.

Even without a heater you can raise many plants in a greenhouse. You will simply have to sow later. For instance, tomatoes can be sown in late winter if you can provide moderate heat for germination; without heat, you must delay sowing until mid spring.

Sowing in a coldframe can begin at the same time as in a cold greenhouse. Conserve warmth as much as possible, ventilating at midday on warm days and covering with bubblewrap, greenhouse insulation or other material on cold nights. A soil-heating cable may be installed in a coldframe, in which case sowing times are as for a heated greenhouse.

Sowing small seeds in pots

Fill the container to the rim with seed compost and press it down

with the bottom of a similar container until it is 1cm (½in) below the rim. Sprinkle seeds thinly and evenly, spacing larger seeds, such as tomatoes and pelleted seeds at least 1cm (½in) apart.

Cover the seeds with a very thin layer of compost and firm the surface evenly. Water lightly, preferably using a fine rose pointing upwards. Or place the pot or tray in a shallow water bath (the kitchen sink is ideal) until the surface looks damp but not soaking wet. This will prevent the seeds being displaced by a heavy shower of water from above.

Label the tray with the name of the variety and the date of sowing.

Sowing without a propagator

If germinating the seeds in a greenhouse, but without a propagator, cover the container with a sheet of glass or clear plastic to conserve moisture and put a sheet of cardboard on top.

If growing on a windowsill, place each tray in a polythene bag, tying it tightly to retain moisture, but enclosing as much air as possible.

Remove the covering as soon as the first shoots emerge. If left in the dark seedlings can become drawn and worthless in 24 hours. In a heated propagator, remove the tray as soon as the seedlings break the surface and put them somewhere warm and light.

Sowing large seeds in pots

Seeds of marrows, cucumbers, melons and sweetcorn are best sown in potting compost in 7.5cm (3in) plastic, clay or fibre pots and grown on without disturbance until their final planting.

Sow two seeds 1cm (½in) apart and 1cm (½in) deep in the centre of

SOWING SEEDS IN A TRAY

Sow seeds thinly Use a tray filled with moist seed compost. For easier control fold the open flap to form a spout and carefully tap them out of the packet.

Put in a heated propagator Alternatively put the tray into a plastic bag and fold it under. Stand in a warm shady place or even the airing cupboard.

Pricking out When the first true leaves appear, prick out seedlings into another tray. Prise them up with a plant label, pencil or pointed stick, and hold seedlings by a leaf, not by the fragile stem.

the pot, inserting the seeds of marrows, melons and cucumbers on edge. Keep covered with glass and brown paper until they germinate. If two seedlings appear, remove the weaker one.

Give french and runner beans a good start by sowing them in moist seed compost in large plastic cream or yoghurt cartons, in which drainage holes have been punched. Put five or six seeds 2cm (1in) deep in each carton. Seal them in a plastic bag and put pots in an airing cupboard for a few days until the seeds germinate.

Pricking out

Seedlings in trays must be given room to develop by spacing them out in other trays or planting them singly in pots. Do this 'pricking out' as soon as the seedlings are large enough to handle. Fill trays or pots with John Innes No. 1 and lift each seedling with the point of a pencil or plastic plant label, holding it by a leaf and not by the stem. Use a pencil or stick to make a hole in the compost and plant the seedling with its stem covered to just below the seed leaves – the leaves that appear first as the seedling breaks the surface.

Water the seedlings and keep them out of direct sunlight for two days, then place them close to the glass to encourage sturdy, short-jointed growth. Water regularly and shade the glass on sunny days.

Hardening off

Plants raised in a greenhouse or indoors must be acclimatised before being planted outdoors. Ideally, put them in a coldframe or under cloches a week or so before planting out. At first, leave frame lights or cloches open only during

Using a propagator An electric element warms up the compost providing the heat and humidity needed for germination and root growth. Crops started in this way can be harvested days, or even weeks, earlier, yet the propagator costs only a few pence a week to run. Choose a thermostatically controlled one, which will help to prevent a build-up of heat inside on warmer days.

the day. A few days later, give some ventilation at night and, finally, leave the protection off altogether. Alternatively, stand the plants in a porch or verandah by day and take them in for the first few nights. Remember that plants that are growing in small containers exposed to sun and wind need more frequent watering than those under cover.

Transplanting

When transplanting vegetables to their permanent positions after raising them under glass or in a seedbed, choose plants that are stocky, sturdy and well hardened off.

Check that the soil is moist and firm, and allow time for it to settle after digging.

If possible, wait for mild, still, damp weather. Unless the plants are given protection, they may be stunted by strong winds or hot sunshine.

Planting tender crops

Courgettes, cucumbers, marrows, melons and tomatoes are among plants that will not grow when the soil and the air are cold, so timing is crucial when planting outdoors.

In the south, wait until mid spring if these plants are to be protected by cloches, or until the end of spring or early summer if to be planted in the open. In the north, allow at least an extra week or two in both cases.

If the soil is dry, water it thoroughly the day before planting. Water the plants an hour or two before moving them, taking particular care that fibre pots get a thorough soaking. Marrows, cucumbers and melons may suffer a severe check if their roots are disturbed. For this reason they are often grown in fibre pots, which can be planted directly in the soil.

If the plants have been raised in pots, tap them out carefully. Hold the pot upside down in the palm of your hand, with the plant projecting between your fingers.

Tap the rim of the pot smartly against a solid object, such as a trowel, so that the plant slides out with the soilball intact.

Make a hole in the soil about 2.5cm (1in) wider than the fibre pot or soilball. Set the plant in the hole and draw soil round it, firming with the back of the trowel or with your fingers. Give enough water to help the soil to settle.

Transplanting from a seedbed

Move hardy plants, such as Brussels sprouts, from the seedbed to their permanent positions when about 10cm (4in) high. The plants should have short stems and spreading leaves. Make sure also that each has an inner growing point of undeveloped leaves.

During a dry spell, water the seedbed thoroughly the day before planting. At the same time, water the planting site.

Lifting and moving Use either a trowel or a dibber to make the planting holes. Lift the plants with a trowel and set each in a hole, slightly deeper than it was in the seedbed. Make sure there is no cavity below the roots.

Firm each plant by pushing the trowel or dibber into the ground alongside and levering the soil firmly against the roots; water in.

To test if you are planting firmly enough, hold a leaf between finger and thumb and pull. If the leaf tears, the plant is firm enough; but if you pull the plant out of the ground, replant it more firmly and test the other plants.

If you are planting more than one row, stagger the plants in adjacent rows to give them more room to grow.

Protecting young plants When planting during hot spells, shade plants by putting fleece or newspaper over them for two or three days to help them to get established. Use bricks or stones to keep the paper or fleece in place. If you have tunnel cloches, put these over the plants and cover with black polythene or green netting.

Birds sometimes pull newly planted brassicas out of the ground. Net the bed if you don't plan to cover the plants with newspaper or black polythene.

After planting brassicas and lettuces, it is a good idea to protect them from slugs and snails (page 241). And as a precaution against cabbage root fly (page 238), sprinkle bromophos or diazinon granules around the stems of brassica plants. Keep the soil moist, and spray the plants each evening until they are established.

TRANSPLANTING BRASSICAS

Plant firmly Firm planting is vital to prevent roots from drying out and help them to develop.

Test with a tug When pulled, a leaf should tear but the plant stay in. If it lifts, replant firmly.

Buying plants

Generally, it is better to grow your own plants from seed rather than buy the plants from a nursery. You get a better choice of varieties and you are able to produce the plants just at the time you are ready to set them out.

However, if something goes wrong with your own sowing you will have to buy plants. These are the points you should then look for:

Buy sturdy plants Look for short stems and deep green leaves, indicating that they have been well hardened off.

Make sure they are damp Choose pots or trays that are already well watered.

Check suitability Choose plants – such as indoor or outdoor tomatoes – to suit your needs.

Mulching and watering

Soil is a natural reservoir. The more thoroughly it is cultivated, and the more decayed organic material (called humus) it contains, the greater its capacity to store water.

Apart from surplus rainwater, which drains away, soil loses moisture in two ways: evaporation from the surface, and through the action of plants, which take up water in their roots.

In hot, dry spells the moisture content of soil needs to be supplemented by watering, but it can also be conserved by mulching: placing a barrier between the soil and the air. A mulch can be a layer of organic material, polythene, garden compost, weed-barrier sheeting or well-rotted manure.

How hoeing helps Frequent hoeing is also of benefit. Without hoeing, and especially if trodden and compacted when wet, the soil's surface remains dark in colour and may feel moist during dry weather. This is because moisture is being drawn to the surface, where it will be lost by evaporation. Later, the surface will bake hard and crack, increasing the loss of moisture.

This is less likely to happen if you hoe regularly, leaving a fine, grainy surface up to 2.5cm (1in) deep.

The beneficial effect of hoeing can be increased by adding another moisture-retaining layer – proprietary soil conditioner, garden compost or manure – along both sides of rows of crops to a depth of 5–8cm (2–3in).

When to mulch Mulch soft-fruit bushes and canes in spring while the soil is still moist. Begin mulching annual crops of vegetables when they are a few

Get a head start If you don't have space to propagate your own plants from seed, then buy them as trays of plug plants, which are ready to pot on or plant out, in exactly the same way as those you have grown yourself.

inches high. If the ground is dry, water it thoroughly before applying the mulch. Mulches of organic material, such as manure or compost, are valuable because they

ultimately add to the humus content of the soil. But weed-barrier sheeting, black polythene or even old carpet or underlay makes an effective mulch for some crops

– especially for strawberries and bush tomatoes, as it prevents the fruits resting on the soil.

Before laying polythene, ensure that the soil is moist and treat for slugs and snails. Weed-barrier sheeting is usually permeable, so rain can pass through and onto the soil. Cover each edge of the polythene or weed barrier with soil to keep the sheets in position.

You can lay separate strips about 30cm (12in) wide on each side of a row of plants, or cut slits in a broader sheet to match the positions of plants.

Watering When using a hose or can, water the ground thoroughly, giving at least 25 litres per square metre (5 gallons per square yard). If you give too little, water will not reach the roots even though the top layer appears wet. If you continue to apply small amounts, the roots may be drawn up to the moist surface and will suffer even more if this dries out.

Some plants – for example, cucumbers, marrows, melons, pumpkins, runner beans and tomatoes are very thirsty drinkers. They show distress quickly if they do not have sufficient moisture.

Regular watering of these crops is essential during long, dry spells. Spasmodic watering can cause poor setting of the flowers of some crops and ripening fruits may split.

Water in the evening so that the plants get the benefit during the night. Water applied early on hot, sunny days will evaporate before it can reach the roots.

Harvesting and storing

Harvesting is one of the most satisfying jobs in the garden: the time when a gardener gets his or her reward for months of toil.

But, like other stages of food growing, harvesting has its pitfalls. Much of your effort will have been wasted if you don't gather your vegetables until they are past their best or if you store them inappropriately.

Make the most of the advantage you have over commercial growers by picking vegetables while they are young, tender and full of goodness and flavour – and only a few minutes before they are to be cooked or preserved. Check plants daily at times when crops are maturing quickly to make sure that you don't allow them to become overripe.

Pick french and runner beans before the seeds start swelling, or they will be tough and stringy and the plants will stop producing.

Pick peas when the pods are smooth and bright green. If only a few peas or beans are ready, keep picking frequently and put the pods in the fridge until you have enough to make a meal.

Pick perpetual spinach and sea kale beet regularly to discourage them from bolting (going to seed).

Storing vegetables Many summer vegetables can be frozen (page 252) or bottled (page 270). Others, such as marrows, onions, potatoes and root vegetables can be stored for winter use in an airy, frost-free place such as a garage or shed. Ensure that doors and

windows fit well and, in a severe winter, give additional protection with sacking, straw or newspaper.

Do not put sacks or containers directly on the floor and do not lean them against walls.

Never use polythene bags or sacks for vegetable storage or the contents will either start to grow or will rot. Store only undamaged and healthy vegetables, and inspect them regularly.

Potatoes and root crops In the past it was often recommended that potatoes and root vegetables should be stored in an earth clamp outdoors, but few gardeners today grow enough to make this worthwhile. Clamps are, in any case, an inconvenient method of storage as they may have to be opened in wet weather.

Instead, keep long-rooted beetroot, carrots and celeriac in boxes of damp sand (page 108) or old potting compost to prevent them from shrivelling. Before storing, twist off the leaves of beetroot and trim the foliage of carrots and celeriac with a knife.

Leave potatoes to dry on the ground before storing them in large, unsealed paper bags or hessian sacks. Potatoes in store need air but not light, so make sure light cannot enter the bags or sacks at any point. Put the sacks on upturned boxes to keep them off the ground.

Either hang onions, shallots and garlic in nets, or tie them to lengths of rope. Store marrows and pumpkins in nets, or old nylon stockings or tights, hanging from a beam or the shed roof. Leave parsnips, swedes and leeks in the soil until they are needed, as they will withstand frost.

GATHERING THE HARVEST

Green gooseberries Put gooseberries into a colander, discarding any that are squashy or damaged. Use fresh, freeze or make into jams and jellies.

Store potatoes in sacks Leave potatoes to dry on the ground and check them for damage before storing them in large, unsealed paper bags (below) or hessian sacks

Handfuls of leeks Lift leeks with a fork as required – they will keep growing through winter. Give them a good shake to get the bulk of the soil off the roots.

Twist gently Don't be tempted to pull ripe apples off the tree as this will cause others nearby to drop. Instead lift and gently twist.

Forced rhubarb The beautiful vivid stalks of forced rhubarb are ready for pulling in spring. Don't force the same crown the following year as it will need time to recover its vigour.

Water and watering

Attitudes towards watering have changed greatly in recent years. Water metering, frequent periods of drought and recurring national water shortages have made people much more conscious of the need to conserve both tap and rainwater.

Being thrifty with this precious commodity is an easily acquired habit that can be beneficial both to the environment in general and your own crops in particular.

Conserving water

Always collect as much rainwater as possible. Not only is it free, but it is much more beneficial to plants than that out of the tap.

Most properties – even garden sheds and summerhouses – have gutters. If these are connected to a soakaway or the mains drainage system, a diverter can be quickly and easily installed to divert rainwater into a tub or tank. When the butt is full, the rainwater is automatically rerouted back into the soakaway or drain.

There is a whole range of water butts available, from small ones holding a few hundred litres to tanks with a capacity of 1000 litres or more. Where space is at a premium, many of these larger tanks can be installed below ground – even below the vegetable garden itself.

Modern rainwater containers are usually made of plastic, which is easily cleaned, and have lids or are closed tanks that keep larger debris and insects out.

One small butt is not adequate during a long, dry spell. It is often easier to join together several such receptacles with specially designed connectors than replace the original butt with a larger one.

When installing a water butt, always stand it on bricks or a compatible stand so you can fill a watering can from the tap.

An electric pump makes watering easier, and there are several on the market designed for the domestic garden. By connecting a hose to the tap at the bottom of the tub or tank and turning on the pump, the pressure will be high enough to water efficiently.

Automatic watering systems

Watering with a watering can or hose is not always the best way of watering. An automatic drip system is the best way of getting the water to container plants, for example. A length of perforated hose laid along a row of vegetables or looped around the base of a tree will get the water straight to the roots, while reducing evaporation to a minimum. Such systems can be manually operated, or connected to a timer – great for busy gardeners.

Conserving soil moisture

A humus-rich soil holds water much longer than one deficient in organic material. Mulching with manure, compost or weed control sheeting will allow rainwater to penetrate the soil without it

The gentlest spray When watering seedlings fit a fine rose to your watering can. If you point the rose upwards, the spray is even softer – though watch out for the 'running tap' effect that can occur if the rose isn't a really tight fit.

Irrigation system A garden irrigation system uses far less water than an ordinary hose, as it delivers water only where it's needed. It can be adapted to provide a spray instead of trickle-feeding water, by fitting a special micro sprinkler attachment to the nozzle.

evaporating immediately, and regular hoeing will also conserve moisture by breaking capillary attraction at the surface.

In general, a healthy, established crop or plant should only be watered during a severe drought as where the roots are, deep in the soil, there should be enough moisture to see the plants through till the next rain. Inadequate watering often does more harm than good by encouraging the roots to grow up to the surface.

When watering is a must

Newly planted fruit trees and bushes and plants like strawberries must be watered in hot, dry spells, but it is better to water thoroughly once or twice a week than a dribble every day. Newly sown vegetable crops will usually survive without watering – if the drills were watered when the seed was sown – until germination starts. Then the seedlings will show signs of stress if the ground dries out and must be watered immediately. Covering the crop with fleece after sowing until it is well established will reduce evaporation and also transpiration from the leaves.

Young fruit trees and bushes need watering from the time the crop is setting until the fruit is fully developed in all long periods without rain, otherwise much of the fruit will drop prematurely and what is left will be much smaller than it should be.

Crops in greenhouses and covered coldframes will always require regular watering – daily in summer, less frequently the rest of the time, but must never dry out.

Weeds and weedkillers

If you do not control weeds they will, at first, compete with vegetables for plant foods and water, and may later overrun the crop altogether. However, their abundant presence in your kitchen garden does at least show that the soil is fertile.

There are four ways of getting rid of weeds: pulling them up by hand; treating them with chemical weedkiller; hoeing when they first appear; or covering the ground with an impermeable membrane, such as heavy-duty black polythene or one of the proprietary weed control materials sold in garden centres and builders' merchants.

Hoe regularly – at least weekly throughout spring and summer. A few minutes of regular attention are more effective than hours spent in clearing a badly overgrown plot.

The aim of hoeing is to sever the tops from the roots of all seedling weeds so they will not regrow, therefore it is important to keep the hoe blade sharp. A less sharp blade will uproot some weeds; if this is happens in showery weather, be sure to rake up the weeds so that they do not get a chance to re-establish themselves, and put them on the compost heap.

In dry weather, you can leave uprooted weeds between the rows, as they will soon die. Your choice of hoe depends partly on the task and partly on your personal preference.

There are four main types: the draw hoe, which is especially useful for earthing-up potatoes; the Dutch hoe, which is ideal for destroying weeds between rows of vegetables; various types of patent hoes, which are mostly improved forms of the Dutch hoe; and the short-handled, or onion, hoe, which is excellent for accurate weeding close to plants (see pages 12–13).

Whatever type of hoe you use, make the most of hot, dry days – when uprooted weeds wilt and die almost immediately – and hoeing leaves the surface of the soil loose and crumbly.

Hand weeding However carefully you use a hoe, some weeding will still have to be done by hand among close-growing plants, such as peas. Deal with the weeds when they are small, because if left too long their removal will disturb the roots of the vegetables.

Even in a well-tended garden, deep-rooted perennial weeds may get a hold among permanent crops such as asparagus, or among summer vegetables at holiday time. Get rid of them by easing the soil away with a trowel so that enough of the roots are exposed to pull them out cleanly by hand.

Such hand weeding is necessary where perennial weeds grow through a mulch. Otherwise, spot-treat carefully with the chemical weedkiller glyphosate (see below).

Weeding a seedbed In a seedbed, vegetable seeds and weed seeds have exactly the same conditions for germination. The seedlings may therefore, emerge at about the same time, and you may be confronted with a bewildering green carpet in which vegetables are hard to distinguish from weeds. Anticipate this problem at sowing time by inserting small canes at the ends of each row. When growth is about 2.5cm (1in) high, tie string between the canes, so marking the seed row, and hoe to within 2.5cm (1in) on each side.

Hand weed when the vegetables are clearly distinguishable, and thin them at the same time.

When sowing slow-germinating parsnips, sprinkle radish seeds in the drill. The quick-germinating radishes will mark the row for weeding, and provide a crop by the time you need to thin the parsnips.

Using chemical weedkillers Chemical weedkillers are most effective in clearing paths, waste ground and the soil beneath fruit trees and bushes. Their use is more limited in the vegetable garden. Here, periodic digging and regular hoeing keep down both perennial and annual weeds.

The best weedkiller for use in the vegetable and fruit garden is glyphosate. Sprayed on to the leaves, it is translocated to the roots, which are killed.

Careful application If applied with care, glyphosate can be used to weed between vegetables and ornamentals but it can cause damage to any green part of a plant, so it is not easy to apply to just the weeds. It is best used to clear ground before replanting with vegetables and fruit, and for keeping the ground around fruit trees and bushes free from perennial weeds.

Two strengths are available to the home gardener – one which will clear most soft weeds, and a stronger formulation for controlling nettles, brambles and other woody and persistent weeds.

Most weeds will be destroyed with one application, but persistent ones, like bindweed, couch grass, ground elder and horsetail may need two or more applications.

When to apply Glyphosate should be applied in warm weather, when no rain is forecast for at least 6 hours, and may take three weeks or more to kill the weeds completely. Early removal of treated weeds may cause the roots to regrow.

The chemical is neutralised as soon as it touches the ground, which means that you can replant immediately the weeds have died.

Identifying garden weeds Both annual and perennial weeds are relatively easy to control in ground that is cultivated regularly. But sometimes a gardener takes over a neglected plot or faces an invasion by a seemingly indestructible perennial weed from a neighbour's garden.

Among the hardest of these intruders to eradicate are perennials that multiply by rhizomes – creeping underground stems that spread out from the parent plant and throw up fresh shoots to form a new plant.

However carefully and diligently you think you have cleared an area by digging, you could well discover, the following spring, that small pieces that you missed are throwing up new vigorous shoots.

Chemical control with glyphosate is the quickest and most effective way of dealing with such persistent weeds, but if you are trying to achieve an organic garden, or if time is not of the essence, you could instead cover a badly weed infested area with black polythene or weed control membrane. This will clear most weeds within 12 to 18 months providing no light is allowed to get through any rips or tears in the covering.

For this reason it is important to be able to recognise weeds so that the most effective treatment can be given to destroy them. The illustrations on the following pages show some of the most common weeds found in vegetable gardens or under fruit bushes and trees.

WARNING

- **Store weedkillers out of the reach of children.**

- **Never put liquid weedkillers in containers where they may be mistaken for something else.**

- **Read the makers' instructions and carry them out carefully.**

- **Do not use weedkillers in a high wind.**

- **Keep the outlet of the can or spray close to the weeds being treated.**

- **Wash out sprays and watering cans thoroughly after use and use these types of containers specifically for weedkillers.**

Perennial weeds

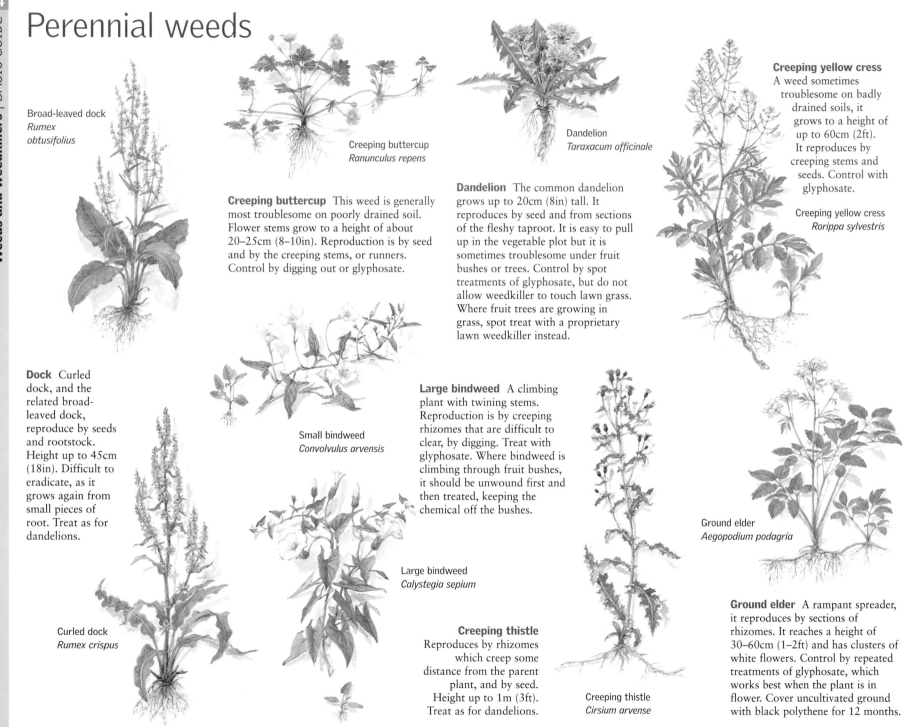

Broad-leaved dock
Rumex obtusifolius

Creeping buttercup
Ranunculus repens

Dandelion
Taraxacum officinale

Creeping yellow cress
A weed sometimes troublesome on badly drained soils, it grows to a height of up to 60cm (2ft). It reproduces by creeping stems and seeds. Control with glyphosate.

Creeping yellow cress
Rorippa sylvestris

Creeping buttercup This weed is generally most troublesome on poorly drained soil. Flower stems grow to a height of about 20–25cm (8–10in). Reproduction is by seed and by the creeping stems, or runners. Control by digging out or glyphosate.

Dandelion The common dandelion grows up to 20cm (8in) tall. It reproduces by seed and from sections of the fleshy taproot. It is easy to pull up in the vegetable plot but it is sometimes troublesome under fruit bushes or trees. Control by spot treatments of glyphosate, but do not allow weedkiller to touch lawn grass. Where fruit trees are growing in grass, spot treat with a proprietary lawn weedkiller instead.

Dock Curled dock, and the related broad-leaved dock, reproduce by seeds and rootstock. Height up to 45cm (18in). Difficult to eradicate, as it grows again from small pieces of root. Treat as for dandelions.

Small bindweed
Convolvulus arvensis

Large bindweed A climbing plant with twining stems. Reproduction is by creeping rhizomes that are difficult to clear, by digging. Treat with glyphosate. Where bindweed is climbing through fruit bushes, it should be unwound first and then treated, keeping the chemical off the bushes.

Ground elder
Aegopodium podagria

Curled dock
Rumex crispus

Large bindweed
Calystegia sepium

Creeping thistle
Reproduces by rhizomes which creep some distance from the parent plant, and by seed. Height up to 1m (3ft). Treat as for dandelions.

Creeping thistle
Cirsium arvense

Ground elder A rampant spreader, it reproduces by sections of rhizomes. It reaches a height of 30–60cm (1–2ft) and has clusters of white flowers. Control by repeated treatments of glyphosate, which works best when the plant is in flower. Cover uncultivated ground with black polythene for 12 months.

Perennial nettle
Urtica dioica

Annual weeds

Groundsel Reaching 8–45cm (3–18in), its heads develop many seeds, which are carried by the wind. Seeds germinate throughout the year. Clean up hoed-off plants as seed heads continue to mature.

Groundsel
Senecio vulgaris

Hairy bitter cress
Cardamine hirsuta

Hairy bitter cress This low-growing weed grows in dry ground and between rocks. It flowers from spring to late summer.

Chickweed
Stellaria media

Chickweed A low-growing weed, this thrives in moist soil. It will flower and forms seeds even in winter.

Nettle Reproducing by rhizomes and seeds, pull out with a gloved hand among vegetables; among fruit trees and bushes control by repeated treatments of 2,4-D – 2,4,5-T, or mecoprop. On waste land treat the whole area with glyphosate or sheet with black polythene.

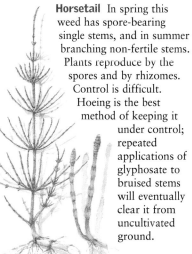

Horsetail In spring this weed has spore-bearing single stems, and in summer branching non-fertile stems. Plants reproduce by the spores and by rhizomes. Control is difficult. Hoeing is the best method of keeping it under control; repeated applications of glyphosate to bruised stems will eventually clear it from uncultivated ground.

Horsetail
Equisetum arvense

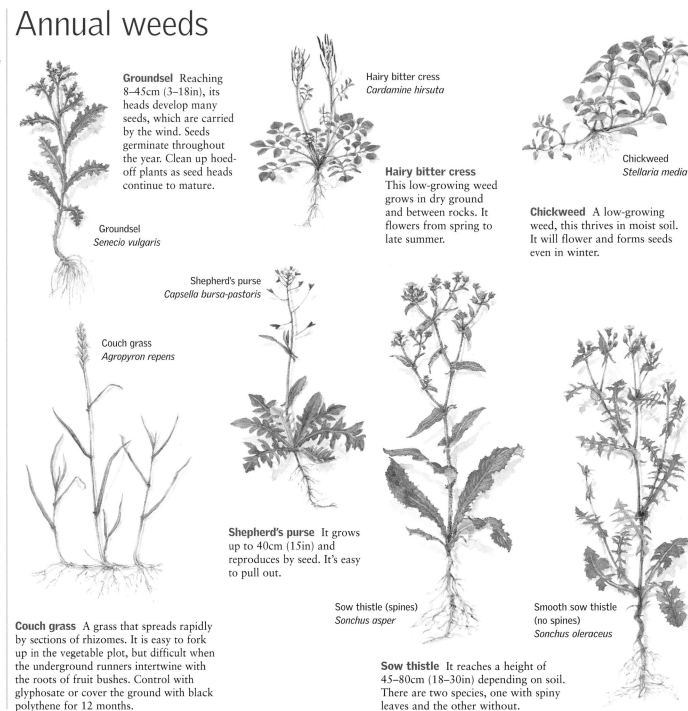

Shepherd's purse
Capsella bursa-pastoris

Couch grass
Agropyron repens

Shepherd's purse It grows up to 40cm (15in) and reproduces by seed. It's easy to pull out.

Couch grass A grass that spreads rapidly by sections of rhizomes. It is easy to fork up in the vegetable plot, but difficult when the underground runners intertwine with the roots of fruit bushes. Control with glyphosate or cover the ground with black polythene for 12 months.

Sow thistle (spines)
Sonchus asper

Smooth sow thistle
(no spines)
Sonchus oleraceus

Sow thistle It reaches a height of 45–80cm (18–30in) depending on soil. There are two species, one with spiny leaves and the other without.

The fruit garden

Few home gardeners nowadays have space for an orchard. Fruit bushes, and certainly fruit trees, have to be fitted in as best they can, often at the expense of ornamental plants or part of the vegetable plot.

Fortunately, fruit trees are attractive as well as productive. If trained as cordons, espaliers or fans, they make effective screens and, to save space, they can be grown in these forms against walls and fences.

Even a small garden can yield heavy crops of fruit. But think ahead before you plant, as fruit trees and bushes could be in the ground for the next half century.

Ready for winter Pruned and staked with sturdy supports, the trees in this little orchard will withstand winter's onslaught.

The choice of what to grow is governed not only by the family's tastes, but also by the amount of space you have available. When making your plans, bear in mind the area a tree will occupy at maturity, not at the time of planting – use the chart on this page to guide you.

In the early years, grow salad crops or strawberries between trees and bushes to make the best possible use of the ground. As the trees mature, they will cast too much shade for you to grow crops between them.

You will also have to decide, again according to taste and available space, on a balance between soft fruits and tree fruits, which include apples and pears, apricots, cherries, peaches and nectarines, and plums and gages.

Soft fruits, produced on bushes, canes or low-growing plants, include black, red and white currants, gooseberries, loganberries and strawberries. They bear crops sooner after planting than fruit trees and often give a better return for the area they occupy.

Fruit trees, however, eventually produce heavy yields in good seasons, and if you have a surplus, you can store it, bottle it, make it into jam or freeze it.

Drawing up a plan

To help to decide what fruits to grow, and where best to plant them, draw up a plan in the manner suggested for an overall garden design (page 8).

Make a list Make a list of fruits in order of preference by your family. Fit these into the plan, working out how many trees and bushes you need by looking at the

pages for each specific fruit (see Growing and Cooking, pages 66–225), and checking planting distances against those shown in the chart (below).

Avoid planting fruit trees in the vegetable garden itself, where they will shade other plants and complicate your cropping plans. If soft-fruit bushes or canes are to be planted in this area, form a block at one side of the vegetable plot so that they do not interfere with rotation of crops.

Choose a sunny wall or fence for a fan-trained apricot, peach or nectarine. If you have additional wall space, use it to grow cordons or espaliers of apples and pears,

and cordons of gooseberries and red or white currants. Alternatively, trees and bushes trained to these forms make excellent screens.

Decide on the fruits to grow as feature trees beside the lawn or at the back of flowerbeds. Apples, pears and cherries on dwarfing rootstocks are probably the best for this purpose, though a plum on dwarfing stock would be suitable for a large garden.

Whatever the fruit, be sure to choose a self-fertile variety if you are planting a tree on its own.

Soft fruits Finally, fit soft fruit bushes, canes and plants into your plan. You will probably find that

you do not have enough room for some of the fruits at the bottom of your list of preferences. However, don't be tempted to plant trees, bushes and canes too close together in order to squeeze them in.

Choose varieties to suit your taste, your region and the specific site you have chosen.

Do not, for example, choose a 'Bramley's Seedling' apple if you have only a small garden as it grows too vigorously and will occupy too much space. Choose instead, one of the recommended culinary apples and check with the supplier that it has been grafted on to dwarfing rootstock.

USEFUL FACTS ABOUT FRUIT TREES AND BUSHES

FRUIT	FORM OR VARIETY	DISTANCE BETWEEN TREES AND BUSHES	BEST AGE TO PLANT (YEARS)	TIME UNTIL CROPPING (YEARS)	EXPECTED LIFE (YEARS)
Apples	Bush	3.6–6m (12–20ft)	2–3	2–4	30–50
	Dwarf pyramid	1.5–1.8m (5–6ft)	2–3	2–4	30–50
	Cordon	75cm–1m (2½ft–3ft)	2–3	2–4	30–50
Apricots	Fan-trained	3.6–4.5m (12–15ft)	3	2–3	15–20
Blackberries	'Himalaya Giant'	3.6–4.5m (12–15ft)	1–2	1–2	10–12
	Other varieties	2.5–3.6m (8–12ft)	1–2	1–2	10–12
Cherries	On dwarfing stock	4.5–6m (15–20ft)	2	4–5	30–50
Currants	Black	1.5–1.8m (5–6ft)	2	2	12–15
Currants	Red and white bush	1.5m (5ft)	2	1–2	15
	Single cordon	40cm (15in)	2	1–2	15
Gooseberries	Bush	1.5m (5ft)	2–3	1–2	10–15
	Single cordon	40cm (15in)	2–3	1–2	8–12
	Triple cordon	1m (3ft)	2–3	1–2	8–12
Loganberries		3.6m (12ft)	1	2	10
Peaches	Bush or fan-trained	3.6–4.5m (12–15ft)	1–3	3–4	15–30
Pears	Bush	3.6–4.5m (12–15ft)	3–4	2–4	40–60
	Dwarf pyramid	1.2–1.5m (4–5ft)	2–3	2–4	40–60
	Cordon	75cm–1m (2½ft–3ft)	2–3	2–3	40–60
Plums	Bush	3.6–4.5m (12–15ft)	2–3	2–4	30–50
	Pyramid	3–3.6m (10–12ft)	3	3	30–50
Raspberries		45cm (18in)	1	1	6–10
		1.8m (6ft) between rows			

Which form of tree?

The traditional orchard tree, known as standard or half standard, is too large for most modern gardens, but there are other forms and sizes to suit smaller gardens. These include bush, dwarf pyramid, cordon, espalier and fan-trained trees.

Bush The largest of these is the bush, with a height and spread of 2.6–5.8m (8–18ft). The size varies according to the type of fruit and, with apples and pears, to the vigour of the rootstock on which the tree has been grafted.

Shoots of varieties of apples are grafted on to the rootstock of derivatives of wild apples, and pears onto those of quince. The various types of rootstock affect the eventual size of the tree and how it will crop. When buying apple or pear trees, always check that they are on dwarfing stock.

Apples, pears, cherries and plums can be grown as bush trees.

Dwarf pyramid In a small garden, apples and pears are better grown as dwarf pyramids which, because of the dwarfing stock on which each variety is grafted and the way you prune them, will grow to only 2.1m (7ft), with a spread of about 1.2m (4ft).

Cordon Most economical in terms of space is the cordon, which consists of a main stem with short, fruiting spurs. It is grown diagonally against a wall, or in the open supported by posts and wires.

Apples and pears can be grown by this method. Although the yield per tree is small, a row of cordons, set only 80cm–1m (2½–3ft) apart, is very productive for the amount of space occupied. Also, several varieties can be grown in a comparatively small space.

Espalier Apples and pears can also be grown as espaliers, which carry fruit on a number of tiers, or horizontal branches. An espalier can be planted against a wall or fence, or trained on wires supported by posts to form a screen between your garden and your vegetable plot.

You can even grow espaliers as a form of ornamental and productive fence to surround your entire garden – an ideal solution on many new estates where only post-and-wire fences are provided.

'Step-overs' are single-tier espaliers sometimes used to edge a border or path. A fan-trained tree is the best form for growing peaches, nectarines or apricots against a sunny wall.

Family tree In a very small garden where there is room for only one tree, you could grow a 'family tree' on which three varieties of apples, or three varieties of pears, are grafted on to a single rootstock.

This means that the selected varieties pollinate each other and give a succession of fruit over an extended season.

Again, it's important to check that dwarfing stock has been used, or the tree may grow so large that it defeats its original purpose of saving space.

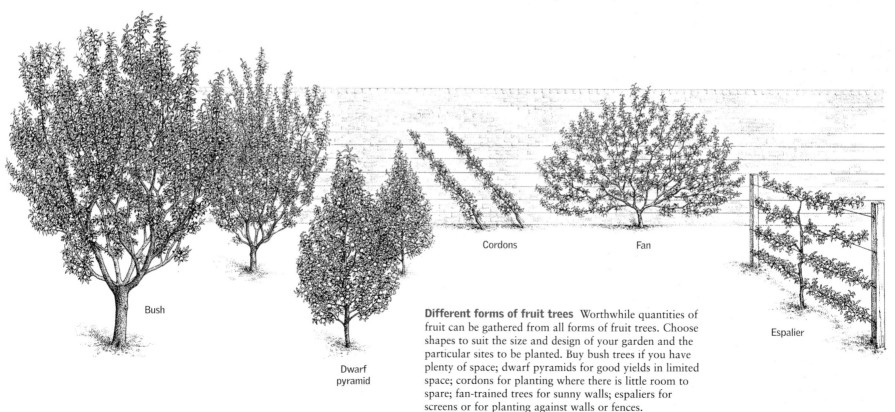

Bush

Dwarf pyramid

Cordons

Fan

Espalier

Different forms of fruit trees Worthwhile quantities of fruit can be gathered from all forms of fruit trees. Choose shapes to suit the size and design of your garden and the particular sites to be planted. Buy bush trees if you have plenty of space; dwarf pyramids for good yields in limited space; cordons for planting where there is little room to spare; fan-trained trees for sunny walls; espaliers for screens or for planting against walls or fences.

Heeling in Provided the ground is neither frozen nor too wet, trees or bushes can be set in a trench temporarily – with their roots well covered – until you are ready to plant them.

Buying and planting fruit trees

Plant bare-root and rootballed fruit trees and bushes while they are dormant – from late autumn to just before growth begins again in early spring. The earlier they are planted the better.

Rootballed trees have their roots enclosed in soil or compost held in place with elastic mesh; this keeps the roots in good condition until you are ready to plant. Some nurseries recommend that the net should not be removed, but the trees generally establish better during the dormant period if it is cut off and the trees or bushes planted like bare-root specimens.

It is essential that you avoid planting when the ground is waterlogged or frozen. Fruit trees and bushes grown and sold in pots or similar containers may be planted at any time of year, except during periods of waterlogging, severe frost or drought.

When ordering or buying, choose two or three-year-old trees for bush, cordon and dwarf pyramid forms of apples and pears. Do not buy maidens or one-year-old trees, or you will then have to do the initial shaping, which is best left to an expert. If you are a keen and experienced gardener, you might prefer to do this for yourself.

Buy espaliers with two tiers, or sets of horizontal branches, and fan trees with four ribs. Buy currant bushes at two or three years old and cane fruits at one year old.

Preparing for planting

Prepare the ground according to the individual needs of each type of fruit. (See Growing and Cooking, pages 66–225.)

Do not take bare-root bushes or trees out of their wrapping if they are delivered at a time when the weather and ground are unsuitable for planting.

Keep them instead in a cool but frost-proof shed or garage. The day before planting, unpack the trees or bushes and, if the roots are dry, soak them in water for 12–24 hours. Thoroughly water containerised specimens and allow to drain before planting.

Heeling in

If the ground is suitable but you have no time to plant the trees in their permanent positions, unwrap them and heel them in – that is, lay them close together in a trench, lightly firming soil over their roots.

Place trees at an angle, away from the prevailing wind. They may be left like this for several weeks.

Supporting

If you are planting bush trees or dwarf pyramids, you need to drive

a short stake support into the planting hole before you plant the tree. Tie the tree to the stake with strong string, wrapping sacking round the stem; or use adjustable ties, which can be bought at garden centres.

Before planting a fan-trained tree against a wall or fence, fix horizontal support wires with vine eyes, sold at garden centres and DIY stores. Stretch the wire tightly, preferably with straining bolts.

Plant with the stem about 25cm (9in) from the wall; leaning the stem slightly towards the wall. This will allow plenty of room for subsequent growth. Before planting cordons and espaliers against a

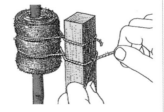

Staking For bush trees and dwarf pyramids, drive a short stake into the planting hole before putting the tree in position.

SECURING TREES TO SUPPORTING STAKES

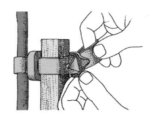

Adjustable tie This is the best method. Slacken the tie as the trunk swells.

Twine and sacking Wrap sacking round the trunk to prevent damage to the bark.

SUPPORTING WIRES FOR FANS AND ESPALIERS

Vine eyes For a secure fixing, drill holes and screw the eyes into wall plugs.

Straining bolts Turning the nut tightens the wire and prevents subsequent sagging.

wall or fence, fix the support wires in the same way as for a fan-trained tree but space the lowest 80cm (2½ft) above the ground, with 60cm (2ft) intervals between this and subsequent wires.

Cordons and espaliers When growing cordons or espaliers in the open, sink stout posts at 2.7m (9ft) intervals to carry the support wires. Treat the posts with wood preservative – or, better still, buy them pressure treated – and sink them at least 60cm (2ft) in the ground, leaving 2m (7ft) above the ground.

Brace each post with a 2m (7ft) length of wood, setting it at an angle with about 60cm (2ft) in the ground. Use straining bolts to make the wire taut, and adjust these later if necessary.

Raspberries Erect similar supports for raspberries (see page 195), but the posts need be only 1.7m (5½ft) above the ground for most varieties, and 2m (6ft) for more vigorous varieties. Set the bottom wire 80cm (2½ft) above the ground, with the middle and top wires at 45cm (18in) intervals.

Planting

Before planting, use a pair of secateurs to cut back damaged roots to the undamaged part and shorten long roots. This is not necessary with a containerised tree, but you may need to tease out a few of the outer roots if the tree was pot-bound.

Hold the tree upright on the planting site with its roots spread out on the ground. This will indicate the size of the hole needed. Dig the hole deeply enough for the tree to be planted at its previous

Pruning fruit trees and bushes

Planting a bare-root tree Make a hole large enough to spread the roots; fork over the base and add compost. Hold the tree in the hole and back-fill, shaking it down as you go. Tread firmly and water well. Then apply a mulch.

depth, which you can see from the soil mark on the stem. Fork the soil at the bottom to improve drainage, adding well-rotted compost if the soil is poor. For bush and pyramid trees, drive in the stake.

Stand the tree about 10cm (4in) from the stake – or 25cm (9in) from the wall – spread out the roots and sift in fine soil. Shake the stem vigorously up and down so that soil settles between the roots and there are no air pockets. Firm the soil carefully with your feet.

Plant cordons with the stems leaning towards the north, if possible, so that they receive maximum light. Allow 2.5m (8ft) between the base of the last cordon in a row and the end of the wires or wall.

With all forms of tree, ensure that the graft between the stock and the tree is at least 10cm (4in) above soil level after planting, otherwise the tree may put out its own roots and override the dwarfing effect of the rootstock.

This graft or union looks like a knobbly projection between the stem and the roots.

Fruit bushes are planted in much the same way, except that a supporting stake is usually unnecessary. Plant them at the same depth as they were in the nursery, again as shown by the soil mark on the stem.

After planting
The roots of trees and bushes are often disturbed by frost in the winter after planting. Check every week or so and firm any cracked ground with your feet.

Water the ground copiously during dry spells throughout the year after planting.

Pruning is a task that frightens many beginners. You can allay your fears by understanding a few simple principles.

In the first few years of the life of a tree or bush, the aim is to create the desired shape: to encourage the tiers, or horizontal branches of an espalier, for example, or produce the open-centre 'goblet' form of a bush tree.

After the framework of the main branches has been established, often about the fourth year after planting, the aim is to keep a balance between new growth and fruit production.

These aims are achieved in different ways and at different times of the year, according to the type and form of the fruit tree or bush. The calendar on page 51 will remind you when to prune, while detailed pruning instructions are given for each fruit between pages 66 and 225.

Hard pruning usually results in strong growth. A shoot that is cut back severely will quickly produce vigorous leaf-bearing shoots, which become non-fruiting stems. This is the aim in the early stages, when building up the formative framework of the tree, but it is a disadvantage when the aim is to produce fruit buds. To achieve this, prune lightly or not at all.

If a tree has been neglected, spread the pruning over three years so that the shock of heavy pruning is lessened.

First take out diseased wood and branches that cross or rub against each other. In the case of a bush tree, the final stage is to remove branches in the centre.

Carry out this pruning at a time to suit the particular type of fruit.

Tools for pruning
A sharp pruning knife can be used surely and cleanly by a nurseryman or woman or an experienced gardener. In the hands of a beginner, however, it may cause more harm than good by tearing the bark or making jagged cuts, which can let in disease.

Most of us are much better off with a good pair of secateurs. There are two types:

Bypass or parrot-bill These have curving blades and a scissors-like action. Most modern pruners are a variant of this design.

Anvil secateurs These have a thick edge, or anvil, against which a single blade does the cutting.

The two types are equally effective and which you choose is entirely a matter of preference. Both can be used to prune stems up to 1cm (½in) in diameter. Do not try to cut stems thicker than this or the blade and joint may suffer permanent damage.

For stems up to about 4cm (1½in) in diameter use either long-handled loppers, which have sturdy, secateur-like blades and long handles to give extra leverage, or a pruning saw.
For branches thicker than 4cm (1½in), use only a pruning saw.

Get cutting blades sharpened every year or two, according to how much they are used. This is a job best done by a professional grinder or you risk damaging the cutting edge.

Oil tools carefully after use before putting them away.

Secateur options
Many gardeners manage with only a pair of secateurs: a saw and long-handled loppers are needed mainly for renovating neglected trees. Choose from bypass, scissor-like secateurs (far left) or anvil-type (left).

How to prune

When pruning for new growth, cut just above a healthy growth bud, pointing in the direction the new shoot is to grow.

Start the cut opposite to, and level with, the base of the bud and slant it upwards to finish just over the bud. Cut cleanly, using a steady pressure, so that the blade does the work. Do not twist the secateurs, otherwise the cut may have a ragged edge.

When pruning to remove an unwanted shoot, make the cut flush with the bark of the major branch from which it was growing, leaving no stub.

Lopping When removing a large branch, first cut it about 25cm (10in) from the trunk. Saw from the bottom until a quarter of the way through, then complete the cut from the top. Finally, remove the stub close to the bark of the trunk.

This method reduces the risk of the wood and the bark splitting.

Always paint large wounds with a wound compound to prevent the entry of disease spores.

Notching It is sometimes necessary to stimulate the growth of dormant buds after pruning. This may, for instance, be helpful when training espaliers, in order to stimulate the two buds that will develop into the next tier. You are unlikely to need to do this with vigorous varieties.

This encouragement to growth is given by notching the bark just above the bud. Use a sharp knife designed for the job.

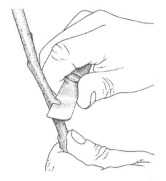

Notching To encourage a growth bud to develop, use a sharp knife to make a shallow notch in the bark immediately above the bud.

WHERE TO MAKE PRUNING CUTS

Correct cut, cleanly made and close to the bud.

Too close This cut may damage the bud.

Too far This stub is too long and will die – when it may harbour disease.

Make pruning cuts just above, but not too close to growth buds. Then new shoots develop without a stub of dead wood beyond.

Leader The leading shoot of a branch, which is allowed to grow until it reaches the desired length. The harder it is pruned, the more vigorous will be the new growth.

Spur A short lateral branch bearing clusters of fruit buds. On old fruit trees spurs may become overlarge, and need drastic pruning.

Growth buds They are smaller and more pointed than fruit buds and lie flat on the stem. Leaves or new shoots are produced by growth buds.

Fruit buds These plump, rounded buds – much more prominent than growth buds – produce blossom, then fruit.

Certain parts of the tree – shown above – are referred to repeatedly in pruning instructions. Try to learn these terms before attempting practical work. Trees differ in their fruiting habits and this, too, affects pruning. Spur-fruiting trees, such as 'Cox's Orange Pippin', fruit only on spurs. Tip-bearing trees, such as 'Worcester Pearmain', fruit on the tips of the previous summer's growth as well as on spurs.

UNDERSTANDING THE TERMS USED IN PRUNING

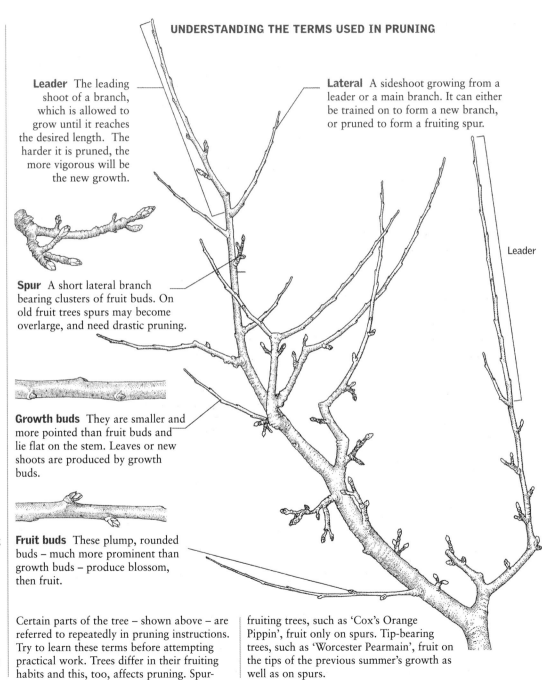

Lateral A sideshoot growing from a leader or a main branch. It can either be trained on to form a new branch, or pruned to form a fruiting spur.

Leader

REMOVING A BRANCH

Step 1 Cut from beneath Make the first cut about 25cm (10in) from the trunk. Saw from the underside, cutting about a quarter of the way through.

Step 3 Remove the stub Cut close to the trunk. Again, first saw from the underside and then complete the cut from above.

Step 2 Then cut from above Complete the cut from the top of the branch. Cutting in two stages prevents the wood and bark splitting as the branch falls.

Step 4 Clean and dress Pare away any rough edges with a sharp knife. Apply a wound compound to the cut to prevent disease spores from entering.

MONTH-BY-MONTH PRUNING REMINDERS

Timing is a vital factor in pruning fruit trees and bushes. Follow this guide, because correct pruning is essential to keep a balance between fruit production and the growth of new wood. Some trees may also be put at risk of infection by being pruned at the wrong time of year. Detailed instructions are given on pages 66–225.

Late winter
- Start the programme of rubbing out and pinching back **apricots**, **peaches** and **nectarines** after growth begins.
- Prune **apples** and **pears** (bush and half-standard), if not completed earlier; also cut back autumn-fruiting **raspberries** to within a few inches of the ground.

Early spring
- Cut back newly planted autumn-fruiting **raspberry** canes.
- Prune **gooseberries**, and red and white **currants**, if not done in winter, and bush **plums**.

Mid spring
- Prune pyramid **plums** during the formative period, for four or five years after planting.
- Pinch back unwanted growth buds on **peaches**.

Late spring
- De-shoot wall-trained **peaches** and **nectarines**.
- Shorten leaders of mature **apple** and **pear trees** grown as cordons, dwarf pyramids or espaliers.

Early summer
- Remove shoots growing towards or away from a wall from fan-trained **cherries** and **plums**.
- Pinch out young growth of **figs**.

Midsummer
- Prune **gooseberries** and bush and cordon white **currants** after fruiting.

Late summer
- Summer-prune cordon, espalier and dwarf pyramid **apple** and **pear** trees, and pyramid **plums** when new growth is mature.
- Cut out **raspberry** canes after fruiting.

Early to mid autumn
- Prune **blackcurrants**. Prune **cherries**, **damsons** and **plums** after fruiting. Prune wall-trained **peaches** and **nectarines** after fruiting.
- Cut down **blackberry** and hybrid **berry** canes that have fruited. Cut back shoots of trained sweet **cherries** that were pinched back in early summer.

Late autumn
- Prune, if not already done, black, red and white **currants**, **blackberries**, **gooseberries** and hybrid **berries**. If there is a likelihood of bullfinch attacks, delay pruning of red and white **currants** and **gooseberries** until early spring.

Early winter
- Prune established bush and half-standard apple and pear trees.
- After planting, cut back red and white **currant** and **gooseberry** bushes, and **apple** and **pear** trees.
- Prune dwarf pyramid, cordon and espalier **apple** and **pear** trees for three or four years after planting.

Mid winter
- Continue pruning **apples** and **pears** (bush and half-standard); also **gooseberries** and red and white **currants**, if not completed earlier.
- Cut back newly planted **blackberry**, hybrid **berry** and **raspberry** canes.
- Protect buds from birds.

Protecting fruit from birds

Having lavished months of care and devotion on your fruit bushes, nothing is more exasperating than to see birds gorging themselves on your just-ripening crops.

The problem is on the increase, since less soft fruit is grown nowadays than a few years ago.

It is of little use to erect scarecrows, old CDs or sticks bearing rattling lengths of silver foil, because within a short time, the birds get used to them and the deterrent effect is lost.

One measure worth taking is to place shallow dishes of water near the bushes in hot weather: there is no doubt that thirst adds to the birds' determination to get at the fruit. But the only real protection is some kind of netting enclosure.

Temporary protection

If you have only a few canes or plants, it is hardly worth building a permanent fruit cage around them. Protect them instead with a cheaper, temporary structure which you can easily remove at the end of the fruiting season.

This is most economically achieved by using plastic netting supported on stakes or canes. To prevent the mesh from tearing, it's a good idea to cover the tops of the sticks with inverted jam jars, choosing jars to suit the diameter of the posts.

Even when firmly seated in the soil, the sticks should be long enough to support the netting well above the tops of the plants or bushes you wish to protect. Make sure you allow for the plants growing taller during the season.

Insert the canes or stakes in the ground no more than 1.2m (4ft) apart, and put the jam jars on top. Peg the netting along one side of the plants, then carry the other edge up and over the stakes. Pull the netting taut so that it rides clear of the top of the plants, and peg it down firmly all round – including an overhang at each end of the structure.

TEMPORARY CAGE

Top the canes with jam jars
Insert canes on either side of a row of plants. Fasten the netting on one side and pull it over.

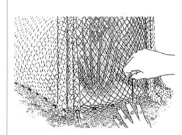

Peg down the net Use wire or wood pegs to anchor the edges of the netting, or weigh it down with stones or bricks.

Firm pegging is particularly important, since blackbirds and thrushes generally look for an entrance at ground level.

Protecting wall fruit

Blackberries and hybrid berries, as well as peaches, nectarines, apricots and other fruits grown against a fence or wall, also require protection.

This is best provided by fixing a 5cm x 2.5cm (2in x 1in) batten along the wall above the tops of the fruit trees or canes. Stud the upper edge of the batten with small nails spaced not more than 15cm (6in) apart and hook the upper edge of the netting onto them. Bring the lower edge forward and pass it over stakes set in the ground in front of the fruit.

These forward supports need only be high enough to keep the netting clear of the fruit when pulled taut and pegged down at the front and ends.

Remove the netting as soon as the fruits are harvested.

The framework can be used in late winter with a waterproof cover to keep rain-borne peach leaf curl spores (page 245) off peaches, apricots and nectarines.

Protecting strawberries

These succulent fruits are a favourite target for almost every bird in the neighbourhood, and you have little hope of keeping many for yourself unless you protect the plants. Many gardeners simply spread nets over them, but this is quite useless. The birds sit on the mesh and peck the berries through it as it sinks beneath their weight.

In addition, some fruits always grow through the mesh and it is difficult to avoid pulling them off when lifting the net during picking.

The answer is to construct a temporary fruit cage by placing jar-capped canes around the perimeter of the bed and drawing the net tightly over them. A height of 60cm (2ft) is sufficient, but if the bed is a wide one you will need extra rows of supports to prevent the net sagging onto the plants.

Permanent enclosures

The ideal, though rather more expensive, way of protecting your soft fruit against birds is by constructing a permanent fruit cage. Its size depends on how much space you are prepared to allocate to soft-fruit growing; but an area of, say, 6m x 4.5m (20ft x 15ft) or more, would probably justify the building of a permanent enclosure – perhaps against a wall.

To make the best use of it, plant your bushes or canes as close together as you can without overcrowding. Expense can also be saved by using plastic or nylon mesh for the walls of the cage rather than the more traditional wire netting. Support the netting on posts spaced no more than 1.8m (6ft) apart. In order to give plenty of headroom, the tops of the posts should be 1.8m (6ft) from the ground, but allow an additional 60cm (2ft) to give a firm footing in the soil.

Your cage should last for a long time if you use 5cm x 5cm (2in x 2in) pressure-treated timber for intermediate posts, and 7.5cm x 5cm (3in x 2in) braced posts at the corners. Alternatively, use metal piping. Link the post tops with heavy-duty wire stretched taut.

Further wires stretched from side to side across the cage should be enough to keep the roof netting from sagging unless the cage is wider than 5.4m (18ft), when an additional row of supports up the centre is advisable.

Lay plastic or nylon netting over the roof and take it down the sides to the ground. Fix the net to the posts with brass hooks or pastic cable ties and metal eyes and peg the bottom firmly to the ground, or secure with bricks or large stones.

If there is a risk of bullfinches stripping the dormant fruit buds during winter, leave the netting up throughout the year. Shake the snow off as necessary, otherwise the weight of a heavy accumulation may cause the entire structure to collapse or become distorted.

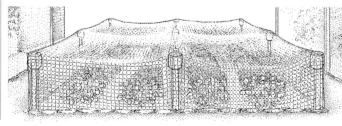

Strawberry patch You can net a larger patch of strawberries by spacing your jam jar-topped canes all over the bed in between the plants. Make sure the tops are at least 30cm (12in) higher than the plants. Peg the sides and ends to the ground to keep birds out.

Raising your own fruit bushes

The grafting techniques needed for propagating tree fruits, such as apples and pears, are beyond the scope of most amateur gardeners. But even beginners can increase their stock of soft fruits.

It is important to use healthy wood. Where a soft fruit bush is showing signs of disease, or yield and vigour have started to decline, it is best to dig up and dispose of the old bush and replace it with healthy stock, ideally elsewhere in the garden.

Propagation can be done in three ways.

Cuttings Pieces of new growth are cut into lengths and inserted in the soil to root. Gooseberries, and all three types of currants, can be propagated by this method.

Layering To increase blackberries and loganberries, either bend over the tips of young canes and cover with soil to induce the tip to root and new canes to spring up or layer from pliable young shoots.

Root division Raspberry canes push out underground suckers which become the new canes. These new plants can be severed from the parent and planted in a permanent position.

Blackcurrants

Take cuttings of straight, firm stems of blackcurrants in autumn. Trim back with a pair of secateurs any soft growth at the top to just above a bud. Cut at the base below a bud, leaving a cutting 20–30cm (8–10in) long. Remove any leaves, but leave all the buds.

Dig out a trench in well-cultivated soil, making one side vertical by pushing the spade straight down. Stand the cuttings 15cm (6in) apart against the straight wall, with not more than three buds showing above the surface. Buds in the ground will produce new basal shoots.

Fill in the trench carefully, firming the soil round the cuttings with your hand or by treading. If the soil is heavy, sprinkle a little coarse sand round the cuttings as you fill in. Inspect the cuttings every few weeks, and firm soil cracked by frost.

Blackcurrants root easily, and about nine out of ten should show growth in spring. If growth is good during summer, move the bushes to their permanent positions in autumn. If it is poor, leave the cuttings in the trench and, during the winter, cut all shoots to a few inches above ground level to promote vigorous growth in the next season.

Gooseberries

A gooseberry bush is grown on a single stem, or 'leg', and this requires a different preparation from that given to blackcurrant cuttings.

In autumn, remove well-ripened shoots about 30cm (12in) long and rub off all but the top three or four buds from each. These will eventually grow into the main branches.

Bury the cutting to a little over half its length, leaving an exposed stem with the buds at the top.

Treat afterwards as for blackcurrants. Results, however, are unlikely to be as good.

Red and white currants

In mid to late autumn, prepare cuttings, 25–40cm (10–15in) long as for gooseberries. Cut off any unripened wood, just above a bud. No trimming is necessary, however, if the cutting is brown at the tip.

Trim the lower end to just below a bud, and rub off all but the four or five buds at the top. These will eventually form the branches. Dip the lower end of each cutting in hormone rooting powder.

Set cuttings 15cm (6in) apart in a trench, with the top 13cm (5in) above soil level.

Cuttings of red and white currants root readily and they can be planted in their permanent positions the following autumn.

Raspberries

During the growing season, raspberry plants produce new canes at the base of the parent plant, and other canes, called suckers, that spring directly from the roots that spread out beneath the soil.

Those at the base are trained as fruiting canes for the following season, while suckers are generally destroyed by hoeing.

You can, however, increase your stock by allowing the sucker canes to grow and using the strongest of these as new plants.

In late autumn or early winter, lift the suckers with a fork and sever them from the parent cane with secateurs. Lift them carefully with their roots intact and replant immediately. Grow these new canes only from healthy parent stock. Always buy raspberry canes which are certified to be virus free. You can safely take new plants from them for the next two or three years, but you risk spreading virus disease to take them after that.

Blackberries and hybrid berries

The easiest method of raising blackberries and loganberries is to 'layer' shoots so that they root in the soil. Between the middle of summer and mid autumn – though not before it has developed fully – bend down a shoot that has formed during the season, strip back the leaves and make a nick in it with a sharp knife. Dig a hole about 10cm (4in) deep where the cane will touch the ground and fill it with seed compost. Angle the split cane over the hole and peg in place with galvanised wire bent into two hairpin shaped staples. Alternatively, anchor the growing tip of a cane into the compost-filled hole (below). It will root within weeks and a shoot will spring up.

In early winter, sever the new plant from the parent by cutting about 30cm (12in) from the base. Transfer the plant to its permanent position the following spring.

Peaches

You can grow peach trees from stones. In early autumn, set a stone in a pot of potting compost. Seal the pot in a polythene bag and put in a cool spot – about 10°C (50°F). When a shoot appears put the pot in a sunny window. Move it to the garden when 15cm (6in) high and plant in its permanent position when a year old.

TIP-LAYERING FOR BLACKBERRIES

In summer Bend a new shoot down to the ground, tie it to a cane and bury the tip in a pot of seed compost sunk into the ground. Keep the compost moist.

Check the new plant The tip should begin to root and a new plant develop in a few weeks: scrape away some of the compost to check for new roots. In autumn, sever the new plant from its parent and replant into its permanent position.

Greenhouse gardening

A greenhouse helps to lengthen the gardening year, turning late winter into spring and coaxing summer to linger into autumn. For this reason alone, a greenhouse is worth having.

For a gardener keen on growing food, it is also a sound investment. The initial cost can be returned in a few years by the savings on plants raised from seed, and by harvesting vegetables when they are at their most expensive in the shops.

As a greenhouse is a long-term investment, spend some time looking at the pros and cons of different types before making your decision.

How big a greenhouse?

If you want to grow vegetables, such as early lettuces, tomatoes, cucumbers, sweet peppers and aubergines, as well as raising seedlings, a glazed greenhouse 3m x 2.5m (10ft x 8ft) is ideal.

If you cannot afford this, either buy a similar-size greenhouse made of polythene or buy a smaller glazed greenhouse and use it to raise early plants and to grow a summer crop of tomatoes.

When deciding on the size, consider the cost of heating if you plan to grow plants much earlier than their normal season. The larger the area of glass, the more expensive the greenhouse will be to heat, although you can divide larger greenhouses into different temperature zones, using polythene sheeting or bubble insulation.

Types of greenhouses

Although greenhouses are made in many shapes and sizes, there are four main types:

Vertical-sided Free-standing buildings with a span roof and vertical side walls – or walls set at only a slight angle – are the most popular type of garden greenhouse. Some have timber cladding up to the staging, or are designed to be built on low brick walls, but for food growing buy one with the glass extending to the ground on at least one side. Then you can plant tomatoes, melons or cucumbers directly in the greenhouse border.

Dutch light Large panes and angled side walls let in the maximum amount of light. Greenhouses of this type are ideal for growing plants directly in the soil because the glass extends to the ground.

You can put up temporary staging in late winter and spring for trays of seedlings, and remove it in summer to make space for growing plants in the ground.

Lean-to As its name implies, this type of greenhouse is erected against a wall of a building, preferably facing south where it will get most sunlight. It is warmer than a free-standing greenhouse, and you may even be able to heat it by extending your household central heating. Depending on your house, and the size of the structure, you may need local authority approval.

Circular This shape of greenhouse has many advantages. Light is let in evenly and little floor space is wasted because working in the

centre allows you to reach all the plants without having to walk up a path. The flow of air is controlled by ventilators at ground level and an adjustable dome at the top.

Wood or metal?

The choice of cedar wood or an aluminium-framed greenhouse is again a personal one. Cedar blends more happily into the garden background, and needs to be treated with a wood preservative only every two or three years. Some metal greenhouses are now powder-coated in a green or white finish, which looks good in a traditional setting.

Wooden greenhouses are generally delivered in prefabricated sections. The sides, gable ends and roof sections are easily bolted together, but the glazing may take several days to complete.

Here an aluminium greenhouse has an advantage, because its panes can be clipped into place in a few hours. Another advantage of an aluminium model is that it needs no maintenance.

However, a wooden one tends to be slightly warmer as timber retains heat better than aluminium.

Polythene greenhouses

The big advantage of a polythene greenhouse, sometimes called a polytunnel, over a glazed one is its lower initial cost. A polythene house 6m x 3m (20ft x 10ft), for

example, may cost only half as much as a glazed house measuring 3m x 2m (10ft x 6ft). So you could put a substantial part of your vegetable plot under cover for a relatively small outlay. This is fine if you have plenty of space, but if you have a small plot, a small greenhouse used mainly for raising seedlings might be more practical.

A polytunnel consists of a framework of tubular steel hoops covered by special horticultural polythene. The hoops are driven directly into the soil or into tubes set in the ground. Foundations are unnecessary and the greenhouse can be erected and dismantled quickly: a mobility that can be exploited in a crop-rotation plan.

CHOOSING A GREENHOUSE TO SUIT YOUR NEEDS

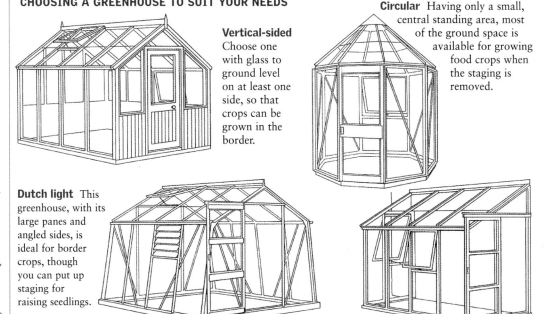

Vertical-sided Choose one with glass to ground level on at least one side, so that crops can be grown in the border.

Circular Having only a small, central standing area, most of the ground space is available for growing food crops when the staging is removed.

Dutch light This greenhouse, with its large panes and angled sides, is ideal for border crops, though you can put up staging for raising seedlings.

Lean-to Built against a south facing wall, this saves space and is warmer than a free-standing greenhouse.

MINIATURE LEAN-TO

The combination of rising costs and small gardens has created the need for a really small greenhouse. The mini-greenhouse is basically a coldframe, turned on end to form a small lean-to against a house or garage wall. Sliding or hinged doors give access to shelves that can be placed at any height. You work from outside the lean-to – a bit of a disadvantage in bad weather.

Though of limited value for growing food crops, the mini-greenhouse is useful if you have restricted space. If you live in a flat, you can put one on a sunny balcony or patio. It is ideal for raising seedlings, and the wall against which it is sited will help to retain day-time warmth for dispersal during the night.

The greenhouse could be used, for example, for growing tomatoes on one part of the plot one year and moved to another part where the tomatoes are to be grown the following year.

In late winter and spring, seedlings can be raised in pots or trays on a trestle table or on staging sold by the greenhouse manufacturers.

Problems with polythene The main disadvantage is condensation, producing a high humidity which can cause a number of plant disorders. This problem varies with the make and design, so choose a greenhouse with ventilators on the door and the far gable.

Heating, combined with good ventilation, will also reduce condensation, but the choice of heater is important – natural gas or paraffin heaters only make the problem worse.

An electric heater is better, and the ideal is an electric fan heater, which drives warm air to all parts of the greenhouse. In summer, the fan can be switched on without the heating element to keep the air moving.

A second drawback with polythene is that it is not as efficient as glass in keeping out frost. During frosty spells, therefore, shut the ventilators

Polytunnels This tunnel shape is typical of polythene greenhouses. More important than its shape is the ventilation provision. Check that there is a free flow of air to minimise condensation. Double-skinned versions provide better insulation and heat retention.

Ventilation Opening windows are essential to aid air flow. Automatic ventilation brackets are available to open and close vents according to temperature or humidity within the greenhouse.

during the afternoon to increase the humidity. Condensation will then act as an insulator and slightly reduce the loss of heat.

A third disadvantage is that the polythene needs replacing at least every two to four years and this regular expense must be balanced against the initial cost of the greenhouse.

The polythene used in most greenhouses is treated with an ultra-violet light inhibitor to slow down deterioration caused by

Greenhouse thermometer Choose a maximum-minimum thermometer to record the daily range of temperatures, especially in a propagator where the right heat is critical for germination.

sunlight. Wind is also a problem, not so much for wear and tear as for the loss of heat.

Siting a greenhouse

Choose a position where the greenhouse catches the most sunlight, especially in late winter and early spring when seedlings are beginning to grow. Avoid low-lying ground, which may get waterlogged or become a frost pocket, and choose, if possible, a position sheltered from cold winds.

It does not matter whether you align the greenhouse north-south or east-west – but try to position the door on a side away from icy winds. If you plan to lay electricity and water supplies, then don't site it too far from the house.

Wherever you site it, lay a path to the door, and if it's near a fence or wall, allow space all round for glazing and maintenance.

Insulate Insulating a greenhouse in winter and early spring with bubble wrap acts very much like double glazing. Buy it off the roll from garden centres, along with all necessary fixings.

Greenhouse management

Correct ventilation, watering and temperature control are necessary for success with greenhouse crops.

Ventilation Fungus diseases flourish in a warm, stagnant atmosphere. At least two roof ventilators, as well as one or more at a lower level, are needed to ensure an adequate air flow in hot weather. If necessary, the door can be propped open, or an opening hatch fitted in the lower half of a wooden door. An electric fan heater, with the heating element switched off, is also an efficient method of keeping the air flowing.

The guesswork and constant attention can be relieved by installing automatic ventilation. There are two kinds. One is a vent opener sensitive to temperature changes, which automatically opens or closes the ventilator

GREENHOUSE SHADING

Greenhouse plants must be protected from direct sunlight in the height of summer, and seedlings need shade even on a bright spring day.

• Ideally, shading should be on the outside of the roof, an inch or two above the glass. Slatted wooden blinds that can be rolled up and down are the most efficient, but they are expensive.

• Less costly alternatives are adjustable green plastic blinds inside the greenhouse, sheets of green polythene for clipping to the inside bars of the roof and fine-mesh plastic netting that also allows air to circulate. Horticultural fleece, particularly in a green colour, can also be draped in front of the glass rather like net curtains.

• The cheapest form of shading is by painting the glass with a white, opaque shading paint specially formulated for greenhouses. Always paint the outside of the glass. Shading the inside keeps out sunlight without reducing the temperature.

• Shading paint can make the greenhouse too dark on very dull days, but a paint is now available that turns opaque in bright sunlight but becomes more transparent on dull days. Some external shading paints turn transparent in rain but do not wash off until the glass is cleaned at the end of the season.

Golden delight Tomatoes, such as this yellow cherry variety, are a popular greenhouse choice, and can produce much better crops inside than grown outdoors.

according to the temperature in the greenhouse. It does not need electricity to operate it.

The other is an electric extractor fan, which is thermostatically controlled to provide a continuous gentle movement of air and also to reduce condensation. These fans are easy to install and cheap to run but they need a mains supply.

Watering A regular supply of water is essential at all stages of plant growth, but sometimes watering by hand is not possible or practical. There are two methods of automatic watering which not only save a good deal of work, but also result in better plants.

The first, capillary irrigation, works on the principle that if a pot plant sits on a bed of wet sand the

compost in the pot will soak up enough water to keep the plant healthy. A number of capillary systems are available.

In one, mains water is taken from a tank fitted with a ballvalve. The water runs into a trough on one side of the staging and is drawn by a glass-fibre wick into the sand tray. In another system, pots stand on a highly absorbent mat, which again takes water from a mains-supplied trough.

Capillary watering is suitable only for seedlings and for plants small enough to be grown on the greenhouse staging.

An entirely different system – suitable for plants of all sizes – is trickle irrigation, in which a pipe is laid near the plants and drip nozzles release a steady supply of water. Liquid fertiliser can be added so that plants are watered and fed at the same time. More sophisticated greenhouse irrigation systems are also available, often with timing devices, and usually electronically controlled. Check the internet to see what is available.

Temperature control

It is a challenge trying to keep a greenhouse warm enough for seedlings to thrive in spring, and cool enough to prevent plants from getting scorched in a summer heatwave.

The biggest problem with artificial heating is the cost, but vegetables and fruits do not need such high temperatures as ornamental plants, and you can grow worthwhile crops even in an unheated greenhouse. If you are trying to economise, wait until late winter or early spring before making your first sowings.

The only time when fairly high temperatures are needed is when sowing seeds of some tender vegetables. But even then there is no need to heat the whole greenhouse. Either use an electric propagator for raising the seedlings, or put the greenhouse heater under the staging and erect a polythene canopy over the top to trap the warmth.

A saving on heating bills can also be made by insulating the greenhouse in winter and early spring with bubble wrap. This is sold off the roll in garden centres, along with all necessary fixings. You can choose small or large 'bubbles' – the larger bubble insulation is more efficient. Insulating a greenhouse in this way can save up to 20 per cent of

Greenhouse staging You can buy purpose-built shelving – or staging – which helps you to maximise the use of space in the greenhouse.

heating costs. If you decide to warm the whole greenhouse – so you can enjoy a variety of crops while shop prices are very high – the choice of heaters is wide.

Gas Designed to burn mains or bottled gas, this type of heater has accurate temperature controls and costs less to run than most other forms of heating.

Heaters running on mains or piped bottled gas (from large cylinders situated outside the greenhouse, for example) have to be installed by law by an approved, qualified (CORGI) fitter, so the initial outlay for the heater and for having it installed may be high, especially if the greenhouse is some distance from the house.

Bottled gas running costs are higher than mains gas.

Paraffin Portable paraffin heaters give reasonable frost protection, but they have limitations as the sole source of heating. Water vapour produced during combustion creates excessive condensation unless you provide constant ventilation.

Running costs are lower than for electricity but higher than mains gas. Few types have automatic temperature control.

Paraffin heaters need regular maintenance to reduce fumes; a badly maintained flame can also produce sooty smoke, which can be a disaster in a greenhouse.

Electricity This is the most expensive form of heating, and the most versatile. Once an electricity supply has been connected, you can run not only heaters, but also a propagator, lighting and a fan extractor. You must employ a qualified electrician for the wiring. There are two main forms of electrical heaters: tubular and fan.

Tubular heaters are fixed to the sides or floor of the greenhouse, and take up little room. Fan heaters move the air more vigorously, as well as raising the temperature.

Whatever the form of heating, it is worth hanging a maximum-minimum thermometer in the greenhouse, to keep track of how the system is behaving when you are not there.

Staging

Manufacturers supply staging – slatted benching – to fit their greenhouses. Alternatively, you can make it yourself using 50mm x 50mm (2in x 2in) timber for the legs, and 50mm x 25mm (2in x 1in) timber for the top framework. Nail 50mm x 12mm battens to this frame to form the slatted bench.

Cross-bracing (made of 50mm x 25mm timbers) between the legs and upper frame will keep the structure steady, provided you stand the legs on bricks or slabs.

Greenhouse hygiene

A greenhouse provides ideal conditions for plant growth, but these can be just as encouraging to pests and diseases. Keeping the greenhouse tidy will cut down on a lot of trouble. If you have a shed, keep pots and similar items there rather than in the greenhouse when not being used.

Inspect plants daily during the growing season and deal with trouble promptly. See individual crop entries (pages 66–225) and the section on pests and diseases (pages 238–49). Remove diseased, dying and dead plant material immediately.

Use biological controls or yellow sticky traps to reduce pests, but do not use both at the same time or

Wood-framed greenhouse The glass is held in place by a timber framework, supported on solidly constructed block walls. Gutters collect rainwater from the sloping roof.

Strawberries under glass If you pot up some healthy strawberry runners in autumn and move them into the greenhouse for winter, you should be able to enjoy early fruits when shop prices are high.

the traps will catch your controls as well as the pests.

Check new plants before putting them in the greenhouse. If possible, 'quarantine' them first. Raising your own plants will prevent accidental infection. Keep plants strong by potting on when necessary, feeding regularly and watering carefully.

In late autumn, when growth has stopped, wash down the interior with hot, soapy water or a disinfectant. A pressure washer is a good piece of equipment for blasting dirt from crevices.

Before sowing in late winter, clean the glass inside and out to let in as much light as possible.

Maximising productivity

To get the best value out of your greenhouse, aim to have crops at various stages for at least ten months of the year. The table alongside will help you to decide what to grow and when to make the sowings.

The growing programme can be divided into two periods. During the first, from mid winter to late spring, sow crops that will continue to maturity in the greenhouse, and others that will eventually be transplanted in the open.

During the second, overlapping period – from early spring through autumn – grow a selection of plants, such as tomatoes, in pots, grow bags or in the greenhouse border (marked * in the table).

During summer, you can almost double your growing space if you dismantle the staging and store it elsewhere. Do this in late May, when the last of the tender young plants are moved outdoors.

GROWING FOOD CROPS IN A GREENHOUSE

VEGETABLE OR FRUIT	TIME TO SOW	MINIMUM TEMPERATURE	REMARKS
Aubergines	Late winter–very early spring*	18°C (64°F)	Grow on at a minimum temperature of 16°C (61°F)
Broad beans	Mid–late winter	Unheated greenhouse	Plant out in mid spring
French beans	Early–mid spring	Unheated greenhouse	Transplant cloches about 6 weeks later
	Mid spring	Unheated greenhouse	Plant outside late spring
Runner beans	Mid spring	Unheated greenhouse	Transplant cloches about 6 weeks later
	About 2 weeks later	Unheated greenhouse	Harden off and plant outdoors end of spring
Cauliflowers	Mid–late winter	10°C (50°F)	Harden off in early spring and plant out
Chicory	Force roots early winter–early spring	7–16°C (45–61°F)	
Cucumbers	Frame varieties*: late winter	21°C (70°F)	Grow in greenhouse. Minimum night temperature: 16°C (61°F)
Lettuces	Early autumn	Unheated greenhouse	Transplant to greenhouse border
	Mid autumn–late winter	10–12°C (50–54°F)	Transplant to greenhouse border Min. 10°C (50°F)
Marrows and courgettes	Mid spring	Unheated greenhouse	Harden off and plant out late spring
Melons	Casabas*: Early–mid spring	16°C (61°F)	Grow on in greenhouse
	Cantaloupes: mid spring	16°C (61°F)	Transplant to frames or cloches from late spring
Pumpkins	Late spring	18–21°C (64–70°F)	Harden off and plant out early summer
Rhubarb	Force under staging, early winter–early spring	7–16°C (45–61°F)	
Sweetcorn	Spring	Unheated greenhouse	Harden off and plant out in late spring
Sweet peppers	Early spring*	16–18°C (61–64°F)	Grow in the greenhouse with minimum night temperature of 7°C (45°F), or harden off after about 6 weeks and plant out at end of spring
Tomatoes	Mid winter*	15°C (59°F)	Grow on in heated greenhouse
	Early spring*	15°C (59°F)	Grow on in unheated greenhouse
	Spring	15°C (59°F)	Harden off and plant in open late spring-early summer

Greenhouse crops The asterisk * indicates plants, such as tomatoes and cucumbers, that you can grow to fruition in the greenhouse, whether in pots, grow bags or in the greenhouse border.

Coldframes

The small area covered by a coldframe is often the most intensively cultivated part of a vegetable plot. With careful planning, you can grow a succession of food crops in a coldframe throughout the year.

If you have a greenhouse, or if you plan to germinate seeds indoors, the coldframe is a useful halfway house in which to harden off plants before they go to their permanent positions outdoors.

A coldframe should never be empty. For instance, during winter it can be used for protecting cauliflower plants that will be set outside in early spring, or for lettuces to heart up in spring when they are expensive in the shops.

Seeds of onions and lettuces can be sown in winter, two months earlier than in open ground.

After the onions and lettuces are planted out, their places can be taken in late spring by french and runner beans. These, in turn, will be planted in the open, to be replaced by cucumbers or melons that will grow to maturity in the coldframe during summer.

When harvesting is complete, it's time to restart the cycle and sow cauliflowers and lettuces to overwinter in the frame.

If you decide to lay electric soil-warming and air-warming cables, your coldframe can become a miniature greenhouse and your scope is widened even further.

Types of coldframe

Coldframes are sold in a variety of sizes and materials. There are wooden frames with glass tops (called lights); metal frames with

MAKING A COLDFRAME

Step 1 Marking out Saw the plywood sheet in half lengthways. On one half mark the two sides, each 1.2m (4ft) long, 50cm (20in) high at the back, 38cm (15in) at the front. On the other half mark out the back 1.2m (4ft) by 50cm (20in), and the front 1.2m (4ft) by 38cm (15in). Cut all four panels.

Step 2 Reinforce Frame the inside of each panel by cutting, glueing and nailing four battens round the perimeter.

You will need
- 2.4m x 1.2m (8ft x 4ft) sheet 1cm (½in) thick treated exterior plywood
- 21m (70ft) of 5cm x 2cm (2in x ¾in) treated battening
- 1.2m x 1.25m (48in x 50in) rigid plastic panel (or polythene sheeting)
- 4cm (1½in) galvanised nails, 6cm (2½in) countersunk screws, four 5cm (2in) angle brackets and screws, pair 10cm (4in) brass butt hinges and screws, waterproof wood glue, weatherproof adhesive tape or staplegun, white woodstain, wood preservative and paintbrush
- Pencil, tape measure, straight edge, saw, hammer, drill, screwdriver

Step 3 Join front to sides Drill five evenly spaced holes 2–3cm (1in) in from the edges and screw in place. Repeat for the back panel. Measure both diagonals to check that frame is square – they must both be equal.

Step 4 Make a frame for the lid Cut and assemble four lengths of batten on edge for the lid frame. Butt join with glue and screws; then reinforce the inside corners with angle brackets.

Step 5 Strengthen the lid Fix a central batten from front to back with glue and screws. Then cut four short battens as glazing bars and space evenly, two in each half of the lid.

Step 6 Paint the inside white Use the white woodstain to paint the inside of the frame as this will help to improve light levels.

Step 7 Attach the lid Use the brass hinges and screws to fit the lid to the back edge of the frame.

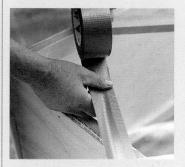

Step 8 Glaze the lid You can use rigid panels, drilled and screwed to the lid, sealing the edges with tape, or stretch a sheet of thick polythene over the lid and staple in place underneath.

Step 9 Preserve it Paint the outside with wood preservative. Make a notched pole to act as a lid stay.

glass or uPVC lights and frames made completely of transparent plastic. Each type has advantages and disadvantages.

Wooden frames Fitted with glass lights, these are the most efficient in conserving heat. Most are made from cedar, which has natural resistance to rot and insect attacks. They can last for many years but they are slightly more expensive than other types.

Metal frames These can be fitted with glass or acrylic lights. Acrylic is cheaper and a better option in a garden where children play ball games. Aluminium frames are light and easy to move from one part of the garden to another. They need no maintenance. Galvanised-iron frames are about the same price as aluminium and, though a little heavier, can be moved easily.

Plastic frames In addition to being the cheapest, they let in the most light. They lose heat quickly

at night, however. This makes them of more use in the shorter, warmer nights of spring than in the winter.

DIY coldframes A simple frame can be made from odd pieces of wood, some chicken wire and a sheet of heavy-gauge polythene. A practical size is about 1m (3ft) square with the back wall 40cm (16in) high and the front 30cm (12in) high. Staple the chicken wire tautly to the top and fix the polythene over this with drawing pins. The wire will prevent the polythene from sagging under the weight of rainwater. To get to your plants, lift the frame to one side.

Siting and management
Choose a sunny, sheltered spot. If the frame has a single, sloping light, face this towards the south.

Prepare the ground thoroughly some weeks before planting by digging in well-rotted manure or compost at the rate of a bucketful to the square metre (square yard). Just before planting, rake into the top a general fertiliser at 90g per

square metre (3oz per square yard), together with about half a bucketful of moist peat substitute (often sold as 'soil conditioner').

The manure and peat substitute will ensure that the ground is moist enough for overwintering crops, which should not be watered until they start to develop in spring.

During late winter and early spring conserve heat in metal frames either by lining the inside walls with polystyrene tiles or by drawing up soil round the outside.

During frosts, cover the lights of any type of coldframe with sacking or similar, removing this during the day. In warm spells open the light to let in air, and close it again in the evening.

Protect against slug damage (page 241) in the coldframe after sowing and planting, and keep a look out for other pests while plants are growing.

Growing in heated frames
If you don't have the money or the space for a greenhouse, a heated coldframe is a good alternative. Use along with an unheated frame or cloches, where you can harden off plants before putting them in their permanent positions.

Soil-warming cables laid under the surface will hasten early crops and allow sowing at least a month earlier than in the open. However, this won't provide full protection against frost. On cold nights, cover the lights with several layers of fleece or other insulating material.

Alternatively, install air-warming cables on the inside walls of the frame, to supplement those under the soil, to give frost protection.

Timber or metal? Wood, which helps to conserve warmth, needs treating with preservative every year or two. Most timber frames have sliding lights, but some are hinged. In an aluminium coldframe, the sides may be metal-clad or glazed. Glass sides are ideal for spring and summer crops, but are colder in winter.

Crops under cloches

Gardeners discovered many years ago that a plant could be forced into early growth by protecting it with a glass cover. A French designer came up with a practical and efficient shape for forcing individual plants. It was a bell-shaped glass dome and it became known as a cloche, which is the French word for bell.

The name has persisted, although most cloches are no longer bell-shaped and they now protect whole rows instead of individual plants. Because of its cost, glass has largely been replaced by rigid plastic or polythene.

Lantern cloches These heavy glass-and-iron cloches look beautiful and work well. For ventilation, simply angle the lid.

Since most vegetables are grown in straight rows, a number of cloches set in a line, with the ends closed to exclude draughts, are ideal for producing early crops and for protecting tender plants.

Generally, sowing and planting are possible about a fortnight earlier in cloches than in the open. This early start, resulting in earlier harvesting, makes it possible for more than one crop to be grown on the same ground in a season.

As an example of a cropping programme lettuces, sown in late autumn, may be cut in mid spring, to be followed by early fruiting dwarf tomatoes. These in turn, may be succeeded by spring cabbages planted in the open. The cloches, meanwhile, are transferred to another part of the plot to restart the cycle.

This mobility enables a gardener to use a cropping technique whereby cloches are moved from one row to another as the season progresses.

Early carrots, for example, may be given a good start by being covered at the beginning of spring. They then go on to mature in the open and the cloches are moved four to six weeks later to enable newly planted tomatoes to become established. Three to four weeks later still, the cloches are again moved, this time to protect heat-loving plants, such as aubergines and peppers, for the rest of summer or until they are too tall to fit underneath.

Types of cloches
Cloches are obtainable in a variety of sizes, shapes and materials – some much more expensive than others. Costs, naturally, are related to the size of the cloche, so it is a

good idea to decide what crops you intend growing under cloches before buying them.

If you plan to grow only early lettuces, a cloche 30cm (12in) wide and 25cm (9in) high is adequate. For growing melons to the fruiting stage, however, you will need cloches about 45cm (18in) wide and 30cm (12in) high.

Measure the row, then buy enough cloches to form unbroken protection over it. Remember to buy two end panels, as the cloche is not fully effective until these are placed in position. Each type of material used for cloches has advantages and disadvantages.

Solid plastic Moulded plastic cloches are cheaper than those made of glass but, initially, are more expensive than polythene. They have a greater life expectancy than glass, which is easily broken, or polythene, which must be replaced every few years.

DIFFERENT TYPES OF CLOCHE

Tunnel Takes a little longer than others to erect. Inexpensive, and easy access. Versatile, as basic structure will support polythene, netting or fleece.

Moulded plastic Easy to use, but some types are expensive. Check expected life span.

Barn (glass) Four panes are secured in a wire frame. Good protection, but costly.

Corrugated PVC Simple and long lasting. Cloche is secured in wire hoops.

Tent (glass) Patent clips enable odd panes to be used. Restricted height and width. Plastic tents are also available.

Other cloches Plastic bells, available in several different sizes (page 62), are good for protecting single plants; glass-and-iron lanterns can be used to shelter a tray of seedlings or an individual plant (facing page).

Bell jars These plastic bell jars have adjustable vents on top and holes around the bottom for ventilation.

Plastic cloches can be made of corrugated PVC, uPVC, polypropylene, clear polystyrene or a number of proprietary materials.

Makers have taken advantage of the flexibility and lightness of the plastic. You can, for example, buy cloches that are 1.8m (6ft) long – a size that would be far too heavy and cumbersome to handle in glass. Only three of these cloches are needed to cover a row 5.5m (18ft) long, so simplifying the task of moving them from crop to crop.

Widths of cloches vary from 20cm (8in) for growing seedlings, to 80cm (30in), in which two or three rows of vegetables can be grown to maturity.

Heights vary from 10cm (4in), for seedlings, to 40cm (15in),

for fully grown plants such as bush tomatoes.

Solid plastic cloches are available with straight sides, or curved into hooped tunnels. Both designs are equally effective, but some straight-sided models have the added refinement of ventilation flaps to reduce condensation and promote air circulation. Condensation in solid plastic cloches is not, however, as serious as in polythene tunnels.

Polythene These cloches are obtainable either as separate units, which are then put end to end, or as a complete tunnel cloche (sometimes called a polytunnel) made from a length of polythene draped over wire hoops.

Polythene is obtainable in various gauges, or thicknesses. The thinnest, 150 gauge, is the cheapest, but it will last only a year or two. Heavy-duty 500 gauge is more expensive but will last three or four years, if you look after it.

Polythene treated with an ultraviolet inhibitor to slow down deterioration is available from horticultural suppliers. This lasts longer than untreated material.

Condensation can be a problem with polythene as it can provide optimum conditions for the spread of fungal diseases. It is therefore important to ventilate the cloches to clear the condensation and get air circulating.

As polythene is light and unbreakable it has a big advantage over glass when being moved from one crop to another. Its lightness can be a disadvantage, however, in areas subject to high winds. If gales are forecast, anchor individual cloches with bricks, or form an inverted 'V' over them with canes driven into the ground. Tunnel cloches are anchored by their method of construction.

Glass Cloches made from glass have proved their worth for many years, but the cost of glass and delivery has made them an expensive investment. Many garden centres now carry only a restricted stock, while firms that sell by mail order sell only the wire supports – it's up to you to buy the glass from a local glazier. If you want to go down this route, order horticultural glass, which is cheaper than window glass.

Breakages also add to costs, but glass has some advantages over rigid plastic and polythene. When kept clean, glass cloches let in the maximum amount of light, and on cold, clear nights they retain heat better than polythene. Ventilation is good and on exposed sites their weight makes them more secure than lighter materials.

There are three shapes of glass cloches – the tent, the low barn

Traditional glass bells These old glass cloches show exactly how 'cloches' got their name.

CONSTRUCTING AND USING TUNNEL CLOCHES

The cheapest form of cloche is a '**tunnel**' made from a series of galvanised hoops pressed firmly into the ground and covered with a sheet of light-gauge polythene. A second hoop holds the polythene in place.

Kits containing hoops and about 10m (30ft) of 150–gauge polythene are obtainable from garden centres. The hoops will last for many years, but the polythene deteriorates in sunlight and needs to be replaced with new sheeting every year or two. The tunnels can be fixed in place or moved from row to row in a matter of minutes.

There is no need to move the cloches to gain access for sowing or planting, or to provide ventilation. Simply slide back one side of the polythene cover.

Insert wire hoops Set the hoops about 1m (3ft) apart, using a garden line as a guide to ensure a straight row.

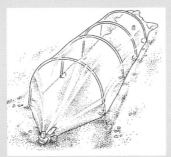

Knot one end of cover Tie the end to a peg inserted 60cm (2ft) beyond an end hoop. Draw cover over the hoops.

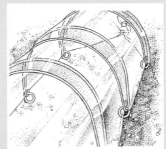

Secure other end of cover Tension the cover by clipping the outer hoops onto loops in the supporting hoops.

and the high barn. A tent cloche consists of two sheets of glass about 60cm x 30cm (24in x 12in) fixed at the top by a galvanised-iron clip to form a pitched roof or tent. Tent cloches are useful for raising seedlings or for single rows of crops such as lettuces, carrots and beetroots.

Barn cloches have four panes of glass, two forming sides and two the pitched roof. A low barn cloche is 60cm (2ft) long and 30cm (12in) high. With a width of about 60cm (2ft), it is possible to grow a central row of lettuces and outer rows of carrots or beetroot. The lettuces will be harvested first, leaving the other crops to mature. A high barn cloche is as wide and long as a low barn but the height is about 50cm (20in). A row of these cloches is useful for getting plants such as aubergines, tomatoes and peppers to a fairly advanced stage before high summer, when protection is no longer necessary.

Growing under cloches

If possible, prepare the ground at least a month before sowing or planting to give the soil time to settle. Dig in well-rotted manure or compost at the rate of a bucketful to the metre run. About a fortnight before sowing or planting, rake into the surface soil a dressing of general fertiliser at about 50g to the metre (2oz to the yard) run.

Mark a row with a line, leave this in position, and cover the row with the cloches to warm up the soil. Secure the end panels with two canes driven into the ground. The cloches must be removed at sowing or planting time and the purpose of leaving the line is to centre the row where the plants will get most headroom.

After sowing or planting, take action to prevent slug or snail damage (page 241) and replace the cloches in exactly the same positions as they were when the ground was being warmed.

Sowing and growing Sow small seeds about 5mm (¼in) deeper than in the open because the surface dries during the warming-up period. Do not water until the seeds germinate. Water the soil after setting out young plants, however.

After that, cultivation is the same as for growing in the open. Although the surface soil may look dry, a few inches down it will have about the same moisture content as the uncovered soil alongside. Capillary action ensures that water reaches the plants' roots.

Climate management Although any type of cloche provides artificially benign growing conditions, you may need to take action when there are sudden changes in the weather.

If spring days are unusually warm, open up some continuous

cloches or slide back the polythene of a tunnel cloche, to allow air to circulate. Replace or close the cloches an hour before sunset.

If late spring frosts are forecast, cover tender plants, such as tomatoes, with four or five sheets of newspaper or a double thickness of fleece in the evening and remove them in the morning.

A week before moving cloches from one row to another, harden off, or acclimatise, the protected plants that are about to be left in the open. To do this, leave off some cloches during the day and replace them in the evening.

Fruit under cloches

Melons and strawberries are usually the only fruit grown under cloches, but the results are usually highly successful.

Cloches serve a dual purpose when covering strawberries (page 52). They make it unnecessary to net against bird attacks and, if put in position in late autumn or early winter, will provide an earlier crop than outside, generally in May.

PROGRAMME FOR SOWING AND PLANTING UNDER CLOCHES

VEGETABLE OR FRUIT	TIME TO SOW *ONLY IN HEAT	TIME TO PLANT UNDER CLOCHES	TIME UNDER CLOCHES
Aubergines	Early spring*	Late spring	Late spring–autumn
Broad beans	In the north, winter		In the north, winter–spring
French beans	Spring		Early–late spring
Runner beans	Middle of spring	Middle of spring	Middle–late spring
Carrots	Early spring		Early–mid spring
Lettuces	Late summer	Autumn	Autumn
	Autumn		Winter
	Late winter		Autumn–spring
			Winter–late spring
Marrows	Spring*	Late spring	Late spring
Melons	Mid spring*	Late spring	Late spring–early autumn
Onions	Winter		Winter–early spring
Peas	Autumn		Autumn–spring
	Late winter		
Peppers	Early spring*	Early–mid spring	Early spring–autumn
Radishes	Autumn		Autumn–early spring
	Winter–early spring		Autumn–early spring
Strawberries		Early winter–late spring	late spring
Sweetcorn	Mid spring	Late spring	Mid–late spring
Tomatoes	Mid spring*	Late spring	Late spring
Turnips	Late winter		Late winter–late spring

When to sow The asterisk * indicates sowing periods that only apply in heated propagation conditions.

GROWING CROPS UNDER CLOCHES

Soil preparation Dig the soil several weeks before sowing, so that it settles. Rake in fertiliser a fortnight before sowing.

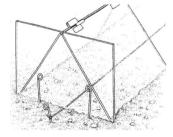

Warming the soil A fortnight before sowing, place cloches centrally over a garden line. Close each end of the row with glass.

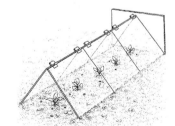

Planting – and after Set the plants, or sow seeds, along the line and replace cloches. Take action to prevent slug damage.

Frost precaution On clear evenings in spring, place layers of newspaper over the glass. Remove next morning.

GROWING and COOKING

Angelica

This tall, flowering herb is a member of the parsley family. It makes an imposing display at the back of a herb garden or flowerbed, especially when it reaches its full height of 2–3m (7–10ft).

Angelica is a biennial that dies after it has produced seeds. However, if the stems are cut back before they flower it can be kept alive for several years.

Add the aniseed flavoured stems and leaves when stewing apples or rhubarb; pick young stems and side-growths to preserve in sugar; or infuse the leaves to make a refreshing herbal tea.

Angelica has always been surrounded by superstition and is credited with having magical and medicinal powers. It takes its species name, *Angelica archangelica*, from Michael the Archangel. Legend has it that a monk praying for a cure for the plague had a vision in which the archangel showed him the herb. Thereafter, it was said that each year, on May 8th – the day the archangel appeared – angelica would come into bloom.

Planning the crop
Angelica does best in deep, rich, moist soil in a sunny or partly shaded position.

How much to grow These plants grow vast and most gardens would be overwhelmed by more than one or two plants.

Growing tips
Whether you buy seeds or keep seeds from one of your own plants, sow them as soon as possible, because they will grow only if planted within three months of ripening. Sow straight into the ground or in seed-plug trays and leave outdoors – the hardy seedlings can survive frost and should be exposed to winter weather. Transplant seedlings to their final positions in spring in deep moist soil – ideally with the roots in shade and tops in the sun.

Pests and diseases
Aphids (page 238) are the pests most likely to occur on angelica. Otherwise, it is generally disease-free.

Harvesting stems, leaves and seeds
Pick the young, soft leaves to use fresh in late spring. Use the stems of the second year's growth to cook with stewed fruit or preserve as candied angelica – familiar as those bright green crystallised strips used to decorate cakes and desserts. Collect ripe seeds in autumn.

Preparing and cooking
Add slices of raw, peeled stems – chopped like celery – to salads. The chopped stems also give a novel flavour to stewed fruits, such as apple or rhubarb, or to fruit pies and crumbles. They're also used in jams and preserves. Angelica stems are not suitable for freezing.

Candied angelica is made by boiling the stems in sugar syrup.

The tender leaves are slightly bitter, with a mild liquorice flavour, that goes well with fish or adds a kick to green salads.

The seeds have a mild aniseed flavour and are used in Middle Eastern and Moroccan dishes. An extract from the root is used to flavour aperitifs and liqueurs.

AT-A-GLANCE TIMETABLE
SOWING
AUTUMN
Sow newly ripened seeds in September and keep outdoors
SPRING
Transplant to final growing positions
HARVESTING
LATE SPRING AND SUMMER
Tender leaves for salads; stems for using in stewed fruit dishes
EARLY AUTUMN
Ripe seeds for cooking/sowing

Apples

'Cox's Orange Pippin'

'Bramley's Seedling'

Apple trees do best in an open, sunny, but sheltered site. They will grow in most soils, except those that are waterlogged or have a high lime content. Apples thrive inland throughout the British Isles but don't do well in coastal areas exposed to salt-laden winds. In the north there is a greater risk of blossom being destroyed by spring frosts.

The earliest apples are ready for picking and eating in August; the latest can be stored for eating until as late as the following May.

Bush tree

Dwarf pyramid

Originally growing wild in Europe and the Near East, the apple is one of the oldest fruits known to man, and also one of the most widely cultivated.

Although many of the apple trees planted in long-established gardens require a good deal of space, trained and dwarf forms can now be grown in even the smallest town garden.

You can also buy 'family trees', in which three or four varieties are grafted on a single rootstock to provide a succession of fruits.

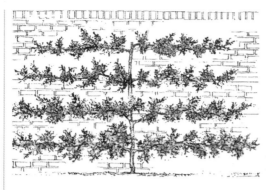

Espalier

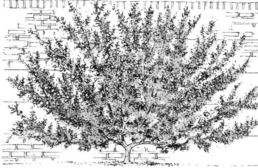

Fan-trained

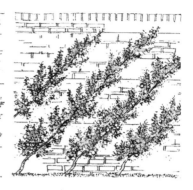

Cordon

Planning the crop
Prepare the site in autumn by forking in plenty of well-rotted manure or garden compost. Leave to settle for at least a month before lightly forking and levelling the soil prior to planting.

Tree shapes You may already have apple trees in your garden, but if you've decided to plant new trees, you can choose forms and varieties best suited to the site.
Bush trees A good choice if you have plenty of room; plant these 4–6m (12–20ft) apart. A single, bush tree may produce 90kg (200lb) or more of fruit, depending on the variety, with an average yield of 35–45kg (80–100lb).
Dwarf-pyramid trees These are suitable where space is more restricted; set them about 2m (6ft) apart. One tree may produce 7kg (15lb) or more of apples, with an average yield of 4–5kg (8–10lb).
Single-stemmed cordons Trained on wires (page 69) and planted 1m (3ft) apart, with 2m (6ft) between rows, cordons enable you to grow several varieties on a very small plot. An established cordon will yield about 1.5–2.5kg (3–5lb).

Espaliers With a spread of 3–4.5m (10–15ft), these are ideal grown against a fence or wall in full sun or with a little shade. Alternatively, grow them in the open and train on wires (page 68).
Step-over apple trees Essentially a single tier espalier, this type of tree can be used to edge a border or flank a garden path.
Patio apples If you have a little courtyard garden, grow apple trees in large containers of soil-based compost. You can train them as bushes or dwarf pyramids.

Varieties The varieties listed on pages 72–73 are widely available. When choosing trees, think about what position and type of soil they'll be growing in; staff at the nursery or garden centre should be able to advise you about what's best for your garden.

Fruit trees are available on a range of rootstocks. The rootstock determines the vigour of the tree and how big it will grow. If you don't want your apple tree to get too big for the garden, then choose the right rootstock – and if the rootstock is not stated on the label, then don't buy the tree. The three

apple rootstocks are: m27 – 1.2–1.8m (4–6ft), m9 – 2.5–3m (8–10ft), m26 – 3–4.5m (10–14ft).

Most apple trees cannot self-pollinate, so you'll need to plant at least two trees that will blossom at the same time. Discovery and Early Victoria, for example, will happily cross-pollinate. Alternatively, you can buy a 'family tree', as its

AT-A-GLANCE TIMETABLE

PLANTING

LATE AUTUMN – EARLY SPRING
Container-grown young trees may be planted at any time, except in conditions of drought, waterlogging or severe frost

PRUNING

LATE AUTUMN – EARLY SPRING
• Winter pruning
SECOND HALF OF SUMMER
(JULY/AUGUST)
• Summer pruning

HARVESTING

LATE SUMMER – LATE AUTUMN
Depends on variety. Test ripeness by gently lifting and twisting

varieties will have been chosen for simultaneous flowering.

How to grow apple trees
Apple trees are sold as bare root, root-balled or in large pots. The best time for planting is during frost-free weather between autumn (October) and early spring (mid March), though you can plant those bought in containers year round during suitable weather. Dig a hole big enough to hold the roots or rootball comfortably. When planting a bush tree, first hammer in a supporting stake and then plant the tree close against it.

With all forms of tree, make sure that the union between the stock and the scion is at least 10cm (4in) above soil level. Back-fill the hole and firm the soil gently before securing the tree to the stake with a tree tie.

Keep the tree well watered, especially during dry spells, in the first growing season. For the first two or three springs after planting, mulch around the tree with manure, compost or bark to help to retain moisture in the soil. In winter or early spring each year, apply a top dressing of a balanced

tree fertiliser, sprinkled over an area a little larger than the spread of the branches.

Training and pruning During the first four years of a tree's life, your aim is to create a strong framework of branches. The way you train and prune the tree depends on the shape you require. If you buy a young apple tree with only a single stem, you'll need to prune it carefully each winter to create the shape you want. Alternatively, you can buy a more mature tree, which has already been partly trained at the nursery, and is easier to shape.

Ideally, buy bush trees, cordons and trees for training as dwarf pyramids at two or three years old; choose an espalier up to four years old.

SUMMER PRUNING A CORDON APPLE TREE

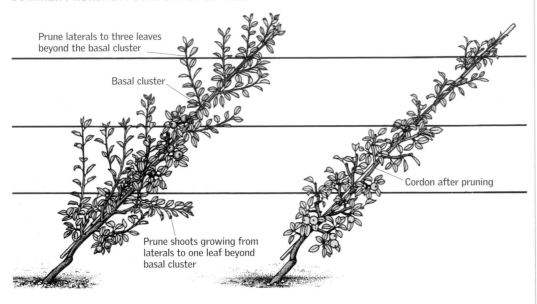

Prune laterals to three leaves beyond the basal cluster

Basal cluster

Cordon after pruning

Prune shoots growing from laterals to one leaf beyond basal cluster

Summer training Prune cordons when new growth matures, in late summer to early autumn. Cut back laterals growing from main stem to three leaves from the basal cluster (where growth began in the spring) and cut back shoots from existing laterals or spurs to one leaf. You can also use this method for espaliers and dwarf pyramids.

Training a cordon

After planting a cordon apple tree (right) no pruning is necessary except for tip-bearing varieties. Shorten the leader of these by a quarter. From then on, prune the trees in summer using a technique known as the modified Lorette system – which also works for other restricted tree shapes.

Modified Lorette system Prune when the new summer growth matures – that is, when the shoots are at least 25cm (9in) long, the leaves are dark and the base is woody. Cut back shoots from the main stem to three leaves beyond the basal cluster. Prune shoots

from existing laterals or spurs to one leaf beyond the basal cluster. Delay pruning laterals less than 23cm (9in) long until they reach that length. Any new shoots that grow after summer pruning should be cut back to one bud on well-ripened wood in September or early October.

When a cordon grows beyond the top support wire, untie the tree and re-fasten it at a sharper angle – but not lower than 35 degrees from horizontal. Adjust its neighbours so they remain parallel.

When the cordon reaches its final height, cut back new growth on the leader to 1cm (½in) in May. Cut above a bud and repeat this

operation every May. As the tree gets older, thin out overcrowded spurs during winter while the tree is dormant.

Pruning a neglected cordon

Start to improve the shape of the tree in winter, first sawing back some of the thicker vertical branches to within 3–5cm (1–2in) of the main stem. Cut long spurs back according to their thickness – the heaviest ones the hardest. Spread this pruning over two or three years.

During the following summer, prune using the modified Lorette system, removing some of the growth completely.

Training an espalier

If you'd like to grow an espalier, but have little pruning experience, then buy a three-year-old tree. This will have two tiers, or horizontal branches, already trained. There are two stages to annual pruning:
Winter pruning is done in the early years to produce extra tiers, if wanted, and to thin overcrowded spurs later.
Summer pruning is the same as for cordons, using the modified Lorette system (below left).

Forming new tiers Once you've planted the tree and tied its branches to the support wires, cut back the main stem to a bud just above the wire that will support the next tier.

When growth begins, choose two good buds below the cut, on opposite sides of the stem, to grow into side branches. Rub out any buds between these three.

Tie a cane vertically to the support wires. As the centre shoot grows, tie it to the cane.

Fasten two more canes to the wires on each side of the first cane, setting them at an angle of 45 degrees. Tie the sideshoots to these as they grow. If one grows more vigorously than the other, lower the angle of its cane and raise the cane of the other shoot to a more vertical position.

The following winter, remove the side canes, bend the branches down and tie them to the wire supports. Repeat the process yearly until you have as many tiers as you want. When you form the top tier, cut back the main stem to two side buds, leaving no upper bud.

Don't prune vigorous leaders on the tiers until they have grown as long as you want them. Then, cut

PLANTING CORDON TREES

Create the framework Drive in a sturdy upright every 3m (10ft) and staple taut horizontal wires to the posts about 60cm (2ft) apart. Space cordons 60cm (2ft) apart, inserting a cane at 45° for each tree. Tie the canes securely to the horizontal wires.

Plant the trees Plant a cordon beside each cane at the same angle and attach the main stem to the cane with adjustable tree ties. Prune now or wait until spring. Here, the low sideshoot on the first tree has been retained to fill the empty triangular space.

TRAINING AN ESPALIER

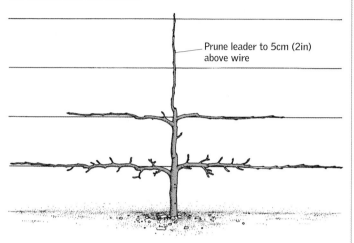

Prune leader to 5cm (2in) above wire

After planting Tie branches to support wires and cut back main stem to a bud about 5cm (2in) above the wire that will support the next tier of horizontal branches.

back the previous year's growth to 1cm (½in) in late spring. Repeat this treatment every year. Otherwise, all you need do is summer prune using the modified Lorette system (facing page).

Training a dwarf pyramid

Dwarf pyramids are trained to a shape rather like a Christmas tree. Choose a two-year-old tree, and having planted it shorten the central leader to leave about 25cm (9in) of last summer's growth. To keep the leader straight, cut back to a bud pointing in the opposite direction from that chosen when the tree was pruned the previous winter.

Shorten branch leaders to about 20cm (7in), cutting back to an outward-pointing bud.

In late summer or early autumn, prune using the modified Lorette system (see opposite). Also shorten mature new growth on branch

leaders – but not the central leader – to five or six leaves above the basal cluster of leaves.

Each winter, shorten the central leader by the method used at planting time. Once the tree reaches about 2m (7ft), you can restrict its growth by cutting back half the previous summer's growth on the central leader in May. Then, every May, shorten the previous summer's growth to just 1cm (½in).

You can also shorten branch leaders in May if they are crowding a neighbouring tree.

Shaping and pruning a bush apple tree

Having planted your two-year-old bush apple tree, shorten branch leaders by about half to two-thirds so that the tips of the branches are roughly level. Prune to an outward-facing bud.

Over the following summer, several lateral shoots will grow

from the branches. The next winter, choose some pointing upwards and outwards to form more branches.

As a rule, prune back to an outward-facing bud, but if the variety has a slightly drooping habit, you can also prune branches to an inward-facing bud.

Shorten vigorous new growth by a third; weaker new growth can be shortened by half. After pruning, the tips of the branch leaders should be at least 45cm (18in) from their nearest neighbour and more or less level with each other.

Cut back any laterals not chosen to form main branches to four buds from the base – these will become future fruiting spurs. Shorten or remove any laterals crowding the centre. This pruning establishes the basic shape of the tree, though you may need to carry out a little more formative pruning over the next two or three years. From then on, the way you prune will depend on

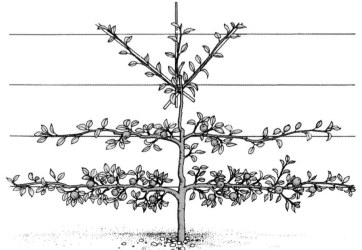

The next summer As growth begins, choose two buds, one pointing left and one right, below the cut made at planting. As these shoots grow, tie them to canes set at an angle of 45 degrees.

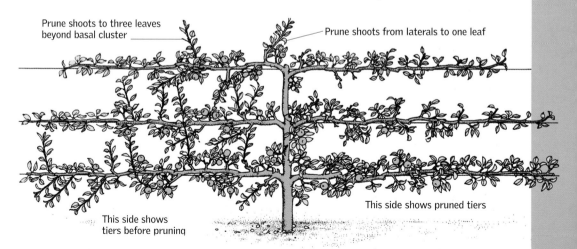

Prune shoots to three leaves beyond basal cluster

Prune shoots from laterals to one leaf

This side shows tiers before pruning

This side shows pruned tiers

An established tree When the tiers have reached the desired length, cut back the previous year's growth to 1cm (½in) each May. In late July or August, prune shoots from tiers to three leaves from the basal cluster, and shoots from laterals to one leaf.

PRUNING A YOUNG TREE

Thin fruiting spurs Where fruiting spurs have become crowded or cross each other, cut some of them off either at the base or where they branch.

Remove awkward shoots Cut off young shoots and buds that emerge close to main branches or point in the wrong direction.

whether your tree is a spur-bearer or a tip-bearer. A spur-bearer, such as Grenadier or Cox's Orange Pippin carries all its fruit on spurs. A tip-bearer, like Worcester Pearmain or Bramley's Seedling, bears its fruit on spurs and at the tips of shoots.

Pruning a spur-bearing bush

The easiest way to prune a spur-bearing tree is known as the regulated system. Light pruning each winter keeps the centre of the tree open. First, cut out dead and diseased wood and either remove shoots that cross or crowd each other, or shorten them so that they no longer cross. Likewise, shorten any shoots competing with the branch leaders.

In the early years only, shorten branch leaders by cutting away a quarter of the previous season's

Let in the air Aim to leave an open, balanced arrangement of sideshoots to admit plenty of air and light; clear away all prunings when you have finished.

growth if they are vigorous, but by only a third if they are weaker.

This pruning encourages heavy cropping, but as the tree gets older the size of fruits will get smaller. If this happens, cut out some of the fruiting laterals and thin some of the fruiting spurs in winter.

Pruning a tip-bearing bush

Tip-bearing apple trees produce much of their fruit on the tips of shoots formed in the previous year, and some on spurs. The proportion differs with each variety. Those

that are mainly tip-bearing require comparatively little pruning.

Every winter, cut back branch leaders to a growth bud to induce lower buds to break and form more tip-bearing shoots. Don't prune laterals with fruit buds at their tips, or you'll lose potential fruit.

If growth is crowded, cut out some of the previous summer's growth to three or four buds.

Restoring a neglected tree

You can revive a neglected apple tree with a bit of care and

attention. This involves pruning, fertilising and some spraying against pests and diseases.

Neglected trees generally fall into two categories – those that have grown too vigorous and are producing fruit well out of reach for picking, and those that have weak growth and are producing only small fruits.

With both kinds, cut out dead and broken wood and treat cankers. Protect major pruning cuts with a fungicidal wound product to prevent re-infection.

TRAINING AND PRUNING A DWARF PYRAMID

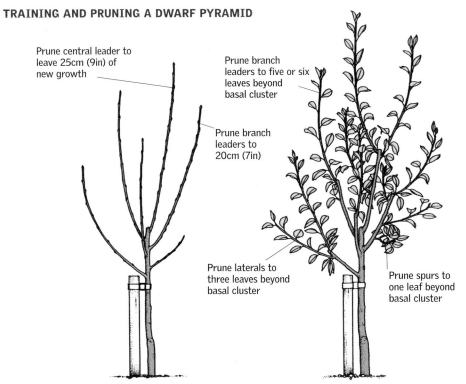

Prune central leader to leave 25cm (9in) of new growth

Prune branch leaders to 20cm (7in)

Prune branch leaders to five or six leaves beyond basal cluster

Prune laterals to three leaves beyond basal cluster

Prune spurs to one leaf beyond basal cluster

After planting Prune the central leader to a bud on the opposite side to that chosen during the previous winter, leaving 25cm (9in) of new growth. Shorten each of the branch leaders to 20cm (7in).

Summer pruning Shorten mature growth on branch leaders to five or six leaves above the basal cluster. Prune laterals in the same way as that advised for cordons (page 68).

Pruning an over-vigorous tree

If a tree has grown too tall, cut it back gradually over three or four winters to reduce the shock of severe pruning. Known as 'de-horning', this opens up the centre of the tree and reduces the height of branches to make fruit-picking easier. First cut back high branches in the centre to the main trunk. Prune back outer, tall-growing branches to a lower branch. Lightly thin out smaller laterals and young growth. The process will take three or four years

Pruning a weak tree

Improve the size of fruit and encourage new growth, by reducing the length of long spur systems in winter. This will cut out some fruit buds so that those that remain will produce larger fruit. Cut out the weakest spurs and leave those carrying the plumpest fruit buds.

Thinning the crop

Bearing a heavy crop puts a strain on a tree and can result in poor-quality fruit. You can start to thin a heavy crop in early June, before the natural 'June drop'. Remove badly shaped fruits, then wait until after the natural drop before making a final thinning.

Cut through the stalk with scissors or hold the stalk between two fingers and press the apple away with your thumb.

You shouldn't need to thin cordons, espaliers or dwarf trees much at all, but the fruit on large bush trees should be spaced out. Thin dessert varieties to 10–15cm (4–6in) apart, and large cooking varieties 15–25cm (6–9in) apart.

Pests and diseases

Pests include aphids, codling moth grubs and winter moth caterpillars. Apples are also attacked by apple sawfly, capsid bugs, red spider mites, tortrix moths and woolly aphids. Main diseases include apple canker, bitter pit, brown rot, fire blight, honey fungus, magnesium deficiency, papery bark, powdery mildew, scab and silver leaf (see Pests and Diseases, pages 238–49).

Harvesting and storing

To test whether an apple is ready for picking, place the palm of your hand beneath it, lift and twist. It should come away easily. Eat early varieties soon after picking, as they don't keep. If you wish to store apples (right), you'll need a frost-free garage or cool spare room.

Preparing and cooking

Both cookers and eaters can be made into purées for sauces, soups and puddings – try topping apple purée with fluffy meringue. Apple rings sautéed in a little butter are delicious with pork, while sharp apples can be used to stuff goose or duck. Core whole, unpeeled apples and roast around a pork joint for the last 20 minutes. Cubes of crisp eating apples can be added to salads, such as the classic Waldorf with celery and walnuts. Make warming crumbles, perhaps adding a handful of blackberries or some slices of scented quince.

See also bottling (page 309); chutneys (page 335); drying (page 343); freezing (page 294); fruit cheeses and butters (page 323); jams (page 314); jellies (page 320); pickles (page 328); sauces, ketchups and relishes (page 339) and wine-making (page 357).

Protect apples for storage Wrap apples in specially oiled paper or layers of newspaper; or stack them on fibre trays or keep in clear, plastic bags with the tops unsealed or the sides perforated.

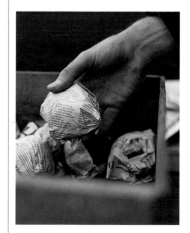

Stack carefully Handle apples gently and keep them in a frost-proof garage or spare room where the temperature is stable but cool. Check the apples from time to time and remove any brown or rotting fruits.

TRAINING AND PRUNING A BUSH APPLE TREE

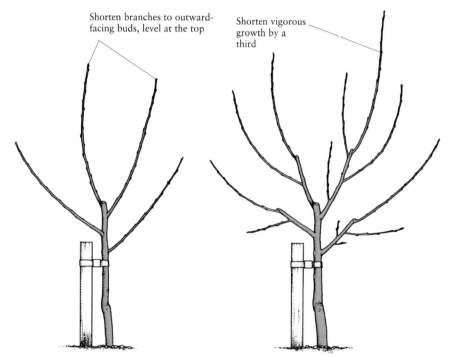

Shorten branches to outward-facing buds, level at the top

Shorten vigorous growth by a third

After planting When pruning a bush tree, aim for a goblet shape – open in the centre. Shorten branches by about a half to two-thirds to outward-facing buds so that their tips are level.

The next winter Choose well-placed shoots as new branches and prune back to outward-facing buds. Shorten vigorous growth by a third, the rest by half. Tips of branch leaders should be about level.

Apple varieties

Varieties in the same pollination group – such as the early George Cave and the late Idared, which are both in group A – blossom at the same time and will cross-pollinate.

EARLY APPLES

George Cave (dessert)
Pick: early August
Use: early to end August
Pollination group: A
Sweet, aromatic flavour; regular cropper; suitable for the north; spur-forming and tip-bearer.

Grenadier (cooker)
Pick: early August to early September
Use: August to September
Pollination group: B
Firm flesh; acid flavour; regular cropper; suitable for the north; spur-forming.

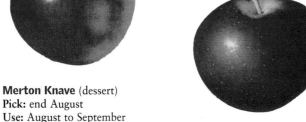

Merton Knave (dessert)
Pick: end August
Use: August to September
Pollination group: B
Crisp, white flesh; sweet; good flavour; regular cropper; spur-forming.

Discovery (dessert)
Pick: mid to end August
Use: mid August to September
Pollination group: B
Crisp, sweet and juicy; some scab resistance; spur-forming.

MID-SEASON APPLES

James Grieve (dessert)
Pick: early September
Use: September to October
Pollination group: B
Tender, juicy, excellent flavour; hardy and reliable but prone to canker; spur-forming.

Worcester Pearmain (dessert)
Pick: early September
Use: September to October
Pollination group: B
Crisp and sweet; hardy, reliable cropper; resistant to mildew; tip-bearer.

Laxton's Fortune (dessert)
Pick: mid September
Use: late September to October
Pollination group: B
Sweet, rich flavour; some resistance to scab; hardy; tends to bear biennially; spur-forming.

Ellison's Orange (dessert)
Pick: mid September
Use: September to October
Pollination group: C
Sweet, aromatic flavour; tends to bear biennially; suitable for the north; spur-forming.

St Edmund's Russet (dessert)
Pick: mid September
Use: mid September to October
Pollination group: A
Very fine flavour but fruits inclined to be small; compact growth; spur-forming.

Lord Lambourne (dessert)
Pick: late September
Use: October
Pollination group: A
Crisp, moderately sweet; some resistance to scab; hardy; spur-forming.

Egremont Russet
(dessert)
Pick: late September
Use: October to December
Pollination group: A
Sweet, nutty; some resistance to scab; best russet for the garden; spur-forming; upright growth.

Sunset (dessert)
Pick: end September
Use: October to December
Pollination group: B
Crisp, excellent flavour; compact growth; attractive blossom; hardy; spur-forming.

Kidd's Orange Red
(dessert)
Pick: early October
Use: November to January
Pollination group: B
Crisp and sweet, with very good flavour; reliable cropper; spur-forming.

Cox's Orange Pippin
(dessert)
Pick: early October
Use: November to December
Pollination group: B
Excellent flavour but needs good cultural treatment; susceptible to scab, mildew and canker; spur-forming.

LATE APPLES

Idared (dessert)
Pick: mid to end October
Use: December to April
Pollination group: A
Crisp, juicy; recommended for its keeping qualities; regular cropper; hardy; spur-forming.

Orlean's Reinette (dessert)
Pick: late October
Use: November to February
Pollination group: C
Crisp, yellow flesh with sweet, rich flavour; may shrivel in store; spur-forming; vigorous growth.

Spartan (dessert)
Pick: early October
Use: November to January
Pollination group: B
Crisp flesh with juicy, wine-like flavour; prone to canker; hardy; spur-forming.

Golden Delicious
(dessert)
Pick: mid October
Use: November to January
Pollination group: C
Crisp, sweet and juicy; easy to grow; reliable cropper; hardy; spur-forming.

Lane's Prince Albert (cooker)
Pick: early October
Use: December to March
Pollination group: C
Crisp flesh; acid; regular cropper; compact habit; grows well in a garden; hardy; spur-forming.

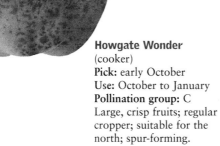

Golden Noble (cooker)
Pick: late September
Use: September to January
Pollination group: C
Tender, yellow flesh; acid; an excellent cooker; recommended for the garden; spur-forming.

Howgate Wonder
(cooker)
Pick: early October
Use: October to January
Pollination group: C
Large, crisp fruits; regular cropper; suitable for the north; spur-forming.

Bramley's Seedling
(cooker) **Pick:** early October
Use: November to February
Pollination group: B
(must be grown with two other varieties in group B).
Our best cooker, but suitable for the garden only when grafted on to dwarfing stock; spur forming and tip-bearer.

Crab Apples

Although grown mainly as ornamental trees, many species of wild apples, and their cultivated varieties, can be used for making preserves and wine.

They need little pruning, and so are less trouble to grow than dessert and cooking apples. Some crab apples are too big to plant in a small garden, but many are grown on dwarfing stock and one of these planted in a lawn will provide blossom in late spring and colourful fruits in September for making into jellies.

Planning the crop

Crab apples will grow in any fertile, well-drained soil. A dressing of rotted manure or compost will help the tree to get started, but from then on, no feeding is necessary.

Choose a variety on the most suitable stock to suit the site. Check the size of varieties offered by the nursery – standards can spread up to 7.5m (25ft), and you don't want to overwhelm your garden.

Crab apples are generally self-fertile, so only one tree needs to be grown to provide fruit. Even a dwarf tree will yield about 10kg (20lb) when established. Crab apples are also useful pollinators for a wide variety of cooking and eating apples.

Varieties

Crab apples can be divided into two main types – those with ornamental flowers and fruits, such as *Malus* **Profusion**, and those that bear pretty blossom and much larger fruits, like **John Downie** – which makes great jelly.

Growing tips

Plant a bare root or rootballed tree during autumn or winter, and secure the tree to a stake for a few years until well rooted. Container grown trees can be planted all year round as long as the weather is suitable. Keep well watered if the weather is dry in the spring following planting.

Pruning

No regular pruning is needed except to remove dead, diseased or crossing branches. Do this in winter.

Pests and diseases

As for cultivated apples (see page 71).

Harvesting and storing

The apples ripen in mid to late autumn. The fruits of some varieties will stay on the tree all winter and are attractive to many birds when other food is scarce. If you wish to use them, they are best preserved soon after picking.

Preparing and cooking

All crab apples make superb jelly (page 277). The fruit is high in pectin so the jelly sets easily, and whatever colour the apple, cooks to a warm pinky-orange. It's delicious served with any roast meat or poultry, with sausages and with pork pie. You can also use herbs with crab apples to make flavoured jellies – try mint, sage or thyme.

See also pickles, page 285 and wine-making, page 304.

AT-A-GLANCE TIMETABLE

PLANTING
LATE AUTUMN TO EARLY SPRING
(Containerised ones may be planted throughout the year)

PRUNING
WINTER
Prune dead, weak or crossed branches if necessary

HARVESTING
MID TO LATE AUTUMN

Apricots

The apricot is relatively difficult to grow in this country, because of its early blossoming – generally in February – when there are few insects about to assist pollination.

In the north, apricot trees cannot produce fruit unless they are grown under glass. In the south, you can grow

Fan-trained bush apricot.

apricots successfully as fan trees if you choose a south-facing wall in a sheltered position. If your garden is very warm and sheltered, you may be able to grow apricot as a bush but, by and large, fan-training on a sunny wall is more reliable.

Apricot trees grow best in a well-drained, limy loam. Dwarf varieties can be grown in large pots or tubs of soil-based potting compost on a sunny patio during summer and moved into the greenhouse or conservatory in winter.

The apricot – a native of China – is believed to have been first grown in this country in the 16th century by one of Henry VIII's gardeners. Its name comes from the Latin *praecox*, meaning 'precocious', a reference to its early blossoming.

Planning the crop
If the soil is heavy, put a layer of rubble at the bottom of the hole before planting. Apricots don't like an acid soil, but you can improve alkalinity by spreading lime at the rate of 60g per square metre (2oz per square yard) in late autumn or winter each year.

How many trees to grow Few gardens have space for more than one tree: an established fan on a 2.5m (8ft) wall will have a spread of at least 3.5m (12ft) and a bush could spread up to 4.5m (15ft).

Varieties The most reliable outdoor variety in the UK is

Moorpark, which ripens in mid to late August; it has well-flavoured, orange flesh and is a heavy cropper.

Growing tips
Choose two or three-year-old trees, which should produce fruit in their fourth year. Bare-rooted trees can be planted at any time from late autumn to early spring; you can plant containerised trees all year round if weather and soil conditions are suitable.

Training To form the framework of the tree, train as for peaches (page 178) but prune in early spring as growth begins. Once the framework is established, prune fans in the same way as plums (page 187); train bush trees as for sour cherries (page 117). Patio varieties need little regular pruning.

Feed and water Each winter, apply as a top dressing 90g bonemeal and 30g sulphate of potash per square metre (3oz and 1oz per square yard) over the rooting area, which is roughly the same as the spread of the tree. Alternatively, top-dress with a slow-release, compound fertiliser according to manufacturer's instructions in early spring. Every third year, omit the bonemeal but spread a 7.5cm (3in) layer of rotted compost or manure instead.

In June apply 30g of sulphate of ammonia per square metre (1oz per square yard). Water thoroughly during dry spells.

Frost protection Apricots can blossom as early as February, so you might want to protect the tree from frosts by covering with a double thickness of 2.5cm (1in) plastic netting. Because of this

early blossoming, when few insects are about, you can improve the fruit yield by using a fine paintbrush to transfer pollen from one flower to another.

Never allow an apricot tree to bear too heavy a crop. In April or May, thin the growing fruits to about 10cm (4in) apart.

Pests and diseases
Pests that commonly affect apricots include **aphids** and **caterpillars**, **glasshouse red spider mites** and **scale insects**. The most likely disease is **die-back**, while apricots grown outdoors are prone to **peach leaf curl**. This disease is rain-borne in winter and early spring, and can be prevented by erecting a cover over the tree during this period so the branches do not get wet. Pot-grown apricots can be protected from peach leaf curl by overwintering in a cold greenhouse. Pick off any diseased leaves immediately, as the spores overwinter on the twigs and bark. If a tree has been infected, spray it with Bordeaux mixture just after leaf fall in autumn, and again as the buds start to swell in late winter and early spring. (See Pests and Diseases, pages 238–49.)

Harvesting and storing
Apricots soften some time before they are fully ripe. Leave them on the tree for as long as possible to ripen – from late July to late August depending on variety. When ripe they are well coloured and part easily from the tree. You can keep apricots for up to a month in a cool, well-ventilated place.

Preparing and cooking
Fresh, just-ripe apricots are excellent as dessert fruits – on

their own or with cream, ice cream or custard. Overripe fruits become mealy and are then better used in purées and sauces.

Wipe apricots carefully with a damp cloth – they bruise easily – cut in half along the indentation in the skin and twist the two halves apart. Remove the stone with the tip of a knife. Poach for about 8 minutes in water with sugar added to taste. Poached apricots make good pie and flan fillings; puréed apricots can be folded into whipped cream to make a delicious fool or made into a sauce for steamed puddings and ice creams. An apricot glaze is traditionally used beneath almond paste on iced Christmas and wedding cakes.

Finely chopped fresh or dried apricots, mixed with diced celery, butter, breadcrumbs, herbs and eggs, make a perfect stuffing for rich meats.

See also bottling (page 270); chutneys (page 292); drying (page 300); freezing (page 252); jams (page 271); pickles (page 285) and syrups and juices (page 283).

AT-A-GLANCE TIMETABLE

PLANTING
• **Bare root**
LATE AUTUMN TO EARLY SPRING
• **Containerised**
all year in favourable weather

PRUNING
EARLY SPRING

HARVESTING
LATE SUMMER TO EARLY AUTUMN

Temperamental fruit Apricot yields can be unpredictable, so making preserves and jams will see you through times of lean pickings.

Artichokes, Globe

Their delicate yet unmistakable flavour makes artichokes one of the most prized of garden vegetables. They are not only delicious but also strikingly beautiful, their silvery-grey leaves providing a perfect foil for summer flowers. For this reason, they are often grown in herbaceous borders.

Globe artichokes need an open sunny position where the soil is rich and well drained. Each mature artichoke will yield up to six heads during June and July, and you can expect a plant to grow and flower for about six years, though the globes will grow progressively smaller and tougher.

History has not recorded the name of the adventurous gourmet who discovered that the base of the flower scales of the thistle-like globe artichoke – and also the base of the flowers themselves – could be eaten. But, whoever it was, he made a fine discovery.

Planning the crop

Except in the south of England, artichoke plants will not always survive the winter and it is best to grow it in a sheltered, but sunny, part of the garden.

In the winter before planting, dig in some well-rotted compost or manure and leave the ground rough until spring. Then rake soil to a fine tilth and spread on 90g of general fertiliser per square metre (3oz per square yard).

How many plants to grow The number grown will depend on how popular artichokes are in your household – and how much space you have. They need to be set 1m (3ft) apart in each direction, but if space is tight, you can plant singly at the back of a herbaceous or mixed border. They will reach a height of 1.2–1.5m (4–5ft).

Varieties Green Globe and Purple Globe are the most widely available varieties. **Purple Globe** is hardier than **Green Globe** and is the best choice for cooler counties.

Growing tips

Although artichokes will grow and flower for around six years, the heads get smaller, and sometimes tougher, after the third or fourth years. It's a good idea to replace a few each year so that you always have new plants maturing and some old ones dying down.

To start a crop, buy young plants or suckers in April and plant in well-manured soil to the same depth as they were in the nursery bed or pot. In May, apply a liberal mulch of manure or compost.

In dry periods, especially when plants are growing strongly, make sure that they are well watered.

The new plants will provide some heads by August or September, but it is better to encourage growth in the first year by removing the buds as soon as they appear. This will give you larger heads in subsequent seasons.

In their second and third years, allow each plant to develop only four to six stems. Leave the flower on the main stem – called the king head – and several others at the end of lateral shoots. Nip off any extra buds on sideshoots to ensure a good crop.

AT-A-GLANCE TIMETABLE

PLANTING
SPRING

MULCHING
LATE SPRING TO EARLY SUMMER

DISBUDDING
(1st year)
LATE SUMMER TO EARLY AUTUMN

HARVESTING
(2nd and 3rd years)
SUMMER (JUNE–JULY)

CUTTING BACK
(2nd and 3rd years)
LATE AUTUMN TO EARLY WINTER

DIVIDING
(2nd and 3rd years)
LATE AUTUMN OR SPRING

In November, cut the main stems down almost to ground level, draw the surrounding soil around them and cover the soil with a layer of straw. Enclose this with wire netting and cover with a double layer of horticultural fleece.

Raising new plants In spring or late autumn, select strong shoots about 25cm (9in) high on plants that are at least three years old. Cut vertically alongside each shoot, using a spade or sharp knife, retaining part of the rootstock beneath it. Discard the rest of the plant after removing the shoots.

Shoots removed in April can be planted out immediately in their permanent positions. If you remove

Producing chards Before finally discarding a three or four-year-old plant, its blanched shoots, called chards, can be eaten. After harvesting the heads, cut back the foliage and allow fresh shoots to grow to a height of 60cm (2ft).

Blanch by enclosing in a collar of black polythene or brown paper. When blanched, eat raw or cooked, like celery.

RAISING NEW PLANTS FROM OLD STOCK

Dividing Use a spade or a sharp knife to remove strong shoots in spring or late autumn, each with a piece of rootstock attached.

Transplanting Plant the shoots 1m (3ft) apart in each direction. If removed in autumn, overwinter them in a coldframe.

shoots in November, pot them in potting compost and keep in a coldframe during winter. Plant out in their final positions in spring.

Pests and diseases

Artichokes are generally free from pests, although in damp conditions **slugs and snails** may sometimes be a problem; they may also become infested with blackfly. The major disease is **petal blight** (page 245).

Harvesting and storing

Mature plants produce ripe heads in June or July. Pick them, starting with the king head, when they are still green and tightly wrapped. Use secateurs to cut off the heads, then cut back each stem to about half its original length. The flower heads on the lateral shoots are best picked when about the size of a hen's egg. Very small, young heads can be cooked and eaten whole. **See also** freezing (page 252).

Preparing and cooking

The artichoke head, at the top of a tough stalk, is composed of stiff scales, or bracts, closely compressed round a shallow base known as the heart. A thick cluster of silky hairs – the choke – is embedded in the heart. The edible parts of a globe artichoke are the fleshy, half-moon shape at the base of each scale, and the heart.

Covering for winter Protect with straw, enclosing this with netting and covering with fleece.

Preparation To prepare an artichoke for cooking, trim the stalk level with the base of the head, cut off any damaged outer scales. If you wish, you can slice off the top of the head and trim off the points of the remaining scales with scissors, though this is not strictly necessary. Wash well and stand upside-down to drain.

Rub all cut surfaces with lemon to prevent discoloration.

The choke can be removed before or after cooking. Spread the outer scales apart and pull out the small inner scales until the choke is revealed. With a teaspoon, scrape off the hairs adhering to the heart. If the heart only is to be used, remove all the outer scales before discarding the choke, and rub the heart with lemon.

Cooking Fill a large pan with water to which salt and 2 tablespoons of lemon juice have been added. Bring to the boil; add artichokes and boil for 40–50 minutes or until tender – when a scale can easily be pulled away. Drain upside down.

Serving and eating Serve boiled artichokes either hot with melted butter or Hollandaise sauce, or cold with a French dressing. Pull off each scale; dip the fleshy base in the butter or dressing and scrape it off with your bottom teeth. Once you get to the middle, carefully remove the silky hairs and eat the heart dipped in the sauce.

HARVESTING THE HEADS

King head

Lateral head

Remove the largest bud, or king head, first, then the smaller heads on lateral shoots.

Harvesting Use a sharp knife or secateurs to cut through stems.

PREPARING FOR COOKING

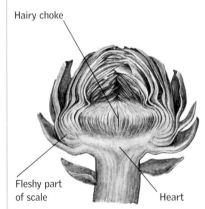

Hairy choke

Fleshy part of scale

Heart

Parts of an artichoke, showing how the flower scales are joined to the heart at the base.

Trim You can, if you wish, trim the points off the flower scales.

Remove the choke Before cooking you can remove the choke by scraping it off the heart with a spoon.

Artichokes, Jerusalem

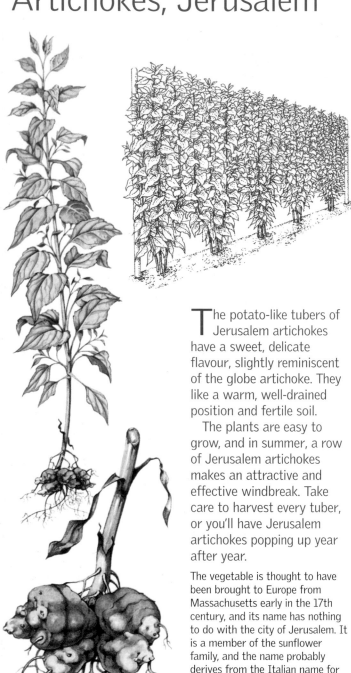

The potato-like tubers of Jerusalem artichokes have a sweet, delicate flavour, slightly reminiscent of the globe artichoke. They like a warm, well-drained position and fertile soil.

The plants are easy to grow, and in summer, a row of Jerusalem artichokes makes an attractive and effective windbreak. Take care to harvest every tuber, or you'll have Jerusalem artichokes popping up year after year.

The vegetable is thought to have been brought to Europe from Massachusetts early in the 17th century, and its name has nothing to do with the city of Jerusalem. It is a member of the sunflower family, and the name probably derives from the Italian name for that plant: *girasole*.

Planning the crop

Choose a sunny position, ideally where brassicas were grown the previous season. If the land is reasonably fertile, you don't need to add manure; otherwise, to produce large tubers, enrich the soil with well-rotted manure or compost in the autumn or winter before planting.

How many to grow Each seed tuber should yield 1.5kg (3lb) – that is 19kg (42lb) per 6m (20ft) row.

Varieties The traditional small knobbly tubers that used to be grown have been superseded by varieties like **Fuseau** and **New White**, which is smooth-skinned and has a fuller flavour.

Growing tips

In February or March, use a draw hoe to make a furrow 15cm (6in) deep and plant the tubers 45cm (18in) apart in the bottom. Alternatively, plant single tubers at this depth with a trowel.

Allow 1m (3ft) between rows. When you cover the tubers, leave a ridge about 5cm (2in) high over their tops. Spread a dressing of general fertiliser along this at 60g per square metre (2oz per square yard) and hoe it into the surface.

When the stalks of the plants are 15cm (6in) high, draw up another 5cm (2in) of soil. Repeat every couple of weeks or so until there is a 15cm (6in) ridge.

Now drive a 1.8m (6ft) stake or cane 60cm (2ft) into the ground at each end of the row. Run wires between the stakes and tie the plants to the wires with soft string as they grow, so that wind will not rock them and expose the tubers.

Pests and diseases

Jerusalem artichokes may be attacked by **cutworms**, **root aphids** and **swift moth**. Their principal ailment is **sclerotinia disease** (see Pests and Diseases, pages 238–49).

Harvesting and storing

The tubers will be ready for lifting by the end of October, when the top growth begins to turn brown. Cut the stems back to within 30cm (12in) of the ground.

You can leave the tubers in the ground until needed during winter – their cut stems will tell you where they are. Unless you want to establish a permanent Jerusalem

RIDGING AND SUPPORTING

First ridging Form a shallow ridge using a hoe along each row when plants reach 15cm (6in).

Follow-up ridging Draw soil up round plants every two weeks until ridge is about 15cm (6in) high. As plants get taller, support them using canes with wire stretched between them.

artichoke bed, then be sure to dig up even the smallest tubers to prevent regrowth.

Preparing and cooking

In the kitchen, you can treat Jerusalem artichokes like potatoes; but, as the creamy-white flesh discolours quickly, add lemon juice to the rinsing and cooking water.

Scrub the tubers and peel thinly with a stainless-steel knife or use unpeeled, causing less work and giving a better flavour.

Cook in boiling salted water, with lemon juice for 20 to 30 minutes, depending on size. Drain and serve tossed in melted butter.

You can also sauté parboiled Jerusalem artichokes in butter or cut them into slices and deep fry in hot oil. They can be roasted round a joint for 30 minutes, and their sweet, nutty flavour is also good in soups and casseroles.

AT-A-GLANCE TIMETABLE

PLANTING
LATE WINTER TO EARLY SPRING
Set tubers 45cm (18in) apart in a furrow 15cm (6in) deep

RIDGING
LATE SPRING TO EARLY SUMMER
When plants reach 15cm (6in) start earthing up

HARVESTING
FROM LATE AUTUMN

Asparagus

Asparagus, prized for the delicate flavour of its young shoots, is a luxury if you have to buy it. In some ways it is even a luxury to grow at home, because its cropping season lasts only six weeks, but being a perennial, it takes up space all the year round.

If you only need a few spears, you can grow it in a flower border; its fern, later in the year, is very attractive.

Planning the crop

Asparagus does best in a fairly open position, sheltered from wind. It needs a rich, well-drained soil, so initial preparation of the bed is vital to its future success.

In the autumn before planting, dig a bed 1.2m (4ft) wide to accommodate two rows. Dig well-rotted manure or compost into the topsoil at the rate of a bucketful to the square metre. Lighten heavy soil by adding gritty sand, or if the soil tends to become waterlogged, grow it in a raised bed.

The following spring, rake the bed level and work in 120g of general fertiliser per square metre (4oz per square yard).

How much to grow Six mature plants – those more than four years old – should yield one average helping of spears a week during the six-week season.

Varieties Connovers Colossal was traditionally the most popular variety and is still widely grown, but the plants are either male or female and the female ones, which produce berries, are less productive and can spread seedlings all over the garden. In recent years, a range of all-male hybrids has been introduced, starting with **Lucullus** and now including disease-resistant varieties like **Cito**.

The spears of most asparagus varieties are green with a purple tinge to the tips that varies in intensity according to variety, but there are also all-purple forms which generally have a finer flavour and can be eaten raw.

All-male hybrids from a breeding programme in Limburg in Holland are sometimes known as white asparagus because the stems of the spears are whiter than other varieties; these have the suffix 'lim' and include **Franklim** and **Gijnlim**.

Growing tips

You can grow asparagus from seed, but for quicker results, buy one or two-year-old plants. Don't try to transplant roots older than this.

One-year-old crowns are best, but they will not yield spears large enough to eat for two years.

Plant in spring Use a spade to make trenches 20cm (8in) deep, 1m (3ft) apart, and wide enough to take the plants' roots when spread out flat. Put back about 5cm (2in) of soil to create a low ridge all the way along the base.

Remove plants from their packing and set them 45cm (18in) apart in the trenches. Spread out their roots (see right) and cover them as quickly as possible with soil to stop them from drying out.

Cover the plants with an 8cm (3in) layer of soil, and firm the surface. Fill the trenches up gradually by drawing soil from the sides as you hoe during summer. By October the bed should be level.

The first two years For the first two years, lightly hoe to keep weeds down. Water thoroughly in dry spells. In late October or early November, when the stems turn yellow, cut down ferns to within 3cm (1in) of the soil and mulch with rotted manure or compost.

Keep well nourished Each spring, dress the rows with a general fertiliser at the rate of 60g per square metre (2oz per square yard). Follow this routine of organic manuring in autumn, and fertiliser application in spring.

Ridges or flat? The third spring after planting, you'll need to decide whether to grow in ridges – which will produce longer, blanched spears – or on the flat, where the stems will be shorter but may be cut earlier.

To make ridges, draw up the soil to a height of 13cm (5in) just before the crop is ready to be cut. Level out the ridge in autumn. On the flat, leave the soil as it is.

When the bed is established, cut back the foliage to 15cm (6in) from the ground when it changes colour each autumn, and burn it.

Raising new plants

Asparagus can be raised from seed, but it will take an extra year to produce spears for cutting. In April, soak seeds overnight in lukewarm water and sow in drills 1cm (½in) deep and 30cm (12in) apart. When the seedlings are about 15cm (6in) high, thin out to 15cm (6in) apart.

Water well during summer and plant out in their permanent bed the following spring.

Pests and diseases

The pests most likely to occur are **asparagus beetle**, **cutworms**, and **slugs and snails**. The principal diseases and disorders of

PLANTING ASPARAGUS CROWNS

Dig a trench Crowns should be planted in a 45cm (18in) deep trench, enriched with plenty of well-rotted compost or manure. Make a ridge down the middle. Set the crowns 45cm (18in) apart along the ridge.

Spread the roots, crabwise To prevent drying out, place sacking over them until you are ready to cover with soil. Then cover with an 8cm (3in) layer of fine soil. Fill the trench gradually as the plants grow during summer.

Cutting the ferns In late autumn or early winter, cut down the yellow foliage to 15cm (6in).

asparagus are frost damage and **violet root rot** (see Pests and Diseases, pages 238–49).

Harvesting and storing
Do not harvest shoots grown from one-year-old crowns during the first two seasons. In the third year take only one or two spears from each plant.

In subsequent years, harvest for only six weeks, allowing the later shoots to grow into ferns. If the plants are encouraged to grow in this way, the bed should continue

Harvesting Use a sharp, serrated knife to cut the spears up to 10cm (4in) below soil level.

to produce good crops for at least 20 years.

Harvest the ripe spears when their tips are about 10cm (4in) above the soil. Use either a special asparagus cutter or a serrated knife, cutting the base of the spear up to 10cm (4in) below soil level.

If you aren't going to use them straight away, then stand the spears in iced water for a few hours, then wrap and store in the fridge until they are needed. That way, you can cut several spears

AT-A-GLANCE TIMETABLE

SOWING
- Year before planting
SPRING
1cm (½in) deep, 30cm (12in) between rows

THINNING
- Year before planting
SUMMER
when 15cm (6in) high

PLANTING
- First year
SPRING
45cm (18in) apart 1m (3ft) between rows

FIRST HARVEST
- Third year
LATE SPRING TO EARLY SUMMER

CUTTING BACK
- Third year
15cm (6in)
LATE AUTUMN – EARLY WINTER
- Fourth and subsequent years
EARLY WINTER

MAIN HARVEST
- Fourth and subsequent years
LATE SPRING TO EARLY SUMMER

each day, saving them until you have enough for a meal. This is better than allowing them to become too large.
See also freezing (page 252).

Preparing and cooking
Few vegetables can compare in flavour with tender, home-grown asparagus. In their prime the small heads, or spears, should be tightly compressed; the stems, whether green or white, moist and glistening. The slightest trace of brown on the cut edge indicates that the asparagus is past its best, and is beginning to lose its succulence.

Boiled asparagus Wash the asparagus carefully so as not to damage the tender tips. Trim the woody parts from the bases of the stems. Green stems need only washing, but white stems have a bitter and hard skin which must be peeled off, always from the tip downwards.

Trim the spears so that they are of uniform length, and tie in small bundles with fine string or cotton tape. Stand the bundles upright in a pan – or better still, a tall, narrow asparagus steamer – of boiling salted water for about 8 minutes, depending on the thickness. Keep the asparagus tips above the water level so that they cook in the rising steam.

This delectable vegetable is served hot or cold and is delicious served whole with salt and melted butter, and perhaps a squeeze of lemon juice, or a hollandaise sauce. It can be used in omelettes and risottos, soups and pasta dishes, sauces, salads and soufflés.

Asparagus peas

The asparagus pea is confusingly named, because it is neither asparagus nor even a true culinary pea. Nevertheless, it is a member of the pea family, and takes its name from the asparagus-like flavour of the pods, which are cooked whole.

It is also known as the winged pea because of the four wavy flanges, or wings, on the pod.

Planning the crop
Asparagus peas grow best in well-drained, fertile soil in a sunny position. The plant is half-hardy and therefore vulnerable to frost.

In the autumn or winter before sowing, prepare the bed by digging in some well-rotted manure or compost. Before sowing, apply a general fertiliser at 60g per square metre (2oz per square yard).

How much to grow A 6m (20ft) row will provide regular pickings for a family of four during August. There is only one species of asparagus pea.

Growing tips
In the south, sow the seeds in the second week of May, 20cm (8in) apart in drills 5cm (2in) deep. The drills should be 45cm (18in) apart.

Sow two seeds in each position and remove the weaker one if both germinate.

In the north, sow the seeds 3cm (1in) deep in pots of seed compost in a greenhouse or frame, or on a sunny windowsill indoors, at the end of April, and plant out 20cm (8in) apart in early June when the danger of frost is past.

In each case a second sowing can be made a few weeks later to give a succession. Support the plants with twiggy sticks.

Pests and diseases
Normally disease-free, asparagus peas may suffer from the same pests as peas (page 182).

Aubergines

Harvesting and storing
Pick the pods when they are only 2–4cm (1–2in) long. If they are allowed to grow longer, they become stringy and lose their delicate flavour.

Go over the plants daily, because regular picking will help to maintain supplies.

Preparing and cooking
Use the pods as soon as possible after picking, topping and tailing them as for young French beans. Cook the prepared peas in the minimum of boiling water for about 5 minutes. Drain and toss in melted butter and sprinkle with chopped parsley, dill, marjoram or basil. Grated nutmeg and ginger also go well with asparagus peas.

AT-A-GLANCE TIMETABLE

SOWING (SOUTH)
Rows 45cm (18in) apart
Seeds 20cm (8in) apart
5cm (2in) deep
LATE SPRING
Sow outdoors
and thin when necessary

SOWING (NORTH)
SPRING AND EARLY SUMMER
Sow in pots in spring
Plant out in early summer

HARVESTING
LATE SUMMER TO EARLY AUTUMN
Pick regularly when pods are 2–4cm (1–2in) long

Aubergines tend to do best grown in a greenhouse in the British Isles – although modern varieties will give good results outdoors if planted in pots or growing bags in a warm, sunny and sheltered position. Indoors, you can expect up to about 12 fruits on each plant; outdoors, you'll get up to four.

The aubergine is a native of tropical Asia, though it is widely cultivated elsewhere. It is used in dishes such as moussaka and ratatouille. Its alternative name, eggplant, comes from its smooth skin and ovoid shape.

Planning the crop
In a greenhouse, grow aubergines in 20cm (7in) pots, growing bags (three plants per bag) or plant them in the border. If grown outdoors, choose a position that is open to the sun for most of the day. Plants require well-drained soil, liberally dressed with manure.

How many to grow This really depends on how much room you have. The pots or outdoor plants should be spaced about 45cm (18in) apart.

Varieties Always choose varieties that are described as early. Compact forms are available that are particularly suited to patio growing. Although the most popular varieties are black-skinned, you can also buy pink, striped and white-skinned aubergines. Look for newer varieties described as bitter-free to cut down on the preparation time needed when cooking. Together with their attractive, mauve flowers, modern aubergines can make ideal ornamental plants for a garden or a summer patio.

Growing tips
For growing in a greenhouse or outdoors, sow aubergines in small pots or trays of seed compost in late winter. The temperature needs to be 18°C (64°F), so place in a propagator or close to the heat source in the greenhouse, or on a windowsill in a warm room.

When large enough to handle, prick the plants out singly into 8cm (3in) pots of John Innes No. 1 compost or a soil-less potting compost. Grow them on in a temperature of about 16°C (61°F).

Transplanting If the plants are to be grown indoors, transfer them to 18cm (7in) pots of John Innes No. 2 compost or a proprietary soil-less potting compost when they are 10–15cm (4–6in) tall, or plant three in a grow bag. Alternatively, plant them in the border.

Outdoor protection Harden off outdoor plants during late spring and plant them outside when the temperature is warm enough and all risk of frost has passed, spacing them 45cm (18in) apart. Protect with a cloche or coldframe until they are established. For growing on a patio, plant in 18cm (7in) pots or in grow bags.

If you don't have access to a greenhouse, you can buy aubergine plants from garden centres in spring – although the choice of varieties will be limited.

Encouraging fruit When the plants are about 23cm (9in) high, pinch out the tops to encourage them to bush.

On indoor plants, allow up to three fruits to form on each of the three or four lateral branches that will develop. Outdoors, pinch out

AT-A-GLANCE TIMETABLE

SOWING
LATE WINTER

PRICKING OUT
SPRING
When seedlings are large enough to handle

TRANSPLANTING
EARLY SUMMER
• **Greenhouse plants**
When 10cm (4in) high
• **Outdoor plants**
When risk of frost is past

PINCHING OUT
SUMMER
When 25cm (9in) high

HARVESTING
LATE SUMMER TO MID AUTUMN

STOPPING AND PINCHING OUT

Stopping Remove the growing point of each plant when it is 25cm (9in) high. This encourages side-branches to develop.

Pinching out Outdoors, allow only one fruit to develop on each branch by pinching out the tip, three leaves beyond the fruit.

the tips of each branch once a fruit has formed on it, leaving three leaves beyond the fruit. Indoors and out, remove sideshoots that form on laterals. However, some patio varieties are naturally bushy and require no pinching out.

Feeding and watering Water generously and give weekly feeds of a proprietary soluble tomato fertiliser once the fruits are visible. Regularly spray leaves with water to keep down red spider mites.

Pests and diseases
Aphids (page 238) and **glasshouse red spider mites** (page 239) are the pests most likely to affect aubergines. The plants are generally disease-free.

Harvesting
Aubergines are ripe when they have turned black-purple (depending on variety) all over – usually late summer or mid autumn, a little earlier for greenhouse crops and a little later for those grown outdoors.

Handle the fruits carefully and remove by snipping through the

stems with scissors or secateurs. Aubergines can be kept for about a fortnight after harvesting.
See also freezing (page 294).

Preparing and cooking
This vegetable is usually fried in oil to be served as an accompanying vegetable, or stuffed with a variety of fillings and baked. The oval fruits keep fresh for longer than most vegetables, especially if they are stored in the bottom of the fridge.

To prepare aubergines, wipe them clean with a damp cloth and trim off both ends. Cut them cross-ways into thin slices and sprinkle the slices with salt; leave to stand for 30 minutes to draw out the bitter juices. Rinse the slices in cold water and dry. Bitter-free varieties do not need this treatment.

Fry in butter or oil until golden-brown. Drain on kitchen paper and serve with grilled or roast meat or a yoghurt and herb dip.

Chopped basil or marjoram go well with fried aubergine slices, or they may be sprinkled with black pepper, ground ginger or paprika.

Balm

The lemon-scented balm is a good herb to grow near fruit trees, because it attracts bees, which help pollination. This hardy perennial is used to flavour salads, soups, sauces and cold drinks.

In the past, it was used medicinally to cure stomach ailments, improve the memory and heal wounds.

Golden and variegated varieties of balm are available. They have the same lemon fragrance but are more decorative and are a useful addition to herb containers, window boxes and hanging baskets.

Planning the crop
Balm tolerates light shade and thrives in most average soils. The plant has tubular white flowers and some coloured varieties, and one or two plants can make a decorative addition to a perennial border. If you do, bear in mind that it is a fairly tall, bushy plant – up to 1.2m (4ft) high, and with a spread of 50cm (20in) – and so needs ample space. It also seeds freely and can become somewhat invasive unless the seedlings are removed regularly. Alternatively, remove the flowers before they start to set their seed.

How much to grow Bearing in mind its size and relatively limited uses, one plant should be enough.

Growing tips
Sow the seeds 1cm (½in) deep in late April or early May where the plants are to grow. Thin seedlings to 15cm (6in) apart. Alternatively, buy small plants from a garden centre. Balm grows well in pots and other containers.

Keep the plants well watered during their first summer, and pick the leaves sparingly until they are well established.

In subsequent years, cut the stems back to about 15cm (6in) from the ground each June to encourage the growth of new shoots. Each October, cut them back to just above ground level.

Raising new plants Divide in mid autumn and plant pieces of root with three or four buds. Otherwise pot up self-sown seedlings and grow on until large enough to plant out in their permanent positions.

Pests and diseases
Balm is usually trouble free.

Harvesting and storing
Gather the leaves and young shoots throughout summer for immediate use. For drying (page 300), pick leaves before the plant starts to flower in June and July.
See also freezing (page 252).

Preparing and cooking
Use the lemon-scented leaves, finely chopped, in salad dressings, or as flavourings for white sauces to accompany delicate white fish, such as plaice and sole.

Finely chopped leaves can be used as a substitute for grated lemon peel in sweets, sorbets, cakes, sauces, mayonnaise and fresh-fruit salads.

Rub chicken portions for grilling with bruised leaves, or use the chopped leaves as a stuffing.

AT-A-GLANCE TIMETABLE

SOWING
LATE SPRING
1cm (½in) deep

THINNING
SUMMER
When large enough to handle thin to 15cm (6in)

CUTTING BACK ESTABLISHED PLANTS
SUMMER
Cut back to 15cm (6in)
AUTUMN
Cut down to just above ground level

Basil

Basil, an annual herb, is used to flavour soups, pasta sauces and salads. The leaves go particularly well with tomatoes.

The herb is related to balm and, like other plants in this family, it is attractive to bees, and worth growing near plants that need pollinating.

There are several species of basil, with different flavours, colours and leaf shapes. Sweet basil, the kind sold in supermarkets, is the most widely used in cooking and to make pesto sauce. Purple basil has a warm, pungent flavour that complements rice dishes.

Planning the crop
Basil needs a warm, sheltered site and grows best in well-drained, fertile soil. If you are growing basil outdoors in the north of Britain, or if the only available site outdoors is exposed, you'll need to protect the plants with a cloche.

How much to grow This really depends on how much your household is likely to eat. One meal of pasta with pesto sauce will use up several handfuls of leaves, but a dozen or so leaves are enough to add flavour to a tomato salad.

Six plants of any type should provide plenty of fresh leaves from July to September, as well as dried leaves for use in winter, but the plants are so attractive that they can be used in mixed or annual borders as bedding plants – so plant as many as you like.

Varieties There are several species of basil, including **bush, sweet green, lemon, lime, purple** and **Siam**, all with different flavours. In addition, there is now a wide range of varieties with distinctive flavours and coloured or unusual shaped leaves.

All can be grown from seed, either from indoor sowings during early spring or from outdoor sowings made during late spring.

How to grow basil
For early plants, sow the seeds in spring at a temperature of 13°C (55°F) in a pot or tray of seed compost. Prick out the seedlings into small pots of multipurpose compost when they are large enough to handle.

Harden off the plants in late May and plant them out 30cm (12in) apart at the end of the month.

DIVIDING A SUPERMARKET-BOUGHT POT OF BASIL

Acclimatise the plant Stand the pot in its plastic sleeve in a cool, well-lit place. Gradually turn down the sleeve a little more each day. Water gently if dry.

Remove the sleeve When you can take off the sleeve without the stalks flopping over, gently tap out the contents of the pot.

Split the rootball Use a sharp knife to divide the rootball into several segments. Pot up each one into a 10cm (4in) pot of soil-based compost.

Let them recover Stand the pots in a lightly shaded place and water gently. Once the plants recover you can grow and pot them on as necessary.

Keep the soil moist until the plants are well established.

You can raise seedlings of bush basil for growing in pots in the same way, and transfer them to 13cm (5in) pots of John Innes No. 2 compost.

You can also sow basil seed outside in late spring, once all danger of frost has passed, in the position where the plants are to grow. Sow in a very shallow drill 5mm (¼in) deep, and thin out the seedlings, eventually allowing about 30cm (12in) between plants.

Water the plants during dry spells, and pinch out the flower buds at an early stage to encourage leaf growth.

Harvesting and storing
If you are picking the leaves for immediate use, harvest them as required until the first autumn frosts. To harvest larger numbers of leaves at a single picking, for drying or freezing or making into bulk batches of pesto sauce, cut the plants down once or twice to

AT-A-GLANCE TIMETABLE

SOWING (OUTDOORS)
5mm (¼in) deep
LATE SPRING
SOWING (UNDER GLASS)
EARLY SPRING
Keep above 13°C (55°F)

THINNING/PRICKING OUT
When large enough to handle. Harden off plants to be moved outdoors once risk of frost has passed
SPRING

HARVESTING
EARLY SUMMER TO EARLY AUTUMN

Bay

encourage fresh young growth.
See also drying (page 300) and
freezing (page 252).

Preparing and cooking

Traditionally, this herb is used in
the preparation of tomato dishes.
Tear the leaves or use them whole,
rather than cutting them.

The fresh young leaves are
added, torn, to salads; also to
garnishing butters and to white
sauces served with fish or poultry.

Never cook basil for very long or
the unique flavour will be lost.

Basil leaves are used in savoury
and sweet omelettes, added to
soups as flavouring or garnish, and
form the basis for the Italian pesto,
a thick sauce of pounded basil,
garlic, salt and oil, cheese and pine
nuts, served with pasta dishes.

Tricolore salad The best way to
appreciate the subtle, spicy
flavour of fresh basil is in the
tricolore salad – where the herb is
served with fresh tomatoes,
mozarella cheese and olive oil.
The salad gets its name – which
means three colours – from the
Italian flag, which is also red,
white and green.

The sweet bay, or bay
laurel, is grown for its
aromatic leaves, which are
used to flavour fish dishes,
soups and sauces. Although
native to countries around
the Mediterranean, the bay
survives as a hardy shrub in
all but the harshest of
British winters. If protected
from cold north and east
winds, it will flourish even in
coastal areas.

The bay can be allowed
to grow to its natural height
of 6m (20ft) or more.
Otherwise, you can grow it in
a tub and restrict its growth
by pruning.

A single shrub, even when
kept small by pruning, should
provide more than enough
leaves for a family.

Growing tips

The bay grows well in any ordinary
garden soil in a sunny, sheltered
position. No pruning is needed for
unrestricted trees grown in the
open garden.

In a tub, use John Innes No. 3
compost. Plant in spring.

When growing in a tub, you can
plant either a shrub already trained
from a garden centre or nursery, or
buy a young plant and train it
yourself. Nursery-trained shrubs
are comparatively expensive, and it
can be very satisfying training your
own bay tree.

If you decide to do so, you have
the choice of maintaining the
shrub's natural shape, or of
growing it with a bare stem
beneath a more formal ball-shaped
head of leaves.

When young, the natural growth
form of a bay tree is roughly
pyramidal. To maintain this shape
in a compact form, trim all actively
growing shoots in late summer to
maintain the desired outline. This
usually means cutting them back
by half.

To train a ball-headed standard
tree, see illustrations (right).

Raising new plants In late
summer or early autumn, take
10cm (4in) cuttings of lateral
shoots, with a heel (page 31), and

AT-A-GLANCE TIMETABLE

PLANTING
SPRING

PRUNING
SUMMER

CUTTINGS
LATE SUMMER TO EARLY AUTUMN

insert them in equal parts of peat
substitute and sand or perlite in a
coldframe. In spring, set the rooted
cuttings in 10cm (4in) pots of
multipurpose potting compost, and
in the following October set the
plants out in a nursery bed with
other young plants or in their final
positions.

If you plant them in a nursery
bed, allow them to grow for a
further 18 months before planting
out the strongest trees in their
permanent positions or in a
container, in spring.

Pests and diseases

The stems and underside of leaves
may be attacked by **scale insects**
(page 241). The leaves can be
attacked by **bay sucker**, a sap-
sucking insect that causes leaves to
curl at the margins and turn yellow,
and later, brown. Pick off and burn
infested leaves. If an insect
infestation causes the tree to
develop sooty mould, wash this off
with warm, soapy water.

Harvesting and storing

Once the shrub is established, pick
the leaves as required at any time
of the year.
See also drying (page 300)

Cooking with bay

Bay leaves are invaluable in
cooking. The highly aromatic leaves
are used freshly dried, to flavour
marinades, pickles, stocks and
sauces, casseroles, pâtés and
terrines. Milk custards and
puddings are greatly improved by
the addition of a partly dried bay
leaf, but its main use is in the
classic bouquet garni.

TRAINING A STANDARD BAY

Remove the leading shoot's tip
Snip out when 1.2–1.5m (4–5ft)
high. Keep lateral shoots pinched
back to two or three leaves.

Cut back new shoots The
following summer, cut shoots at
the top of stem to 15cm (6in) and
lower laterals to three leaves.

Trim the head shoots A year
later, trim these to four or five
leaves and remove lower shoots.
From then on, prune annually to
maintain a tidy ball shape.

Beans, broad

The flavour of broad beans is best when the beans are small and before the pods become tough. Commercially grown beans are often twice this size, and the bean may then have a leathery skin. Don't discard the leafy tops of the plants – they can be picked and cooked like spinach.

The broad bean is said to have been brought to Britain by the Romans, and is known to have been an important crop during the Middle Ages.

Planning the crop

Broad beans thrive in fertile, well-drained soil enriched with manure. In general, spring-sown beans do best in medium to heavy soil; autumn-sown beans are more likely to thrive in lighter soil.

If you think your soil is too heavy, work some coarse sand or soil conditioner into the top 15cm (6in) just before sowing.

How much to grow A double row 6m (20ft) long will provide about 18kg (40lb) of broad beans.

Varieties There are two classes of broad bean – **longpods** and **windsors** – which further divide into green and white types. Green-seeded beans are the better choice for freezing.

Longpods have kidney-shaped seeds in pods which can be as long as 35cm (14in). Windsors produce round seeds in short, broad pods. The longpod varieties are hardier, and are therefore more suitable for autumn sowing, but the windsors are sweeter.

Recommended longpod varieties include **Aquadulce**, the best variety for autumn sowing, **Express** and **Exhibition Longpod** (also known as **Bunyards Exhibition Longpod**).

Recommended windsors include **Green Windsor** and **Jubilee Hysor** – with, respectively, green and white seeds. **The Sutton** is a dwarf, white-seeded, windsor type suitable for small gardens, raised-bed cultivation and exposed areas. It is suited to both autumn and spring sowing.

Growing tips

Except in the north of Britain, sow in late autumn for an early crop, and early to mid spring for the main crop.

Set the seeds 15cm (6in) apart and about 5cm (2in) deep in a double row, with 25cm (9in) between rows. If more than one double row is sown, space each pair of rows 80cm (30in) apart.

Plant some reserves Sow a few extra seeds in a clump at the end of the rows to provide replacement plants for any that do not germinate or develop properly.

Sowing indoors In the north, particularly where the garden is exposed, it is not worth trying to sow beans outdoors at the end of the year. Instead, sow in mid to late winter in a cold greenhouse or frame, and plant out in early spring. Sow the main crop in mid spring.

When sowing in a coldframe or greenhouse, set the seeds 5cm (2in) apart in both directions in trays of seed compost. Cover with

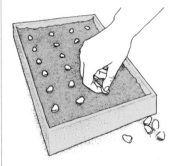

Sowing in a seed tray Set the seeds 5cm (2in) apart each way and 2.5cm (1in) from the tray's edge. An average tray will hold about 24 seeds.

Protecting broad beans In spells of very cold weather inspect autumn-sown beans and protect with a covering of fleece.

a 3cm (1in) layer of compost and lay a sheet of glass and a newspaper over the box. Remove the glass and paper when germination begins – usually after about two weeks. Plant the beans out in their final position, 15cm (6in) apart in a double row with 25cm (9in) between rows, in April.

In an exposed garden the beans need support. Insert 1m (3ft) high stakes or canes along both sides of the row, and tie two strands of string at suitable heights all round to 'frame' to support the bushy plants. Hoe the rows regularly to keep down the weeds, and give plenty of water during dry weather.

When the lowest pods are 8cm (3in) long, pinch out the plant's growing points. This encourages pod growth and development, and removes the part of the plant most likely to harbour the bean's

AT-A-GLANCE TIMETABLE

SOWING
15cm (6in) apart, 25cm (9in) between rows, 5cm (2in) deep
- **Early crop**
LATE AUTUMN TO EARLY WINTER
- **Main crop**
EARLY TO MID SPRING

PINCHING OUT
- **Early crop**
When lowest pods are 8cm (3in) long
- **Main crop**
When lowest pods are 8cm (3in) long

HARVESTING
- **Early crop**
LATE SPRING ONWARDS
- **Main crop**
EARLY SUMMER ONWARDS

Pinching out the tops For larger pods, and to reduce trouble from blackfly, pinch out the growing point when the lowest pods are 8cm (3in) long.

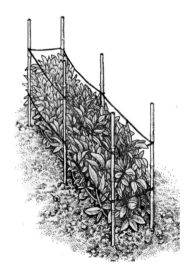

Supporting the plants In exposed gardens, support tall varieties by tying string to a double row of canes. Two strands will give adequate support.

greatest natural enemy – black bean aphid, or blackfly.

Pests and diseases
The principal pests of broad beans are **bean seed fly**, black bean **aphid** and **slugs and snails**. Diseases that may affect the crop are **chocolate spot** and **foot rot** (see Pests and Diseases pages 238–49).

Harvesting and storing
The earliest crops are ready in late spring. Start to pick them when the pods are no more than 5cm (2in) long and cook them whole. In all other cases pick the beans as required, feeling the pods to get an idea of the size of the beans inside. **See also** freezing (page 252).

Preparing and cooking
Young beans, no thicker than a finger and 8cm (3in) long, are the most delicious. They are cooked in their pods. Larger broad beans must be shelled before cooking, and served as an accompanying hot vegetable or in a salad.

Mature beans, which tend to be floury, should also be shelled. After boiling, remove the outer tough skin of the beans, too – pinch a cooked bean between your thumb and forefinger and the bright green inner bean will pop out.

Then, you can mash the beans to a purée with olive oil, garlic, salt and pepper and serve as a paté. Or leave the beans whole and dress them still warm with good olive oil, a squeeze of fresh lemon and a seasoning of salt and freshly ground black pepper. This salad is delicious sprinkled with chopped fresh herbs.

Beans, french

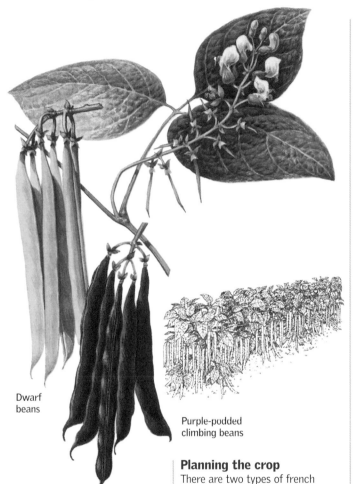

Dwarf beans

Purple-podded climbing beans

French beans are worth growing even on the smallest plot. They are ready for picking two or three weeks earlier than the first runner beans, and you don't even have to stake them if you grow dwarf varieties – though you'll get a bigger yield from climbers.

Planning the crop
There are two types of french beans – dwarf beans, which can even be grown in tubs or window boxes; and climbing beans, which may be grown up poles like runner beans, or like peas up tall bushy twigs or sturdy netting.

Both types need the same growing conditions and general cultivation. They like a light, well-drained soil in a sunny position. It is helpful, though not essential, to choose a sheltered site, as the plants are rather vulnerable to wind damage.

Dig the ground in the autumn before sowing, adding well-rotted manure or compost at the rate of a bucketful per square metre.

How many to grow A double row of dwarf beans 9m (30ft) long may yield up to 10kg (20lb) of beans. A similar row of climbing beans should yield double that amount. A 9m (30ft) row of haricot beans will provide several pickings of fresh beans, and a winter's supply of dried beans (see Beans for drying, page 92).

Varieties French beans come in dwarf and climbing varieties.

Dwarf french beans
Cropper Teepee, **Purple Teepee** and **Golden Teepee** Green, purple and yellow, stringless pods respectively; easy to pick because flowers and beans are carried above the dark foliage.
The Prince Flat-podded; a good exhibition variety.
Delinel A newer, heavy cropping 'filet' type, with pencil-thin pods and good disease resistance.

Climbing french beans
Blue Lake Consistent cropper; good flavour.
Cobra High-yielding variety; its attractive mauve flowers make this suitable for growing in the ornamental border.

Growing tips
By sowing in succession, fresh beans can be picked from late midsummer to autumn. French beans are not hardy, so to be sure of success don't sow outdoors until late spring – not more than a week or so before the risk of frost has passed.

However, sowing a week or two earlier may, with luck, yield an earlier crop. If a late frost kills your seedlings, you can make a fresh sowing. Successional sowings may in any case be made until the second half of summer.

Sow the seeds 5cm (2in) deep, with the rows spaced 18in (45cm) apart. Set the seeds in pairs, 25cm (9in) apart, and remove the weaker of the two if both germinate.

When sowing, you can form a drill with a draw hoe to the required depth, or you can plant the beans with a trowel. In each case, allow 2–3cm (1in) between the seeds in each pair so that removing one does not disturb the roots of the other.

You can produce an earlier crop if you have a greenhouse, coldframe or cloches. To raise early plants in a greenhouse or frame, sow two or three seeds in small pots of seed compost. Sow in mid spring if the plants are to be set out under cloches; a week or two later if they are to be planted direct into open ground. They should germinate without

AT-A-GLANCE TIMETABLE

SOWING
LATE SPRING TO LATE SUMMER
25cm (9in) apart, 5cm (2in) deep, 45cm (18in) between rows

THINNING
Remove the weaker of each pair of seedlings

HARVESTING
Eight weeks after sowing; pick often to encourage production

Harvested beans A colourful summer crop includes French, runner and flageolet beans.

artificial heat. Remove the weaker seedlings when large enough to handle to leave one plant per pot.

To plant under cloches, transfer the plants from the pots in late spring. Delay planting in the open until the start of summer and harden the plants off first. Plant the beans 25cm (9in) apart in rows spaced 45cm (18in) apart, or in hanging baskets, window boxes, tubs or troughs on the patio or balcony.

You can also sow french beans under cloches in mid spring, at the same spacings as for unprotected sowings, and then leave the cloches in position until the beans outgrow them.

Give support to climbing beans, using stakes or netting, when they are about 10cm (4in) high.

Pests and diseases
Common pests of french beans are **bean seed fly**, black bean **aphid** and **slugs and snails**. Diseases most likely to occur are **anthracnose** and **foot rot** (see Pests and Diseases pages 238–49).

Harvesting and storing
Dwarf beans start to crop within eight weeks of sowing, and many produce pods for up to eight weeks after that. The more they are picked, the more they produce – so look over the plants every day or two and pick pods while they are young and tender.

If they are left too long, the pods become stringy and the plants stop producing.

To make sure that you do not pull the whole plant out when harvesting, hold the stem steady with one hand and pull the pods downwards with the other.

Whether cooked immediately or frozen (see page 252), French beans should be used as soon as possible after gathering.

Preparing and cooking
These are at their most delicious when young and tender. There's no need to string them; just take off the stalks (the tails can be left on) and rinse. Lightly cooked and refreshed in cold water, they make a tender summer salad dressed with oil and lemon juice, salt and garlic. Cook them with tomatoes for a fabulous accompaniment to fresh fish or as a pasta sauce; steam and serve with a knob of butter to accompany any meat or fish dish. French beans can also be added to stir-fries for the last minute or two of cooking time. French beans are also a major ingredient of the summer dish, **Salade Niçoise**, which combines tuna, eggs, french beans, waxy new potatoes, anchovies and black olives in a robust, mustardy, oil-and-vinegar dressing.

Purple pods These stunning dwarf french beans will lose much of their glorious hue when cooked. If you want to retain the colour, don't boil them. Instead, stir-fry them briefly until just tender, or steam them in an unlidded pan.

Beans, runner

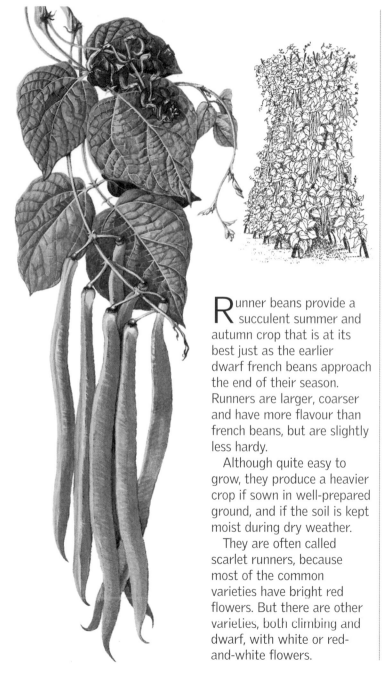

R unner beans provide a succulent summer and autumn crop that is at its best just as the earlier dwarf french beans approach the end of their season. Runners are larger, coarser and have more flavour than french beans, but are slightly less hardy.

Although quite easy to grow, they produce a heavier crop if sown in well-prepared ground, and if the soil is kept moist during dry weather.

They are often called scarlet runners, because most of the common varieties have bright red flowers. But there are other varieties, both climbing and dwarf, with white or red-and-white flowers.

Planning the crop

Runner beans grow best in a sunny position, though with as much shelter as possible to encourage the insects needed to pollinate the flowers. They will grow in most garden soils, but do best in rich, well-drained ground. Runner beans need a deep, well-manured bed to allow maximum root development.

They can also be grown in large tubs of multipurpose compost, supported by a cane wigwam, and dwarf varieties are ideal both for containers and small raised beds. A row of fully grown plants makes a good privacy screen.

A month or two before sowing, dig a trench 45cm (18in) wide where you plan to sow the crop. Remove the top layer of soil and fork a generous dressing of rotted compost or manure – at least a bucketful per square metre – into the 15cm (6in) of soil beneath. Replace the topsoil, first marking the centre of each end of the trench so that you will know where to sow. Bank up any surplus soil along each side of the trench, where it will help to retain water.

If you plan to grow the beans in a circle, bury the manure accordingly and mark the site with pegs.

How much to grow A 6m (20ft) double row of climbing runners, grown on well-manured ground, should produce up to 36kg (80lb) of beans from summer through into autumn. The yield will be much lighter if you dwarf the plants by pinching out their tips.

Varieties There's a vast choice available; here are some of the best:
Enorma An improved strain of

Prizewinner; long pods of fine flavour.
Lady Di Stringless runner bean with a good flavour.
Hammonds Dwarf Scarlet The first dwarf runner bean, and still good to grow in windy sites where climbers might blow over.
Painted Lady Old variety with red-and-white flowers; pretty enough to grow at the back of a border.
Riley Rose-pink flowers make this another candidate for the ornamental garden.
Sun Bright Yellow leaves and bright red flowers; ideal for a dual-purpose garden screen.
Hestia Similar to Painted Lady, only dwarf; excellent in window boxes and large pots on the patio.
Snow White Another dwarf, but with white flowers; it sets early and does well even in less than perfect conditions.

CANE SUPPORTS FOR BEANS

Plant out in spring Seeds sown under glass can be planted in their final growing positions in spring, 15cm (6in) apart in double rows 60cm (2ft) apart.

Build a sturdy cane support
Canes or rustic poles work equally well. Tie to a horizontal pole where poles cross.

Guide young plants Once they are tall enough, begin guiding the plants up the canes from inside the structure.

Growing tips

Sow outdoors in late spring. Under cloches, you can sow three to four weeks earlier. For an even earlier crop, raise the seedlings indoors, or in a coldframe or greenhouse, by sowing in small pots of seed compost in mid spring. After hardening the plants off, plant them out at the end of spring or very early summer.

If you plan to plant the beans out under cloches, you can sow about a fortnight earlier.

Supporting the plants To grow plants up poles or canes, push the supports into the ground in two rows about, 45cm (18in) apart. Set the poles in facing pairs, with 30cm (12in) between adjacent supports, and insert them at an angle so that each pair of poles crosses. Tie additional poles horizontally at the crossing-point to brace the structure (see page 89).

You can also support runner beans on netting – plastic, string or wire – and in this case plants should be grown in single rows about 80cm (30in) apart. Staple the netting to 50mm x 50mm (2in x 2in) timber uprights, spaced about 90cm (3ft) apart along the row, with a length of heavy-gauge wire along the top.

Another way to support runner beans is on a maypole. Insert a 2.5m (8ft) stake in the centre of each circle, and attach strings from the top of the stake to pegs hammered into the soil about 60cm (2ft) from its base. Allow 60cm (2ft) between pegs, and tie the strings in a half-bow so that they are easy to undo if they become slack and need tightening. You can use canes instead of the strings, if you prefer, leaving out

Netting support A plastic mesh, supported by strong posts, is easy to erect and will last for years if stored carefully.

the centre post. Tie the tops of the canes together, wigwam fashion.

Sowing the seeds Whichever method of support you choose, sow two seeds 5cm (2in) deep beneath the foot of each pole or string, or at 30cm (12in) spacings along the netting, and remove the weaker of the pair if both germinate. Use surplus seedlings to fill gaps where neither seed germinates.

Alternatively, sow only one seed in each position, but sow a few extra at the end of each row for filling gaps.

Protect from slugs (page 241) immediately after sowing or planting out.

Watering and spraying

You'll need to water frequently to keep runner beans growing during dry spells, and it is important not to let the soil dry out completely once the flowers appear. A thick mulch of compost or lawn mowings, applied when the ground is wet, helps to retain soil moisture. While the plants are flowering, spray them daily with water during dry weather – preferably in the evening.

When they reach the tops of the poles or netting, pinch out the growing tips to encourage the formation of sideshoots and to prevent the heads of the plants developing into a tangled mass.

After the crop has been harvested, cut down the stems but leave the roots in the ground as they add nitrogen to the soil. As runner beans are perennial you may find some plants regrow the following spring or summer from the old root, which has formed a tuber rather like that of a dahlia. These plants are usually weak and are best removed.

Pests and diseases

Runner beans may be attacked by **bean seed fly**, black bean **aphid**, and **slugs and snails**. The most

---

AT-A-GLANCE TIMETABLE

SOIL PREPARATION
EARLY SPRING
Dig a trench 45cm (18in) wide; enrich soil with manure

SOWING
LATE SPRING
Pairs of seeds, 30cm (12in) apart and 5cm (2in) deep

THINNING AND SPRAYING
Remove the weaker seedling; spray daily in dry weather

HARVESTING
SUMMER ONWARDS

Beans, soya

likely diseases are **chocolate spot** and **foot rot** (see Pests and Diseases pages 238–49).

Harvesting and storing
Pick the beans while they are still young and tender, before the seeds begin to swell in the pods. The more they are picked, the more the plants will produce. For this reason, always remove large beans that have been overlooked.

If you can't use pods immediately, stand them in a cool place with the ends of their stems in shallow water.

See also drying (page 300) and freezing (page 252).

Preparing and cooking
Maturing shortly after french beans, runner beans can be used in much the same way. To prepare them for cooking, wash thoroughly, cut off the tops and tails and peel off any stringy edges. Discard any discoloured or damaged parts.

Chop larger beans into 3cm (1in) diagonal lengths; small ones can be cooked whole.

Cook in a small amount of boiling water for 5–7 minutes. Drain thoroughly in a colander, and serve at once with a pat of butter. Or try them lightly tossed in cream and a handful of fresh chopped herbs. Prepared and cooked runner beans can be served cold in a salad with finely sliced red onions. They taste very good with a lemony vinaigrette, too – toss them in a mixture of olive oil and lemon juice plus zest and a good sprinkling of salt and pepper.

Don't throw away big, old beans. Instead, discard the pods and cook the mature seeds like broad beans (page 87).

A mong the most nutritious of all the legumes, soya beans are an especially valuable source of protein for vegetarians. Birds like them too, so this crop is well worth netting.

If you delay sowing part of the crop until midsummer, you can extend the cropping period well into autumn.

Planning the crop
Soya beans need a warm site – in a good summer their yield can be twice as heavy as that in a cool season. Prepare the soil during the previous autumn or winter by digging in a bucketful of manure or compost per square metre. A couple of healthy 6m (20ft) rows will provide plenty of pods.

Variety The only variety available for amateur growing is **Untie**.

Growing tips
Sow in the open in late spring in the south. In the north, it is better to wait until early summer. In light soil, sow in drills about 5cm (2in) deep; in heavy soil, make the drills only 3cm (1in) deep. Set the seeds 8cm (3in) apart. Allow 25–30cm (9–12in) between rows. This close sowing is fine because soya plants form only a single stem, instead of branching like french beans.

Cover the rows with netting or fleece to protect them from birds. The seedlings will appear about three weeks after sowing, depending on the temperature and the amount of moisture in the soil.

Alternatively, start the seeds in pots. This prevents them from being eaten by mice and wood pigeons, although the plants get off to a slower start than those sown where they will eventually grow. Put four seeds to an 8cm (3in) pot of seed compost – indoors or in a coldframe – in late spring. Set plants out singly in their final positions, 8cm (3in) apart, in early summer. Water in, and make sure that they do not dry out during the first few days while they are forming new roots. The plants will need supporting with twiggy sticks to keep them upright.

Pests and diseases
Bean seed fly (page 238), black bean **aphids** (page 238) and **slugs and snails** (page 241) are the most likely pests. Soya beans are generally disease free.

AT-A-GLANCE TIMETABLE

SOWING OUTDOORS
LATE SPRING TO EARLY SUMMER
5cm (2in) deep; 8cm (3in) apart; 25–30cm (9–12in) between rows

SOWING INDOORS
MID SPRING

TRANSPLANTING
EARLY SUMMER
8cm (3in) apart

MAIN HARVEST
LATE SUMMER TO EARLY AUTUMN

LATE HARVEST
AUTUMN

Harvesting and storing
Soya beans may be picked at two stages – first, for eating fresh, either shelled or cooked in the pod, and later for drying and storing.

In late summer or autumn, pick the pods while they are still green but when the seeds inside can be seen and felt. Usually, the pods on a single plant are ready at the same time, and it may be easier to cut the stem at the base and remove the pods in the kitchen.

As the season progresses, the pods look more cream-coloured and the foliage takes on autumn tints. Shelled beans can still be cooked at this stage, but not the whole pod.

By the time the seeds are ripe the foliage will have died away. Pull up the plants, complete with their roots, tie them together and hang them in an airy place such as a shed or garage to complete the drying off.

Shell them when the pods are absolutely dry, and store the beans in tins or bags for use as needed.

Preparing and cooking
Young, immature green pods can be cooked and eaten just like sugar snap peas, with butter and chopped fresh herbs. Later, they need to be shelled like broad beans. This is not as easy as with other beans. First, you must blanch the pods in boiling water for about 5 minutes before cooling and breaking in half. Then you can cook the shelled beans, again in boiling water, for 10–15 minutes until tender. Serve tossed in butter and sprinkled with parsley.

Beans for drying

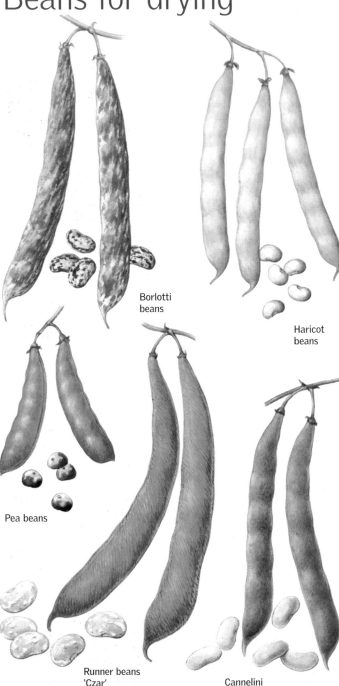

Borlotti beans

Haricot beans

Pea beans

Runner beans 'Czar'

Cannelini beans

Some beans that are technically french beans are grown mainly for drying, although when young the whole pod can be eaten in the same way as other french beans. A few varieties used for drying are really runner beans producing flat, white beans. These, too, are dual-purpose beans, eaten whole when young and tender, or podded, dried and cooked as butter beans.

Look out, too for borlotti, lima, cannellini and other types of bean listed as suitable for drying.

Borlotti beans generally have striking, brightly coloured pods and attractive, white seeds with dark red streaks. Other beans for drying include cannellini, flageolet, lima, black-eyed, haricot and a climbing bean known as the pea bean, which has interesting, white-and-brown seeds that can be used in most recipes calling for dried beans.

Planning the crop
Most borlotti and other drying beans are cultivated in the same way as other french beans (pages 87–88).

Those varieties described as runner beans should be grown like runner beans (pages 89–90).

How many to grow A 9m (30ft) row of borlotti and similar bean varieties will yield some beans for picking young, and enough beans to last an average family until the following season.

Varieties Choose from these recommended varieties:

Borlotti beans
Centroflamme (100 Flames); **Rosso**; **Lingua di Fuoco** (Firetongue). Other varieties are often offered in specialist seed catalogues.

Other beans for drying
Czar A white-seeded runner bean which is eaten as a butter bean.
Canadian Wonder Red-seeded french bean for cooking in chilli con carne.
Soissons Climbing flageolet/french bean.
Dolico-dall'occhio Black-eyed/french bean.
Comtesse de Chambord Haricot/french bean.
    Lima, **cannellini** and **pea beans** are usually listed under these generic names.

Growing tips
Beans for drying are grown and cared for either as french or runner beans according to type (pages 87–90). The main difference is that to get the maximum mature crop for drying, a long growing period is desirable, so the ground where the beans are to be sown should be warmed by covering with black polythene or cloches from late winter. When the soil temperature has reached 13°C (55°F) the seeds can be sown, but should, themselves, be covered with fleece or cloches until late spring to protect them from late frosts and keep them growing strongly.

Otherwise, sow two seeds in small pots of multipurpose compost in the greenhouse in mid spring and plant out when the seedlings are well-developed

(usually early summer). These plants will, by this time, be at the same stage as those sown earlier outdoors. Do not pick too many pods fresh for cooking green, as this will delay the plants' maturity.

Pests and diseases
See french beans (pages 87–88) and runner beans (pages 89–90).

Harvesting and storing
Leave the pods on the plants until they have ripened and turned white in autumn. Choose a dry day to pull up the plants whole, and hang them in a dry, airy place.

When the pods feel crisp and dry, shell the beans and spread them out on trays to dry thoroughly. When you are confident that the seeds are completely dry, store in airtight tins or jars until you want to use them – in any recipes requiring dried beans.

Preparing and cooking
Dried beans can be used in soups, stews, casseroles and many ethnic dishes. It's vitally important to soak dried beans overnight, drain and rinse thoroughly.

All types contain a large amount of the chemical lecithin, a poison that can cause severe stomach upsets but this is destroyed by thorough boiling. To cook, place beans in a pan of cold, unsalted water, bring to the boil and boil hard for at least 10 minutes, before turning down to a simmer and cooking until tender. Home-dried beans do not need as long a cooking time as shop-bought ones.

Use cooked beans in warming winter casseroles – they combine superbly with pork or bacon when cooked in a thick, sweet, tomato-based sauce.

Beetroot

Long-rooted beetroot

Globe beetroot

These sweet-tasting roots will succeed in most gardens that are fertile and not waterlogged.

There are two main types of beetroot. Globe varieties are generally grown for eating freshly boiled in summer and autumn; long-rooted kinds are more suitable as a main crop for harvesting in autumn and storing for winter use.

Beetroot is generally a deep crimson, but you can also grow golden yellow, striped or white varieties.

The ancient Greeks used to eat beetroot leaves, while the root has been popular in Britain since Tudor times.

You can eat the root raw, grated in salads, or cooked, although this diminishes its vitamin C content. Beetroot can make your urine red – many parents have panicked at the sight of pink nappies after feeding beetroot to their babies.

Planning the crop

Like most vegetables, beetroot need an open, sunny site. Although the roots do best on a light, sandy loam they can be grown on heavier soil if this is suitably prepared. Dig the plot in the autumn or early winter before sowing and, if the soil is heavy, fork in sieved garden compost or soil conditioner at the rate of a bucketful per square metre.

Do not grow beetroot on freshly manured ground or the beets will tend to divide into small, forked roots. Before sowing, rake in a dressing of general fertiliser at 60g per square metre (2oz per square yard).

How many to grow A 6m (20ft) row should produce about 10kg (20lb) of globe beetroot, or 20kg (40lb) of a long-rooted variety for winter use.

Globe-rooted varieties
Boltardy – fine-textured, deep-red root; highly resistant to bolting; can be sown earlier than most other varieties.

AT-A-GLANCE TIMETABLE

SOWING
• Globe beet
SPRING TO MIDSUMMER
• Long-rooted beet
LATE SPRING

THINNING
MIDSUMMER TO LATE SUMMER
• **First thinning** 5cm (2in) apart when 2.5cm (1in) high
LATE SUMMER TO EARLY AUTUMN
• **Second thinning** Thin when roots are half golf-ball size. Leave strongest seedling in each group and eat the babies

HARVESTING
FROM LATE AUTUMN THROUGH WINTER, AS REQUIRED
Pull before roots exceed cricket-ball size

Crimson Globe – can be sown for succession from late April to July to give roots for winter use.
Detroit – sweet, crisp flesh.
Golden Ball – golden-yellow flesh; excellent sweet flavour.

Intermediate and long-rooted varieties
Chioggia – orange-pink outside, pink and white rings inside. **Albina Vereduna** – white flesh, mild flavour.

Cylindrical and long-rooted varieties
Cylindra – deep red, good flavour. **Cheltenham Green Top** – very long roots; stores well.

Growing tips
In sheltered positions in the south, sow bolt-resisting varieties from mid March onwards. In the north, delay sowing until mid April. For a succession of roots in summer and autumn, sow globe varieties from spring to midsummer (July).

Sow long-rooted varieties in late spring or early summer for winter storage.

For globe varieties draw the drills 30cm (12in) apart; for long-rooted varieties allow 45cm (18in) between rows. In both cases, make drills about 2cm (¾in) deep.

A beetroot 'seed' is, in fact, a fused cluster of up to four separate seeds. As these will germinate as a group, sow sparingly to make subsequent thinning easier. Single seeds, such as **Monopoly** are also available. These reduce the need for thinning, but must be sown closer together.

Space seed clusters of globe varieties about 5cm (2in) apart. For long-rooted maincrop varieties, sow two clusters every 20cm (8in)

HARVESTING AND STORING BEETS

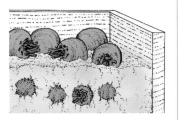

Lift the roots Pull globe beetroot by hand; lift long-rooted types with a fork, taking care not to damage the roots.

Remove the leaves Known as 'topping', all you have to do is screw off the foliage, leaving the leaf stalks attached to the root so that it doesn't 'bleed'.

Pack in a box Store maincrop roots by layering with sand or old potting compost. The material should be slightly damp.

Protect Cover each layer of roots with sand before adding the next, finishing with sand.

along the drill, later thinning to a single seedling.

When the seedlings of globe varieties are about 3cm (1in) high, remove the weakest from each group to leave a row of single seedlings about 5cm (2in) apart. You can eat the leaves of these thinnings raw in salads; cook larger leaves like spinach.

When the roots are about half the size of a golf ball, start thinning so that those left to grow on are about 10cm (4in) apart. Boil the baby beets you pull up to eat as a delicious vegetable. Pull the rest of the crop as you need them, but don't let any grow above the size of

a cricket ball, as they become woody and lose flavour.

Pests and diseases
Aphids (page 238) may attack young shoots; beetroot can also be affected by **violet root rot** (page 247).

Harvesting and storing
Pull globe beetroot by hand as required. Once out of the ground, hold the base of the leaves with one hand and twist off the root with the other. Cutting leaf stems, or twisting them off too close to the root, will cause the root to 'bleed' when cooked.

Lift long-rooted beetroot in early winter by putting a fork alongside the row and easing the soil so that the roots can be pulled out without damage. After twisting off the tops, store the roots in boxes of sand or peat in a frost-proof shed or garage.

Now that winters are getting milder, you can leave maincrop beetroot in all winter to pull when required; just give them some protection with straw or fleece.
See also chutneys (page 292); freezing (page 252); pickles (page 285) and wine-making (page 304).

Preparing and cooking
At its best when pulled young, before the flesh becomes stringy, you can peel and grate raw beetroot to eat as a salad – perhaps adding some zesty freshly grated horseradish.

If you wish to cook the beets, don't peel them, and be sure to leave the stringy root and 3–4cm (1–2in) of leaf stalks intact. This will help to prevent the colour and flavour leaching out into the cooking water.

Boil the beets until tender; this can take an hour or more depending on their size. Then, put them into a bowl of cold water and rub the skins off with your thumbs – it will come away easily.

Make a warming soup by cooking grated raw beetroot and onion in stock; whizz it all in a blender, season well and top with a dollop of crème fraîche.

Cooked, then grated and served hot, beetroot is a great accompaniment for pork or poultry. Puréed and mixed with potatoes and a little grated cheese, it's the perfect baby food.

Blueberries, cranberries and lingonberries

In the wild, these berries grow in acid, moorland soil. In the garden they need a moist, peaty, very acid soil and an open, sunny position. If your garden is on limey soil, grow the bushes in pots or tubs of ericaceous (lime-free) compost.

The cultivated blueberry originates in America but is related to our native wild bilberry, whortleberry or lowbush blueberry, which has smaller fruits.

The cranberry is a close relative of the blueberry, and requires similar conditions and cultivation. The lingonberry (also known as cowberry, mountain cranberry or lowbush cranberry) is sometimes grown as an alternative to the cranberry.

Planning the crop
Don't try growing these bushes in your garden unless you have a damp, acid soil. Prepare the soil a few weeks before planting by digging a hole about 1–1.2m (3–4ft) square. Break up the subsoil with a fork, but be careful not to bring it to the surface. Mix an equal amount (by volume) of damp peat substitute or sieved leafmould with the topsoil, and fill in the hole so that the ground has time to settle before planting. Do not manure the ground.

How many to grow Blueberries may grow to 1.8m (6ft) high with a spread of up to 1.2m (4ft). Each bush will produce 2.5–5kg (5–10lb) of fruit, depending on weather and soil conditions. Plant at least two bushes, preferably of different varieties, to ensure pollination.

Varieties These bushes have good autumn colour, so could be planted among ornamental shrubs; they also look good in containers.
Blue Crop vigorous; grows to a height of 1.5m (5ft) with a similar spread; it bears large sweet berries and is a reliable cropper.
Earliblue grows to a height of 1.4m (4ft 6in) with a 1.5m (5ft) spread; its large berries ripen from mid July.

Growing tips
Plant blueberry bushes in the prepared ground 1.5m (5ft) apart at any time from late autumn to early spring. Container raised plants may be planted at any time providing the weather is suitable.

AT-A-GLANCE TIMETABLE

PLANTING
LATE AUTUMN TO EARLY SPRING
1.5m (5ft) apart

PRUNING
LATE AUTUMN TO EARLY SPRING

HARVESTING
SUMMER TO AUTUMN

After planting, apply a 15cm (6in) mulch of peat substitute, leafmould, shredded bark or sawdust. Commercial growers find that sawdust gives more successful results than peat substitutes.

In early spring, apply a general fertiliser at the rate of 60g per square metre (2oz per square yard). About one month to six weeks later, apply sulphate of ammonia at the rate of 30g per square metre (1oz per square yard).

Except for removing stems lying on the ground, pruning is unnecessary until the third winter.

Lowbush blueberries, cranberries and lingonberries can be grown in individual pots or as ground-cover on suitable soil, planted initially 30cm (1ft) apart.

Pruning Each winter, from the third winter onwards, cut back old, dry stems either to the ground or to a vigorous new shoot close to the ground.

Blueberries, which fruit on the tips of the previous season's growth, first produce sideshoots soon after flowering in spring; then in July vigorous growths push up from the base of the bush. Hard pruning in winter will encourage this renewed growth and result in larger, earlier fruit.

RAISING NEW BLUEBERRY BUSHES

Layering Select one or two long shoots in early autumn, and cut a tongue in each where it can be bent to touch the ground (left). Peg down with bent wires. Sever the plant and set it in its permanent position when well rooted, after one or two years.

Cuttings Take cuttings of semi-ripe shoots, with a heel of old wood (left), in midsummer. Remove the soft tip, dip the heel in rooting powder, and plant in equal parts (by volume) of peat and sand, or perlite, in a coldframe. Spray frequently with water until rooted.

Lowbush blueberries, cranberries and lingonberries These need very acid, boggy conditions to succeed in open ground. They produce horizontal shoots across the surface of the soil, with short, upright shoots coming from these. The shoots flower in summer and set berries that are ready for picking in autumn. Little regular pruning is needed. Simply clip back the shoots after fruiting and remove dead wood. Feed these in the same way as blueberries.

Pests and diseases
These plants are generally trouble free.

Harvesting and storing
Pick the berries from the middle of summer to mid autumn as they ripen. Go over the bushes a number of times.
See also chutneys (page 292); freezing (page 252); jams (page 271); jellies (page 277) and wine-making (page 304).

Healthy eating Blueberry muffins are a tasty way to keep up fibre levels.

Preparing and cooking
Blueberries, and our native bilberries, are used chiefly for jams and jellies; but cleaned, and with the stalks and blossom ends removed, they may also be eaten fresh as dessert berries.

Blueberry muffins Mix together 200g self-raising flour, a teaspoon of baking powder, 85g caster sugar, the zest of a lemon, an egg, 100ml milk and 50g blueberries. Spoon into a nonstick muffin tray and cook in an oven preheated to 220°C (425°F, gas mark 7) for about 15 minutes. Cool the muffins on a wire rack.

Cranberry sauce This traditional Christmas sauce is easily made by stewing 300g fresh cranberries with the juice and zest of four clementines, 120g white sugar and a small glass of Port. Simmer for about 15 minutes until the skins split and the fruit becomes pulpy. It will store in a covered pot in the fridge for a couple of weeks.

Borage

The young leaves of borage, an annual herb, taste like cucumber. They can be used to flavour salads and soups or chopped finely and stirred into crème fraîche or yoghurt. Try serving a yoghurt and borage 'raita' with curry or dipping crudités or prawns into the crème fraîche mix.

Its bright blue, star-shaped flowers, borne from June to September, can be used to garnish salads or frozen in ice-cube trays and used in summer drinks. Borage flowers, like those of balm, are attractive to bees and useful for encouraging pollinating insects.

The plant grows 45cm to 1m (18in–3ft) high, and has a similar spread, so plant it near the front or centre of a flower border or in clumps at the top of a sunny bank, as well as in the herb garden.

Planning the crop
Borage will grow in almost any type of soil, but it does best in well-drained ground in a sunny position.

How many to grow Five or six plants will provide plenty of leaves throughout summer.

Growing tips
Sow seeds in spring in their growing positions, setting them about 1cm (½in) deep and 30cm (12in) apart, in groups of three. Remove the weakest seedlings, leaving the strongest to grow on unchecked.

Borage seeds germinate readily and the seedlings grow rapidly,

AT-A-GLANCE TIMETABLE

SOWING
SPRING
A pinch of seeds, 30cm (12in) apart, 1cm (½in) deep

THINNING
LATE SPRING
When large enough to handle

HARVESTING
EARLY SUMMER TO AUTUMN
Tender young leaves and blue, star-shaped flowers

making this one of the easiest herbs to grow. Borage also seeds itself freely, so in subsequent years you should be able to get all the plants you need by transplanting self-sown seedlings. Transplant the seedlings before they develop their hairy leaves, otherwise they tend to wilt and may die or do poorly.

Pests and diseases
This herb is sometimes attacked by **aphids** (page 238), but it is generally free of disease.

Harvesting and storing
Borage plants grow very fast and the young leaves are ready for picking about eight weeks after sowing. They are covered in fine hairs, which can irritate the skin.

Borage can be dried for winter use, but this is more difficult than with many other herbs because the leaves tend to turn black if the ventilation is inadequate or the temperature too high. However, they may be frozen.
See also drying (page 300) and freezing (page 252).

Preparing and cooking
Besides being used in salads, the flowers and leaves are also added to summer punches, to which they bring a cucumber-like coolness. Tea made from freshly chopped leaves is refreshing, and the flowers can be candied and used for cake and sweet decorations.

Broccoli and calabrese

Broccoli

Calabrese

If you want to be able to harvest fresh vegetables all year round, then plant sprouting broccoli in your vegetable patch. Its purple or white heads help to fill a lean period in late winter and early spring, when Brussels sprouts have almost finished and the spring cabbage season has yet to begin.

What we buy as 'broccoli' in the supermarket is, in fact, calabrese, which produces larger, green heads in autumn. This is much less hardy than broccoli and will not stand the winter, so do not sow for spring use.

Sprouting broccoli does not produce a single, large head in the same way as a cauliflower. Instead, it grows spears – many small heads, which are cut with a length of stem and cooked in a bunch. As you cut the spears, more will develop over a period of four to six weeks.

Planning the crop

Broccoli and calabrese grow best in fertile, loamy soil in a sunny position. It is helpful, but not vital, to choose a site sheltered from winter winds for sprouting broccoli. Failing this, they may need supporting with sturdy canes.

If the soil has not been manured for a previous crop, dig in some well-rotted manure or compost during the autumn or winter before planting.

Feed the soil In spring, give all soils, unless already alkaline, a top dressing of garden lime at a rate of 120g per square metre (4oz per square yard). A fortnight before setting out the plants, hoe in a general fertiliser at 90g per square metre (3oz per square yard).

How many to grow Sprouting broccoli occupies a good deal of space – about 60cm (2ft) between plants – for as long as eight months of the year. These two factors will determine how many you want to grow in the area available. Ten plants in a row 6m (20ft) long should yield at least 7kg (15lb) of spears.

Varieties Grow a few plants of an early sprouting broccoli such as **Early White Sprouting** and a late one like **Late Purple Sprouting** for plenty of spears from the second

half of winter to well into spring. Every year new – and possibly improved – varieties of calabrese seed are offered for sale. Check your seed catalogues for the latest introductions.

Growing tips

Sow calabrese seeds in early spring, and those of sprouting broccoli about four weeks later, in drills 1cm (½in) deep in a seedbed or in a coldframe or in seed trays in an unheated greenhouse. Allow 30cm (12in) between drills outdoors.

Thin the seedlings to 5cm (2in) apart. Pot up indoor-raised seedlings into 9cm (3in) pots when large enough to handle. When the plants are about 10cm (4in) high, plant them in their permanent positions.

Calabrese Allow 50cm (20in) between plants and 60cm (2ft) between rows.

Sprouting broccoli Set plants 60cm (2ft) apart, and allow 80cm (2ft 6in) between rows. Firm both well with your feet.

Keep weeds down with a hoe and water thoroughly during dry spells.

Sprouting broccoli plants may get rocked by winter winds, which loosens their roots. Drive stakes in on each side of the row, and tie strings between the stakes to support the plants.

Pests and diseases

Pests that may occur include **aphids**, **cabbage root fly**, **cabbage whitefly**, **caterpillars** and **flea beetle**. **Club root** and **whiptail** are the most likely diseases. See Pests and Diseases, pages 238–49.

Harvesting and storing

Calabrese Cut the heads of calabrese with about 2.5cm (1in) of stalk in late summer and early autumn when the flower buds are green and tightly closed. After the main head is cut, sideshoots will grow and further heads will be produced.

Broccoli When harvesting sprouting broccoli, cut about 10–15cm (4–6in) of stem and cook this with the heads. Cut back the stem to a point just above a pair of sideshoots, which will then produce fresh spears.

Both calabrese and sprouting broccoli can be frozen (page 252).

AT-A-GLANCE TIMETABLE

SOWING
• Calabrese
EARLY SPRING
• Sprouting broccoli
MID SPRING
1cm (½in) deep in rows 30cm (12in) apart

THINNING
• For both
When seedlings are large enough to handle
5cm (2in) apart

TRANSPLANTING
• For both
When plants are about 10cm (4in) high
50–60cm (20–24in) apart
Rows 60–80cm (24–30in) apart

HARVESTING
• Calabrese
LATE SUMMER TO AUTUMN
• Sprouting broccoli
LATE WINTER TO SPRING

Preparing and cooking

Sprouting broccoli White, green and purple sprouting broccoli are related to the cauliflower, but in flavour they are more reminiscent of asparagus. The fresh spears, on brittle stalks, may in fact be cooked and served in the same way as most asparagus dishes.

To prepare broccoli, wash the spears carefully in cold water, strip off the leaves and trim off any tough parts from the base of the stalks. Traditionally, broccoli is cooked in boiling, lightly salted water. However, boiling broccoli almost halves its vitamin C content, so it is better to microwave, stir-fry or lightly steam it. Tender stems should be cooked in a couple of minutes – test with the tip of a knife. Sprouting broccoli makes a delicious starter or side vegetable; cook until tender and serve with melted butter. Or dip spears like soldiers into soft-boiled egg yolk.

Calabrese This vegetable has a milder flavour than sprouting broccoli. Chop up the florets and add them to pasta water 5 minutes before the end of cooking. Drain and stir in some crème fraîche and grated parmesan for a fast and delicious family meal. Calabrese is great in stir-fries and curries, or served raw in a selection of crudités and dips. Or simply cook whole to serve with roast meat or a hearty stew.

Don't discard the stalks of broccoli or calabrese; these can be chopped up and sweated in butter or oil with onions and other vegetables and blended with stock to make a nutritious soup.

Brussels sprouts

This hardy vegetable is rich in vitamin C, and will provide a crop during autumn and winter if both early and late varieties are planted. However, if you have a freezer it may be easier to make a single sowing of either type and freeze surplus sprouts to extend their period of use.

Brussels sprouts occupy a fair amount of space over a longer period (about eight months) than most crops. For this reason they may not be a wise choice for very small gardens, and in any case they do better in rather more open conditions than those provided by the average fenced-in plot.

It is thought that Brussels sprouts, a descendant of the wild cabbage, were first grown in Belgium – hence their name.

Planning the crop

Sprouts grow well only in fertile, reasonably limey soil. Dig the following season's bed during winter, so that it has plenty of time to settle. Ideally, it should have been well manured for a previous crop; otherwise, add compost or manure when you dig. Then spread lime on the surface (page 20).

How many to grow Each 3m (10ft) row of plants should yield about 7.5kg (16lb) of sprouts.

Varieties The introduction of F1 hybrid varieties has greatly improved the quality and yield of Brussels sprouts. Only the best of the ordinary varieties give equal results. **Bedford Fillbasket** is perhaps the best of the old varieties. For a tried and tested F1 hybrid, consider **Topline** or **Peer Gynt**. **Rubine** is an interesting variety in that it is a red sprout that keeps its colour when cooked.

Growing tips
Although you can produce very early sprouts by sowing in a cold greenhouse, these will mature when there are still plenty of summer vegetables around. Better to sow outdoors and fill the winter

dearth. With that in mind, make your first sowings of early varieties in early to midspring in a sheltered seedbed.

Sowing Brussels sprouts Sow the seeds 1cm (½in) deep in drills 25cm (10in) apart, thinning the seedlings to at least 5cm (2in) apart when they are about 2cm (1in) high.

Early varieties will be ready for harvesting from autumn to the turn of the year.

Sow maincrop varieties in mid spring, with similar spacings to early varieties. They will mature from early winter till spring.

Transplanting When plants of both early and maincrop varieties are about six weeks old and 10–15cm (4–6in) tall, transplant them into their final bed and give a

top dressing of a slow-release, general fertiliser, according to manufacturer's instructions.

Select only healthy, strong-looking plants, making sure each has a growing point, and plant them firmly 45–60cm (18in–2ft) apart – the closer spacing for compact varieties – in rows the same distance apart.

The best way to plant is with a dibber, first making the planting hole with the tool and then, after planting, stabbing it in again close to the plant to firm the soil against it. If you use a trowel, firm the soil afterwards with your heel.

In windy areas, it is a good idea to plant in a shallow trench and draw the soil up to the stems as the plants develop – they will make more roots into the extra depth of soil so they will be less likely to rock about in a wind. Loose

planting is the most likely cause of 'blown' (open) sprouts.

Water the sprouts thoroughly in dry weather.

Stake the plants individually if they seem to rock in strong winds.

Pests and diseases
The pests most likely to affect Brussels sprouts are **aphids**, **cabbage root fly**, **cabbage whitefly**, **caterpillars** and **flea beetle**. Diseases include **club root** and **leaf spot**.
See Pests and Diseases, pages 238–49.

Harvesting and storing
The best time to pick sprouts is when they are small. Harvesting standard varieties after frost improves the taste, but newer F1 varieties have been bred to taste sweet from the outset.

Pick the lower sprouts first. Sprouts at the top of the plant can be encouraged to swell by removing the cabbage-like head – called sprout tops – which can be cooked as a separate vegetable.
See also freezing (page 252).

Preparing and cooking
Pick the sprouts when they are not much larger than walnuts, and with their leaves still tight and firm. Old Brussels sprouts with loose leaves are practically flavourless.

Pick the sprouts just before cooking, peel off any ragged outer leaves and trim the base. You can, if you wish, cut an X in the stalk, though this is not necessary. Rinse the prepared sprouts in cold water.

Cook or steam in the minimum of boiling salted water for 6–8 minutes. The cooked sprouts should still have some bite, not be watery and squashy. Drain and serve.

Shredded leaves Pests may strip the leaves of Brussels sprouts but this will have no detrimental effect on the sprouts themselves.

The flavour is enhanced if you boil the sprouts for just 5 minutes, and then braise them with finely sliced onions in a little butter, stock and seasoning for a further 3–4 minutes.

Sprouts with chestnuts This is a traditional accompaniment to roast turkey at Christmas. Go for a weight ratio of about two to one sprouts to chestnuts. Cook the sprouts for 5–7 minutes. Meanwhile, sauté cooked, peeled chestnuts in a little butter in a separate pan. Toss the two together and season with a good grind of fresh black pepper.

Sauteed sprouts Fry some diced bacon until it turns golden brown. Add a large handful of trimmed and halved Brussels sprouts, along with some grated orange rind, a slab of butter and a dollop of wholegrain mustard. Cook for 5 minutes, until the sprouts are crisp. Add a few water chestnuts, roughly chopped, and cook for another 3–4 minutes. Season and serve.

Treating the soil Use only garden compost to fertilise the ground, as using manure will lead to open heads instead of tight-budded sprouts.

AT-A-GLANCE TIMETABLE
SOWING
• **Early varieties**
EARLY SPRING
• **Maincrop varieties**
SPRING
Sow 1cm (½in) deep in rows 25cm (10in) apart
THINNING
• **Both early and maincrop varieties**
5cm (2in) apart when seedlings about 2cm (1in) high
TRANSPLANTING
• **Both early varieties and maincrop**
45–60cm (18in–2ft) apart both ways
LATE SPRING (EARLY)
EARLY SUMMER (MAINCROP)

Cabbages

Savoy cabbage

Winter cabbage

Summer cabbage

Red cabbage

Spring cabbage

The cabbage is hardy and easy to grow, and if different varieties are planted it will provide a succession of crops throughout the year.

In shape, cabbage heads, or hearts, may be round, conical or drumhead (round, with a flattened top); in colour they range from dark and light green to pink and purple.

Long reviled as the most abhorred vegetable of school dinners, the cabbage even lent its name as a term of contempt for a dull, stolid person. But if grown and cooked properly, cabbage is a delicious vegetable and one rich in nutrients.

Spring cabbages have bright green, loose-leaved heads and are in season from early to late spring. The small varieties may be cut early, before they mature – when they are known as spring greens.

Summer cabbages have larger, more compact heads. They are ready in late summer and autumn.

Autumn and winter cabbages, which have solid heads like the summer varieties, are ready for cutting from autumn to late winter.

Savoy cabbages are round-headed, with crisp, crinkled leaves. They are hardy and easy to grow, and with successional sowings will provide a crop of fresh green vegetables from early autumn right through winter and spring. Red cabbages, which are often grown for pickling, have solid heads of crisp leaves. They are another good autumn and winter crop.

Planning the crop

Cabbages need a sunny, open site in well-drained, alkaline soil. This applies to both the seedbed, in which they are raised, and to the main growing site.

When cabbages follow pod-bearing crops and salads in a crop rotation, the plot should not require manure or compost; instead, apply a general fertiliser at planting time. If you are growing vegetables for the first time, and therefore establishing a rotation, dig in a dressing of manure or compost during the previous winter.

Whether or not manure is needed, spread lime on the surface after digging (page 20) unless the soil is chalky or has recently been limed. If you don't apply lime after digging, then rake it into the surface of the soil at planting time.

How much to grow A 3m (10ft) row will yield about 5kg (10lb) of spring cabbages, 6.5kg (14lb) of summer cabbages or 5.5kg (12lb) of autumn, winter, savoy or red.

Varieties Cabbages are available to harvest in spring, summer, autumn and winter, according to variety and you can choose to grow summer cabbages with rounded or pointed heads. Other common types are the crinkle-leaved Savoy and tight-headed red cabbage.

Summer cabbages with round heads

Golden Acre Early; medium-size; good flavour.

Minicole (F1 hybrid) Small hard heads that will not go to seed for several months.

Summer cabbages with pointed heads
Greyhound Medium-size, with few outer leaves.
Hispi (F1 hybrid) Large, solid, crisp heads.

Autumn and winter cabbages
Christmas Drumhead Dwarf and compact; very hardy.

Savoy cabbages
January King Very hardy; suitable for the north.
Savoy King (F1) Matures in late summer to autumn.

Spring cabbages
April Crops heavily; firm hearts.
Durham Early Early, reliable and hardy.

Red cabbages
Blood Red Matures early; pickles well.
Red Drumhead Compact heads suitable for the smaller plot.

Growing tips
Cabbages of all types are raised in a seedbed or in trays under glass, and then transplanted to their growing positions. In both cases you'll need to have dug the ground and applied a dressing of lime, if necessary (page 20). Before sowing or planting, tread the bed firm and rake it to a fine tilth. Apply a general fertiliser at 60g per square metre (2oz per square yard).

Summer cabbages Sow seeds in mid spring in a prepared seedbed at the same depth and distance as for spring cabbages (right). Or sow in an unheated greenhouse or coldframe in trays of seed compost.

Thin overcrowded seedlings, and transplant those that are left to a permanent bed in late spring or early summer, setting them 45cm (18in) apart in rows the same distance apart. Prick out those raised under glass into 9cm (3in) pots and plant out in late spring. Plant firmly. Hoe regularly during summer, and keep well watered.

Autumn and winter cabbages Sow seeds in mid to late spring in a prepared seedbed, as for spring and summer cabbages. For a regular supply through the winter months, sow two or more batches.

Transplant the seedlings between late spring and the second half of summer. Set them 45cm (18in) apart in rows 60cm (2ft) apart. Keep the bed weed-free by regular hoeing until late autumn, and water freely during dry spells.

Savoy cabbages Sow the seeds as for other cabbages. Seeds sown in mid spring will produce a crop from early autumn to the middle of winter; those sown in late spring will provide cabbages from mid winter till spring; a summer sowing will give a crop the next spring.

Transplant the seedlings after six weeks, planting them 45cm (18in) apart with 60cm (2ft) between rows. Hoe regularly and keep the soil damp.

Spring cabbages Draw shallow drills 5mm (¼in) deep and 15cm (6in) apart, in a prepared seedbed, during mid to late summer. Sow the seeds thinly in the drills.

It is important to sow spring cabbages at the right time. Too early, and the plants may grow too large to withstand a hard winter; too late, and they won't develop beyond seedling stage before the days become shorter and colder.

Garden larder Winter cabbages can stay in the ground until you need them. This is a winter savoy; its leaves are characteristically crinkled.

Keep the bed watered, and thin seedlings to 5cm (2in) apart. Six weeks after sowing, move seedlings to their permanent bed. Space plants for use as spring greens 30cm (12in) apart. Allow 40cm (15in) between those you will leave to form hearts. In both cases, leave 45cm (18in) between rows.

After planting, firm the soil around the young cabbages with the dibber or with your heel, then water the plants.

Keep the plot weed-free by hoeing. In spring, dress the soil with 15g of nitrate of soda per square metre (½oz per square yard) and hoe into the surface.

Red cabbages Sow the seeds in early September in the same way as for other cabbages. Leave the seedlings in the seedbed throughout autumn and winter, protecting them with cloches during severe weather.

Transplant young cabbages into their permanent bed in April, setting them 60cm (2ft) apart in rows the same distance apart. Remove weeds regularly with a hoe, and water during dry spells.

Pests and diseases
Cabbages are subject to the same pests as other brassica crops, namely **aphids**, **cabbage root fly**, **cabbage whitefly**, **caterpillars** and **flea beetle**. Diseases and disorders include **club root**, **damping off**, **downy mildew**, **leaf spot** and **wire stem**. See Pests and Diseases, pages 238–49.

Harvesting and storing
Cut cabbages when their heads are firm and fleshy. Savoy cabbages are best eaten after a slight frost, which brings out their flavour.

Dig up cabbage stumps after the crop is over. They will take a long time to rot if placed whole on the compost heap, so either burn them or put them through the shredder before composting.

If you don't need the plot for another crop, leave a few stumps in the ground to provide a further crop of greens. Clusters of leaves will sprout from the stems; cut and eat them while young and tender. **See also** freezing (page 252).

Preparing and cooking
Although the cabbage has been widely grown for centuries, it has suffered from incorrect, prolonged boiling, resulting in a flavourless, soggy mass, an unpleasant pervading institutional smell and a bad reputation.

Prepare cabbages for cooking by removing the outer coarse leaves, cutting into quarters and cutting out the hard centre core and the base. Wash thoroughly and drain, and cook either in wedges or shredded. Use the minimum of boiling, lightly salted water – just enough to prevent sticking.

Cook shredded cabbage for 3–4 minutes; wedges will take a little longer. Drain and add a knob of butter and some fresh ground pepper or caraway seeds.

Braised red cabbage To make this winter warmer, finely shred a large cabbage and gently fry for a few minutes in a flameproof casserole with a chopped onion. Add half a bottle of red wine, a couple of tablespoons soft dark brown sugar, some grated apple, salt and pepper. This is best cooked in a slow oven as it won't stick. Give it at least 2 hours and serve with a fatty meat – duck, goose or shoulder of lamb.

Chinese Cabbage and Pak choi

New varieties of Chinese cabbages and pak choi have made them much easier for the home gardener to grow as they are hardier and less likely to run to seed.

Both leaves have a delicate flavour, and absorb other flavours well, making them especially useful in stir-fries and soups. The increased popularity of oriental cooking has seen a huge rise in the availability of these, and other exotic leaves.

Chinese cabbage – also known as Chinese leaf – looks more like a cos lettuce than a conventional cabbage; pak choi has fleshy white stalks and tender, smooth green leaves. Nevertheless, both are members of the brassica family. Unlike other cabbages, both pak choi and Chinese cabbage must be sown where you want them to grow, not transplanted.

Planning the crop
Prepare the ground in late spring. Spread a light dressing of manure or compost and work it in. If you have acid soil, sprinkle lime on the surface, but allow a few weeks between manuring and liming.

How many to grow Up to ten cabbages can be grown in a 3m (10ft) row. A single cabbage is sufficient for six people, so a single row of this length should be ample for most families. Succession planting of fast-growing pak choi in a single 3m (10ft) row should provide plenty of leaves – bearing in mind that many other garden vegetables are also ready to eat in summer and early autumn.

Varieties All seed companies offer good modern hybrid varieties – look for Chinese cabbages described as having a short internal stalk. Some Chinese cabbages can also be sown in a cold greenhouse for winter and spring cropping.

Some varieties of pak choi have purple-tinted leaves; choose these if you want colour in your salads, or if you are growing in a border, as they make for an attractive display.

Other seed mixtures Seed companies often offer Oriental leaf mixes, including **Mizuna**, **Oriental mustards** and **coriander**. These can

SOWING
- Pak choi
Outdoors in cropping position
SUMMER TO EARLY AUTUMN
- Chinese cabbage
Outdoors in cropping position
MID TO LATE SUMMER

THINNING
Remove the weakest when large enough to handle

HARVESTING
- Pak choi
Baby leaves and thinnings for salads; larger ones when ready for stir-fries
- Chinese cabbage
Tie leaves with twine if hearts seem loose as they grow. Cut hearts at the base with a knife
LATE SUMMER TO MID AUTUMN

be sown from late spring and throughout summer and autumn. Harvest while the leaves are small and tender, or use as a cut-and-come-again crop.

For best results, sow little and often, ideally in a pot, small tub or window box. Thinning is not necessary as picking the leaves will thin the crop. You can also sow the seeds under glass or in a cool conservatory for winter salads. **See also** Salad leaves and stir-fry mixes (page 200).

Growing tips
From mid to late summer, sow the seeds in the prepared ground 1cm (½in) deep, spacing cabbage rows 60cm (2ft) apart, and pak choi rows 45cm (18in) apart, if you are sowing more than one row. As soon as the seedlings are large enough to handle, thin them out to 30–40cm (12–15in) apart.

Water the plants well during dry spells and hoe the bed regularly to kill weeds. Watch out for slugs in late summer. If cabbage hearts seem loose, you can raise the outer leaves round them and tie them in place with garden twine, but with most modern varieties this should not be necessary.

Pests and diseases
Chinese cabbages and pak choi are subject to the same pests that afflict other brassicas. The most likely are **aphids**, **cabbage root fly**, **cabbage whitefly**, **caterpillars** and **flea beetle**. Disorders include **club root**; **damping off**, **leaf spot** and **wire stem**.
See Pests and Diseases, pages 238–49.

Harvesting and using
Although Chinese cabbages should

be left to grow until they are mature and have firm hearts, they will be inedible if they are allowed to run to seed. The crop generally matures from late summer to mid autumn. Pak choi thinnings can be used in mixed green salads. When mature, pak choi forms a dense head – cut and eat as required.

Preparing and cooking
Both these cabbages can be eaten raw in salads – shred Chinese cabbage and leave pak choi leaves whole. Serve them with a vinaigrette or lemon dressing, or with an exciting mix of lime juice, garlic, fresh chilli, honey and oil. These greens also form the basis of many stir-fries and make excellent soup. Or you can lightly steam them and serve as a vegetable with grilled fish or light poultry dishes.

Sesame greens and bean sprouts
Stir-fry an onion and 2 chopped garlic cloves, until softened. Add 1 shredded savoy cabbage and ½ head of Chinese cabbage. Fry for 2–3 minutes, then add a cup of bean sprouts. Pour 4 tablespoons of oyster sauce and 2 of water into the middle of the frying pan. Stir until hot. Mix all the ingredients together. Season if necessary and serve sprinkled with dry-fried sesame seeds.

Chinese cabbage with stir-fry strips
Stir-fry some mangetout, spring onions and pak choi, cut into the sizes you want, for a minute in some groundnut oil. Add some pork, chicken or beef strips, which have been marinated in sherry, sesame oil and soy sauce and fried once already. Cook until piping hot and serve with noodles.

Cardoons

This handsome plant, with its great purple flowers and silvery leaves, closely resembles the globe artichoke and may, in fact, be its ancestor. Despite this, cardoons are grown not for their globes but for the midribs and stalks of the young leaves. These have a distinctive flavour, similar to that of globe artichoke.

Like celery, the stalks are blanched and cooked on their own, or in soups and stews.

For centuries an established favourite in French kitchen gardens, the cardoon's distinctive taste deserves greater popularity in Britain, although there has been an upsurge of interest in recent years.

Planning the crop
Cardoons need a rich, moisture-retentive but well-drained soil, and are best grown in trenches similar to those used for celery. These large plants make a useful screen in summer for the vegetable plot, but make sure they do not cut all the light from smaller plants nearby. If you only want one or two plants, try growing them at the back of an ornamental border. Alternatively, plant along a boundary as a privacy screen for the summer.

Varieties Improved White and Ivory White are recommended, but seed companies and nurseries often do not specify variety.

How much to grow
Cardoons are still a novelty in Britain, and it's a good idea to grow only two or three plants to begin with. Then, if you decide you like them, you can plant more. About twelve plants should provide plenty for most families.

Growing tips
More adventurous garden centres offer young cardoon plants for sale, or you can raise them from seed.

In spring, dig a trench 30cm (12in) wide and 30cm (12in) deep, leaving the excavated soil on each side. Fork a generous layer of well-rotted manure into the soil at the bottom of the trench and leave it for a few weeks.

Sow the seeds in late spring in groups of three, 50cm (20in) apart and 1cm (½in) deep. Put cloches or fleece over the trench during the first month, and remove the two weaker seedlings from each group, when large enough to handle.

Cardoons need generous watering throughout summer, together with a dose of weak liquid fertiliser once a week.

Blanching the stems The cardoons will have finished growing by about mid September, and this is when to blanch the stems. On a

AT-A-GLANCE TIMETABLE		
TRENCHING		
SPRING		
30cm (12in) deep and wide		
SOWING		
LATE SPRING		
In groups of three seeds 50cm (20in) apart		
THINNING		
Remove the two weakest when large enough to handle		
EARTHING UP		
MID AUTUMN		
HARVESTING		
LATE AUTUMN		

Carrots

BLANCHING THE STEMS

Tie with string Choose a dry, sunny day, when the leaves are dry, to tie the stems together firmly with raffia or soft string.

Wrap the leaves Wrap brown paper or black polythene round the leaves. Secure with raffia or string before earthing up.

Earth up Draw soil round the plants. Though not vital, this gives extra protection.

---

sunny day, when both the foliage and the earth are dry, tie the leaves firmly together with string and wrap black polythene sheeting around each plant from the bottom to the top. Tie the polythene in place, and earth up the plants, as for potatoes, using the earth left on each side of the trench. The soil provides extra protection from frost and strong winds. In a month, blanching should be complete, and you can dig up the plants for use.

Pests and diseases
Cardoons may be affected by **aphids** (page 238), but otherwise they are relatively trouble free.

Harvesting and storing
Dig up the plants as needed, when blanching is complete.

Alternatively, dig up several plants and store them, wrapped in polythene, in a cool, dry place.

Preparing and cooking
The edible stems, with their artichoke flavour, can be prepared and cooked like celery, but are not suitable for eating raw.

Remove the outer hard stems, which in some varieties are bristly, and trim off the root ends and any pieces of damaged stem. Separate the individual stems and scrub clean. Leave them in a bowl of water to which some lemon juice has been added; this will help to stop them discolouring. Cut into chunks and at the same time pull any stringy bits from the stems.

Cook in boiling, lightly salted water for about 20 minutes, or until tender, drain and serve tossed in butter, or with a cheese or Hollandaise sauce. Cooked and cooled, cardoons can also be served in an oil-and-vinegar dressing.

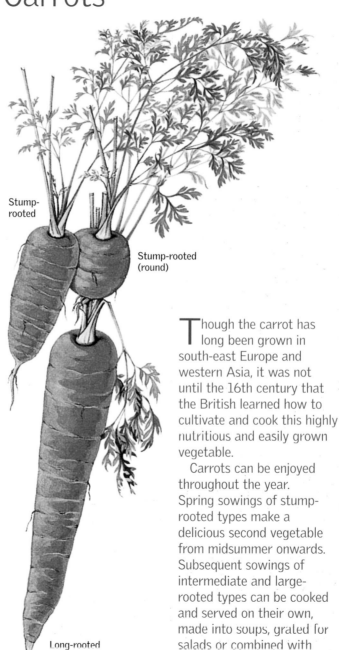

Stump-rooted

Stump-rooted (round)

Long-rooted

Though the carrot has long been grown in south-east Europe and western Asia, it was not until the 16th century that the British learned how to cultivate and cook this highly nutritious and easily grown vegetable.

Carrots can be enjoyed throughout the year. Spring sowings of stump-rooted types make a delicious second vegetable from midsummer onwards. Subsequent sowings of intermediate and large-rooted types can be cooked and served on their own, made into soups, grated for salads or combined with other vegetables to provide a variety of dishes.

Planning the crop
Cloches or a frame are needed for the earliest spring sowings – and also for a late crop of 'new' carrots in autumn. But no protection is needed during the main growing season, and satisfactory crops can be grown on a variety of soils.

Carrots are traditionally orange or orange-yellow in colour, but the modern trend towards eating vegetables raw has led to the introduction of many unusual colours, such as purple, yellow and white. The flavour does not differ much from their orange cousins, although it may be more delicate.

Site and situation Carrots do best in light, well-drained soil in a sunny situation, or one with only minimal shade. Early crops, in particular, do best in full sun. Clay is unsuitable.

Do not sow carrots in soil that has recently been manured. In a rotation scheme they should follow brassicas, such as cabbages and Brussels sprouts.

Short-rooted carrots also grow successfully in pots, tubs, growing bags and window boxes.

How much to grow A 3m (10ft) row will yield up to 6kg (13lb) of early carrots, or 7kg (15lb) of maincrop carrots, in fertile soil.

Varieties Carrot varieties can be grouped into three main types for different situations: round, intermediate and long-rooted. Whichever you grow, where carrot fly is known to be a problem, look for a variety with some resistance.

Round or short-rooted These non-tapering varieties are best for very early crops grown under cloches or in frames: **Early Scarlet Horn; Nantes; Amsterdam Forcing; Sytan** (carrot fly resistant); **Kundulus** (round-rooted).

Intermediate or stump-rooted
For open sowings on shallow soils: **Autumn King; Berlicum; Chanteray Red Cored; James's Scarlet Intermediate; Fly Away.**

Long-rooted Tapering long-rooted varieties are best on deep, rich ground: **Scarlet Perfection; St Valery.**

Growing tips
You can sow short-rooted carrots in a frame or under cloches in early spring. Put cloches in position at least two weeks before sowing to warm up the ground. Just before sowing, break down the soil and apply 120g of general fertiliser per square metre (4oz per square yard).

Short-rooted Sow seeds thinly in 5mm (¼in) deep drills, 25cm (9in) apart. Pelleted seeds are an advantage as they can be placed individually, making subsequent thinning much easier. Replace the cloches or frame lights until the seedlings are growing strongly.

If space allows, make another sowing of a short-rooted variety two or three weeks later, either under cloches or in the open.

A late summer sowing, grown fast under cloches, will provide tender carrots in early winter.

Intermediate/long-rooted
From mid spring until the second half of summer, sow intermediate or long-rooted varieties in rows 30cm (12in) apart. These later sowings do not need cloche protection.

Thinning When the seedlings are large enough to handle, thin them to 2.5cm (1in) apart then later to about 5cm (2in) for short-rooted varieties and 7.5–10cm (3–4in) for intermediate or long-rooted crops. You can use the larger thinnings in salads or for cooking.

Ideally, all thinning should be done on dull days or in the evening. Sun brings out the smell of the carrot foliage, which attracts the carrot fly. To avoid this, thin as little as possible and water the plants after thinning.

Pests and diseases
Carrot fly (page 238) is the principal pest to watch out for. The most likely diseases and disorders are **sclerotinia disease** (page 246), **splitting** (page 247) and **violet root rot** (page 247).

AT-A-GLANCE TIMETABLE

SOWING
Rows 25–30cm (9–12in) apart and 5mm (¼in) deep
- **Short-rooted varieties**
EARLY–MID SPRING AND LATE SUMMER
- **Intermediate/Long-rooted**
MID SPRING TO SECOND HALF OF SUMMER

THINNING
When large enough to handle.
- **First thinning** 2.5cm (1in)
- **Final spacing** 7.5–10cm (3–4in)

HARVESTING
- **Short-rooted varieties**
EARLY–MIDSUMMER AND EARLY WINTER
- **Intermediate/Long-rooted**
SUMMER THROUGH AUTUMN

Harvesting and storing
Pull up early, short-rooted varieties in early and midsummer, easing them with a fork if the ground is hard. Harvest maincrop carrots in mid autumn, using damaged carrots immediately and storing the rest in boxes (see right) for use during the winter. Always use a fork to loosen intermediate and long-rooted varieties before you pull them up.

Many modern maincrops can be left in the ground until needed, or until spring. Cover the tops with leaf-mould, compost or fleece to prevent weather damage. **See also** freezing (page 252); pickling (page 285); syrups and juices (page 283) and wine-making (page 304).

Preparing and cooking
Carrots are used as flavouring for stocks, casseroles and stews, as the base for soups, served as a cooked vegetable on their own, or eaten raw in salads, with dips together with other crudités, such as sticks of cucumber, or as a garnish.

To prepare carrots, trim off the tip of the tapering root end and the leaves, complete with any woody or discoloured pieces. Scrape young carrots under cold running water, but peel older carrots thinly.

Before cooking, cut older carrots into quarters, slices, batons or chunks. Leave young, small carrots whole, or cut them in half.

Cook carrots in boiling, lightly salted water, or a light stock, for 10–30 minutes – depending on their age and the method of preparation. They can be finished off in melted butter, sprinkled with finely grated cheese, parsley, mint, ginger or coriander or glazed with melted butter and honey. They can also be served in a Béchamel sauce

TRIMMING AND STORING CARROTS

Getting ready for storage
Before storing carrots, wash off the soil and trim away the foliage close to the crown.

Bed carrots in sand Store the carrots in boxes. Lay them flat, in single layers, between layers of damp sand.

or tossed in cream or roasted alongside a joint of meat. Mash old carrots, or a mixture of carrot and swede, with butter and seasoning, in the same way as potatoes.

Carrot and ginger soup Making soup is a good use for a glut of carrots; a large batch can be frozen in portions to use later. In place of the traditional coriander, try carrot with ginger to give a fabulous kick to a familiar ingredient.

Gently cook one chopped onion, a crushed or chopped clove of garlic and a finely chopped 5cm (2in) piece of root ginger in 2 tbsp olive oil for 3–4 minutes. Add 600g (1lb 5oz) peeled and chopped carrots and cook for a further 5 minutes. Add 700ml (1¼ pints) vegetable stock, the zest and juice of 2 large oranges, season and cover and simmer for 30 minutes, or until the carrots are soft. Purée until smooth then reheat to serve.

Cover and put them away
Finish with a final layer of sand and store the box in a cool, frost-free shed.

Cauliflowers, Broccoli and Romanesco

Cauliflowers are the most difficult of the brassica family to grow, but, given the right conditions and choice of varieties, they can be harvested all year round.

Winter cauliflowers – confusingly also known as broccoli – have large white heads similar to summer cauliflowers, and can be harvested throughout winter and spring. Don't confuse them with sprouting broccoli (see page 100) which have many small, sprig-like heads instead of a single curd.

Romanesco is becoming increasingly popular as a late summer to early winter crop. They resemble cauliflowers with pointed heads, and many tightly packed, pointed lime-green florets.

Planning the crop

To be successful, cauliflowers need an open position and rich soil, and must be kept growing quickly. A setback, such as a spell of drought or a serious check in growth, can result in failure.

Cauliflowers grow best in rich, loamy soils. In an established crop-rotation scheme, grow them on land manured the previous year for pod-bearing crops, applying a general fertiliser at 100g per square metre (3oz per square yard) at planting time. Unless the soil is alkaline, give a top dressing of garden lime at 120g per square metre (4oz per square yard) during the winter or spring before planting.

On a new vegetable plot, dig in manure or compost during the winter before planting cauliflowers, and top-dress with lime after about six weeks.

How much to grow About 14 cauliflowers can be grown in a 6m (20ft) row. If you try to grow more than this you are unlikely to be able to eat them while they remain in prime condition.

Varieties Hearting broccoli are classed as winter cauliflowers, so when buying cauliflower seeds you can choose from three main categories: **summer-heading**; **autumn-heading**; and **winter and spring-heading**. Aim to grow a selection of different varieties to get a succession of curds, rather than planting a large number of a single variety that will all mature at the same time.

Cauliflowers for home cultivation have benefited greatly in recent years from the extensive breeding programmes designed to improve commercially grown crops. New varieties are introduced into seed catalogues every year, so check regularly for the best varieties.

Growing tips

For the earliest summer-heading cauliflowers, ready for cutting in late spring and early summer, sow in a coldframe in mid autumn or in a slightly heated greenhouse during the second half of winter.

In a coldframe prepare the soil in the same way as for an outdoor seedbed (page 35). Scatter the seeds lightly and cover with seed compost or sifted soil to a depth of 5mm (¼in). Keep the frame closed until the seeds have germinated, then open it slightly to allow a little ventilation during mild weather.

Thin the seedlings to about 5cm (2in) apart when they are large enough to handle. If hard night frosts are forecast, cover the frames with sacking or old carpet. Keep the plants in the frame, ventilating as necessary, until they are planted out in spring.

In a greenhouse sow the seed in late winter in seed trays at a

Romanesco broccoli This has a delicate flavour and texture. It is good eaten raw or lightly steamed and served like asparagus.

temperature of 10°C (50°F). When the seedlings are large enough to handle, prick them out into small pots of potting compost.

In early March, put the tray into a coldframe to harden off the plants for several days.

To plant out into the young plants' permanent bed, use a trowel to make holes 45cm (18in) apart in the prepared bed. Space rows 45cm (18in) apart.

Choose plants that have about six leaves and a good ball of soil around the roots. Check that each plant has a strong growing point – a small half-folded leaf at the tip of the stem. Place the roots in the hole and firm the soil well by pressing with your heel close to the stem.

AT-A-GLANCE TIMETABLE

Cauliflowers under glass

SOWING
• **In a frame**
AUTUMN
• **In a greenhouse**
SECOND HALF OF WINTER

PRICKING OUT
Thin or prick out to 5cm (2in) apart when large enough to handle

TRANSPLANTING
Space 45cm (18in) apart
• **In a frame**
SPRING
• **In a greenhouse**
EARLY SPRING

HARVESTING
In a frame or greenhouse
LATE SPRING TO SECOND HALF OF SUMMER

Water well, and keep watering if necessary. Never allow the plants to dry out, or they will produce undersized heads.

How to grow cauliflowers outdoors
For a later crop of summer-heading cauliflowers sow outdoors in spring. The same method of sowing, thinning and planting out is suitable also for autumn-heading and winter-heading cauliflowers.

Sowing Prepare the seedbed in a sunny, sheltered spot by raking the soil until it is fine and level. Sow the seed in a drill 5mm (¼in) deep, spacing drills 30cm (12in) apart. If you sow more than one variety, mark the names of the varieties on labels as each is sown – they will be indistinguishable otherwise.

Cover the drills with soil and firm; keep the seedbed moist.

Thinning and transplanting Thin to 5cm (2in) spacings when the seedlings are large enough to handle. Plant out when the plants are 10–15cm (4–6in) high, following the method advised for the early crop raised under glass, but spacing these larger-growing, later plants 60cm (2ft) apart, with the rows also 60cm (2ft) apart.

Maintenance Keep the plants well watered, and give a dressing of a high nitrogen fertiliser once or twice during the growing season to improve the quality of the plants and curds.

When the curds of white-headed varieties begin to form, break two or three of the large outside leaves over them. This will help to keep the curds pure white: sunlight turns

them yellow and frost can make them turn brown. Many modern varieties have incurving leaves, which naturally shelter the developing curds.

Pests and diseases
Like other brassicas, cauliflowers and broccoli are subject to attack by **aphids**, **cabbage root fly**, **cabbage whitefly**, **caterpillars** and **flea beetles**.

The principal diseases and disorders are **club root**, **damping off**, **downy mildew**, **leaf spot**, **whiptail** and **wire stem** (see Pests and Diseases, pages 238–49).

Harvesting and storing
Cut the heads when they are firm. If left too long the curds break up as the plant begins to flower. If a number mature at the same time, pull up the plants and hang them upside down in a cool shed. They will keep for up to three weeks.

AT-A-GLANCE TIMETABLE

Cauliflowers outdoors

SOWING
5mm (¼in) deep in rows 30cm (12in) apart
EARLY-LATE SPRING

THINNING
Thin to 5cm (2in) apart when large enough to handle

TRANSPLANTING
Space 60cm (2ft) apart
SPRING TO SECOND HALF OF SUMMER

HARVESTING
SECOND HALF OF SUMMER – LATE SPRING

Rainbow effect Purple, orange and green-headed varieties of cauliflower are also available. Some seed companies offer collections of a few seeds of each. Where space is limited, grow a few of these novelty varieties in the flower border.

Cauliflowers can also be frozen and are delicious pickled.
See also freezing (page 252) and pickling (page 285).

Preparing and cooking
Cauliflowers are too often overcooked, so take care to watch the clock and test as they cook: they should be tender, yet remain crisp. Make sure that they are thoroughly drained and not soggy.

Before cooking, cut off the coarse, outer leaves. There is no need to remove the inner, tender leaves or the pale green leaves at the base. Trim the end of the stalk flush with the base of the head of the cauliflower, and cut a cross in it with a sharp knife to help to make the stalk tender.

You can cook the cauliflower whole, in boiling, lightly salted water for 12–15 minutes; or for 8–10 minutes if divided into florets. A little lemon juice in the water helps to preserve the white colour.

Cauliflower may be served on its own or with a white, cheese or parsley sauce. Cauliflower cheese is a warming main course, served with jacket potato. Cauliflower makes creamy soups, but its crisp, nutty texture and taste are also perfect for serving raw with dips.

Purple headed cauliflowers turn green when cooked, but individual florets of the different coloured varieties (above) make an eye-catching addition to mixed salads.

Celeriac

Celeriac has a flavour reminiscent of celery – not surprisingly, as the two plants are closely related. However, its roots, not its stalks, are eaten. It can be mashed, roasted, boiled, steamed, made into soup or used to flavour stocks. It is also eaten raw in salads.

Celeriac is easier to grow than trenched celery, which perhaps accounts for its popularity on the Continent.

As celeriac needs a long growing season, germinate the seeds in a warm place in early spring and plant outdoors in late spring or early summer.

It is essential to keep the plants growing steadily throughout spring and summer, otherwise they will not form decent-sized roots. The first should be ready for lifting by mid autumn.

Planning the crop
Grow celeriac in a sunny position in well-drained soil, that you have enriched in the winter before planting with rotted manure or compost, at the rate of a bucketful per square metre (square yard).

How much to grow A 6m (20ft) row should yield 10kg (20lb) or more of roots – enough for most families during autumn and winter.

Varieties Most catalogues list only one or two varieties. Look for those described as having smooth skin, or being easy to wash.

Growing tips
Sow celeriac seeds in early to mid spring at a temperature of 10–13°C (50–55°F). A greenhouse is the ideal place, but seeds can also be germinated in an airing cupboard and the seedlings grown on a sunny windowsill.

Sow the seeds in a seed tray. Press down the compost to make it level and firm, and sprinkle the seeds thinly over the top. Cover thinly with compost.

When the seedlings are about 1cm (½in) high, prick them out about 4cm (2in) apart in each direction into a tray of potting compost, or in individual small pots. Keep them in the greenhouse or

AT-A-GLANCE TIMETABLE

SOWING
EARLY TO MID SPRING

PRICKING OUT
When seedlings are 1cm (½in) high, prick out 4cm (2in) apart or individually into small pots

TRANSPLANTING
30–40cm (12–15in) apart both ways
LATE SPRING OR EARLY SUMMER

HARVESTING
AUTUMN TO EARLY WINTER

indoors for three to five weeks, then put them in a coldframe for a week to harden off.

When setting out the plants in their final bed, set them at 30–40cm (12–15in) intervals in rows the same distance apart. Plant the seedlings so that the roots are buried and the leaves are just resting on the soil surface. Keep the plants well watered in the early stages, and hoe frequently to kill weed seedlings, otherwise the plants may suffer impaired growth.

A fortnightly feed of liquid fertiliser will help to keep the plants growing steadily. Apply this just before or just after watering.

Throughout late summer and autumn, when the roots are swelling, remove any side-growths. If you fail to do so, the roots may not develop fully.

Pests and diseases
Carrot fly and **slugs and snails** are the principal pests of celeriac. **Leaf spot** is the disease most likely to occur. **See Pests and Diseases**, pages 238–49.

Harvesting and storing
Use the roots as required during autumn and early winter. Leave them as long as possible, however, so that they attain maximum size. There is no advantage in using them while they are immature.

At the end of this period, lift those that remain, remove the foliage and store in damp sand or peat substitute in a cool shed or cellar.

Preparing and cooking
This root vegetable is rapidly gaining popularity in Britain. The sweet celery flavour is most pronounced in young roots

weighing up to about 500g (1lb). Older roots tend to become woody and hollow.

To prepare celeriac for cooking, trim off the upper leafy part. Do not discard the leaves, however, as they are excellent for flavouring soups and sauces; in France they are considered an essential part of a fresh bouquet garni.

Slice off the root end and scrub the celeriac under cold running water. Peel fairly thickly, and as the celeriac is prepared drop it in a bowl of cold water with 1–2 teaspoons of lemon juice to prevent discoloration.

Cut the celeriac into slices, chunks or narrow strips and cook in boiling salted water for 10–20 minutes depending on the size of the pieces.

Serve celeriac as an accompanying vegetable – on its own, in a white sauce, or mashed and creamed like potatoes. Or make a robust celeriac-and-potato mash to accompany game.

Celeriac makes an excellent soup, and is equally delicious eaten raw as a crisp salad.

Celeriac remoulade This classic salad is sold in delicatessens all over France. Slice half a celeriac into matchstick thin strips and coat with the juice of half a lemon – this will stop the celeriac discolouring. Mix 3 tablespoons of good-quality mayonnaise with 2 or 3 teaspoons of Dijon mustard and stir into the celeriac. Season to taste with salt and pepper and chill in the fridge for at least 2 hours or overnight so that the flavours develop.

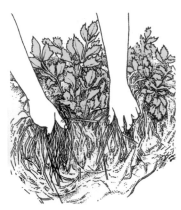

Blanching outer plants During the second half of summer, pack straw round a block of self-blanching celery to help blanch the outer plants.

or early summer. Just after midsummer is the right time for a second batch.

Plant the seedlings 25cm (9in) apart each way to form a block. Use a trowel to loosen and lift the plants from the box, and to plant them. Keep soil-balls intact while transplanting, and water in well.

Remove side-growths from the base as they appear. If the celery is grown in a frame without a top there is little else to do. If it is being grown in an open bed, pack straw round the outside plants in the second half of summer to blanch the outer rows.

Growing celery in trenches
Raise the seedlings in the same way as for self-blanching varieties, but delay sowing for two to three weeks. Make a second sowing in a frame in mid spring.

Plant out the first sowing in late spring. Follow that with a second sowing a few weeks later, spacing

the seedlings for a single row 25cm (9in) apart along the centre of the prepared trench.

If planting double rows, allow 45cm (18in) between the rows and set the plants 25cm (9in) apart. Keep well watered, especially during dry spells.

Earthing up Begin earthing up when the plants are 30–40cm (12–15in) high. This will be in late summer for the late spring-planted celery, and early autumn for those planted in early summer.

Before drawing soil round the plants, cut off any suckers that grow from the base and tie black polythene or paper round the stems. Water thoroughly, and draw some soil from the ridges on each side into the trenches to form a slight slope reaching about halfway up the stem of each plant.

Three weeks later, draw more earth round the plants to the base of the leaves.

After three more weeks make the final earthing up, sloping the soil to form a ridge (see right).

Pests and diseases
Celery is liable to be attacked by the **carrot fly** (which eats the roots), **celery fly** (which burrows into the leaves) and **slugs and snails** (which can shred the foliage). Diseases and disorders that may affect celery plants include **bolting, boron deficiency, leaf spot** and **splitting** (see Pests and Diseases pages 238–49).

Harvesting and storing
In late summer, start lifting self-blanching celery with a fork, piling up the straw against newly exposed plants. All must be cleared before severe frosts set in.

Lift celery grown in trenches from mid autumn – that is, about eight weeks after the first earthing up.

Open the ridge from one end, remove the plants with a fork, then earth up again as a protection against frost.

In extremely severe weather, spread bracken or straw on top of the ridge to prevent damage to the stems.

See also freezing (page 252); pickles (page 285); sauces and relishes (page 296); vinegars (page 299) and wine-making (page 304).

Preparing and cooking
Although mainly used as a fresh salad ingredient, celery is equally good as a cooked vegetable. Prepare a head of celery, either for eating raw or for cooking, by trimming off the lower end and removing entirely any damaged outer stems. Don't discard undamaged ones, but remove the strings from the tougher outer branches using a potato peeler.

Cooking celery For cooking, cut each head in half lengthways, trim off the leaves (which are excellent

STAGES IN GROWING TRENCH CELERY

Preparing the trench In winter, dig a trench 30cm (12in) deep and – for a single row – 40cm (15in) wide and work in well-rotted manure or compost.

Planting Set plants 25cm (9in) apart in the trench during late spring or early summer. Water thoroughly until the plants are established.

Tying and earthing Start the blanching process by tying black polythene round the plants and drawing soil against them.

Final earthing The earthing-up process is completed in three stages, the last leaving only the leaves exposed above the ridge.

AT-A-GLANCE TIMETABLE

Trench-grown celery

SOWING
• First crop
EARLY TO MID SPRING
• Second crop
MID SPRING

PRICKING OUT
• First crop
Prick out 5cm (2in) apart into a tray when large enough to handle.
• Second crop
Prick out 5cm (2in) apart into a tray when large enough to handle.

TRANSPLANTING
• First crop
LATE SPRING
• Second crop
MIDSUMMER

FIRST EARTHING
• First crop
LATE SUMMER
• Second crop
EARLY AUTUMN

SECOND EARTHING
• First and second crops
Three weeks after first earthing

THIRD EARTHING
• First and second crops
Three weeks after second earthing

HARVESTING
• First crop
AUTUMN
• Second crop
LATE AUTUMN TO LATE WINTER

for flavouring stocks and stews or as an attractive garnish) and rinse the stems under cold running water. Alternatively, separate the stems and scrub them in water, peeling off any stringy bits.

Cook celery, cut into 5–10cm (2–4in) lengths, in a small amount of boiling, lightly salted water for 15–20 minutes, or steam for 20–30 minutes. Serve boiled or steamed celery in a cheese or parsley sauce, or smother it in melted butter and sprinkle with toasted almonds or grated nutmeg.

Celery can be cooked slowly in stock with other vegetables – onions or carrots, for example, or with lentils and bacon to make a satisfying stew.

Cut into chunks or short sticks, celery adds great flavour and texture to stir-fries.

Raw celery Celery to be eaten raw should not be left in water longer than necessary, or the stems will lose their characteristic crispness. Fresh, undamaged leaves may be left on the stems of celery to be served with a cheese board.

Chopped into small chunks, celery can be mixed with cooked, beetroot cubes, or with fresh apple and walnuts. Creamy textured dressings, such as mayonnaise or blue cheese, go especially well with celery-based salads.

Serve raw celery, carrot and cucumber sticks with dips such as hummous and taramasalata.

Cherries

Sweet cherry

Morello (acid) cherry

Many sweet cherry trees require a great deal of space; unless you have a large garden, look for a cherry tree grafted on to a dwarfing rootstock. Older varieties of cherry have to be cross-pollinated by another variety; if you have space for only one tree, then choose one of the newer, self-fertile cultivars.

You can grow acid Morello cherries, used mainly for bottling and jam making, as bush or fan-trained trees. As they are self-fertile, they can be grown singly. They grow well in cool conditions, such as on a north-facing wall.

Choosing a cherry tree

A fan-trained tree on a non-dwarfing rootstock grown against a wall will attain a span of 4.5–6m (15–20ft). Slightly more space than this is needed between bush trees.

A fan-trained tree on the semi-dwarfing Colt rootstock will span approximately 4m (12ft), and grow to 4–5m (12–15ft).

A fan-trained tree on the dwarfing Gisela 5 rootstock will span 2.5–3m (8–10ft) and reach an average bush height.

Varieties The two distinct types of cherry – sweet and sour – derive from our native *Prunus avium* and *P. cerasus* and from forms brought from eastern Europe by the Romans.

The following sweet cherries are self-fertile, and therefore may be planted singly: **Lapins**; **Stella**; **Summer Sun**; **Sunburst**; **Sweetheart**.
Morello, the only acid cherry usually available, is also self-fertile.

Growing tips

A deep, well-drained soil in sun will give the best results with sweet cherries, but aspect is unimportant for acid ones.

Plant bare-rooted trees between late winter and spring. Pot-grown trees may be planted at any time of year as long as the weather is suitable to do so.

When planting a bush tree, drive a supporting stake into the hole and tie the tree to it. Unless the tree is secured in this way it will have a tendency to be rocked by high winds, and this will lead to the loosening of the roots and a delay in the tree's development.

Feed and water

Each winter, feed the trees with 15g of sulphate of potash per square metre (½oz per square yard) over an area roughly equivalent to the spread of the tree. In March, apply 30g of sulphate of ammonia per square metre (1oz per square yard).

Every third year, apply 90g of superphosphate per square metre (3oz per square yard). Alternatively, top-dress with a slow-release compound fertiliser each year in early spring.

Water the ground under trees thoroughly during dry spells in summer.

Pruning sweet cherries If the trees are growing as fans against a wall, they only need light pruning. In mid spring, rub out all new shoots growing towards or away from the wall, but leave unpruned the leaders of shoots that will become part of the main framework. Follow this up during summer by pinching out the growing tips of all other new shoots after they have produced five or six leaves.

When shoots have reached the top of the wall, shorten them to just above a weak lateral shoot, or

AT-A-GLANCE TIMETABLE
Morello (acid) cherries
PLANTING
LATE AUTUMN TO EARLY SPRING
HARVESTING
SUMMER TO AUTUMN
PRUNING
After fruiting

Don't give them away Pick cherries as soon as they ripen, or they'll end up being feasted on by birds.

bend them over horizontally and fasten to the top wire. Tie all new shoots to fit into the fan shape.

In autumn cut away any dead wood and shorten the shoots that were pinched out in summer, cutting them back to three or four buds.

Limit the pruning of standard sweet cherries to removing dead or diseased branches, and branches that rub against one another. Paint the cut ends with a proprietary sealing compound to keep out silver-leaf infection.

Pruning acid cherries For the first three years, train and prune bush trees in the same way as bush apples (page 71) and fan-trained trees as fan peaches (page 178).

Established acid cherries fruit only on wood that developed during the previous summer. Your objective is to stimulate plenty of new growth each year by heavy feeding and by pruning to produce renewal shoots.

In spring, rub out shoots on fan trees that are growing towards the wall, and either tie back or remove outward-growing shoots. Tie in

AT-A-GLANCE TIMETABLE

Established sweet cherries

RUBBING OUT
SPRING

PINCHING OUT
SUMMER

HARVESTING
SUMMER

PRUNING
AUTUMN

PRUNING FAN-TRAINED SWEET CHERRIES

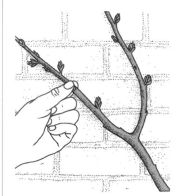

Rubbing out A proportion of new shoots will grow towards or away from the wall. Rub these out with your thumb during spring, but leave the leaders of main branches.

Pinching out Within a few weeks the remaining shoots will have five or six leaves. Now pinch out growing tips of new shoots, other than branch leaders.

Limiting the length When shoots reach the top of the wall, shorten to a weak lateral rather than stopping them abruptly.

Pruning new growth In autumn, cut back shoots that were pinched back earlier. Reduce to three or four fruit buds.

young shoots that are growing parallel with the wall.

In late summer, after fruiting, cut back a proportion of the older shoots – those up to three years old – to a young replacement shoot. Keep the tree in balance by pruning the same amount off either side of the fan.

Bush trees need similar treatment. After fruiting, cut out some of the less productive branches – but leave those that are more than three years old, otherwise the wound will be too severe. Seal all cuts with bituminous tree paint to prevent disease spores entering the vulnerable, raw, bare surfaces.

Pests and diseases
Birds love cherries – especially sweet varieties – so if you want to enjoy the fruit yourself, you'll probably have to net the tree. If the tree is very large, you can keep at least some of the fruit safe by netting the lower branches; trees on dwarfing rootstocks are easier to cover completely.

Birds are attracted less to acid cherries than to sweet cherries, but netting Morello cherries is still a good idea. Apart from birds, the pests most likely to attack cherries are **aphids** and **caterpillars**. The more troublesome diseases are **bacterial canker**, **chlorosis**, **honey fungus**, **shothole** and **silver leaf** (see Pests and Diseases pages 238–49).

Harvesting and storing
Sweet cherries may be pulled off by hand. They do not keep well, and should be eaten soon after picking. Pulling off acid cherries, which mature between summer and mid autumn, can wound the spurs and allow the diseases to which the trees are susceptible to enter. Stop this happening by cutting off the cherries with sharp scissors.
See also freezing (page 252); pickles (page 285) and wine-making (page 304).

Preparing and cooking
Serve sweet white, red and black cherries fresh as a dessert fruit on their own, or add them to fresh fruit salads and summer drinks. You can buy a gadget called a cherry stoner, which removes the stone without breaking the cherry. They are often incorporated into the handle ends of garlic crushers.

Easy cherry clafoutis Remove stones from 750g sweet cherries. Beat 6 eggs with a pinch of salt and then stir in 100g flour and 90g caster sugar – ideally flavoured with a vanilla pod. Add 250ml milk, a little at a time. Pour the smooth batter into a greased flan dish; sprinkle the cherries all over and cook for about 45 minutes in a preheated oven at 190°C (374°F, gas mark 5) until puffy and golden. Dust with icing sugar and serve warm.

Morello cherries Mouth-puckeringly sharp when eaten raw, Morello cherries make superb preserves and are also excellent poached and in pies and flans.

Remove the stalks, wash and drain. Stone cherries over a plate to catch any escaping juice.

Sour cherries work well in stuffings, especially for fatty meats like lamb or goose. Use them combined with onion, breadcrumbs, herbs and seasonings.

Chervil

G rown mainly for its bright green, feathery leaves, chervil is a hardy biennial herb, normally gown as an annual.

The plant looks rather like parsley and its fresh leaves are used in much the same way – chopped for adding to salads, garnishing soups and delicately flavoured fish, sprinkling over new potatoes and using in fines herbes. Frozen leaves can be used in the same way.

Successional sowing and growing under glass in winter will provide you with a year-round supply of fresh chervil leaves.

The plant grows to a height of 30–45cm (12–18in) and bears clusters of white flowers from June to August. A native of south-eastern Europe and western Asia, chervil has long been naturalised in Britain and elsewhere.

Planning the crop
Early and late-sown plants will thrive in full sun, but those grown in summer benefit from partial shade in hot, dry areas. The herb will do well in any soil, provided the drainage is good.

How much to grow The best way to grow chervil is as a short-term crop, making four to six sowings at intervals during the year and using only tender young leaves. Following this method, you'll have plenty of leaves if you grow five or six plants at any one time. Chervil will grow well in pots, window boxes and other containers.

How to grow chervil
Sow the seeds 5mm (¼in) deep in an open seedbed at any time between spring and late summer. Allow 30cm (12in) between rows if you are sowing more than one row, and thin the seedlings to about 30cm (12in) spacings. Water the plants in dry weather and remove flowering stems as soon as they appear. This will not only encourage the growth of young, tender leaves for a longer period, but will also prevent self-sown seedlings from growing like weeds in the surrounding soil.

However, if you want to collect seeds for later use, then let one of the heads mature and gather the ripe seeds before they fall.

Herbs for winter Chervil can also be grown indoors between autumn and late winter. Plant two or three seeds in a 15cm (6in) pot filled with seed compost. Remove the weaker plants and grow the remaining one on the kitchen windowsill for a supply of fresh leaves in winter.

Pests and diseases
Chervil is normally trouble free.

Harvesting and storing
Cut or pick the leaves six to eight weeks after sowing. The leaves are too tender for successful drying, but they can be preserved by freezing (page 252).

Preparing and cooking
This aromatic herb is similar to parsley, although the lacy leaves are a paler green and have a more delicate flavour. It is one of the traditional herbs for an omelette au fines herbes; it is also used to flavour cream sauces and soups, salads and vinegars, and is attractive as a garnish.

The slight aniseed taste combines well with some vegetables, such as baby carrots, and tiny new potatoes are delicious when tossed in butter and sprinkled with finely chopped chervil. You can also stir chopped chervil into a mayonnaise sauce to serve with cold asparagus.

Sprinkle chopped chervil over scrambled eggs, poached white fish and grilled tomatoes, and use it to give colour and extra flavour to creamy mashed potatoes.

Add a couple of teaspoons of chopped chervil to a white cream sauce, Bearnaise or Hollandaise, to accompany roast poultry, poached and baked fish or boiled cauliflower.

Chervil butter This butter goes well with grilled salmon steaks, roast veal and escalopes. Soften 100g (4oz) of butter and blend thoroughly with 2 teaspoons of blanched, finely chopped chervil. Season to taste with salt and white pepper, and roll into a sausage shape in damp greaseproof paper.

Chill in the refrigerator until firm, then cut into slices. Stamp out fancy shapes with a small biscuit cutter and use as a garnish.

Vary the chervil butter by adding any of the following flavours: 2 teaspoons lemon juice; a crushed clove of garlic; salt and freshly ground pepper; or additional herbs, such as finely chopped chives, tarragon or dill.

Chervil soup

This soup, topped with a poached egg and served with fresh crusty bread, is a meal in itself.

Clean and prepare 2 or 3 leeks, 3 carrots, 2 medium potatoes and 2 sticks of celery. Dice all the vegetables and put into a pan with about a litre (2 pints) of chicken stock.

Bring to the boil and simmer gently for 10–12 minutes until the vegetables are tender. Season to taste with salt, pepper and sugar.

Then knead together a tablespoon each of butter and flour to form a paste and add this to the soup in small pieces, whisking well until it thickens.

Pour boiling water over a large bunch of fresh chervil, drain immediately and chop finely. Stir the herb into the soup but do not allow to boil, or the chervil will lose both flavour and colour.

Pour the soup into bowls, and gently float a poached egg on top of each one.

Variation If you prefer a smooth soup, sweat the chopped vegetables in the butter before adding the stock; simmer until tender and then blend in a liquidiser.

Chicory

Chicory in summer

Chicory chicons

A hardy perennial, native to Europe, chicory is first grown outdoors, then forced and blanched inside to produce a conical head of crisp, white, faintly bitter leaves known as chicons.

Chicory is easy to grow, and is a valuable winter vegetable. It makes a crunchy raw salad, when it combines particularly well with citrus fruits. As a vegetable dish, it can be boiled, steamed or braised and served with melted butter or a cream or egg-based sauce.

The leaves of one variety, Sugar Loaf (Pain de Sucre), can be eaten unblanched, in summer. The other varieties may be forced, a few roots at a time, to give a continuous supply of chicons throughout winter and early spring.

Planning the crop

Chicory is deep-rooting and needs a rich soil – either one manured for a previous crop, or one into which you have incorporated plenty of well-rotted compost or manure, before sowing.

How much to grow A 3m (10ft) row should yield up to 3kg (6lb) of chicons.

Varieties The most popular varieties are **Sugar Loaf**, whose leaves can be picked in summer and cooked like spinach or used raw in salads, and **Witloof**, also known as **Brussels Chicory**.

Growing tips

Sow the seeds in the open in the second half of spring and first half of summer. Sow them thinly in drills 5mm (¼in) deep and 45cm (18in) apart.

When the seedlings are large enough to handle, thin them to about 25cm (9in) apart.

Keep weeds under control by hoeing, and water the bed thoroughly during dry spells.

Lifting the roots In late autumn or early winter, cut the leaves off about 2–3cm (1in) above the roots and lift carefully with a fork. The roots should be 30cm (12in) or more long, about 5cm (2in) across the top and parsnip-shaped.

STAGES IN BLANCHING CHICORY

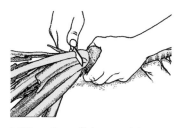

Lifting Cut off the remaining foliage 2–3cm (1in) above the roots before or after lifting in late autumn or early winter. Lift the roots carefully with a fork.

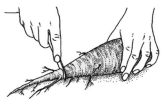

Trimming Before storing the roots, reduce the length of each to about 20cm (8in) by trimming off the lower end. Rub off any sideshoots.

Forcing Plant four or five roots in a 25cm (9in) pot of soil. After watering, cover with another pot to exclude light.

Harvesting Given sufficient warmth, the chicons will be 15cm (6in) high a month later. Cut them off at the base.

Rub out any sideshoots, leaving only the main crown. Trim the roots to a length of about 20cm (8in) and store them in a cool, frost-proof shed or in a shallow trench beneath a layer of soil – marking this so that you can find them later.

Forcing the roots Force the roots in batches as you need them (they take about four weeks). To do this, pack them upright, four or five at a time, into a 25cm (9in) pot filled with soil. The roots should be about 5cm (2in) apart.

Water the pots and cover them with inverted pots of the same size, or with cardboard boxes, to keep out the light.

Put the pots in a warm place, such as a greenhouse or kitchen, where the temperature will be between 7° and 16°C (45–61°F). The darkness and warmth will induce chicons to sprout up from the crowns.

Pests and diseases

Cutworms (page 239), **slugs and snails** (page 241) and **caterpillars of the swift moth** (page 241) are

A splash of colour For colourful winter salads, try growing some red chicory as well as the white varieties.

the principal pests likely to affect your crop. Chicory is seldom attacked by any disease.

Harvesting and storing

The plants are ready for use when the chicons are about 15cm (6in) high, which generally takes four weeks. Cut off the chicons just before using them.

When all the chicons have been picked, you can simply put the roots onto the compost heap, or you can water the pots and leave the plants to grow a second – but inferior – crop of chicons.

Preparing and cooking

Use this delicate vegetable while the blanched chicons are still young and firm, before the leaves begin to turn yellow and the tops show pale green. The central, hard core of chicory is bitter, and this bitterness becomes more pronounced with age. If you plan to eat chicory fresh in a salad, you can reduce the bitterness by blanching it in boiling water for a minute or two. Add a

little lemon juice to the water to preserve the chicory's whiteness.

Prepare chicory by removing the outer leaves. Trim the root end clean and cut out the core with a sharp, narrow-bladed knife.

Chicory and grapefruit salad

This slightly sharp salad goes well with rich meats. Prepare two heads of chicory and cut them crossways into thin slices. Squeeze the juice from half a grapefruit. Peel the skin from the other half and remove all the white pith.

Divide the grapefruit into segments and cut each segment in half. Mix with the chicory.

Whisk together the grapefruit juice, 2 tablespoons of white wine vinegar and 8 tablespoons of good olive oil. Season with salt and pepper and a few drops of Tabasco sauce. Pour the dressing over the salad and toss well.

Edible boats Because of their shape, chicory leaves provide an elegant, edible way to serve a salad, such as this one made with chunks of pink salmon and pale green avocado.

Chives

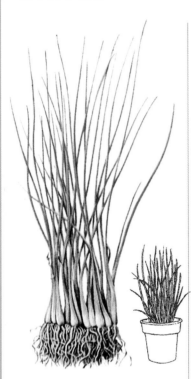

The fine, tubular leaves of this hardy, perennial herb are used to give a delicate onion flavour to a wide range of dishes.

It is an extremely versatile herb, combining well with omelettes, salads, soups, stews and numerous sauces and salsas. You can make a delicious herb bread by mashing chopped chives into butter, and spreading the mixture into a French loaf before baking it in the oven.

Chives need little attention and are among the easiest of all garden plants to grow.

Chives are in season outdoors from March until autumn; you can enjoy a winter supply of fresh chives by growing them in pots on the kitchen windowsill.

Planning the crop

Chives will grow in any good garden soil in a sunny or semi-shaded position. They may also be grown in pots and window boxes.

How much to grow Three large clumps should supply plenty of chives for the season. Chives can also be used to make an attractive and useful edging to the vegetable plot, and when in flower they attract pollinating insects.

Growing tips

The easiest way to grow chives is to buy plants from a nursery. Plant them in the herb bed about 30cm (12in) apart and allow them to multiply. Within a few months they will grow into good-sized clumps, if you remove the flowers.

Chives can also be grown from seed. Sow these outdoors in March, in groups of three or four at 30cm (12in) intervals and 5mm (¼in)

AT-A-GLANCE TIMETABLE

SOWING
EARLY SPRING
30cm (12in) apart 5mm (¼in) deep

THINNING
Remove the weakest seedlings

HARVESTING
SPRING TO AUTUMN

deep. When they have germinated, remove the weakest seedlings. From then on you can increase your stock by dividing the plants in autumn.

Even if you don't need extra plants, it's a good idea, every three years, to dig up the clumps in autumn and divide them into groups of half-dozen shoots. Replant these 30cm (12in) apart in fresh ground that has been dressed with well-rotted compost.

For a winter supply take one or two small clumps, put them into 10cm (4in) pots of potting compost and keep them on a windowsill.

Pests and diseases

Chives are seldom troubled by pests. The only disease likely to affect them is **rust** (page 246).

Harvesting

Cut the leaves close to the ground as required. Cut all the leaves from a clump before moving to the next; in turn, each plant will soon grow a new crop of leaves.

Preparing and cooking

The finely chopped, dark green leaves are much used as a garnish for salads and sauces, and for flavouring egg and cheese dishes. Chives are a necessary ingredient in tartare sauce to serve with fish, and are used as flavouring in salad dressings.

The easiest way to chop them is by holding a small bunch in one hand and snipping it with kitchen scissors.

Try sprinkling tomato and egg sandwiches with chopped chives. Fold chopped chives into ricotta or cottage cheese, creamy mashed potatoes and dips, and mix with vegetables and cucumber salads.

If you really like onion flavours, include the pink chive flowers along with the chopped leaves in your salad – they look delicate and pretty but have a robust flavour, so don't use too many.

Chive butter Garnish meat, fish and poultry dishes with a simply made chive butter. To make this, stir 100g (4oz) butter until soft, and blend in 4 tablespoons of blanched, finely chopped chives. Roll the butter into a sausage shape, wrap it in damp greaseproof paper and chill the roll in the refrigerator. To use, cut into narrow slices.

Flowering chives The pretty pink flowerheads will attract pollinating insects to the garden.

Chive omelette Gently mix 2 eggs and a tablespoon of chopped chives. Melt a little butter in an omelette pan and add the egg and herb mixture. While the eggs are still runny, add a further tablespoon of chopped herbs before you fold the omelette. The warmth of the eggs will bring out the flavour of the herb. You can use other fragrant herbs with the chives; try parsley, tarragon or chervil.

Coriander

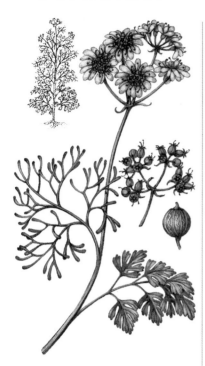

This hardy annual herb, a native of south-east Europe that now also occurs in Britain, is grown for its fresh leaves and seeds.

Before ripening, the seeds have an unpleasant smell; but, as the small fruits mature, this gives way to a warm spicy aroma – a sure indication that they are ready to harvest.

The pungent leaves have long been widely used in Oriental cookery. Today, their distinctive flavour lends excitement to fresh salsas and green leafy salads. Remember that a little coriander leaf goes a long way, and also that most children find its powerful flavour quite unpalatable.

Coriander seeds are used whole or pounded in a pestle and mortar to flavour curries, soups and breads.

The plant is easy to grow, and requires little attention.

Planning the crop
Coriander needs a sunny position. It will grow satisfactorily in any well-drained soil, but does best in one enriched with well-rotted manure or compost. Grow it in small pots on the windowsill for a supply of fresh leaves.

How much to grow If you enjoy the flavour of coriander leaf and you also intend to harvest the ripe seeds, then you will need at least a dozen plants. Coriander plants grow to about 45cm (18in) high, with a spread of 15–25cm (6–9in). There is only one species.

Growing tips
Sow the seeds 5mm (¼in) deep in an outdoor seedbed in mid to late spring. Thin the plants to 25cm (10in) spacings as soon as they are large enough to handle. Use these thinnings as fresh leaves in salads and Asian cookery. Otherwise sow a small pinch of seed in a plant pot.

Pests and diseases
Coriander is normally trouble free.

Harvesting
Use thinnings or pick leaves when required. For the seeds, your nose is the best harvesting guide. When the seed heads emit a pleasant, spicy odour – following their previously disagreeable smell – cut them off and leave them to dry on trays, either in the sun or indoors.

When they are dry, shake out the seeds, or rub them off, and place in airtight containers.

You can freeze the leaves (page 252) for use in cooked dishes.

Cooking with coriander
This bitter-sweet, aromatic herb is becoming increasingly popular, and is widely available fresh in British supermarkets. Add the leaves to curries just before serving. Or make a zingy salsa for serving with fish or poultry by combining any or all of the following: lime juice and zest; spring onions, chopped; tomatoes, chopped; avocado chunks; fresh chillis, chopped; plenty of coriander leaves and a good splash of extra virgin olive oil.

Use the dried seeds, picked in late summer, in a curry spice mix. Whole or ground, coriander seeds are suitable for flavouring chutneys and pickles. In eastern Europe, the seed is widely used in cakes, breads and cheeses. Try adding ground coriander to rice pudding or bread-and-butter pudding in place of the usual nutmeg and cinnamon.

AT-A-GLANCE TIMETABLE

SOWING
MID TO LATE SPRING
5mm (¼in) deep

THINNING
25cm (10in) apart, when large enough to handle

HARVESTING
LATE SUMMER

Corn salad

Also known as lamb's lettuce, this salad vegetable can be grown throughout the year, but is generally sown as an autumn and winter crop to use when fresh salad leaves are scarce.

Corn salad is a good substitute for lettuce, and can be used in the same ways. It gets its other name, lamb's lettuce, from the fact that the leaves are at their greenest and crispest when lambing starts, at the end of winter.

The plant is completely hardy, but will receive less of a check in severe weather if you protect it under cloches. This will help to ensure a continuous supply of tender young leaves.

Planning the crop
Grow corn salad in sunny, well-drained soil containing plenty of well-rotted manure or compost.

How much to grow A 3m (10ft) row will provide about 20 plants.

Varieties Seed companies don't usually offer a choice of varieties.

Growing tips
If you sow corn salad in early to mid spring, then in late summer and finally in mid autumn, you should have fresh supplies growing all the year round.

If you want only a winter crop, make sowings in late summer and autumn.

Sow seeds in drills 1cm (½in) deep, with 25cm (9in) between rows, and thin seedlings to 15cm (6in) apart. Keep the ground well watered during the first few weeks after sowing and hoe frequently to keep weeds down. Cover with cloches to minimise growth check during cold spells.

AT-A-GLANCE TIMETABLE

SOWING
EARLY TO MID SPRING; LATE SUMMER; MID AUTUMN
1cm (½in) deep

THINNING
25cm (10in) apart, when large enough to handle

HARVESTING
ALL YEAR IF SOWN IN SPRING AND AUTUMN

Courgettes and marrows

Pests and diseases
Apart from **slugs and snails** (page 241), corn salad is generally trouble free.

Harvesting
The plants are ready for use after they have produced their fourth pair of leaves.

Either use the entire plant after cutting off the roots, or pick a few of the larger leaves from each mature plant. They tend to be rather short-lived, so it's best to start using the leaves as soon as they are ready.

Preparing and cooking
This salad plant is ideal for use when ordinary lettuce is scarce and lacking in flavour.

Because the leaves grow close to the ground they tend to be muddy or gritty when picked, and need careful washing.

Use the leaves whole in green or mixed salads. Toss them in a slightly sweet dressing of oil, mustard, vinegar or lemon juice, and season to taste with salt, pepper and sugar or honey.

Corn salad can also be cooked like baby spinach and works particularly well in pasta sauces and in stir-fries.

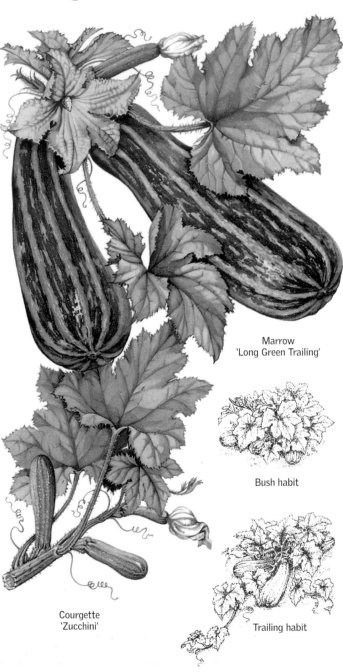

Marrow
'Long Green Trailing'

Bush habit

Courgette
'Zucchini'

Trailing habit

Although not especially nutritious, courgettes and marrows provide a considerable yield from a modest area. You can even plant them on a compost heap, as long as you don't need to disturb it before autumn.

Courgettes, which are basically small marrows, are increasingly popular and have a range of uses. They can be eaten with a wide range of dishes, and because so many courgettes mature at more or less the same time, they are an excellent crop for the freezer.

Marrows can be served as a side vegetable, often coated in a white sauce, or stuffed with mince and vegetables as a main course. They absorb other flavours well which makes them a good choice for using in spicy chutneys and pickles, or jams such as the traditional marrow-and-ginger.

Planning the crop
Courgettes and marrows both require a sunny position and a deep, rich soil. They can be sown or planted directly in the soil, or on an old heap of thoroughly rotted manure or compost if this will not be needed for a time.

You can grow courgette varieties described as 'compact' in large pots or in growing bags – one or two per bag, maximum.

When planting in soil, in late spring, take out a good spadeful where each plant is to be grown and work in a bucketful of manure or compost at the bottom of the hole. Return the topsoil, and form a ridge about 5cm (2in) high surrounding each planting site to help to retain moisture when watering the plants.

On a compost heap, mix a little soil into the planting position and make sure that the heap does not dry out during spells of sunny weather.

Trailing courgettes are more suitable than bush varieties for growing in this way.

How many to grow Four to six plants should provide plenty of courgettes (or marrows) for a family, for both immediate use and for freezing. Bush varieties take up far less room than trailing varieties.

Varieties
All Green Bush A bush courgette producing medium size fruits; dark green; good flavour.
Golden Zucchini An F1 hybrid courgette; slender, golden fruits with a fine, delicate flavour.
Zucchini An ever-popular F1 hybrid; this courgette classic is extremely early and prolific; tender and tasty flesh.
Long Green Trailing This marrow produces very large fruits; dark green with paler stripes.

Growing tips
Both courgettes and marrows are raised in the same way. Prepare the beds, as already described above, in late spring. If you want to make an earlier start to preparing the site and ensure prolific courgettes later on, then try the following tip.

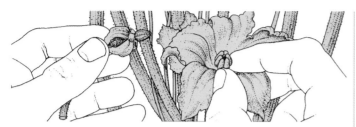

Pollinating courgettes If insects are scarce, you can use a soft brush to transfer pollen from male to female flowers; or, as here, rub the male flower directly onto the open blooms of the female flowers.

In late autumn decide exactly where you want your courgette plants to grow. Dig a pit for each one and line it with newspaper or cardboard. Every time you have raw organic kitchen waste to compost (such as peelings), put this into your pits instead of onto the compost heap. In spring, cover the pits with a layer of topsoil and mark them with canes.

Sow seeds in pairs 2.5cm (1in) deep in fibre pots filled with seed compost. Put the pots in a coldframe or on a shaded windowsill indoors. When leaves appear, remove the weaker of the two plants from each pot. At the end of spring, plant out the seedlings in their fibre pots.

Plant bush varieties 60cm (2ft) apart and trailing plants 1–1.2m (3–4ft) apart. Water well after planting, and throughout the growing season during dry spells.

Courgettes and marrows produce both male and female flowers. Females have an embryo fruit behind the bloom; males have no swelling behind it. Insects usually pollinate courgettes, but in dull, cold or wet weather, when there are few insects about, it is a good idea to pollinate the flowers by hand to make sure that the fruits form (see above).

Pests and diseases
Aphids, glasshouse red spider mites and glasshouse whitefly are the pests most likely to give trouble. Diseases that may occur are cucumber mosaic virus and powdery mildew (see Pests and Diseases, pages 238–49).

Harvesting and storing
Ideally, you should begin cutting and eating courgettes when the fruits are 4in (10cm) long.

Marrows are best if eaten in summer when the fruits are 25–30cm (9–12in) long and when the skins yield to gentle pressure of

AT-A-GLANCE TIMETABLE

PREPARING THE BED
MIDDLE OF SPRING (OR DIG PITS IN WINTER)

SOWING
LATE SPRING
In pairs in fibre pots of compost. Thin weaker plants

HARVESTING
• Courgettes
Cut when 10cm (4in) long
• Marrows
Cut when 25–30cm (9–12in) long

the fingers. Leave a few late marrows on the stalk to ripen in autumn. Harvest these just before the first frosts are expected and hang them in nets in an airy, frost-free place. Stored in this way, they will last for several weeks.

See also chutneys (page 292); freezing (page 252); fruit cheeses and butters (page 281); jams (page 271) and pickles (page 285).

Preparing and cooking
Marrow skins are tough; leave them on when cooking but don't eat them. Remove the large seeds from marrows before cooking. The entire courgette can be eaten – skins, seeds and even flowers.

Prepare courgettes by washing and trimming both ends. Cut off any discoloured or bruised patches. Slice, cube or cook whole. Steam or boil until tender, or sauté in a little olive oil and butter.

Courgettes are one of the main ingredients of ratatouille – a vegetable stew that also includes tomatoes, aubergines, onions and peppers. When you have a glut of tomatoes and courgettes, make a batch and freeze it.

Courgette flowers are beloved of television chefs. Pick perfect flowers, dip them in a light batter and deep fry until crisp and golden; baby courgettes are also delicious cooked like this.

Grated garlic courgettes Wash the courgettes and grate them coarsely – a food processor is ideal for this. Warm some olive oil in a large pan or wok and add one or two cloves of garlic. Stir-fry the courgettes in the garlicky oil and season with salt and pepper.

Harvesting courgettes Use a knife to cut through the courgette stalks. The white markings on these leaves are powdery mildew; this doesn't affect fruit production but do not compost any plant remains.

Cucumbers

Indoor (frame) cucumber

There are two main categories of cucumbers – outdoor and indoor. These are traditionally described as ridge and frame, and may be listed as such in seed catalogues. The outdoor 'ridge' cucumbers were so called because for many years gardeners grew these varieties on ridges of loam and compost.

The indoor 'frame' cucumbers, as their name suggests, have to be grown under glass, whether in a heated or cold greenhouse or in a coldframe. Today these are often listed as greenhouse cucumbers.

Outdoor (ridge) cucumber

Apple-shaped cucumber

Today, you can also buy all-purpose varieties that can be grown under glass or in a sunny spot outdoors.

Mini-cucumbers are increasingly popular; one variety of mini outdoor (ridge) cucumber is the gherkin, whose fruits are good for pickling.

If you have a heated greenhouse, you can produce cucumbers ready for eating in late spring and early summer, long before those grown in a cold greenhouse or outdoors are ripe.

Cucumbers, which probably originated in Africa, have graced salad dishes for thousands of years. They were in great demand in ancient Rome, and were grown in the vegetable gardens of the city, using techniques similar to those used today.

Planning the crop
Outdoor cucumbers Many gardeners nowadays have abandoned the practice of growing outdoor cucumbers on ridges. The original purpose was to prevent wet soil from rotting the stems, which can happen when drainage is poor. But just as many casualties are caused by ridge-grown plants becoming too dry, and it is probably better to grow them on level ground, with pockets of rich soil beneath the plants.

Prepare planting pockets
Choose a sunny, yet sheltered position in spring, a week or so before planting time. Dig a square hole for each plant 30cm wide and 30cm deep (1ft x 1ft), allowing about 60cm (2ft) between holes. Fill the holes with a mixture of

AT-A-GLANCE TIMETABLE

Outdoor cucumbers

SOWING
• In pots/growing bag
MID SPRING
• In the ground
LATE SPRING

TRANSPLANTING/THINNING
• In pots
LATE SPRING TO EARLY SUMMER
• In the ground
Remove weakest seedling

PINCHING OUT
• In pots/growing bag
Remove growing tip when plant has 6–7 leaves
• In the ground
Remove growing tip when plant has 6–7 leaves

HARVESTING
• In pots/growing bag
SUMMER TO AUTUMN
• In the ground
SUMMER TO AUTUMN

Outdoor cucumber The skins of standard outdoor varieties are often knobbly, but still edible. Tough skins can be peeled.

well-rotted compost or manure and fine soil, and scatter some general fertiliser over the surface.

Alternatively, grow two plants to a growing bag on a sunny patio.

Indoor cucumbers The problem with growing cucumbers in the average greenhouse is that, ideally, they require a night temperature of about 16°C (61°F), together with a high level of humidity. This makes them uneasy company for other greenhouse vegetables that like it cooler and less humid. However, as a rule you only need to heat the greenhouse in spring, as summer night temperatures are likely to be above the recommended minimum without the help of a heater.

As with outdoor cucumbers, provide a rich mixture of soil and compost. Prepare planting 'pockets' as described above for outdoor cucumbers – though leaving the surface mounded over the planting positions. Alternatively, fill 25cm (10in) pots with John Innes No. 3

Compost or a good-quality, soil-less compost, or grow the plants in growing bags.

However you choose to grow your cucumbers, you should shade the glass from spring onwards to prevent damage from scorching.

Indoor cucumbers can also be grown in coldframes – hence the name 'frame' cucumber – though they will crop later than those grown in a warm greenhouse.

Dig the growing pockets beneath the higher end of the frame, and use some form of shading – an old dust sheet would do fine – to shield young cucumbers from scorching on sunny days.

How many to grow The average yield from one indoor cucumber plant is less than 10 fruits, though an expertly grown plant may produce as many as 20 cucumbers. Two or three outdoor plants, and perhaps a single indoor one, together with one or two gherkin varieties should be plenty.

Varieties Always grow all-female varieties when growing indoor (greenhouse) cucumbers. These do not produce male flowers, which can pollinate the crop and make the fruits bitter and misshapen. They have a smooth skin and seed catalogues always have a good choice of disease-resistant, all-female forms. Most garden centres also offer all-female plants for sale in spring.

Outdoor (ridge) cucumbers also have all-female varieties, but standard varieties, like **Long Green Ridge** are still popular.

Most standard outdoor varieties have a rough, knobbly skin and tend to be shorter and fatter than indoor cucumbers, or you could try growing a round 'apple' variety, like **Crystal Apple**.

Growing tips: outdoor cucumbers and gherkins

In mid spring, sow two or three seeds 1cm (½in) deep in 8cm (3in)

GROWING OUTDOOR (RIDGE) CUCUMBERS

Preparing the soil Make planting stations, 60cm (2ft) apart, by filling spade-depth holes with a mixture of well-rotted compost or manure and soil.

Pinching out laterals If any laterals show no signs of fruiting, pinch out the tip beyond the sixth or seventh leaf.

Pinching out leaders Shortly after planting, when six or seven leaves have developed, pinch out each plant's growing tip to encourage the growth of fruit-bearing laterals.

fibre pots filled with seed compost. The seeds need a temperature of 21°C (70°F) to germinate, so put the pots in an airing cupboard or in the greenhouse near a heater. Remove the weakest seedlings to leave only one in each pot.

Harden off the seedlings during late spring and plant them out in the prepared beds, when there is no danger of frost.

Alternatively, in late spring, sow three or four seeds 2–3cm (1in) deep and 8cm (3in) apart from each other in the centre of each planting pocket – which are themselves at 60cm (2ft) spacings. Once they have germinated, remove the weaker seedlings and leave the strongest to stand alone. Whichever method you follow, pinch out the growing tip of each plant after six or seven leaves have appeared. This will encourage fruit-bearing shoots to develop.

Unlike indoor cucumbers, the female flowers of some outdoor varieties require fertilising by the

male – so don't remove male flowers. Your nursery or the seed packet or catalogue should have advice on this.

Pollination is normally carried out by insects, but if few are about, wait until the male flowers are fully developed, then transfer male pollen to the female flowers with a fine paintbrush.

If a lateral fails to show any sign of fruit production by the time the sixth or seventh leaf appears, nip off its tip.

Keep the soil moist by watering round the plants. Feed regularly with a liquid fertiliser, and protect them against slugs. As the fruits swell and ripen, keep them off the soil with pieces of board or glass.

Growing tips: indoor cucumbers and gherkins

Heated greenhouse The main snag about growing cucumbers in this way is the high temperature required if they are grown early in the season to fruit before those

grown in coldframes or outdoors. All indoor varieties need at least 21°C (70°F) to germinate, and though in most cases this can be lowered as the seedlings grow, they must be housed in a greenhouse where the night temperature does not drop below 16°C (61°F) throughout the growing period.

One way round this is to buy young plants from a garden centre that have been acclimatised to lower temperatures.

Begin sowing at any time from late winter, placing the seeds in compost-filled 8cm (3in) fibre pots.

Insert a single seed edgeways 1cm (½in) deep into each pot and place the pots in a propagator, above the greenhouse heater or in an airing cupboard.

While the seeds are germinating, rig horizontal wires across the end of the greenhouse from one glazing strut to another. These will be used to train the laterals. Rig the wires about 30cm (12in) away from the glass.

TRAINING GREENHOUSE CUCUMBERS

Pinching out leaders Remove the tip of each leader, or main shoot, when it reaches the roof. Lateral shoots will develop.

When the seedlings have developed two rough leaves – in other words the leaves that follow the initial seedling leaves – transplant them to the prepared greenhouse bed, or into the large pots, or into growing bags. Fix a vertical stake beside each plant.

When the plants have grown up to the height of the roof, pinch out the tips of the leading shoots. This will encourage the growth of the lateral shoots, which should then be attached to the horizontal wires with twine.

It is often recommended that male flowers should be removed to prevent the fruits from becoming bitter due to pollination, but this is generally unnecessary. Natural pollination of greenhouse varieties is fairly uncommon, and fruits picked when young, as they should be, will not be seedy or bitter.

If no cucumbers have appeared on the laterals by the time they are 60cm (2ft) long, pinch out the

Pinching out laterals Pinch out laterals just beyond the second leaf after the fruit. Restrict to 60cm (2ft) if no fruits form.

growing tips. Even when laterals do produce fruit, pinch them out just beyond the second leaf after the first cucumber.

Laterals frequently put out fruit-bearing sideshoots. When this happens, treat them in the same way as the laterals themselves by pinching out the growing tips two leaves beyond the first cucumber.

Shade the plants from strong sunlight, and water them well. Keep the air humid by spraying the greenhouse floor twice a day, and ensure it is well-ventilated.

Once the fruits begin to swell, give the plants a fortnightly feed of liquid fertiliser.

Coldframe cucumbers Prepare the planting stations by early May, so that the plants can be set out at the end of the month.

Sow seeds in fibre pots in the same way as for greenhouse cultivation, but leave them to germinate within the coldframe.

When the seedlings are growing well, transplant them to their final growing situation – that is, a single plant beneath each frame light at the highest point of the frame.

Replace the lid of the frame and cover the glass with greenhouse shading or a coat of limewash. Open the lid 5cm (2in) on the sheltered side on warm days, but close it to a small crack at night, using a thin wedge.

Water the plants frequently, and spray the inside of the frame twice a day during hot weather. This will help to maintain the necessary degree of humidity.

When the plants have developed about six leaves, pinch out the growing tips to promote the development of laterals. Spread these evenly over the frame floor. Remove the male flowers (easily identified by their slender stalks) before they open, and pinch out all fruiting shoots two leaves beyond the first cucumber.

You should also pinch out any shoot that climbs over the front edge of the frame.

Pests and diseases

Aphids, **glasshouse red spider mites** and **glasshouse whitefly** are the pests most likely to occur.

Diseases to which cucumbers are susceptible include **cucumber mosaic virus**, **grey mould**, **powdery mildew** and **soil-borne diseases** (see Pests and Diseases pages 238–49).

Harvesting and storing

It may be tempting to discover how big your cucumbers will grow if left on the plant, but they will taste much better if you harvest them before they have reached their maximum size. It is just as

GROWING IN FRAMES

Pinching out leaders Remove growing tip of each plant when six leaves have formed. Fruit-bearing laterals will develop.

Pinching out laterals Spread shoots evenly over frame floor. Pinch out each tip just beyond the second leaf after the fruit.

important, however, not to cut the fruits too early. As a rough guide, a mature cucumber should have parallel sides. If the sides dwindle to a point, the fruit is not developing properly and may have a bitter flavour. This usually occurs towards the end of the cropping season.

Depending on the variety, outdoor cucumbers can be harvested from the middle of summer to at least the middle of autumn. Indoor plants have a

longer season, from midsummer through most of autumn. However you grow them, cucumbers are best eaten soon after cutting. **See also** pickles (page 285); sauces, ketchups and relishes (page 296) and vinegars (page 299).

Preparing and cooking

Cucumbers are usually eaten cold in salads. Wash and dry the cucumber and slice off both ends. You don't need to peel unless the skin is rough or bruised. Slice into thin rings or, if very seedy, cut in half lengthways, scoop out the seeds with a teaspoon and chop into chunks.

Chilled cucumber soup This refreshing summer soup is made in a blender. Chop up a cucumber and sprinkle with salt. Leave for half an hour, rinse and drain. In a large bowl mix 300ml natural yoghurt with 150ml single cream, a clove of garlic, crushed, 2 tablespoons each of olive oil and white wine vinegar. Season with salt and pepper and fold in the cucumber. Tip the whole lot into the blender and whizz until smooth. Chill for 2 hours. This soup looks pretty garnished with mint leaves and a swirl of cream.

Cucumber in dill dressing Slice the cucumber into paper-thin rounds. Lay out flat and sprinkle with salt to let the water drain out. Rinse and dry on kitchen paper. Mix 75ml soured cream or crème fraîche with 75ml natural yoghurt and a heaped tablespoon of fresh, finely chopped dill. Fold in the cucumber slices, season with salt and pepper and serve at once.

Currants, black

These hardy shrubs do well in any part of the country. They are easy to grow and long lived.

The dark, acid berries are richer in vitamin C than any other garden fruit, and for this reason have long been used in health-boosting cordials. Blackcurrants are a versatile fruit that can be used to make jam, jelly, fruit syrup, pies, puddings and other desserts, as well as ice creams and water ices. They also freeze well.

Planning the crop

Blackcurrants thrive in full sunshine, but will also do well in slightly shaded positions. Avoid pockets and hollows subject to late spring frosts.

Blackcurrants will grow in any soil – from sandy loam to heavy clay, but they don't like to be waterlogged. Whatever the soil, it should be well-manured.

How many bushes to grow

A mature bush will yield about 5–7kg (10–15lb) of fruit. Fully grown bushes can take up a fair amount of space. Even a compact bush will need an area roughly equivalent to a 1.5m (4–5ft) diameter circle on the ground.

Varieties

The Ben varieties have revolutionised blackcurrant growing in recent years, bringing heavy crops, disease resistance and a more compact habit to the soft-fruit garden. However, if space is no problem, these three older varieties are worth considering:

Wellington XXX Mid season; heavy cropper; sweet fruits; do not spray with lime-sulphur.

Baldwin Late; medium-size currants; compact bush.

Mailing Jet Very late; also flowers late and so escapes frost.

Growing tips

Buy certificated disease-free plants from a reputable nursery. Enrich the soil with garden compost or farmyard manure.

Most plants are now sold in containers, so may be planted in their permanent positions any time the weather is right. However, planting is still best done in autumn, while the soil is still warm enough to get the roots growing but watering is not usually necessary.

Plant the bushes 1.5–1.8m (5–6ft) apart in each direction. Compact varieties may be positioned slightly closer than this. Put them into the ground a little deeper than they were in the container or nursery bed, using the soil mark on the stem as a guide.

After planting, prune all the shoots to about 2–3cm (1in) above ground level, cutting just above a bud. This means that the bushes will yield no fruit the first summer; instead, their energy will be used to produce vigorous new growth that will provide a crop during the second summer after planting.

After this pruning, mulch the plants with a layer of compost, manure or other organic material. Repeat this mulch every spring, at the rate of two buckets per square metre (square yard), to feed the plants and to conserve moisture in the soil.

Dress the soil in mid winter with 30g sulphate of potash per square metre (1oz per square yard), and in early spring with 30g sulphate of ammonia. Every third year, apply a dressing of 60g of superphosphate per square metre (2oz per square yard). Alternatively, top-dress each spring with a compound bush fruit fertiliser, following manufacturer's instructions.

After spells of hard frost, ensure that the bushes – which are shallow-rooted – have not been lifted. If they have, firm them in with your feet. Do not disturb the roots by weeding with a fork or hoe; regular mulching should keep down weeds.

Water the plants regularly during dry periods. In the first autumn after planting, cut down the weakest of the current season's shoots to just above the soil. During the following autumn, cut out a few of the weaker shoots to stimulate new growth. In

AT-A-GLANCE TIMETABLE

- **Year of planting**
PLANTING
AUTUMN-SPRING

PRUNING
- **End of first year**
AUTUMN
Prune the weakest shoots to ground level

- **Second year onwards**
HARVESTING
EARLY TO LATE SUMMER

PRUNING
LATE SUMMER TO AUTUMN

ESTABLISHING BLACKCURRANTS

Planting Dig a hole broad enough to spread the roots. Set the bushes slightly deeper than they were in the nursery.

Pruning Cut each shoot of the newly planted bushes to within 2–3cm (1in) of ground level, above an outward-facing bud.

PRUNING BLACKCURRANTS

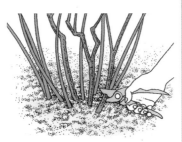

Annual pruning From the second autumn onwards, remove some older wood each year to make way for younger shoots that will produce fruit the following year.

Neglected bushes To restore untended bushes, remove crowded shoots from the centre and cut out older shoots – the darkest-looking ones – elsewhere.

succeeding autumns remove a proportion of the older wood to make way for replacement shoots.

Cut low down to promote new growth from near ground level. Aim to cut out between a quarter and a third of the old wood. If you have inherited untended blackcurrant bushes, cut out the old wood from the centre to let in

RAISING NEW BUSHES

Preparing a cutting Choose long straight stems of this year's growth on healthy plants. Cut off the thin growing tip just above a bud, and trim the base just below a bud to leave a cutting about 20–30cm (8–12in) long.

Rooting the cuttings Set the cuttings in a V-shaped trench about 15cm (6in) deep. In heavy soils cover the base of the trench with sharp sand. Replace the soil and firm it with your foot.

light and air, then the oldest-looking (darkest) remaining shoots. Really hard pruning is needed to stimulate new growth.

How to raise new bushes You can easily increase blackcurrants from hardwood cuttings. In mid autumn, take cuttings from current season's shoots that are well-ripened and healthy looking. Cut off the unripened tip just above a bud, and the bottom just below a bud, to make a cutting about 20–30cm (8–12in) long.

Dig a 15cm (6in) deep, V-shaped trench. If the soil is heavy, put a 5cm (2in) layer of sand in the trench to improve drainage.

Push the cuttings into the trench, 15cm (6in) apart, with two buds showing above ground. Fill in the trench and tread the soil firm.

By the following autumn the cuttings should have rooted and be ready for their permanent positions. Remove them carefully with a fork and replant them, cutting them back hard, as described for planting young plants that have been bought from a nursery.

Pests and diseases

The principal pests of blackcurrants are **aphids**, **blackcurrant gall mite** and **capsid bugs**. Diseases most likely to occur are **American gooseberry mildew**, **grey mould**, **honey fungus**, **leaf spot** and **reversion** (see Pests and Diseases pages 238–49).

Harvesting and storing

Pick blackcurrants only when they are properly ripe – that is, a week or so after they have turned black. The fruits at the top of each cluster generally ripen first.

See also bottling (page 270); drying (page 300); freezing (page 252); fruit cheeses and butters (page 281); jams (page 271); pickles (page 285); syrups and juices (page 283) and wine-making (page 304).

Cooking blackcurrants

Blackcurrants are cooked and used as pie and pudding fillings, for flavouring ice creams and sorbets, and for making jam and fruit syrups. In recipes like summer pudding they are mixed with redcurrants and other soft fruits. Always use the berries as soon as possible after harvesting as they deteriorate fast.

Handle carefully to avoid bruising. The easiest way to strip the berries from the stalks is to hold a bunch above a colander and 'comb' off the currants with a table fork. Then wash the currants by

dipping them, in their colander, in several changes of cold water. Drain the fruit before using it.

Summer pudding Line the base and sides of a 1 litre pudding basin with slices of stale, white, crustless bread cut to shape so as to fit together neatly. Fill the middle with about 750g black and redcurrants and other soft fruits – blueberries, raspberries and blackberries, for example – that have first been gently simmered with 100g sugar until the sugar dissolves and the juices begin to run. Keep back a couple of tablespoons of juice. Make a 'lid' out of bread; fit a saucer inside the basin over the pudding and put a heavy weight on top. Chill for 8 hours. Turn the pudding out onto a serving plate and pour the reserved juice over any bits of still-white bread. Serve with softly whipped cream.

Summer pudding Use black and redcurrants and other soft summer fruits in this juicy classic.

Currants, red and white

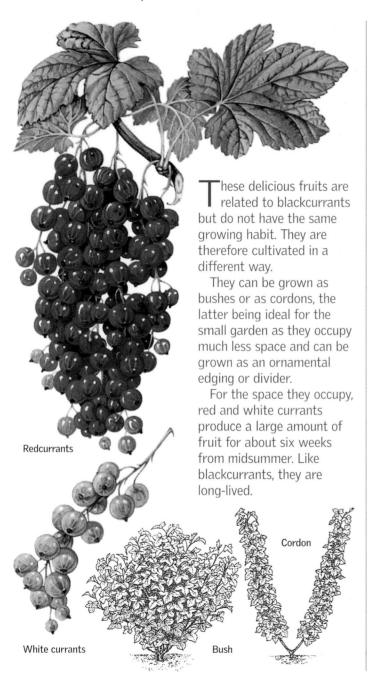

Redcurrants

White currants   Bush   Cordon

These delicious fruits are related to blackcurrants but do not have the same growing habit. They are therefore cultivated in a different way.

They can be grown as bushes or as cordons, the latter being ideal for the small garden as they occupy much less space and can be grown as an ornamental edging or divider.

For the space they occupy, red and white currants produce a large amount of fruit for about six weeks from midsummer. Like blackcurrants, they are long-lived.

Planning the crop
An open site in full sun or semi-shade is best for currants, but you can grow cordons successfully against walls of any aspect.

Whatever the position, it should not be subject to late frosts, because the plants flower early.

Red and white currants grow well in any moisture-retaining soil, as long as it doesn't have a tendency to waterlogging.

How many bushes to grow
Red and white currant bushes yield about 4–5kg (8–10lb) of fruit, and cordons about 1–1.5kg (2–3lb). Each mature bush occupies about 2.3 square metres (25 square feet). Eight single cordons can be planted against a wall 3m (10ft) long.

Varieties Rovada is thought by many to be the best modern redcurrant introduction, but **Laxton's No 1** and **Red Lake** are also good.

The most easily available white currant variety is **White Versailles**.

Growing tips
Red and white currants, like gooseberries, are susceptible to a deficiency of potash. Before planting, apply a general fertiliser at 120g per square metre (4oz per square yard), together with a dressing of well-rotted manure or compost if the soil is low in humus.

The best time to plant is autumn, but as most bushes are container grown, they can be planted at any time of year as long as the weather is suitable. Space bushes 1.5m (5ft) apart in each direction, and cordons 40cm (15in) apart. Alternatively, grow in containers of John Innes No. 3 compost.

After planting a bush, cut back all the branches to four buds above the base of the stems. The top bud should point outwards.

Setting out cordons Before planting cordons, stretch support wires between end posts or along a fence. Set the bottom wire 45cm (18in) from the ground and two more spaced 60cm (2ft) apart above the bottom wire.

Canes tied to these will support the cordons.

After planting a cordon, choose the strongest shoot to become the leader; this will eventually become the main stem. Cut off all others to within 2.5cm (1in) of the base. Prune lateral shoots that grow from the main stem to two buds.

Secure the cordon to the cane with soft string, and fasten the cane to the wires.

Feed bushes and cordons
Mulch the bushes and cordons in winter with a 5cm (2in) layer of well-rotted compost or manure and feed them with 30g of sulphate of potash per square metre (1oz per square yard).

In spring, a further feed of 30g of sulphate of ammonia per square metre (1oz per square yard) will promote growth.

Every third year apply 60g of superphosphate per square metre (2oz per square yard). Alternatively, apply a balanced bush fruit fertiliser every spring.

PRUNING AFTER PLANTING

Bushes Immediately after planting, cut back each shoot to an outward-pointing bud – about the fourth above the base of the shoot. Fruiting stems will grow from these.

Cordons Choose the strongest shoot – two shoots for a double cordon – and cut the remainder back to the base. Fasten the stem to the stake with soft string.

AT-A-GLANCE TIMETABLE
• **First year** **PLANTING** AUTUMN TO SPRING
• **Succeeding years** **SUMMER PRUNING** MIDSUMMER
HARVESTING SUMMER
WINTER PRUNING LATE WINTER

Summer promise Tiny white currants begin to form in spring.

Pruning
Bushes and cordons both need to be pruned in winter and summer. Leave winter pruning, in which growth is always cut back to an undamaged bud, until late in the season.

Bushes During the second winter shorten each branch by half, cutting to an outward-facing bud.

In succeeding winters cut back leading shoots halfway, and laterals to two buds. You want to have a bush that is goblet-shaped, with an open centre.

From about the fifth winter onwards, cut back all the current season's shoots by about 2.5cm (1in). Remove congested old wood from the centre of the bush, aiming to replace it with new growth.

In midsummer, cut back laterals to three or five leaves.

Cordons Winter pruning of cordons involves shortening the leading shoots by a third and laterals to one bud. Do not let the leader grow longer than 1.8m (6ft).

In midsummer cut back laterals to three or five leaves, as you would with bushes.

Raising new bushes
Red and white currants can be raised from cuttings of the current year's growth. In autumn, cut off some well-ripened shoots. Trim the soft wood off the top, just above a bud, and some wood off the bottom, just below a bud, to produce cuttings 25–40cm (10–15in) long. Rub off all except the top four buds, and then plant the cuttings in the same way as blackcurrants (page 138).

When you move the plants to their permanent positions, plant them at the same depth as they were while rooting, and remove any low, unwanted sideshoots so that the bush has a clean stem about 10–15cm (4–6in) long.

Cut back all upper branches halfway to an outward-facing bud. After that, prune them as already described.

Pests and diseases
Look out for **aphids**, **blackcurrant gall mite**, **blackcurrant leaf midge** and **capsid bugs**. Diseases include **coral spot**, **grey mould**, **honey fungus** and **leaf spot** (see Pests and Diseases, pages 238–49).

Harvesting and storing
Pick the fruits as soon as they are ripe and use them immediately, since they do not keep for long.

WINTER AND SUMMER PRUNING

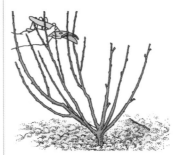

Bushes: second winter Halve the length of each shoot. Cut back to just above an outward-facing bud to ensure an open structure.

Bushes: succeeding winters Cut back leading shoots to half their length, and laterals to two buds. You want to achieve an open-centred, goblet-shaped bush.

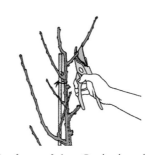

Cordons: winter Cut back each leading shoot by a third, and reduce each of the lateral shoots to a single bud.

Bushes and cordons: summer Around midsummer, prune lateral shoots on red and white currants to three or five leaves.

See also bottling (page 270); freezing (page 252); jams (page 271) and jellies (page 277).

Preparing and cooking
Red and white currants may be served as fresh dessert fruits, left on the stalks after rinsing and draining. Redcurrants are also used in fresh-fruit salads and cooked in compôtes, pastries, jams and jellies. Before cooking, strip currants from their stalks. This is easily done by running the prongs of a fork down the length of the stalk to 'comb' off the berries.

Use frosted redcurrants to garnish fruit mousses, trifles and ice creams or serve on their own as a dessert fruit. Rinse and drain clusters of currants, brush berries with lightly beaten egg white and dredge heavily with sugar. Leave on a wire rack to dry before use.

Damsons

The fruit of the damson is the smallest in the plum family, but what this species lacks in size it makes up for in hardiness. A damson tree will succeed in exposed, wet districts where plums are difficult to grow and gages may not survive.

Planning the crop
Damsons do best in deep, well-drained heavy loams, but they can be grown in most soils.

Damsons are self-fertile so that only one tree needs to be planted to produce a crop.

How many trees to grow One tree is generally sufficient to supply the average family.

Varieties There are two self-fertile varieties that are generally easy to obtain:
Merryweather Produces large, black, fine-flavoured fruits in late summer and early autumn.
Prune The small, tapering, blue-black fruits of this variety have a good flavour and are ready slightly later than Merryweather.

Growing tips
Damsons can be grown as a bush or may be fan-trained on a wall. If more than one tree is to be grown, set them 3.5m (12ft) apart. Plant two-year-old trees in late autumn or early winter.

Container-grown trees may be planted at other times of the year if the weather is suitable.

To establish the framework of the tree, prune and train basically as for apples (see pages 66–74), but prune in early spring as growth

begins – not in winter. Another difference is that a damson should be allowed a more crowded and compact head than an apple tree.

When the tree is established little pruning is needed, as damsons fruit on both old and new wood. The general cultivation of damsons is the same as that of plums (see page 186).

Pests and diseases
Among pests attacking damsons are **aphids**, **caterpillars**, **fruit tree red spider mites** and **plum sawfly**.

Diseases include **bacterial canker**, **brown rot**, **honey fungus**, **rust**, **shothole** and **silver leaf**
See Pests and Diseases, pages 238–49.

Harvesting and storing
Damsons are ripe enough to harvest when they part easily from the tree. Pick the fruit by the stalk to avoid bruising.

See also bottling (page 270); freezing (page 252); fruit cheeses and butters (page 281); jams (page 271); jellies (page 277); pickles (page 285); syrups and juices (page 283) and wine-making (page 304).

Preparing and cooking
These small plums are rarely used as fresh dessert fruits, being more

AT-A-GLANCE TIMETABLE

PLANTING
LATE AUTUMN–EARLY WINTER

PRUNING
SPRING

HARVESTING
AUTUMN

Getting results It will take five to ten years, depending on the variety, for a damson tree to produce a substantial yield of fruit.

often used for pie and pudding fillings and for the classic preserve, damson cheese. To prepare damsons for cooking, wash and dry them and remove any stalks. Cut with the point of a knife along the indentations on the skin and twist the damson into two halves. Carefully prise out the stone with the point of a knife, doing this over a plate.

For purées, cook damsons in just enough water to prevent sticking. Cook for 15–20 minutes, depending on the ripeness of the fruit.

Damson and apple pie
Make an apple pie extra special by adding damsons. Place 375g (¾lb) apples, peeled and cut into chunks, into a pie dish. Add the same weight of prepared damsons. Sprinkle with 75g (3oz) sugar and add three tablespoons of water. Roll out 250g (½lb) shortcrust pastry and use to cover the pie. Bake in the oven at 200°C (400°F, gas mark 6) for about 35 minutes, until golden brown. The pie is best served warm with fresh cream or custard.

Dill

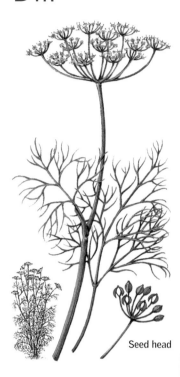

Seed head

Fresh or dried leaves of dill, a hardy annual, add an aniseed flavour to fish, poultry, soups and stews. The feathery, pale green leaves are attractive as a garnish.

Planning the crop
Dill can be grown in any well-drained soil in an open, sunny position. The plants grow to a height of 1m (3ft). Sow at monthly intervals in spring and summer for a constant supply throughout the summer and into autumn.

Growing tips
Sow in shallow drills, about 5mm (¼in) deep, leaving 25cm (9in) between rows.

For a harvest of seeds, thin the first sowing to leave 25cm (9in) between plants. Use the thinnings to provide tender young leaves. Subsequent sowings, for leaves only, need to be thinned to only 10cm (4in) apart.

Pests and diseases
Dill is usually trouble free and is actually a useful companion plant for growing between rows of carrots. Its strong aroma helps to deter the dreaded carrot fly.

Harvesting and storing
The leaves will be ready for picking about eight weeks after sowing.

Pick leaves for using fresh as needed, and those for drying (see page 300) or freezing (see page 252) before the plants start flowering.

Leave plants from the earliest sowing to provide seeds for winter. Pick the seeding heads when they have turned brown, and complete the drying-out process by spreading the seeds on a tray in a warm, dry place. Store the seeds in air-tight jars.

Preparing and cooking
This pungently aromatic herb, with its aniseed flavour, combines

(see page 300) or freezing (see page 252)

AT-A-GLANCE TIMETABLE

SOWING
5mm (¼in) deep
SPRING–SUMMER

THINNING
25cm (9in) apart, when large enough to handle

HARVESTING
LATE SPRING–EARLY AUTUMN

particularly well with both hot and cold fish dishes, and is also useful for salads, cold sauces and dressings. Both the leaves, fresh and dried, and the dried seeds are used in cooking. They are also used to flavour vinegar and as a pickling ingredient with gherkins and cucumbers.

Use the leaves chopped in salad dressings or sprinkle them on buttered new potatoes; on egg, tomato and cucumber sandwiches; on fish and tomato soups; and on grilled and baked fish. The seeds, too, can be added to salad dressings, creamed cabbage and chicken stews.

The feathery, pale green leaves feature particularly in Scandinavian cooking. Raw, smoked and pickled salmon are traditionally served with a strong mustard and dill dressing, which can also be served with smoked mackerel and trout.

Mustard and dill dressing Beat 2 tablespoons of French mustard with 1 tablespoon of sugar and an egg yolk until smooth. Take 6 tablespoons of oil and 2 tablespoons of white wine vinegar, adding them alternately little by little, and beating thoroughly after each addition. Finally fold in a heaped teaspoon of fresh, chopped dill and season with salt and pepper to taste.

Dill sauce Blanch a few dill sprigs, drain and dry before chopping the leaves. You will need about 2 tablespoons when chopped. Lightly whip 150ml (5fl oz) double cream and fold in the chopped dill. Season with salt and pepper to taste and chill for at least an hour before serving.

Endive

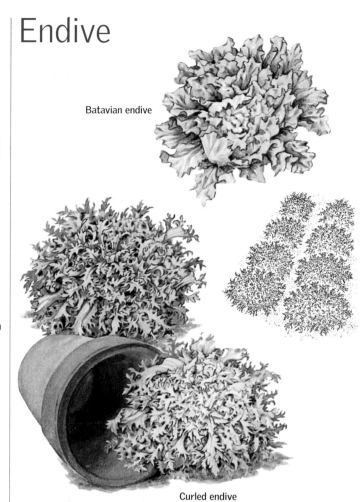

Batavian endive

Curled endive

Endives have been gaining popularity in recent years as an alternative to lettuce. The curly variety is sown in June and July to provide leaves from September to November, while the hardier, wavy-leaved Batavian type is not sown until August. This will give fresh leaves for the table until well into winter, when lettuces have finished. Curly endive has long been used in salads on the Continent, and is known in France as *chicorée frisée*.

Endives may be served raw in salads, or braised with white or cream sauce. They are an ideal accompaniment to grilled steak.

Planning the crop

Endives do best in a light, well-drained soil containing plenty of rotted manure or compost. Plants sown in July or later may be grown in beds from which early potatoes or peas have been harvested. Endives grown for mid-winter eating should be sown in a sheltered position.

How much to grow Nine or ten plants can be grown in a 3m (10ft) row. Two such rows, one containing early and the other late endives, should be sufficient for most families.

Varieties Most seed catalogues list only one or two varieties, but these will be the most reliable and best flavoured.

Growing tips

Sow the seeds thinly in drills 1cm (½in) deep, 40cm (15in) apart, in the position where the plants are to grow. Water them thoroughly, keep them well-weeded and thin the seedlings to 30–40cm (12–15in) apart.

To save seeds, sow groups of three or four seeds at 30–40cm (12–15in) intervals and remove the weakest after germination.

It is inadvisable to sow endives before midsummer because early plants have a tendency to run quickly to seed.

Pests and diseases

Slugs and snails (page 241) may attack the plants. Endives are generally disease-free.

Harvesting and storing

Batavian endives should be blanched to get rid of the natural bitterness in the leaves. Make sure

BLANCHING ENDIVES

Secure with string Choose a sunny or windy day, when the leaves of mature plants are dry, to tie them loosely with soft string.

Cover with a flowerpot Place an upturned flowerpot, or similar lightproof cover, over each plant. Place a stone over the drainage hole to keep out light.

the leaves are completely dry then bind them in the same way as for hearting cos lettuces (page 155).

Cover each endive with an upturned flowerpot, blocking the drainage hole. Alternatively, use a specially designed endive blancher,

which can be obtained from specialist garden supply shops.

After seven to ten days in early autumn, or three weeks in winter, the centres of the plants turn to a creamy-white shade and are then ready for eating. Use the endives as soon as possible after lifting, as even a short period of storage will cause the leaves to toughen.

Modern frisée types tend to be less bitter, and can often be used without blanching.

Preparing and cooking

The curly, pale green leaves of this salad vegetable are excellent for winter salads. They are best tossed in a piquant or sweet dressing on their own.

To prepare endives for use in salads, cut off any outer damaged leaves, trim off the root base,

AT-A-GLANCE TIMETABLE

SOWING
1cm (½in) deep, in rows 40cm (15in) apart
• Curly leaved types
MID-SUMMER
• Batvian types
LATE SUMMER–EARLY AUTUMN

THINNING
30–40cm (12–15in) apart, when large enough to handle

BLANCHING
• Batavian types
EARLY WINTER

HARVESTING
• Curly leaved types
When mature
• Batavian types
Three weeks after starting to blanch

Taste and texture The frilly leaves of endives make them an attractive crop to grow at the edge of a bed or in an ornamental border and an interesting addition to a green salad.

separate the spears and divide into small sprigs complete with sections of white stalk. Wash thoroughly and dry on a tea towel.

For cooking, trim the root bases, leave the endives whole or cut large ones in half lengthways. Wash and drain.

Endive and olive salad Arrange the prepared leaves of one endive and 100g (4oz) green olives in a bowl. Make a dressing by beating an egg yolk with a pinch of salt until smooth and adding a tablespoon of olive oil drop by drop, then stirring in a tablespoon of lemon juice and 50ml (2fl oz) single cream. Mix the dressing well and season with a little mustard powder and sugar. Pour over the endive and toss thoroughly. This simple salad goes well with roast meat or poultry.

Braised endive Take two or three endives and divide each head into two. Blanch for 3 minutes in a pan of boiling, salted water, then refresh under cold, running water and drain. Remove the fat and rind from 50g (2oz) streaky bacon and fry in a casserole dish.

Add a peeled, chopped carrot and a finely chopped onion and cook gently for a few minutes. Lay the endives on top of the vegetables and pour over 300ml (½ pint) chicken or vegetable stock. Season with salt and pepper, cover with a lid, and cook in an oven at 180°C (350°F, gas mark 4) for 45 minutes.

Serve the endives straight from the dish, sprinkled with finely chopped parsley. They are an excellent accompaniment to roast or grilled lamb.

Fennel

The are two distinct varieties of fennel: the tall, perennial herb that is cultivated in the herb or ornamental garden for the fine flavour of its feathery leaves, seeds and stems; and the usually smaller Florence fennel (see facing page), a biennial that is grown mainly for its swollen stem base and is used as a vegetable.

The leaves of both plants, dried or fresh, impart a delicate aniseed flavour to fish, cheese dishes, sauces, pickles and chutneys. The seeds of common fennel, whose aniseed taste is particularly pronounced, may be used to flavour soups, bread and cakes.

Planning the crop

Fennel grows well in a warm, sunny position in any reasonably well-drained garden soil.

How much to grow

Unless a regular supply of seeds is needed, or stems and stalks for cooking, three plants of common fennel – which can reach a height of 2.5m (8ft) – would be adequate for the needs of all but the most fervent fennel lovers. The statuesque plants are attractive enough to grow at the back of a herbaceous or mixed border.

Growing tips

When growing the plants for seeds, sow in spring to allow time for the seeds to ripen in autumn. Sow them thinly in 1cm (½in) drills, or in seed trays in an unheated greenhouse or coldframe. If growing the plants for their leaves and stalks, sow in late spring. In both cases, thin the seedlings to 30cm (12in) spacings.

AT-A-GLANCE TIMETABLE

SOWING
1cm (½in) deep
• For seeds
SPRING
• For leaves and stalks
LATE SPRING

THINNING
30cm (12in) apart, when large enough to handle

HARVESTING
• For seeds
AUTUMN
• For leaves and stalks
JUNE ONWARDS

Pests and diseases

Fennel is generally trouble free.

Harvesting and storing

Pick the leaves as required from June onwards, pinching off the flowerheads as they form unless you wish to harvest the seeds.

Gather the seed heads on a dry day in early autumn, when they have turned pale brown. Hang them in a warm place for a week or two, with a tray underneath to catch any seeds that fall.

Make sure that the seeds are dry before storing them in air-tight containers.
See also drying (page 300) and freezing (page 252).

Preparing and cooking

The blue-green leaves of fennel are most attractive as a garnish. They are sweetly aromatic, with an aniseed flavour that is reminiscent of dill, but less pungent.

Both the leaves and the seeds are used for the same cooking purposes as dill. But while dill is traditionally used in northern European cooking, the flavour of fennel is more usually found in Mediterranean dishes. Bass and other oily fish are often grilled on a bed of fennel leaves.

The dried seeds are used chiefly in pickles, seed cakes and herbal teas. The fresh leaves, finely chopped, are added to dressings for cucumbers and green salads, to fish soups and stews, and to young buttered vegetables.

Fennel, Florence

The stem base of Florence fennel, also called finocchio, may be chopped raw into salads; but it is more usually simmered in a stock or added to stews.

The ferny leaves of Florence fennel make an attractive backdrop to the herb or vegetable bed.

Planning the crop

Florence fennel requires more attention than the common species. Dig well-rotted manure or compost into the ground during winter, and rake in a dressing of general fertiliser at 60g per square metre (2oz per square yard) shortly before sowing the seeds in spring.

Choose a sunny position in well-drained soil.

How much to grow

As a general rule, half a stem base of Florence fennel per person is sufficient for one meal. Since it is generally only eaten as a vegetable for special occasions, a 3m (10ft) row, yielding 10–12 plants, should be enough for most families.

Growing tips

Sow the seeds thinly in a 1cm (½in) drill in spring, thinning the seedlings to 30cm (12in).

Keep the plants well-watered and, when the stem bases begin to swell, draw earth around them in the same way as for potatoes.

Pests and diseases

Florence fennel is generally trouble free.

Harvesting and storing

Gather the swollen stem bases for cooking in late summer or early autumn. Use the leaves for flavouring or as a garnish.
See also freezing (page 252).

Preparing and cooking

This delicate vegetable has the same sweet aniseed flavour as common fennel. It is made up of tightly compressed fleshy leaves,

---

AT-A-GLANCE TIMETABLE

SOWING
1cm (½in) deep
MID SPRING

THINNING
30cm (12in) apart, when large enough to handle

HARVESTING
EARLY–MID AUTUMN

like an onion, and is used as a vegetable or salad ingredient.

Trim away the leafy top stems close to the root. Do not discard the leaves, which can be added to the cooking liquid for extra flavour or used, finely chopped, as a garnish. As the fleshy leaves are more pungent than the leaves of common fennel, use them with discretion.

Trim the root base and wash the fennel roots in cold water. For salads, cut the fennel roots in half lengthways and then across into thin slices. For cooking, leave fennel roots in halves and cook in a small amount of boiling, lightly salted water for 15–20 minutes, depending on size.

Drain thoroughly, sprinkle with ground coriander or nutmeg and serve with melted butter. Cooked fennel may also be covered with finely grated cheese, and melted butter poured over it.

Figs

Gardeners have tried to grow figs in Britain since the time of Henry VIII. Some have been successful, but many have been discouraged after severe winters or dismal summers have ruined their crops.

Figs are natives of Mediterranean countries, but they can be grown in southern parts of Britain with some special care and attention. They need a south-facing wall, which will capture the sun and warmth. They also do well in large containers on a sunny patio.

Figs harvested during summer were formed during the previous year, and are present during winter as embryo fruits next to the terminal growth buds on young shoots. It is these shoots and tiny fruits that require protection during cold winter weather.

Planning the crop
The root system of figs must always be restricted to encourage fruiting, so dig a hole about 1m (3ft) square and 1m (3ft) deep and line with bricks or stone slabs. Add rubble to a depth 30cm (12in) and ram it down hard.

Fill the hole with two parts of good, but not rich, garden soil mixed with one part of mortar rubble to which 1kg (2lb) of bone meal has been added.

Figs may also be grown on the patio in 40cm (15in) pots of John Innes No.3 potting compost.

Varieties There are two varieties of figs that give the best results when grown in this country.
Brown Turkey Produces brown-green fruits; grown against a wall.
White Marseilles Produces pale green fruits; can be grown as a bush tree in a warm, sheltered spot.

Growing tips
You will probably buy container-grown young plants, which you can plant at any time of the year when the weather is fine and the ground is not frozen or waterlogged.

Make a hole in the prepared bed just big enough to take the roots. Spread these out and cover with soil, firm the ground with your feet and give a light mulch of well-rotted manure or compost.

For the first three winters, train the trees in the same way as bush apples (page 73) or fan peaches (page 177). In subsequent summers pinch out sideshoots to five leaves from their base.

If grown as a fan, train in further branches where there is room. Early in the season, rub out shoots growing towards or away from the wall.

Feeding is unnecessary during the three years the framework is being built up. In subsequent years, mulch with rotted manure or compost at the rate of a bucketful per m² (square yard) in spring. In autumn, remove all immature figs larger than peas that have grown during the summer, as they will not survive the winter. The smaller fruitlets left towards the end of the shoots will mature the following year.

Protect these in winter by covering with fleece. Gradually remove the protection in spring as the danger of hard frost lessens.

Raising new trees
Take 10–15cm (4–6in) heel cuttings of semi-ripe wood in early autumn. Insert them in 7.5cm (3in) pots of equal parts (by volume) of peat and sand, and place them in a coldframe. Plant out 18 months later, when they should have strong roots.

Mediterranean origins Figs are unusual in that the fruit has to survive winter on the tree, before being harvested in its second summer. This is fine in mild climates, but not so easy in the cold, wet winters of Britain.

Pests and diseases
Figs are generally free of pests. Diseases liable to attack fig trees are **coral spot, fig canker** and **grey mould** (see Pests and Diseases, pages 238–49).

Harvesting and storing
Leave the fruits to ripen on the tree, which will usually be between late summer and mid autumn. The fruit is ripe when it hangs down, the stalk softens and the skin splits.
See also bottling (page 270) and drying (page 300).

Preparing and cooking
The few home-grown figs that ripen in Britain are a rare delicacy and best savoured as a fresh dessert fruit.
　Wipe the figs carefully, cut them in half and serve with a spoon. The sweet seeds and the juice are easily scooped out, leaving the purple-green skins. Fresh cream or vanilla ice cream make delicious accompaniments, but this is not really necessary.

For more sophisticated occasions, fresh figs can be dressed with delicate sweet sauces, flavoured creams or yoghurt.

Figs in brandy
Place eight figs, with stalks removed, in a bowl and cover with boiling water. After a minute the figs can be easily peeled and cut into quarters. Place in a fresh bowl and add 4 tablespoons of brandy sweetened with a little honey. Chill in the fridge for an hour. When ready to serve, drain off the brandy and whisk it into 150ml (5fl oz) double cream until the cream is stiff enough to pipe. Now layer four serving dishes with cream, add six fig quarters to each; add another dollop of cream and top each with two fig quarters.

Flowers, edible

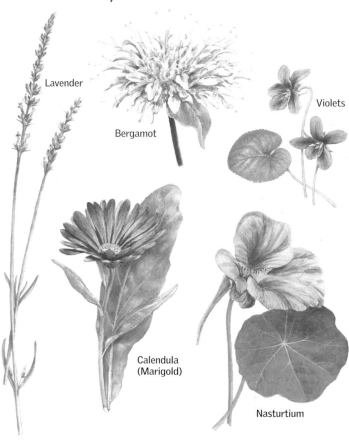

Lavender

Bergamot

Violets

Calendula (Marigold)

Nasturtium

STAGES IN GROWING FIGS

Planting To restrict the roots, dig a hole 1m (3ft) square and deep. Line with bricks or stone slabs. Place rubble on the bottom.

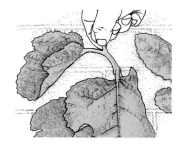

Pinching out shoots Stopping young growths after the fifth leaf during early summer, will encourage new fruit-bearing shoots to form.

Removing fruits Only the smallest embryo fruits will survive the winter. In mid autumn, remove any that are larger than peas.

Many plants have edible flowers that can be used to decorate or flavour all kinds of food. They are usually eaten raw and just a few brightly coloured blooms can transform a fairly ordinary dish into something rather special.

　It is worth remembering, however, only to use flowers that you know are edible – many flowers are toxic, and eating them can cause nasty symptoms from a stomach upset to something much more serious.

　Most edible flowers are attractive enough to plant in any sunny position in the garden, from beds and borders to all kinds of containers. They can also be grown in the vegetable garden, where they will attract pollinating insects and add a splash of cheering colour for much of the year.

Planning the crop

Most culinary herbs have edible flowers. Herbs can be grown in hanging baskets and pots, as well as in beds. They need a sunny position and good drainage, but apart from that are undemanding.

A few wild flowers, herbaceous and bedding plants have edible flowers. If you want to eat native plants, grow them yourself instead of taking them from the wild.

How much to grow

You do not need many plants – one of each variety may be sufficient – and you may be able to utilise what is already growing in the garden.

Varieties

There are many plants in the herb garden and ornamental border with edible flowers.

Herbs

The following herbs are particularly useful: **anise hyssop** (agastache), **basil, bergamot** (monarda), **borage, chives, feverfew, fennel, hyssop, lavender, marjoram, mint, rosemary, sage, salad burnet, savory** and **thyme**.

Bedding plants and wild flowers

Grow a few of these for their edible blooms: **nasturtium, pelargonium, marigold** (calendula), **sweet rocket, violets** and **wild pansy (heartsease)**. Roses also have edible petals.

Growing tips

Position in full sun with good drainage. Most herbs do not need well-manured or fertilised soil. In pots, use John Innes No. 1 or No. 2 compost and make sure there is good drainage in the bottom. Plant herbs from mid spring to late summer, so they can become established before winter arrives.

Edible bedding plants and wild flowers need a sunny position. Bedding plants require good soil or compost and regular liquid feeding throughout their growing and flowering period. Wild flowers, on the other hand, don't like heavily manured and fertilised soil.

Bedding plants are planted in spring or autumn depending on variety. Plant roses bare-root from late autumn to early spring.

Pests and diseases

In general, if properly planted and maintained, there should be no serious problems.

Harvesting and storing

Edible flowers are best picked and used immediately before serving. Some, such as rose petals and sweet violets, can be crystallised by dipping first into beaten egg and then icing sugar. Then put them somewhere warm and dry, for 24 hours until they are crisp. Store them between sheets of paper in an airtight tin. They look fantastic on top of cakes and puddings.

Serving

Flowers from sage, savory, basil, marjoram, thyme and fennel can be sprinkled over cooked savoury dishes, or added to salads. Borage flowers can be floated in summer drinks and cold consommés.

Flowers for salads Mint or chives flowers, hyssop, salad burnet, anise hyssop, feverfew petals and marigolds (calendula) are used to decorate salads. Nasturtium flowerheads can be eaten whole.

Flowers for puddings For a pretty decorative flourish, sprinkle pelargonium and sweet rocket petals over cold puddings and scatter rose petals onto the top of a trifle. Add lavender to homemade ice cream or egg custard.

Adding colour Nasturtium flowerheads, used whole, in a green salad add bright tones and a peppery flavour.

Garlic

A key ingredient in French and Mediterranean cooking, garlic has gained in popularity with the British over the past few decades, probably as a side effect of the Continental holiday boom. Its unique flavour is powerful, and so it should be used with caution. Nevertheless, garlic is indispensable in the modern kitchen and is easy to grow.

Planning the crop

Grow in a sunny position, in a soil that is light and well-manured.

How much to grow

A single clove – the name given to the small divisions of the garlic bulb – goes a long way when used to flavour dishes, and there are a dozen or more cloves in each bulb. About 12–15 plants should be ample.

Varieties

Seed companies offer a wide range of varieties that have been specially bred for the British climate and garden centres stock prepacked bulbs from autumn to spring. Flavours range from very strong to mild. You may also find elephant garlic on sale, which is related to the leek family, although its big cloves have a mild, garlic-like flavour which some people find preferable to that of true garlic. Cultivation is similar.

Growing tips

Garlic needs a long growing period, so plant it either in autumn or early spring in ground that has been raked to a fine tilth. Strip the papery outer skin from a garlic bulb, carefully separate the cloves and plant them 15cm (6in) apart, pointed end upwards and only just covered by soil. Allow 30cm (12in) between rows.

Pests and diseases

Onion eelworm sometimes attacks garlic. The disease most likely to occur is **white rot** (see Pests and Diseases, pages 238–49).

Harvesting and storing

Lift garlic when the foliage dies down in late summer, easing the plants out of the ground with a fork to avoid damaging them.

Dry the bulbs thoroughly in the sun and store them in a cool, dry place – never in the kitchen. Put aside a few bulbs for planting the following year.

See also drying (page 300); freezing (page 252); pickles (page 285) and vinegars (page 299).

Preparing and cooking

To prepare garlic, simply peel the cloves, which can then be crushed, chopped or used whole. The pungent aroma and flavour of garlic is unique, and while shallots are often recommended as a substitute the two flavours cannot really be compared. Used with discretion, garlic gives heightened flavour to almost any savoury dish. A sliced clove rubbed over the inside of the salad bowl, over chops, steaks and fish fillets leaves a faint but distinct flavour. Raw, chopped garlic in butters, salad dressings and marinades, in vinegars and crushed with salt has a similar effect.

For stronger flavours in stews and casseroles, and as larding strips in joints of lamb and pork, use whole or halved cloves and cook with the ingredients.

Garlic may be crushed in a special garlic press, or finely chopped and fried with other vegetables for a braising base. Many cookery experts maintain that a garlic press results in loss of flavour, due to the juices escaping.

For cooked dishes that will be frozen and stored for any length of time, it is best to omit garlic at the initial stage and add it to the dish when reheating it.

Garlic bread

Take six peeled cloves of garlic and crush or chop finely. Mix in to 175g (6oz) unsalted butter. Take a French loaf and cut into thick slices, stopping each cut just short of the bottom crust. Spread each slice liberally with the garlic butter, wrap the whole loaf in tin foil and heat in the oven at 180°C (350°F, gas mark 4) for about 25 minutes until crisp. This simple dish is a great accompaniment to pizzas and spicy meat dishes.

Gooseberries

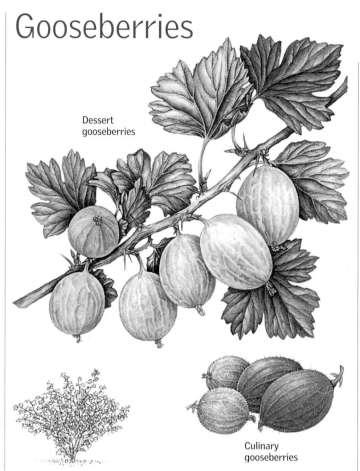

Dessert gooseberries

Culinary gooseberries

Though gooseberries are native to northern Europe, only in Britain are they truly popular. Ever since Tudor times, gooseberry pies, fools, tarts and jellies have been appearing on tables.

Gooseberries are easy to grow and do well throughout Britain. By planting a selection of varieties, you will be able to harvest berries from late spring to late summer. The different varieties may be sweet or acid, yellow, white, green or red. The sweet fruits can be eaten raw for dessert, while the acid ones are more suitable for cooking, as well as for making jam and wine.

Planning the crop

Gooseberries do well in semi-shade or full sun. They need protection from cold winds and late frosts. Any moist, well-drained soil is suitable, but a deep, well-manured loam is preferable. Make sure that the soil is free from perennial weeds. If possible, use a fruit cage to keep birds off.

How many bushes to grow

A mature, well-tended gooseberry bush will yield up to 5kg (10lb), and cordons about 2.5kg (5lb).

Varieties There are many types to choose from, including cooking and dessert varieties:
Keepsake Early; green; dessert or cooking. **May Duke** Early; red; dessert or cooking (when green). **Careless** Mid season; white; cooking. **Jubilee** An improved form of 'Careless', with bigger and better flavoured fruit, a better-shaped bush and good resistance to American gooseberry mildew. **Golden Drop** Mid season; yellow; dessert. **Leveller** Mid season; yellow; dessert or cooking. **Invicta** A vigorous grower with good mildew resistance and huge crops of fruit. **Whinham's Industry** Late; red; dessert or cooking.

Growing tips

Before planting, work manure or compost into the soil, at least a bucketful to the square metre (square yard). This is essential if the soil is light. It also makes heavy soil easier to work and improves drainage. At the same time, apply 25g of sulphate of potash per square metre (1oz per square yard).

Planting out Buy two or three-year-old plants. Planting time is between late autumn and early spring for bare-rooted plants, but those bought in containers can be planted at any time, in favourable weather. Plant bushes 1.5m (5ft) apart, single cordons 40cm (15in), double cordons 60cm (2ft) and

THINNING GOOSEBERRIES

Picking at the right time
Overcrowded stems encourage disease and produce smaller fruit. Start thinning when fruit are roughly the size of grapes.

Creating growing space Leave small clusters of fruit at intervals of about 7.5cm (3in). The thinnings can be used in cooking or to make jam.

triple cordons 1m (3ft). Leave 1.5m (5ft) between rows. Plant firmly.

Grow cordons against a fence. Staple three horizontal support wires at 30cm (12in) intervals. Tie each cordon to a cane with string and secure the cane to the wires.

Standard gooseberries can be bought from nurseries for growing in tubs, but young plants may be trained as standards by removing

sideshoots until the desired stem height is reached. Tie the stem to a cane and provide a stake. Prune the head as with a bush gooseberry.

In winter, firm any plants loosened by frost. Drape netting or fleece over the plants from late winter. This will give developing buds some protection against frost and birds. To encourage pollinating insects, remove the fleece during the day. Remove any suckers, and never let the plants dry out during hot weather.

Feeding Every spring, feed the plants with 20g of sulphate of potash per square metre (³⁄₄oz per square yard) and give them a mulch of well-rotted compost or manure. Alternatively apply a top dressing of a slow-release balanced fertiliser before mulching. Remove by hand any weeds; using a hoe may damage the roots.

Pruning

Prune the bushes in winter. If birds are likely to damage the buds, wait until the buds start to swell.

It is best to prune spreading, drooping bushes to an inward-pointing bud; upright varieties to an outward-pointing one.

The first year Shorten the strongest three or four shoots on a one-year-old bush by about three-quarters and remove the others at their base. Cut out any low shoots to create a clean stem about 10–15cm (4–6in) long.

The second year Cut off half the new wood growing from the eight to ten best shoots (two-thirds if the new growth is spindly or drooping). Remove all other shoots, cutting just above the bottom bud.

PRUNING GOOSEBERRIES

Cutting back Shorten sideshoots to two buds. Remove any thin or spindly shoots. Aim for a goblet-shaped bush with an open centre.

Established bushes Prune mature plants in the same way as red currants (see page 129).

Raising new bushes

Gooseberries can be raised from cuttings in the same way as for red and white currants (see page 129).

To create a single cordon after planting out the rooted cutting in its permanent position, select the strongest shoot and remove the others flush with the main stem. Tie the young cordon to a cane with soft string. To make a double cordon, choose the two strongest shoots that emerge from the main stem about 25cm (9in) from its base. Until they are 15cm (6in) long, train them horizontally in the same way as for an espalier (see pages 68–69). After that, train them against vertical canes.

For a triple cordon, select the best three shoots 25cm (9in) above the ground. Train the two outside shoots as for a double cordon, and the middle one as for a single.

Taking out old branches Cut out one or two of the old, dark branches where young shoots are growing and tie these in.

Pests and diseases

The worst pests to affect gooseberries are **aphids**, **capsid bugs** and **gooseberry sawfly**.

The most serious diseases are **American gooseberry mildew**, **grey mould**, **honey fungus**, **leaf spot**, **rust** and **scald** (see Pests and Diseases, pages 238–49).

AT-A-GLANCE TIMETABLE

PLANTING
LATE AUTUMN–EARLY SPRING

WINTER PRUNING
LATE WINTER

SUMMER PRUNING
MIDSUMMER

FRUIT THINNING
LATE SPRING–EARLY SUMMER

HARVESTING
LATE SPRING–LATE SUMMER

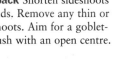

Preparing for new growth
Remove surplus shoots growing from the base. Clear weeds and mulch with straw or manure.

Harvesting and storing

Thin out heavy-cropping plants from late spring onwards, removing berries from each branch so that there are 7.5cm (3in) intervals between those remaining, which will then grow larger. The picked fruit can be used for cooking or preserving. Thinning can be carried out several times.

See also bottling (page 270); chutneys (page 292); freezing (page 252); fruit cheeses and butters (page 281); jams (page 271); jellies (page 277); pickles (page 285); syrups and juices (page 283) and wine (page 304).

Preparing and cooking

Sweet red or yellow gooseberries are served fresh as a dessert fruit. The smaller, harder acid varieties are suitable for cooking only.

To prepare gooseberries, snip off flower and stalk ends with scissors. Wash them and allow to drain; dry dessert berries on kitchen paper.

Grapes

with glass or plastic to aid ripening. Alternatively, grow them in a greenhouse, preferably with some heat in late spring and early autumn.

Vines have been grown successfully in this country since the time of the Romans. The first are believed to have been planted only 70 years after Julius Caesar's invasion in 55 BC. Later, the fortunes of Britain's vines followed those of the monasteries, where they were extensively grown. With the Dissolution of the Monasteries in the 16th century, the number of vineyards rapidly declined.

A revival of grape growing came in the late 18th century. This time the vines were not grown in the open but under glass, mostly on the large estates of landed gentry. Today, British wine growing is in the ascendant once more, with vineyards in Surrey producing wines to rival those of France.

Planning an outdoor crop

Growing grapes can be very rewarding, whether they are used in desserts or for home-brewed wine. Siting the vine is important when growing vines outdoors. Choose a sheltered position in full sun. Avoid frost pockets and sites in even partial shade. A slope facing south or south-west is ideal.

For growing vines on a wall or fence, choose a site facing south, south-west or south-east. Vines grown this way succeed in areas too cold for growing completely in the open. In more favourable areas, extra warmth that radiates from the wall makes the grapes sweeter and better flavoured.

Drainage is vitally important. Vines grow best in a sandy, gravelly soil that warms up quickly in the sun, but they will succeed in any type of soil if the drainage is good.

Preparing the ground On heavy soils dig a trench at least 60cm (2ft) deep, leading away from where the vine is to be planted. Place a layer of rubble, broken bricks or clinker at the bottom of the trench. The deeper the trench and the more rubble the better, because the roots of an established vine go deep and must never be allowed to become waterlogged.

Two or three months before planting, fork in well-rotted manure or compost at the rate of a bucketful per square metre (square yard), plus John Innes base fertiliser at the rate of 90g per square metre (3oz per square yard).

To grow vines on a wall, fix support wires 30cm (12in) apart and held 13cm (5in) away from the wall with vine eyes.

Providing support To grow vines in a row in the open, you will need to set out some support posts 1.5m (5ft) high at intervals of 2.5–3m (8–10ft). The end posts should be at least in 6cm (2½in) in diameter, and intermediate posts about 5cm (2in) in diameter. Allow 1.5m (5ft) between rows.

Staple a single strand of 12–gauge galvanised wire to the posts 45cm (18in) from the ground. Loosely twist two strands together and staple them 80cm (2½ft) from the ground, with another length of twisted wire fixed about 45cm (18in) above this.

If fruiting shoots are trained through the double wire, the twisting will save the trouble of tying them.

Fruit of the vine Grape vines are good-value plants for the garden, producing juicy ripe fruit and a colourful display of foliage in autumn.

How many to grow An established vine in the open will produce at least ten bunches of grapes – about 2.5kg (5lb) – in a good year. A cordon on a wall may produce 7–10kg (15–20lb) or more, depending on its size.

Generally, it is best for a beginner to start with only a few vines, adding more later if sufficient space is available.

Outdoor varieties Choose early ripening grapes for cooler areas. In more favourable districts grow early varieties in the open or on walls, and mid-season varieties on walls only, where the extra protection will hasten ripening.

Generally, white grapes can be grown more successfully than red, except in the hottest summers.
Cascade (Seibel 13/053) Small bunches of deep purple grapes are

Growing grapes in Britain depends mainly on locality. South of a line roughly from Pembroke to the Wash, grapes can be grown in the open on wire supports, or against a sunny, south-facing wall. They may also be grown in an unheated greenhouse, which should be reserved for the best varieties of dessert grapes.

In sheltered places north of the line, grapes can be grown against a south-facing wall if given some protection ready mid season. It is a heavy cropper ideal for wine-making.

Madeleine Sylvaner 28/5 An early white that is a consistent cropper, producing a fair wine grape.

Siegerrebe An early ripening, deep golden grape with a fine muscat flavour. It is a good all-rounder,

TRAINING A SINGLE CORDON

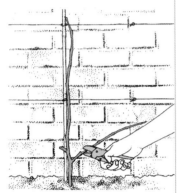

After planting Choose the strongest leader as the rod, and cut the others to one bud. Tie the leader to a cane and to the wires.

The following summer Pinch out all flowers. In late summer, cut back laterals as part of the training to produce fruiting spurs.

recommended as a dessert grape and for making wine.

Growing grapes on a wall

Training a vine up a wall is the easiest way of growing grapes. The wall provides shelter and warmth, ensuring a good crop. The vine itself, with its colourful autumn foliage, also has decorative appeal.

Vines are best planted while they are dormant, generally between late autumn and early spring, although containerised specimens may be planted any time of year when the weather is suitable. For the beginner, spring is probably best, as the risk of long periods of severe frost is then over. Nurseries generally supply vines that are one year old.

If planting must be done in autumn, pile a layer of organic material such as well-rotted compost over the lower buds to protect them from frost, and draw it back from the plant when growth begins in spring.

When planting, dig a hole wide enough for the roots to be spread out evenly and deep enough for the vine to be at the same level as it was in the nursery. The soil mark on the stock will indicate this.

The simplest method of growing grapes on a wall is to train them on a single cordon, or rod. Set the vines 1.2m (4ft) apart, and 25cm (9in) away from the wall.

After planting, choose the strongest leader to grow on as the rod and cut the others to one bud. Tie the leader to a cane and secure the cane to the wires.

During the following growing season pinch out flowers as they appear and in late summer, cut back laterals to five leaves. In early winter, remove immature

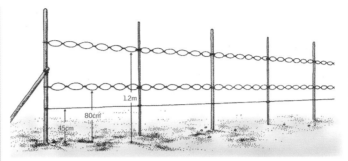

Preparing support wires for outdoor grapes Drive in support posts, and staple three lengths of wire to them at the distances shown. Use a single strand at the bottom and two loosely twisted strands in the centre and on top.

wood on the stem by cutting back to ripe, nut-brown wood of not less than pencil thickness.

Repeat this sequence during the second year after planting, but during summer pruning also cut back sub-laterals to one leaf.

This training should produce a well-spurred cordon for providing a limited harvest in the following season. In the first cropping year allow only three bunches to a cordon. In the following year allow four or five.

Thereafter, allow only one bunch per foot run, which usually means that you will harvest a bunch from each spur.

Growing grapes in the open

If wall space is limited, or you want to produce a more substantial crop, you can grow grapes in the open, as long as you give the vines decent support. Preparation and planting is the same as when growing against a wall. Before planting, drive a stout cane into the soil so that 1.8m (6ft) is left above ground level. This will provide a support for tying in replacement shoots. Alternatively, plant the vine

against a fence post. Space the vines 1.2m (4ft) apart – or 1.5m (5ft) if the soil is fairly rich.

Allow only the strongest shoot to grow in the first year. Tie this to the support, and pinch out all other shoots at one or two leaves.

In early winter the vine will be ready for training by the double Guyot system (see below), one of the simplest ways of growing vines in the open. By this method, grapes are grown on laterals from stems produced in the previous year while, at the same time,

Preparation for planting Before planting drive a stout cane into the hole, leaving 1.8m (6ft) above ground. Tie the cane to the wires.

replacement stems are trained for fruiting in the following year.

Guyot system of training After leaf-fall, but before Christmas, cut the vine down to three or four buds. The following summer, allow the three strongest shoots to grow, and pinch out any others. In early winter, tie two of the shoots along the bottom wire. Cut the third shoot back to three buds.

In the following summer, train the fruiting laterals from the two horizontal stems through the double wires. In late summer, cut the tops of the laterals to two or three leaves above the top wire and remove all sub-laterals. Tie the three replacement shoots to the cane, and pinch back the laterals growing from them to one leaf.

AT-A-GLANCE TIMETABLE

Growing outdoor grapes
• **First year**

PLANTING
LATE AUTUMN–EARLY SPRING

TRAINING
Tie strongest shoot to supporting wire

ANNUAL PRUNING
EARLY WINTER–LATE SUMMER

• **Succeeding years**

TRAINING
LATE SUMMER

THINNING FRUITS
MID–LATE SUMMER

HARVESTING
EARLY–MID AUTUMN

In early winter, remove completely the two shoots carrying the laterals that have fruited that year. Tie two replacement young shoots to the bottom wire and cut back the third shoot to three buds. Repeat this system of training each year.

Restrict the crop to four bunches in the first fruiting year, six in the second, and allow full cropping thereafter. Always keep the vines well-watered, especially in the year after planting. Dress the rows generously with well-rotted garden compost or spent mushroom compost every spring. This acts as a mulch to keep moisture in and weeds out.

Feeding In late winter, apply a general fertiliser along each side of the row at the rate of 60g per square metre (2oz per square yard). In spring, apply magnesium sulphate (Epsom salts) as a top dressing at 60g to the square metre (2oz per square yard).

How to grow grapes in a greenhouse

Greenhouse vines are usually grown as single-stem cordons, like those trained against walls. However, a gardener who moves into a home with an established greenhouse vine may find that it has a number of spaced-out rods. Each of these should be treated in the same way as a single cordon.

Preparation Before planting a vine, decide whether to plant it inside the greenhouse or whether to set it in an outside border and train it indoors through an aperture. Although the gardener has less control over the management of a vine in an outside border, watering is easier.

Prepare the soil by mixing 10 parts of good loam with 1 part crushed bricks and old mortar. Two weeks before planting, for each cubic metre, add 5kg (10lb) John Innes-based fertiliser, 2.5kg (5lb) bone meal and 2.5kg (5lb) dried blood.

TRAINING VINES ON SUPPORT WIRES IN THE OPEN

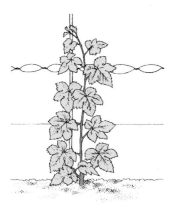

First summer after planting
Tie the strongest shoot to the support. Pinch out other shoots to one or two leaves.

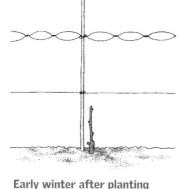

Early winter after planting
Cut the vine down to three or four buds. Cover with leaf-mould or straw to protect against frosts.

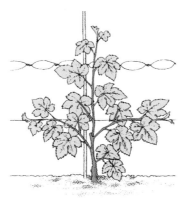

Next summer Allow the three strongest shoots to grow. Train them to the support wires and pinch out any other shoots.

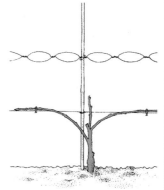

Following early winter Tie two of the following shoots along each side of the bottom wire; cut the third shoot back to three buds.

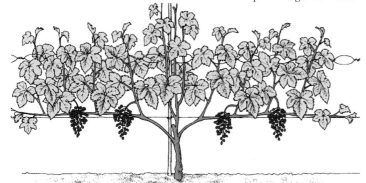

Subsequent summers Train the laterals from the horizontal stems through the twisted wires. Remove sub-laterals and, in late summer, cut the lateral tips to two or three leaves above the top wire. Tie replacement stems to the cane and pinch back laterals to one leaf.

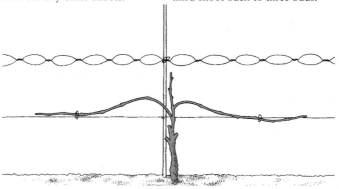

In early winter every year Cut back to the base the two stems that have carried fruit. Tie two of the replacement shoots to the bottom wire and prune the remaining shoot to three buds. These buds will provide the following season's shoots. Repeat this training every year.

AT-A-GLANCE TIMETABLE
• **Established greenhouse vines**
PRUNING/CLEANING
EARLY WINTER
TOP DRESSING
MID WINTER
RESTRICTING SHOOTS
SPRING
POLLINATING
LATE SPRING
THINNING FRUITS
SUMMER
HARVESTING
AUTUMN

Greenhouse grapes If you live in the north of England, you will need to grow grapes in a greenhouse, which may need heating in colder months.

In the greenhouse, set up support wires 30cm (12in) apart and held 45cm (18in) from the roof by vine eyes screwed into the glazing bars or by securing them to the gable ends of the greenhouse.

How many to grow The minimum size of a greenhouse for growing grapes is 2.5m (8ft) long, 2.1m (7ft) to the ridge and 1.5m (5ft) to the eaves. Single-stem cordons are set 1.2m (4ft) apart, so the number planted depends on the length of the house.

Greenhouse varieties The amount of artificial heat required in a particular locality generally dictates which varieties you can grow. The first two varieties listed can be successfully grown in a cold greenhouse.
Black Hamburgh Large black berries with good flavour ripen in mid season; reliable and hardy.

Buckland Sweetwater The best general-purpose white grape. Produces an early crop of large, sweet berries.
Muscat Hamburgh Black, medium-sized berries with an excellent muscat flavour are ready from mid to late season. Needs heat in northern parts.
Muscat of Alexandria Large white berries with superb muscat flavour crop from mid to late season. Requires artificial heat and cross-pollination to set well.

Looking after greenhouse grapes For the first two or three years after planting, train the cordon in the same way as when growing a vine on a wall (see previous page). For an established vine follow this annual routine.

Early winter Prune the previous summer's growth back to one bud. After pruning, scrub the rods gently with tar-oil winter wash, diluted according to the manufacturer's instructions.

After pruning, wash the glass and superstructure with a suitable disinfectant, which you can buy from a horticultural supplier.

Mid winter to early spring Keep the ventilators open. The vines are dormant at this time and frost hardy.

Top-dress the rooting area in mid winter with a mixture of 120g per square metre (4oz per square yard) of John Innes-based fertiliser, plus an equal amount of dried blood. Follow with a light dressing of well-rotted manure or compost.

Mid spring Close the ventilators to increase the temperature and induce the buds to break. Spray the rods, soil and path with water twice daily.

The buds will swell quickly. Select the strongest shoot from each spur, and rub out the others with your thumb.

Two weeks later, keep the longest-flowering trusses, stopping these at two leaves beyond the bunch. Pinch out the others at the fourth or fifth leaf, and sub-laterals at the first.

Late spring As the laterals reach 25cm (9in), tie them to the supporting wires. When the flowers open, use a camel-hair brush to distribute pollen between them. When the flowers have set, give a weekly liquid feed, according to the manufacturer's instructions.

Keep the temperature high and the humidity fairly low until the flowers have set, then increase ventilation in the greenhouse over a period of weeks to lower the temperature.

Regularly damp down the border and path around the vines.

Summer Ventilate freely. As the berries swell, thin them over seven to ten days. With a free-setting variety remove half the berries from the inside of the bunch, leaving more on the shoulders.

When the grapes begin to show colour, reduce watering to a mere dampening of the border. Stop applications of liquid feed.

Early to mid autumn Cut the bunches of grapes as they ripen. Increase the temperature by closing the greenhouse ventilators until the last bunches are cut.

Pests and diseases The most common pests attacking grapes are **glasshouse red spider mites**, **mealy bugs** and **scale insects**. Diseases and disorders that may occur include **grey mould**, **honey fungus**, **magnesium deficiency**, **powdery mildew**, **scald**, **shanking** and **splitting** (see Pests and Diseases, pages 238–49).

Harvesting and storing Grapes are ripe when they swell and change colour. Use scissors to cut the bunch from the vine. If not bruised, grapes will keep in a cold place for two months.

VITAL EARLY TREATMENT TO ENSURE GOOD CROPS IN THE GREENHOUSE

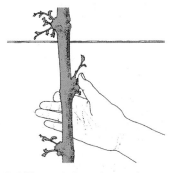

Rubbing out In spring, as the buds swell, select the strongest shoot from each spur and rub out the others with your thumb.

Pinching out About a fortnight after rubbing out the unwanted buds, stop the shoots with the longest-flowering trusses at two leaves beyond the bunch. Pinch out the others at the fourth or fifth leaf, and sub-laterals at the first. Tie laterals to supporting wires.

HOW TO PRODUCE LARGE, EVEN BUNCHES OF GRAPES

Pollinating When the flowers open in late spring, assist pollination by stroking along the trusses with a soft camel-hair brush.

First thinning As the berries swell, usually in early summer, begin thinning by removing some of the berries from inside the bunches.

Final thinning Spread thinning gradually over seven to ten days. Leave more on the shoulders to give the bunch a good shape.

Harvesting When grapes are ripe they change colour and often develop a bloom. Cut with secateurs or sharp scissors.

See also drying (page 300); pickles (page 285); sauces, ketchups and relishes (page 296) and wine-making (page 304).

Preparing and serving
Most luscious of all dessert fruits, the juice and sweetness of grapes are best enjoyed in the fresh berries. They can be eaten on their own, in fresh fruit salads, as edible garnishes to savoury and sweet dishes or as an accompaniment to a cheeseboard.

For special occasions, grapes can be sugar-frosted. Brush the berries with lightly beaten egg white, dredge with sugar and leave on a wire rack for about 15 minutes before serving.

Grapes are seldom cooked, but they are sometimes peeled for garnishes and fruit salads, when they should have the pips removed. Most grapes can be peeled by pulling the skin away with the fingertips, beginning at the stalk. If the skins are tough, dip a few grapes at a time in boiling water for 30 seconds, then plunge them into cold water.

The simplest way to remove the pips is to cut the grapes in half and ease the pips out with the tip of a knife.

Grape salad
Perhaps best reserved for special occasions, this rather indulgent dish is a novel accompaniment to the cheeseboard. Peel 375g (¾lb) black or white grapes and remove the pips. Dissolve 100g (4oz) sugar in 4 tablespoons of hot water and stir in the juice and grated rind of one lemon. Pour this syrup over the grapes and chill for an hour.

Meanwhile make a mayonnaise by gradually adding 200ml (7fl oz) olive oil to one egg yolk. Fold in 150ml (5fl oz) of lightly whisked double cream. Drain the grapes then fold into the mayonnaise and cream mixture, setting a few aside for use as decoration.

Grapes in French dressing
The unusual combination of sweet grapes and French dressing works well with cold ham or baked fish.

Strip about 250g (½lb) of seedless grapes from the stalks. Rinse and drain, discarding any that may be bruised or mouldy.

Make up the dressing by stirring 2 teaspoons of French mustard with 1 teaspoon of caster sugar and gradually adding 6 tablespoons of olive oil followed by 3 tablespoons of white wine vinegar. Season to taste.

Put the grapes in a bowl, pour the dressing over them and toss well. Chill in the fridge for at least 30 minutes. Drain the grapes from the dressing and serve on a bed of lettuce.

Horseradish

Y̶ou can find this hardy herb growing wild along roadsides, field boundaries and railway embankments in many parts of Britain. It is easy to grow in the garden, but can become invasive. Watch out for this, because once spread, it is difficult to get rid of. This is because the roots are deep and tough and if even a small piece is left in the ground a new plant will grow.

A sauce made from freshly grated horseradish root makes an unsurpassable accompaniment to roast beef and to some fish dishes.

Planning the crop
Grow horseradish in any odd corner of the garden, but preferably one that is sunny or in only partial shade. The plants do best in rich, well-drained soil.

How much to grow Horseradish roots grow to a length of 30cm (12in) or more, and to a thickness of 2cm (¾in). Three or four plants should be ample, spaced about 60cm (2ft) apart.

Growing tips
Roots for planting can be obtained either by digging them up from waste ground in late summer and storing them until the following spring, or by buying them from a good nursery or herb supplier.

Dig the patch deeply in winter, working in plenty of compost.

In early spring, drive holes in the ground with a crowbar or sharp stake to a depth of 35cm (14in), spacing the holes 60cm (2ft) apart. Drop a piece of root into each hole.

AT-A-GLANCE TIMETABLE
PLANTING
EARLY SPRING
35cm (14in) deep
HARVESTING
LATE SUMMER–EARLY AUTUMN

Ideally, the pieces should be about 30cm (12in) long with crowns (tufts of new foliage) at the top. Roots 7.5–10cm (3–4in) long will do, but in a shallower hole.

Raising new plants
Keep some of the autumn-harvested roots for planting in the following year.

Pests and diseases
Although seldom troubled by pests, horseradish may be affected by **leaf spot** (page 245), **shothole** and (page 246).

Harvesting and storing
Horseradish plants grown from small pieces of root should be left in the ground for at least two years. If grown from large pieces, dig up the plants from late summer onwards. Store in boxes of sand.

See also sauces, ketchups and relishes (page 296) and vinegars (page 299).

Preparing and cooking
Horseradish sauce is as traditional with roast beef as is Yorkshire pudding, but a major drawback lies in the preparation. The skin and flesh emit fumes more powerful than those of the strongest onion.

Some people counter these eye-watering effects by wearing glasses, while others resort to the old folklore remedy of holding a piece of bread in the mouth as they peel and grate it.

Grating can be made easier by putting the horseradish through the mincer or shredder attachment of an electric food mixer. Once grated, horseradish should be used immediately as it quickly loses its pungent flavour.

Grated horseradish is used in creams, sauces and mayonnaises to flavour roast beef, fish (especially smoked), boiled poultry, and with tomato salads or as a stuffing for hard-boiled eggs. Grated horseradish is also used as a garnish with roast meat and with steak tartare.

Horseradish sauce
Fold 3 rounded tablespoons of grated horseradish into 150ml (5fl oz) soured cream and season to taste with salt, black pepper and mustard. Serve with hot or cold roast beef, cold ham, smoked trout or salmon.

Horseradish cream
Whisk 150ml (5fl oz) whipping cream until it holds it shape and fold in 2 rounded tablespoons of grated horseradish. Take 50g (2oz) cooked and cooled macaroni and fold into the cream. Season to taste with vinegar, salt and sugar.

Serve in a small bowl sprinkled with paprika and garnished with a few sprigs of watercress. This is a classic accompaniment to cold roast beef. You can turn it into an unusual salad by adding a little diced ham or beef to the mixture and serving on a bed of lettuce, garnished with sliced tomatoes.

Hyssop

Hyssop, a hardy evergreen herb, was once widely grown for its minty leaves which were used to flavour stews, soups, meat stuffings and salads. Nowadays it is rarely grown, possibly because many people find it too bitter. But it is still used in making the liqueur Chartreuse.

Throughout summer and autumn hyssop bears pretty spikes of blue, pink or white flowers, according to variety, so it can make an attractive, low ornamental hedge around a herb garden. It grows to a height of about 45cm (18in).

Planning the crop
Hyssop grows best in a sunny position and on well-drained soil.

How much to grow Unless you are growing hyssop for decorative purposes, a single plant is sufficient. Only a few of the pungent leaves are needed in each dish.

Varieties Seed sold as hyssop is generally the common blue-flowered species, but specialist seedsmen may stock vigorous varieties
Albus A white-flowered form.
Roseus Has pale pink flowers.

Growing tips
Sow the seeds outdoors in late spring in drills 5mm (¼in) deep. When the seedlings are large enough to handle, thin them to intervals of 7.5cm (3in).

Set them in their permanent positions at any time between autumn and early spring. If you intend to grow more than one plant, space them at 30cm (12in) intervals.

To encourage the plants to bush out, remove the tips of the main shoots. Once plants are established, trim them with shears each spring.

AT-A-GLANCE TIMETABLE

SOWING
MID–LATE SPRING
5mm (¼in) deep

THINNING
7.5cm (3in) apart, when large enough to handle

HARVESTING
All year round

Raising new plants
An existing stock of plants can be increased by taking 5cm (2in) cuttings of sideshoots from mid to late spring. Remove the lower leaves and insert the cuttings in equal parts of peat substitute and sand or perlite, in a coldframe, shading the glass in hot weather.

Plant the rooted cuttings directly into their permanent site, or grow them on in 7.5cm (3in) pots and plant out in autumn.

Large and bushy plants can be divided in spring.

Pests and diseases
Hyssop is usually trouble free.

Harvesting and storing
Pick the leaves at any time of year, as needed. For salads they are at their best in early summer.

See also drying (page 300) and freezing (page 252).

Preparing and cooking
Finely chopped hyssop leaves may be used instead of mint and can be sprinkled over vegetables, salads, meat stews and vegetable soups.

Hyssop is also added to fruit salads and cups, sprinkled over grapefruit and added to apple and apricot pies and flans.

To make a herbal tea with hyssop leaves, steep 25g (1oz) of fresh leaves in 600ml (1 pint) of boiling water for 5–10 minutes and strain the infusion. The herb has traditionally been used to treat stomach and chest disorders, having a calming effect.

Kale and rape kale

Plain-leaved kale

Curled-leaved kale

Both kale and rape kale are valuable winter vegetables. Descended from the wild cabbage, they provide greens from mid winter to the middle of spring when other greenstuff may be scarce.

The kales are extremely hardy, surviving conditions that will harm broccoli and Brussels sprouts. Indeed, it is generally thought that frosts improve their flavour.

The leaves of kale, which is also known as borecole, may be either curled or plain. Rape kale, too, has plain or curled leaves. It is sown later than true kale and produces a later crop.

Planning the crop
Kales are best grown on well-drained, medium or heavy loam, which has been well manured for a previous crop. Two weeks before planting kale – or sowing rape kale – dress the surface with a general fertiliser at a rate of 60g per square metre (2oz per square yard). Like all brassicas, kale thrives in an alkaline soil, so apply lime after digging the plot during the previous winter.

How much to grow A 9m (30ft) row will yield an average of 8.5kg (18lb) of kale or rape kale. The amount you need may to some extent depend on the quantity of summer vegetables you have stored in the freezer.

Curled-leaved kale varieties
Dwarf Green Curled A hardy variety; fine quality; tightly curled.
Pentland Brigg Very hardy; young shoots and flower stalks may be eaten.
F1 Red Bor A heavy cropper with decorative purple-red, heavily crinkled leaves.

Plain-leaved kale varieties
Cottager's The leaves are purple tinged and it produces abundant sideshoots in spring.
Thousand Headed The hardiest plain-leaved variety; pick shoots in late winter and spring.

Rape kale varieties
These are sold under different names, although there is not much to choose between them in terms of cropping and flavour. They include **Asparagus Kale**, **Favourite**, **Hungry Gap** and **Ragged Jack**.

Growing tips for kale
Sow the seeds in a 1cm (½in) deep drill in mid spring. Thin the seedlings to about 5cm (2in) apart so that they have space to form sturdy plants.

Transplant them to the prepared permanent bed in summer, spacing them 60cm (2ft) apart in each direction. Firm the plants in with your feet or with the dibber, and keep them watered until they are well established.

Growing tips for rape kale
Delay sowing rape kale until just after midsummer. If sown earlier it will put on too much foliage and the large, succulent leaves may fail to survive winter.

Sow directly into the permanent bed in drills 1cm (½in) deep and 45cm (18in) apart. Thin the seedlings in stages until they are 30–45cm (12–18in) apart.

Alternatively, to save seed, sow in groups of three or four at 30–45cm (12–18in) spacings, removing all but the strongest seedling in each group when large enough to handle.

Hoe frequently to destroy weeds, and tread the ground around the plants occasionally to prevent winds rocking them. If they become excessively large and floppy, push a bamboo cane into the soil alongside each plant and tie the plant to it.

Pests and diseases
Pests that may attack kales include **cabbage root fly**, **cabbage whitefly**, **caterpillars** and **flea beetle**. The disease most likely to give trouble is **club root** (see Pests and Diseases, pages 238–49).

Harvesting
The leaves of kale are ready for cutting from mid winter onwards. Cut the centre of each plant first to encourage the production of fresh sideshoots.

Start cutting rape kale either in late winter or when the true kale has finished.

When either type starts to flower, pull up the plants. Chop the tough stems into small pieces, to speed rotting, before putting them on the compost heap.

Preparing and cooking
This much-neglected winter vegetable is useful for its crisp, curly leaves which are rich in antioxidants, iron and vitamin C. It is more popular in the north of England and in Scotland than in the south, being used as a vegetable, for soups and in purées.

Raw kale is also suitable for a winter salad. Toss the freshly chopped leaves in a well-peppered lemon dressing and garnish with quartered hard-boiled eggs.

AT-A-GLANCE TIMETABLE
SOWING
1cm (½in) deep
• Kale
MID SPRING
• Rape kale
SUMMER
THINNING
• Kale
Thin to 5cm (2in) apart, when large enough to handle
• Rape kale
Thin to 30–45cm (12–18in) apart, in stages
PLANTING
• Kale
SUMMER
• Rape kale
Do not transplant
HARVESTING
• Kale
WINTER–MID SPRING
• Rape kale
LATE WINTER–LATE SPRING

To prepare kale for cooking, strip the long leaves from the tough stems and then shred them away from the white midribs. Wash thoroughly in cold, running water.

For cooking, boil kale in the minimum amount of boiling lightly salted water for 10–15 minutes. Drain in a colander and chop the leaves roughly, then heat through with a little butter and season with pepper and ground cloves. Alternatively steam the leaves for about 20 minutes.

Its rather strong taste makes kale an excellent vegetable to accompany fatty and smoked meats, such as pork and bacon.

Colcannon

This dish, which originates in Scotland and Ireland, is good for using up leftover mashed potatoes. You'll need a quantity of kale to match the amount of mashed potato, in this case 375g (¾lb). Place the prepared kale into a pan of lightly salted, boiling water and cook for 15 minutes. Alternatively you can steam the kale, which should take about 10 minutes. Drain thoroughly and chop finely. Meanwhile peel and chop an onion and put it in a pan with 150ml (5fl oz) milk. Bring to the boil, then remove from the heat, cover and leave to infuse. Blend the mashed potatoes with the chopped kale. Heat through over a gentle heat, adding as much of the milk and onion as it will absorb to give a creamy consistency. It makes a great accompaniment to any roast, grilled or fried meat dishes.

Kale soup

Boil or steam 250g (½lb) kale until tender. Drain and chop finely and set to one side. Peel and chop an onion, three carrots and three potatoes. Clean three leeks and cut into narrow slices. Lightly fry the vegetables for a few minutes until softened, then add a litre (2 pints) of stock and season well with salt and pepper. Bring to the boil and simmer for about 25 minutes, until all the vegetables are cooked. Blend the soup in a liquidiser then return to the pan adding enough milk to give the desired consistency. Fold in the chopped kale and season to taste with salt, pepper and sugar. Pour into soup bowls and garnish with chopped hard-boiled eggs.

Kale and potato cakes

Another kale-and-potato combination, this is a quick and easy dish. Blanch 250g (½lb) kale in boiling salted water for two minutes. Drain and when slightly cooled chop finely and stir into 500g (1lb) mashed potatoes. Blend in two eggs and then gradually add breadcrumbs until the mixture reaches a fairly stiff consistency – you'll need about 50g (2oz). Season with salt and black pepper then shape into flattened, egg-sized balls. Melt 50g (2oz) butter and fry the kale and potato cakes for about 8 minutes, turning them once or twice until brown and crisp. Serve hot or cold with a mixed grill.

Kiwi fruit

The kiwi fruit is an attractive, perennial climber, with furry stems and large, heart-shaped leaves. The showy, fragrant flowers are creamy-white, turning yellowish as they mature.

The kiwi fruit is hardy in warmer areas, but does best grown on a sunny wall or fence, as the fruit needs a warm summer to ripen properly. If you live in a colder area, you will need to grow the vine in a frost-free greenhouse.

In the past, you needed a large plot to grow kiwis because varieties were either male or female and you had to have at least one of each to ensure cross fertilisation. Today's self-fertile varieties mean that you can grow kiwi fruit on a much smaller plot.

The plant was discovered in China in the 19th century, hence its alternative name, Chinese gooseberry. Growers in New Zealand coined the name kiwi fruit because the shaggy fruits resembled their national bird, the kiwi.

The kiwi is a woody deciduous vine, that can reach 9m (30ft) in length. It produces egg-shaped, brown fruits covered in short stiff hairs. The bright green flesh surrounds a white core and is studded with tiny black seeds.

Planning the crop

A well-drained, deep, preferably sandy loam is the best growing medium, but the plants will cope with many other soil conditions.

Pot-grown plants can be planted at any time the weather is favourable, but early spring planting will get your kiwi off to the best start. Choose a warm,

---

AT-A-GLANCE TIMETABLE

PLANTING
- **Container-grown plant**
EARLY SPRING
Most kiwis are sold as pot-grown plants and can be planted all year round. For the best start, plant in spring

PRUNING
- **Immediately after planting**
Cut down to 30cm (1ft) above ground level
- **First and second years**
EARLY SUMMER
Cut back shoots when growth passes top wire
WINTER
- **Third year onwards**
Cut back laterals to two beds beyond where the last fruit was produced

HARVESTING
AUTUMN
Fruiting will not begin until the vine is 5 years old. Pick the fruits as they ripen

sunny wall or fence and attach a trellis or wires to give support.

If you don't have a spare wall or fence, then construct a system of posts and wire supports in full sun, with the horizontal wires fixed 30–40cm (12–16in) apart.

Dig the ground thoroughly the previous autumn or early winter, and incorporate plenty of manure, compost or other organic material.

Add coarse bone meal at a rate of 120 to 180g per square metre (4–6oz per square yard) and work in thoroughly. If the soil is very heavy, incorporating sharp sand will improve texture and drainage.

How many to grow
Choose a self-fertile cultivar; one vine should produce enough fruit for most families.

Varieties In the past, Hayward or Bruno were considered to be the best choices but self-fertile forms have been developed and are now widely available. A self-fertile form such as **Jenny** or **Duo** will fit into most plots. Although the individual fruits are usually smaller, these will usually produce a good crop.

Growing tips
Always buy a named variety, not a seedling. Seedlings, although less expensive, can be extremely rampant and variable in performance.

Alternatively take cuttings of named varieties in late summer, or layer plants to make new plants in spring, and plant on the following early autumn or spring.

Prepare the ground thoroughly and ensure the supports are in place before planting. The soil at the base of a sunny wall may be dry, even after preparation; if so,

give a good soaking and leave the site to settle down before starting to plant.

Water the plant in its pot and allow to drain. Dig a hole large enough to accommodate the rootball comfortably, fill with water, and wait until the water has drained away before planting.

Remove the kiwi fruit from its pot, place in the hole so that the soil is level with the compost, backfill the hole and firm gently.

Cut the plant back to 30cm (12in) above ground level.

Keep well-watered until the plant is mature, especially when growing against a warm wall. Feed in spring with a balanced fertiliser. A fortnightly liquid feed with a tomato fertiliser throughout summer will encourage fruiting.

Pot-cultivated kiwi fruit should be planted in John Innes No. 3 Compost and fed regularly throughout the growing season every year. If growing in a greenhouse, plant in well-prepared border soil or in large pots.

Training and pruning
First and second years
In early summer, cut back the shoots when the growth has passed the top wire of the support. This will encourage the growth of lateral canes and produce a main framework.
Summer Train one new cane along each wire. Pinch out the shoots when they have filled the allotted space. Stop any sub-lateral at five leaves.

Third and subsequent years
Summer The fruit is produced on laterals from the main framework. Pinch these back to seven leaves beyond the last fruit.

Winter Cut back the laterals to two buds beyond where the last fruit was produced. On mature plants cut back some of these laterals harder to a dormant bud.

The Kiwi fruit is a self-supporting, twining vine, and does not need tying in, although some shoots may need a little help in getting them to grow in the right direction.

Pests and diseases
Kiwi fruit plants are not usually troubled by pests and diseases.

Harvesting and storing
Pick the ripe fruit in mid to late autumn. Store in single layers in trays and boxes for about six weeks before eating, when the flavour will have developed fully.

Preparing and eating
Although the whole of the fruit is edible, its surface hairs can irritate the throat so it is normally peeled. The fruits are usually eaten fresh in desserts or salads. They contain very high levels of vitamin C – much higher than most citrus fruits – and one fruit can provide an adult's daily recommended intake.

You can serve kiwi to children in an egg cup; slice off the top and give them a teaspoon to scoop out the juicy flesh.

Don't try using the fruit in jellies – it contains an enzyme that prevents setting (and that is also used to tenderise meat).

You can store kiwi fruits for up to six weeks in the fridge; they are ready to eat when the surface yields slightly to the touch.

If you want to hurry the ripening process, then put unripe fruits in a sealed plastic bag with a banana or an apple.

Kohlrabi

Kohlrabi's nutty and turnip-like flavour help to make it a favourite vegetable on the Continent.

It deserves to be more widely grown and eaten in this country because it matures in only 10–12 weeks from sowing, withstands autumn frosts, and can be stored for several weeks.

Planning the crop
Kohlrabi grows best in fertile, well-drained soil. If the ground is poor, fork in some well-rotted compost and hoe in a general fertiliser at the rate of 60g per square metre (2oz per square yard).

How much to grow If your family enjoys root vegetables, sow rows about 3m (10ft) long at four-week intervals from early spring to late summer for a constant supply.

Varieties Although the flesh is white in all varieties, some may have green or purple skins.
Purple Vienna Has a purple skin with hard white flesh.
White Vienna Has a pale green skin and especially delicate flavour.

Growing tips

Sow the seeds in a drill about 1cm (½in) deep where the plants are to grow, spacing the rows 40cm (15in) apart. Thin seedlings to 25cm (9in) intervals. Keep them well-watered.

Pests and diseases

The pests most likely to affect this crop are **aphids**, **cabbage root fly**, **cabbage whitefly**, **caterpillars** and **flea beetle**.

The principal diseases and disorders are **club root**, **damping off**, **downy mildew**, **leaf spot**, **whiptail** and **wire stem** (see Pests and Diseases, pages 238–49).

Harvesting and storing

Pull the plants out of the soil when the bulbous stems are about the size of a tennis ball.

Although the final autumn crop can be left in the ground until needed, it is better lifted when mature. Trim the leaves and roots, and store in a dry, cool place.

Preparing and cooking

This root vegetable resembles a turnip in appearance, and is also similar in taste. The roots are white or purple and should be used while young, before they become coarse. They are suitable for cooking as a side vegetable, and may also be used raw in salads.

To prepare koh-rabi, cut off the leafy tops and trim away the root base and any fibrous roots. Scrub thoroughly in cold running water, and peel rather thickly. Cut the roots crossways into 1cm (½in) slices, or finger-width strips.

Cook kohlrabi, either in slices or strips, for 10–15 minutes in a very small amount of boiling, lightly salted water, adding butter at the

rate of about 75g (3oz) to every pound of vegetable. Serve the kohlrabi with a little of the cooking liquid poured over it, or in a white sauce. Alternatively, mash with butter and a little milk.

For a fresh salad, cut the raw peeled kohlrabi into narrow strips, or grate the roots on the coarse side of a grater and toss in French dressing.

Kohlrabi casserole

Peel and finely chop an onion then fry in a little oil until soft and golden, but not brown. Remove from the pan and set aside. Fry up 250g (½lb) diced streaky bacon (rind removed) until crisp and then set aside. Next take 500g (1lb) potatoes, peeled and sliced, and an equal amount of prepared kohlrabi strips (cut in half). Line a casserole dish with a layer of diced potatoes, followed by a layer of kohlrabi. Add a layer of onion and bacon, seasoning the layers with salt and black pepper. Continue with the layers until ingredients are used up, finishing with potatoes. Pour in 150ml (5fl oz) of stock, cover and cook at 180°C (350°F, gas mark 4) for an hour.

AT-A-GLANCE TIMETABLE

SOWING
EARLY SPRING–LATE SUMMER
1cm (½in) deep
40cm (15in) between rows

THINNING
25cm (9in) apart, when large enough to handle

HARVESTING
LATE SPRING–MID AUTUMN

Land cress

Land cress, an annual also known as American cress or winter cress, is one of the few vegetables that will thrive in a damp, shady part of the garden. It is also hardy, so it is worth growing to provide watercress-flavoured leaves for winter salads and garnishes. A variegated form is available that is just as tasty, but also looks attractive in mixed containers or ornamental beds and borders.

Planning the crop

Choose a site that is moist and, preferably, shaded. When digging, add well-rotted manure or compost to the soil at the rate of a bucketful per square metre (square yard).

How much to grow Sow in March for use in summer, and in September for winter use. About six to eight plants in summer, and eight to ten in winter, will give a constant supply of leaves.

Varieties Seed merchants sell the seed simply as land cress or American cress.

Growing tips

Sow the seed in a drill about 5mm (¼in) deep. If the ground is even slightly dry, water the site thoroughly before sowing.

When the seedlings are large enough to handle, thin them so that they are 20cm (8in) apart.

Keep the ground well watered, particularly during dry spells, and mulch with well-rotted manure or compost, or with dampened peat.

Land cress can also be grown in 18cm (7in) pots of multipurpose compost. Sow three or four seeds to a pot and remove all but the strongest when the seedlings are large enough to handle. Put the pots in a partially shaded place and water regularly.

Pests and diseases

Slugs and snails (page 241) may cause problems. Land cress is generally disease-free.

Harvesting and storing

The cress grows quickly, and you can expect to make the first pickings about eight weeks after sowing. Pick the outer leaves first,

leaving the centre to produce more. As the plant gets older, discard the tougher, outer leaves and pick only from the centre. The cress doesn't store very well, so pick just enough for your needs.

Preparing and cooking

Land cress resembles watercress, although the green leaves are smaller and have a less delicate flavour. For this reason, pick them while they are young.

Land cress may be used as a substitute for watercress garnishes, particularly with roast chicken and game. It may also be used as a basis for soups (see Watercress soup, page 225).

Pick the leaves just before they are needed and prepare in the same way as watercress.

Use land cress as an ingredient in mixed or green salads, or combine with segments of orange and toss in French dressing.

AT-A-GLANCE TIMETABLE

SOWING
5mm (¼in) deep
• **Winter crop**
AUTUMN
• **Summer crop**
SPRING

THINNING
20cm (8in) apart
• **Winter and summer crops**
When large enough to handle

HARVESTING
• **Winter crop**
LATE AUTUMN–EARLY WINTER ONWARDS
• **Summer crop**
LATE SPRING ONWARDS

Leeks

Traditionally leeks were used to make soups and stews during Lent, at a time of year when other vegetables were scarce. This highlights one of the qualities for which the leek is still valued – its ability to survive the hardest of winters.

It is also an easy vegetable to grow, provided it is sown sufficiently early to give it a long growing season.

Quick-maturing varieties can be sown thickly, left untransplanted and used throughout summer in salads as an alternative to spring onions.

The leek has been the national emblem of Wales ever since AD 640, when Welsh forces under King Cadwallader wore the vegetable as a badge of recognition and defeated an invading Saxon army. The leek is a popular winter vegetable all over Britain and in the Newcastle area in particular, the growing of exhibition leeks has become a passion. With the aid of closely guarded techniques and fertilisers, experts raise 4.5kg (9lb) giants, with blanched bases measuring 51cm (20in) or more.

These are massive compared with the specimens that most of us manage to grow, but leeks of more modest size remain one of the most worthwhile vegetable crops.

Planning the crop
Leeks will thrive in any well-drained soil, even in the coldest areas, provided it is well manured during the winter before planting.

How much to grow A 3m (10ft) row will yield an average of 5kg (10lb) of leeks. Two rows should be sufficient for most families.

Varieties
Musselburgh Improved A very hardy, a long-stemmed Scottish variety.
King Richard Slim and quick maturing. Suitable for growing in raised beds.
Lyon A very hardy variety, producing solid, white stems of excellent flavour.

Planting out Leek seedlings that are spaced close together (as shown) will be small and can be used as baby vegetables, or as substitutes for spring onions.

Earthing up During autumn use a hoe to draw soil up around the base of the plants. This will increase the length of the blanched stems.

Growing tips
Sow leeks 1cm (½in) deep in an outdoor seedbed during early spring. In midsummer, when the seedlings will be about 20cm (8in) high, transplant them into their final bed, first trimming the tops to reduce water-loss.

With a dibber, make holes 15cm (6in) deep and 25cm (9in) apart, leaving 40cm (15in) between rows. Drop the young leeks into the holes. Do not replace the soil, but water the seedlings thoroughly. The amount of soil carried into the holes by the water will set the leeks in place without settling between the leaves. The holes will soon fill up as you water and hoe.

During the rest of the summer, hoe the bed regularly to keep down weeds, and water thoroughly during dry spells. During autumn, draw soil around the developing stems (known as earthing up) to increase the length of the blanched part.

Pests and diseases
Onion fly (page 240) is the most likely pest. **Rust** (page 246) and **white rot** (page 247) are the principal diseases.

Harvesting and storing
To extend the harvesting period, start lifting the leeks when they are about 2cm (¾in) thick. Ease them out of the soil with a fork, otherwise they may break.

Continue lifting the leeks during the winter as they are needed. They will keep growing throughout winter, though only slowly during the coldest months.

See also freezing (page 252).

Preparing and cooking
Together with potatoes and onions, leeks are one of the most versatile and popular of vegetables. They are used to flavour soups and stews, and a few leaves wrapped round sprigs of parsley and thyme make a quick bouquet garni.

Leeks are also used as an accompanying vegetable, and may be boiled, steamed, braised or fried. They may be cooked whole and served hot, lukewarm or cold as an appetiser. Young leeks, finely chopped, can be used in a salad and dressed with oil-vinaigrette. They are also delicious par-boiled,

AT-A-GLANCE TIMETABLE

SOWING
EARLY SPRING
5mm (¼in) deep

TRANSPLANTING
MIDSUMMER
25cm (9in) apart with 40cm (15in) between rows

EARTHING UP
AUTUMN

HARVESTING
LATE AUTUMN–SPRING

wrapped in ham and baked in a cheese sauce.

Leeks for cooking should be cleaned thoroughly to remove any grit or dirt that may have lodged in among the leaves. Begin by slicing off the root base and trimming off the upper green leaves, removing any tough or damaged outer leaves. If the leeks are to be cooked whole, as for braising, make a downward slit into the white part, long enough to prise the leaves apart but not so deep that the stem splits in two. Rinse the leeks thoroughly under cold, running water, washing away all traces of soil and grit.

Alternatively, cut the leeks in half lengthways and rinse them well; or wash them first, then cut crossways into 2.5–5cm (1–2in) pieces, or into even thinner slices.

Braised leeks

Put 750g (1½lb) prepared whole leeks in a heavy-based pan. Pour 600ml (1 pint) of vegetable stock over the leeks until just covered. Season with salt and pepper and add a bouquet garni. Bring to the boil over a high heat then cover and simmer gently for 45 minutes until the leeks are tender and most of the liquid evaporated. Serve the leeks with a garnish of parsley. They go well with roast poultry and beef, or with grilled steak.

Protecting the roots

A cardboard tube placed around the leek at transplanting time helps to keep the soil out of the developing white base.

Lettuce

Winter butterhead
'Valdor'

Bronze-tinted butterhead
'Continuity'

Cos
'Little Gem'

Summer butterhead
'All the Year Round'

Loosehead
'Salad Bowl'

Miniature butterhead
'Tom Thumb'

Crisp-heart
'Webb's Wonderful'

There are two main types of lettuce grown in Britain: cos or Romaine, which are generally oblong with crisp leaves; and cabbage lettuces, which are further divided into butterhead and crisphead or iceberg types.

There are also loose-leaf or cut-and-come again types, which produce a profusion of leaves but no heart and will produce new leaves if a few are picked on a regular basis. Some seedsmen also sell packets of mixed seeds, giving lettuces which mature over an extended period.

Although lettuces were popular with the Romans and Greeks, they are believed to have a much longer history, and may have been grown thousands of years earlier in the Far East. In Britain, the lettuce was already popular by the 16th century, and today it is the most widely grown salad vegetable.

Although lettuces are easy to grow in summer and early autumn, they need the protection of glass, polythene coldframes or cloches if their season is to be extended into the first half of winter. A frost-free greenhouse or frame will be necessary for harvesting lettuces from the middle of winter to early spring. If you intend to grow early or late crops, choose only varieties recommended for this purpose by seed merchants.

In a small garden, lettuces need not occupy a special bed. They can be planted as a catch-crop between

Green ruffles Looseleaf lettuces have appealing frilly-edged leaves that can be harvested singly or as a whole lettuce. This vibrant green would make an attractive edging plant for a vegetable bed or a border.

slower-maturing vegetables, such as parsnips. The lettuces will be out of the ground before the other crop needs the space.

Planning the crop
Lettuces grow best on a fertile, well-drained soil. Before sowing or planting apply a general-purpose fertiliser at the rate of 60g per square metre (2oz per square yard). Alternatively you can use grow bags.

How many to grow Avoid the risk of summer gluts alternating with shortages by sowing a 3–3.5m (10–12ft) long row every three weeks in the open from mid spring

to the second half of summer. This should give a steady supply.

Varieties These are listed by type in the order of sowing. A careful selection will give you lettuces from March to early December. As well as the varieties recommended below, seed companies often bring out new varieties so check the catalogues for what is available.

Butterhead varieties
• For sowing in autumn in the open and ready in mid spring:
Arctic King Extremely hardy with a large head and good flavour.
Valdor Very hardy with a large, solid head.

• For sowing in a cold greenhouse, coldframes or under cloches in late autumn; ready in spring:
May Queen This variety may also be sown in the open in early spring to mature in June.
• For sowing in a cold greenhouse, coldframes or under cloches in mid winter, transplanting outdoors in spring to mature in late spring and early summer:
Tom Thumb Quick-growing – its head is no larger than a tennis ball. May be grown to maturity under glass, or sown outside in early spring.
Unrivalled May also be sown in the open from March to July.
• For successional sowings outside from March to July with plants maturing in 10–12 weeks:
All the Year Round A lettuce with a solid, pale green heart, it is reliable even in dry summers with minimal watering.
Continuity A compact and long-standing, bronze-tinted variety; one of the best for light soils.
Suzan Pale leaves and large hearts. May also be sown under glass in January.

Crisphead or iceberg varieties
Lakeland Bred to grow well in the British climate and will withstand poor conditions.
Webb's Wonderful Large-hearted lettuces that are slow to run to seed.
Windermere A smaller lettuce than Webb's Wonderful, but quicker to mature.

Cos or Romaine varieties
Little Gem A dwarf and compact lettuce; one of the earliest maturing cos.
Lobjoits Green Grows to about 25cm (9in) tall; dark green heart.

Winter Density Has a dark green heart; may be sown outdoors in September for cutting the following May.
• Forcing varieties to sow in coldframes, cloches, or a cold greenhouse, in the first week of August to crop in November and December:
Emerald A hardy variety with a large, solid heart.
Kwiek Has a large heart.

Looseleaf lettuces
Salad Bowl Produces numerous tender, curled leaves; practically non-bolting; an excellent choice for trouble-free cropping over a long period. Often sold in mixtures with the equivalent red-leaved variety, **Red Salad Bowl**.
Lollo Rossa Red, frilly leaves; good decorative lettuce. Can be grown in a mixed ornamental border.

Growing outdoor lettuces
From spring to the second half of summer sow seeds in drills about 5mm (¼in) deep and 30cm (12in) apart. Thin the seedlings to 7.5cm (3in) apart as soon as they are large enough to handle.

Thin finally according to variety. For instance, space the dwarf 'Tom Thumb' 15cm (6in) apart, most butterheads 25cm (9in), and large iceberg varieties such as 'Webb's Wonderful' 30cm (12in) apart.

The second thinnings can be used in salads, or transplanted in another bed. Space them as necessary, and plant with a dibber or trowel. After firming the soil, water the roots well.

Do not transplant outdoor lettuces after the middle of spring because during long dry spells the plants are likely to bolt (run to seed prematurely).

Keep the plants well-watered and hoe regularly to keep down the weeds. Most modern cos varieties will form a compact heart without

AT-A-GLANCE TIMETABLE

Outdoor lettuces

SOWING
5mm (¼in) deep
• Summer varieties
SPRING–MIDDLE OF SUMMER
• Overwintering varieties
AUTUMN
• Forced varieties
LATE SUMMER

FIRST THINNING
7.5cm (3in) apart, when large enough to handle

TRANSPLANTING
• Summer varieties
SPRING (Use thinnings if required)
• Overwintering varieties
Do not transplant
• Forced varieties
AUTUMN (Under glass)

SECOND THINNING
15–30cm (6–12in) apart
• Summer varieties
When plants touch. Space to suit variety
• Overwintering varieties
EARLY SPRING
• Forced varieties
No second thinning

HARVESTING
• Summer varieties
EARLY SUMMER–LATE AUTUMN
• Overwintering varieties
MID-LATE SPRING
• Forced varieties
First half of winter

any assistance. If any do not, slip a rubber band over the leaves, or tie them with soft string.

Overwintering varieties Sow fully hardy varieties in their permanent bed in early autumn. A month later, thin to only 7.5cm (3in) apart; then, if severe weather kills some plants, enough will survive to yield a good crop.

In early spring, thin to 15–20cm (6–8in) apart and give a top dressing of general-purpose fertiliser at the rate of 60g to the metre (2oz to the yard).

Greenhouse lettuces
Sow suitable varieties in late summer to produce a crop during the first half of winter. Sow the seeds in a bed prepared as for the outdoor summer sowings. In September, transplant the seedlings to a coldframe, cloche or to a bed in a cold greenhouse, setting the plants 25cm (9in) apart.

For a crop in spring, sow a forcing variety in autumn directly in the coldframe or under cloches. Sow three or four seeds 1cm (½in) deep in groups about 7.5cm (3in) apart in each direction.

When the seedlings are about 1cm (½in) high, remove all but the strongest plant from each station. Water sparingly or not at all during winter, and make a final thinning to 15cm (6in) spacings at the end of winter when the plants start to grow again.

Pests and diseases
The main pests are **aphids**, **cutworms**, **slugs and snails** and **wireworm**. The principal diseases of lettuces are **damping off**, **downy mildew** and **grey mould** (see Pests and Diseases, pages 238–49).

Harvesting
Start using a crop of lettuces as soon as the first hearts form. They should be taken as needed.

Morning is the best time to gather them. Either cut the lettuces with a sharp knife just above ground level, or pull the whole plant and cut the root off afterwards. Pick leaves from 'cut-and-come-again' types as required.

Preparing and cooking
Prepare lettuce leaves by washing lightly in cold water and drying in a salad spinner or on a soft towel.

Lettuces can be cooked as a vegetable or as a soup, but they are used chiefly in salads. It is the dressing that gives a salad its distinctive taste. Oil-vinaigrette or French dressings are the most often used, with added fresh herbs such as chives, parsley, dill, fennel or marjoram.

Make a salad up at the last possible moment and, ideally, do not toss it in its dressing until it is served. Use only enough dressing to coat the ingredients.

Lovage

Lovage, a many-purpose perennial herb, is believed to have been brought to this country by the Romans. From the Middle Ages its leaves have been used in medicines and for giving a musky, celery-like flavour to soups, stews, sauces and salads.

The herb can be difficult to get hold of and is virtually never sold in supermarkets. So it is best to grow your own supply.

Planning the crop
Lovage grows best in a well-drained soil in a sunny position or partial shade. It reaches a height of 1.5m (5ft).

How many plants to grow Just two or three plants will provide enough fresh and dried leaves for flavouring dishes. You will need to grow additional plants if you intend to use them for candying.

Growing tips
Sow the seeds in autumn or spring in a drill about 1cm (½in) deep, either in a seedbed or where the plants are to grow. When the seedlings are large enough to handle, thin them to 30cm (12in) apart; or transplant them in their permanent positions at 30cm (12in) spacings.

During summer, remove any flowering stems to promote the growth of young leaves and to stop the plant from setting seed.

Young lovage plants are usually obtainable from the herb sections of garden centres.

Raising new plants
An existing stock of plants may be increased by dividing the roots in early spring and replanting the divisions at 30cm (12in) spacings.

Pests and diseases
Lovage is generally trouble free.

Harvesting and storing
Pick the leaves as required from early summer into autumn.

See also drying (page 300), freezing (page 252).

Preparing and cooking
This perennial herb has almost disappeared from general use, although it was extremely popular in medieval herb gardens. It resembles a giant celery in shape and provides a distinctive feature in any herb garden.

The taste is also similar to that of celery, though it is much stronger and has a slightly lemony, yeasty flavour. In southern Europe the stems are candied in the same way as angelica, and the dried seeds are used like caraway seeds in breads and biscuits.

The roots, too, are edible, but few gardeners would wish to grow sufficient plants to use them for this purpose.

In general, it is the glossy, dark green leaves that are used for flavouring, especially in vegetable soups and in stews, where they give an impression of substance and body due to their distinctive yeasty taste. Add a little dried lovage to a bolognese sauce and you will almost certainly receive compliments and enquiries about your 'secret ingredient'.

Use the washed and finely chopped leaves to flavour stock, fish chowders and cooked vegetables. The leaves may also be used in omelettes, salad dressings and cream sauces, or they may be mixed sparingly in salads.

Marjoram and oregano

Sweet marjoram

Pot marjoram (oregano)

Two types of the herb marjoram are grown for their aromatic leaves and flowers, which are used to flavour a variety of dishes. One, called sweet marjoram, is usually grown as a half-hardy annual. It has a finer flavour than the other type, pot marjoram, which is a hardy perennial and is more often referred to as oregano.

Planning the crop
Like most herbs, marjoram grows best in full sun and in a well-drained, fertile soil.

How much to grow
Two or three plants of each type of marjoram will provide a plentiful supply of leaves through summer and autumn. Leaves can be frozen for use during winter, when the plants are dormant.

Both sweet marjoram and pot marjoram can be grown in containers indoors and outdoors for decoration as well as cookery. Pot marjoram has several attractive variegated forms.

Varieties
Seed is sold as sweet marjoram or pot marjoram.

Growing tips
Sow seeds of sweet marjoram in a tray of seed compost under glass in early spring at a temperature of 10–13°C (50–55°F).

Prick out the seedlings when they are large enough to handle and place in 6cm (2½in) pots of potting compost. Put a single seedling in each pot.

Harden off before planting out 30cm (12in) apart in their permanent positions in late spring.

Clusters of flowers appear from summer to early autumn from knot-like bracts. This is the inspiration for the plant's alternative common name, knotted marjoram.

For winter pot plants, take cuttings of basal shoots in late summer (see page 31).

Sow pot marjoram in mid to late spring in 5mm (¼in) deep drills in the open. Thin to 30cm (12in) apart. The plants grow to a height of about 30cm (12in).

Raising new plants
Propagate established plants of pot marjoram by taking 5cm (2in) cuttings of basal shoots in mid to late spring. After removing the lower leaves, insert them in equal parts (by volume) of peat substitute and sand, or perlite, in a shaded coldframe (either directly into the bed of the frame or into pots containing this mixture).

Plant out in their permanent positions when rooted.

Pests and diseases
Marjoram is generally trouble free.

Harvesting and storing
Pick the leaves and flowers of sweet marjoram when needed during summer. For freezing (see page 252), pick before the flowers open – generally in midsummer.

The leaves of pot marjoram can be picked from spring to autumn, as required.

Preparing and cooking
The hairy leaves of sweet marjoram have a flavour reminiscent of thyme, although they are sweeter,

Bunch of herbs Tie sprigs of marjoram, rosemary and sage together in a bouquet garni for use in soups and stews.

and are often used as a substitute for this herb. They are excellent for flavouring roast or grilled meat, in stuffings for meat, poultry and oily fish, and to flavour omelettes, soups and stews.

Pot marjoram has the same culinary uses as sweet marjoram, but the leaves lack the sweetness and often have a bitter taste.

Use marjoram in a bouquet garni for soups and stews, and to flavour minestrone, tomato and chicken soups. Oily fish, such as mackerel and trout, can be stuffed with marjoram leaves prior to grilling or baking. Wrap a few leaves in muslin and add them to beef and

pork stews, casseroles, and to braised chicken, duck, pheasant and other game birds.

Sprinkle tomato salads with finely chopped marjoram, or mix with sugar to flavour bread-and-butter and rice puddings. The leaves can also be used to flavour homemade vinegars.

Pizzaiola sauce
Finely chop 2 onions and 2 garlic cloves and gently fry in a little oil until softened. Remove the stalk, pips and pith of a green pepper and dice the flesh. Add to the onions and cook on a gentle heat for a further 15 minutes. Add 50g (2oz) chopped mushrooms and 500g (1lb) skinned, chopped tomatoes. Stir in a tablespoon of freshly chopped marjoram along with 150ml (5fl oz) stock.

Cover and allow to simmer for 10 minutes. Season to taste with tomato paste, chilli sauce, salt and black pepper. The sauce can accompany pasta or can be served with grilled or fried sausages, beefburgers or meatloaf.

Medlars

Medlars are somewhat out of fashion nowadays, and the trees are too large for planting in most modern gardens. They attain a height and spread of about 4.5–6m (15–20ft), which would overwhelm the average suburban plot.

However, if you inherit one in a garden that you take over, or if you have a garden large enough to plant one, you will find the medlar a most attractive tree.

The branches are gnarled and twisted, and large pink or white flowers are borne in early summer. In autumn, the leaves flare into brilliant colour and, of course, the tree bears it distinctive fruit.

Planning the crop
A well-drained loam suits medlars best. They need an open, sunny position, preferably with some shelter from brisk northerly and easterly winds.

Varieties Two varieties are generally available.
Dutch Has widely spreading branches and bears large fruits.

Nottingham The branches are more erect. The fruits are smaller and more richly flavoured.

Growing tips
Buy a three or four-year-old standard or half-standard from a nursery. Plant it in well-manured soil between late autumn and early spring, though the earlier the better. Otherwise buy a containerised young tree and plant at any time the weather is suitable. Support a young tree with a sturdy stake.

Prune back the leaders of the main framework branches by half each winter for two years, then by a quarter for the next two years. Cut strong sideshoots to about 15cm (6in). Mature trees require little or no pruning.

Pests and diseases
Medlars are generally trouble free.

Harvesting and storing
The fruits part easily from the tree in late autumn or early winter, and this is the time to pick them.

Gather the fruits on a dry day and store them, eye downwards, in a single layer in a cool place.

After three or four weeks, the colour of the fruits will deepen to

AT-A-GLANCE TIMETABLE

PLANTING
LATE AUTUMN-EARLY SPRING

PRUNING TREES
LATE AUTUMN-EARLY SPRING

HARVESTING
LATE AUTUMN-EARLY WINTER
Store for about three weeks before eating

dark brown, and they will become soft to the touch – a process commonly known as 'bletting'. The fruits may then be eaten raw, or cooked – they should not be eaten straight from the tree.

Preparing and cooking
Medlars were popular after-dinner dessert fruits in Victorian days, their flavour often being complemented by a glass of port. But there are other ways of enjoying their distinctive taste.

Ripe medlars can be cut across and their soft flesh scraped out with a teaspoon, sweetened to taste with soft brown sugar and mixed with thick cream. Or try beating the fresh, sweetened pulp to a fine purée and blending it with cream and cider, to make a delicious fool.

Medlars can also be roasted in the oven, like apples. Stick a whole clove in each cleaned fruit and set in a shallow, buttered, ovenproof dish. Bake in the oven at a temperature of 180°C (350°F, gas mark 4) for about 10 minutes, or until soft but not mushy. Serve lukewarm with a bowl of sugar and cream, or with a caramel or cider sauce.

An accompaniment for meat
Try using medlar sauce as a delicious change from apple sauce to serve with fatty meats, such as pork and goose.

To make it, spoon the flesh from a sufficient quantity of ripe medlars and cook to a pulp with very little water and 1 or 2 tablespoons of lemon juice. Simmer over a low heat, stirring frequently until quite soft, then sweeten to taste with brown sugar and add a little ground cloves or cinnamon.

Medlar jelly provides a rose-coloured and distinctive accompaniment to game dishes. Make the jelly as for crab-apple jelly (see page 280), letting the fruit cook for a fairly long time over a low heat to extract all the juices and flavour.

Medlars need the addition of lemon juice to obtain a good set. Allow the juice and pared rind of a medium-size lemon to each 500g (1lb) of medlars.

Medlar fool
Scrape the pulp from 750g (1½lb) ripe medlars and beat to a smooth purée with a fork. Stir in 4 tablespoons of sweet cider and sweeten to taste with sugar – about 100g (4oz). Lightly whip 150ml (5fl oz) double cream and fold it into the medlar purée. Spoon the mixture into serving dishes or wine glasses and chill in the fridge for about 2 hours.

Decorate with candied violets or toasted hazelnuts. As a variation, the purée can be blended with 300ml (½ pint) thick custard and chilled. Pipe a little cream over the top and sprinkle on decorations.

Melons

Casaba melon

Cantaloupe melon

Melons are fairly easy to grow under cloches, in coldframes or in an unheated greenhouse, though results vary from year to year with the amount of sunshine. Most gardeners begrudge the amount of greenhouse space needed, so cloches and coldframes are the usual choice.

It is essential to choose a variety that is suited to cool conditions – not a hothouse melon.

Planning the crop

Melons require a warm situation and a moist, fertile soil. The usual method is to grow them in large pots of multipurpose compost or in grow bags. However, if you are going to grow them in a greenhouse border, in a coldframe or under cloches, you should prepare the ground well in advance by making up the soil from good-quality turves that have been stacked for at least four months, or by working in a proprietary humus-adding soil conditioner.

Do not dig in manure, as this tends to produce over-luxuriant growth.

How many to grow Three or four plants will yield about a dozen melons. It is a good idea to raise the plants in two batches so that they do not all ripen at the same time.

Varieties Two types of melon are grown in this country: cantaloupes, which are comparatively hardy and can be grown in coldframes; and casabas, which have larger fruits and are always grown in the greenhouse. Cantaloupes have more flavour than casabas.

For ease of cultivation, choose cantaloupes. These are often sold as young plants in late spring by garden centres. The most reliable varieties include:
Ogen Green fleshed.
Sweetheart An F1 hybrid, with scarlet flesh.

Good varieties of casabas include the following:
Blenheim Orange Orange fleshed
King George Orange fleshed
Superlative Orange fleshed
Honeydew Green fleshed
Hero of Lockinge White fleshed.

GROWING MELONS UNDER CLOCHES

Planting Water before removing the plant from its pot, to keep the soil intact. Plant with the root-ball just above the surface.

Pinching out Encourage fruit-bearing sideshoots to form by pinching out the tip when the plant has four or five leaves.

Growing melons under frames and cloches

While it is possible to sow seeds beneath cloches or a frame in late spring, results will be more reliable from an indoor sowing, with artificial heat, in mid spring.

Sow the seeds in 7.5cm (3in) fibre pots containing John Innes seed compost or a multipurpose compost. Press a single seed edgeways into each pot 1cm (½in) deep, water the pots well and enclose in a plastic bag. Leave in the airing cupboard, or near the heater in a greenhouse, until the seeds germinate.

To provide a succession of plants and ultimately a longer fruiting season, sow a second batch of seeds two or three weeks later.

When the seedlings appear, place them on a warm windowsill or near the glass in a greenhouse. Do not allow the roots to become cramped. Pot on, if necessary, into 20cm (8in) pots.

Plant them out in frames or under cloches from the middle of May onwards. Place frames or cloches in position a fortnight before planting so that the soil beneath them warms up.

Set the plants 1m (3ft) apart with one plant in the centre of an average-size garden frame.

Disturb the roots as little as possible when planting, and water the plants to ensure that their growth is not interrupted. Plant so that the top of the root-ball is just above the surface. This will lessen the chances of collar rot.

As each plant develops four or five rough leaves – that is, excluding the original seed leaves – pinch out the growing point to encourage sideshoots to form.

In due course, select the four strongest shoots and pinch out any others that form. In a frame, direct these towards the corners; under cloches, train two in each direction.

For the best-sized fruit, allow only one melon to form on each shoot. Remove any other fruits that develop, leaving similar-size fruits on each shoot. Pinch out the tip of the shoot two leaves beyond the fruit.

Growing melons in a greenhouse

Different methods are needed for growing melons indoors, mainly because they require supporting. They are usually grown as double-stemmed cordons.

Sow in early spring if you are able to maintain a minimum temperature of 16°C (61°F) while the seedlings are growing. Otherwise wait two or three weeks, and sow as for frame or cloche crops. When the young plants have developed four or five leaves, transplant them to their final growing positions – either in the greenhouse border, in growing bags (two per bag) or in 25cm (9in) pots filled with John Innes No. 3 Compost. Set the plants, or pots, 80cm (2½ft) apart.

Insert two, eave-height canes, 26cm (10in) apart, alongside each plant. Fasten horizontal wires, using vine eyes, to the glazing bars on the side wall of the greenhouse and to the underside of the roof, at 30cm (12in) intervals. The eyes

prevent the melon leaves from touching the glass.

Pinch out each plant's growing point when it is 15cm (6in) high. Pinch out all but the two strongest of the sideshoots that will then form; tie to the canes.

Continue tying-in the two shoots, first to the canes and then to the wires, until they are 1.5–1.8m (5–6ft) long. At this stage, pinch out their growing points.

Laterals will develop from the two stems as soon as the tops are pinched out. Tie these to the wires, and pinch out their tips when they have developed four or five leaves. Pollinate the flowers that grow on sub-laterals; remove flowers that grow on the main stems.

The aim is to produce four female flowers on each stem for simultaneous pollination.

Pollination Melons produce both male and female flowers, the latter being distinguished by the swelling of the embryo fruits behind the blooms. In half-open frames or

TRAINING GREENHOUSE MELONS

Securing two laterals After removing the growing tip when 15cm (6in) high, train the two strongest sideshoots to canes.

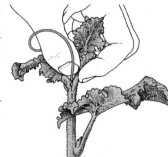

Pinching out the tips After training each pair of shoots up the canes and wires, pinch out when 1.5–1.8m (5–6ft) long.

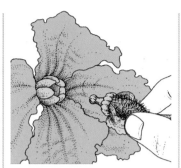

Assisting pollination When growing melons under glass, you will need to aid pollination by pressing male flowers (petals removed) to female flowers.

open-ended cloches, the chances are that bees or other insects will pollinate the plants. In enclosed greenhouses, however, or in cold weather, you will need to pollinate the flowers by hand.

When the young fruits begin to swell, remove the largest and the smallest, leaving only those of the same size on each plant. Any large fruit remaining will develop at the expense of the others.

Pests and diseases

The pests most likely to affect melons are **aphids**, **glasshouse red spider mites** and **glasshouse whitefly**. The chief diseases are **cucumber mosaic virus** and **soil-borne diseases** (see Pests and Diseases, pages 238–49).

Harvesting and storing

Cut melons from the stalks only when they are completely ripe. The best way to test this is to press the end of the fruit furthest from the stalk. If the skin yields to the touch, the melon is ripe.

See also freezing (page 252).

Preparing and serving

Cool, refreshing melons are equally suitable as a starter or a dessert. Casaba melons are larger, firmer and have paler flesh than the cantaloupe melons. The latter are sweeter and for the most part have orange-yellow flesh.

Melon is usually served lightly chilled, but bear in mind that prolonged refrigeration destroys the delicate flavour. An hour's chilling is sufficient.

Prepare a melon for serving in sections by cutting it in half lengthways, and then cutting each half lengthways into segments.

Scoop out the pips and loose fibres with a spoon. The skin may be left on, or the melon detached from it by running a sharp knife blade between flesh and skin, leaving the skin in position.

Serve melon segments with sugar and a squeeze of lime or lemon juice. For a first course, melon combines well with smoked meat. Or the flesh may be diced, and tossed with cubes of mild cheese in a French dressing.

For a simple dessert sprinkle the melon segments with ground ginger or fill half melons with soft fruits, sprinkled with liqueur or white wine.

Mint

Apple mint

Spearmint

Peppermint

One of the features of this indispensable herb is the wide range of flavours and scents provided by its many varieties. Ginger mint, spearmint, peppermint, apple mint, bergamot mint and pennyroyal were all grown in the old-fashioned herb garden (the latter with an odour so pungent that it was said to drive fleas away).

Though these varieties are still available today, there are two types that dominate: spearmint and apple mint. This is mainly due to their usefulness as kitchen herbs. A handful of freshly picked leaves are famed as accompaniments to a wide range of dishes, from roast lamb, new potatoes or young peas, to cream cheese sandwiches and chutneys.

All mints are grown in the same way and need the same conditions. The challenge with mint lies not in obtaining a crop, but in preventing it from spreading to surrounding areas.

Planning the crop
Plant mint in a deep, moist soil in a semi-shaded position, although mint will grow almost anywhere, including damp, dark corners where few other plants survive.

Mint may also be grown in a window box or large pot, and those with variegated leaves look attractive in hanging baskets.

If you grow mint in a herb or vegetable bed, sink an old, bottomless bucket into the soil and plant the roots inside. This will help to prevent them spreading. Alternatively, confine the roots with a plastic bag (see below).

How much to grow
Mint grows rapidly, so three or four plants of your chosen variety should provide an ample supply for both cooking and storing.

Varieties
Some of the more unusual varieties have already been mentioned, but it may be necessary to enquire at several nurseries or specialist herb farms to obtain a particular sort.

However, the two most commonly used in the kitchen – apple mint and spearmint – are readily available.

Growing tips
Prepare the ground in late winter and dig a spadeful or two of well-rotted compost or manure into the planting site. Obtain a few roots in

Bag it up You can control invasive plants such as mint by planting them inside a plastic bag filled with soil. The bag will prevent the roots from spreading.

early spring from a neighbour, and plant them 5cm (2in) deep and 15cm (6in) apart. Alternatively, buy potted plants from a nursery and set them 15cm (6in) apart.

Whether growing from roots or plants, water the soil well so that the mint becomes established. Thereafter, it requires little attention other than ensuring that it does not spread beyond its allotted space.

Raising new plants
Mint can be propagated from early spring to late autumn by digging up pieces of root or by taking cuttings of young shoots.

For a fresh supply of mint during winter, place young plants or pieces of root in pots of potting compost in autumn and stand them on the kitchen windowsill.

Pests and diseases
Mint is seldom troubled by pests. **Rust** (page 246) is the most likely disease.

Harvesting and storing
Pick the fresh, green leaves at any time, from late spring until early autumn, as needed.

You can maintain a supply of mint sauce throughout winter by chopping a bunch of mint leaves, placing them in a jar and covering them with golden syrup. Take out a few teaspoons as required and mix them with white vinegar.

See also drying (page 300); freezing (page 252) and vinegars (page 299).

Preparing and cooking
This most traditional of British herbs is associated with fresh summer vegetables, lamb and mutton, as well as salads. It has been of culinary importance for hundreds of years.

Gather the leaves while they are young. Add whole sprigs when cooking new potatoes, young peas and carrots, beans and spinach. You can also add sprigs to fruit and wine punches.

Mint refreshers Iced mint tea makes a refreshing summer drink. Pour boiling water over freshly gathered leaves, allowing the liquid to cool before chilling in the fridge.

A classic mint julep consists of a few mint leaves placed in a glass with crushed ice, a little sugar syrup and 2 tablespoons of whisky. Fill the glass with crushed ice, pour more whisky over the ice and decorate with a sprig of mint.

Flavour and garnish Finely chopped mint gives additional flavour to salads and dressings, soups, cream and cottage cheeses, stewed fruit and apple sauces.

Sugar-frosted mint leaves make an edible garnish with summer fruits such as melon or peaches. Brush small sprigs or individual mint leaves lightly with beaten egg white, dredge with caster sugar and leave to dry. Use the frosted leaves the same day.

AT-A-GLANCE TIMETABLE

PLANTING

EARLY SPRING
5cm (2in) deep and
15cm (6in) apart

HARVESTING

LATE SPRING–AUTUMN
Pick the fresh, green leaves as needed

Mulberries

Mulberry trees mature into very large specimens, so are not suitable for a small garden. But if you do have the space, the mulberry is well worth considering. It has a graceful, elegant habit, attractive foliage and produces an abundance of delicious fruits, from which you can make excellent jams and wines.

Mulberry trees were first planted in Britain at Syon House, Brentford, in 1548, and during the next two centuries were widely grown throughout the London area. Like their ancestors from the Far East, they were grown not so much for their fruits as for their leaves, which are the sole food of silkworms.

The London silk-weaving industry was relatively short lived, but many of the original trees survive to this day. Several trees planted by James I in 1610 can still be seen in the grounds of Buckingham Palace.

Planning the crop
Mulberries will grow almost anywhere in Britain where there is a deep, moist soil, though in the north of England and in Scotland they will do better if protected by a south-facing wall.

They can be grown either as bushes or standard trees, the latter eventually achieving a height of 10m (30ft) or more, which is too big for most modern gardens.

How many to grow Mulberries are self-fertile, and a single tree would be ample for most families.

Varieties There are two species, the black mulberry that produces fine, dark fruits, and the white type with pale fruits that are relatively tasteless. When fed to silkworms, the leaves of the white mulberry produce better silk than those of the black. This fact is unlikely to concern gardeners today, and the best choice is the black mulberry.

Growing tips
The usual way to acquire a mulberry is by purchasing a young tree from a nursery. Most are now grown in containers, so may be planted at any time the weather is favourable.

Plant the young tree in an open, sunny position in well-manured ground, taking particular care not to damage the roots.

Raising new plants Take a cutting from a friend's tree in either autumn or early spring, preferably a 30cm (12in) cutting that has some older, two-year-old wood at the base. Plant the cutting deeply so that all but two or three buds are buried below ground.

Even longer branches can be rooted with a good chance of success, though any lateral branches should be trimmed off and about half the main branch buried in the soil.

Large branches can be planted in the position where the tree is to grow, but shorter cuttings are better grown in a nursery bed for a year or two until they are well rooted.

Avoid using any shoots that are growing from near the base of the tree. The more desirable black mulberry was sometimes grafted on to a white species, and the basal shoots may therefore be of the less desirable white sort.

Pruning Mulberries tend to bleed when cut, so avoid heavy pruning. You will need to remove dead wood, or inward-growing branches that rub against their neighbours. Do this in late autumn to spring.

Pests and diseases
Birds are fond of the ripe fruits, and may strip much of the crop unless the tree can be netted. The principal disease of this tree is **canker** (page 242).

Harvesting and storing
The best way to gather mulberries is to wait until the fruit ripens in late summer, then spread a cloth or large sheet of plastic beneath the branches and shake the tree gently.

Any unripe fruits can remain on the tree to be gathered later.

Mulberries may be eaten fresh, or used in cooked dishes.

See also bottling (page 270); freezing (page 252); fruit cheeses and butters (page 281) and wine-making (page 304).

Preparing and cooking
When the blood-red mulberries become ripe in early to mid autumn the fruits should be gathered and used as soon as possible. They may be used for jams but, as their pectin content is low, you will need to add lemon juice.

The slightly acid, juicy berries may also be served as fresh dessert fruits with sugar and cream. Handle the berries as little as possible. Wash them if necessary, and remove calyces and damaged parts. Note that both berries and juice stain badly, and the stains are almost impossible to remove.

Mulberry with junket was a popular dish in the 17th century. Today, a similar dessert is made by arranging layers of sweetened mulberries with layers of natural yoghurt in serving glasses, sprinkling the top with soft brown sugar and leaving them to chill.

All recipes for raspberries and loganberries are also suitable for mulberries, and they are excellent for fruit pies.

Baked mulberries
Place 500g (1lb) mulberries in a deep pie dish. Dredge with 100g (4oz) brown sugar and bake in the oven at 180°C (350°F, gas mark 4) for 15–20 minutes, until the juices begin to flow from the fruit. Meanwhile prepare a custard sauce. Gently heat 600ml (1 pint) milk with half a vanilla pod. When almost boiling, remove from the heat, cover and leave to infuse for 10 minutes. Remove the vanilla pod and stir in 2 tablespoons of caster sugar. Beat 4 egg yolks in a large bowl and gradually whisk in the warm vanilla milk. Strain the mixture into a clean saucepan and stir constantly over a low heat until the custard thickens. Serve the baked mulberries straight from the oven with a jug of warm custard. You can also serve the dish with fresh cream instead of custard.

AT-A-GLANCE TIMETABLE

PLANTING
LATE AUTUMN–EARLY SPRING

PRUNING
LATE AUTUMN–EARLY SPRING

HARVESTING
EARLY–MID AUTUMN

Mushrooms

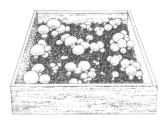

M ushroom is a term used to describe several edible fungi. The familiar button or white mushroom is a close relative of the wild mushrooms that grow in pastureland and open woods in autumn and spring. It is the one most commonly cultivated, although there are several other species that are readily available to buy, particularly the chestnut, oyster and shiitake types.

Planning the crop

Mushrooms can be grown in the garden. They require a shady corner of the lawn that has been enriched with very well-decayed manure or compost, yet contains no fungicides or weedkillers.

The chief disadvantage of such a site is that cropping is rather uncertain and of limited duration, and it will not be possible to cut the grass once the mushrooms start to appear.

Indoors, mushrooms may be grown in any dimly lit corner of a shed or cellar, where a fairly steady temperature of 10–13°C (50–55°F) is assured. It is necessary first to prepare the compost.

Use fresh, damp, strawy manure if possible. Mix it thoroughly and pile it in a heap to generate heat. After a week, turn the heap over and repeat the process every two or three days until the manure becomes crumbly and has lost its smell. It is then ready for use. Pack it firmly into open boxes or tubs to a depth of 25–30cm (10–12in).

If no manure is available, you can buy ready-mixed mushroom compost from a nursery or a commercial grower.

How much to grow Mushrooms tend to crop in flushes. Large quantities may spring up within a few days, while at other times only a few may appear. Even so, a single box – say, 1m x 60cm (3ft x 2ft) – or one of the mushroom-growing kits, should be sufficient.

Varieties There are several varieties to choose from:
Agaricus bisporus albida The well-known white cap mushroom.
Agaricus bisporus The brown-capped chestnut mushroom.
Oyster mushrooms These belong to the **Pleurotus** genus.
Shiitake mushrooms Sometimes listed as **Lentinus edodes**.

There are many lesser-known mushrooms available to grow from specialist suppliers and it is worth checking the Internet to see the latest varieties on offer.

Growing tips

To grow mushrooms outdoors, choose a warm, damp day between late spring and early autumn and lift small squares of turf about 5cm (2in) thick and at 30cm (12in) spacings. Insert a walnut-size piece of spawn into each hole and replace the turf afterwards.

The best means of raising mushrooms in boxes is to wait until the natural heat of the decaying manure drops to a temperature of 24°C (75°F). When this occurs, insert the small pieces of spawn about 5cm (2in) deep into the compost, allowing 25cm (10in) between each piece.

Water the compost lightly, and within a few days the spawn will start to spread fine threads, or hyphae, throughout the box. The interwoven mat that soon develops is called the mycelium, and is the main part of the fungus. The mushrooms that we harvest and eat are the 'fruiting bodies' of the fungus, which pop up above the soil from time to time.

Ten days after planting, cover the compost with a layer of sterile subsoil to help to maintain the temperature and to prevent loss of moisture. Mushrooms will generally appear about eight to ten weeks after planting, and will continue to do so for three months afterwards.

Mushroom kits

In recent years, kits have become available for growing mushrooms, and this is probably the easiest way of raising a crop at home. The white cap and chestnut mushroom kit generally comprises a box or bucket of sterilised, straw-based compost, a bag of a soil-like material ('casing'), and the

STAGES IN GROWING MUSHROOMS

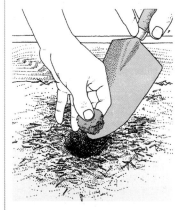

Planting the spawn Insert the pieces of spawn 5cm (2in) deep when the compost temperature falls to 24°C (75°F)

Covering with soil Use subsoil, dug from 30cm (12in) below ground, to cover the compost ten days after planting the spawn.

Ready to eat Pearl oyster mushrooms can be grown from a mushroom log kit, such as this poplar. They also grow on birch, willow, beech and sycamore, preferring still-rooted stumps.

appropriate amount of mushroom spawn. Other kits are available for growing winter varieties of mushroom. These come in self-contained bags or pots that can be left outdoors in a shady spot and will withstand frosts.

AT-A-GLANCE TIMETABLE

• **Outdoor mushrooms**

PLANTING SPAWN
LATE SPRING–EARLY AUTUMN
Place under small squares of turf 5cm (2in) deep and 30cm (12in) apart

HARVESTING
From 8 weeks after planting, for up to three months

Oyster, shiitake, chicken-of-the-woods and some other, more-unusual mushrooms, such as lion's mane, can be raised on logs. You can buy logs that have already been inoculated with the fungus. All you have to do is simply place them in a shady spot in the garden and wait for the mushrooms to sprout. Suppliers also sell 'plugs' or 'dowels' of spawn and special wax for sealing them in the log. You can use your own log, either a cut log of about 30cm (12in) diameter and about 60cm (2ft) high, or one that is still rooted in the ground. The species of tree that you can use depends on the type of mushroom you wish to grow, and the packs provide instructions.

After drilling holes into the log, the spawn plugs are pushed in and the hole is sealed with wax. The crop of mushrooms will usually appear around 12 to 18 months later, depending on the species.

Pests and diseases

The larvae of various species of mushroom fly may tunnel into the stalks and caps, rendering the plants inedible. A variety of

mushroom diseases may occur; contact your local garden centre or supplier for specific advice.

Harvesting and storing

Mushrooms taste best if cooked and eaten immediately after picking. They will store for a few days in the salad compartment of the refrigerator, but should be used as soon as possible. If you want button mushrooms – which can be eaten raw – pick them before the membrane between the cap and stalk separates to reveal the gills.

See also drying (page 300); freezing (page 252); pickling (page 285) and sauces, ketchups and relishes (page 296).

Preparing and cooking

Mushrooms are a versatile ingredient and kitchen staple. Just a few mushrooms can add a special touch to the most ordinary dish. They are delicious on their own sautéed in butter and served on toast. Serve them grilled or fried with breakfast bacon, sausages or kidneys, fold them into an omelette, or use as a savoury topping to scrambled eggs.

Add chopped, lightly fried mushrooms to a white sauce and serve with grilled fish or left-over chicken, or fold them into a brown sauce to go with roast lamb or beef, chops or steaks. Alternatively, blend chopped, sautéd mushrooms into forcemeat stuffing for a roasting chicken or crown of lamb.

Finely chopped mushrooms blended into softened butter make an attractive garnish to steaks and chops – as an alternative to grilled mushrooms – and to plain omelettes. They may also be used to enrich and flavour white sauces.

Prepare mushrooms for cooking, salads or garnishing by trimming away the dirty base of the stalks. Do not peel unless the edges are ragged or discoloured. Although mushrooms may be cleaned in cold water, less loss of flavour occurs if they are simply wiped with a clean cloth dipped in milk.

For grilling, mushrooms may be left whole and brushed with melted butter or oil. Grill under a moderate heat for 6–8 minutes, turning them once.

Fry small whole or sliced mushrooms in butter over a gentle heat for 3–5 minutes, and use them as a garnish. When frying large mushrooms, either quarter them or cut them into narrow slices.

Today the more exotic species of mushrooms are becoming increasingly popular. Chestnut mushrooms can be used in much the same way as field or button mushrooms, but they have a much more intense flavour. Use them in stews and risottos to add flavour.

Shiitake and oyster mushrooms are a main ingredient of Chinese

stir-fries. Their rich and meaty flavour also works well in stews and vegetarian dishes.

Mushroom risotto

This Italian dish is a mushroom-lover's delight. Try substituting different varieties to enjoy subtle variations in texture and flavour.

Soak some dried porcini mushrooms, about 15g (½oz), in warm water. Once plumped up, slice the mushrooms and retain the liquid. Gently fry a finely chopped onion and 2 finely chopped garlic cloves in a little olive oil. When softened, add 500g (1lb) sliced fresh mushrooms with the porcini mushrooms and cook for 5 minutes. Stir in 375g (12oz) Arborio rice with the reserved liquid from the porcinis. Cook gently until the liquid has been absorbed and then gradually add 1 litre (1¾ pints) vegetable stock. Stir well as you add the stock a little at a time,

Mushroom medley There is a great variety of exotic mushrooms on the market for growing at home, so you can have your own constant supply.

until the dish has a creamy consistency and the rice is cooked. Season with salt and black pepper to taste and serve with a sprinkling of freshly grated Parmesan cheese.

Mixed mushroom pasta

Cook 350g (12oz) tagliatelle or other type of pasta in plenty of boiling water. Meanwhile gently fry a small, thinly sliced onion in a little butter until softened. Add 25g (1oz) pine nuts and cook for about a minute until golden.

Next add a selection of sliced mushrooms to the pan, such as 100g (4oz) shiitake, 100g (4oz) oyster and 100g (4oz) brown-capped mushrooms. Fry for 2 minutes, then stir in 50g (2oz) chopped sun-dried tomatoes, a tablespoon of lemon juice and a tablespoon of chopped fresh basil.

Drain the pasta and then add the mushroom mixture to it, mixing together well.

AT-A-GLANCE TIMETABLE

- **Indoor mushrooms**

PLANTING SPAWN
ALL YEAR ROUND
Subject to suitable temperature

COVERING COMPOST
Ten days after planting

HARVESTING
From eight weeks after planting for three months

Nuts

Several species of nut-bearing trees grow in Britain, but they tend to be too large for most gardens, or produce only minimal crops. The hazel, on the other hand, is relatively neat and reliably delivers an abundant harvest of nuts.

Hazel is the name given to trees of the genus *Corylus*, which includes cobnuts and filberts. The only differences between them are small variations in the shape and size of the nuts, and slight subtleties of flavour.

Even when grown as a bush, a hazel occupies a good deal of space; but if you have the room it is well worth planting one both for its decorative value in spring,

when the branches are covered with long, pale yellow catkins, and for the protein-rich nuts that ripen in early to late autumn.

Unfortunately, squirrels are just as aware as humans that the nuts are excellent for winter storage. There is no simple defence against them.

Planning the crop
Hazels do equally well in open sun or partial shade; but grow them, if possible, in a position that is sheltered from the north and east winds. Any well-drained soil is suitable, including chalky soils.

How many to grow Even if pruned into bush form, a mature hazel stands 1.8m (6ft) high and has a spread of 3.5m (12ft). Unless your garden is considerably larger than average, a single bush should

be enough. Where space is scarce, a well-pruned hazel makes an attractive specimen tree in a lawn.

Varieties Somewhat confusingly, it is cobnuts that are most generally known as hazels, while one variety of filbert is called a Kentish Cob.
Cosford (cobnut) Produces large, smooth, oval nuts in small husks; plenty of spring catkins; a good pollinator.
Kentish Cob (filbert) The large, long nuts have a good flavour; crops heavily when interplanted with a suitable pollinator, such as 'Pearson's Prolific'.
Red Filbert (filbert) One of the best-flavoured varieties; its small, narrow nuts are cased in reddish husks; a poor catkin producer and needs a pollinator to crop heavily.
White Filbert (filbert) Similar to 'Red Filbert', but lacking the red skin and with distinctive, pale green foliage.

Growing tips
A bush is the best form in which to grow a nut tree in the average-sized garden. Its main stem will have been pruned to 45cm (18in) at the nursery.

AT-A-GLANCE TIMETABLE
PLANTING
AUTUMN
PRUNING
First four or five years:
NOVEMBER
Subsequent years:
SPRING
HARVESTING
AUTUMN

Plant the young bush in autumn. After planting, and for three or four subsequent autumns, reduce the previous season's wood by half, cutting back to an outward-pointing bud. This will help to build up the bush.

Cobnuts and filberts are self-fertile. Pollen from the male catkins, which are borne on twigs grown in the previous season, is blown on to the tiny female flowers, which grow on shoots formed the previous year. To ensure that this fertilisation takes place, pruning of bushes that have begun flowering – generally when they are four or five years old – should be left until spring.

Cut back any shoots that have borne fruit during the previous season to two or three buds; this will help to encourage renewed growth. In late summer, cut out entirely all strong growth at the centre of the bush. Remove all suckers at their point of origin.

Mulch the bush with well-rotted compost or farmyard manure in autumn or spring.

Pests and diseases
Hazelnuts are subject to attack by nut weevil, and to damage caused by a number of caterpillars, including those of the winter moth.
Honey fungus (page 244) is the principal disease.

Harvesting and storing
Pick the nuts when they have turned brown. Put them in a warm place for a few days to dry out, then store them in containers in a cool place.

Preparing and cooking
These small, sweet-tasting nuts are a traditional feature of the Christmas fruit basket. They are apt to dry out in their shells, but you can prevent this by packing them in layers of salt and storing them in air-tight jars.

A nutty gift Hazelnuts can be made into deliciously sweet truffles, laced with coffee, cocoa and rum. They make a thoughtful and welcome homemade gift, especially at Christmas.

Hazelnuts are used as a garnish, and also in making confectionery. They are also a common ingredient of cakes and biscuits.

The shelled nuts can be used with their brown skins intact, but for confectionery purposes the brown skins should be removed. This is done by spreading the nuts over a grill pan and leaving them for a few minutes under a moderate heat. When the skins begin to split, remove the nuts from the heat. Once the nuts have cooled, rub off the papery skins.

Hazelnut truffles

Take 50g (2oz) of shelled hazelnuts and remove the skins. Beat 50g (2oz) unsalted butter until it is soft and work in 100g (4oz) porridge oats, 100g (4oz) caster sugar and 2 or 3 tablespoons of cocoa powder until well blended. Add a few drops of rum essence and enough black coffee to bind the mixture without making it too sticky (you'll need about 3–4 tablespoons). Leave the mixture to firm slightly then take small pieces and shape into balls between the palms of your hands. Set one hazelnut on top and press down. Alternatively chop the hazelnuts and use them to coat the balls. The truffles can be stored in an air-tight container in the fridge for a few days.

Other nuts

The other well-known nut-bearing trees are less widely grown domestically than the hazel due to problems with small crops or because the mature trees are too large to grow comfortably in most gardens. But if you are keen on a particular type of nut, you may wish to persevere.

Gardeners often have trouble harvesting **almonds** from an ornamental *Prunus* tree. This is because the tree originates from the warm climate of the Middle East. In Britain frost may damage the blossom or cool weather in summer may prevent the formation of sweet, edible nuts. You may be successful if you fan-train a young tree against a warm south-facing wall, in a similar way to the apricot (page 75), but you are unlikely to ever have a bumper harvest.

The same is true of seed-raised **walnuts** (*Juglans*), the main reason being the length of time before you can hope to harvest your first crop – you are likely to need to wait at least 15 years from planting. Another disadvantage is the massive size of the mature tree. If you want to grow a walnut, choose a cultivar specially bred for early cropping, such as **Broadview**.

Sweet chestnuts (*Castanea*) are really only suitable for the largest gardens. The chestnut normally grown in Britain is the Spanish chestnut (*C. sativa*), which prefers a fertile, slightly acid soil and makes a very large tree in time. The variety **Marron de Lyon** is the one usually grown for its nuts.

Winter warmer If you have a sweet chestnut tree you will be able to enjoy a seasonal treat of roast chestnuts. Place them under a grill until their skins split.

Olives

Unripe olives

Ripe olives

The olive (*Olea Europaea*) is a small tree native to the coastal Mediterranean region. The recent shift towards warmer average temperatures in Britain means that it is now possible to keep olive trees outdoors all year round, although in cooler areas they may do better in large pots as summer patio plants and taken into a cool greenhouse or conservatory for winter. By and large, an olive tree will survive the average British winter, providing the temperature does not drop below –10°C (14°F).

The olive is an attractive tree, with silver, elliptical leaves and small, whitish, fragrant flowers. In its native environment, it is very long lived, and old trees have a picturesque, gnarled appearance.

Once established, the olive is drought-resistant and tolerant of poor, infertile soils, but if you want it to produce good fruit, you need to give it the same care as any other fruit tree.

With the increasing interest in Mediterranean food and garden design has come a demand for home-grown olives, and while you are unlikely to produce an enormous crop, there is something very satisfying about picking olives off your own tree.

Planning the crop

Olives need a warm, sheltered situation in full sun. However, they will usually only produce flowers when at least two months during the year have average temperatures below 10°C (50°F). They also need a 12 to 15 week period during which temperatures fluctuate between day and night. This means that olives can be grown reasonably successfully in the open garden in many parts of the UK, but in colder areas they are best grown in large pots or tubs, and in very cold places they will need the year-round protection of an unheated greenhouse.

To set fruit, a warm summer is necessary, so in many years your olive tree may have little more than ornamental value.

You can buy young olive trees and bushes from many nurseries and garden centres, or by mail order, and via the internet. The trees don't begin fruiting until they are about six years old, so the larger the specimen, the sooner it will produce fruit.

Olive trees are invariably container grown, so may be planted at any time of the year when weather conditions are suitable. It's best to plant in spring, however, so as to allow the tree to become established before the cold weather sets in.

Olive trees are often sold as topiary specimens. However, the hard pruning and clipping involved in shaping the tree produces unproductive shoots, which means that topiary specimens will not be much good for fruit production.

A semi-mature tree grown in the ground will have quite a large spread, and this should be taken into account when deciding where to plant. Restricting the roots by growing in a pot will slow down growth, and will also encourage flower and fruit production, given the right conditions. Positioning the pot on paving near a sunny wall also helps to ripen the fruit.

How many to grow Cropping is still uncertain in this country, and home-grown olives are still very much a novelty. Furthermore, young olive trees are expensive, so your budget might govern how many to grow. It's a good idea to start with just one or two trees or bushes. You can always buy more if they are a tremendous success.

Varieties Although there are specific varieties of olive trees in commercial cultivation, you are unlikely to find anything other than the European olive species, **Olea Europaea** offered for sale in Britain.

Growing tips

If you are planting in the ground, prepare the site in the previous autumn by thorough digging, adding plenty of farmyard manure,

---

AT-A-GLANCE TIMETABLE

PLANTING

SPRING

Container-grown bushes and trees can be planted year round, but do best if put in the ground in spring

---

TRAINING

As branches grow longer, weight them down or tie to main trunk instead of pruning

---

HARVESTING

LATE AUTUMN–WINTER

If you wish to preserve your own olives, wait until they turn purple before picking garden compost or other organic material, and work in coarse bone meal at the rate of 120 to 180g per square metre (4–6oz per square yard).

Olives prefer a limey soil, so a top dressing of garden lime, according to the degree of acidity, should be given to soils with a pH value of less than 6.5.

In spring, dig a large hole to accommodate the rootball and fill with water; then water the olive tree thoroughly. When the water has drained from the hole, plant the tree firmly. The trunk or stem should be staked up to the crown (see photograph) to keep it straight and prevent wind rock. Keep the tree well-watered, adding a liquid feed once a week, until it is established. Top-dress with a slow-release, balanced fertiliser every year in spring.

Growing in a pot If you choose to grow the tree in a large pot, fill it with John Innes No. 3 Compost. Each year in spring, remove the top few centimetres of compost and replace with new. Regular liquid feeding, from spring to late summer, is essential for pot-grown olive trees if they are to produce fruit regularly.

Pruning and training
Rather than cutting back the branches, which will reduce any crop, they can be weighted down or bent over and tied into the main trunk. This technique, known as festooning, will encourage more regular and heavier cropping, as well as controlling the spread of the head.

Pests and diseases
An olive tree growing in good conditions is rarely troubled with pests and diseases. Pot-grown olives may sometimes be attacked by scale insects (page 241).

Sometimes a disease called verticillium wilt can affect olive trees – so it's worth checking with your supplier that the tree you are buying has been grafted on to a verticillium-resistant rootstock.

Harvesting and storing
Commercially grown olives can either be harvested in early autumn, while still green, or left on the tree until winter to turn purple. The green fruit has to undergo a chemical treatment process to remove the worst of the bitterness before being bottled in brine.

The olives turn purple when fully ripe; these don't need treating with chemicals and can be home pickled in brine to give you black olives.

Preparing and using
Preserving your own olives is a laborious process, and success cannot be guaranteed as home pickling is an imprecise science.

Italian classic Ripe, black olives add a delicious salty tang to a simple cheese and tomato pizza.

If you want to have a go, then first thoroughly wash your ripe, purple olives. Put them in a bowl of cold water – weighing them down to keep them submerged. Rinse the olives and change the water every day for ten days.

Now comes the brine process. You need to use non-iodised salt at a rate of about a cupful to every 4 litres of water. Submerge the olives in the brine and renew the solution every week for four weeks. Thereafter, use a half strength brine solution, again replacing it every week until the olives are edible – you'll only discover that by tasting them, but don't try to rush it: this process can easily take as long as three months.

Store the olives in the weaker brine in a cool, dark place and keep them covered; don't worry about the scum that forms on the top of the brine. Scoop it off and discard any olives that have gone soft. A good olive is firm and unspoiled.

Olives can be eaten on their own as an accompaniment to drinks – classically a chilled fino or Manzanilla sherry, or added to numerous salads and cooked dishes. You can make a simple spread, called tapenade, for melba toast or thinly sliced ciabatta, baked until crisp in the oven. Using a mini food processor or pestle and mortar, blend stoned black olives with anchovy fillets, extra virgin oil and some ground black pepper and garlic if liked.

Arrange olives on a pizza before baking or add a handful to a chicken bake or a simple tomato sauce for pasta for extra bite.

A natural spread Although olive trees are often clipped into topiary balls, they will only fruit if allowed to grow to their natural shape.

Onions

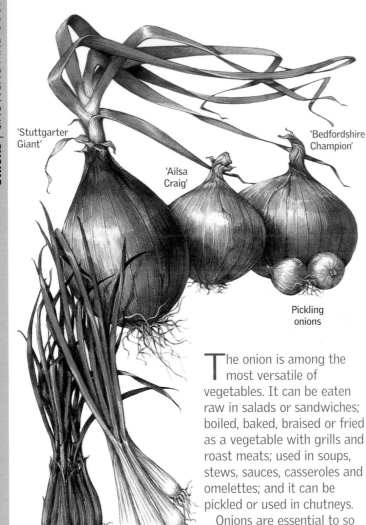

'Stuttgarter Giant'

'Ailsa Craig'

'Bedfordshire Champion'

Pickling onions

Welsh onions   Spring onions

The onion is among the most versatile of vegetables. It can be eaten raw in salads or sandwiches; boiled, baked, braised or fried as a vegetable with grills and roast meats; used in soups, stews, sauces, casseroles and omelettes; and it can be pickled or used in chutneys.

Onions are essential to so many recipes that the gardener faces a challenge in trying to keep up with all the demands from the kitchen. However, most of these may be met by careful planning, and by planting the right varieties of onions at the right time.

Apart from onions grown specially for salads and pickling, there are four groups grown from seed:

Japanese varieties Sow these in late summer in their permanent bed for harvesting the following midsummer.

Early autumn-sown varieties
The bulbs are larger than those of the Japanese varieties. Sow the seeds in early autumn, transplant the seedlings to their permanent bed in spring, and pull and store the bulbs in the second half of summer.

Winter-sown varieties
Germinate under glass and transplant to the permanent bed in spring for an autumn crop.

Spring-sown varieties Sow directly in the permanent bed for harvesting in autumn. They will keep well into the following spring.

In addition to onions grown from seed, onion sets – immature

AT-A-GLANCE TIMETABLE

• **Japanese onions**
SOWING
LATE SUMMER
1cm (½in) deep in drills
40cm (15in) apart

THINNING
SPRING
5cm (2in) apart

BENDING
Bend leaves when they turn yellow

HARVESTING
EARLY-MIDSUMMER

bulbs ripened during the previous summer – may be planted in spring to produce an autumn crop to ripen at the same time as the winter-sown varieties. Onion sets are sold by seed merchants and garden centres. Sets of Japanese onions are also available, which are planted about six weeks later than the seed is sown.

Planning the crop
Onions need a site in full sun, and do best on a light, deep loam. Maincrop onions require soil that has been well manured. Dig the plot deeply in autumn, even as early as mid September, and work in two buckets of well-rotted manure or compost per square metre (square yard).

Spring onions, pickling onions and Welsh onions will grow satisfactorily on any fertile, well-drained soil.

Onions of all types grow best in firm ground, so prepare the bed well in advance to give it a chance to settle.

In late winter apply a dressing of 120g of bonemeal and 60g of sulphate of potash per square metre (4oz and 2oz per square yard). Alternatively, rake in 90g (3oz) of general fertiliser before sowing or planting.

How many to grow A 9m x 1m (30ft x 3ft) bed should produce about 100 onions weighing at least 12kg (25lb); but with good feeding and care the yield may be twice as great. This applies to both onions grown from seeds and those grown from sets.

If sown in succession, rows of spring onions only a few feet long should keep the family supplied. The number of pickling onions to

grow is very much a matter of taste. A 3m (10ft) row will yield 100–150 small onions.

Varieties The gardener is spoilt for choice when it comes to varieties of onions. A selection of recommended varieties follow, but it is always worth checking the latest seed catalogues for new

Planting onion sets In spring plant onion sets outside in rows at intervals of 15cm (6in). Where mice are a problem, start them off in pots and plant them out when they are bigger.

varieties, and also for onion sets. The first four groups, comprising maincrop onions, are described in the order that the bulbs will ripen.

Japanese varieties:
Express Yellow Dark yellow skin; quicker maturing than 'Kaizuka'.
Kaizuka Extra Early Flat, pale yellow bulbs.

For late-summer sowing:
F1 Hygro High yielding; globe shaped; good keeper.
Ailsa Craig large, globe-shaped bulbs; mild flavour.

For winter sowing under glass:
Kelsae One of the largest varieties; golden and globe shaped; good for showing.

For spring sowing:
Bedfordshire Champion Large, globe shaped; heavy cropper; good keeper.
Ailsa Craig An old favourite, reliable to grow but its keeping qualities are not as good as some other varieties.

Red Baron A popular red onion, but can run to seed in some seasons.

Spring onions:
White Lisbon Quick growing; mild flavour.

Pickling onions:
Paris Silver Skin Very quick growing; early ripening.

Growing tips

It is important to choose a sowing date and method of cultivation suited to the particular type of onion you are growing.

Japanese varieties Sow in early autumn in drills 1cm (½in) deep, with the rows 40cm (15in) apart, in the prepared permanent bed.

Do not transplant, but in the spring thin to 5cm (2in) apart. Water in dry spells, and hoe frequently to keep down the weeds until the bulbs are ready for pulling in early to midsummer. Use them to fill the period before maincrop varieties ripen.

Early autumn sowing (maincrop) Prepare a seedbed on well-drained soil that has been raked to a fine tilth. Sow the seeds fairly thickly in drills 1cm (½in) deep and 25cm (9in) apart.

Early the following spring, as soon as the soil can be worked easily, transplant the seedlings to the prepared permanent bed. The bed must be firm, and on light soils it is helpful to tread it before raking, or to firm it with a roller.

Use a trowel to plant the seedlings, leaving about 1cm (½in) of white stem covered with soil. Space the seedlings 15cm (6in) apart in rows 30cm (12in) apart.

Keep the plants watered, and hoe regularly between the rows. Hand-weed between the onions in the rows.

Winter sowing (maincrop)
Sow in trays or pots of seed compost. Firm the compost level 1cm (½in) from the top of the container. Dust the surface with lime to make the seeds easier to see, and sow them at 2.5cm (1in)

spacings. Press each seed just under the surface with the point of a pencil, or tap the side of the tray so that the seeds settle into the compost. Sift a little compost over them and water through the fine rose of a can, or with a sprayer.

Cover with glass, then a folded sheet of newspaper, and place in a cold greenhouse, a coldframe or under cloches.

Alternatively, place uncovered in an unheated propagator. Remove the newspaper as soon as the seeds germinate, and take off the glass or remove the propagator cover before the seedlings reach it.

Harden off the seedlings in early spring and plant out 2–4 weeks later. Treat them in the same way as autumn-sown seedlings.

Early spring sowing (maincrop) Sow the seeds directly into the prepared permanent bed in early spring, or as soon as the soil can be raked to a fine tilth. Sow 1cm (½in) deep in drills 30cm (12in) apart.

When the seedlings are 5cm (2in) high, thin them to 2.5cm (1in) apart. When they are 10–15 cm (4–6in) high, thin them again to 10cm (4in) apart. Use the thinnings in salads. Lift the bulbs in autumn for storing.

Onion sets Plant the sets in the prepared permanent bed in early to mid spring, or late autumn for Japanese varieties. Make drills about 2cm (¾in) deep and 30cm (12in) apart. Space the bulbs 15cm (6in) apart in the drills, and cover with soil so that only the tips are showing.

Firm the soil and cover the bed with netting to prevent birds from lifting them out. Check frequently

and replace any bulbs that have been forced out of the soil as the roots grow. Cultivate as for early autumn-sown onions.

Spring or salad onions
Thinnings of maincrop onions can be used when they are about 10–15cm (4–6in) high for salads, but for a regular supply it is better to grow the mild, quick-growing variety called 'White Lisbon', or a similar, non-bulbing salad variety.

Sow the seeds thinly in a 1cm (½in) drill in autumn for the first crop to be pulled during spring. In late winter, a second sowing can be made in a coldframe or under cloches for pulling in midsummer. There is no need to thin the crop.

Further sowings can be made at four-weekly intervals from early spring to the second half of summer to provide a constant supply through summer and into autumn.

Pull the onions when they are about 15cm (6in) high. Any left-overs that start to form bulbs can be left for pickling.

Onions for pickling Unlike maincrop onions, pickling onions do best on light soil that has not recently been manured, as it is necessary to keep them small. If the soil is very fertile, sow the seeds more thickly than usual.

Sow the seeds in spring in a bed raked to a fine tilth. Either scatter the seeds, or sow them 1cm (½in) deep in drills 15–20cm (6–8in) apart.

Little thinning is necessary, provided the plants have space to form small bulbs, and the crop will be ready for pulling in the second half of summer.

AT-A-GLANCE TIMETABLE FOR MAINCROP ONIONS

SOWING
EARLY AUTUMN
1cm (½in) deep in drills 25cm (9in) apart
WINTER
In pots, 2.5cm (1in) apart
EARLY SPRING
1cm (½in) deep in drills 30cm (12in) apart

THINNING
• Early autumn sowing
No thinning
• Winter sowing
No thinning

• Spring sowing
When 5cm (2in) high

TRANSPLANTING
15cm (6in) apart
• Early autumn sowing
EARLY SPRING
• Winter sowing
MID SPRING
• Spring sowing
No transplanting

BENDING
• Early autumn sowing
Bend leaves when yellow

• Winter sowing
Bend leaves when they turn yellow
• Spring sowing
Bend leaves when they turn yellow

LOOSENING
Two weeks after bending the leaves, loosen plants with a fork

HARVESTING
The onions can be lifted two weeks after loosening

Welsh onions These hardy, non-bulbous perennials are also known as ciboules or green onions. They grow to a height of 30cm (12in) and resemble multistemmed salad onions.

The pencil-thick shoots grow together in close tufts. The shoots are used as salad onions, and the leaves in the same way as chives (see page 120).

Prepare the ground as for maincrop onions and sow throughout spring where the plants are to mature, thinning to give 25cm (10in) spacings between the plants. Lift and divide the clumps every three years.

Pests and diseases

Pests which may attack plants of the onion family include **onion eelworms** and **onion flies**.

Diseases include **downy mildew**, **neck rot** and **white rot** (see Pests and Diseases, pages 238–49).

Harvesting and storing maincrop onions

When the outer leaves begin to turn yellow, bend over the tops to encourage early ripening. Two weeks later, push a fork under the bulbs to loosen the roots.

After another fortnight – or sooner if the weather is particularly wet and the onions show any sign of splitting – lift the bulbs and spread them out in a greenhouse or shed to ripen fully. This will take some days – or even weeks with large bulbs. Complete the ripening in a cool, dry place.

At all stages handle bulbs carefully to avoid the risk of bruising, as this will encourage diseases. Do not trim off the withered tops at this stage, as they will be needed if you string the onions.

To store, secure the onions one above the other to a length of rope or strong string and hang them in a

cool, dry place. Alternatively, hang them in bags of nylon or string netting.

Preparing and cooking

Onions have been used as a flavouring in cooking since earliest times, being gathered in the wild long before the development of the first kitchen gardens. Today's ploughman's lunch is simply a version of the farm worker's traditional midday meal, which consisted of a hunk of coarse bread, a couple of onions and a mug of weak ale – plus a lump of cheese when times were good.

As a flavouring, onion is invaluable in stocks and soups, casseroles and sauces. Shallow or deep-fried, it makes an edible garnish; raw and finely chopped, it adds a crunchy texture and flavour to tomato and green salads and to sandwich fillings.

Onions are also excellent as an accompanying vegetable, either boiled and served in a white or cheese sauce, or glazed and sprinkled with parsley. They may be served as a first course – stuffed or baked – or used in flans and pies they make excellent main courses.

To prepare onions for cooking, cut off the upper part with the stalk attached. Trim off the roots, but do not remove the root base entirely as this holds the onion together, making slicing and chopping easier; some cooks say that keeping it on while you chop also reduces the stinging vapours given off. Peel off the dry, outer layers of skin.

To slice an onion, lay it on its side and make a series of close cuts, starting at the neck end. Discard the root end when the onion has been sliced.

For chopping, cut the onion into halves, from neck to root base, then cut each half into thin vertical slices. Finish each cut just short of the root base, so that the onion does not disintegrate. Place the sliced halves cut sides down and cut across the previous cuts.

To dice an onion or chop it finely, cut a third time across the two sets of cuts made previously.

Clean salad onions by trimming the green stalks to just above the white part, trimming off the roots and peeling off the thin, outer layer.

It is advisable to keep a special chopping board for onions, as the pungent flavour may otherwise be passed on to other foods.

Onion sauce

Peel and finely chop one large onion. Fry in 1½ tablespoons of butter over a gentle heat until soft but not coloured. Blend in 2 tablespoons of flour; cook for a few minutes, then blend in 300ml (½ pint) milk, stirring continuously. Keep stirring until the sauce thickens and is free of lumps. Season to taste with salt and black pepper and simmer gently for 5 minutes. The sauce is excellent served with lamb or fried herrings.

Onion quiche

Peel and slice 500g (1lb) onions, Melt 50g (2oz) butter in a pan and add the onions plus a light seasoning of salt and pepper. Cover the pan and leave the onions to 'sweat' over a low heat for about 30 minutes, until they are soft and golden but not brown. Drain and set to one side to cool.

Meanwhile, prepare about 175g (6oz) shortcrust pastry, which you will use to line a 20cm (8in) flan dish. Once rolled and laid over the flan dish, allow the pastry to chill in the fridge.

Now make the filling. Beat 3 eggs and season with salt and pepper. Beat in 3 tablespoons of dry white wine, 300ml (½ pint) soured cream and 1 tablespoon finely chopped basil. Fold the cooled onions into the mixture and spoon into the flan case. Lay 4 bacon rashers over the top and bake for 40 minutes at 200°C (400°F, gas mark 6) until the filling is firm.

Storing onions When they are completely dry, bind the onions to a length of rope for hanging in the kitchen. Start at the base; trim off surplus leaves afterwards.

Oranges and lemons

Orange

Lemon

Grapefruit

In most areas of Britain, citrus fruit trees need winter protection. The exception is the warmer western coastal areas affected by the Gulf Stream, where they may survive outdoors in winter. For this reason, the traditional way of growing citrus fruits in temperate climates is in pots in a warm, sunny, sheltered place on the patio, moving them into a frost-free greenhouse or conservatory when the weather cools down. The bushes will also grow quite happily under glass all year round, but bear in mind that they need good ventilation, even in winter.

Ripening depends more on heat than sunshine. For a good crop, the fruit needs six months after flowering when the night temperature does not drop below 16°C (61°F). This means that you may need some extra night-time heat in autumn.

All citrus fruits are thought to have originated from just three species, those now in cultivation having been developed from them by hybridisation. The original species are native to South-east Asia and the Pacific islands, but commercial cultivation today takes place in tropical and sub-tropical regions across the world, from Florida and California to the Mediterranean coast and southern Brazil.

The fruit has also been cultivated in cooler climates for hundreds of years. The Romans had orangeries in the 1st century AD, and later this fashion moved to more northerly parts of Europe, including the British Isles.

Early orangeries had large windows in the outside walls, but it took until the 19th century to realise that citrus fruit required as much light as possible, and orangeries attached to stately homes had glass roofs added.

The trees grown at that time were large, and took many men to move them in and out of the orangeries at the appropriate times of the year – as it was believed they must have a period outdoors in summer. In fact, an annual spell outdoors is not strictly necessary.

Since the introduction of more manageable and easily cultivated varieties in recent years, growing citrus fruit is now within the reach of any gardener.

Planning the crop

You'll need a frost-free greenhouse or conservatory to house your trees in winter, and if you want to bring them outdoors in summer, a sunny, sheltered patio or terrace.

It's best to buy trees from a specialist supplier, which you can find via the internet or the RHS *Plant Finder*, an annual publication.

How many to grow Growing citrus is fun, and the only limits to the number of trees is the space available and cost, as good trees can be expensive. Young grafted trees are often available at more reasonable prices, but they will take a year or two to bear fruit.

One plant each of a reliable orange, lemon, grapefruit and lime is a good number to start with, as long as there is room, particularly in the conservatory or greenhouse.

Varieties A number of different citrus fruits are available, including lemons, oranges and more unusual crossed varieties.

Lemons A good variety to start with is **Meyer**. This is easy to grow and hardier than most. **Rosso** has attractive red flesh. **Four Seasons** – as its name suggests – produces flowers and fruits all year round.

Crosses Try **Pursia**, a lemon-mandarin cross that produces fruit like lemons, but sweeter. **Bergamot** is an orange-lime cross; its fruits are large and juicy and the peel is used for bergamot oil.

Oranges **St Michael's** produces large, well-flavoured, thin-skinned fruit. **Calamondin** bears small, acid fruits in profusion, which are good for making marmalade. An ornamental, variegated form is available. Look also for clementine, mandarin, tangerine and satsuma.

AT-A-GLANCE TIMETABLE

PLANTING
Citrus bushes are sold in containers and available year round

PRUNING
• **Young bushes**
During growing season
• **Fruit bearers**
Once the bushes begin bearing fruit no pruning is needed

HARVESTING
As the fruits ripen

Grapefruit **Star Ruby** bears sweet fruits with a good flavour.

Growing tips
Plant in large tubs of soil-based compost such as John Innes No. 2. Good ventilation is essential, even in winter, when the minimum temperature should be about 7°C (45°F), although it can drop below this for very short periods. Lime trees are the exception, requiring a minimum temperature of 10–13°C (50–55°F). Shade the greenhouse from late spring to early autumn if it is in full sun, to prevent scorch.

If the tubs are not too heavy, you can move them outdoors once the danger of frost is passed, until autumn, as they will benefit from fresh air. Using sturdy pot stands on casters can help with this, unless you have steps to negotiate.

Flowers and fruits The main flowering period is in spring, although flowers may be produced at other times. The fruits take 12 months to mature, so established bushes will often bear flowers as well as fruits in various stages of development all at the same time. The grapefruit can take up to 17 months to ripen.

The best flavours are produced at higher temperatures, and ripening depends more on heat than sunshine. For a good crop, citrus needs six months after flowering when the night temperature does not drop below 16°C (61°F), so in autumn some additional night-time heat may be necessary.

Feeding and watering
Throughout the growing season, feed at fortnightly intervals with a liquid feed. Specific citrus feeds are

available, but a general liquid fertiliser or a tomato feed without calcium is fine. Remove the top centimetre or two of compost once a year in spring and top-dress with John Innes No. 3 Compost to which a balanced fertiliser containing trace elements, particularly zinc, has been added.

Water regularly; never allow the plants to dry out, or they will drop, first the flowers and fruit and, later, the leaves – although once regular watering is begun again new leaves will grow. Be careful not to overwater in winter.

Pruning
Young citrus bushes should be pruned to form a good shape. Prune during the growing season, first removing any low-growing branches so the bush is growing on a single stem. Next, remove or cut back any shoots higher up that are badly placed or will spoil the shape as the bush matures.

After the bushes have started to bear fruit, no regular pruning is necessary. Sometimes you may feel you should cut back over-vigorous branches, but this can promote the production of 'water shoots' – strong, vertical shoots that can crowd the head of the bush and spoil the shape. A good option in this situation is to try a technique known as 'festooning'. Instead of cutting, this involves looping vigorous, pliable branches over and tying the tips into the main trunk, which will encourage fruiting.

Don't let young bushes set more than four fruits; remove surplus fruitlets. Older plants can be allowed to set as many fruits as the plants can support; they will drop the rest at flowering time or just after.

Pests and diseases
Aphids, **mealybugs**, **scale insects** and **whitefly** may be a problem, especially when the bushes are permanently grown under glass. **Caterpillars** sometimes eat the leaves. **Chlorosis** is a disorder that sometimes affects citrus plants watered regularly with very hard tap water. The leaves may turn yellow or an unhealthy pale green and growth will be stunted. Give an ericaceous plant tonic according to instructions until the leaves start turning a better colour, and switch to watering with rainwater (see Pests and Diseases pages 238–49).

Harvesting and storing
Let the fruits grow as large as possible and change colour before you pick them. They can be used immediately. Ripe fruits can be left on the bushes for several weeks before they start to deteriorate, and this is, in fact, the best way to store them. In a fruit bowl they will soon start to lose their juiciness. Always cut the fruits off with scissors – don't try to pull them off the bush or you may damage the branches.

See also Jams (page 271) and jellies (page 277).

Preparing and cooking
All citrus fruits have a high concentration of vitamin C and calcium and, eaten regularly, can help to boost your immune system and fight off colds and flu. They are great for cooking, adding zest to sweet and savoury dishes and in marinades. Of course, they are also essential in making marmalade, but you are unlikely to be able to harvest a sufficient quantity at home to make a batch.

You can add any citrus fruit to vegetables, salads or meat dishes to give a bit of zing. Lemon goes particularly well with lamb; oranges or grapefruit make a terrific salad when combined with baby spinach leaves, avocado and crispy bacon; and most fish dishes benefit from a good squeeze of fresh lemon or lime juice.

Clementine, mandarin, tangerine and satsuma Delicious eaten raw, these fruits can also be used to make a speedy warm dessert. Peel and slice into thick rings with a sharp knife, sprinkle with a little sugar and warm through under the grill or in the oven. Serve with a spoonful of crème fraîche or creamy Greek yoghurt.

Oranges can be sliced in half, unpeeled, and roasted with duck or goose for the last half hour of cooking time. Serve one half per person, to be scooped out and eaten with the meat.

Acidic citrus juices are used to enhance many foods; the zest, once lifted from the bitter white pith, adds a mouthwatering fragrance to sweet and savoury dishes. Try adding finely grated lemon zest to mayonnaise, or to the skin of a chicken before roasting. Fresh citrus fruit forms the basis for perfect jellies and sorbets, while all citrus fruit has an affinity with butter, eggs and cream – the perfect example being lemon meringue pie.

Parsley

provide leaves through winter into spring. Parsley can also be grown in a pot kept indoors on a windowsill for year-round use.

In the garden, parsley need not take up space in the vegetable plot. Instead, it can form an attractive edging to a path or add a splash of greenery to a flower border.

Parsley had widely different reputations among the ancient Greeks and the Romans. At banquets, the Greeks wore sprigs of parsley on their heads in the belief that it created both gaiety and a good appetite. The Romans, however, planted it on graves. This association with death persisted until the Middle Ages, and people believed that to transplant parsley invited death and crop failure.

Planning the crop
Parsley needs a well-drained, fertile soil in a sunny or partly shaded position. Prepare the soil by working in a moderate dressing of well-rotted compost or manure during the previous winter.

Grow the winter crop in a sheltered, south-facing position.

How much to grow Since parsley is a cut-and-come-again herb, about six plants will give an adequate and constant supply.

Varieties The most widely grown variety is **Champion Moss Curled**, although some chefs believe that the flat-leaved varieties have a better flavour.

P arsley is widely used for garnishing hot and cold dishes and for flavouring sauces and stuffings. It is also an essential component of a bouquet garni.

Although a biennial, parsley is best grown as an annual, since it produces fewer and smaller leaves on the flowering stems in the second year. To ensure a constant supply, make two sowings – one in spring for summer and autumn use, and another in midsummer to

AT-A-GLANCE TIMETABLE

SOWING
5mm (¼in) deep
• Summer crop
SPRING
• Winter crop
SUMMER

THINNING
• Summer crop
Thin first to 7.5cm (3in); later to 25cm (9in)
• Winter crop
Thin first to 7.5cm (3in); later to 25cm (9in)

TRANSPLANTING
25cm (9in) between plants
• Summer crop
MID SPRING (If sown under glass)
• Winter crop
No transplanting

HARVESTING
• Summer crop
EARLY SUMMER–MID AUTUMN
• Winter crop
EARLY WINTER–LATE SPRING

Growing tips
Sow in drills 5mm (¼in) deep where the plants are to grow. The seed is slow to germinate – sometimes taking up to five weeks – so help germination by watering through a fine rose to keep the soil moist until the seedlings appear.

So that you can keep on top of weeds, removing them even before the parsley germinates, you will need to mark the rows by mixing a few lettuce or radish seeds with those of the parsley. The seedlings of these crops will generally appear within a week and you will clearly see the line of your crop. You will

then be able to pull up weeds as they appear on either side.

When the parsley seedlings are large enough to handle, you can remove the marker crop and thin the seedlings to 7.5cm (3in) apart. When they are well established, thin them again to 25cm (9in) spacings.

If the weather in early spring is severe, sow the seeds in a box of seed compost and place in a cold greenhouse, coldframe or cloche. Plant the seedlings outside, 25cm (9in) apart, when the weather warms up.

Provide partial shade for summer-sown seeds and seedlings, keeping the ground moist to encourage germination and growth. In cold districts, cover the summer-sown parsley with cloches to encourage continued growth during winter, or transfer one or two plants to pots for growing indoors.

Pests and diseases
Parsley is occasionally attacked by **aphids** and **carrot flies**.

It is also susceptible to **leaf spot** and to certain **virus diseases** (see Pests and Diseases, pages 238–49).

Harvesting and storing
Cut only one or two sprigs at a time from each plant until the parsley is well established. Cut out all stems that are going to seed, otherwise the plants will not produce new growth.

From midsummer onwards, sprigs of parsley can be cut for drying (page 300) and freezing (page 252).

Preparing and cooking
Parsley is the most commonly used of all British-grown herbs, indispensable in cooking and as a

colourful garnish. Parsley is essential in a bouquet garni and as a flavouring for many soups and stocks. Chopped parsley is added to white sauces, used in omelettes, and is often blended into salad dressings, mayonnaises, stuffings and forcemeats.

Sprinkle fresh, finely chopped parsley over cooked vegetables, cream soups, tomato salads, fricassées of chicken, grilled kidneys, grilled and fried fish – in fact, over almost any type of savoury dish. Sprinkle some finely chopped parsley over the lemon wedges served with fish.

Small new potatoes are often tossed in butter and finely chopped parsley before serving. As an alternative, heat the boiled potatoes in a little butter, add a few tablespoons of white stock and the juice of half a lemon. Serve the potatoes in this sauce, liberally sprinkled with finley chopped parsley.

Whether for use in cooking or as a garnish, parsley should be used absolutely fresh. Wash it carefully under cold running water and shake well to dry. Shorten the stems and, if it is to be kept for even a few hours, stand the parsley in a jar of water.

For garnishing, divide parsley into small sprigs and use fresh, or deep-fry the sprigs in hot oil for a minute and use to garnish fried or grilled fish.

Small wooden chopping bowls with a two-handled, curved blade are excellent for chopping all types of fresh herbs, as are miniature moulis. Large quantities of parsley are best chopped on a board, using a sharp knife, but small amounts are more easily snipped with scissors.

Parsley, Hamburg

Planning the crop
Hamburg parsley grows best in well-drained, fertile soil, preferably enriched with well-rotted manure or compost during the winter before sowing.

How much to grow
This depends on how much you like the root's celeriac-like flavour. About 40 roots can be grown in a 9m (30ft) row to provide the average family with vegetables for around 20 meals.

Growing tips
Sow the seeds in spring in a 5mm (¼in) deep drill, leaving 30cm (12in) between drills if you sow more than one row. Thin the seedlings when they are large enough to handle, leaving them 25cm (9in) apart. Hoe regularly.

Pests and diseases
Hamburg parsley is generally free from pests, but crops are occasionally attacked by parsnip canker (see page 245).

Harvesting and storing
The roots, about 15–18cm (6–7in) long, will be ready to lift and use from mid autumn. They are hardy and may be left in the ground until needed, or they can be lifted and stored in boxes of moist sand for use as required during winter.

Preparing and cooking
The flavour of Hamburg parsley is reminiscent of both kohlrabi and celeriac. On the Continent it is used to give extra flavouring to thick meat and vegetable soups, rather as the English use turnips. Unlike both kohlrabi and turnips, which taste best when pulled young, the roots of Hamburg parsley should be left to mature before being harvested.

Prepare them like other root vegetables, peeling off the skin and trimming the roots and tops. Cut into even chunks and cook in boiling, lightly salted water for about 25 minutes, or until tender. They can also be steamed. Serve tossed in butter and finely chopped parsley, or coat them with a Béchamel or cheese sauce.

Hamburg parsley can also be creamed and made into a purée with butter, cream and eggs and flavoured with paprika.

Alternatively, use Hamburg parsley instead of celeriac or parsnips in the recipes given for these crops. (See page 111 for celeriac and page 176 for parsnips.)

Home-grown parsley Parsley is easy to grow and brings a splash of lush green to the vegetable patch. Its many uses in the kitchen warrant giving it plenty of space in the garden.

Parsley butter
Make grilled and fried fish dishes a little special with this easy-to-make accompaniment. Use a tablespoon of chopped parsley to 100g (4oz) butter. Soften the butter in a bowl using a wooden spoon and then blend in the parsley. Incorporate the herb thoroughly and season to taste with salt, pepper and a few drops of lemon juice. Roll the butter flat between two sheets of greaseproof paper and chill until firm. Use fancy biscuit cutters to cut the butter into shapes.

Parsley dip
Put 100g (4oz) cream cheese into a bowl and stir in a few tablespoons of lukewarm water until smooth and soft. Blend in 1–2 tablespoons chopped parsley and season to taste with Worcestershire sauce, tabasco, lemon juice, salt and pepper. Spoon into its serving bowl and chill for at least an hour.

Serve the dip with cauliflower sprigs, celery, carrot sticks or savoury biscuits. For a variation use chopped chives instead of parsley – or a mixture of the two.

Hamburg, or turnip-rooted, parsley is grown for its roots, which are cooked like parsnips. The tops can be eaten, but they are coarser and not as tasty as those of parsley.

The vegetable provides a welcome change of flavour in winter, either on its own or as an addition to stews and soups.

AT-A-GLANCE TIMETABLE

SOWING
5mm (¼in) deep, in rows 30cm (12in) apart
SPRING

THINNING
25cm (9in) apart, when large enough to handle

HARVESTING
AUTUMN ONWARDS

Parsnips

Long variety

Short-rooting variety

Parsnips have a long growing season. The seeds are sown outside at the beginning of spring, if the weather is favourable, and the roots are not harvested until the following winter. This means that the crop occupies ground for almost a year. But in exchange for the ground they occupy, parsnips demand little attention once the seedlings have been thinned. They are harvested when fresh vegetables are scarce, and are very hardy.

Planning the crop

Parsnips will grow in almost any soil, but they do best in deep, rich, fairly light ground. Choose an open, sunny position and use a bed that has been well manured for a previous crop. Do not use fresh manure, or the parsnips will 'fork', or split up into several roots, rather than making one long, clean root.

When planning where to site your parsnip crop remember that parsnips have a long growing season and will be in place for most of the year. One way to get a little extra out of the parsnip bed is to sow a catch-crop of compact lettuces between the rows when sowing the parsnips. The lettuces mature and are cut before the parsnips need all the space.

Alternatively, sow radish seeds in the drills with the parsnips. They will grow quickly to show the line of the drill for early hoeing, before the parsnips germinate. The radishes will be ready for use when the parsnips are thinned.

How many to grow As the germination of parsnips can be unreliable, the seeds must be sown fairly thickly. About 50 parsnips can be grown in a 9m (30ft) row to provide vegetables for perhaps 25 meals for a family of four.

Varieties Long varieties for good, deep soil include **Improved Hollow Crown** and **Tender and True**. **White Gem** and **F1 Gladiator** are medium varieties. Short-rooting varieties for shallow soil include **Avonresister** and **Offenham**.

Many newer varieties now have good resistance to parsnip canker. Consult seed catalogues for these.

Growing tips

Sow the seeds in early spring as soon as the soil is dry enough and the most severe of the winter weather had passed. First prepare the soil by raking into the surface a general fertiliser at the rate of 60–90g per square metre (2–3oz per square yard).

Make drills 1cm (½in) deep and 40cm (15in) apart. Give the seedlings a preliminary thinning when they are about 2.5cm (1in) high, then continue thinning until they are 15–25cm (6–9in) apart.

Alternatively, sow three or four seeds in groups 40cm (15in) apart, and remove the weakest seedlings.

Hoe regularly between the plants to keep down the weeds.

Pests and diseases

The pests most likely to attack parsnips are **carrot flies** (page 238). The most common disorders are **parsnip canker** (page 245) and **splitting** (page 247).

Harvesting and storing

Parsnips can be used as soon as the leaves die back in autumn, but it is better to wait until sharp frosts improve their flavour. When lifting the roots take care not to damage them with the fork.

Parsnips are best left in the soil until they are needed, but the last of the crop should be dug up in late winter, before the roots start to produce new leaves. Put them in a cool place and cover with soil.

Preparing and cooking

This sweet root vegetable was eaten by our ancestors in the same way as potatoes are today, and did not lose favour until long after the introduction of potatoes. Parsnip was the traditional vegetable with roast beef and boiled cod.

Prepare the roots for cooking by cutting off the tops and the tapering roots. Peel the parsnips thinly and cut lengthways into thick slices. Cut large roots into quarters and take out the woody cores.

Parsnips may be boiled in lightly salted water for about 20–25 minutes, depending on the size, or they may be steamed. They can also be poached in milk.

Parsnips are excellent when roasted, in the same way as potatoes, and served with roast chicken or beef. They are often boiled and mashed and made into a purée with butter and nutmeg, either on their own or mixed with equal amounts of mashed carrots or potatoes.

Parsnips also make a velvety soup that is especially good spiced with a little chilli.

The natural sweetness of parsnips has led them to be used, as a purée, in tarts and cakes.

Parsnip purée

Boil or steam 875g (1¾lb) prepared parsnips until tender. Drain and mash to a purée. Return the purée to the pan and beat in 50g (2oz) butter. Beat in the yolk of an egg and a tablespoon of honey. Season to taste with salt, pepper and cinnamon. The purée is an ideal accompaniment to roast meat and baked ham.

AT-A-GLANCE TIMETABLE

SOWING

EARLY SPRING
1cm (½in) deep, in rows
40cm (15in) apart

THINNING
Thin gradually until
15–25cm (6–9in) apart

HARVESTING
AUTUMN–LATE WINTER

Peaches and nectarines

'Peregrine' (peach)

'Lord Napier' (nectarine)

Peaches have been grown in England since long before the Norman Conquest. The Anglo-Saxons called the peach tree Perseoctreou – the Tree of Persia – a name that is still reflected in its botanic title *Prunus persica*.

Because of their origins, peach trees require mild, sunny conditions to thrive in Britain. They do best when fan trained against a south-facing wall. They are also widely grown in greenhouses.

Planning the crop

Peach trees will thrive only in a sheltered, sunny position. If you do not have a south-facing wall or fence place it against one facing west or south-west. A temporary shelter from winter rain can be erected over a wall-trained tree during winter to control peach leaf curl, the spores of which are carried in winter rain.

In warmer parts in the south, peaches can be grown as bush trees in sunny, sheltered gardens.

Peaches and nectarines do well under glass, but before planting a tree in a large greenhouse you should consider whether the space could be used more economically for short-term crops. In a lean-to greenhouse, a tree can be fan-trained against the back wall and other crops grown in front of it.

Compact varieties, grown on dwarfing rootstocks and often referred to as patio varieties are widely available from larger garden centres and fruit nurseries. These may be grown in large tubs of John Innes No. 3 Compost in a sunny, sheltered spot on a patio or similar.

An advantage of patio plants is that you can easily control peach leaf curl by moving them into a greenhouse or cool conservatory for winter, when the spores are present. They can be outside again the following spring.

Peaches succeed only in well-drained soil. If the soil is heavy, dig a trench 1.8m (6ft) long, 1m (3ft) wide and 1m (3ft) deep along the wall where the tree is to be fan-trained. Place a layer of broken bricks or mortar at the bottom, cover this with chopped turfs, and fill with good-quality loam. Add nitro-chalk to the loam at the rate of 30g to the square metre (1oz to the square yard).

Before planting, secure horizontal wire supports to the wall or fence at 15cm (6in) spacings. Secure the wires with vine eyes, obtainable at garden shops and centres.

Blossom bonus An added benefit of growing a peach tree is the exquisite blossom, produced in profusion in spring.

How many to grow A single tree will provide enough fruit for the average family. Both peaches and nectarines are self-fertile, so you will need only one tree.

Peach varieties For growing outdoors in the south, choose varieties that ripen by early autumn; in the north, plant those that ripen earlier, in late summer.
Duke of York Hardy; large fruits with greenish-white flesh, ripens in late summer.
Peregrine Hardy; crimson fruits with yellowish-white flesh; ripens in late summer.
Rochester Hardy; large, fine-flavoured fruits with yellow flesh; ripens in late summer.
Garden Lady A patio peach for tub cultivation; ripens in late summer.
Bonanza A patio peach with large fruits heavily flushed red. Ripens in late summer.

Nectarine varieties As the nectarine is less hardy than the peach, choose varieties that ripen early outdoors in the south. In the north nectarines must be grown in an unheated greenhouse.
Early Rivers Rich flavoured; pale yellow flesh; ripens in midsummer.
Lord Napier Large, rich-flavoured fruits with pale green flesh; ripens in late summer.
Nectarella Dwarf nectarine, suitable for a patio or balcony or where space is limited; orange-red flesh; ripens in late summer.

Growing tips

Young peach trees are usually sold in containers, so they may be planted at any time if the weather is right. Nonetheless, autumn planting will get them off to the best possible start. Patio varieties may be planted in large tubs at any time. Space fans 3.5–4.5m (12–15ft) apart and bushes 4.5m (15ft) apart.

Dig a hole so that the roots can spread out, and plant to the same depth as the trees grew in the nursery or container. This can be seen by the soil mark on the stem. Set the stem about 25cm (9in) from the wall and incline it slightly.

FAN-TRAINING A YOUNG TREE

Securing the side branches In late winter, before growth begins, cut both the side branches back to 30–45cm (12–18in), making each cut just above a growth bud. Secure the canes to the wires at about 40 degrees and tie the branches to these.

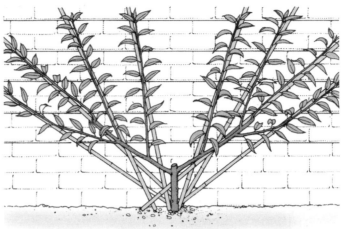

Securing additional shoots During the summer after planting, tie in the shoots that will grow from each end bud. Allow two well-spaced shoots to grow upwards from each branch, and one from the lower side. Tie these to canes and rub out other buds.

In late winter, feed with 30g of sulphate of potash per square metre (1oz per square yard). Every third year add 60g of super-phosphate per square metre (2oz per square yard). Alternatively, use a slow-release balanced fertiliser each year in early spring. Apply 30g of nitro-chalk per square metre (1oz per square yard) in spring, and mulch with well-rotted manure or compost.

Pollination is essential, but often the flowers open before insects are about in sufficient numbers to pollinate them. In years like this and always when growing under glass, you will need to pollinate the plants artificially. Dab each flower with a camel-hair paintbrush at about noon every day during the flowering period.

Protect the flowers against frost by covering the trees with small-mesh netting, but remove this during the day so that pollinating insects can reach the flowers.

Keep the ground moist through the growing season. The ground near a wall dries out quickly, and after a hot day 135 litres (30 gallons) of water may be needed by a mature tree carrying a full crop.

Start thinning the fruits when they are about the size of a marble. Reduce clusters to single fruits, and remove all fruits growing towards a wall and any that do not have room to develop properly. Thin the fruits out to a final spacing of 25cm (9in) when they are about the size of a golf ball. Nectarines should be spaced 15cm (6in) apart.

Growing from a stone Peaches are among the few fruits that can be grown successfully from seed. In autumn, set the stones singly in 13cm (5in) pots of John Innes No. 1 potting compost.

Plant the resultant seedlings in the garden when they are about 15cm (6in) high. In the second winter transplant them to their permanent positions, treating them as you would a grafted tree.

Formative pruning
A two-year-old tree trained at a nursery will have at least two side branches, or ribs. After planting, cut these back to 30–45cm (12–18in), making the cut just above a growth bud. Tie the ribs to canes with soft string and secure the canes to the support wires at an angle of about 40 degrees. During summer, tie shoots from the end buds to the canes.

Select two evenly spaced shoots on the upper side of each branch, and one on the lower, to train on as ribs. Rub out all other shoots. As the selected shoots grow, tie them to canes and space them evenly.

In the following winter prune the leader (last year's summer growth) of each of the eight ribs back to a triple bud, leaving about 60–80cm (2–2½ft) of well-ripened wood. A triple bud is easily recognised because it has one growth bud, which is pointed, accompanied by two blossom buds, which are round. This pruning will stimulate the tree into producing more strong shoots that can be trained on to form additional ribs and so fill the available wall space.

A three-year-old fan tree bought from a nursery will have about the same number of ribs, and should be pruned in the same way after planting.

Pruning a mature tree
Established trees need pruning twice each year: first in spring and summer, and again after the fruit has been harvested.

Spring and summer pruning consists of rubbing out, pinching back and tying in. As growth begins, usually in mid spring, rub out shoots growing outwards or towards the wall.

Last year's laterals, carrying blossom, should have a number of growth buds. Select one or two of these at the base of the laterals to form replacement shoots for the following year. Pinch back all others to one leaf. Leave the leader unpruned at this stage.

In early summer, thin out the many new laterals which will be produced along the extension growth so that the remainder are 10–15cm (4–6in) apart along the upper and lower sides of the ribs. These shoots will become next year's fruiting laterals. Next, pinch back to six leaves the present fruit-carrying laterals, unless they are required as additional framework branches. Pinch back replacement shoots to about ten leaves.

Tie shoots, especially the fruit-carrying laterals, to supporting wires. Carry out the second part of annual training after the fruits have been harvested, from midsummer to mid September. Cut back laterals that have fruited – unless they are wanted as part of the framework to the replacement shoots which are tied in. After this pruning the ribs, radiating out parallel to the wall, should carry shoots spaced out about 10–15cm (4–6in) apart, all tied to the wires.

Pests and diseases
Peaches and nectarines are vulnerble to attack from many pests and diseases. The most likely pests are **aphids**, **caterpillars**, glasshouse **red spider mites** and **scale insects**.

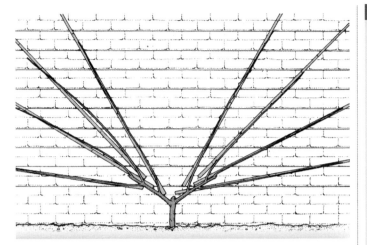

Final shaping of a young tree During the second winter, prune each of the eight branches or ribs back to a triple bud, leaving 60–80cm (2–2½ft) of well-ripened wood. This will encourage more ribs to develop, so providing even growth, and making the most of the wall space covered by the tree.

The principal disorders are **bacterial canker**, **brown rot**, **chlorosis**, **honey fungus**, **peach leaf curl**, **powdery mildew**, **shothole**, **silver leaf** and **split stone** (see Pests and Diseases, pages 238–49).

Harvesting and storing

Peaches and nectarines are ready for picking when the flesh around the stalk yields to gentle pressure from the fingers. Pick the fruits carefully to avoid bruising.

For the many uses to which peaches and nectarines may be put, see also bottling (page 270); chutneys (page 292); drying (page 300); freezing (page 252); fruit cheeses and butters (page 281); jams (page 271); pickles (page 285) and wine-making (page 304).

Preparing and serving

Peaches and nectarines are at their best served fresh as a dessert. They need no peeling. Simply cut them into halves along the indentations of the flesh, then twist the two halves to separate them. Remove the stones – you may need to use a sharp knife.

Peaches and nectarines can also be used fresh in fruit salads, and as a fresh purée, they can form the basis for ice creams and sweet soufflés. Slices of fruit, lightly poached in sugar syrup, are excellent as fillings for pies and flans and go particularly well with raspberries.

For cooked desserts, the fruit should be peeled. To make this easier, dip them first in a bowl of boiling water for 1–2 minutes and then immerse them in cold water. Peel the skins downwards in strips, using a small knife.

AT-A-GLANCE TIMETABLE

- Young tree
PLANTING
MID–LATE AUTUMN

PRUNING
LATE WINTER

- Established tree
TRAINING
MID SPRING

FRUIT THINNING
MIDSUMMER

HARVESTING
LATE SUMMER–MID AUTUMN

PRUNING
LATE SPRING AND
LATE SUMMER–MID AUTUMN

Peach compôte Peel four peaches, cut in half and remove stones. Put 125g (4oz) caster sugar in a pan with 300ml (½ pint) water with the pared rind and juice of one small lime. Slowly bring to the boil so that the sugar dissolves, then add the peach halves, rounded sides down. Poach gently for about 10 minutes until the peaches are tender, but still retain their shape. Lift the peaches out of the syrup and allow to cool. Turn up the heat and boil the syrup rapidly until it has reduced and thickened, be careful not to let it caramelise. Cut the peach halves into segments and chill for at least 2 hours.

Just before serving whisk 150ml (5fl oz) whipping cream until stiff enough to retain its shape. Fold in 2 tablespoons of the cooled syrup and 50g (2oz) crushed macaroons. Spoon a layer of cream into four serving dishes, add the peach slices

TRAINING REPLACEMENT AND FRUITING SHOOTS

Spring Pinch back growth buds on last year's laterals to one leaf – leaving one or two buds at the base. These will provide replacement shoots.

Late spring Pinch back fruit-bearing laterals to six leaves, unless needed as replacements. Pinch back replacement shoots to ten leaves.

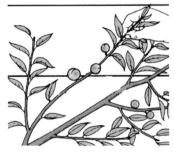

Late spring Thin out new laterals on the upper and lower sides of ribs to 10–15cm (4–6in) apart. These will fruit next year.

After harvesting Cut out fruited laterals, unless needed as part of the framework, to the replacement shoots already tied in.

and then decorate each dish with a swirl of cream. As an alternative you can substitute nectarines for peaches, but they will generally need less poaching time.

Curried peaches This dish makes an unusual accompaniment for roast pork, a meat that goes particularly well with many fruits, not just the traditional apple sauce.

Peel four peaches, cut them in half and remove the stones. Cut the flesh into thin slices and arrange them in a buttered ovenproof dish. Mix 25g (1oz) demerara sugar with a teaspoon of curry powder and sprinkle over the peaches. Dot with flakes of butter – about 15g (½ oz), then bake at 180°C (350°F, gas mark 4) for 15 minutes until the peaches are golden brown.

Pears

Espalier   Dwarf pyramid

P ears, which are native to Europe and western Asia, have been cultivated in Britain since the earliest times. There are hundreds of varieties, though not more than a dozen are generally available from nurseries.

Wherever apples grow, pears will grow too, but they need slightly different conditions and treatment. They need watering more frequently during dry spells, for example, since they are less able than apples to withstand drought.

Few pears are self-fertile, so you will need to buy two different varieties that flower at the same time to allow cross pollination.

Planning the crop

Plant pears in a sunny, sheltered position, preferably in deep, loamy soil that will retain moisture in summer. If the soil is free-draining and sandy, dig two or three buckets of well-rotted farmyard manure or garden compost into the planting area. Before planting, fork in general fertiliser at the rate of 90g per square metre (3oz per square yard).

During subsequent years, in the second half of winter, feed with 30g of sulphate of potash per square metre (1oz per square yard). In early spring apply 30–45g of sulphate of ammonia per square metre (1–1½oz per square yard). Every third year add 45–60g (1½–2oz) of superphosphate to the sulphate of ammonia dressing.

Alternatively, apply an annual top dressing of a slow-release, compound fertiliser according to manufacturer's instructions in early spring.

As most pear trees are not self-fertile, you will need to grow at least two trees. Bush trees will need to be within 3.5–4.5m (12–15ft) of each other; half standards, 4.5–6m (15–20ft); cordons, 80–90cm (2½–3ft); espaliers, 3.5–4.5m (12–15ft); and dwarf pyramids, 1.2–1.5m (4–5ft).

Space permitting, by choosing early, mid-season and late varieties it is possible to have pears from late summer until the New Year.

How many to grow Yields of pears vary each year according to the weather – that is, the incidence of spring frosts and the amount of rainfall. About 1.5–2.5kg (3–5lb) may be expected from an established cordon; 2.5–3kg (5–6lb) from a dwarf pyramid; 10–12kg (20–25lb) from a three-tier espalier, and 18–23kg (40–50lb) from a bush tree. A tree planted when three years old should fruit within two or three years, depending on weather and position.

Varieties All the following are dessert varieties, although any may be cooked if picked while still firm and not completely ripe.

William's Bon Chrétien Generally regarded as the best-flavoured early pear, but keeps only a short time. Pick in late summer to ripen in early autumn. Pollinated by 'Conference'.

Concorde A comparatively new hybrid of 'Conference' and 'Comice' with all the good attributes of both but none of the problems. Pick in late autumn for eating in early winter. Pollinated by 'Winter Nelis' but partly self-fertile.

Conference A regular cropper that is excellent for bottling. Pick the fruits in early autumn for eating in late autumn and early winter. A suitable pollinator is 'William's Bon Chrétien' but it will set a crop of pears without pollination.

Doyenné du Comice This is widely considered the best-flavoured pear; needs a sheltered position with rich soil and regular mulching. Pick in late autumn for eating from the first half of winter; excellent for bottling. Pollinated by 'Winter Nelis'.

Winter Nelis Pick in late autumn to ripen at a temperature of 16°C (61°F) in December. Pollinated by 'Doyenné du Comice'.

Growing tips

A bare-rooted pear tree should be planted between late autumn and early spring, although most specimens are now sold in containers for year-round planting. Nevertheless, planting the tree in November will ensure the best possible start.

Before planting a bush tree, drive a stake at least 60cm (2ft) deep into the soil so that the tree can be tied to it by plastic strap ties. Plant to the same depth as it was in the nursery – as indicated by the soil mark on the stem. Ensure that the union between stock and scion is above soil level. Spread the roots out evenly and firm the soil as it is put back.

During winter, firm any trees that have been lifted by frost. In spring, water the trees during dry weather to help them to become established. Throughout the tree's life, water during dry spells, giving not less than 18 litres per square metre (4 gallons per square yard). Mulch with well-rotted compost or manure.

Pear fruitlets need less thinning than those of apples. In a good year, however, reduce each cluster to one or two fruitlets at the time they begin to turn downwards.

AT-A-GLANCE TIMETABLE

PLANTING
LATE AUTUMN–EARLY SPRING

SUMMER PRUNING
JUST AFTER MIDSUMMER

THINNING FRUIT
As fruits begin to turn downwards

HARVESTING
LATE SUMMER–AUTUMN

WINTER PRUNING
EARLY–LATE WINTER

Pruning and training Prune and train pear trees in the same way as apples (see pages 66–73). Established bush pear trees can, however, be cut back harder than apples, so do not hesitate to remove overcrowded branches, particularly in the centre of the tree, during winter pruning.

Summer pruning of cordons, espaliers and dwarf pyramids is earlier than for apples, starting when the summer growth matures – usually just after midsummer in the south, but later in the north.

As the tree matures it will produce fruiting spurs more freely than apples, and these should be thinned in winter.

Pests and diseases

Among the pests that may attack pear trees are **aphids**, **caterpillars**, **codling moths**, **fruit tree red spider mites**, **pear leaf blister mites** and **tortrix caterpillars**.

The principal diseases and disorders are **boron deficiency**, **brown rot**, **fire blight**, **honey fungus**, **scab**, **splitting** and **stony pit** (see Pests and Diseases, pages 238–49).

Harvesting and storing

Most varieties of pears ripen off the tree. Harvest early varieties, such as 'William's Bon Chrétien', by cutting the stalk when the fruit is mature but still hard. Pick mid-season fruits (for eating in late October or early winter) and late varieties (for use thereafter) when the stalk parts easily from the spur after a gentle twist. Store the fruit in a cool room or shed at a temperature of 2–4°C (36–40°F).

Do not wrap the pears, but lay them on a tray or shelf in a single layer. Make sure the fruits do not touch each other. Check frequently, and when they approach maturity – which is shown by a slight softening of the flesh close to the stalk – bring them into the house for two or three days to finish off the ripening. Pears can be put to many uses.

See also bottling (page 270); chutneys (page 292); drying (page 301); freezing (page 000); fruit cheeses and butters (page 281); jams (page 271); pickles (page 285) and wine-making (page 304).

Preparing and cooking

Dessert pears, which should be just ripe, may be served as a dish on their own, as part of a fresh-fruit salad or as an accompaniment to the cheeseboard. They may also be cooked, preferably poached in a sugar syrup and served chilled with, for example, a chocolate or custard sauce.

Prepare pears for cooking by first peeling them with a stainless-steel knife to prevent discoloration. If they are to stand for any length of time before cooking, brush them with lemon juice to prevent browning.

Pears may be poached whole, first removing the blossom end but leaving the stalk intact and scraping it clean with a knife. Alternatively, cut the peeled pears into halves and use a pointed teaspoon to scoop out the centre cores and the woody filaments running towards the stalk ends.

'Conference'

'Louise Bonne of Jersey'

'William's Bon Chrétien'

'Doyenné du Comice'

'Fertility'

'Joséphine de Malines'

'Winter Nelis'

Peas

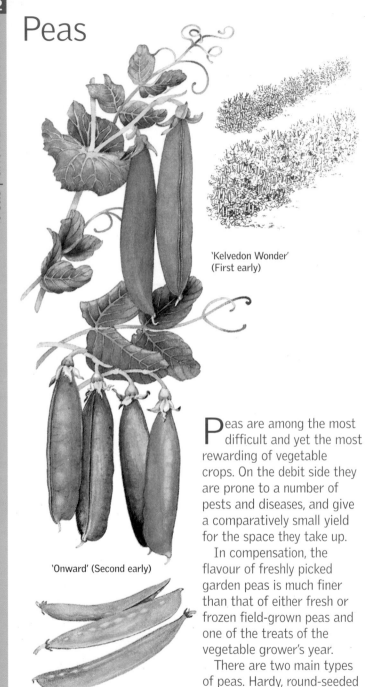

'Kelvedon Wonder'
(First early)

'Onward' (Second early)

Sugar peas, or mangetout

Peas are among the most difficult and yet the most rewarding of vegetable crops. On the debit side they are prone to a number of pests and diseases, and give a comparatively small yield for the space they take up.

In compensation, the flavour of freshly picked garden peas is much finer than that of either fresh or frozen field-grown peas and one of the treats of the vegetable grower's year.

There are two main types of peas. Hardy, round-seeded peas are sown in late autumn and early spring for picking in late summer and early autumn; the wrinkled type, which have a sweeter flavour, can be sown only from spring to the middle of summer for harvesting from June onwards.

There are also sugar peas, known as mangetout, which are grown in the same way as garden peas but are picked before the seeds have fully developed.

Planning the crop

Peas grow best on rich, well-drained soil. Good drainage is particularly important for early varieties, as the seeds will rot in cold, wet soil.

Dig the plot at least three or four weeks before sowing, working in two buckets of compost or well-rotted manure to the square metre (square yard). A week before sowing, rake in a top dressing of a general-purpose fertiliser at 60–90g per square metre (2–3oz per square yard).

In a small kitchen garden it is best to grow only one or two rows of early peas to be harvested with the first carrots, french beans and turnips. As soon as the peas are finished, the ground can be used for growing leeks or cabbages.

On a larger plot, peas can be grown in succession for picking from late spring until well into autumn if the right varieties are sown at the right time.

Depending on the variety, peas grow to heights varying from 45cm (1½ft) to 1.8m (6ft). The ultimate height will affect the type of supports you will need to provide.

Sowing peas Stagger the seeds about 7.5cm (3in) apart in three rows. Sow overwintering varieties closer together to allow for losses.

How much to grow A packet of seed is usually sufficient to sow a row 4.5m (15ft) long, but the yield from this will vary, depending on the height of the plant and the growing conditions.

A row of dwarf early peas, for example, may provide a family of four with enough helpings for only four meals, whereas three times this yield may be expected from a tall, maincrop variety.

Varieties Choose from these recommended varieties of round, wrinkled, early, maincrop and late peas, sugar peas and petit pois.

First-early round-seeded

varieties for sowing in early winter (late autumn in the north) or late winter-early spring include:

Feltham First 45cm (1½ft).
Meteor 45cm (1½ft).
Pilot 1.1m (3½ft).
First-early wrinkled varieties for sowing in early spring.
Kelvedon Wonder 45cm (1½ft).
Little Marvel 45–60cm (1½–2ft).
Early Onward 60cm (2ft).

Second-early wrinkled varieties for sowing in mid spring.
Onward 60cm (2ft).
Hurst Green Shaft 60–80cm (2–2½ft).

Maincrop varieties, for sowing in mid–late spring
Lord Chancellor 1–1.2m (3–4ft).
Gradus 1.2m (4ft)
Alderman 1.5m (5ft).

Late crops for sowing in summer for picking in autumn.
Kelvedon Wonder 45cm (1½ft).
Progress No. 9.

Sugar peas for sowing from early spring to midsummer.
Oregon Sugar Pod 1–1.2m (3–4ft).

Petit pois small-seeded peas for sowing from early spring-mid-summer.
Gullivert 1m (3ft).

Growing tips

If you wish to grow a number of rows of peas, allow 60cm (2ft) between varieties that will reach 45cm (1½ft) high; 1m (3ft) between those reaching 1.2m (4ft) high, and so on.

In a small garden where only one row of peas is to be grown, allow a reasonable distance between peas and the neighbouring crop. Onions, beetroot or lettuces, for example, can be grown successfully on the southerly or

sunny side only 45cm (1½ft) from a row of tall maincrop peas. But about double this space is needed on the shaded side, especially when growing the taller varieties of peas.

Use a swan-neck hoe or onion hoe to draw a flat-bottomed drill 10cm (4in) wide and 4–5cm (1½– 2in) deep. In spring and summer sow seeds 5–7.5cm (2–3in) apart in three staggered rows in the drills.

Sow overwintering varieties more thickly to compensate for losses that can happen in bad weather. Draw the soil over the drills with a rake to level the surface . Protect recently sown seed from birds by covering the rows with netting, or with clusters of twigs. Overwintered crops should be protected with cloches until the following spring.

As soon as the seedlings are through, hoe on each side of the rows to get rid of weeds. When the seedlings are 7.5cm (3in) high, push in small, twiggy sticks to encourage the plants to climb. Do this as soon as the plants are tall enough: plants left to straggle on the ground may be attacked by slugs.

Once the plants are growing strongly, put in the final supports. These can be twiggy branches, wire strung between bamboo stakes, or netting tied to posts, but must be at least as high as the ultimate height of the variety being grown.

Make sure the peas get a constant supply of moisture and mulch the rows with damp leaf-mould, garden compost or other organic material.

Pests and diseases

Aphids, **bean seed flies** and **pea moths** are among the most troublesome pests. Likely diseases and disorders include **damping off**, **foot rot**, **manganese deficiency** and **soil-borne** diseases (see Pests and Diseases, pages 238–49).

Harvesting and storing

When the pods seem to have reached their full length, check daily to feel if the peas are swelling inside. Aim to pick the pods when the seeds are well developed but before they are fully mature.

To harvest your crop, pull the pod upwards with one hand while holding the stem with the other.

Harvest sugar peas, or mangetout, when the pods are about 5cm (2in) long and the seeds only just beginning to develop inside. If insufficient of these small pods are available at a single picking, keep the first gathering in the fridge until you can pick more.

As soon as the plants have been cleared of pods, cut the haulms down to ground level and put them on the compost heap.
See also Freezing, page 252.

SUPPORTING THE PEAS

Short, twiggy sticks These will start the peas climbing, and so discourage slugs and snails, when they are about 7.5cm (3in) high.

Taller canes Later on, provide taller sticks, wires or plastic mesh to suit the height of the variety that is being grown.

Preparing and cooking

Top and tail mangetout peas as for french beans. They are young and tender and so do not require stringing. Wash them in cold water and cook for no more than 5 minutes in boiling, lightly salted water, or steam for a few minutes.

The tiny petit pois, like other garden peas, are shelled from their pods. Do not throw the pods out, as they can be used for vegetable stocks; or, if quite young and fresh, as a vegetable on their own. After shelling, break the pod near the blossom end and pull off the thin waxy covering. Cook the pods in butter for about 10 minutes, or until tender but still crisp.

Petit pois may be boiled in salted water, but they are much tastier if only par-boiled and then finished off in butter, under a cover, and sprinkled with chopped mint. Alternatively they can be steamed.

Shell full-sized peas and steam or cook in boiling, lightly salted water with a sprig of mint, a teaspoon of sugar and a little lemon juice to preserve the fresh green colour. They will need to boil for 15–20 minutes, depending on size. Serve them tossed in butter and sprinkled with mint, parsley, dill or basil.

Use cold, cooked or tiny fresh peas as an ingredient in mixed salads, particularly rice salads. Or arrange buttered peas in grilled or fried mushroom caps and serve as an edible garnish with fish, meat or poultry.

Buttered mangetout

There is nothing quite as delicious as freshly picked mangetout straight from the garden. Top and tail 500g (1lb) of mangetout and steam for 4–5 minutes. Melt 50g (2oz) butter in a large saucepan and add the peas. Cover and cook over a gentle heat for 5 minutes, shaking the pan from time to time to prevent sticking and to ensure the peas are evenly covered with the butter. Stir in a dessertspoon of finely chopped fresh parsley and mint at the end of the cooking time. This simple dish goes well with grilled or baked fish.

AT-A-GLANCE TIMETABLE

SOWING
4–5cm (1½–2in) deep, in 10cm (4in) wide drills
- **Early round-seeded**
  EARLY WINTER
- **Early wrinkled**
  EARLY SPRING
- **Main crop**
  MID–LATE SPRING
- **Late crop**
  SUMMER
- **Sugar and petit pois**
  EARLY SPRING–MID-SUMMER

FIRST SUPPORTS
5–7.5cm (2–3in) apart
- **Early round-seeded**
  When seedlings are 7.5cm (3in) high
- **Early wrinkled**
  When seedlings are 7.5cm (3in) high
- **Main crop**
  When seedlings are 7.5cm (3in) high
- **Late crop**
  When seedlings are 7.5cm (3in) high
- **Sugar and petit pois**
  When seedlings are 7.5cm (3in) high

MAIN SUPPORTS
- **Early round-seeded**
  When plants are growing strongly
- **Early wrinkled**
  When plants are growing strongly
- **Main crop**
  When plants are growing strongly
- **Late crop**
  When plants are growing strongly
- **Sugar and petit pois**
  When plants are growing strongly

HARVESTING
- **Early round-seeded**
  LATE SPRING–EARLY SUMMER
- **Early wrinkled**
  EARLY SUMMER
- **Main crop**
  SUMMER–AUTUMN
- **Late crop**
  AUTUMN
- **Sugar and petit pois**
  EARLY SUMMER–AUTUMN

Peppers and Chillies

Sweet pepper

Chilli

S weet peppers, or capsicums, are often grown under glass in Britain, although many modern varieties will grow outdoors. The fruits can be eaten when green, or allowed to ripen to yellow or red, according to the variety. Chillies are related to sweet peppers and are grown in exactly the same way. The hot-flavoured fruits are used in curries, pickles and sauces.

Planning the crop
Grow indoor plants in 25cm (9in) pots of potting compost, or plant three in a grow bag. Otherwise, plant them in the greenhouse border after digging in a moderate dressing of well-rotted manure.

In the garden, prepare a bed against a south-facing wall or fence by digging in manure or compost – a bucketful to the square yard – some weeks before planting. Rake in 60g per square metre (2oz per square yard) of a general-purpose fertiliser before planting. They can also be grown outside in large pots or grow bags. Dwarf varieties will succeed in window boxes.

How many to grow Outdoors you should be able to pick at least three peppers from each plant – more in a good summer, and perhaps twice as many indoors. Between four and six outdoor plants or two or three greenhouse plants should be sufficient.

Varieties Most garden centres stock a selection of seeds. You can sometimes buy small plants.
Canape (F1 hybrid) An early variety that does well outdoors and under glass.
Bell Boy Popular for growing in the greenhouse or outside.

Apache Compact and decorative chilli pepper that makes a good pot plant for a sunny window.
Jalapeno A good variety for use in pizza toppings; fruits turn fiery red when ripe.

Growing under glass
Sow a few seeds in a pot of seed compost during early spring at a temperature of 16–18°C (61–64°F). When the seedlings are large enough to handle, prick them out individually into 7.5cm (3in) pots of potting compost. Grow the pepper plants at an average daytime temperature of 16–27°C (61–81°F), with a night-time minimum of 7°C (45°F). Make a final potting in 25cm (9in) pots of John Innes No. 3 potting compost.

Alternatively, transplant the seedlings from the 7.5cm (3in) pots directly into the greenhouse border, setting them 45cm (1½ft) apart.

Insert 1m (3ft) canes into the pots or soil, and secure the growing plants to them with string. Shade the glass during hot weather.

Water the plants daily during the flowering period. Apply liquid fertiliser every ten days after the first fruits appear.

Growing outdoors
Sow and prick out into individual pots as for growing under glass. In mid spring, harden the plants off in a coldframe before planting out 45cm (1½ft) apart in late spring or early summer. Tie to a cane.

Dwarf varieties should be planted in large pots, growing bags or window boxes. As they are usually short and bushy, they do not need staking.

Water regularly. After the first fruits set, give the plants a liquid feed every ten days.

AT-A-GLANCE TIMETABLE

SOWING
• **Under glass**
EARLY SPRING
• **Growing outdoors**
EARLY SPRING

PRICKING OUT
• **Under glass**
When large enough to handle
• **Growing outdoors**
When large enough to handle

TRANSPLANTING
• **Under glass**
Into 25cm (9in) pots, grow bags or greenhouse border
• **Growing outdoors**
LATE SPRING–EARLY SUMMER

HARVESTING
• **Under glass**
MID-SUMMER–EARLY AUTUMN
• **Growing outdoors**
LATE SUMMER–AUTUMN

Pests and diseases
Caterpillars (page 238) are the pests most likely to occur. The plants are liable to attack by **grey mould** (page 244).

Harvesting and storing
Green peppers are ready for picking during the second half of summer in the greenhouse, and in late summer and autumn outside.

See also chutneys (page 292); freezing (page 252); pickles (page 285) and sauces, ketchups and relishes (page 296).

Preparing and cooking
In spite of their common name, the large red, green or yellow vegetable peppers have a sweet rather than a spicy flavour. Use them as soon as possible after harvesting, before they become limp, and remove the seeds before cooking and serving.

Peppers are ideal in salads, their crunchy texture giving body and substance to softer vegetables. In cooking, peppers combine well with aubergines and tomatoes and are essential ingredients of such classic dishes as Hungarian goulash and ratatouille. They can also be stuffed and baked.

Prepare peppers by first washing and drying them. Slice off the stalk and remove the seeds. Use a small knife to cut out the pale membranes inside, taking care not to break the skin if the peppers are to be stuffed. The peppers can now be cut cross-ways into slices.

Red and green chillies are used for flavouring chutneys, marinades, meat stews and casseroles as well as in Indian and Chinese dishes.

Little but strong Green chillies are an essential ingredient of Asian and Mexican dishes. Take care when using home-grown chillies as they can be very hot.

Plums and Gages

'Victoria'

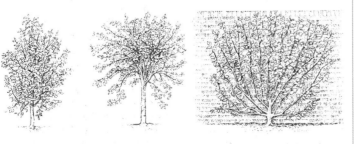

'Denniston's Superb'

Since plums are one of the more expensive fruits to buy, they are well worth growing in your garden. But before you buy your tree, you will need to plan carefully where to plant it and what variety to grow. Always check which rootstock has been used for grafting. A bush tree needs considerable space, but there are dwarf rootstocks that produce a more suitable tree for the

Pyramid   Bush   Fan-trained

average garden. You can even grow plums as a fan tree against a wall. If space is limited, consider growing a self-fertile variety, so avoiding having to plant another tree.

Plums were introduced to Britain from France and Italy in the 15th century and became a staple fruit in Britain up until the Second World War. Then, unaccountably, the popularity of the plum suddenly declined, and many acres of orchards were turned over to other crops. Though plums may have waned in popularity there are still plenty of varieties available to the home gardener. Plums have much to offer in terms of culinary use and deserve a place in the garden.

Planning the crop

Before growing plums think about the space available. A bush or half standard tree on the most widely used rootstock – St Julian A – may have a spread of 4.5m (15ft) or more, and many varieties also require a nearby tree of a different variety for cross-pollination. However, the newer, semi-dwarfing rootstock – Pixy – will reduce the spread by up to half.

The gardener with restricted space should choose a tree grafted onto Pixy, or plant either a pyramid on St Julian A, that can be restricted by pruning to 2.7m (9ft) high, with a spread of 2.5–3m (8–10ft), or a fan-shaped tree.

If there is space for only one tree, choose a variety that is self-fertile (which means it is capable of setting fruit without being pollinated by another tree).

Both plums and gages grow best in full sun. It is essential to avoid frost pockets, as plums flower early. They succeed in most well-drained soils, but on very acid soils top-dress with garden lime at the rate of 240g per square metre (8oz per square yard) after planting.

How many to grow Provided you choose a self-pollinating variety, a single tree should yield sufficient fruit for an average family. An established pyramid may produce 13.5–34kg (30–75lb) of fruit, according to the variety. A bush or half-standard on Pixy will yield up to half this quantity. If you intend to plant more than one, space pyramids on St Julian A and bushes and half standards on Pixy, about 3–3.5m (10–12ft) apart.

A fully grown, fan-trained tree will produce an average of 12–13.5kg (25–30lb) of plums, and much more in a good year. Plant fans 4.5–5.5m (15–18ft) apart. Fans are sometimes available on Pixy rootstock, in which case space about 3m (10ft) apart.

Where space is plentiful, plant bush trees on St Julian A about 4.5m (15ft) apart. Each tree, when established, will produce an average of 23–45kg (50–100lb), according to the variety.

Varieties If you have room for only one plum or gage tree, choose from the following self-fertile varieties:
Early Transparent Gage Apricot yellow; late summer.
Denniston's Superb Greenish-yellow dessert plum; late summer.
Victoria Bright red plum suitable for bottling, jams and desserts; susceptible to silver leaf; late summer–early autumn.

Marjorie's Seedling Purple plum for cooking and bottling; mid autumn.

If there is room for more than one plum tree, so that there can be cross-pollination, choose from:
Early Rivers Small fruits from a small, compact tree; pollinator 'Victoria'; late summer.
Kirke's Purple-black dessert plum; pollinator 'Early Transparent Gage' or 'Laxton's Gage'; mid autumn.

Growing tips

Bare-rooted plum trees can be planted at any time from late autumn to early spring, but the earlier the better. Container-grown trees may be planted at any time of year, if the weather is suitable.

To plant, dig a hole slightly wider than the spread of the roots. Make it sufficiently deep to allow the soil mark on the stem of the tree to be level with the surrounding soil after planting.

When planting a bush or dwarf pyramid, first hammer in a support stake and place the tree against it. Secure the trunk to the stake with a tree tie, or with soft string tied round a piece of cloth to protect the bark from chafing.

AT-A-GLANCE TIMETABLE
PLANTING
LATE AUTUMN–EARLY SPRING
PRUNING
SPRING–EARLY AUTUMN
THINNING FRUITS
MIDSUMMER
HARVESTING
LATE SUMMER–MID AUTUMN

Before planting a fan tree, prepare the wire supports on walls as for peaches (page 178). Place the trunk about 25cm (9in) from the wall and slope it slightly inwards while replacing the soil. Spread out the ribs of the fan evenly and tie them to the support wires with soft string.

Every spring apply sulphate of ammonia or dried blood at the rate of 15g per square metre (½oz per square yard) plus a similar amount of sulphate of potash.

Every third year add a dressing of superphosphate at the rate of 60g per square metre (2oz per square yard).

Alternatively, top-dress annually each spring with a slow-release fertiliser according to manufacturer's instructions.

After applying the fertiliser, mulch with well-rotted compost or manure at the rate of a bucketful to the square metre. Apply the compost mulch and the dressings of fertiliser to the soil covered by the spread of the branches.

When weeding, be careful not to disturb the roots, or the tree will throw up suckers. If suckers do appear, pull them up rather than cut them off.

Prune during warmer weather (between spring and autumn). During colder weather, there is a risk that silver leaf disease may enter the pruning cuts.

Training a fan tree Prune as for fan-trained peaches (page 178) for the first two or three years after planting. This will establish the framework of the tree. Thereafter, the treatment differs because plums, unlike peaches, fruit on both old wood and on shoots produced the previous summer.

PRUNING A FAN-TRAINED PLUM TREE

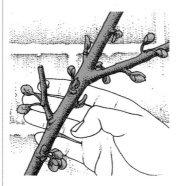

Rubbing out buds In spring, as soon as growth begins, rub out all buds that are growing towards or away from the wall.

Pinching out shoots In summer, pinch out the tips of sideshoots not needed to form new branches. They will have six or seven leaves.

Shortening the shoots After the crop has been harvested, shorten by half the sideshoots that were pinched out in summer.

As soon as growth begins in the spring you will need to restrict growth (see above). In midsummer, pinch out branches that aren't needed. Shorten remaining shoots after the crop has been picked (see above).

Cut out dead wood and prune back any unwanted shoots flush with the wood from which it springs. Brush the wounds with tree paint.

Tie down any vertical-growing shoots so that they are trained horizontally.

Training a pyramid If you decide to train a pyramid from a maiden or one-year-old tree, cut back the stem to 1.5m (5ft) above the ground in early spring after planting. Cut off flush with the stem any branches lower than 45cm (1½ft) from the ground. Prune back any other branches to half their length. In the second half of summer, shorten branch leaders to 20cm (8in) to a downward or

outward-facing bud. At the same time, prune laterals to 15cm (6in).

If you do not want to spend time on this early training you can plant a two-year-old tree. In either case, future care of the tree is the same.

In the middle of the spring following planting, and in subsequent years, shorten the central leader by two-thirds, cutting back to just above a bud. Cut out any shoots that are competing with the leader. In summer, prune new growth as in the previous summer.

When the tree reaches a height of 2.7m (9ft) shorten the last year's growth on the central leader to about 2.5cm (1in). Do this in late spring each year. Try to keep branches at a maximum length of 1.2–1.5m (4–5ft), pruning back just after midsummer.

Training a bush tree You generally buy bush plum trees as either two or three-year-old trees. After planting a two-year-old tree,

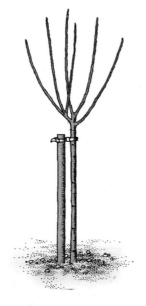

Pruning a bush tree In early spring, reduce each primary leader on a newly planted two-year-old tree by half. Cut to an outward-facing bud.

prune each of the four or five primary leaders by half to an outward-facing bud in mid spring.

A three-year-old tree will have six to eight leaders. Prune these in early or mid spring by a third to an outward-facing bud. Repeat this treatment in the next two years.

Thereafter, restrict pruning to the cutting out of any dead wood and crossing shoots. Do this as soon as possible after the crop has been harvested, and well before leaf-fall.

Thinning the crop Plum-tree branches are often brittle and they may snap under the weight of fruit, giving silver leaf or other diseases a chance to enter the wounds. To avoid this, start thinning a heavy crop in early summer, but do not complete the final thinning to 5–7.5cm (2–3in) apart until after the natural fruit fall in June.

When thinning, curl a finger round the stalk and snap off the fruitlet with your thumbnail, leaving the stalk still on the tree. If branches are still overladen, support them by tying them to stakes driven into the ground.

Pests and diseases

Common pests of plums and gages include **aphids**, **caterpillars**, **fruit tree red spider mites** and **plum sawflies**. The diseases most likely to occur are **bacterial canker**, **brown rot**, **honey fungus**, **rust**, **scald**, **shothole** and **silver leaf** (see Pests and Diseases, pages 238–49).

Harvesting and storing

Pick plums for cooking, bottling or freezing before they are quite ripe. If plums are intended for eating, leave them on the tree as long as possible so that they ripen.

PRUNING AN ESTABLISHED PYRAMID

Spring pruning Each spring, cut back the central leader by approximately two-thirds. Make the cut just above a bud.

Summer pruning In the middle of summer, shorten the growth on branch leaders to eight leaves. Cut back laterals to six leaves.

Go over the tree a number of times, choosing only the plums that are ready at each picking. Pick plums and gages so that the stalk comes away with the fruit.

In wet weather pick gages before they are quite ripe or their skins are likely to split.

For the various methods of preserving plums, see also bottling (page 270); chutneys (page 292); freezing (page 252); fruit cheeses and butters (page 281); jams (page 271); pickles (page 285) and wine-making (page 304).

Preparing and cooking

Sweet, juicy plums are excellent as fresh dessert fruits. Together with the cooking varieties, they are also used for cooked desserts including tarts, pies and cakes.

Wash plums and greengages, and wipe them dry before serving. Serve them whole as dessert fruits, but remove the stones before cooking. Cut along the indentations on the flesh, twist the halves apart and remove the stones with the tip

of a knife. Use halved in fresh fruit salads, for compôtes, as fillings for pies, flans and turnovers, and in steamed, sweet suet dumplings.

Baked plum custard

Arrange 500g (1lb) halved plums (stones removed) in a lightly buttered ovenproof dish. Sprinkle over 1 or 2 tablespoons of demerara sugar. Separate 3 eggs and beat the yolks with a tablespoon of sugar and the grated rind of half a lemon until light and fluffy. Heat 200ml (7fl oz) single cream to just below boiling point and add slowly to the egg mixture, stirring all the time. Strain into a new pan and heat without boiling until it thickens. Whisk the egg whites with a pinch of baking powder until stiff and fold into the custard. Pour over the plums. Set the dish in a roasting tray with about 2.5cm (1in) cold water and bake for 35 minutes at 180°C (350°F, gas mark 4). Serve warm.

Potatoes

POPULAR VARIETIES

'Majestic' (maincrop)

'King Edward' (maincrop)

'Kerr's Pink' (second early)

'Home Guard' (first early)

'Golden Wonder' (maincrop)

Potatoes are a staple of the British diet, whether boiled, roasted, mashed or served as chips. Apart from being indispensable in the kitchen, potatoes also help the gardener because the frequent moving of the soil during their cultivation helps to clear the plot of annual weeds, giving them a reputation as a cleansing crop. So unless space is at an absolute premium, it is a good idea to grow at least a few potatoes – preferably of an early variety. After the tubers have been harvested, the ground can be used for planting late crops such as cabbages, leeks and peas.

Despite the legends, it seems unlikely that Sir Walter Raleigh had much to do with the introduction of the potato to England, though he may well have planted some on his Cork estates in 1588, the year of the Armada. There is some evidence that the potato was brought to England some two years earlier in the holds of Sir Francis Drake's ships, fresh from their profitable raids on South America, where the vegetable originated.

Surprisingly, more than 150 years were to pass before the British regarded the potato as anything more than a novelty or as cattle food. It was only after the Irish and Scottish famines of the 18th century, that its true value was realised. Today it remains a British staple.

Planning the crop

Potatoes grow best in an open position. If grown in shade, the haulm, or green top, becomes lank and spindly as it reaches upward towards the light.

Potatoes grow reasonably well in most soils, but the best results are obtained from land that has been well manured. Dig the ground in autumn or winter, working in compost or well-rotted manure at the rate of a bucketful to the square metre (square yard).

A fortnight before planting, dress the ground with a mixture of two parts superphosphate, one part sulphate of ammonia and one part sulphate of potash, using the mixture at the rate of 120g per square metre (4oz per square yard).

Alternatively, apply a general-purpose fertiliser at the rate of 60–90g per square metre (2–3oz per square yard).

How much to grow Potatoes take up a lot of space, so the amount you grow depends on how valuable these vegetables are to the family economy. A bed 6m x 6m (20ft x 20ft), for example, might produce about 200kg (4 cwt) of maincrop potatoes, which could keep a family of four supplied for six months or more.

A bed of this size, however, is as big as the whole vegetable plot in many gardens, and such a yield would require good manuring and cultivation. Early potatoes give a much smaller yield, but are

harvested from early summer when prices are still comparatively high.

Varieties Not all potatoes are suitable for every district, so seek local advice before settling on a particular variety. It is advisable to buy seed potatoes, which are grown in an area free from disease-carrying aphids, and not to plant those sold for eating.

First early varieties (for harvesting in early summer)
Swift; Rocket; Maris Bard; Pentland Javelin.

Second early varieties for harvesting in midsummer
Nadine; Marfona; Wilja; Estima.

Maincrop varieties (for harvesting in early autumn)
Desirée; Cara; King Edward; Majestic; Pentland Crown; Pentland Dell.

Preparing seed potatoes for planting

Buy seed potatoes in winter and at once take them from their bags and place in a cool, well-ventilated room. After a week or two, set them in seed trays with their 'eyes' (from which the sprouts will grow) uppermost. Place the trays in a cool room or greenhouse. In four or five weeks the sprouts should be sturdy and, ideally, 1–2.5cm (½–1in) long. Sprouted, or 'chitted', in this way, the potatoes have a longer growing season and produce a heavier crop.

Growing tips

Plant first-early potatoes as soon as the weather starts to warm up in spring. Plant second-earlies two to three weeks later, and maincrop varieties about two to three weeks

Planting potatoes You can plant your sprouted (or 'chitted') potatoes in a 10cm (4in) deep trench at 30cm (12in) intervals; or you can plant them in individual holes at the same depth and distance.

after this. Use a draw hoe to make drills 10cm (4in) deep and 45cm (1½ft) apart for early potatoes, and 60cm (2ft) apart for maincrop varieties. Alternatively, use a trowel to plant the potatoes in holes 10cm (4in) deep.

Select well-sprouted tubers and set them at the bottom of the drills or trowel holes about 30cm (12in) apart for early varieties and 45cm (1½ft) apart for maincrop potatoes. Place them carefully so that the sprouts are uppermost and are not damaged during planting.

The ideal seed potato for planting is about the size of a hen's egg and has at least two sprouts. A larger tuber may be cut in half before planting, leaving at least one sprout on each piece.

Return the soil to the drill, or fill each hole, and draw up a little more soil from between the rows to make a slight ridge over the line of planted potatoes.

When the first shoots appear draw soil over them with a hoe, increasing the height of the ridge, as protection from late frosts. Earth up the plants again when they are about 25cm (9in) high, and again a fortnight or so after that. Continue earthing at regular intervals until the foliage meets between the rows. During a dry spring, you will need to water early potatoes frequently to ensure that the crop matures.

Pests and diseases

Potato blight may infect main-crop potatoes between late spring and late summer if a spell of warm weather coincides with high humidity. The middle of summer is the most likely period for this to happen, but regular spraying (see page 245) will prevent infection.

Some of the newer varieties on the market, such as **Sarpo Mira**, are blight resistant and may not be

AT-A-GLANCE TIMETABLE

SPROUTING
- First-early varieties
MID WINTER
- Second-early varieties
MID WINTER
- Maincrop
MID WINTER

PLANTING
10cm (4in) deep, at 30–45cm (12–18in) intervals in rows 45–60cm (1½–2ft) apart
- First-early varieties
EARLY–MID SPRING
- Second-early varieties
MID SPRING
- Maincrop
MID SPRING

EARTHING UP
- First-early varieties
Start earthing when young growths appear
- Second-early varieties

Start earthing when young growths appear
- Maincrop
Start earthing when young growths appear

FINAL EARTHING
- First-early varieties
Earth fortnightly until tops meet between rows
- Second-early varieties
Earth fortnightly until tops meet between rows
- Maincrop
Earth fortnightly until tops meet between rows

HARVESTING
- First-early varieties
EARLY–MIDSUMMER
- Second-early varieties
LATE SUMMER–MID AUTUMN
- Maincrop
THROUGHOUT AUTUMN

affected at all in a normal year. **Aphids**, **potato cyst eelworms**, **slugs** and **snails** and **wireworms** are common pests of the potato. The diseases most likely to occur are **black leg**, **gangrene**, **potato blight**, **powdery scab**, **scab** and **wart disease** (see Pests and Diseases, pages 238–49).

Harvesting and storing
Potato-lifting time varies from one part of the country to another, depending on the prevailing climate. In the south-west, and in other mild and sheltered areas, the earliest varieties may be ready for harvesting in early summer, while in other districts they may not reach maturity until several weeks later.

As a rough guide, you should be able to gather a few new potatoes about 12–14 weeks after planting. To gather the first few early potatoes before the whole crop is ready, brush away a little soil from the sides of a ridge and remove any potatoes that have grown to the size of a hen's egg. Replace the soil over the smaller tubers and leave them to grow. They should at least double in size during the next two or three weeks, after which the crop can be lifted as required. When lifting potatoes, insert the fork at least 15cm (6in) away from the stems to avoid impaling the tubers. Push it well into the side of the ridge so that the plant can be lifted and thrown between the rows in a single action.

Maincrop potatoes, on the other hand, take at least 20 weeks to come to full maturity – that is, to be ready for storing.

Some may be dug a few weeks earlier, but they will have to be used immediately since the skins

Earthing potatoes As the crop grows, use a rake to pull up loose soil, making a ridge, so that the tubers are always covered.

will not have set yet. Before lifting the entire crop, test one or two potatoes by rubbing the skin with your thumb. If the skin of the tuber does not rub off, the crop is ready.

Store potatoes in a dry, cool, but frost-free place. Place them in light-proof but ventilated boxes or hessian sacks, or pile them on a dry floor and cover with straw.

Preparing and cooking
Home-grown new potatoes have unequalled flavour and a firm texture. They should be scrubbed or scraped – never peeled – or boiled in their skins. They are excellent served cold in salads, but are probably most delicious when boiled whole in lightly salted water, with a sprig of mint, until just tender. Serve them tossed in butter, and sprinkled with chopped parsley, dill, chives or coarse salt. Maincrop potatoes should be

scrubbed clean, peeled, and any eyes cut out, then cut into even-sized pieces. Place in cold water and boil for about 20 minutes.

Potatoes of even size may also be boiled without peeling, and the skins removed after cooking and draining. This method wastes the absolute minimum amount of flesh – far less than you will remove when peeling.

Boiled potatoes can be mashed with a fork or a potato masher. Mashed potatoes may be creamed with butter and a little milk and seasoning. Add a touch of green by folding in chopped parsley, chives, freshly chopped kale or spinach, or brighten with roughly chopped tomato or crisp-fried onions.

Duchesse potatoes are made from creamed potatoes enriched with egg. Pipe the potato into small heaps about 5cm (2in) high on a baking tray, or place them as a border round a cooked dish, and bake in a hot oven for about 25 minutes, or until golden.

For fried or sautéed potatoes, boil the potatoes until almost tender, cut them into 5mm (¼in) thick slices, and shallow-fry in hot oil over a moderate heat until golden-brown and crisp. Serve sprinkled with coarse salt, parsley, chopped marjoram or chives.

To make chips, peel maincrop potatoes, cut them into 1cm (½in) slices and cut these into strips. Heat fat in a deep-fryer to smoking point – 196°C (385°F) – and lower the basket with a single layer of chips into the hot fat for 4–6 minutes. Drain thoroughly on absorbent paper.

For roasting, peel the potatoes and cut them into even-sized chunks, then par-boil for 5 minutes before coating in oil and placing round a

roasting joint for 50–60 minutes.

To bake potatoes in their jackets, first scrub them clean, then pierce in several places with a knife (to enable steam to escape as the potato cooks). For a crisp skin, rub in some olive oil. For a softer skin, wrap the potato in tin foil. Bake at 190°C (375°F, gas mark 5) for at least an hour.

A good dish for using up old potatoes is 'Anna potatoes'. After peeling, cut the potatoes into thin slices and arrange them in overlapping layers in a buttered, ovenproof dish. Sprinkle with salt, dot with butter and bake, covered, in the oven for an hour at 190°C (375°F, gas mark 5).

Bulgarian potato pie
Peel 1kg (2lb) potatoes and cut into 1cm (½in) slices and dry with absorbent kitchen paper. Heat 5 tablespoons of oil in a pan and fry the potato slices for 2 minutes. Lift out and drain off the oil, resting the slices on kitchen paper. Add a finely chopped onion to the pan and fry for 3 minutes. Stir in 4 tablespoons of tomato purée and 174ml (6fl oz) dry white wine. Bring to the boil and boil rapidly until the liquid has reduced by a third. Place half the potato slices into a buttered ovenproof dish, sprinkle with salt, black pepper and paprika and pour half the sauce over them. Add the remaining potatoes and the rest of the sauce. Top with 2 tablespoons of breadcrumbs and a tablespoon of oil sprinkled over the top. Alternatively add a little grated cheese. Cover and bake on the lower shelf in the oven at 180°C (350°F) for an hour. Remove the lid for the last 15 minutes of cooking, to give a brown crispy topping.

Growing potatoes in containers
Potatoes will grow successfully in a variety of containers, even a black plastic rubbish sack. But for more consistent results it is better to invest in a large plant pot or a purpose-built potato barrel with a side panel that conveniently slides up so that you can access the crop a few tubers at a time.

Use quick-maturing, early varieties such as **Swift** and **Rocket**. In early spring, or late winter if you are growing them in a cold greenhouse, cover the base of the container with a shallow layer of soil-less potting compost, and space five or six tubers on top for a potato barrel. A large pot will take no more than one or two tubers.

Cover with about 5cm (2in) compost. The tubers will start to sprout. When the shoots appear through the compost, cover with more and repeat until they have reached the top of the container.

Keep the compost damp but not soggy, and feed weekly with a liquid fertiliser.

New tubers will be produced all up the covered shoots; the first, near the bottom, should be ready for harvesting after about 12 weeks. Leave small tubers to grow bigger.

It is possible to grow new potatoes for Christmas in this way, using a few of your early crop and planting in August in a cold greenhouse.

Pumpkins and Squashes

Pumpkins and squashes are closely related to the more familiar marrow. They make an interesting addition to the vegetable patch, with large attractive leaves and curiously shaped orange, yellow and piebald fruits.

There are two types of plant: bushes and trailers. Both occupy a good deal of space in the vegetable patch for a fairly long growing season. But in their favour the fruits store very well, lasting throughout winter. Another advantage for the lazy gardener is that once established their large leaves shade out all but the most tenacious weeds.

Planning the crop
Pumpkins thrive in full sun in rich, well-drained soil. The top of a compost heap would be ideal.

Otherwise, dig holes about 40cm (15in) square and fill with well-rotted compost, leaving a shallow depression at the top.

How many to grow Two or three plants should be adequate.

Varieties There are many different types of squash, pumpkin and edible gourd available, producing fruit that differ in size, shape and colour. Look out for seeds of new varieties at garden centres. Recommended squashes:
F1 Butternut Winter squash. Produces handy-sized fruit that is relatively easy to peel and has a good nutty flavour.
Patty Pan Summer squash. Produces plenty of small fruits with scalloped edges, which are harvested when immature at about 5cm (2in) across.

Recommended pumpkin varieties include: **Atlantic Giant**; **Mammoth**; and **Hundredweight.**

Growing tips
Sow one or two seeds in 7.5cm (3in) pots of seed compost in mid spring. Germinate at a temperature of 18–21°C (64–70°F) and harden off the seedlings in a coldframe.

Transplant to the final growing positions in late spring or early summer, setting the plants at least 1m (3ft) apart. Alternatively, grow one plant in a tub or grow bag.

Pinch out the growing point of each plant when it has about five leaves. Keep well watered in the early stages of growth and during any dry spells.

Larger fruits may be grown by heaping soil over the axis of fruit-bearing laterals, the point where they emerge from the main stem. The plant will then send out roots to obtain more food and moisture.

Pests and diseases
Aphids, glasshouse red spider mites and **glasshouse whiteflies** are the principal pests.

Possible diseases include **cucumber mosaic virus, powdery mildew** and **soil-borne diseases** (see Pests and Diseases, pages 238–49).

Harvesting and storing
Cut small-fruited varieties as they mature in summer. Leave large-fruited types on the plants until late autumn. Bring them in if the weather is excessively wet as the fruit can rot where they touch the ground. Store for winter use in a frost-free shed.

Preparing and cooking
Both vegetables belong to the same family as marrows and courgettes. The smaller varieties, which often have crooked necks, may be cooked like courgettes after the thin skin has been removed. Young, ripe squashes are also suitable for steaming in butter or for baking whole with a savoury filling. There is no need to peel them when they are young.

Pumpkins, which are a large type of squash, mature in early autumn. They are an extremely popular vegetable in America, where they are associated with hallowe'en and used in two classic dishes: pumpkin pie and pumpkin soup.

They can also be used as an accompanying vegetable. For this purpose, cut the pumpkin in half crossways, and remove the seeds and stringy bits. Put in a roasting tray, shell side up, round a joint of meat and bake in the oven at a temperature of 160°C (325°F, gas mark 3) for about an hour, or until the flesh is tender. Scrape the pulp from the shell, mash to a purée and cream with butter and seasoning.

Pumpkins may also be cut into small chunks, peeled and divested of seeds, and boiled in lightly salted water for 20–30 minutes. Serve with a cheese sauce. Cut into chunks and roasted first, pumpkins and squashes make a delicious risotto ingredient.

Pumpkin soup
Boil or steam 1kg (2lb) pumpkin (peeled, deseeded and cut into chunks) until tender. Drain thoroughly and mash to a purée. Melt 100g (4oz) butter in a large pan and fry one large finely chopped onion for about 5 minutes until soft and transparent. Add the puréed pumpkin and heat through for 10 minutes, stirring continuously to prevent burning. Gradually add 1 litre (2 pints) milk and season to taste with salt and pepper. For a smoother soup, strain through a sieve, return to the pan and heat through. At this stage you can add 150ml (5fl oz) cream, or serve as it is with a sprinkling of finely chopped fresh dill or chervil.

Pumpkin pie
Make 500g (1lb) of pumpkin purée as above and set aside to cool. Meanwhile roll out 250g (½lb) shortcrust pastry and use it to line a 26cm (10in) flan ring set on a baking sheet. Bake this blind at 200°C (400°F, gas mark 6) until brown. Beat 300ml (½ pint) cream lightly with 3 eggs, a tablespoon of grated lemon peel and 150g (5oz) caster sugar. Stir this mixture into the pumpkin purée, adding ½ teaspoon of salt, 1 teaspoon of ground ginger and ½ teaspoon of ground mixed spice. Combine thoroughly, then spoon into the pie shell and bake at 180°C (350°F, gas mark 4) for about 1¼ hours until set and brown. Serve warm or cold with whipped cream.

AT-A-GLANCE TIMETABLE

SOWING
MID–LATE SPRING

TRANSPLANTING
1m (3ft) apart
LATE SPRING–EARLY SUMMER

HARVESTING
SECOND HALF OF SUMMER–
LATE AUTUMN

Quince

The quince has been grown in Europe for so long that its place of origin has been forgotten, though it probably derived from somewhere in central Asia.

The tree lives to a great age and, as it matures, puts out wide, contorted branches. These, and the large white or pale rose flowers that are produced in June, make the tree a picturesque backdrop for any large garden.

Quinces require a good deal of space. Even in bush form they grow to a height of 3–3.5m (10–12ft) with a spread of 3m (10ft), while as standard trees they may reach a height and spread of 4.5m (15ft).

Planning the crop

Quinces will succeed in any good garden soil, but do best in a moist loam and in an open, sunny site.

In the North, however, they require some protection, such as a sunny corner bounded by two walls. Unless grown in such a sheltered place, it is unlikely that the fruits will ripen on the tree.

How many to grow Quinces are self-fertile, so it is unnecessary to grow more than a single tree.

Varieties There isn't a great deal of choice available, though most garden centres stock **Vranja**. This popular variety produces large pear-shaped fruit in early autumn.

Growing tips

Buy two-year-old plants for bushes, and three or four-year-olds to grow as standards. Bare-root specimens should be planted between late autumn and early spring; containerised plants can be planted any time the weather is suitable.

Each February apply bonemeal at the rate of 120–150g per square metre (4–5oz per square yard) to the area beneath the branches. In May, apply a mulch of compost, farmyard or stable manure over the same area.

For the first three or four years, winter-prune the one-year-old growths by half. In following years no pruning is necessary, except to cut out diseased wood or badly placed branches.

Pests and diseases

The pests most likely to occur are **aphids**, **capsid bugs**, **caterpillars**, **codling moths** and **fruit tree red spider mites**. The most likely disease is **powdery mildew** (see Pests and Diseases, pages 238–49).

Harvesting and storing

Pick the fruits in mid autumn and store in a cool, dry, frost-proof place. Fruits continue to ripen after harvesting, and generally last for six to eight weeks.

Keep them away from other fruits, such as apples and pears, which may become tainted by the strong aroma of the quinces.

See also freezing (page 252); fruit cheeses and butters (page 281); jams (page 271); jellies (page 277).

Preparing and cooking

This hard fruit, which is ready for picking in autumn, is not suitable for eating raw. For this reason it is usually made into a sparklingly clear, rose-pink jelly which is an ideal accompaniment to fatty meats and roast game (see recipe below). Because of their high pectin content, quinces also make excellent jams.

Quinces require long, slow cooking – about 1½ hours – to reduce them to a pulp for jam and jelly-making, but only about half that time for use as pie fillings. They combine particularly well with apples, but need a lot of sweetening with sugar or honey.

Quince honey is a form of confectionery favoured by the ancient Greeks. To make it, boil chopped quinces until pulpy, rub them through a sieve, and add 750g (1½lb) sugar to every 1kg (2lb) of quince purée.

Bring to the boil and simmer for about 15 minutes, until quite thick, as for making fruit cheeses (see page 281). Pour the mixture on to a flat, wet dish and leave to dry in a warm place for about a week; then cut into squares and roll in raw brown sugar. Store in airtight tins.

Quince jelly

Take 2kg (4lb) quinces, scrub clean and cut into small pieces. Put the quince in a large pan with the juice of 2 lemons and about 2 litres (4 pints) water. Bring to the boil and simmer until quite tender. Strain for a good 15 minutes, retaining the liquid. Return the pulp to the pan with another 1 litre (2 pints) of water, bring to the boil and simmer for 30 minutes. Strain and combine the liquid with the liquid collected. Measure the liquid, transfer to a fresh pan and bring to the boil, adding 750g sugar for every litre (or 1lb per pint). Boil until the setting point is reached.

Quince and apple pie

Melt 25g (1oz) honey and 25g (1oz) butter in a heavy-based pan. Stir in about 100ml (4fl oz) water and then add 250g (½lb) quinces (peeled, cored and cut into chunks). Cover the pan and simmer over a gentle heat until the quinces are just tender. This will take about 45 minutes. Leave to cool.

Take 375g (¾lb) apples (peeled, cored and cut into chunks) and mix with the quince pieces in a pie dish. Sprinkle with 50g (2oz) sugar and add 4 tablespoons of the quince cooking liquid or water. Roll out 175g (6oz) pastry and use it to cover the pie, trimming off the edges. Brush the pastry with milk and sprinkle lightly with sugar then make a small slit to allow steam to escape and bake at 200°C (400°F, gas mark 6) for 35–40 minutes. Serve warm or cold with cream or custard.

AT-A-GLANCE TIMETABLE
PLANTING
LATE AUTUMN–EARLY SPRING
PRUNING
During winter, for first 3–4 years
OCTOBER
HARVESTING
MID–LATE AUTUMN

Radishes

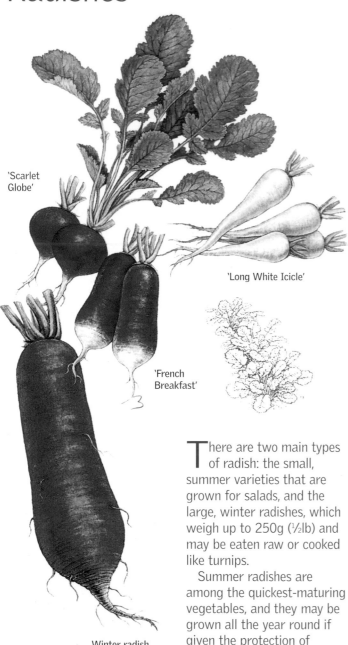

'Scarlet Globe'

'Long White Icicle'

'French Breakfast'

Winter radish

There are two main types of radish: the small, summer varieties that are grown for salads, and the large, winter radishes, which weigh up to 250g (½lb) and may be eaten raw or cooked like turnips.

Summer radishes are among the quickest-maturing vegetables, and they may be grown all the year round if given the protection of coldframes and cloches during winter.

Planning the crop

Summer radishes do not need deeply dug soil because they are not in the ground for more than a few weeks, but they grow best – especially in hot weather – if sifted compost is worked into the top 7–10cm (3–4in) at the rate of a bucketful to the square metre.

Well-drained soil is needed for the first sowings under glass in late winter. Winter radishes, like other root crops, grow best in soil that was manured for a previous crop.

In spring, sow radishes in a sunny but sheltered spot. In summer, choose a position in partial shade to help to prevent the plants going to seed prematurely.

How much to sow For a continuous supply of summer radishes, sow a row 2.5m (8ft) long every three weeks.

Varieties Numerous types of winter and summer radishes are available from garden centres. You can buy mixed packets of summer radish seeds, which are useful for adding interest to a salad.

• For sowing under glass
Rougette Quick maturing with a bright red skin.
Saxerre An early, round-rooted variety.
• For outdoor sowing spring–autumn
French Breakfast Tender, with a mild flavour; long rooted.
Long White Icicle The best of all white radishes.
Scarlet Globe A brilliant red radish, with delicate white flesh.
• Winter radishes
Black Spanish Long and **Black Spanish Round** Both varieties have black skin and white flesh.

China Rose Long, blunt-ended roots; rose-coloured skin.

Mooli radishes produce roots up to 30cm (12in) long, which can be eaten raw or cooked. Treat them as either summer or winter radishes.

Some radishes, such as **Rat's Tail** and **Munchen Bier** grow taller than average and are cultivated for their edible pods, which can be eaten cooked or raw. Basic cultivation is the same as for summer varieties.

Growing summer radishes

Make the first sowings under glass in a coldframe or under cloches in the second half of winter. Put cloches in position a fortnight before sowing, to warm and dry the soil. Sow thinly in drills 5mm (¼in) deep and 15cm (6in) apart. Do not sow thickly or the plants will produce foliage at the expense

AT-A-GLANCE TIMETABLE

SOWING (Outdoors)
5mm (¼in) deep, in rows
15cm (6in) apart
• Summer radishes
SPRING–AUTUMN
• Winter radishes
MID–LATE SUMMER

THINNING
• Summer radishes
No thinning if sown 2.5cm (1in) apart
• Winter radishes
Thin to 15cm (6in) when large enough to handle

HARVESTING
• Summer radishes
4–6 weeks later
• Winter radishes
From 10 weeks later

of the roots. Instead, aim at sowing about 1–2.5cm (½–1in) apart in the drills. Keep the soil moist so that the radishes grow quickly.

From spring onwards, sow outdoors at the spacings advised for early crops. Frequent sowings will ensure a continuous supply of tender young radishes. If left for more than a week or two when mature, they will become woody and lose their flavour.

Growing winter radishes

Sow the large-rooted winter varieties from mid to late summer in drills 30cm (12in) apart, and thin the plants to 15cm (6in) spacings when large enough to handle.

Keep the soil moist during dry weather, otherwise the plants will not make sufficient growth.

Pests and diseases

Radishes may be attacked by **flea beetles** (page 239). They are generally disease free.

Harvesting and storing

Pull summer radishes when they are young and tender. The roots of winter radishes may be left in the ground until required. Alternatively, lift them in late October and store in boxes of sand in a cool place.

Preparing and serving

All summer radishes may be used in salads or served with cheese or as a garnish. Trim the roots and tops off, wash and dry, and cut away any blemishes on the skins.

Prepare large radishes and winter radishes as above, leave them whole and cook in boiling, lightly salted water for about 10 minutes. Serve with parsley sauce.

Raspberries

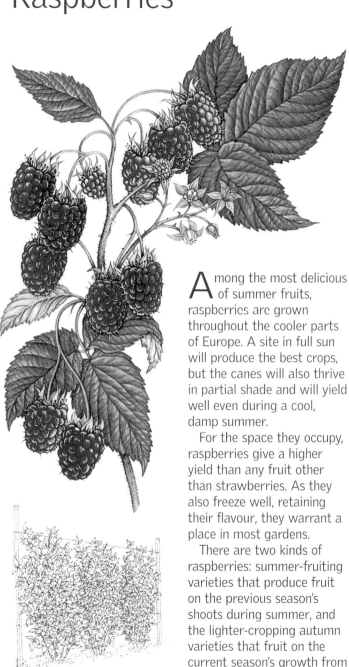

Among the most delicious of summer fruits, raspberries are grown throughout the cooler parts of Europe. A site in full sun will produce the best crops, but the canes will also thrive in partial shade and will yield well even during a cool, damp summer.

For the space they occupy, raspberries give a higher yield than any fruit other than strawberries. As they also freeze well, retaining their flavour, they warrant a place in most gardens.

There are two kinds of raspberries: summer-fruiting varieties that produce fruit on the previous season's shoots during summer, and the lighter-cropping autumn varieties that fruit on the current season's growth from early autumn onwards.

Planning the crop

Choose a sunny site if possible, or one that is in shade for a few hours each day, but not exposed to strong winds. Raspberries need a moisture-retaining but well-drained soil. Ideally, it should be slightly acidic.

Prepare the bed a few months before the canes are to be planted. Dig in a generous layer of well-rotted manure, compost or alternative sources of humus. This is particularly necessary if the soil is alkaline.

Rake in a surface dressing of 60g of general fertiliser per square metre (2oz per square yard).

How many to grow
A 3.5m x 2.7m (12ft x 9ft) plot will support three rows of seven canes, which should eventually yield over 10kg (20lb) of berries in a season – plenty for the average family.

Varieties
Among the best summer-fruiting varieties are:
Glen Moy Early; heavy cropper; small to medium fruits.
Malling Admiral Late; heavy cropper; good flavour.
Malling Jewel Early to mid season; heavy cropper; excellent flavour.
Malling Promise Early; heavy cropper; fair flavour.
The following autumn-fruiting raspberries are recommended:
Fallgold Good yellow colour and flavour.
Autumn Bliss The best autumn-fruiting raspberry today. Produces well-flavoured fruit on strong canes that do not need supporting.

Growing tips
Raspberries are highly susceptible to virus diseases, and it is important to start by purchasing

PLANTING RASPBERRIES

Prepare the ground Dig a strip about 1m (3ft) wide and a spade blade deep (top left) and fork in a bucketful of compost or rotted manure per plant.

Planting After soaking the roots in water for a few hours, dig a hole for each cane, keeping the plants adequately spaced. Spread the roots out as you plant them. Firm the soil gently with your foot (above left). Prune each cane to about 25cm (9in) high to stimulate growth (above right). They will produce fruit the following year.

one-year-old canes, that have been certified disease-free, from a reputable nursery.

If possible, plant the canes in late autumn or early winter. Otherwise, plant at any time up to early spring.

For each row dig a trench about 25cm (9in) wide and 7.5cm (3in) deep. Set the raspberry canes in this, 45cm (18in) apart. The exception is 'Malling Jewel', which produces fewer canes and should be planted 40cm (15in) apart.

Golden berries The variety 'Fallgold' offers a surprising yellow alternative to the traditional deep pink berries, but is just as tasty.

Cover the roots with soil, and firm this down with your heel. Space rows 1.8m (6ft) apart.

After planting, cut back each cane. This will prevent fruit being borne the following summer, but the vigour of the plant will be increased to ensure better fruiting in following years.

Apply a mulch of shredded bark, peat substitute, well-rotted lawn mowings or compost around the plants each spring to help to feed them and to conserve moisture. You can also improve yields by applying 30g of sulphate of potash per square metre (2oz per square yard) in winter, and 15g of sulphate of ammonia or dried blood per square metre (½oz per square

yard) in early spring. Control unwanted suckers, as well as weeds, by shallow hoeing or by smothering with rotted straw or compost. Give the plants plenty of water in summer.

The first summer after planting, insert a 2.5m (8ft) post into the ground at both ends of each row, sinking the posts 60cm (2ft) into the ground. For summer-fruiting varieties, space three 12–13 gauge galvanised wires 80cm, 1.1m and 1.7m (2½ft, 3½ft and 5½ft) from the ground, and stretch them between each pair of posts. Tie the canes to the wires with soft string.

Each summer, after picking summer-fruiting varieties, remove the canes that have carried berries

TRAINING SUMMER-FRUITING CANES

 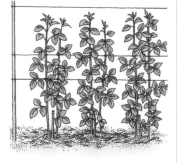

Pruning After harvesting the crop, cut down to ground level the canes that have fruited. Also remove any spindly new growths.

Tying in Use soft string to tie the new canes to the support wires, in place of those that have fruited. Space the canes evenly.

by severing them just above soil level. Select the strongest current-year canes and tie to the wires, spacing them 7.5–10cm (3–4in) apart. Cut out the remaining new shoots; pull out suckers well away from the rows. In late winter, cut each cane down to a good bud a few inches above the top wire.

Autumn-fruiting canes do not grow as tall as summer varieties. Space two parallel support wires, 80cm and 1.2m (2½ft and 4ft) from the ground, and set cross-ties every 30cm (12in) so that the canes are supported without being tied. Cut down the canes of autumn-fruiting plants in February.

Raising new plants
If the canes are virus-free, take suckers in early winter to increase the area of the bed. They begin to deteriorate from the eighth year and it is then better to buy in new stock. Burn the old plants or take them to the local recycling centre for disposal – do not compost. Set out new plants on a fresh site.

Pests and diseases
The commonest pests are **aphids**, **leaf-hoppers** and **raspberry beetles**. The most troublesome diseases are **cane blight**, **cane spot**, **chlorosis**, **crown gal**, **grey mould**, **honey fungus**, **mosaic virus**, **spur blight** and **virus diseases** (see Pests and Diseases, pages 238–49).

Harvesting and storing
Pick raspberries when they are well coloured all over. At this stage they will come away easily from the stalk, leaving the core behind.

Raspberries do not keep well, so eat or freeze them as soon as possible after picking.

See also bottling (page 270); freezing (page 252); fruit cheeses and butters (page 281); jams (page 271); jellies (page 277) and wine making (page 304).

Preparing and cooking
Like strawberries, raspberries are at their most enjoyable when served fresh with plenty of cream

and sugar. Use them as soon as possible after picking. Wash carefully as the fruits bruise easily. For most desserts, raspberries are made into a purée. One way is to rub the berries through a nylon sieve, pressing the fruits down with a wooden spoon. It is easier to purée the raspberries in a liquidiser, then sieve to remove the pips.

AT-A-GLANCE TIMETABLE

- New canes
PLANTING
45cm (18in) apart, in a 25cm (9in) wide trench
- Summer fruiting
LATE AUTUMN–EARLY SPRING
- Autumn fruiting
LATE AUTUMN–EARLY SPRING

STAKE AND TIE
- Summer fruiting
SECOND HALF OF SUMMER
- Autumn fruiting
SECOND HALF OF SUMMER

- Established canes
HARVESTING
- Summer fruiting
SUMMER
- Autumn fruiting
AUTUMN

PRUNING
- Summer fruiting
After harvesting
- Autumn fruiting
LATE WINTER

FINAL TRAINING
- Summer fruiting
Snip canes to the top wire
LATE WINTER
- Autumn fruiting
Tie in new growth
SPRING–SECOND HALF OF SUMMER

Rhubarb

Maincrop stems

Forced stems

Forced

Unforced

Rhubarb gives gardeners an early foretaste of the fruit season to come. Its pale pink stems can be used as a dessert as early as January – nearly five months before any other fresh fruit is ready.

By various methods of forcing and cultivation, it can be encouraged to yield heavily throughout the spring and summer months. Once established, a rhubarb bed needs little attention – simply apply an annual mulch of well-rotted manure or compost in spring.

Planning the crop

Rhubarb does best in an open position and can be grown in most types of soil. But, since it is likely to be in the same bed for five years or more, it is vital to prepare the ground correctly before planting.

Rhubarb roots penetrate deeply, so start by working in well-rotted manure or compost to about twice the depth needed for most vegetables. A month or two before planting, dig a hole 60cm (2ft) square where each root is to be planted. Fork a bucketful of well-rotted manure or compost into the soil at the bottom of the hole. Work in a further bucket of manure or compost into the topsoil and return to the hole.

If more than one root is to be planted, space the prepared holes 1m (3ft) apart and mark each one with a stake.

How much to grow Three or four plants will provide sufficient stems for an average family.

Varieties

Champagne Early Reliable cropper with red stems.
Timperley Early Thin-stemmed variety suitable for forcing; matures early.

Growing tips

Spring is the best time for planting rhubarb crowns, though late winter is satisfactory provided the ground is not frozen. They can also be planted in late autumn.

Container-grown rhubarb may be planted at any time when the weather is suitable.

In the prepared ground, earlier marked with a stake, dig a hole deep enough to take the whole of the woody part of the rootstock, leaving any new shoots just protruding. Tread the soil round the roots, and water freely.

Mulch the bed with well-rotted manure or compost, and water freely in dry spells. Feed regularly through the first summer with a general liquid fertiliser. Cut off any flowering spikes as soon as you see them.

During the second half of summer, dress the ground with a general-purpose fertiliser at the rate of 120g per square metre (4oz per square yard).

Forcing rhubarb After the rhubarb has been growing for three years, some of the vigorous clumps can be selected for forcing.

For a very early crop, use a spade to lift one or two strong plants in early winter and turn them over to expose their roots to frost. This has the effect of producing a false 'winter', to make the plants dormant.

After the roots have had some frost, put the plants the right way up in boxes, cover with moist peat substitute or old potting compost and place the boxes in a dark shed. If the shed is not dark, cover the boxes with black polythene.

Alternatively, place the boxes under a greenhouse bench, using a sheet of black polythene as a curtain to keep them dark. The plant starts growing vigorously in the dark. Rhubarb that has been forced in this way can be replanted, but will take two or three years to crop heavily again.

For a second-early crop, force one or two of the crowns outdoors, without moving them, by covering with a barrel or large bucket in late winter. Bank straw or leaves round the box for extra protection.

For a third crop, cover rhubarb in the permanent bed with straw, which will advance it a week or two ahead of the main crop.

Raising new plants

With regular feeding each spring, a rhubarb bed may be left undisturbed for years.

When you need new plants, dig up a large clump in late winter or early spring. Divide the roots with a spade, leaving at least one growing point on each, and replant the pieces.

Plants can also be raised by sowing seeds outdoors in spring.

Pests and diseases

Among pests attacking rhubarb are stem and bulb **eelworms** and caterpillars of **swift moths**.

The diseases most likely to occur on rhubarb are **crown rot**, **honey fungus** and **leaf spot** (see Pests and Diseases, pages 238–49).

Harvesting and storing

Do not pull any of the stems in the first year. In the second and third years pick only a few stems. In following years, pull fully grown stems as needed.

Cut off the leaves, which are poisonous, and put them to rot on the compost heap.

See also bottling (page 270); freezing (page 252); fruit cheeses and butters (page 281); jams (page 271); pickles (page 285); sauces, ketchups and relishes (page 296);

AT-A-GLANCE TIMETABLE

- **First year**
PREPARING THE GROUND
WINTER

PLANTING
EARLY SPRING

- **Subsequent years**
FORCING (Outdoors)
LATE WINTER

HARVESTING
FROM EARLY SPRING

syrups and juices (page 283) and wine-making (page 304).

Preparing and cooking

The tender, pink rhubarb forced for use in late winter and early spring has a more delicate, less acidic flavour than the thicker and coarser maincrop stalks.

The acidity of rhubarb can be diminished by blending it with ginger, cinnamon and the juice and rind of an orange. The clean taste of rhubarb makes it an ideal dessert to follow fatty or stodgy main courses.

Apart from its uses in cooked desserts, rhubarb is also an excellent filling for pies and baked puddings and as a base for fools and other creamed desserts. It is also used for jams, either on its own or in combination with soft fruits such as redcurrants and raspberries.

Prepare young, forced rhubarb simply by trimming off the leafy tops and the pale pink root slivers at the base of the stalks. Wash and dry carefully.

Older rhubarb often develops a stringy covering which must be peeled off, together with any bruised or damaged parts, as the stems are being cut into pieces.

When cooked, stems often have a pale, uninteresting colour, but this is easily improved by adding a few drops of cochineal.

Poached rhubarb

Wash and trim 1kg (2lb) rhubarb, removing any stringy bits and blemishes on maincrop stems. Cut into 1cm (½in) lengths.

Put 100g (4oz) sugar in a pan with 3 tablespoons of cold water, 2 tablespoons of orange juice, a cinnamon stick and the peel of half

PLANTING AND HARVESTING RHUBARB

Planting rhubarb Set each crown so that the roots are covered but the new shoots just protruding. Replace the soil and firm with your feet.

Harvesting Pull the largest stems from each plant by placing your thumb inside the stem as far down as possible and twisting it away from the crown.

an orange. Bring to the boil over a gentle heat, stirring until the sugar has dissolved. Cover with a lid, remove from the heat and allow to stand for 10 minutes.

Strain the syrup into a fresh pan, add the rhubarb pieces and simmer gently, uncovered, for about 10 minutes, until the rhubarb is tender.

This simple rhubarb dish is usually served warm with custard or cream. The poached rhubarb can also be used as a filling for pies and puddings.

Rhubarb crumble

Wash and trim 750g (1½lb) rhubarb, removing any stringy bits on maincrop stems. Chop into 1cm (½in) pieces and place in a deep, buttered, ovenproof dish. Sprinkle with 75g (3oz) sugar and add 2 tablespoons of orange juice.

Cut 75g (3oz) unsalted butter into small pieces and rub it into 175g (6oz) flour until the mixture resembles fine breadcrumbs. Mix in 75g (3oz) sugar and ½ teaspoon of ground ginger.

Spoon the crumble mixture over the rhubarb, pressing it down well with the back of a spoon. Bake in the centre of the oven at 190°C (375°F, gas mark 5) for 35 minutes, or until the topping is crisp and golden.

This classic winter dessert is best served warm with custard.

Rosemary

Rosemary, a hardy, evergreen shrub, originally came from the shores of the Mediterranean, where it is still collected for use in medicines and ointments. It is sometimes planted as a hedge.

In the kitchen, its sweetly fragrant leaves are used, fresh or dried, to flavour roast lamb, pork, chicken, rabbit and grilled fish.

The pretty blue flowers, which appear from early spring through to autumn, make a fragrant garnish for a fruit cup.

Planning the crop

Rosemary thrives in any well-drained soil in a sunny position, given shelter from cold winds.

How much to grow Since rosemary can grow up to 2.1m (7ft) high – although it is usually shorter – one bush is sufficient to provide a supply of leaves throughout the year.

Growing tips

Rosemary in several different varieties is readily available in pots from garden centres, or you can raise your own from seed.

Sow the seeds in seed compost in a 7.5cm (3in) pot or in a seed tray under glass in spring. When the seedlings have grown large enough to handle, prick them out into individual pots.

Set the plants out in their permanent positions in late spring or early summer. If you wish to grow more than one plant, space them 1m (3ft) apart, or 40cm (15in) if you are growing a hedge.

Alternatively, sow the seeds 5mm (¼in) deep in an outdoor seedbed in mid spring. Thin to 5cm (2in) spacings when they are large enough to handle, and plant

AT-A-GLANCE TIMETABLE

SOWING
SPRING

PRICKING OUT
When large enough to handle

TRANSPLANTING
LATE SPRING–EARLY SUMMER

HARVESTING
ALL YEAR ROUND

out in their permanent positions in summer.

Raising new plants
Take 10cm (4in) cuttings of half-ripe shoots from early summer to the middle of autumn, and insert them in equal parts (by volume) of peat substitute and sand, or perlite or vermiculite, in a coldframe.

Shade the frame until the cuttings root, then pot them in 7.5cm (3in) containers of potting compost. They will be ready for planting out in their permanent positions during the following spring. Hardwood cuttings, 15–20cm (6–8in) long, can be planted in autumn in the positions where the plants are to grow.

Pests and diseases
Rosemary is a robust plant and generally trouble free.

Harvesting and storing
Pick the young leaves and stems fresh for immediate use. To dry the leaves for winter use, or sprigs for a bouquet garni, see page 300.

Preparing and cooking
This evergreen Mediterranean herb is used freely in Italian cooking to flavour almost any kind of savoury dish. Wash the sprigs, which are sometimes used whole, or else the tiny leaves are pulled off the woody stems. Small sprigs of rosemary give an aromatic flavour when inserted into slits cut in lamb, pork or veal that is to be roasted. Alternatively, use fresh rosemary in stuffing.

Sage

The wrinkled, grey-green leaves of the hardy sage bush can be picked all year round for making stuffing to flavour pork, duck and goose.

The attractive evergreen plants, growing to at least 60cm (2ft) high, and maybe much more, produce spikes of small, violet-blue flowers in summer. Sage is therefore an appealing plant for growing in the flower border, containers and window boxes, as well as in the herb garden.

Planning the crop
Sage grows best in a warm, dry position. It thrives in any well-drained garden soil, except the most acid.

How much to grow One or two plants will provide more than sufficient leaves for the kitchen all through the year, although you may choose to grow more for their decorative value.

Growing tips
Sow the seeds in a pot or tray of seed compost in a coldframe or greenhouse in early spring, just covering the seeds with sifted compost. Prick the seedlings out when the first true leaves show, placing them singly in 7.5cm (3in) pots. Plant them out 30cm (12in) apart when the roots fill the pots.

Alternatively, sow the seeds outdoors from mid to late spring. Prick out the seedlings into a nursery bed, and transfer them to their final positions in autumn.

Raising new plants
Take 7.5cm (3in) heeled cuttings (see page 31) between early summer and mid autumn, and insert in equal parts (by volume) of peat substitute and sand, fine perlite or vermiculite in a coldframe. When the cuttings have rooted put them in their own individual 7.5–10cm (3–4in) pots of potting compost and overwinter them in the frame.

Nip out the growing tips, and plant out in spring.

Alternatively, 15–20cm (6–8in) hardwood cuttings, similar to those of gooseberries and currants (see pages 140 and 128), may be planted in autumn in their final growing positions.

Pests and diseases
Capsid bugs (page 238) sometimes attack the leaves and young shoots. **Grey mould** (page 244) is the disease most likely to attack sage.

Harvesting and storing
Pick the fresh leaves as and when required. They have the best flavour in high summer, just before flowering.

Sage can be dried (see page 300) but, since the leaves can be picked all the year round, it is hardly worth the trouble.

Preparing and cooking
This is one of the few herbs to have been in fairly constant use in English cookery since the Middle Ages. Today, however, sage is chiefly an ingredient of stuffings for fatty meat and poultry, and sometimes in country-style pork sausages. It is much favoured by German and Norwegian cooks to counteract the richness of oily fish.

The finely chopped leaves give a distinctive flavour to meat loaves and similar dishes made from pork, ham or sausage meat.

Mix them into the covering for Scotch eggs, or sprinkle the chopped leaves over liver when frying or grilling.

Add sage to cream cheese, omelettes, meat and vegetable soups, stews and casseroles, to bouillon for oily fish and marinades for hare and venison.

Sage-and-onion stuffing
Peel and finely chop 4 onions. Fry in a little oil until soft and transparent, but not brown. Remove from the heat and mix with 100g (4oz) fresh breadcrumbs and a tablespoon of freshly chopped sage leaves. Season well with salt and black pepper. Add a lightly beaten egg to bind the ingredients together.

Use the stuffing with roast pork, chicken or goose. As an alternative, substitute half the onions with finely chopped cooking apples, and mix in a tablespoon of fresh thyme with the sage.

AT-A-GLANCE TIMETABLE

SOWING
SPRING

PRICKING OUT
When first true leaves have formed

TRANSPLANTING
When roots fill the pot

HARVESTING
ALL YEAR ROUND

Salad leaves and stir-fry mixes

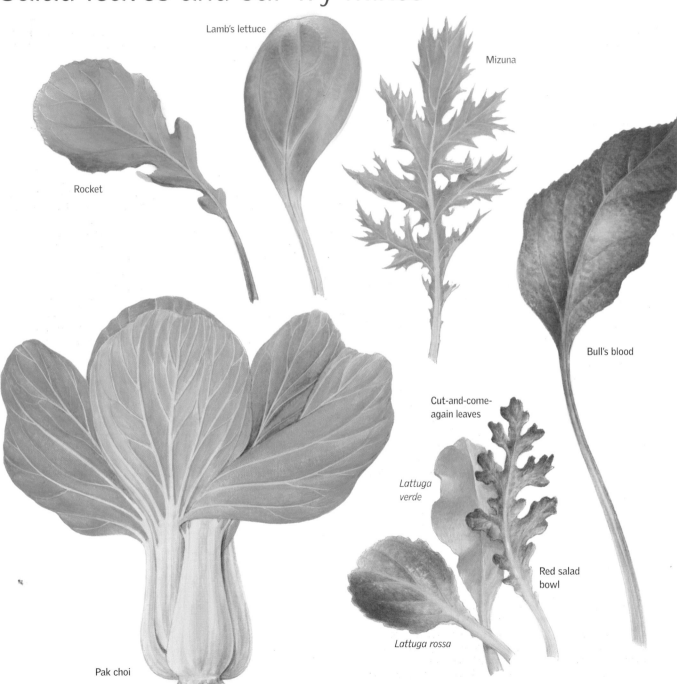

Lamb's lettuce

Mizuna

Rocket

Bull's blood

Cut-and-come-again leaves

Lattuga verde

Red salad bowl

Lattuga rossa

Pak choi

A green salad need no longer be restricted to a few limp lettuce leaves, although supermarkets charge high prices for an interesting mix of ready-prepared, good-quality, fresh salad leaves.

In fact, many young vegetables and herbs can be grown and eaten in the same way as cut-and-come-again lettuce, and seed catalogues offer an increasingly wide range of suitable varieties.

Many seed companies make the job even easier by supplying their own salad leaf mixtures, but there is a lot of fun to be had in experimenting with your own combinations.

The more varieties you include in your collection, the more flavours you can add to your salads. Easy to grow, and taking up little space, salad leaves can be grown in the smallest gardens, or on a patio, balcony, or even in a windowbox, for a fraction of the supermarket cost.

Planning the crop

For the best results, salad leaves should be grown quickly. They need a fertile, well-worked, well-drained soil, or they can be grown in pots of multipurpose compost, growing bags or window boxes.

The more colourful kinds make an interesting and attractive edging to a border.

It is possible to have a year-round supply by growing leaves in a cold greenhouse, under cloches, or in a coldframe during winter.

Prepare the ground for growing the leaves by digging in a general fertiliser at a rate of 60g per square metre (2oz per square yard) three or four weeks before sowing. Prepare soil in the same way for growing under cloches or in the greenhouse border or coldframe.

How much to grow Salad leaves should be sown little and often. A row no longer than 2m (6ft) will provide enough leaves for daily salads. Allow enough space for successional sowings – two 4m (12ft) rows will be enough to keep the crop in production, including a 2m (6ft) row that can be covered with cloches in autumn.

Shelter from the cold Use cloches to protect early and late salad leaves and so extend the cropping period.

Varieties Leaves that you are likely to find in catalogues include Oriental mustards such as **Red Giant**, **Red Feather** and **Pizzo** leaf radish; leaf carrot; land and water cress; rocket; kale **Red Russian**; red amaranth; salad burnet; komatsuma; mizuna; beet **Bull's Blood**; lamb's lettuce; cos and cut-and-come-again lettuce varieties; pak choi; spinach; tat soi; sorrel; chicory and purslane.

Any or all of these combine well together in salads and many can be added to stir-fries just before the end of cooking, to give colour and texture. Mizuna, pak choi, red mustards, texel greens and cavalo nero are ideal for stir-fries.

Mustard **Giant Red**, sorrel **Blood Veined**, beet **Bull's Blood**, variegated land cress and red-leaved lettuce make attractive edible additions to containers and as border edgings.

Young leaves of herbs such as coriander, dill, parsley, chives and chervil give a distinctive and piquant flavour to a green salad.

Growing tips

Make the first sowings in early to mid spring, covering with cloches in colder parts of the country. Sow at three-week intervals until mid autumn and cover the later sowings with cloches; otherwise sow in a cold greenhouse or coldframe. Pots sown in autumn can be placed in a sunny spot on the patio and covered with a bell cloche.

Sow thinly in drills 5mm (¼in) deep, with 20–30cm (8–10in) between rows. If sown thinly enough, there should be no need to thin out. If sowing in pots and other containers, scatter the seed sparingly over the surface of the

SOWING

EARLY SPRING TO MID AUTUMN
Sow at three week intervals for a succession of leaves

THINNING

If you sow seeds thinly, they shouldn't need thinning. If they do, pull up the seedlings as the leaves are ready to eat

HARVESTING

Pick leaves as required for eating; young leaves are more tender

compost and cover with 5mm (¼in) of finely sifted compost.

If the seedlings appear rather close together, then it's best to pull up a few completely when you first start to gather, rather than just picking the leaves.

Each sowing should give at least four pickings of leaves, and if left to recover while the next sowing is being cropped, it will yield a final picking or two before it is cleared.

To encourage the leaves to grow rapidly, keep the seedlings well watered, and add a liquid fertiliser once a week.

Always pick when the leaves are just large enough to be added to a salad. If there is a surplus, it can be made into soup similar to lettuce or watercress, or added to stir-fries and other vegetable dishes just before serving.

Some ingredients in a mixed salad-leaf packet will run to seed (bolt) quickly if short of water or allowed to grow too big; others quickly become tough, stringy or too strongly flavoured. Growth will slow down, even under

cloches, from late autumn until early spring, but if you have sown enough, you should still be able to brighten up your winter salads.

Pests and diseases
The pests likely to affect salad and stir-fry leaves are **slugs and snails** (page 241), **cutworms** (page 239) and **wireworm** (page 241).

Diseases are relatively few, as most varieties sold for salad leaves and stir-fries are modern ones, bred to resist problems associated with this kind of intensive cropping.

Damping off may be a problem with container-grown leaves, especially under glass; **downy mildew** can affect leaves of older lettuce varieties included in mixed leaves collections, and **grey mould** may affect young plants, especially during colder weather (see Pests and Diseases, pages 238–49).

Harvesting and storing
Pick the leaves for salads when they are young and tender. Cut the outer leaves near the base, or pick off carefully so as not to pull up the whole plant. Ideally use straight

away. Any surplus leaves will keep in the salad drawer at the bottom of the fridge for a day or two.

Older but still tender leaves can be harvested and used in stir-fries.

Preparing and serving
Wash the leaves gently in cold water, and dry carefully in a clean tea towel.

Always use in salads at the last moment, so they remain crisp and fresh. Do not add dressing until you are about to serve; within a short time of being dressed the leaves will wilt or become translucent, almost as if they've been cooked.

Stir-fries Leaves used in stir fries require the shortest possible cooking time to keep their crispness and colour. Add them for a few seconds, after everything else is cooked and ready to eat.

Fresh to the plate Baby leaves, picked straight from the garden, make a sweet and tender salad full of flavour and texture.

Salsify

Salsify is also known as the vegetable oyster, or the oyster plant, because of the flavour of its long, fleshy roots. This makes it a distinctive vegetable for use in late autumn and winter.

It has the disadvantage on a small vegetable plot, however, of taking up space over a long growing period. A gardener with space problems could compromise by growing only a short row, and catch-cropping with lettuces or radishes during early spring.

Planning the crop
Salsify grows best in light loam, although it will succeed in any soil except the heaviest clay. Do not grow on recently manured soil.

In autumn or winter, dig a shallow trench where the salsify is to grow and break up the soil at the base. Leave the trench open throughout winter to let the frost break up the soil further.

Varieties Only two varieties are usually obtainable.
Mammoth Long-tapering roots, sweet flavour.
Sandwich Island Vigorous grower, large roots.

Growing tips
Sow the seeds thinly into the prepared ground in spring in drills 1cm (½in) deep. If you wish to grow more than one row, allow 30cm (12in) between them. When they have grown large enough to handle, thin the seedlings to allow 25cm (9in) between them. Hoe lightly between the rows, drawing the soil up to the plants rather than away from them.

Pests and diseases
Salsify is generally free of pests. One of the few diseases to attack it is white blister. This fungal disease attacks the leaves, covering them with blisters full of white, powdery spores. There is no treatment other than to remove and burn any diseased plants.

Harvesting and storing
The roots are ready from mid autumn. They are hardy and can be left in the ground until needed.

When lifting, avoid damaging the roots or they will bleed like beetroot. To prevent this, break up the soil on each side of the row with a fork, then ease it away to expose the roots. Be sure to insert the fork to its full depth.

Leave some roots in the ground to produce the tender shoots, called chards, that will be ready for picking throughout spring. These can be blanched by drawing soil over them as they grow. The pale, tender leaves can then be eaten raw in salads. Alternatively, they can be left unblanched and cooked as a green vegetable.

Preparing and cooking
Salsify is similar to another root vegetable called scorzonera (see page 204). Both are long and slender, but salsify has a light brown soft skin while scorzonera's skin is black. Both have soft, white, sweet flesh, that of salsify having a faint oyster flavour.

Prepare both vegetables in the same way. Brush the soil off under cold running water. Cut off the base of the roots and the leafy tops, and remove the skin by peeling thinly or scraping. Rinse quickly and cut into 2.5–5cm (1–2in) lengths.

Put in a pan with just enough boiling, lightly salted water to cover the vegetables and add 1 tablespoon of lemon juice or white wine vinegar to preserve the white colour. Boil for 20–30 minutes, or until tender.

The rinsed and dried, finely chopped leaves may also be used fresh in salads or cooked like spinach. The white shoots, known as chards, produced by salsify towards the end of winter, can be cooked like asparagus.

Both salsify and scorzonera roots are also excellent for winter salads. Clean the roots, grate them on the coarse blade of a grater, sprinkle with lemon juice and fold into a dressing of mayonnaise, soured cream or oil-vinaigrette.

Salsify with cheese
Take 500g (1lb) prepared salsify and cut into 5cm (2in) chunks. Put in a pan of lightly salted boiling water to which a tablespoon of lemon juice has been added. Simmer gently for 25–30 minutes, or until tender. Drain thoroughly and keep warm.

Melt 75g (3oz) butter in a large pan. Add the salsify and toss quickly until thoroughly coated with the butter. Sprinkle with nutmeg. Spoon into a serving dish and cover with 50g (2oz) finely grated cheese. Serve with any type of grilled meat, ham or bacon.

As an alternative, flavour a white sauce with nutmeg and cheese and fold the salsify into this.

Salsify with mousseline sauce
Take 500g (1lb) prepared salsify and cut into 2.5–5cm (1–2in) pieces. Put in a pan of lightly salted boiling water with 1 tablespoon of lemon juice. Simmer gently for 25–30 minutes, or until tender. Drain thoroughly and keep warm.

Meanwhile put the juice of a lemon with 1 tablespoon of cold water in a bowl. Stir in 2 lightly beaten egg yolks and set the bowl over a pan of simmering water.

From 100g (4oz) butter, break off a knob and add to the eggs. Whisk until the mixture thickens. Take the bowl off the pan and gradually whisk in knobs of the remaining butter, beating thoroughly between each addition. Season to taste with salt and pepper and fold in 4 tablespoons of lightly whipped double cream. Heat the sauce over the pan of simmering water.

This creamy dish takes a little effort, but is good for entertaining. It should be served with roast or grilled meat, fish or poultry. Recipes for salsify and scorzoneras (see page 204) are interchangeable.

AT-A-GLANCE TIMETABLE
SOWING
1cm (½in) deep
SPRING
THINNING
25cm (9in) apart
When large enough to handle
HARVESTING
LATE AUTUMN

Savory

Summer savory   Winter savory

The spicy-flavoured leaves of savory are excellent as a flavouring for stuffing and meat dishes. Two types are grown. Summer savory is an erect bushy annual which grows to a height of about 30cm (12in). Winter savory is a hardy, evergreen perennial that grows to about the same height as summer savory but has a

more spreading habit. Its base becomes so woody that plants need to be replaced every two or three years.

The dried leaves of summer savory are generally considered to have a better flavour than those picked fresh from winter savory.

Planning the crop

Grow summer and winter savory in a sunny position in any fertile, well-drained soil. Alternatively, the plants can be grown in large pots of John Innes No. 1 Compost.

How much to grow Three or four plants of summer savory, and one or two of winter savory, should supply plenty of leaves all the year round for most families.

AT-A-GLANCE TIMETABLE

SOWING
- Summer crop
SPRING
5mm (¼in) deep
- Winter crop
EARLY AUTUMN

THINNING/POTTING
- Summer crop
When about 5cm (2in) high, thin to 15–25cm (6–9in) apart
- Winter crop
When large enough to handle, prick out into 7.5cm (3in) pots

HARVESTING
- Summer crop
ALL SUMMER
- Winter crop
EARLY WINTER–EARLY SPRING

Growing tips

For a summer supply of either type of savory, sow the seeds in drills 5mm (¼in) deep in mid spring. When the seedlings are about 5cm (2in) high, thin them to 15–25cm (6–9in) apart.

For a winter supply of summer savory, sow a few seeds in a pot in early autumn. When the seedlings are large enough to handle, prick them out into 7.5cm (3in) pots of potting compost and grow on either indoors, or in a greenhouse heated to 7–10°C (45–50°F).

Pests and diseases

Savory is generally trouble free.

Harvesting and storing

Pick fresh leaves and young shoots of summer or winter savory as needed. For drying (see page 300) pick the shoots of summer savory in late summer. The leaves and shoots may also be frozen (see page 252).

Preparing and cooking

Fresh savory, both the summer and the winter types, should be picked while the leaves and shoots are quite young. They may be used, sparingly, to flavour peas or beans in the same manner as mint.

The leaves of both types dry well, losing little of their sharp flavour. The dried leaves may be used like sage to flavour stuffings and sausage meat and to give a distinctive flavour to a variety of meat dishes.

Scorzoneras

Scorzoneras are hardy, winter vegetables grown for their black-skinned, delicately flavoured roots. They are believed to have been named after 'scurzon', the Catalonian for serpent. At one time scorzoneras were used in Spain to treat snakebites.

Planning the crop

Scorzoneras thrive in any fertile, well-drained soil, in a sunny, open position. Choose ground manured for a previous crop because fresh manure may make them fork into a number of separate roots.

In shallow soil, dig a trench during the previous winter in the position where they are to grow, and break up the soil at the bottom with a fork. Do not bring the subsoil to the surface.

How much to grow Scorzoneras take up ground for a long period, so a single row – say 6m (20ft) long – may have to suffice where space is limited. This would provide sufficient roots for about five meals for an average family.

Variety There isn't a great deal of choice for this vegetable. **Russian Giant** is an established variety that you can buy from most garden centres.

Growing tips

Sow the seeds in mid to late spring in drills 1cm (½in) deep. If you wish to grow more than one row, draw the drills 40cm (15in) apart. Thin the seedlings in two or more stages until they are 20–30cm (8–12in) apart.

Alternatively, sow the seeds in groups of two or three, 20–30cm (8–12in) apart, and then remove all but the strongest seedling in each group.

Hoe regularly to keep down weeds. Water thoroughly in dry spells or there is a risk of the plants running to seed.

Pests and diseases
Scorzoneras are generally free of pests. White blister is one of the few diseases that may occur. See the description in the salsify entry (page 203).

Harvesting and storing
The roots are ready by the second half of autumn. Lift them as needed, as scorzoneras are very hardy and may be left in the ground throughout winter.

When digging them up be careful not to snap the slender roots. Break up the soil on each side of the row with a fork and gently ease the roots out of the ground by inserting the fork to full depth alongside the plants.

Preparing and cooking
This winter root vegetable is similar to salsify, and prepared and cooked in the same way (see page 203). Recipes for scorzoneras and salsify are interchangeable.

AT-A-GLANCE TIMETABLE

SOWING
1cm (½in) deep, in rows 40cm (15in) apart
MID-LATE SPRING

THINNING
Thin gradually to 20–30cm (8–12in) apart

Seakale

Plant in summer

Forced shoots

S eakale, a hardy perennial, is grown for its blanched shoots, which are forced in winter and spring and cooked like asparagus. It requires a permanent bed, so a gardener with a small plot should consider whether the yearly crop of succulent stems will compensate for the amount of space taken up in the vegetable plot.

Don't confuse seakale with seakale beet, also known as Swiss chard or silver beet, a type of spinach grown for its leaves (page 218).

Planning the crop
Seakale grows best on a sandy loam containing plenty of lime, but will succeed in most soils that are suitably prepared. It is worth going to some trouble, since the crop will occupy the same piece of ground for some years.

Dig the ground deeply in autumn, working in a bucketful of well-rotted manure or compost to each square metre. Leave the ground rough and apply a dressing of garden lime at the rate of 60–120g per square metre (2–4oz per square yard).

In spring, apply a top dressing of general-purpose fertiliser at a rate of 120g per square metre (4oz per square yard).

How much to grow A double row 6m (20ft) long will provide an average family with enough for one meal a week from mid winter until mid spring, provided successive methods of forcing are adopted to ensure a continuing supply.

Varieties Named varieties are not usually available.

Growing tips
Thongs – sometimes available at good nurseries – can be planted during winter, but early spring is the best time. Set them 60cm (2ft) apart in rows spaced 60cm (2ft) apart. Plant so that the tips are 5cm (2in) below soil level. Water and feed the plants liberally. Mulch with well-rotted, strawy manure in late spring. In early summer, add a

Planting the thongs Use a trowel to plant the thongs, spacing them adequately. Bury their tops to encourage them to produce strong shoots.

top dressing of agricultural salt at the rate of 30g per square metre (1oz per square yard).

Remove all flowering stems as soon as they appear because they reduce the plants' strength and diminish the crop.

To raise plants from seed, sow the seeds 1cm (½in) deep in spring. Thin to 15cm (6in) spacings and leave the plants to grow for a year. The following spring, replant them 60cm (2ft) apart. In the autumn, dress the bed with well-rotted compost and leave the plants for a further year before forcing them.

Forcing the shoots There are three ways to obtain blanched shoots throughout winter and early spring: by digging up roots and bringing them indoors for the early pickings; by forcing them outdoors under flowerpots – although this depends on having a supply of fresh manure; and by blanching plants in their permanent bed to provide a later crop.

For early shoots, lift some roots in early winter after the leaves have withered. Cut off the pencil-thick side roots, or thongs, for planting the following spring (as described above).

Pack the main roots for forcing in boxes or large pots of soil, leaf-mould or spent potting compost and keep them in a dark place, such as a cellar or shed, at a temperature of about 7°C (45°F) as forcing proceeds. Do not allow the temperature to exceed 16°C (61°F). In mid winter start off more roots in the same way to get a steady succession of shoots.

Alternatively, force plants in the open by covering them with 25cm (10in) flowerpots in autumn and

FORCING SEAKALE SHOOTS

Trimming the roots Lift roots from late autumn, trimming off the side roots or thongs. These can be kept for planting.

Potting the roots Pack the main roots, which are to be forced, in boxes or pots of soil, peat substitute or leaf mould and keep in the dark.

Forcing and harvesting With gentle warmth – about 7°C (45°F) – the forced shoots will be ready in seven weeks, or less.

Forcing outdoors Alternatively, force shoots by placing a large pot over the roots. Cover first with leaves and rotting manure.

piling leaves round them. In winter, raise the temperature by replacing the leaves with fresh, rotting manure packed in a 30cm (12in) layer round and over the pots.

Forced shoots will be ready for picking in six or seven weeks during winter, but this period becomes progressively shorter as spring approaches. By early spring, only about three weeks is needed.

Raising new plants

When preparing the roots for forcing in autumn, select the best of the thongs, or side roots. Cut

them into pieces 13–15cm (5–6in) long, making a straight cut at the upper end, nearest the main root, and a slanting one at the other. This helps you to know which way up to position the root section when replanting.

Tie the thongs in bundles and place them under about 7.5cm (3in) of sand or soil in a coldframe during winter. By spring the thongs will have developed buds at the end that was cut straight. Keep the strongest bud to form the new shoot and rub out the rest.

Plant the thongs in the same way as the parent crowns, straight end uppermost, just covering the bud or developing shoot.

Pests and diseases

Seakale is subject to the same pests as other brassicas – **cabbage root flies**, **cabbage whiteflies**, **caterpillars** and **flea beetles**.

Club root and **violet root rot** are the diseases most likely to occur (see Pests and Diseases, pages 238–49).

Harvesting seakale

Cut the shoots when they are about 15cm (6in) high. When all the blanched shoots have been cut, discard roots forced indoors as they will not grow again satisfactorily if replanted.

Outdoors, fork the ground around roots that have cropped and allow them to grow again. They can be forced outdoors, year after year, if the ground is kept well manured.

Use the shoots as soon as possible after cutting as they soon lose both texture and flavour. The leaves from any stems that have not been forced can also be gathered for eating raw or cooked.

Preparing and cooking

This vegetable can be used in two quite different ways. Cook and serve the blanched leaf shoots in the same way as celery; use the fresh leaves from unforced stems in salads, or cook them like spinach.

To use unforced leaves, wash, dry and shred them, then toss in a lemon or oil-vinaigrette dressing. Alternatively, put the washed leaves in a pan with the absolute minimum of boiling, lightly salted water and simmer for about 10 minutes. Drain thoroughly, chop the leaves finely and reheat with a little butter. Alternatively the leaves can be steamed.

To prepare the blanched stalks for cooking, trim off the roots and tops, wash in cold water and tie the stems in small bundles with soft string. Place them in a pan of boiling, lightly salted water, adding a little lemon juice to preserve the leaves' white colour. Boil gently for 25 minutes, or until tender, or steam them. Drain, and serve with melted butter, chopped parsley or with a white sauce.

AT-A-GLANCE TIMETABLE

PLANTING
• Seakale
EARLY SPRING
60cm (2ft) apart
Rows 60cm (2ft) apart

REMOVING FLOWERS
Cut off flower stems as they appear

FORCING
EARLY WINTER ONWARDS

HARVESTING
WINTER–MID SPRING

Seakale salad

Trim the roots and tops off 500g (1lb) seakale. Wash the stalks and tie them in bundles and put in a large pan of boiling, lightly salted water with a little lemon juice. Simmer gently for 25 minutes, then drain thoroughly and leave to cool. When cold, cut the stems into 5cm (2in) sections.

Prepare the dressing while the seakale is cooling. Put 175g (6oz) mayonnaise in a bowl and blend in 2 teaspoons of chopped parsley plus a teaspoon each of chopped chives, mint, chervil and tarragon. Add a tablespoon of lemon juice and season with salt and pepper to taste. If necessary, you can add a little soured cream to give the mixture a pouring consistency.

Arrange the seakale in a serving dish and spoon over the mayonnaise dressing. Chill for 30 minutes. This salad goes well with poached fish and cold meats.

Braised seakale

Trim the roots and tops off 500g (1lb) seakale. Wash the stalks in cold water and cut into 10cm (4in) lengths. Melt 25g (1oz) butter in a heavy-based pan and add the seakale, tossing it so that it is evenly coated in butter. Pour 300ml (1 pint) of milk into the pan, bring to the boil and season with salt and pepper.

Cover and simmer over a gentle heat for 25 minutes, by which time the seakale should be tender and the cooking liquid reduced to a glaze. Spoon the seakale and liquid into a serving dish and garnish with finely chopped parsley. Seakale can also be served in a Bechamel or Bearnaise sauce.

For a final crop, to be cut in mid spring, prepare the bed in autumn as soon as the foliage has died down, by piling soil from the side of the rows to 20cm (8in) deep over the remaining plants.

Shallots

I n France, many cooks consider the flavour of shallots to be finer than that of onions. In Britain, the bulbs are used mostly for pickling, but there is a compromise that should suit the cook, the gardener and the gourmet. This is to use the largest bulbs as a substitute for onions, medium-sized bulbs as seed for the following year, and the smallest for pickling in spiced vinegar.

After planting, each shallot splits up to form a cluster of bulbs. Their final size depends largely on the richness of the soil. The biggest shallots may be up to 4cm (1½in) across – an excellent size for cooking.

Planning the crop
Shallots do best in a sunny position on land previously manured for another crop. Like onions, shallots grow best on firm soil so prepare the bed well in advance, allowing the ground time to settle. See the advice for onions (page 168).

How many to grow Seed merchants sell shallots by weight, and there are 20–30 bulbs in half a kilo. Thirty shallots planted in a 4.5m (15ft) row will produce a crop of 2–2.5kg (4–5lb) – perhaps more on a rich soil.
When grown for pickling, about 250g (½lb) of shallots will fill a 500g (1lb) jam jar.

Varieties Most garden centres only stock one or two varieties for sale by weight. There is a bigger choice in pre-packed shallots sold through mail order.
Native de Niort is a large variety that is popular with exhibitors.

AT-A-GLANCE TIMETABLE

PLANTING
LATE WINTER
15cm (6in) spacings, in rows 30cm (12in) apart

HARVESTING
LATE SUMMER

DIVIDING AND STORING
When tops have withered

How to grow shallots
Plant shallots in late winter or early spring. If the soil is light, push the bulbs in firmly so that they are three-quarters buried. On firmer soils, make a hole with the tip of a trowel or draw a drill with a hoe. In each case leave only the tip of the bulb protruding. Allow 15cm (6in) between the bulbs and 30cm (12in) between rows.
After a week or two, replant any bulbs that have become dislodged. Hoe regularly to keep the weeds down throughout spring and early summer.

Pests and diseases
Onion eelworms and **onion flies** are the principal pests of shallots.
The most likely diseases are **downy mildew**, **neck rot** and **white rot** (see Pests and Diseases, pages 238–49).

Harvesting and storing
When the foliage dies back in summer or early autumn, lift the clusters of shallots and lay them out to dry for a few days.
When the foliage has withered completely, split the clumps into single bulbs and leave them to ripen for a few days longer. Finally, store them in a net or a basket in a cool, dry place.

Preparing and cooking
These small onions are used for flavouring rather than as a vegetable. Their mild flavour enhances stocks, soups and marinades.
Prepare shallots by peeling away the outer layers of dry skin, then dicing the bulb or cutting it crossways into thin rings.

Hung up to dry Ripe shallots can be stored in a cool dry place until you need them. Keep them in a basket or use their foliage to tie them in a string, as you might for onions (see page 170).

Spinach

Summer spinach

New Zealand spinach

The lush green leaves of spinach are bursting with nutritional value. The most popular type is summer spinach which provides an abundance of leaves in summer, the surplus of which can be frozen for later use.

New Zealand spinach tolerates drought and grows well in dry, poor soils where other types of spinach will fail. But it is killed by frost.

Planning the crop

As summer spinach needs to be grown quickly in order to produce large, succulent leaves, sow the seeds in soil that has recently been dressed with manure or compost. The crop takes only a few weeks from sowing to harvesting, so it is a good idea to grow some between rows of other vegetables.

Summer spinach will also benefit from the shade cast by the leaves of neighbouring plants.

New Zealand spinach remains in the ground for considerably longer and must therefore be allocated a place in the cropping plan. It, too, needs well-manured soil.

Two weeks before sowing any type of spinach, rake a general-purpose fertiliser into the soil at the rate of 60g per square metre (2oz per square yard).

How much to grow
Sow a 3.5–4.5m (12–15ft) row of round-seeded summer spinach every three weeks if you want to be able to harvest a succession of leaves throughout summer.

One 6m (20ft) row of New Zealand spinach will be sufficient to provide an average family with regular pickings over many weeks.

Varieties
Round-seeded summer spinach varieties include:
Long Standing Round Quick growing with dark leaves.
Sigmaleaf Does not run to seed as quickly as most other varieties.

New Zealand spinach is sold under this name.

Growing tips
Make the first sowing of round-seeded spinach in early spring in the south and three to four weeks later in the north. Continue sowing at three-week intervals until just after midsummer. Sow New Zealand spinach in spring.

Sow the seeds of summer spinach in drills 2.5cm (1in) deep and 30–40cm (12–15in) apart. As soon as the seedlings are large enough to handle, thin them to 15cm (6in) apart, and finally to 30cm (12in). The second thinnings can be used in cooking.

Sow seeds of New Zealand spinach 2.5cm (1in) deep, in groups of two or three, with 60cm (2ft) between groups and 1m (3ft) between rows. Remove the weakest seedlings in each group.

Water all spinach plants liberally, especially during dry spells, to reduce the risk of the plants running to seed. This is one of the main hazards of the crop during spells of hot weather.

AT-A-GLANCE TIMETABLE

SOWING
2.5cm (1in) deep, in rows 30–38cm (12–15in) apart
• **Summer spinach**
SPRING–MIDSUMMER
• **New Zealand spinach**
MID SPRING (In groups)

THINNING
30cm (12in) apart
• **Summer spinach**
When large enough to handle
• **New Zealand spinach**
Leave strongest seedling in each group

HARVESTING
• **Summer spinach**
EARLY SUMMER–AUTUMN
• **New Zealand spinach**
EARLY SUMMER–MID AUTUMN

Pests and diseases
Spinach may be attacked by **aphids**. **Cucumber mosaic virus, downy mildew, leaf spot** and **shothole** are the most likely diseases (see Pests and Diseases, pages 238–49).

Harvesting and storing
With all types of spinach, pick the leaves when they are ready. Even when not required in the kitchen, the leaves of New Zealand spinach should be picked regularly to encourage further growth. (See also freezing, page 252).

Preparing and cooking
Spinach deteriorates quickly after picking and should be used as quickly as possible, while still crisp. Immerse the leaves in a large bowl of cold water, lift them out and repeat with fresh water – once or twice more – until the water is quite clear of sand and grit.

Spinach does not need additional water for cooking. It is sufficient to put the leaves in a large pan with only the water that adheres to the leaves from the last rinsing. Cook over gentle heat for 7–10 minutes, until soft. Alternatively steam for 5 minutes. Drain thoroughly, using a saucer to squeeze excess water out of the leaves in a colander.

Torn and tossed in towards the end of the cooking time, spinach leaves will wilt and make a delicious addition to many curries. They also make a quick and simple pasta sauce: wilt the spinach leaves, cooked with just their washing water clinging to them, then stir in a small tub of crème fraîche and a crumbled vegetable stock cube. Mix with the pasta and serve with black pepper and grated parmesan cheese.

Sprouting Seeds

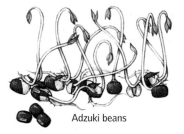

Adzuki beans

Alfalfa sprouts

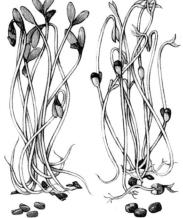

Fenugreek   Mung beans

Mustard   Cress

A lmost all vegetable and cereal sprouts are edible, and may be used in a wide variety of dishes. The sprouting seeds contain a wealth of vitamins, minerals and protein, making them an easy-to-grow, cheap and nutritious food crop.

The most familiar of edible sprouting seeds are, of course, mustard and cress, while Chinese restaurants have done much to popularise bean shoots. But there are many others with subtle differences in flavour.

Seeds for sprouting are available from health-food shops and seed companies. They are also delicious, both in their subtleties of flavour and in the wide range of dishes they enhance.

Methods and equipment
One of the advantages of growing sprouts is that, having bought the seeds, there is almost no further expense. Depending on the method used, all you need is a few jam jars or trays, paper towelling, muslin and some elastic bands.

You can buy specially designed seed sprouters from some garden centres and seed companies, but they are not necessary in order to produce good seed sprouts.

Most seeds will germinate at room temperature and may be grown in the kitchen. Some, however, need a few days in the warmth of the airing cupboard, and some require 'greening' to achieve their full flavour.

Those benefiting from the slightly higher temperature are buckwheat, fenugreek, lentils, sunflowers, triticale and wheat.

Whichever method you choose, there are two basic rules to follow. First, wash the seeds well and soak them overnight in a bowl of lukewarm water, using 4 cups of water to 1 cup of seeds.

Second, drain off the water, rinse the seeds thoroughly and place them in the sprouting container. During the next few days, rinse the seeds again, once or twice daily, depending on variety and the dryness of the weather.

Sprouting Seeds in a tray
Scatter the seeds on damp paper towelling and cover them with similar material. Keep the top paper moist and remove it when the seeds sprout. 'Green' the sprouts if necessary on a shady windowsill.

SPROUTING SEEDS IN A JAM JAR

1 Place soaked seeds in a jar and secure a square of damp muslin over the top. Place the jar on its side, in a bowl, in a warm room.

2 Place the jar in a dark corner or airing cupboard. Rinse the seeds as required (see overleaf) by half filling the jar with water.

3 Replace the muslin, swill the seeds gently and drain through the cover. Continue rinsing until the sprouts have reached the desired length.

4 If the sprouts require 'greening', place the jar on a windowsill for a day or two. After emptying from the jar, rinse well in a colander.

Tray method In some ways this is the easiest method of sprouting (see left), but it is not suitable for all types of seed.

Jar method Use this method (above) for seeds that must be rinsed during the sprouting process. Once the seeds are ready, store them in the fridge for up to a week to stop them growing.

Preparing and cooking
The young sprouts of beans and other seeds need minimal preparation, except for a final rinsing. They are best used as fresh as possible. They can be added, raw, to mixed salads to give a crunchy texture, or served on their own as a salad with an oil-vinaigrette or sour-cream dressing.

Sprouted seeds make an excellent addition to soups, stews, and main dishes, adding a welcome new flavour and texture. They can also be stir-fried or steamed, and served as a side-dish vegetable.

Use the peppery tasting mustard and cress to add punch to green and mixed salads, or as a garnish sprinkled over grilled steaks.

Mustard and cress are often used with egg dishes, as a sandwich filling, and to add colour to any pale savoury dish.

Where a recipe specifies bean sprouts, either mung beans or adzuki beans may be used. Fenugreek is suitable for curries, salads and soups. Buckwheat, triticale and wheat may be added to bread dough, as well as being used to flavour soups and salads. Wheat shoots (also known as wheatgrass) can be processed through a juicer to made a highly nutritious drink.

Mung beans, or Chinese bean sprouts, are the basis for much oriental cooking and are probably the most versatile of the sprouting seeds, either on their own or in combination with other foods.

In Chinese cookery, bean sprouts are stir-fried in a little very hot vegetable oil until cooked through, but still crisp. They must be served at once, otherwise the crunchy texture will be lost.

Mixed sprout salad

Use a selection of sprouts of your own choice, for example: 100g (4oz) mung bean sprouts, 50g (1oz) alfalfa sprouts, 50g (2oz) adzuki bean sprouts. Rinse and drain the sprouts. Peel and grate a large, grated carrot, half a red onion and 2 dessert apples. Clean and chop 2 sticks of celery. Place all the ingredients in a large serving bowl and add 50g (2oz) raisins. Add enough mayonnaise to finely coat the ingredients. As an alternative, use an oil-vinaigrette dressing instead of the mayonnaise.

HOW TO GROW THE MOST COMMON KINDS OF SPROUTING SEEDS

	METHOD	RINSING	SPROUTING TIME
Adzuki beans Crisp, sweet, nutty shoots; often used in Oriental cooking	Jam jar Tray	Four times daily, or damp when necessary	3–4 days. Harvest when 2.5cm (1in) long
Alfalfa Fresh green sprouts; ideal for winter salads	Jam jar	Twice daily	3–6 days, including 'greening'. Harvest when 2.5–5cm (1–2in) long
Buckwheat May be used in breads, soups and salads, or as a cooked vegetable	Jam jar	Once daily	2–3 days. Harvest when 1cm (½in) long
Chick peas A Mediteranean plant, frequently used as an accompaniment to curries	Jam jar	4–5 times daily	3–4 days. Harvest when 1cm (½in) long
Fenugreek A classic ingredient of curries. Also good in salads and soups. Requires 'greening'	Jam jar	Once or twice daily	4–7 days, including 'greening'. Harvest when 7.5cm (3in) long
Lentils May be eaten raw or cooked	Jam jar	2–3 times daily	3–4 days. Harvest when 2.5cm (1in) long
Mung (Chinese bean sprouts) White, crisp shoots; a favourite dish in Chinese restaurants	Jam jar Tray	Three times daily, or damp when necessary	4–5 days. Harvest when 5–7.5cm (2–3in) long
Mustard and cress Pungent, peppery shoots. Sow mustard 3 or 4 days after cress. Requires 'greening'	Jam jar Tray	Twice daily, or dampen tray when necessary	11–14 days, including 'greening'. Harvest when 5cm (2in) tall
Sunflower The shoots are delicious, but become strong-flavoured if grown too long	Jam jar	Twice daily	2–3 days. Harvest when 1cm (½in) long
Triticale A hybrid of wheat and rye. Excellent for soups and salads	Jam jar	2–3 times daily	2–3 days. Harvest when 5–7.5cm (2–3in) long
Wheat Wheat sprouts will add a fresh flavour and texture to soups and salads	Jam jar	2–3 times daily	2–5 days. Harvest when 1cm (½in) long

Strawberries

Alpine strawberry

S trawberries are easy to grow and give a quicker return than any other fruit, because plants set out in late summer will provide a crop by early the following summer.

If you have a large plot, you can pick strawberries from very early summer to mid autumn, if you put in a number of selected varieties, and use cloches to extend the growing season.

There are two types – those that carry a single crop in summer, and perpetual, or *remontant*, varieties that begin to crop slowly in early summer, reach a peak later in summer, and then continue through autumn.

Strawberries are an essential ingredient of both great and small summer treats – whether with cream and a glass of fizz at Wimbledon or a birthday party in the back garden. Yet they are by no means difficult to grow.

Planning the crop

Strawberries need a rich, well-drained soil in a sunny position. They do best in slightly acid soils, but they can be grown successfully in almost any well-drained land. They can also be grown in pots, troughs, window boxes, hanging baskets and growing bags. You can move early varieties into a greenhouse or coldframe, after a period of cold, to produce really early crops.

It's almost impossible to provide strawberries with too rich a soil. Before planting, dig in well-rotted manure or compost at the rate of at least a bucketful to the square metre (square yard). Make sure you don't leave any organic material on the surface as this will encourage slugs and snails.

Afterwards, fork into the surface 60g of general fertiliser per square metre (2oz per square yard).

How many to grow A 3.5m x 1.5m (12ft x 5ft) plot will support about 25 plants – enough for most average families.

Varieties The best way to choose varieties, particularly if you want several different sorts for successional crops, is to visit a garden centre with a good fruit section, or, even better, a specialist fruit nursery. This may mean having to buy mail order, so choose the nursery with care. Buy only plants that are certified free from disease.

Growing tips

Plant as early as possible – from midsummer to early autumn – if the plants are to be protected by cloches from the beginning of winter for an early crop, or if you want a good crop out in the open in the first season.

If you have to delay planting until the following spring, remove the flowers so that the plants have a chance to get established to crop the following year.

Plant perpetuals no later than late summer; otherwise wait until spring. Remove the first flowers from those planted in spring.

Pot-grown strawberry plants can be planted at any time of year they are available providing the weather is suitable. Water the plants thoroughly; dig holes big enough to accommodate the root balls; remove the strawberries from their pots and plant immediately.

Set the plants 45cm (18in) apart in rows 80cm (30in) apart. For each bare-root plant, dig a hole about 5cm (2in) deeper than the root system. Then make a mound at the bottom of the hole and spread the roots over this so that the base of the plant is level with the surface as you replace the soil over the roots.

Water the plants in, and keep watering during dry weather. In late winter, place glass or polythene cloches in position if you are aiming for an early crop.

When the berries start to develop – during late spring for single crop varieties – treat the rows for slugs and tuck fresh straw under each plant to keep the berries off the ground. Alternatively, use black polythene, ground cover fabric or the strawberry mats sold by most

Planting strawberries Mark out planting positions and dig holes to accommodate the root balls, or large enough to spread the roots of bare-root plants. Plant carefully, at the same level as the compost in the pot, firm in well and water regularly in dry weather during the early weeks.

RAISING NEW PLANTS

Pegging runners In summer, use bent wire to peg strong runners directly to the soil or to compost-filled pots set in the soil.

Trimming the end Pinch off the outer end of the runner, but do not sever the stem that joins the new plant to the parent plant.

Severing the runner After 4 to 6 weeks, when the plant has rooted, sever the runner and set the plant in its permanent bed.

Easy propagation Perpetual varieties of strawberry are well worth rooting – these types should be replaced every year because quality deteriorates in subsequent seasons.

horticultural suppliers. At the same time, protect ripening fruit from birds by covering with netting or fleece supported by canes.

When all the fruit has been picked, rake off the straw and cut back plants to remove old foliage. Put the debris in your 'green' bin. In mid autumn, cover perpetual plants with cloches to provide a late crop.

In winter, add sulphate of potash to the soil at the rate of 15g per square metre (½oz per square yard). On light soils, give a dressing of sulphate of ammonia or dried blood at 15g per square metre (½oz per square yard) in spring.

Raising new plants Layering runners is the simplest method of propagation.

In the second half of summer, small plants will appear as runners from the mother plants. Choose four of the strongest runners from each plant and peg them into the soil with pieces of bent wire. If the soil is dry or of indifferent

quality, sink 7cm (3in) compost-filled pots into the soil and push the baby plants into these.

Pinch off the outer end of the runner extending from each pegged plant, but do not cut the new plant from its parent until it is well rooted – after four to six weeks. Give the new plant a gentle tug to check that it is rooted, Once it is growing strongly on its own roots, cut the runner and set the new plant in its final position.

The vigour and yield of strawberry plants soon decrease, and all plants – including those raised from runners – should be renewed at least every five years, with the new plants set on a fresh site. Burn old plants or dispose of in your green recycling bin. Don't put them on your compost heap in case they spread diseases.

Pests and diseases
The most common pests attacking strawberries are **aphids**, **cutworms**, **glasshouse red spider mites**, **leaf eelworm**, **slugs and**

snails and **strawberry beetle**. The disorders most likely to occur are **frost damage**, **grey mould**, **leaf spot**, **powdery mildew** and **virus diseases** (see Pests and Diseases pages 238–49).

Harvesting and storing
Pick strawberries by the stalk to avoid bruising. Eat them as soon as possible after picking.
See also bottling (page 270); freezing (page 252); fruit cheeses and butters (page 281); jams (page 271) and syrups and juices (page 283).

Alpine strawberries
Although seeds of the true wild strawberry are obtainable from seed merchants and garden centres, Alpine varieties are much more widely grown and both seeds and plants can be bought from nurseries, garden centres, by mail order and online.

The flowers and fruits of the Alpine strawberry are much smaller than the usual cultivated varieties. Picking the fruits can be a bit slow and laborious, but connoisseurs who enjoy their sweet, rich flavour consider the effort worthwhile.

Although the Alpine is a perennial, the plants deteriorate after the first year. It is, therefore, better to grow plants from seed each year. Alternatively, buy new plants from nurseries in April and May. One of the best varieties is **Baron Solemacher**.

Alpines thrive in rich soil in a sunny position, although they will tolerate a little shade. They need not take up space in the fruit garden – you can grow them in the front of a flower border, in hanging baskets, windowboxes and pots.

Growing tips
During the winter before planting, prepare the site by digging in well-rotted manure or compost at the rate of a bucketful to the square metre (square yard). About three weeks before planting in late spring, rake into the surface 90g of general fertiliser to the square metre (3oz per square yard).

Sow the seeds in pots or trays of seed compost in early autumn. Sprinkle the very fine seeds on the surface, cover with a dusting of compost and press down lightly. Cover the trays with glass and paper until the seeds germinate.

Germination is erratic, but the seedlings should be ready for pricking out into trays of

AT-A-GLANCE TIMETABLE

Strawberries
PLANTING
- Summer crop
SECOND HALF OF SUMMER
TO MID AUTUMN
- Perpetuals
SECOND HALF OF SUMMER
45cm (18in) between plants

STRAWING
- Summer crop
LATE SPRING
- Perpetuals
LATE SPRING

HARVESTING
- Summer crop
SUMMER MONTHS
- Perpetuals
EARLY SUMMER INTO AUTUMN

CLEANING BEDS
After harvesting, remove straw and debris; cut back old leaves and fork lightly

potting compost by the end of October. Overwinter them in a cold greenhouse or coldframe for planting out in late spring. Alternatively, sow the seeds in pots under glass from late winter to mid spring for planting out in late spring or early summer.

Set the plants 30cm (12in) apart, in rows the same distance apart. Protect autumn-sown plants with cloches if there is a likelihood of frost when they start flowering in May. Keep the soil moist at all times. The plants will stop cropping if the roots dry out.

Alpine strawberries fruit over a comparatively long period. Leave fruits to ripen fully for the most flavour. Picking regularly will encourage more fruit to set.

Preparing and serving
Strawberries are probably at their most enjoyable when served fresh with sugar and thick cream; but they are also excellent used fresh, as fillings for tartlets and cream cakes. They are also easily made into ice creams, mousses or cooked for a compôte.

Serve strawberries whole unless they are very large, in which case

they will be easier to eat if you cut them into halves. Use a stainless-steel blade to prevent discoloration of the fruit. You can leave the pretty green flower calyx on the berry, but usually strawberries are hulled, by removing this and the soft centre stalk.

Rinse the berries carefully in a colander in cold water and drain thoroughly before serving.

A small number of strawberries can be made to go further by sprinkling them with sugar, and perhaps a dash of liqueur or sweet wine, and chilling lightly in the fridge until the sugar has melted.

Arrange the berries in tall glasses on a bed of vanilla ice cream or sweetened whipped cream.

Some people prefer to bring out the flavour of freshly picked strawberries by serving them with freshly ground black pepper and balsamic vinegar.

Eton mess This delicious dessert is traditionally served in summer at Eton College. It is a simple 'mess' of meringue, whipped cream and strawberries folded together, and if you use ready-made meringue, it's prepared in minutes.

Wash, hull and cut into quarters 450g (1lb) of strawberries. Sprinkle them with 1 rounded tablespoon icing sugar and set aside. Whip up 570ml (1 pint) double cream until it stands in soft peaks – not too stiff. Now break about 250g (6oz) meringue (or a box of meringue nests) into small chunks, but don't powder them. Fold together the strawberries, meringues and softly whipped cream and serve. This dish should be eaten as soon as it's been assembled, before the meringue loses its crunch.

Swedes

flavoured roots – which are extremely hardy – that you can harvest as required right through winter.

Planning the crop
Swedes will grow well in any fertile soil except one that is acid. Even an acid soil can be made suitable for swedes by giving a top dressing of garden lime at 180g per square metre (6oz per square yard) after digging the soil in preparation for the crop.

Grow swedes in ground that was well manured for a previous crop, not in freshly manured ground.

How many to grow A 6m (20ft) row will provide about 13kg (30lb) of roots – ample to last most families throughout winter.

Varieties The best swede for most regions and climates is **Marian**, though newer varieties are claimed to surpass it for flavour, yield and disease resistance.

You need a fairly open plot in order to grow swedes successfully. They are worth trying in any position as long as it isn't shaded – and being essentially a field crop, they seem to do best where fences or walls do not restrict the flow of air. Under the right conditions, you'll have a crop of mild, turnip-

Growing tips
Sow the seeds where the crop is to grow, in late spring in the south and in early summer in the north. Sow thinly in drills 1cm (½in) deep and 45cm (18in) apart.

Thin the plants as they grow, spacing them finally at intervals of 30cm (12in) to allow them plenty of room to develop.

Except for hoeing to keep down weeds, little attention is required after thinning.

Pests and diseases
The crop may be attacked by **aphids**, **cutworms**, **flea beetle** and **caterpillars** of the **swift moth**.

Diseases and disorders include **boron deficiency**, **club root** and **splitting** (see Pests and Diseases pages 238–49).

Harvesting and storing
Lift the roots as required from autumn until spring. If a very cold snap is forecast, lift a few and keep them in a cool, airy place such as a garage or shed, to use when the soil is frozen.

Preparing and cooking
Prepare swedes by cutting a thick slice off the top and trimming the root end until the pinky-yellow flesh is revealed. Cut off the tough

peel in a thick layer. Wash peeled roots in cold water, cut them into quarters or large cubes and boil in lightly salted water for 30 to 40 minutes, or until soft. Drain and serve tossed in butter.

Alternatively, parboil quartered swedes for about 10 minutes, drain them and add to a roasting joint for the last 30 minutes. They're also good roasted with leeks and onions.

A wintery mash Although swedes may be cooked and served like turnips, they are even better mashed with butter and cream and seasoned with ground nutmeg or ginger. Mashed swedes may also be blended with mashed potatoes, giving the potatoes a sweet flavour which can be further emphasised by adding ginger and butter to the mixture. Try being inventive and use them in aristocratic vegetable purées blended in a food processor with any of the following: carrots, butternut squash, parsnips or sweet potato. Season with spices and smooth with cream.

A hearty addition to dishes Add peeled and quartered swedes to meat and vegetable casseroles and pies. They are particularly good in curries. They combine well with fatty meats, such as lamb and mutton, or add chunks of cooked swede to a hearty bean soup.

Remember that swedes take much longer to cook than potatoes (25–40 minutes boiling depending on the size of the chunks) so parboil them first before using in soups or stir-fries.

Sweetcorn

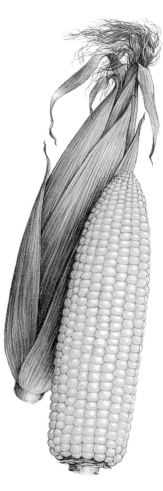

Also known as corn-on-the-cob and maize, sweetcorn is not difficult to grow – as some people believe – and a freshly picked, home-grown cob has a sweeter flavour than you'll ever get from a bought one.

Sweetcorn is believed to have been introduced to Europe from America by Christopher Columbus at the end of the 15th century. It was once considered an unsuitable crop for Britain, but in the past 30 years plant breeders have developed varieties suited to our climate, that will produce reasonable crops even in poor summers.

With its fine foliage and loose, feathery flowers, the plant makes a decorative addition to the garden.

Planning the crop

Sweetcorn needs a sunny, sheltered position. It will grow in any soil, but for good-quality crops enrich the bed with well-rotted compost or manure, at the rate of a bucketful to the square metre (square yard), during the winter before planting.

Just before sowing or planting, apply a general fertiliser at the rate of 60g per square metre (2oz per square yard).

When preparing the bed, remember that sweetcorn does best when grown in a block rather than in a long row. This provides the best chance for the light,

airborne pollen to fall from the male flowers at the top of the plants on to the silky female flower tassels which hang from the tops of the immature cobs.

How much to grow Fifteen plants set in a block measuring about 1.8m x 4.5m (6ft x 15ft) will provide 15 to 25 cobs, depending on the soil and summer weather.

Varieties Every year new, sweeter, easier-to-grow varieties are introduced. Check the seed catalogues and racks to see what is available. You can be sure that all varieties now offered will give good results. If you want to grow baby sweetcorn, make sure you choose a variety specially bred to produce these immature cobs.

Growing tips

Sweetcorn can be grown directly in the open ground in late spring, but success is more assured if seeds are given an early start, whether by sowing in pots under glass in mid spring and setting the plants out later, or by sowing under cloches.

To raise seedlings under glass, sow the seeds two at a time and 1cm (½in) deep in 7–8cm (3in) fibre pots or flowerpots filled with moist seed compost.

Cover the pots with newspaper and glass until the seeds germinate. If you are raising them indoors, enclose the pots in plastic bags and place them in a warm airing cupboard. As soon as the seeds have germinated, discard the weaker of the two seedlings and place the pots in full daylight.

When the seedlings are about 15cm (6in) tall, harden them off. Plant them out in late spring. Set

the plants 40cm (15in) apart in rows 60cm (2ft) apart.

A sowing can be made under cloches in mid spring. Place the cloches in position a week before sowing to warm up the soil. Sow the seeds 1cm (½in) deep in groups of three, spacing the groups 40cm (15in) apart in the rows, with the rows 60cm (2ft) apart.

When the young plants appear, remove the two weakest from each group. Leave the cloches in position until the plants touch the top.

An outdoor sowing can be made in mid spring, placing the seeds in the same way as under cloches. Protect the plot against birds.

Give all plants a regular and plentiful supply of water and a weekly feed of liquid fertiliser. Hoe to keep down weeds, and on windy sites tie young growths to canes.

Cover roots appearing at the base with soil, and do not remove the sideshoots ('tillers') that grow from the base of a plant.

Pests and diseases

Bean seed fly (page 238) and fruit fly are the only common pests. Sweetcorn is usually disease free.

Harvesting and storing

Cobs are ready for picking about six weeks after the silky tassels have appeared at their tops. These will shrivel and turn brown as the seeds develop.

Test by pulling back part of the cob's sheath and pressing one of the seeds with your thumbnail. If it exudes a creamy liquid, the cobs should be picked and used. If the liquid is watery, the cob is not yet ready. If there is no liquid, the cob is well past its prime.

Colour is also a useful guide. The cob is ready to use when the seeds start to turn pale yellow.

Twist the cobs from the plants or snap them outwards, immediately before you cook them – some gardeners advise having the pan of water actually boiling on the stove before you go to pick the corn, so that mere seconds elapse between picking and plunging into boiling water. Stored sweetcorn becomes dry and quickly loses its flavour and sweetness.
See also freezing (page 252) and sauces, ketchups and relishes (page 296).

Preparing and cooking

Corn-on-the-cob is most succulent when the cobs are picked just before the kernels become fully mature, woody and deep yellow. Strip the outer husks from the cobs in a downward direction, trim the stalk close to the cob and pull off the silky tassels from the top.

Corn cobs are easily overcooked. Some super-sweet varieties do not need cooking at all. If cooked, they need, at most, 8 minutes in boiling water. Don't add salt until the cobs are half-cooked – if at all – or the kernels will become tough.

Test the tenderness of the cobs by inserting the prongs of a fork in the corn. When they are ready, drain the cobs thoroughly and serve with plenty of butter.

Special corn-cob skewers are sold for inserting into either end of the cooked corn; alternatively, use two forks. You can use them to hold the cob while biting off the kernels.

You can also strip off the cooked kernels with a fork, or slice them from raw cobs with a sharp knife. Cooked kernels can then be mixed with cream and butter, or folded into a well-flavoured cream sauce and served as an accompanying vegetable.

Corn fritters This popular American breakfast dish is simply made by stirring cooked kernels of sweetcorn into a thick pancake batter – made by whisking together 2 eggs, 125g plain flour, 2 teaspoons baking powder, a pinch of salt and 150ml milk. Fry spoonfuls of the mixture in sizzling hot butter or oil until crisp and golden. These are excellent with crispy bacon and fried eggs.

Sweet potatoes

In warmer parts of Britain, it is possible to grow sweet potatoes outdoors during summer. However, cultivation is not as easy as that of its distant relative, the true potato and the sweet potato's requirement for warmth and sunshine means it is not an economic commercial crop in the British Isles.

Give the plants a sheltered spot in full sun, and you may have some success.

Though cultivated as an annual, the sweet potato is, in fact, a sub-tropical, herbaceous perennial vine. It has attractive leaves and pretty, trumpet-shaped flowers, rather like those of bindweed, and is closely related to the ornamental climber, morning glory.

Sold in greengrocers and supermarkets nationwide, the large, orange-fleshed tubers are versatile, delicious and loaded with vitamins – and not surprisingly are becoming increasingly popular in this country.

Its name was coined by Christopher Columbus when he brought it back from America.

The sweet potato is sometimes erroneously referred to as the yam, which is another plant entirely.

It is thought to have been cultivated as a food crop for at least 5000 years, and is a rich source of carbohydrates, vitamins and minerals.

Planning the crop
Sweet potatoes can be cultivated from supermarket tubers, but it is better to grow varieties sold for cultivation in the United Kingdom, which will be hardier than imported ones.

It's not worth trying to grow sweet potatoes outdoors if you live in the north, or the plot is cold or exposed. But if you have a sheltered spot in full sun, you may be successful. Your soil must be fertile and free-draining, so should be well worked the previous autumn, with plenty of manure or compost incorporated. Heavier soils will need sharp sand added to improve drainage.

If there is a problem with drainage, plant sweet potatoes into ridges, between 15–30cm (6–12in) high according to conditions. But in most parts of the country, it is better to grow the crop entirely under glass, either in the greenhouse border or in large tubs of multipurpose compost.

How much to grow Most suppliers send out cuttings or 'slips' in batches of ten, and as each plant produces a large quantity of tubers, you may find 10 or 20 slips or cuttings is quite enough.

Varieties The variety most likely to be available is **Beauregarde Improved**. This is similar to commercially grown sweet potatoes and has salmon-orange flesh with a distinct flavour and very sweet flavour.

T65 has pale flesh and is the best variety for outdoor cultivation in this country.
Georgia Jet is also reliable in most parts of Britain. This has deep orange flesh and an excellent flavour.

Growing tips
You are not likely to find sweet potato plants in a garden centre, and are more likely to obtain a supply from a specialist mail-order company or via the internet.

Sweet potatoes are grown from cuttings or slips (pieces of the tuber, generally unrooted, which are capable of producing roots given warm, humid conditions) and are dispatched from the nursery by carrier from mid spring to early summer.

Unpack your delivery as soon as it arrives. Plants from cuttings should be potted straight away into small pots of multipurpose compost.

Unrooted slips Cover unrooted slips with an inverted, clear glass jam jar or polythene bag, or place them in an unheated propagator in full light, with the cover on. This will provide maximum humidity until roots appear, at which point they can be planted up.

Grow on the young plants in a light, frost-free place until midsummer, then give a hardening off period of two or three weeks before planting outdoors in a mild area. Even in a mild area, the extra protection of a cloche or fleece for the first few weeks will be beneficial. Space the plants 30cm (12in) apart, with 75cm (30in) between rows. Otherwise, plant in a greenhouse into large tubs of multipurpose compost or direct

into the greenhouse border, 30cm (12in) apart, and 75cm between rows.

The best crops are produced at a temperature of 21–26°C (70–80°F). Keep the plants well watered in dry weather, but do not overwater, as this can cause the tubers to split and may encourage rotting below ground.

The foliage of sweet potatoes grown outdoors can be left to trail

---

AT-A-GLANCE TIMETABLE

POTTING SLIPS OR CUTTINGS
• **Cuttings**
MID SPRING TO EARLY SUMMER
Pot cuttings as soon as they arrive in small pots of multi-purpose compost
• **Slips**
MID SPRING TO EARLY SUMMER
Put under plastic or glass for humidity in a sunny place until roots appear. Then pot

PLANTING OUT
• **Outdoor plants**
MIDSUMMER
Harden off for 2–3 weeks before planting out 30cm (12in) apart, with 75cm (30in) between rows
• **Under glass**
MIDSUMMER
Plant into large tubs of multi-purpose compost or into greenhouse border, using above spacings

HARVESTING
AUTUMN
Tubers mature after 4–5 months. Dig up outdoor ones before soil gets cold and wet; indoor ones are ready when tops begin to yellow

---

over the ground to act as a weed barrier. In a greenhouse, train the foliage up canes or strings attached to the roof, to keep the greenhouse tidy.

Sweet potatoes do not require a lot of fertiliser. If the ground was properly prepared in the previous autumn, this should be sufficient to produce a good crop.

Plants grown under glass in multipurpose compost should be fed weekly with a general liquid feed after six to eight weeks.

Pests and diseases
Sweet potatoes are not usually troubled by pests; however, fusarium **root rot** (page 246) can be a problem if you overwater.

Harvesting and storing
The young leaves can be picked and cooked like spinach at any time once the tops have attained a reasonable height.

Tubers take from four to five months to mature, but will rot if the soil becomes cold and wet, so harvesting is best done as soon as they reach a usable size, which is usually from the end of August. If the crop has been grown under glass, wait until the tops start to turn yellow, which is usually a few weeks later.

Remove the vines (the green tops of the plants) before lifting the tubers. Handle sweet potatoes very carefully as they bruise easily. Do not remove the soil or compost by washing or rubbing until just before cooking.

The tubers will only store for a short period, and should be kept in a warm, humid place for up to a fortnight after lifting. This will help to heal any wounds and reduce shrinkage. It also improves the

flavour of the tubers by converting the starches in the flesh to sugars.

Preparing and cooking
Sweet potato shoots and leaves can be cooked like spinach (page 208) and can be used as a substitute in spinach recipes.

The tubers should be well scrubbed, then can be cooked in the same ways as potatoes (page 190), but you can leave the skins on until after cooking.

Sweet potatoes make a delicious purée, either on their own or combined with other root vegetables. They are also a great baby food, simply boiled and sieved. Babies love the natural sweetness and silky texture.

Roast sweet potatoes Peel and slice a sweet potato into chunky chip-sized pieces and put into a baking tray on top of a layer of sliced onions. The onions give a fabulous flavour and help to stop the sweet potatoes from sticking to the tin. Drizzle the whole lot with olive oil and cook in a medium-hot oven – on the shelf above the joint. They'll take about half an hour. Ten minutes before you want to serve, you can spice up the potatoes: if you like a bit of heat, add some chopped chilli; if you like garlic, add 1 or 2 chopped cloves.

Sautéed sweet potatoes Peel a sweet potato and slice it into rings. Fry in oil in a nonstick pan for 3–4 minutes on each side until lightly browned. These are delicious served with salt and freshly ground black pepper, and a wedge of lemon to squeeze over.

Swiss chard and perpetual spinach

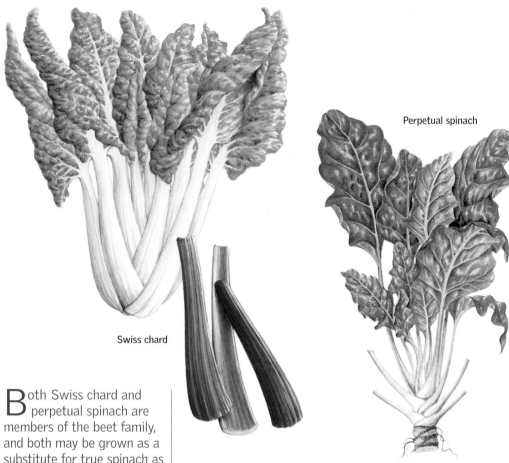

Swiss chard

Perpetual spinach

Both Swiss chard and perpetual spinach are members of the beet family, and both may be grown as a substitute for true spinach as they are easier to cultivate and have a longer cropping period. The word 'Swiss' was originally adopted by 19th-century seed producers to distinguish it from the French charde; it has nothing to do with the country. Swiss chard is sometimes known as seakale beet or silver beet. Swiss chard has spinach-like leaves, but with a broad midrib that can be white, yellow, red or multicoloured according to variety. The leaves can be harvested young and eaten whole, or allowed to mature somewhat, when the midribs themselves become the delicacy. These are removed from the rest of the leaf and cooked like asparagus.

Perpetual spinach leaves resemble those of beetroot, only without the red or purple hue. The flavour of the vegetable, harvested young and cooked gently, is virtually indistinguishable from spinach. More leaves grow to replace those you've picked.

Planning the crop

Swiss chard and perpetual spinach may remain in the ground for up to 12 months. This means that, unlike true spinach, they cannot be grown as catch crops in between other crops, and must be allocated some long-term space in your cropping plan. They need well manured, thoroughly worked soil to thrive. Two weeks before sowing, rake in a general fertiliser at a rate of 60g per square metre (2oz per square yard).

How much to grow One 6m (20ft) row of Swiss card or perpetual spinach will be sufficient to provide an average family with regular pickings over many weeks.

AT-A-GLANCE TIMETABLE

SOWING
• Swiss chard
MID SPRING
• Perpetual spinach
MID SPRING
In drills 2.5cm (1in) deep, 10cm (4in) apart, leaving 40cm (15in) between rows

THINNING
• Swiss chard
30cm (1ft) apart when large enough to handle
• Perpetual spinach
30cm (1ft) apart when large enough to handle

HARVESTING
SUMMER TO EARLY WINTER
Pick outer leaves when large enough for cooking. Raid tender inner leaves for salads, but in moderation. Pull regularly to encourage growth

Swiss chard varieties
Bright Lights Stems in shades of red, purple, orange, yellow, green, violet, gold and striped.
Bright Yellow Yellow midribs.
Lucullus White midribs.
Rhubarb or ruby Scarlet midribs.

Perpetual spinach varieties
Scenic Worth choosing as it seldom runs to seed the first season; tolerates poor conditions.

Growing tips
Sow Swiss chard and perpetual spinach in mid spring, in drills 2.5cm (1in) deep, with 10cm (4in) between seeds. Where more than one row is required, leave 40cm (15in) between rows.

Thin the seedlings to 30cm (1ft) apart when large enough to handle. Keep well watered and hoe regularly to keep the growing area weed-free.

Cover the plants with cloches in autumn to keep the leaves in good shape for picking during late autumn and early winter.

Uncovered plants generally die off in winter, but start producing new leaves in spring. However, during the second season they tend to run to seed, when they should be discarded and replaced.

Pests and diseases
Swiss chard and perpetual spinach are generally problem-free, apart from **slugs and snails** (page 241).

Harvesting and storing
Pick the outer leaves when large enough for cooking. The inner leaves may be picked in moderation and added raw to mixed leaf salads. Perpetual spinach has a somewhat stronger taste than true spinach, so it should be harvested

Pretty on the plate Although standard varieties of Swiss chard have plain pale green to white stems, many brightly coloured varieties are also available, with striking stems in a variety of pinks, reds, oranges and yellows that set off their glossy green leaves.

young. Even when not required for immediate use, the leaves should be pulled regularly to encourage further growth. Put old leaves on the compost heap as they will be tough and strong-tasting.

The leaves are best eaten fresh, but you can wash them and keep them in a polythene bag in the salad drawer of the fridge for up to two days.

See also freezing (page 252).

Preparing and cooking

Both vegetables are used and cooked like spinach (page 208). In addition, the midribs of Swiss chard may be cooked separately like seakale (page 206) or asparagus (page 81).

There is no need to add water when cooking as the leaves have a high water content. For this reason, steaming produces the best results, or wilt them in a saucepan with just the water that clings to them after washing.

The leaves of both plants have a slightly bitter, earthy flavour so tend to be unpopular with children – though try them on tender young leaves, raw, in sandwiches.

You can use them on top of pizzas, just like spinach – wash and shred the leaves and cook them in a dry pan for a couple of minutes until they wilt. Drain well and spread over the tomato sauce before topping with grated mozarella and olive oil.

Add them to stir-fries at the last minute, or fold shredded, wilted leaves along with grated cheese or bacon chunks into beaten egg for filling a quiche.

Tarragon

Tarragon, a hardy perennial herb, is grown for its sweetly aromatic leaves, which are used to flavour fish and meat dishes, and soups. The leaves are also an essential ingredient of fines herbes and are used to make tarragon vinegar.

Tarragon is easy to grow and needs very little attention once established in the garden.

Planning the crop

The herb grows best in a sunny position in light, well-drained soil.

If the soil is heavy, dig in peat or well-rotted manure or compost at the rate of a bucketful to the square metre (square yard) in the autumn before planting.

How much to grow A tarragon plant grows to the height of 60cm (2ft), with a spread of 30cm (12in) or more, so one plant should supply the needs of the average family.

Varieties French tarragon (*Artemesia dracunculus sativa*), which has smooth, dark green leaves, is generally regarded as having a better flavour than Russian tarragon (*Artemesia dracunculus inodora*), which is a fresher green and has less-smooth leaves. However, not all nurseries distinguish between the two.

Growing tips

Since generally only a single plant is needed, the simplest plan is to buy this from a nursery. October or March are the best months for planting, the latter being best on heavy soils. Small, pot-grown plants may be planted at any time if the weather is favourable.

Keep the plant well-watered during dry spells and pinch out the flowering stems as they appear.

Raising new plants Once established, tarragon will keep growing for years. However, it is better to divide and replant old stock every two or three years.

To do this, dig up a plant in spring and pull apart – but do not cut – the underground runners. Replant these 5–8cm (2–3in) deep and 40cm (15in) apart.

AT-A-GLANCE TIMETABLE

PLANTING
Plant pot-grown tarragon in
spring or autumn
AUTUMN OR SPRING

PINCHING OUT
When flowering stems appear

HARVESTING
EARLY SUMMER TO MID AUTUMN

Pests and diseases
Tarragon is usually trouble free.

Harvesting and storing
Pick fresh leaves from midsummer
until mid autumn. Sprigs can be
dried (page 300) or frozen (page
252), but these have less flavour
than fresh tarragon.

Cooking with tarragon
This is one of the classic herbs and
features particularly in French
cuisine as a flavouring for chicken
and other white meats. With its
bitter-sweet flavour, tarragon is
much used in the production of
vinegar, to which it adds a
distinctive taste that comes to the
fore in salad dressings.

It is a traditional herb in *Sauce
Bearnaise*, which can be served
with meat, poultry or vegetables,
and is one of the important
ingredients in *Omelettes aux fines
herbes*, where it is mixed with
other finely chopped fresh herbs,
such as chives.

The fresh, aromatic leaves make
a good flavouring for cream sauces
to accompany fish, for herb butters
and as an addition to creamed
vegetable soups.
Use the finely chopped leaves, too,
sprinkled over green salads and in

stuffings for poultry. Sprinkle
them over sole or other white fish
fillets prior to baking or grilling.
The flavour of tarragon also
complements prawns and other
shellfish.

Sprinkle the chopped leaves on
hot broccoli spears and french
beans, and add them to scrambled
eggs or a creamy sauce for green
vegetables.

Pound fresh tarragon with
parsley, chives and coarse salt and
add to a good wine sauce, with
extra butter, for serving with
chicken, veal or baked fish.

A favourite tarragon-flavoured
dish consists of chicken pieces
browned in butter and then cooked
in dry white wine, in the same pan,
for 30 minutes, with salt, pepper
and sprigs of tarragon added.

Serve the cooked pieces with
chilled tarragon butter.

Tarragon butter Blanch a
handful of tarragon leaves in
boiling water for 1 minute, then
drain them and pat dry. Pound the
leaves to a paste and blend with
100g (4oz) of butter.

Shape into a sausage, wrap in
greaseproof paper and chill in the
refrigerator until firm. Serve in thin
slices on top of grilled steaks or
chicken pieces.

Thyme

Lemon thyme

Common thyme

Although wild thyme
grows profusely on
chalk downs in Britain, the
common thyme used in
cooking is a native of
Mediterranean countries.

The ancient Greeks enjoyed
its mild, slightly sweet
spiciness, and in this country
the evergreen plant has been
used since the Middle Ages
to flavour soups, casseroles
and stuffings for rich meats
and fish.

The wiry-stemmed
common thyme is a bushy,
low-growing herb. Once
established, it can be left for
three or four years.

Lemon thyme, which also
forms a small bush, is
cultivated in the same way
as common thyme.

Planning to grow thyme
The wiry-stemmed common thyme
grows to a height of 20cm (8in),
with a spread of 30cm (12in).
Lemon thyme has a height and

spread of about 30cm (12in). Both
varieties will grow well in a sunny
position in well-drained soil.

How much to grow Two or
three plants will supply leaves for
the average family all the year.

Growing tips
Sow the seeds in a tray of seed
compost in a coldframe in spring.
When the seedlings are large
enough to handle, prick them off
into 8cm (3in) pots of potting
compost. Plant out in autumn.

AT-A-GLANCE TIMETABLE

SOWING
SPRING
Sow seeds in a tray of seed
compost in a coldframe in
spring. Prick out when large
enough to handle

PLANTING OUT
AUTUMN

HARVESTING
Pick as and when the leaves
are needed

Raising new plants Propagate
thyme by taking cuttings of lateral
shoots with a heel (page 31) in late
spring or early summer.

Insert the cuttings in small pots
filled with equal parts (by volume)
of peat and sand, or perlite, and
keep them in a coldframe.

Pot the rooted cuttings singly in
8cm (3in) pots of potting compost
and plant out in autumn.

Alternatively, divide the roots of
established plants in spring and
replant the pieces individually.

Pests and diseases
Thyme is generally trouble free.

Harvesting and storing
Pick the sprigs of leaves when
needed. As thyme is evergreen,
there is little point in drying or
freezing the herb.

Cooking with thyme
This highly aromatic herb is one
of the essential ingredients in a
classic bouquet garni, and it is one
of the most useful kitchen herbs.

Used with discretion, a little
finely chopped thyme adds aroma
and flavour to fruit juices, salads
and salad dressings, to savoury
cream sauces, to all types of
vegetable and meat soups, and to
stews. Use thyme also to flavour
baked, grilled or poached fish.

Rub the leaves on meat before
roasting it, or insert small sprigs
under the skin. Add thyme to
stuffings for poultry, to tomato
sauces and soups and to patés,
terrines and marinades.

A refreshing and health-giving
herb tea can be made from the
leaves of lemon thyme infused with
boiling water for 10 minutes.

Tomatoes

Moneymaker

Big Boy

Golden Sunrise

Tomatoes, whether grown under glass or in the open, are many gardeners' most rewarding – and money-saving – crops.

In an unheated greenhouse ripe tomatoes can be picked from midsummer until autumn, as long as you give them enough water and food and look after them properly.

In the open, tomatoes are more vulnerable to blight, but a good crop will ripen in late summer and autumn in warm summers, and even in cooler years plants will produce a worthwhile crop of ripe tomatoes. Any remaining green fruits can be ripened in a dark cupboard or shoebox indoors or made into green tomato chutney.

You can also grow tomatoes in pots and containers, or grow bags, in sunny, sheltered spots, such as on a patio or balcony. Dwarf tumbling varieties look really pretty when planted in hanging baskets or window boxes.

In the open, bush varieties, which need no de-shooting or staking, produce large numbers of relatively small fruits. Bush tomatoes are excellent for growing under cloches to produce an early crop of high-quality fruits.

Planning the crop

Outdoor tomatoes grow best in a sunny, sheltered position. The soil, whether in the open or greenhouse border, must be rich and moisture-holding. In the preceding winter dig in well-rotted compost or manure at the rate of at least one bucketful to the square metre (square yard).

Before planting, rake in a dressing of general fertiliser at the rate of 90g per square metre (3oz per square yard).

How much to grow An outdoor plant with four trusses of fruit will yield about 2kg (4lb) of tomatoes, depending on the summer and the amount of feeding. A greenhouse plant developing six trusses should produce at least 3kg (6lb) of fruit.

Varieties With the exception of bush varieties, most tomatoes are suitable for growing in greenhouses; but only certain types

AT-A-GLANCE TIMETABLE

Tomatoes under glass
SOWING
MID WINTER TO EARLY SPRING

PRICKING OUT
As soon as seed leaves have developed

PLANTING
40cm (15in) apart when 15cm (6in) high

STOPPING
When tops of plants reach the greenhouse roof

HARVESTING
SUMMER TO AUTUMN

crop reliably outdoors. The fruits of different varieties vary in colour, size, flavour, thickness of skin and earliness, and some are more disease-resistant than others.

Varieties for growing outdoors or under glass
Alicante Smooth-skinned, with exceptionally fine flavour; an early variety.
Big Boy Reliable, beef steak variety. Best grown indoors in colder parts; will grow outdoors in warm areas.
Golden Sunrise Suitable for growing indoors or outdoors; sweet, yellow fruits.
Moneymaker Very popular and reliable tomatoes; grows well under a wide range of conditions.
Shirley A heavy-cropping, disease-resistant variety.

Outdoor bush varieties
Amateur Early and heavy cropping.
Outdoor Girl One of the earliest tomatoes to ripen.
Roma Plum tomato developed for growing in the British climate.
Sigmabush Outstanding for the earliness and quality of its fruits.

Cherry tomatoes
These have become increasingly popular. Among the best are:
Gardener's Delight, **Sungold** and **Sweet One Million**.

Heritage or heirloom tomatoes
These terms are used to describe old tomato varieties that have seen a resurgence in popularity in recent years. One example is **Brandywine**, an early beefsteak variety dating from 1885.

SUPPORTING CORDONS IN A GREENHOUSE

Bury one end When growing tomatoes in a greenhouse border as single stem cordons, anchor one end of a length of string beneath the rootball.
If using grow bags, loop the string under the bag instead.

Tie other end to roof Attach the top end of the string to a roof strut or a strong overhead wire. Twist the growing stem round the string or tie the stem to the string as it grows. You can also use canes or bamboos.

Growing tips

You can buy tomato plants from nurseries, but it is easy, fun, and far cheaper, to raise your own tomato plants from seed.

For plants to be grown in a heated greenhouse sow in mid to late winter; sow those destined for an unheated greenhouse in mid spring; and for planting outside, sow about one or two weeks later.

Sow the seeds about 2.5cm (1in) apart in a tray or pot of seed compost. Sift compost to a depth of 5mm (¼in) over the top and water with a fine rose. Ideally, place the tray or pot, covered with a sheet of paper, in a propagator. Alternatively, put it in a polythene bag in an airing cupboard.

After about four days, keep checking for germination. As soon as the seedlings begin to break the surface, move the container into the light.

When the seed leaves are fully developed, the seedlings are ready for pricking out into 8cm (3in) pots of potting compost, where they can stay until planting time.

Greenhouse cultivation

Tomatoes are ready for planting when about 15cm (6in) tall. Stand the pots in their planting positions for a day or two before setting the plants in the soil. This will give them a gradual transition from the warmer conditions on the greenhouse staging.

Set plants at least 40cm (15in) apart in the greenhouse border or in large pots. In a broad border, you can plant two staggered rows 60cm (2ft) apart. Alternatively, put three plants in a grow bag.

Support each plant with a tall cane or with string tied under a leaf joint near the base of the stem and taken up to a hook screwed into a roof glazing bar or other fastening. If you use canes, tie the developing stems to them loosely every 30cm (12in) or so with soft garden twine.

Keep the plants on the dry side for a week or two after planting, then gradually increase the amount of water to ensure steady growth. You'll probably need to water them every day in warm weather.

Begin weekly feeding with a proprietary tomato feed as soon as the tomatoes on the lowest trusses begin to develop. Pinch out the

AT-A-GLANCE TIMETABLE

Outdoor tomatoes
PLANTING
LATE SPRING TO EARLY SUMMER
45cm (18in) apart

STOPPING
Pinch out top when four trusses have formed

HARVESTING
LATE SUMMER TO LATE AUTUMN

REMOVING SIDESHOOTS

Snap off sideshoots Check your plants regularly for small shoots that grow from the base of the leaves at the angle where they join the main stem. These can appear overnight. Wait until they are about 2–5cm (1–2in) long and then snap them off.

Pinch out the growing tips of indoor plants when they reach the roof; outdoors, remove tips once four trusses have formed.

tops of the stems when they reach roof height. Check cordons regularly and nip off the sideshoots that appear in the leaf axils.

Outdoor cultivation Plant outdoors when the danger of frost is past – late spring or early summer, depending on where you live and the conditions that season. You can plant up to two or three weeks earlier if you use cloches.

Set the plants 45cm (18in) apart, allowing 80cm (30in) between rows. Make the planting hole deep enough for the top of the soilball to sit at least 1cm (½in) below ground level.

Insert a 1.5m (5ft) stake or bamboo alongside each single-stem plant just outside the soilball. Check the plants regularly and tie them to the supports at intervals throughout summer.

Remove sideshoots regularly from the leaf axils of single-stem plants, water the plants frequently in dry weather and apply a liquid tomato fertiliser weekly once the fruits have started to develop.

Pinch out the tops of the plants when four fruit trusses have formed, leaving two leaves above the top truss.

Do not stake or remove sideshoots from bush varieties, but spread black polythene, straw or bark chippings underneath to keep the ripening fruits off the ground.

Ring culture This method of growing tomatoes prevents the plants' roots from coming into contact with the greenhouse soil – this can be an advantage when you suspect that the soil may be contaminated with disease organisms.

Rings are simply bottomless pots, generally made of bituminous felt, in which compost is placed and the tomatoes are planted.

Place the rings on a bed of fine aggregate. The tomatoes send down roots into the aggregate, which should be drenched daily and given a weekly liquid feed once the root system is established.

To set up a ring culture bed, dig a trench 15cm (6in) deep in the greenhouse floor and line it with

polythene. Pierce a drainage hole every 1m (3ft) and spread the aggregate evenly on top to a depth of 15cm (6in).

You can either buy rings or make them yourself by stapling together strips of lino or roofing felt. Each ring should be about 25cm (10in) in diameter and at least 20cm (8in) deep. Stand the rings 45cm (18in) apart on the aggregate.

Growing in grow bags These are plastic bags filled with a mixture of soil-less compost and fertiliser in which you can grow two or three tomato plants. Grow bags are suitable for both indoor and outdoor crops.

After planting, keep the compost moist but do not saturate. Apply liquid fertiliser every week after the first fruits have set.

You can also adapt the ring-culture method described above for growing tomatoes in grow bags. Make rings by cutting the bottoms out of 20–25cm (8–10in) plastic plant pots; then fit these into holes you've cut in the grow bag covering.

Set one plant in each pot making sure its rootball is in the grow bag. Then half fill the pot with potting compost. The hairy lower stems of the tomato plants will put out more roots into this soil and this will improve the plants' access to both water and nutrients. The empty space at the top of the flowerpot makes watering and feeding the plants an easy business.

Growing tomatoes in pots A sunny patio or balcony is ideal for growing tomatoes in 25cm (10in) pots or deep boxes filled with John Innes No. 3 Compost, or a good multipurpose compost.

Leave a 10cm (4in) space between the compost and the top of the container to allow for a top dressing with similar compost when the fruits appear.

Support, remove sideshoots and feed the plants as for tomatoes grown in the soil. They will need more water, however – perhaps even a drenching twice daily during hot weather. Give double the amount of liquid feed recommended by manufacturers for plants growing in the open.

Pests and diseases
Tomatoes are liable to be attacked by **aphids**, **glasshouse whitefly**, **potato cyst eelworm** and **wireworm**.

Diseases and disorders to which the crop is subject are **blossom end rot**, **blotchy ripening**, **damping off**, **foot rot**, **greenback**, **grey mould**, **magnesium deficiency**, **scald**, **soil-borne diseases**, **splitting**, **tomato blight** and **virus diseases** (see Pests and Diseases pages 238–49).

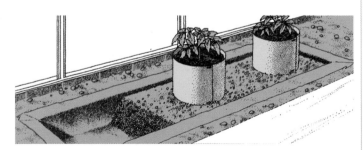

Setting up a ring-culture bed
Dig a trench 15cm (6in) deep and about 30cm (12in) wide, allowing 45cm (18in) for each plant to be grown. Line with polythene, piercing drainage holes every 1m (3ft). Fill with weathered ash, clinker or crushed stone and stand the special bituminous felt rings on top. Plant the tomatoes in John Innes No. 3 Compost.

Harvesting and storing

Fruits can be left to ripen on the plant (which tends to increase their flavour) or removed when they start to change colour. Hold the tomato and press the stalk with your thumb to break it neatly at the joint just above the fruit.

As autumn progresses, you can encourage the ripening of fruits that are already changing colour, under cloches. Place straw along the row, lay the stems horizontally, and cover with the cloches.

Remove green fruits, wrap them separately in newspaper and place in a drawer or lidded boxes indoors. Use fruits as they ripen. Both green and ripe tomatoes make excellent chutneys. Imperfect or overripe tomatoes are ideal for making juices and sauces.

See also **bottling** (page 270); **chutneys** (page 292); **freezing** (page 252); **fruit cheeses and butters** (page 281); **pickles** (page 285); **sauces**, **ketchups and relishes** (page 296) and **syrups and juices** (page 283).

Preparing and cooking

Strictly fruits, but classified as vegetables because of their use in savoury dishes, tomatoes are one of the most worthwhile crops for gardeners. They are brilliant partners with herbs such as basil, chives and marjoram and happily partner strong flavours, such as chilli, onion and garlic.

They can be enjoyed fresh in simple ways – as sandwich fillings; or thinly sliced and turned in a good oil-and-vinegar dressing, sprinkled with chopped parsley or chives, or with finely chopped onion and a touch of garlic.

In cooking, tomatoes are used in soups, added to casseroles for extra flavour and juice, folded into omelettes, or served grilled with scrambled eggs, bacon, grilled meat and baked fish. Try baking tomatoes for 15 minutes, after brushing with oil, or stuffing them with any number of savoury fillings.

How to skin tomatoes Lots of tomato recipes call for skinned tomatoes. To do this, submerge them in a bowl of boiling water for a minute, then cool them in cold water and peel off the skin, beginning at the stalk end.

Bruschetta Remove the skins from about 500g (1lb) ripe tomatoes and cut into quarters. Scoop out the seeds (keep the pulp and seeds to use in soups or casseroles) and chop up the tomato flesh as coarsely or finely as you like. Then add 2 tablespoons of extra virgin olive oil, a small red onion, finely chopped, a squeeze of lemon juice or a tablespoon white wine vinegar and salt and pepper to taste. Serve piled onto grilled slices of ciabatta bread that you've rubbed with garlic and drizzled with olive oil.

You can vary the topping by adding any of the following ingredients: chopped garlic; stoneless black olives, sliced; anchovies, chopped and mixed in, or a fillet laid over the top of each bruschetta; or fresh basil leaves.

Cherry tomato, mozarella and baby leaf salad
This looks really pretty if you use baby mozarellas, which are about the same size as cherry tomatoes. If you are growing your own baby leaves, then use these; otherwise use a small bag of rocket or other small leaves. Onto individual serving plates, arrange the leaves, whole tomatoes and cheeses, and dress with olive oil, lemon juice, salt and black pepper. Serve with warm ciabatta or French bread.

Fresh tomato soup Coarsely chop 1kg (2lb 4oz) of tomatoes. Heat 50ml (2fl oz) olive oil in a pan and add 2 medium onions, chopped and 4–6 cloves of finely chopped garlic. If you like a bit of heat, add half a chilli, chopped or a sprinkling of dried chilli flakes. Sweat gently until the onions are soft and translucent; tip in the tomatoes and cook gently for 10 minutes. Blend the soup in a food processor or push through a mouli to get it smooth and velvety. Warm through gently but do not boil; add salt and sugar to taste and garnish each bowl with fresh basil leaves or finely chopped chives. If the soup is too thick, you can water it down with water or stock.

Basic tomato pasta sauce You can use this as a base for myriad pasta dishes and it freezes, too. It also makes a good pizza topping.

Skin and chop 1kg (2lb 4oz) tomatoes. Cook a couple of medium onions in olive oil until soft and add the tomatoes, 2 teaspoons balsamic vinegar, a glass of red wine, 2 teaspoons sugar and a handful of fresh basil or oregano. Simmer on the hob for up to an hour, stirring from time to time so it doesn't stick. You can leave the sauce chunky or blend it in the food processor – which most children prefer. Check the seasoning and serve spooned over pasta with lots of freshly grated Parmesan cheese.

Variations Ring the changes by mixing the basic tomato sauce with any of the following: mascarpone cheese; chopped black olives; fried bacon; fried aubergine and sun-dried tomatoes; sautéed mushrooms; shredded chicken and sautéed red peppers; fried slices of chorizo; or sliced garlic and fresh chilli. Just cooking any of these in the sauce will change its flavour.

Turnips

Globe-shape turnip

Flat-rooted turnip

Turnips can provide a space-saving bonus for the gardener with a small plot. Because they grow quickly and are picked young, they may be sown between rows of slow-growing crops such as parsnips. The small turnips are harvested before the parsnips develop fully. Different varieties of turnip can be grown to provide roots for most of the year.

Although the turnip has been a favourite since Roman times, its popularity has little to do with its nutritional value. The root consists of about 90 per cent water, with some sugar and pectin – a jelly-like substance which helps jams to set. Nevertheless, it adds a fresh flavour to a dish of vegetables, particularly when accompanied by the season's first peas and carrots.

Planning the crop

Turnips grow best on a light, fertile loam, but they will succeed on most garden soils in an open, sunny position. Do not sow on freshly manured ground, or the roots may split into a number of 'fangs'.

Quick-maturing turnips may also be grown in troughs and windowboxes.

Before sowing, rake in a general fertiliser at the rate of 60g per square metre (2oz per square yard). On an acid soil give a top dressing of garden lime at the rate of 200g per square metre (7oz per square yard) during the winter before sowing.

How much to grow Because turnips grow quickly and are picked young, sow little and often. A row 3m (10ft) long can be expected to yield 5–5.5kg (10–12lb) of roots.

Sow every three to four weeks from early spring to just after midsummer for a continuous supply, and again in late summer to early autumn for winter crops.

Varieties There are several to choose from including:
Purple Top Milan Very early; flat, white roots with purple tops.

Snowball Quick-growing; round roots with white flesh and mild flavour.
Tokyo Cross Quick-growing variety that is sown late. Good for sowing late in the season.
Atlantic Similar to Purple Top Milan (above) but can be forced under cloches early and late in the season.

Growing tips

You can make a February sowing of **Atlantic** or other forcing variety under cloches or in a coldframe, provided there are no hard frosts and the soil is dry enough for you to create a tilth.

Make the first outdoor sowing in a sunny, sheltered bed in early spring in the south, or two weeks later in the north.

Sow again about four and eight weeks later for summer supplies. For autumn and winter crops, sow just after midsummer and in late summer to early autumn.

Sow the seed in drills 1cm (½in) deep, with 40cm (15in) between rows. Thin the seedlings as soon as they are large enough to handle, first to about 8cm (3in) apart, then two or three weeks later to 15cm (6in).

Don't throw away larger thinnings – you can cook them like spring greens.

Keep the ground well watered, or the turnips may go to seed and the roots will become stringy.

Pests and diseases

Cutworms, **flea beetle** and **caterpillars** of the **swift moth** are the principal pests.

Diseases and disorders that may occur are **boron deficiency**, **club root** and **splitting** (see Pests and Diseases, pages 238–49).

Harvesting and storing

Pick the turnips regularly, so that you never allow them to become larger than a tennis ball. Roots smaller than this may be used in salads as a substitute for radishes. Turnips larger than this may be stringy and will have a less pleasant flavour.

Summer harvested turnips may be frozen (page 252). Pull winter turnips when needed, or lift a few and store them in a shed for use during spells when the soil is too frozen for harvesting.

Preparing and cooking

Turnips are at their best in spring and summer if the small, globe-like roots are pulled when about six weeks old. At this stage they will be about the size of tennis balls.

Prepare turnips by cutting off a slice from the leafy top and trimming off the fibrous roots. Many quick-growing varieties do not need peeling, just washing well to remove soil. Peel other young turnips thinly, maincrop turnips thickly, and on the latter also cut out any woody parts. Wash them well, leaving small turnips whole but cutting winter turnips into rough chunks.

Cook young, whole turnips in boiling, lightly salted water for 20–30 minutes. Cook maincrop turnips for 30–40 minutes in boiling, salted water or in clear stock to enhance their flavour.

Serve young boiled turnips tossed in butter and chopped parsley, or is a parsley sauce. Maincrop turnips are more often mashed, beaten with butter and cream and seasoned with salt, pepper, mace and lemon juice, and are known as 'neeps' – a traditional accompaniment to haggis.

AT-A-GLANCE TIMETABLE

SOWING
EARLY SPRING TO LATE SUMMER
1cm (½in) deep in rows 40cm (15in) apart

THINNING
8–15cm (3–6in) apart when large enough to handle

HARVESTING
Pull when tennis-ball size

Watercress

Although the natural environment of watercress is a running stream, this peppery salad leaf can easily be grown in the garden. Under these conditions its main need is copious watering.

There are two types of watercress, one a bronze-green and the other dark green, both of which are native to this country. The bronze-green cress is hardier and has a slightly more pungent flavour.

Watercress is an excellent source of vitamin C and beta carotene and is rich in cancer-fighting antioxidants.

Planning the crop
Grow watercress either in a trench in the vegetable plot or in shallow boxes. Wooden fruit boxes from a greengrocer are ideal.

If you use a box, cover the bottom and sides with a sheet of polythene to ensure that moisture is retained. Fill the box with garden soil or potting compost.

In the open garden, dig a trench 25cm (9in) wide and 60cm (2ft) long. Mix a bucketful of well-rotted manure or garden compost with the soil in the base of the trench, leaving this about 8cm (3in) below the surrounding soil level.

Growing tips
In mid to late spring remove 10cm (4in) shoots from plants bought from a greengrocer and plant them 15cm (6in) apart in the prepared trench. Keep the trench well

watered and the plants will root readily. If you're using boxes, cover these with polythene bags to increase the humidity. Keep them out of direct sunshine.

Alternatively, sow by broadcasting seeds in the trench or box in mid spring. Thin the plants to 15cm (6in) apart when they are large enough to handle.

Remove flowerheads as soon as they appear. If the soil has been well prepared, watercress needs no extra feeding. If however, towards the end of the season, the leaves are getting very small, then feed the plants with general liquid fertiliser to encourage sturdier growth.

You can make a second planting in late summer for a late crop, which you will need to protect in a coldframe or under cloches. Whenever the weather allows, remove the covering to give the plants some fresh air.

Pests and diseases
Watercress is usually free of pests. Plants may sometimes be attacked by **virus diseases** (page 247).

Harvesting watercress
Start picking as soon as the plants are established. Sometimes this can be as early as three or four weeks after planting.

The more the tops are picked, the more new branches will be produced to provide a fresh supply.

Picking can go on into autumn, when boxed plants can be brought indoors or put in a cold greenhouse to extend the season.

Preparing and cooking
Fresh, bright green watercress is used chiefly to garnish savoury dishes and in green salads. Wash

the stems in cold running water, shake them dry and separate into small sprigs. Trim the stalks short and pick off any wilting or yellowing leaves.

Chopped watercress can be mixed into white sauces to accompany vegetables or poultry. It is also excellent blended into mayonnaise or soft creamy cheeses such as ricotta or mascarpone.

Small bunches of watercress are traditionally used to hide the crop end of roast game birds, chicken and duck. The leaves are also incorporated into light, delicate stuffings.

Finally, watercress is used to make one of the oldest of English soups, either served hot or as a creamy chilled soup, perfect for a summer's day.

Hot watercress soup
Cook an onion in a tablespoon of butter in a large saucepan until soft; don't let it brown.

Add 250g (9oz) potatoes, peeled and diced and about 600ml (1 pint) chicken stock. Cook gently for 20 minutes until the potatoes are soft. Then add 3 or 4 big handfuls

(weighing 150–200g (5–6oz)) of washed and chopped watercress and simmer gently for 5 minutes.

Tip the soup into a blender and process until smooth. Pour back into the saucepan and add 50ml (2fl oz) single cream plus some extra milk if the soup is too thick.

Warm through gently, without boiling, season with salt and freshly ground black pepper and serve hot with fresh, crusty bread.

Chilled watercress soup
Melt 2 tablespoons of butter in a heavy saucepan and add 500g (1lb 2oz) leeks, washed and chopped, and 2 potatoes, peeled and diced.

Sweat over a low heat for about 20 minutes, checking from time to time to make sure nothing sticks or burns. Then add a litre (1¾ pints) of vegetable or chicken stock, cover and simmer for 15 minutes or so until the vegetables are tender.

Add 2 or 3 handfuls of washed and chopped watercress and simmer for a further 5 minutes. Season with salt and pepper, and leave to cool before liquidising in a blender until smooth.

Pour the soup into a large bowl and stir in 150ml (¼ pint) double cream. Check the seasoning and then put the soup into the fridge to chill. Serve garnished with a sprig of watercress, a swirl of cream and perhaps an ice cube.

AT-A-GLANCE TIMETABLE

PLANTING
MID TO LATE SPRING
In trenches 25cm (9in) wide, 8cm (3in) deep and 60cm (2ft) long

DISBUDDING
Remove flowerheads as they appear

HARVESTING
From about four weeks after planting

The food-grower's CALENDAR

Late-winter to early spring

The early months of the year can be a bleak time in the garden. Little is actively growing in the chilly weather, although there may still be overwintering crops to harvest, such as root crops left to store in the ground or winter vegetables coming to maturity, such as Brussels sprouts.

But it can be an optimistic time of planning and preparation: digging the ground when frosts allow, warming the soil ready for sowing and even putting your first seeds of the year into the ground as spring begins to emerge from the gloom.

As the sun gets warmer, you may even begin to harvest spring greens and early rhubarb, but keep a weather eye open for sudden spring frosts that can strip fruit trees of their precious blossom.

Protecting fruit from frost
Spring frosts can damage the blossom of early-flowering fruit trees, particularly those trained on a wall rather than growing in the open garden. Drape horticultural fleece over the branches at night, but remove it during the day to allow access for pollinating insects.

Late-winter
(January–February in the south)

Vegetables
● Dig where **beans** and **peas** are to be sown, incorporating well-rotted manure or compost.
● In the open, sow round-seeded **peas**.
● Prepare **celery** trenches.
● Force **chicory** and **seakale** in fortnightly batches.
● Blanch Batavian-type **endives**.
● Lift **Jerusalem artichokes**.
● Place seed **potatoes** in a tray to sprout, or 'chit'.
● In the greenhouse, sow **cauliflowers**, **onions** and **tomatoes** (for growing on in a heated greenhouse).
● Sow **radishes** under cloches,

and **lettuces** in a cold frame or under cloches for planting out in early spring.
● Put cloches in position to warm the soil for early **carrots**.
● Plant **garlic**, **Jerusalem artichokes** and **shallots**.
● In the greenhouse, sow **aubergines**, **cauliflowers** and, later, frame **cucumbers**.
● Order **asparagus** crowns for planting in early spring

Fruits
● Plant **apple**, **apricot**, **medlar**, **pear**, **plum** and **quince trees**; also **blackberries** and **hybrid berries**, **black**, **red** and **white currants**, **blueberries**, **gooseberries** and **raspberries**, unless soil is frozen or waterlogged.
● Continue pruning **grape vines** in

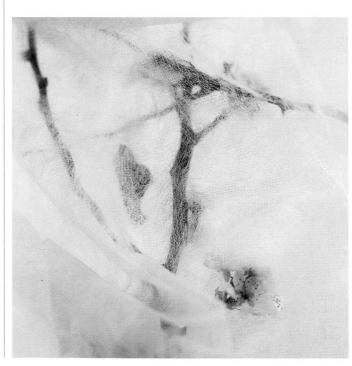

the open. In the greenhouse, prune and tidy the vines, scrub down the glass and framework and replace the top layer of soil.
● Feed and mulch **currant bushes**.
● Force **rhubarb** by putting roots lifted in November in boxes of moist peat.
● Prevent rain falling on **peaches**, **nectarines** and **apricots** by erecting a cover over the top.
● Prepare a bed for planting **rhubarb** in early spring. For an early picking of established plants, cover the crowns with a bucket, box or rhubarb forcer.
● Plant (unless the soil is frozen or waterlogged) **apples**, **apricots**, **medlars**, outdoor **grape vines**, **pears** and **plums**; also **blackberries** and **hybrid berries**, **black**, **red** and **white currants**, **blueberries**, **gooseberries** and **raspberries**.
● Prune **blueberries** and **gooseberries**.
● Cut down the canes of autumn-fruiting **raspberries**.
● Apply fertiliser to **apples**, **cherries**, **peaches** and **pears**.
● Top dress the rooting area of greenhouse **grape vines**.
● Apply fertiliser to **grape vines** in the open.
● Protect **apricot** trees with fleece or netting against frost.

Herbs
● Sow **chervil** in the greenhouse.

In the garden
● Prepare the soil by digging, when weather conditions allow.
● Make a seedbed: break up lumps of soil on the surface then rake it level. Cover the area with plastic sheeting raised on upturned flowerpots to warm the soil for early sowings then hoe off any weeds after two or three weeks.

Early Spring
(Early–mid March in the south)

Vegetables
● Prepare the greenhouse bed for **cucumbers**, and fix support wires.
● Thin Japanese varieties of **onions**, harden off winter-sown seedlings, and plant out maincrop onions sown in late summer.
● Harden off **cauliflowers** sown under glass, and plant out.
● Plant **garlic**, **horseradish**, **Jerusalem artichokes**, early **potatoes** and **shallots**.
● In the greenhouse, sow **celeriac**, **celery**, frame **cucumbers**, **peppers** and **tomatoes** (for growing on under cold glass).
● Sow **carrots** in coldframes or under cloches.
● Outdoors, sow globe **beetroot**, **broad beans**, early **Brussels sprouts**, **calabrese**, **cauliflowers**, **chard** and **spinach beet**, **kohlrabi**, **leeks**, **lettuce**, **onions**, **parsnips**, first-early wrinkled **peas**, **shallots**, **spinach** and **turnips**.

Fruits
● Finish planting bare-root tree fruits, soft fruit canes and **rhubarb**.
● Prune **blueberries**, acid **cherry trees** and fan-trained **plums**.
● Fertilise **apples**, sweet **cherries**, **peaches**, **pears**, **blackberries**, **currants**, **gooseberries** and **raspberries**.
● Pollinate **peach** blossom with a camel-hair brush.

Herbs
● Sow **burnet**, **chervil**, **fennel**, **dill**, **lovage**, **marjoram**, **parsley**, **rosemarry**, **sage** and **thyme**.
● Raise new plants of **lovage** by division of roots.
● Plant **bay** trees and **tarragon**.

The warming taste of winter

Ready to harvest

Crops ready to harvest in the early months of the year include root vegetables, such as **beetroot**, **carrots**, **parsnips** and **swedes**; brassicas, including **broccoli**, Brussels sprouts, winter **cabbages** and **cauliflowers**, and **kale**; winter **radishes** and **spinach**, and the delicious, nobbly **Jerusalem artichokes**. With spring, you may start to harvest early **asparagus**, **salad onions** and spring greens, such as sprouting **broccoli** and **calabrese**. And if you have forced an early crop of **rhubarb** you may be able to pull the first of the pale pink sticks.

Hearty soups, spring greens

Make the most of the earthy flavours of root vegetables by cooking them to a velvety softness in warming soups and casseroles or by roasting slowly alongside a joint of meat until they are tinged with caramel around the edges.

Retain as much of the crisp, freshness of leafy greens as possible by cooking them quickly: steaming them lightly or stir-frying super-fast in a wok.

Sautéed Brussels sprouts

SERVES: 4
1 tablespoon corn oil
75g (2¾oz) rindless smoked bacon
500g (1lb 2oz) Brussels sprouts
1 orange
50g (1¾oz) butter
2 teaspoons wholegrain mustard
115g (4oz) canned whole water chestnuts in water
Salt and black pepper

Heat the oil in a frying pan, dice the bacon and fry it for 2–3 minutes, until golden brown. Rinse the sprouts, trim them if necessary and cut them in half. Wash any wax off the orange and grate the rind into the pan. Add the butter, mustard and sprouts and cook over a moderate heat for 5 minutes, stirring, until the sprouts are crisp.

Drain and roughly chop the water chestnuts, stir them into the sprouts and cook for 3–5 minutes, until the sprouts are golden and the chestnuts heated through. Season to taste.

Aromatic parsnip soup

SERVES: 4–6
850ml (1 pint 10fl oz) vegetable stock
1 large cooking apple
550g (1lb 4oz) parsnips
1 medium onion
1 tablespoon sunflower oil
1 clove garlic
2 teaspoon ground coriander
1 teaspoon ground cumin
1 teaspoon turmeric
Salt
300ml (10fl oz) milk
A few sprigs of coriander and 4–6 tablespoons natural yoghurt to garnish

Warm the stock. Peel the apple and parsnips. Quarter and core the apple, then chop the apple and parsnips into chunks. Peel and chop the onion; Heat the oil in a large saucepan, add the onion and leave it to soften.

Peel and roughly chop the garlic, add it to the pan, then add the spices and cook for 1 minute.

Pour the warmed stock into the pan and add the apple, parsnips and salt. Bring to the boil, then reduce the heat, cover and simmer for 15 minutes. Meanwhile rinse and dry the coriander and strip off the leaves. Remove the pan from the heat and stir in the milk. Process the soup to a smooth purée, then reheat.

Garnish with the coriander and serve, with a spoonful of yoghurt.

Cauliflower and bacon gratin

SERVES: 4
500g (1lb 2oz) cauliflower
250ml (9fl oz) milk
Salt
25g (1oz) butter, plus extra for greasing the dish
1 clove garlic
75g (2¾oz) rindless bacon, diced
25g (1oz) plain flour
100ml (3½fl oz) double cream
50g (1¾oz) Gruyère cheese
Pepper and grated nutmeg
2 tablespoons finely grated Parmesan cheese

Break up the cauliflower into florets and cut the stalk diagonally into 5mm (¼in) slices. Bring a large pan of water to the boil and cook the florets and sliced stalk for 7–8 minutes. Take 75ml of the cooking liquid and mix it with the milk then drain the florets thoroughly. Grate the Gruyère cheese.

Heat the oven to 200°C (gas mark 6). Butter a gratin dish and scatter chopped garlic over the base. Melt the butter in a frying pan and fry the bacon for 5 minutes, or until it releases its fat. While the bacon is cooking, heat the milk mixture. Sprinkle the flour into the bacon pan and stir over a gentle heat for 2–3 minutes without letting it brown.

Remove the bacon pan from the heat and gradually stir in the milk; return to the heat, stirring, until the sauce begins to bubble, then simmer for 5 minutes. Add the cream and bring back to the boil.

Remove from the heat, add half the Gruyère and stir until melted. Season with salt, pepper and nutmeg. Spread the cauliflower in the gratin dish, pour over the sauce, top with the remaining Gruyère and Parmesan cheese and bake for 20 minutes, until the top is bubbling nicely and well browned.

Mid-Spring to early summer

By now, the vegetable garden should be bursting into life; fruit trees and bushes are heavy with blossom as insects buzz from flower to flower pollinating the fruits.

Warm, dry soils are ready for sowing hardier vegetables outdoors and you will soon be rewarded for hard preparation over winter by the sight of seedlings pushing up through the soil.

The garden is full of promise that starts to come to fruition in earnest as spring turns to summer, and the gardener is kept busy watering, harveting, thinning and checking for signs of pests or disease.

Earth-up potatoes As maincrop potatoes grow, pull loose soil up around the stems so that the plants are growing out of a ridge. This prevents the tubers from turning green – and poisonous.

Mid-spring
(Late March–April in the south)

Vegetables
● Outdoors at the start of the period, continue sowing early **Brussels sprouts, calabrese, leeks, lettuce, onions, parsnips,** first-early wrinkled **peas** and **shallots**.
● Prepare the ground and fix stakes for **runner beans**.
● Harden off **cauliflowers** sown under glass, and plant out.
● Plant **asparagus, globe artichokes, cabbages**, winter-sown **onions, onions** sets, and **potatoes** (second-early at the beginning of the period, maincrop at the end).
● Sow ridge **cucumbers** and **tomatoes** (both for growing outdoors) in the greenhouse.
● Sow **celery** in a coldframe; **french beans** and **sweetcorn** under cloches (middle to end of period).
● Outdoors, sow **broad beans,**
maincrop **Brussels sprouts,** summer and autumn **cabbages, carrots, cauliflowers,** globe **beetroot, florence fennel, kale, kohlrabi, lettuce,** second-early **peas, pumpkins, radishes, spinach, Swiss chard, sprouting broccoli** and **turnips**.

Fruits
● Plant containerised fruit trees and bushes.
● Prune **peach** trees.
● Apply fertiliser to **blackberries** and **hybrid berries** and **plums**.
● Give a top dressing of Epsom salts to **grape vines** grown in the open. In the greenhouse, select the strongest vine shoot from each spur and rub out others. Close ventilators and spray vines with water twice a day.
● Thin **apricots** and **gooseberries**.
● Mulch established **fig** trees and **raspberries**. Gradually remove winter protection from fig trees.
● Sow **melons** in the greenhouse.
● Net **strawberries** to prevent birds eating the developing fruit.

Herbs
● Sow **angelica, balm, borage, burnet, chervil, coriander, dill, hyssop,** pot **marjoram, sage** and summer **savory**.

In the greenhouse
● Increase ventilation as temperatures rise and increase humidity by 'damping down' the greenhouse floor whenever you water.

Late spring
(May in the south)

Vegetables
● Prepare the coldframe for frame **cucumbers**, and sow seeds in pots in the frame. Prepare outside beds for **courgettes, marrows** and ridge **cucumbers**.
● Plant summer **cabbages**.
● Harden off **celeriac** and **tomatoes** and plant out towards the end of the month.
● Plant **aubergines** in the greenhouse or under cloches.
● Mulch globe **artichokes**.
● At the beginning of the period, in the greenhouse or under cloches, sow **celery, courgettes, marrows** and **soya bean**. Plant out at the end of the period or in early summer.
● Outdoors, sow **asparagus peas,** long-rooted **beetroot,** winter **cabbages, carrots, french** and **runner beans, cauliflowers, chicory, kohlrabi, lettuce, radishes, spinach, swedes, sweetcorn** and **turnips**.

Fruits
● Plant Alpine **strawberries**.
● Complete summer pruning of **peach** trees. Prune leaders of mature cordon, espalier and dwarf pyramid **apple** and **pear** trees.
● In the greenhouse, tie up laterals of **grape** vines and begin liquid feeding.
● Plant **melons** under cloches or in the greenhouse.
● Hang codling moth traps in the branches of **apple** and **pear** trees, and plum moth traps in **plum** trees.

Herbs
● Sow **chervil, dill,** pot **marjoram** and **sage**.

● Harden off **basil** and **marjoram** in the middle of the period and plant about a fortnight later.

In the greenhouse
● Pot up mail-order plants as soon as they arrive and keep them in a 'quarantine' area for a few days to check for pests and disease.
● Apply shading to the glass ready to protect plants from the harsh summer sun.

Early summer
(Early June in the south)

Vegetables
● Plant frame **cucumbers** in a coldframe.
● Outdoors, plant **Brussels sprouts, cauliflowers, celery, leeks, pumpkins,** ridge **cucumbers,** sprouting **broccoli, sweet peppers** and **tomatoes**.
● Sow **carrots, chicory, chinese cabbages,** curly-leaf **endive, french beans, kohlrabi, lettuces, peas, radishes** and **spinach**.
● Feed **tomatoes** with a liquid fertiliser when the first fruits set. Nip out side-shoots.

Fruits
● Nip back the side-shoots of **figs**. Rub out shoots of fan-trained sweet **cherries** that are growing towards or away from the wall.
● Apply sulphate of ammonia or dried blood to **apricot** trees.
● In the greenhouse, thin **grapes** and reduce watering. Outdoors, restrict the number of branches according to the age of the vine.

Herbs
● Sow **chervil** and **dill** in seed beds outdoors.

Fresh spring produce

Ready to harvest

Through spring you should be able to start harvesting **asparagus**, early **carrots** and **turnips**, overwintered **lettuces** and young seedlings as baby leaves, **radishes**, **spinach**, spring **cabbage**, **spring onions** and **sprouting broccoli**.

Later in this period, you should also be able to pick baby **sweetcorn**, **broad beans**, early **carrots**, **french beans**, **globe artichokes**, **kohlrabi**, an abundance of **lettuces** and **salad leaves**, **peas** and **mangetout**, **shallots**, summer **cabbages** and **cauliflowers** and summer **squash**.

Baby new **potatoes**, served in a little melted butter sprinkled with parsley or chopped chives herald the start of summer for many gardeners and cooks alike.

Soft fruits at their best

As the season turns to summer, check ripening fruits daily to catch them at their peak. Harvest **blackcurrants**, early **peaches**, early **plums**, **gooseberries**, **raspberries**, **red** and **white currants**, late **rhubarb**, **strawberries**, and sweet **cherries** when they are dry – early morning is best – and handle them with care to avoid bruising.

Fresh and simple flavours

Soft fruits – blackcurrants, raspberries and strawberries – are at their best served simply, perhaps with a sprinkling of sugar or with a little cream. Mixed with currants, they make a luscious filling for a classic summer pudding (see page 128) or a topping for pavlova.

Young broad beans and french beans taste sweet and tender in a lightly dressed salad. Make the most of them by serving them alongside tender young salad leaves, or even the thinnings from your crop of lettuces. French beans combine well with finely sliced red onions tossed in a dressing of olive oil, balsamic vinegar and finely chopped garlic for an early summer picnic or lunch.

Early summer casserole
SERVES: 6
500g (1lb 2oz) young carrots
500g (1lb 2oz) new potatoes
500g (1lb 2oz) belly pork
50g (1¾oz) butter
450ml (16fl oz) stock
Salt and pepper
2 sprigs of thyme
1 small cauliflower
250g (9oz) young green peas
Chopped parsley to garnish

Trim, scrape and wash the carrots and chop them into rough slices. Scrape the potatoes and cut any large ones into slices. Remove the rind, bone and gristle from the pork and cut it into cubes.

Melt the butter in a heavy-based pan and fry the meat until golden brown; add the carrots and potatoes and toss well. Stir in the stock, season with salt and pepper and add the thyme. Cover with a lid and simmer for 35 minutes.

Add the cauliflower, broken into small florets, and the peas. Continue to simmer until all the ingredients are tender. Check the seasoning, remove the thyme and thicken if necessary with a little kneaded butter and flour. Serve sprinkled with the chopped parsley.

Broad bean salad
250g (9oz) shelled broad beans
250g (9oz) shelled green peas
2 shallots
6 tablespoons olive oil

2 tablespoons garlic vinegar
Salt and pepper
1 clove garlic
Basil leaves to garnish

Cook the broad beans and peas until tender, drain and leave to cool. Put them in a serving bowl and mix with the finely chopped shallots.

Make a dressing from the oil, vinegar, salt and pepper and crushed garlic.

Dress the salad just before serving, tossing in the dressing until it is well coated and sprinkle with chopped basil.

Potato and green bean curry
SERVES: 4 (as a side dish)
500g (1lb 2oz) small new potatoes
250g (9oz) french beans
15g (½oz) butter
3 tablespoons sunflower oil
2 small green chillis
½ teaspoon each of cumin seeds and ground turmeric
¼ teaspoon garam masala
1 clove garlic
Salt

Scrub the potatoes and cut them into thick slices. Top and tail the green beans, then cut them into 2.5cm (1in) lengths, rinse and drain.

Heat the butter and oil in a wide, shallow pan over a high heat. When they begin to sizzle, stir in the chillis and spices. Peel and crush the garlic and add it to the pan. Fry for 30 seconds. Add the potatoes and a little salt then stir until they are well coated with the butter and oil. Stir in the beans, cover the pan then reduce the heat to moderate and cook for 15 minutes, stirring occasionally.

The curry is ready to serve as soon as the potatoes are tender. Serve it as a side dish or one of a selection of curries along with rice or naan bread.

Midsummer to early autumn

The busiest time of the year for harvesting vegetables, fruits and herbs, summer and early autumn will also keep the gardener busy with watering, feeding and staying vigilant for signs of attack from pests and disease.

But few gardeners begrudge this labour, when it is such a joyous season to be working in the plot enjoying the fruits of their endeavours and the warmth of the long summer days.

What could be better than returning home from the allotment or simply back into the kitchen from the garden laden with fresh home-grown produce for a delicious evening meal?

Mid-summer
(Late June–July in the south)

Vegetables
● Plant **kale**, **leeks** and white **cabbages**.
● Sow curly-leaf **endive**, **kohlrabi**, **lettuces**, **peas**, **radishes**, **rape kale**, **savoy cabbages**, **spinach** and **turnips**.
● Lift **shallots**, and ripen on a path before storing.
● Spray **runner beans** with water to help the flowers to set and check for aphids.
● Feed **peppers** and **tomatoes** with liquid fertiliser when the first fruits form.
● Pollinate **pumpkins and squashes** by hand to ensure a good crop.

Pollinate squashes by hand
Pumpkins and squashes will only fruit if they are cross pollinated, but, in a cool summer, they may be too late for the natural flurry of pollinating insects. Give the plants a helping hand by picking a ripe male flower and pushing it into the centre of a female flower to transfer the pollen.

Fruits
● Plant **strawberries** to ripen under cloches in the spring. Layer runners of established plants.
● Prune **red** and **white currants**.
● Continue to plant containerised fruit trees, bushes and plants unless the weather is dry.
● Prune back growing tips of new shoots on **cherry** trees.
● Prune cordon, dwarf pyramid and espalier **apple** and **pear** trees. Thin the crop of **apples** after the natural ('June') drop.
● In the greenhouse, thin **grapes** and reduce watering. Outdoors, restrict the number of branches according to the age of the vine.
● Prune **blackcurrants** after fruiting.
● Prune fan-trained **plum** trees.
● After pruning fan-trained **peach** trees, tie in replacement shoots.
● Cut back to just above soil level **loganberry**, **raspberry** and **hybrid berry** canes that have fruited.

● Tie autumn-fruiting **raspberries** to support wires.
● Check ties and supports on tree fruits and slacken them if stems are being constricted.
● Stop picking **rhubarb** to allow plants to recover before winter.

Herbs
● Sow **chervil**, **dill** and **parsley**.
● Nip out the growing tips of bushy herbs, such as **basil**, **savoury** and **marjoram** to encourage growth.

Late summer
(August in the south)

Vegetables
● Sow **carrots** (cover with cloches in late autumn), **onions** (Japanese varieties in a permanent bed and maincrop varieties in a seed bed), spring **cabbages** and **turnips**.
● Feed **peppers** and **tomatoes** with liquid fertiliser.
● Earth up trench-grown **celery**. At the end of the period, lift self-blanching **celery**.
● Cut down and burn **potato** tops if leaves show signs of blight.

Fruits
● Plant **strawberries**. Layer runners of established plants.
● Prepare ground for growing **grape** vines outdoors. Train fruiting laterals of vines growin in the open through support wires, and prune.
● Cut back **raspberry** canes, after fruiting, to just above soil level.

Herbs
● Sow **chervil** in a seedbed outdoors.

Early Autumn
(Early September in the south)

Vegetables
● Sow **cauliflowers** under cloches or in a coldframe.
● Outdoors, sow **corn salad**, **land cress**, overwintering **lettuces** and **red cabbages**.
● Remove any side leaves from **celeriac**.
● Earth up **celery**.
● Blanch **cardoons** and curly-leaf **endive**.
● Feed **peppers** and **tomatoes** with liquid fertiliser.

Fruits
● Sow seeds of Alpine **strawberries**.
● Prepare ground for planting bare-root fruit trees, bushes and canes.
● Prune **peach** trees after fruiting and tie in replacement shoots.
● Prune any secondary growth on trained **apple** and **pear** trees.
● Cut away dead wood on sweet **cherry** trees and shorten shoots pinched back in summer.
● Cut down fruited **blackberry** canes to ground level.

Herbs
● Plant **rue** and **thyme**.
● Outdoors, sow **angelica** and **lovage**; under glass sow summer **savory**.
● Gather **fennel** seed-heads for drying.
● Root **sage** cuttings in a cold frame.

The bounty of summer

Ready to harvest

At the height of summer, the fruit and vegetable garden is in full production. You need to check your crops daily to make sure that you pick produce at its best – delicious, young courgettes can turn into mighty marrows overnight, losing much of their best flavour, and soft fruits can overripen and quickly begin to rot.

Fruits of summer and autumn

Early summer's **blackcurrants**, **peaches**, **plums**, **gooseberries**, **raspberries**, **red** and **white currants**, **strawberries** and sweet **cherries** will continue to ripen through the season, joined by **blackberries**, **grapes**, **figs**, loganberries and other **hybrid berries**. As autumn approaches, **apples** begin to ripen, bringing with them the promise of the classic pie-filling combination of blackberry and apple.

Salads and vegetables

Asparagus, **asparagus peas**, **aubergine**, **baby sweetcorn**, **beetroot**, **broad beans**, **calabrese**, **chard**, **carrots**, **courgettes**, **cucumbers**, **florence fennel**, early **potatoes**, **french beans**, **globe artichokes**, **kohlrabi**, **lettuces**, **salad leaves**, **peas** and mangetout, **radish**, **shallots**, **spinach**, **spring onions**, summer **cabbage** and **cauliflower**, summer **squash**, sweet **peppers**, **tomatoes** and **turnips** all reach their peak in summer.

In early autumn you can start to gather **celeriac**, **Jerusalem artichokes**, **kale**, **leeks**, maincrop **potatoes**, **marrows**, **onions**, **parsnips** and **swedes**.

Dealing with gluts

So much produce is ripening at this time of year that you may find you cannot eat it all. Even giving away food parcels to friends may not keep up with the harvest and you will find yourself with a glut.

Fresh tomatoes make a pasta sauce that is hard to beat for flavour (see page 223) or combine them with a bounty of courgettes and maybe sweet peppers to make a tasty ratatouille.

Summer and autumn fruits can be gently cooked in delicious combinations to make compôtes to serve with natural yoghurt, ice cream or as a base for a cobbler or pie. Add cinnamon, ginger and other spices to create your own favourite flavours.

Sicilian caponata

SERVES: 4 (as a first course)
500g (1lb 2oz) courgettes, cleaned, trimmed and sliced
1 green pepper, deseeded and diced
2 onions, peeled and finely chopped
1 aubergine, cut crossways into narrow slices
6 large tomatoes, skinned and roughly chopped
100ml (3½fl oz) olive oil
150ml (5fl oz) dry white wine
Sugar
Salt and pepper

Heat the oil in a heavy-based pan and fry the onions for 3–5 minutes, until soft and golden. Add the courgettes, green pepper and aubergine slices. Stir continuously for about 3 minutes, until the vegetables are softening, then add the tomatoes, olive oil and half the wine. Cook the vegetable mixture over a very gentle heat until the

ingredients are all thoroughly combined, stirring frequently to prevent burning, and gradually adding the rest of the wine.

Season to taste with sugar, salt and pepper and serve with crusty bread.

Fennel and barley risotto

SERVES: 4
1 large head of fennel
Juice of 1 lemon
125g (4½oz) pearl barley
Salt and black pepper
3 tablespoons olive oil
2 slim leeks, sliced
2 cloves garlic, finely chopped
3 tomatoes, skinned and chopped
1 tablespoon chopped parsley

Roughly chop the fennel and put in a bowl with half of the lemon juice. Wash the barley under a cold tap, drain it and tip into a saucepan. Cover with plenty of cold water, bring to the boil, then drain. Rinse the barley and return to the pan with 1 litre (2 pints) of cold water. Return to the boil, add salt and simmer for 30–35 minutes. Drain, mix in the rest of the lemon juice and keep warm in a serving bowl.

Drain the fennel and pat it dry. Heat the oil in a large pan and stir fry the fennel for a few minutes before adding the leeks and garlic. Cook for 2 minutes, add the tomatoes then cook for a further 3–4 minutes.

Mix the vegetables into the barley, season to taste and serve sprinkled with the parsley.

Redcurrant compôte

SERVES: 4
500g (1lb 2oz) redcurrants, rinsed and drained
200g (7oz) caster sugar
1–2 tablespoons brandy
150ml (5fl oz) single cream

Put alternate layers of currants and sugar in a bowl. Leave in a warm room for several hours until the sugar has dissolved, then stir in the brandy. Spoon the redcurrants, with their juice, into serving glasses and chill for about 1 hour.

Mid-autumn to winter

The tradition of the harvest festival in autumn marks the close of the most productive part of the year and signals a shift in activity from growing to beginning to put the garden to bed.

But it's not too late to be sowing crops and bringing them on to ensure an early start in spring, particularly if you have the protection of a greenhouse or coldframe.

As you gather the last of your produce and pull up or prune plants at the end of their season, take time to reflect on your successes and failures and to begin to plan for the new growing season ahead. On cold, wet winter days, time spent mulling over seed catalogues is as productive as that spent digging in the garden.

Mid-autumn
(Late September–mid October in the south)

Vegetables
● Sow **cauliflowers** and **lettuces** under cloches or in a coldframe.
● Blanch curly-leaf **endive**.
● Start lifting trench-grown **celery** at the end of the period.
● Lift and store maincrop **carrots** and **chicory** when leaves die down.
● Harvest and store **marrows** and **tomatoes** when the first frost warnings are given.

Fruits
● Propagate **black**, **red** and **white currants**.
● Protect **fig** trees from frost with straw, bracken or lengths of matting during the second half of the period.
● Remove immature **figs**.
● Close greenhouse ventilators to raise the temperature until the last **grapes** are picked.

Herbs
● Raise new plants of **balm** by division.
● Plant **tarragon**.
● Sow **chervil** under glass for a winter supply.

Late autumn
(Mid October–early November in the south)

Vegetables
● Sow **cauliflowers** and **lettuces** under cloches or in a coldframe.
● Plant Japanese **onion** sets.
● Lift trench-grown **celery**.
● Lift and store maincrop **carrots** and **chicory** when the leaves die down.
● Sow **broad beans** and round-seeded **peas** for late spring crops.
● Blanch curly-leaf **endive**.
● Force **chicory** in batches.
● Lift and store long-rooted **beetroot** and any remaining **celeriac**.
● Cut **globe artichoke** stems almost to ground level and draw soil around them.
● Cut down **asparagus** ferns to within 2.5cm (1in) of the soil.

Fruits
● Plant containerised and bare-root **apple**, **apricot**, **damson**, **hazel**, **medlar**, **peach**, **pear**, **plum** and **quince** trees; also **blackberries** and **hybrid blackberries**, **black**, **red** and **white currants**, **blueberries**, **gooseberries**, outdoor **grape** vines, **raspberries** and **rhubarb**.
● Prune **blackberries** and **gooseberries**.
● Prune **grape** vines in the open. In the greenhouse, prune the vines, tidy the rods, scrub down the house structure and replace the top layer of soil.
● Begin forcing **rhubarb** by lifting one or two plants and exposing their roots to frost to make the plants dormant.

Herbs
● Sow **chervil** under glass for a winter supply.

In the garden and greenhouse
● Remove dead plant remains from the vegetable bed.
● Clean the greenhouse, cloches and coldframes and wash, dry and store pots and trays.
● Insulate the greenhouse to protect overwintering crops.

Early winter
(Late November–December in the south)

Vegetables
● Lift **Jerusalem artichokes**.
● Dig ground where **beans** and **peas** are to be sown next year, incorporating well-rotted manure or compost.

● Prepare **celery** trenches.
● Force **chicory** in batches.
● Blanch Batavian-type **endives**.

Fruits
● Plant **apple**, **apricot**, **medlar**, **pear**, **plum** and **quince** trees; also **blackberries** and **hybrid berries**, **black**, **red** and **white currants**, **blueberries**, **gooseberries**, **grape** vines and **raspberries**.
● Prune **blueberries**.
● Feed and mulch **currant** bushes.
● Force **rhubarb** by putting roots lifted in late autumn in boxes of moist peat substitute or spent potting compost.

Herbs
● Sow **chervil** under glass for a winter supply.

In the garden
● Plan your crops for the coming year and order seeds and potatoes.
● Clean and put away all tools.

Protect next year's harvest
Winter moths can destroy the leaves, blossom and shoots of fruit trees, decimating your next year's crop. Wrap a grease band – a strip of paper spread with grease – around each tree trunk to trap the wingless females as they try to climb the tree to lay their eggs.

Autumn harvest festival

Ready to harvest

As autumn ripens into winter, most green vegetables begin to come to the end of their season, to be replaced by a bounty of root vegetables, pumpkins and squashes and winter varieties of cabbage and cauliflower. Some crops can be left in the ground and picked as you need them, but others should be harvested and stored or preserved to avoid them being spoiled by early frosts.

Windfalls and late berries

Most soft fruits will have been picked by the middle of autumn, but if you have any **blackberries**, **raspberries**, Alpine or perpetual **strawberries** or **blackcurrants** left on the bush, it is worth harvesting them now and using them to make jams or jellies (see pages 271–80) to see you through the winter.

Apples and **pears** will be beginning to fall from the trees, so to avoid your crop being damaged by the fall, collect the fruits and store them carefully (see page 71) in a cool place. Always clear up windfalls and fallen autumn leaves and burn them or compost them to keep pests and diseases at bay.

Root vegetables and Hallowe'en pumpkins

Beetroot, **carrots**, **celeriac**, **celery**, **chinese cabbage**, **florence fennel**, **french** and **runner beans**, **Jerusalem artichokes**, **kale**, **leeks**, late-sown **lettuces**, maincrop **potatoes**, **marrows**, **onions**, **parsnips**, **peas**, **pumpkins** and **squashes**, **spinach**, autumn **cauliflowers**, autumn **cabbages**, **swedes** and **turnips** all come to fruition in the latter part of

autumn. By winter, you will probably only have **Brussels sprouts**, **celeriac**, **Jerusalem artichokes**, **kale**, **leeks**, **parsnips**, **swedes**, winter **cabbage** and **cauliflower**, winter **radish** and winter **spinach** still to harvest.

Make the most of the robust, hearty flavours, by combining your fresh ingredients with meat dishes and enlivening them with the addition of warming spices.

Jerusalem artichoke and smoked haddock chowder

SERVES: 6

3 medium floury potatoes
450g (1lb) smoked haddock
1 onion, roughly chopped
500g (1lb 2oz) Jerusalem artichokes
Juice of ½ lemon
2 sticks celery, destrung and diced
50g (1¾oz) butter
600ml (1 pint) milk
Black pepper
Snipped spring onions to garnish

Peel the potatoes, boil until soft, then drain, mash and set aside. Put the haddock in a pan with the onion and enough cold water to cover, bring to the boil and skim. Simmer the fish for 5–7 minutes, or until it is just beginning to flake.

Drain through a sieve, keeping the liquor and making it up to 500ml (18fl oz) with fresh cold water. Discard the onion. When the fish is cool, skin, bone and roughly flake it. Stir half of the cooking liquid into the potatoes.

Peel the artichokes and slice them thinly into a small bowl of cold water and lemon juice. Fry the celery for 2–3 minutes in butter, then add the milk, drained artichokes and the rest of the fish

stock. Bring to simmering point, then partially cover and cook for 10–15 minutes.

Mix the mashed potato and flaked fish into the vegetable mixture and grind in some black pepper. Heat the soup again, garnish with spring onions and serve with hot toast and butter.

Native American trinity

SERVES: 6

200g (7oz) dried haricot beans, soaked in boiling water for 30 minutes
3 tablespoons olive oil
2 onions, finely chopped
1 teaspoon oregano
1 large butternut squash, about 800g (1lb 12oz)

2 green chillis, deseeded and finely chopped
500g (1lb 2oz) tomatoes, peeled and chopped
2 cobs of corn
Salt and black pepper
3 tablespoons chopped parsley

Drain the soaked beans, put them in a pan of fresh water, bring to the boil and cook fast for 10 minutes. Drain and put the beans into fresh water, bring to the boil then simmer for a further 1 hour 20 minutes, or until tender. Drain and set aside.

Heat the oil in a large pan, add the onions and oregano and cook over a low heat for about 10 minutes, stirring regularly.

Cut the squash into quarters and cut away and discard the seeds and fibre. Peel the flesh and cut into 2.5cm (1in) cubes. Add the squash, chillis and 125ml (4fl oz) water to the onions, cover and simmer for 10 minutes.

Add the tomatoes and simmer again for 20–25 minutes, until the squash is very soft and the tomatoes reduced to a sauce.

Pull away the husks and silk from the corn cobs, strip off the kernels with a strong, sharp knife, holding the cobs upright on a board and cutting downwards.

Add the corn and drained beans to the stew and simmer gently for a further 5 minutes. Season and serve, sprinkled with the parsley.

PESTS
and
DISEASES

Pests

Aphids

Colonies of small insects that suck the sap from new shoots. They can spread viruses and their honeydew excretions encourage sooty mould.

Symptoms Clusters of variously coloured insects on leaves and stems. Distortion of young growth; sticky honeydew on foliage.
Danger Period Spring and early summer outdoors; any time in the greenhouse.
Treatment Spray with derris, imidacloprid or bifenthrin.

Apple sawflies

It is the caterpillars of these ant-like flies that cause the damage, by eating into the hearts of young apples. The flies lay their eggs in the apple blossom and the newly hatched grubs burrow into the fruit.

Symptoms Young fruitlets drop prematurely; superficial scarring on mature fruit.
Danger Period May and June.
Treatment Spray trees thoroughly at weekly intervals when the petals start to fall, using derris or pyrethins.

Asparagus beetles

Reddish-yellow beetles with black-and-yellow wing cases. They lay eggs on asparagus in late spring. Both the beetles and their hump-backed larvae feed on the foliage.

Symptoms One-sided, injured shoots; brown patches on foliage. A severe infestation can literally strip plants bare.
Danger Period May and early June.
Treatment Pick off beetles. Spray with derris or bifenthrin.

Bean seed flies

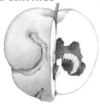

The tiny white grubs of the bean seed fly cause considerable damage to germinating seeds of beans, peas, sweetcorn and other vegetables.

Symptoms Seedlings fail to emerge. Small, white maggots eat into the seeds and young stems.
Danger Period Seed-sowing time and as seedlings emerge.
Treatment Dust along the drill with derris when the seedlings emerge. Cover newly sown seed with horticultural fleece to encourage quick growth.

Blackcurrant gall mites

Serious pests of blackcurrants, not only for the direct damage they do but also because they transmit reversion virus (page 246).

Symptoms Infested buds swell and fail to develop.
Danger Period February and March.
Treatment Remove and burn infested buds in early March. Destroy plants infected by reversion virus.

Cabbage root flies

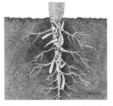

The maggots of this fly attack the roots of recently transplanted cabbages, Brussels sprouts and other brassicas.

Symptoms Outer leaves wilt and develop purple tinge. Young plants may collapse.
Danger Period April to August.
Treatment Protect transplants by covering with horticultural fleece. Alternatively use rubbery carpet underlay, with slits cut for the stems, placed on the soil around the plants.

Cabbage whiteflies

Pests of cabbages, Brussels sprouts and other brassicas.

Symptoms Leaves may be sticky and covered in sooty mould; plant growth is stunted. Clouds of small white flies rise up from the underside of leaves when plants are disturbed.
Danger Period Growing season.
Treatment Spray underside of leaves with bifenthrin or pyrethrum. Burn infected plants after harvest.

Capsid bugs

Several species cause similar damage to a wide range of plants, including apples and currants.

Symptoms Ragged holes appear in younger leaves as adults and nymphs feed on sap; deformed flower buds; misshapen and discoloured fruits.
Danger Period April to August.
Treatment Good garden hygiene, clearing away all garden debris. Spray with hepteophos, permethrin, fenitrothion or malathion in spring, summer and early autumn.

Carrot flies

Maggots burrow into the edible roots of carrots, parsley, parsnips and celery.

Symptoms Reddening of foliage and stunted growth. Mature roots are spoiled by tunnels.
Danger Period June to October.
Treatment Sow seed thinly in May. When thinning, destroy discarded seedlings. Cover crop with horticultural fleece. Intercrop four rows of onions or dill with each row of carrots.

Caterpillars

The larval stage of moths and butterflies. Most eat leaves, but some eat roots, stems or fruit.

Symptoms Ragged holes in leaves. Plants may be destroyed.
Danger Period March onwards outdoors. Any time in greenhouses.
Treatment Pick off by hand or spray with bifenthrin, pyrethins and permethrin or derris as buds open.
See also: Codling moths, page 239; Cutworms, page 239; Pea moths, page 240; Swift moth, page 241 and Tortrix caterpillars, page 241.

Codling moths

Codling moth caterpillars are the major cause of 'maggoty' apples, and may also attack pears.

Symptoms Entry tunnels through the eye of the fruit. Hollow, brown and rotted cores, often with caterpillars inside.
Danger Period June to August.
Treatment Spray in May to June with permethrin or derris and repeat three weeks later. Hang pheromone traps in the trees in May to catch the adult moths before they lay their eggs.

Cutworms

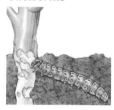

The green or grey-brown caterpillars of several moth species attack root vegetables and lettuces.

Symptoms Fat caterpillars can be seen in the soil. They curl into a C-shape when picked up. Stems of plants cut through at ground level.
Danger Period Dry spells from early spring to late summer.
Treatment Keep weeds in check. Fork soil over in winter to expose the pests to predators, especially blackbirds.

Flea beetles

Pests of seedling cabbages, radishes, swedes, turnips and related plants

Symptoms Young leaves pitted with very small holes made by shiny black beetles that jump in the air when disturbed.
Danger Period Sunny spells in April and May.
Treatment Good garden hygiene. Dust susceptible seedlings with derris. Water plants regularly in hot, dry weather.

Fruit tree red spider mites

Microscopic mites that feed on the sap of apple, pear and plum leaves.

Symptoms Leaves turn yellow-bronze, wither and fall. The mites are invisible to the naked eye and should not be confused with harmless red 'brick spiders'.
Danger Period April to September.
Treatment Spray immediately after flowering with permethrin, derris or a fatty acid spray.

Glasshouse red spider mites

A serious pest not only of greenhouse plants as well as outdoor peaches, strawberries and runner beans.

Symptoms Mottling of upper leaf surfaces, followed by general yellowing. Severely infested plants are covered by a silky webbing.
Danger Period Any time under glass; late summer outdoors.
Treatment Maintain humidity. Spray with permethrin, derris or a fatty acid spray.

Glasshouse whiteflies

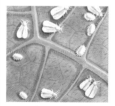

Small white-winged flies that infest many greenhouse plants, especially tomatoes and cucumbers.

Symptoms The small whiteflies and their scale-like larvae are found on the underside of leaves, which become soiled with honeydew and sooty mould.
Danger Period All year round.
Treatment Spray regularly with bifenthrin, fatty acids or permethrin. Alternatively use a systemic pesticide such as imidacloprid.

Gooseberry sawflies

Caterpillars can cause severe damage to gooseberries.

Symptoms Leaves may be stripped to skeletons by 2cm (¾in) long green, black-spotted caterpillars; an entire bush may be defoliated.
Danger Period April to August.
Treatment Spray with pyrethins or derris in early May or when symptoms first appear. Regularly check underside of leaves in the centre of the bush and pick off any sawfly eggs.

Leaf eelworms

These tiny pests attack a wide range of plants, including strawberries and other soft fruits.

Symptoms Brown or yellow discolorations between the main leaf veins. Distortion of buds and young growth.
Danger Period Winter.
Treatment Remove and burn affected leaves; destroy severely infested plants. Maintain good garden hygiene and grow plants in dry conditions.

Leafhoppers

Like aphids, these small creatures feed on the sap of a wide range of plants, both indoors and out.

Symptoms Coarse white flecks on leaves and – often on the underside – the cast-off skins of the insects.
Danger Period April to October outdoors; any time under glass.
Treatment Spray with permethrin, repeating at 14 day intervals. Alternatively use the systemic insecticide imidacloprid.

Leatherjackets

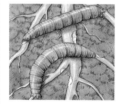

The larvae of craneflies (daddy-long-legs) feed on the roots of a wide range of plants, including brassicas and other vegetables.

Symptoms Plants wilt and occasionally die as the grey-brown, legless grubs attack their roots.
Danger Period April to June.
Treatment Before planting, dig deeply to expose grubs to birds. Fork over soil thoroughly and regularly to continue exposing the pests to predators.

Pests

Mealy bugs

A serious greenhouse pest, especially on grape vines.

Symptoms Patches on leaves and stems of sap-sucking insects covered in woolly or mealy white wax. Stunted foliage.
Danger Period Any time.
Treatment Use a systemic insecticide such as imidacloprid or a non-systemic insecticide such as bifenthrin. The beetle *Cryptolaemus montrouzieri* can be introduced as a biological control agent.

Millipedes

Pests of root crops. They are distinguished from centipedes (which are beneficial) by a greater number of legs, grey-black colouring and slower movement.

Symptoms Tunnels in potato tubers and other root crops.
Danger Period Late summer and autumn.
Treatment Improve garden hygiene and dig deeply, especially in damp, well-manured soil.

Onion eelworms

A pest of onions, shallots, chives and garlic.

Symptoms Bloated, swollen and distorted leaves, stems and bulbs.
Danger Period Growing season.
Treatment Dig up infested plants and burn them. Do not grow onions or related crops on the same site for at least three years. As a prevention, grow onions from seeds rather than sets.

Onion flies

The maggots are a major pest of onions, leeks and shallots.

Symptoms Adult flies lay eggs on the leaves and the larvae hatch out and tunnel into the plants. The leaves turn yellow and the stems and bulbs rot. Small, white maggots feed on the rotting tissue.
Danger Period June and July.
Treatment Burn infested plants and dig over ground to expose any pupating insects to the winter cold and birds. Avoid thinning onions in areas where the fly is prevalent.

Pea moths

The 'maggots' often found in garden peas are in fact the caterpillars of these small moths.

Symptoms The moths lay their eggs in pea flowers and the tiny, pale yellow caterpillars eat the peas inside the ripening pods.
Danger Period May to August.
Treatment Spray with derris or permethrin when the flowers first open. Repeat two weeks later. Alternatively, grow early maturing varieties of peas.

Pear-leaf blister mites

Microscopic mites that feed upon young leaves of pears.

Symptoms Clusters of yellow pustules appear on the upper surface of leaves and gradually turn brown. Young shoots may also be damaged.
Danger Period April to August.
Treatment Pick off and burn infested leaves, or spray with lime-sulphur or fenitrothion at the end of March. The pest is difficult to eradicate yet the tree may still produce a good crop of pears.

Pear midges

Larvae develop within the fruits, rendering them inedible.

Symptoms Young fruits swell rapidly then fail to develop. Black cavities contain small yellowish-white larvae.
Danger Period April to May.
Treatment Spray with fenitrothion just before the blossoms open. Pick off and burn affected fruitlets. Fork over the soil beneath the trees in summer and tidy away fallen leaves and fruit.

Potato-cyst eelworms

The pests can cause serious damage to potatoes and tomatoes.

Symptoms Pinhead-size yellow or brown cysts develop on roots, causing wilting and death of plants.
Danger Period May to August.
Treatment Dig up and burn affected plants and avoid planting tomatoes or potatoes on the same site for at least five years. Grow early potatoes and choose varieties that are resistant to eelworm.

Raspberry beetles

The beetles' grubs tunnel into fruits of the raspberry, loganberry and blackberry.

Symptoms Distorted, grub-infested fruits.
Danger Period June to August.
Treatment Spray thoroughly with derris as soon as flowering ceases. In autumn fork over the soil around raspberries. Remove any mulch and replace with fresh material in spring.

Root aphids

A number of aphid species exist in the soil, where they live on the roots of a wide range of plants, including lettuces.

Symptoms Colonies of white, wax-covered aphids on roots; yellowing, wilting leaves.
Danger Period Late summer and autumn outdoors; any time in the greenhouse.
Treatment Water the non-edible plant roots with imidacloprid or thiacloprid. Grow resistant varieties.

Scale insects

Troublesome in greenhouses, but also a pest of fruit grown outside.

Symptoms Flat or rounded, yellow, brown or white scales, usually on the underside of leaves, beside the veins and on the stems.
Danger Period Any time in the greenhouse. Late spring and early summer outdoors.
Treatment Spray with fatty acids and permethrin, three times at two-week intervals, or use imidacloprid. Alternatively, brush scales off leaves with a toothbrush.

Slugs and snails

Slugs and snails attack many kinds of plants, especially young shoots.

Symptoms Large holes in foliage, tubers, roots and stems. Slime trails may be seen. Slugs and snails are most active at night.
Danger Period Mild wet weather in spring and autumn.
Treatment Scatter metaldehyde pellets or use a slug killer based on aluminium sulphate. A ring of grit, nut shells or crushed eggshells scattered around a plant will deter slugs and snails.

Stem and bulb eelworms

These affect a number of plants, including rhubarb, onions and strawberries. Garden weeds act as hosts to these microscopic pests.

Symptoms Infested bulbs and plants become soft, rotten and distorted. Plants collapse and die.
Danger Period Mainly in spring.
Treatment Dig up and destroy infested plants and avoid replanting in the same soil for at least three years afterwards. Maintain good hygiene in the garden, keeping weeds at bay.

Strawberry beetles

Ripe strawberries may be nibbled by beetles, spoiling the fruit.

Symptoms The damage is similar to that made by birds. The glossy-black ground beetles are 2cm (¾in) long and may be found under the plants.
Danger Period Early summer.
Treatment Remove any debris and garden litter, remove weeds and maintain good hygiene. Spray with bifenthrin or derris, but not when plants are in bloom.

Swift moths

The caterpillars of these moths live in the soil and feed on the roots, tubers and corms of various plants, including carrots and parsnips.

Symptoms Dirty-white caterpillars with brown heads living in the soil; usually seen when digging the soil.
Danger Period Growing season.
Treatment Good garden hygiene and weed control. Thorough winter digging will expose the caterpillars and kill them.

Tortrix caterpillars

The caterpillars of tortrix moths feed upon the leaves of many plants, including pears and apples.

Symptoms Leaves and stems are drawn together by silk webs, housing small grey caterpillars that wriggle backwards when disturbed.
Danger Period May and June outdoors. Any time in the greenhouse.
Treatment Remove caterpillars by hand. Alternatively spray with derris or fenitrothion.

Wireworms

The beetle larvae feed in the soil on the tubers, roots and stems of potatoes, lettuces and tomatoes.

Symptoms Tough-skinned, yellow-brown, worm-like creatures among plant roots.
Danger Period The early years of newly cultivated land.
Treatment Dig thoroughly before planting. Keep weeds under control and maintain good garden hygiene.

Woolly aphids

A common pest on many trees, especially apples.

Symptoms Tufts of white, waxy wool on twigs and branches. Neglected trees may develop woody galls.
Danger Period April to September.
Treatment As soon as wool appears, spray with a high volume of bifenthrin or permethrin. Cut out severely galled branches. A blast with insecticidal soap may dislodge the pests.

Diseases

American gooseberry mildew

A fungal disease that attacks the leaves, shoots and fruits of gooseberries.

Symptoms White mealy powder over fruits, shoots and leaves, which turn brown. Shoots may be distorted. Small, tasteless fruits.
Danger Period April onwards.
Treatment Remove and burn diseased shoots. Spray plants with myclobutanil. Prune bushes to permit free circulation of air. Avoid overuse of nitrogen-rich fertilisers.

Anthracnose

A fungal disease of dwarf beans and, occasionally, runner beans.

Symptoms Dark brown, sunken patches on pods; brown spots on leaves and stems.
Danger Period Growing season, especially in cool, wet summers.
Treatment Destroy all affected plants; sow fresh seed in a new area. If a serious outbreak reappears, spray before flowering with mancozeb.

Apple scab

A fungal disease that only affects trees from the genus *Malus*, spoiling the fruit, leaves and bark.

Symptoms Small blister-like pimples on young shoots and fallen leaves. The blisters later burst the bark and form ring-like scabs.
Danger Period Growing season.
Treatment Cut out and burn diseased shoots in winter. Spray regularly with myclobutanil or mancozeb (except on varieties sensitive to sulphur).

Bacterial canker

A serious disease of cherries, plums, gages and damsons.

Symptoms Elongated lesions exude amber-coloured gum on dying shoots. Leaves wither.
Danger Period Autumn and winter, but symptoms do not appear until spring or summer.
Treatment Cut out and burn infected branches. Spray foliage with Bordeaux mixture in mid August, mid September and mid October. Prune in summer.

Bitter pit

An apple disease that appears on mature fruits.

Symptoms Brown spots beneath the skin of the fruit and throughout the flesh.
Danger Period Growing season, particularly in dry, hot summers.
Treatment Feed and mulch the tree. Never let the soil dry out. In mid June, spray with calcium nitrate at a rate of 8 tablespoons to 23 litres of water. Repeat three times at three-weekly intervals.

Black leg

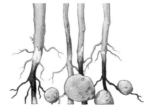

A common disease of potatoes, particularly on poorly drained soil.

Symptoms The leaves turn yellow and the stem softens and dies due to black rot developing at the base of the stem. The rot is caused by fungi or bacteria.
Danger Period June, particularly in cold, wet soil.
Treatment Destroy all affected plants, and replant with healthy tubers. Choose less susceptible varieties. Avoid waterlogged land, or drain it.

Blossom end rot

A disease affecting tomatoes, peppers and aubergines caused by a calcium shortage and drought.

Symptoms Circular brown or black patches form at the blossom end of the fruits.
Danger Period As the young fruits develop.
Treatment Water the plants regularly. The disease is a particular problem with plants grown in pots or grow bags, which dry out easily.

Blotchy ripening

A disorder of greenhouse tomatoes caused by irregular feeding and watering, and periods of over-high temperatures.

Symptoms Hard green or yellow patches on the fruits, often on the lower trusses.
Danger Period Growing season.
Treatment Ensure regular feeding and watering, and maintain even temperatures. A potash feed may help. Grow resistant varieties such as 'Alicante' and 'Shirley'.

Bolting

Plants grow tall and leggy, and flower prematurely before the crop has reached maturity. Lettuces and endives are particularly prone to this; also Chinese cabbages if sown too early in the season.

Symptoms The plants put out long stems, which if left will bear flowers and seeds that are bitter and useless for eating.
Danger Period Growing season, especially during hot weather.
Treatment Avoid late transplanting and overcrowding. Keep the plants well watered, especially at the seedling stage, so that they do not suffer a check in growth.

Boron deficiency

A disorder that afflicts beetroots, swedes, turnips and celery.

Symptoms Edible roots turn brown within; brown cracks on celery stalks.
Danger Period May to August.
Treatment Mix 30g of borax with 10 litres water and distribute over 10m^2 of soil.

Brown rot

A fungus that can attack most tree fruits and nuts.

Symptoms Brown patches and concentric rings of white fungus appear on fruit originally damaged by birds and insects.
Danger Period Summer, and while in store.
Treatment Destroy all damaged or withered fruits, and remove any dead shoots during pruning. Spray fruit with mancozeb before picking to prevent from rotting in store. Do not store damaged fruit.

Cane blight

Raspberries are often afflicted by this fungal disease.

Symptoms Leaves wilt and wither in summer; canes discolour and snap off at ground level.
Danger Period Growing season.
Treatment Cut diseased canes below ground level and burn. Disinfect knife immediately. Spray new canes with Bordeaux mixture. Handle canes with care to prevent damage, which provides an entry point for the disease.

Cane spot

A common disease of raspberries and loganberries.

Symptoms A bacterial infection causes round purple spots, which later form cankers on canes; spots with a whitish centre on leaves; distorted fruits.
Danger Period May to October.
Treatment Cut and burn badly infected canes. Apply copper spray at 14-day intervals, from bud-burst to petal fall.

Chlorosis (lime induced)

A condition affecting raspberries and other acid-loving plants growing in an alkaline soil.

Symptoms Yellowing of the leaves between the veins.
Danger Period Growing season.
Treatment Improve the acidity of the soil by digging in peat, pulverised bark or crushed bracken and by using lime free fertilisers. Add a chelated-iron compound at the rate recommended by the manufacturers.

Chocolate spot

A fungal disease, seldom serious, of broad beans.

Symptoms Dark brown spots on leaves and stems. In severe cases the whole plant may die.
Danger Period June or July on spring-sown beans, while overwintered crops are most at risk during a wet spring.
Treatment Spray with Bordeaux mixture or mancozeb as foliage. appears. Encourage strong growth by liming the soil using a potash fertiliser. Ensure good drainage.

Club root

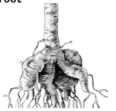

A serious fungal infection of turnips and brassicas.

Symptoms Leaves wilt and turn red, purple or yellow; roots become swollen and distorted.
Danger Period Growing season.
Treatment Little can be done once the soil is infected. Prevent the disease by liming in winter to keep the pH at 7–7.5. Improve drainage, or make raised beds. Rotate the crops and use resistant varieties. Remove and burn any infected plants.

Coral spot

This fungus, normally found on dead wood, may enter living tissue and destroy entire bushes, especially redcurrants.

Symptoms Red, cushion-like masses of spores on dead twigs.
Danger Period Any time.
Treatment Cut out and burn all dead wood and prune 15cm (6in) below the diseased area. Plants are more susceptible when stressed, so identify and rectify any cultural problems. Avoid injury to bark that would allow the disease to enter.

Crown gall

A bacterial disease occurring on fruits, vegetables and other plants.

Symptoms Large hard or soft galls develop on roots and shoots. Plants may appear stunted.
Danger Period Growing season.
Treatment Bacteria enter through wounds, so avoid damage during cultivation. Burn diseased plants. Provide suitable drainage so that the soil is not waterlogged.

Crown rot of rhubarb

A bacterial disease of rhubarb, encouraged by wet soil conditions.

Symptoms Leaves become spindly and discoloured and die early. The main bud rots followed by whole of crown.
Danger Period Growing season.
Treatment Improve drainage and avoid damage to crowns. Dig up and burn entire infected plant. Do not plant rhubarb in the same position again.

Cucumber mosaic virus

Afflicts not only cucumbers, but also marrows and other related plants. It is usually transmitted by aphids but may also be carried on the hands and garden tools.

Symptoms Greenish-yellow mottling of leaves and fruit. Growth is stunted and fruits puckered.
Danger Period Growing season.
Treatment Burn infected plants at first sign of symptoms. Control aphids by spraying. Grow resistant varieties.

Diseases

Damping off

A fungal disease of seedlings; in the vegetable garden, young lettuces are especially susceptible.

Symptoms Seedlings rot and collapse at soil level.
Danger Period From seed sowing to emergence of third pair of true leaves.
Treatment Avoid overcrowding and overwatering. Always use clean pots and sterilised compost. Remove and destroy dead seedlings. Water seed trays with copper or Cheshunt compound.

Die-back

A condition of trees and shrubs caused by disease, frost damage or simply poor cultural conditions.

Symptoms Shoots die back from the tips, often killing larger branches. Foliage turns brown.
Danger Period Any time.
Treatment Cut back to healthy tissue and burn the cuttings. Where disease is the cause, apply appropriate treatment; if no disease is apparent, improve growing conditions.

Downy mildew

Brassicas, lettuces, onions and courgettes may be attacked by this fungal disease.

Symptoms Grey or whitish furry coating on underside of leaves; yellow patches on upper surfaces.
Danger Period Growing season and on onions in store.
Treatment Thin out plants and spray with carbendazim or mancozeb (wait 14 days before harvesting). Always sow seed in sterilised compost, ventilate well and avoid overcrowding.

Fire blight

This serious bacterial disorder strikes suddenly, affecting pears, apples and other trees.

Symptoms Flowers turn black, leaves turn brown and wither. Golden or white slime may exude from the stems.
Danger Period Flowering time.
Treatment Cut back beyond the diseased shoots by at least 30cm (12in). Burn the cuttings. If the disease is extensive, remove and destroy the whole plant.

Foot rot

A disorder of tomatoes, peas and beans, due to fungal attack.

Symptoms Stem bases turn black and rot, usually leading to the death of the plant.
Danger Period Growing season.
Treatment Rotate crops and use sterile compost in peat pots and seed trays. Water young plants with Cheshunt compound when planting out. If necessary, repeat at weekly intervals.

Frost damage

Young leaves and shoots of most plants can be damaged by frost.

Symptoms May include silvering of tomato leaves; cracked tree trunks; puckered distorted leaves; browned or blackened flowers and buds; and die-back of shoots.
Danger Period Mid winter and spring.
Treatment When danger of frost has passed, cut out damaged shoots to prevent entry of fungi. Protect plants with horticultural fleece, straw or sacking.

Gangrene

A fungus that enters potatoes through wounds, generally at lifting time, and appears when the tubers are in store.

Symptoms A slight depression on the skin that enlarges until the tuber is decayed and shrunken.
Danger Period Winter and spring.
Treatment When lifting potatoes, handle them carefully and store them in an airy, frost-free place. Burn any infected tubers. Start again with clean seed potatoes from a reliable source.

Greenback

A condition of greenhouse tomatoes that is brought about by too high a temperature.

Symptoms As fruit starts to ripen, a ring of leathery tissue is left around the stalk end. This area does not turn red.
Danger Period As fruit develops.
Treatment Keep the greenhouse ventilated, and shade the glass in hot weather. Maintain even growth by ensuring that the soil does not dry out. Grow resistant varieties.

Grey mould

Raspberries, strawberries and other soft fruits are particularly susceptible to this fungal blight.

Symptoms Rotting fruit covered by a grey, velvety mould. Also may affect leaves and flowers.
Danger Period Growing season.
Treatment Destroy infected plants. Spray with mancozeb when flowers appear and until just before fruits ripen. In the greenhouse, spray with mancozeb as soon as symptoms appear.

Honey fungus

A widespread parasitic disease on many types of plant.

Symptoms Honey-coloured toadstools growing from dead wood; white, fanned-shaped fungal growths beneath bark; black 'bootlace' threads on roots.
Danger Period Autumn.
Treatment Destroy diseased plants and as many of their roots as possible. The 'bootlaces' do not always spell disaster for your garden since many species of the fungus are not invasive.

Leaf spot

Condition caused by various bacteria and fungi, each specific to one type of plant and unlikely to spread to others.

Symptoms Small brown or black spots of different shapes and sizes. The leaves may fall prematurely.
Danger Period From late spring.
Treatment Remove diseased leaves and burn them. Remove all autumn leaves to the compost heap. Spray diseased plants with mancozeb, penconazole or Bordeaux mixture.

Magnesium deficiency

Lack of magnesium affects the chlorophyll balance of plants, particularly apples and tomatoes.

Symptoms Orange and brown bands between leaf veins. Leaves may fall prematurely.
Danger Period Growing season, and after application of a high-potash fertiliser.
Treatment Spray with a solution of magnesium sulphate (8 tbsp to 11 litres (3 gallons) of water, plus a few drops of detergent).

Manganese deficiency

The disorder mainly occurs in poorly drained sandy soil, and wet areas of low acidity.

Symptoms Premature yellowing between veins of older leaves. Dead patches may appear among the yellow areas.
Danger Period Growing season.
Treatment Spray with a solution of manganese sulphate (2 tbsp to 11 litres (3 gallons) of water, plus a few drops of detergent). Alternatively, apply chelated or fritted compounds.

Mosaic virus

An infection of raspberries, marrows and many other plants.

Symptoms A yellow mottling of the leaves, which sometimes become distorted.
Danger Period Growing season.
Treatment The plants should be dug up and destroyed. There is no chemical control. Buy raspberries that are certified virus-free.

Neck rot

Occurs in stored onions.

Symptoms Grey, velvety mould on the neck of the onion, which then rapidly rots.
Danger Period Growing season, but symptoms not apparent until the onions are in store.
Treatment Destroy diseased onions as they appear. Store only ripened, healthy onions in a well-ventilated, frost-free place. Use a three or four-year rotation system. Do not overfeed with nitrogen-rich fertilisers.

Parsnip canker

Name given to several fungal diseases affecting parsnips.

Symptoms Brown, orange-brown or black cankers on the shoulder of the root. The leaves may develop small black spots with green halos.
Danger Period June onwards.
Treatment Sow seeds early and thinly in deep, loamy soil, adding a balanced fertiliser. Rotate crops regularly, improve drainage and grow resistant varieties. Destroy diseased plants.

Peach leaf curl

A fungal disease of peaches, apricots and nectarines.

Symptoms Leaves develop large red blisters, turn white then brown and finally fall prematurely.
Danger Period Before bud-burst.
Treatment Remove and burn diseased leaves. Spray with mancozeb or Bordeaux mixture in January, repeating a fortnight later and again just before leaf-fall.

Petal blight

A serious disease on several plants; in the vegetable garden it may particularly affect globe artichokes.

Symptoms Dark, saturated spots on petals. Flowers eventually rot.
Danger Period Flowering time, especially in chilly summers.
Treatment Remove and burn diseased flowers.

Potato blight

The most serious of potato diseases; also attacks tomatoes.

Symptoms In damp weather leaves develop yellow-brown patches and a white furry coating underneath; tubers rot. A dry brown rot on tomato fruits.
Danger Period May to August.
Treatment In a wet season especially, spray every 10–14 days with mancozeb. Spray potatoes before the leaves touch other plants, and tomatoes when the first fruits set.

Powdery mildew

General term applied to a number of fungi that produce similar symptoms on a variety of plants, including strawberries and apples.

Symptoms White, powdery coating appears on leaves, shoots and flowers, weakening the plant.
Danger Period Growing season.
Treatment Remove and burn infected growth. Water well and mulch. Spray regularly with mancozeb. Sulphur can be applied as a dust. Plant resistant varieties.

Diseases

Powdery scab

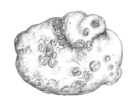

A fungal disease of potatoes.

Symptoms Raised round scabs that later burst to release a brown, powdery mass of spores. Tubers may be deformed and have an earthy taste.
Danger Period Growing season.
Treatment Dig up and destroy affected tubers. Do not plant potatoes on the same site for several years. Improve drainage and grow resistant varieties.

Reversion virus

A viral disease of blackcurrants transmitted by the blackcurrant gall mite.

Symptoms Flower buds are hairless and bright magenta instead of the normal dull grey. Small leaves with fewer lobes than usual. Poor crops.
Danger Period Early summer.
Treatment Control the gall mites (page 238). Dig up and burn diseased plants, and replant with bushes certified virus-free.

Root rot

Any type of plant may be affected due to soil that is too wet or too dry, or a fungal disease such as black root rot or violet root rot (page 247).

Symptoms Discoloured foliage and premature leaf-fall; rotting black roots; collapse of plants.
Danger Period Growing season.
Treatment Destroy infected plants and improve soil conditions. Rotate crops so that the same vegetables are not grown on the same part of the plot in successive years. This prevents a build up of the disease in the soil.

Rust

Mint and plums are particularly prone to this fungal infection.

Symptoms Brown, orange or yellow spore masses gather on leaves and stems. Shoots deformed.
Danger Period Growing season for mint; late summer for plums.
Treatment Cut out and burn diseased shoots and stems. Improve growing conditions; spray with mancozeb at first sign of attack.

Scab

Fungal disease of pears and apples.

Symptoms Dark blotches on leaves, which fall prematurely. Brown-black scabs on fruit, whose skins may crack.
Danger Period Growing season.
Treatment Cut out and burn diseased shoots in winter. Spray regularly with myclobutanil or mancozeb. The disease overwinters on fallen leaves, so clear them away in autumn.

Scald

A condition mainly affecting fruits in overheated greenhouses. It may also occur on outdoor crops during hot summers.

Symptoms Discoloured, sunken patches on grapes, tomatoes, plums and gooseberries.
Danger Period Hot weather.
Treatment Remove damaged fruits before grey mould (page 244) develops. Shade and ventilate the greenhouse, and damp it down early in the day.

Sclerotinia disease

A fungal disease that attacks many plants, including root crops in store.

Symptoms Fungus appears as a white, fluffy mass containing black lumps of spores. Plants may wilt suddenly and collapse. Stored roots soften and decay.
Danger Period Growing season and when crops are in store.
Treatment Burn all diseased material before the spores enter the soil. Store sound roots only. The disease can overwinter in weeds so keep them under control.

Shothole

Holes in leaves of plums, peaches and cherries, also spinach and horseradish. May be due to either bacterial or fungal diseases.

Symptoms Brown patches on leaves develop into holes.
Danger Period Growing season.
Treatment Good feeding and watering. If the disease persists, spray fruit trees with a copper fungicide during summer and at autumn leaf-fall.

Silver leaf

A fungal disease of peaches, plums, cherries, apples and pears.

Symptoms Some leaves become silvered and later turn brown, while infected branches die back.
Danger Period September to May.
Treatment Cut affected branches to at least 15cm (6in) below the fungus. Use tri-sodium orthophosphate to sterilise tools. Prune plums and cherries only in June-August. Try biological control using trichoderma pellets.

Soil-borne diseases

A wide variety of disorders are transmitted through the soil by fungi or bacteria. Beans, peas, cucumbers, melons, pumpkins, squashes and tomatoes are particularly vulnerable.

Symptoms These vary according to the disease. They include the rotting of the roots and tissues at the crowns of all types of plants, and blackening and rotting at the base of stems.
Danger Period Growing period.
Treatment This also varies, but control can be achieved by good garden hygiene and crop rotation. Where disease is persistent, use seed dressings; or water with Cheshunt compound or mancozeb.
See also: Foot rot, page 244; Root rot, page 246; Violet root rot, page 247.

Splitting

A condition affecting all root vegetables as well as apples, pears, plums, gages and tomatoes.

Symptoms Roots split lengthways, often from the shoulder downwards. Fruit skins split to expose inner flesh.
Danger Period Growing season, especially when prolonged dry periods are followed by rain.
Treatment Maintain even growth by mulching heavily and by regular feeding and watering so that soil doesn't dry out.

Spur blight

Fungal disease of raspberries and loganberries.

Symptoms Canes develop purple to silver blotches, spotted with black. Spurs die back.
Danger Period Spring and summer.
Treatment Cut out and burn infected canes after fruiting. When new canes are a few centimetres high, spray with penconazole or mycobutanil. Repeat three or four times at fortnightly intervals.

Stony pit

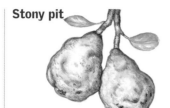

A viral disease affecting old pear trees.

Symptoms Deformed, pitted fruit whose flesh is stony and inedible. The disease spreads gradually over a number of years until the entire tree is infected.
Danger Period Any time.
Treatment Cut down and burn diseased trees. There is no treatment for this disease.

Tomato blight

A serious disorder of outdoor tomatoes.

Symptoms A soft, brown patch spreads rapidly across the fruit, which then shrivels and rots.
Danger Period Wet summers.
Treatment Remove and burn infected plants. In damp weather, especially, spray at roughly fortnightly intervals with Bordeaux mixture. Make sure plants are not overcrowded.

Violet root rot

Carrots, parsnips and asparagus are especially prone to this fungus.

Symptoms Leaves turn yellow and die as violet threads of fungus attack the roots.
Danger Period Growing season.
Treatment Lift and burn infected plants, and isolate the plot by sinking pieces of corrugated iron or plastic 30cm (12in) deep into the soil. Do not grow vulnerable plants there for several years.

Virus diseases
A wide variety of disorders are caused by minute organisms that enter plant tissues through wounds in the outer skin. Some are transmitted through handling the plants, but most are spread by insects such as aphids.

Symptoms These vary according to the plant affected; the same virus will produce different symptoms on different plants. Typical among them are colour changes in leaves and stems, wilting and stunting and the development of outgrowths.
Danger Period Any time.
Treatment Remove and burn badly diseased plants and replant with stock that is certified virus-free. Maintain good garden hygiene and control the pests that spread the diseases.

Wart disease

A serious soil-borne fungal disease of potatoes. By law, it should be reported to DEFRA.

Symptoms Large warty outgrowths on the tubers, causing them to disintegrate.
Danger Period Growing season.
Treatment Remove and destroy all diseased plants. All new potato varieties are certified immune to the disease.

Whiptail

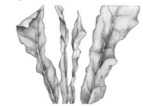

Lack of molybdenum causes this disorder in cauliflowers and broccoli.

Symptoms Leaves become distorted, ruffled and thin, giving a whip-like appearance.
Danger Period Growing period, particularly in acid soils.
Treatment Water with a solution of sodium molybdate (1 tablespoon to 9 litres of water for every 8m² of soil). With acid soils, add lime to bring the pH up to 6.5.

White rot

A fungal disease of onions, leeks, shallots and garlic.

Symptoms White fungus on the edible roots, which quickly rot.
Danger Period Growing season. Spring onions are most susceptible.
Treatment Burn affected plants. Grow onions on a new site each year. Once the disease has struck, the soil remains contaminated for up to 20 years. No chemical treatment is available to amateur gardeners.

Wire stem

A fungal disease that affects many young plants, especially cauliflowers and other brassicas.

Symptoms The base of the stem turns brown, shrinks and easily breaks. Seedlings die or become stunted.
Danger Period Early growth.
Treatment Raise seedlings in sterilised compost. Remove and destroy diseased plants.

Pesticides and fungicides

The list of approved chemicals, and their brand names, is constantly under review by the Department for the Environment, Food and Rural Affairs (DEFRA), but even when trade names change, the chemical contents should be stated on the label. It is always advisable to ask your garden centre for advice about appropriate approved treatments.

Using chemicals safely
Systemic insecticides are absorbed by the plant and treat sap-sucking insects, such as aphids, as well as difficult problems, such as scale, mealy bugs and woolly aphids. Contact insecticides coat the surface over which the insects move or are applied directly to the pest and are effective against chewing pests, such as caterpillars.

Fungicides
Choosing fungus-resistant varieties will help to reduce the need for treatment, but you should also be scrupulous about garden hygiene and make sure plants have enough light, space and food. If your plants do suffer from fungal attack, use fungicides sparingly – an overdose can harm the plant or even kill it. Spray from the bottom of the stem upwards, making sure that you coat the underside of the leaves, where most diseases occur.

Insecticides
Most insecticides kill all insects, so minimise the risk to beneficial creatures, such as ladybirds, by spraying in the early morning or late evening when fewer of them are active. Only treat plants where a pest is visible.
Use a small sprayer and mix no more than you need, or buy ready-to-use products.
Watch the weather and spray only when the it is fine and still.
Spray evenly, particularly on the underside of leaves.

Wear gloves, long sleeves, trousers and stout shoes.
Do not drink, eat or smoke and thoroughly wash your hands and face once you have finished.
Keep children and pets away while you are working.
Safe storage Most garden chemicals have a short shelf-life. Never pour unwanted chemicals down the drain: contact your local council's environmental health department or waste and recycling centre. Store chemicals well away from children and animals.

Homemade cures
You don't always have to use agrochemicals to combat pests.
Repel aphids with garlic Roughly chop 25g of garlic cloves and steep in 1 litre of boiling water for 15 minutes. Strain the liquid and spray undiluted every two to three weeks as an aphid repellant.
Nettle mash Chop 200g of stinging nettle leaves and infuse in 2 litres of cold water for 24 hours. Strain the liquid, dilute (1:5) and spray as soon as you notice a pest.
Treating fungus A simple horsetail decoction works wonders. Chop 500g of horsetail 'needles' and stems and soak in 5 litres of cold water for 24 hours. Transfer it to an old cooking pan and simmer for 15–30 minutes. Cool and strain. Dilute with water (1:5) and use it to spray plants at first sign of fungal infection on three consecutive days.

A-Z OF PESTICIDES AND FUNGICIDES BRAND NAMES

ORGANIC* (or suitable for use by organic gardeners)
BIOLOGICAL CONTROL AGENT **

Aluminium sulphate*
Fertosan slug and snail powder, Growing success, Doff Slug Attack

Amblyseius species**
Thrip control

Anagrus atomus**
Leafhopper parasite

Aphidoletes**
Aphid parasite

Aphidus species**
Aphid parasite

Bendiocarb Doff
Wood Lice Killer

Bifenthrin Doff
Garden Pest Killer, Bayer Bug-free, Bayer Sprayday Greenfly Killer, Scotts Bug Clear, Scotts Rose Clear (with mycobutonil)

Chelated compounds
Chelated Trace Element Mix, Miracle Miracid, Murphy Sequestrene

Copper oxychloride*
Murphy Traditional Copper Fungicide, Copper Tape, Snail Tape, Slug and Snail Rings

Copper silicate Doff Socusil
Slug Repellant

Copper sulphate
Bayer Cheshunt Compound (with ammonium carbonate)

Cryptolaemus**
Mealy bug predator

Deltamethrin Doff
New Ant Killer Spray, Bayer Ant Killer Spray

Encarsia Formosa**
Whitefly predator

Fatty acids*
Bayer Organic Pest Control, Doff Greenfly and Blackfly Killer, BabyBio House Plant Insecticide, Green Fingers Organic Pest Spray

Ferrous sulphate Phostrogen
Moss Killer and Lawn Tonic

Fritted trace elements
Fritted Trace Elements

Grease bands* Bayer Boltac Greasebands, Vitax Fruit Tree Grease, Agralan Glue Bands

Heterohabditis megidis**
Chafer Bug Predator

Hypoaspis**
Sciarid predator

Imidacloprid Bayer Provado
Ultimate Bug Killer concentrate (with sunflower oil), Bayer Provado Ultimate Bug Killer ready to use, Bayer Provado Ultimate Bug Killer aerosol (with methiocarb), Bayer Provado Lawn Grub Killer

Insecticidal soap*
see Fatty Acids

Mancozeb
Bayer Dithane 945

Metaldehyde
Bio Slug Mini-Pellets, Doff Slugoids Slug Killer, Slug Clear!

Metaphycus helvolus**
Scale parasite

Methiocarb Provado Ultimate
Bug Killer aerosol (with imidacloprid)

Myclobutanil Doff Systemic
Fungus Control, Bayer Multiuse, Bayer Fungus Fighter, Scotts Rose Clear 3

Penconazole Scotts
Fungus Clear

Permethrin Bio Kybosh
(with pyrethins), Bayer Ant Killer Dust, Doff New Ant Killer, Doff Foaming Wasp Nest Destroyer (with tetra-methin)

Phasmarhabditis hermaphrodita**
Nemaslug

Phenolic emulsion
Armillatox

Pheromone traps**
Oecas Pagoda Codling Moth Trap, Trappit Codling Moth Trap

Phytoseiulus persimilis **
Red Spider Mite predator

Pyrethrum and pyrethins*
Nature's Answer Natural Bug Killer, Doff All-in-one Bugspray

Rotenone*
Bio Liquid Derris, Doff Derris Dust, Vitax Derris Dust

Steinernema feltiae**
Leatherjacket predator

Steinernema kraussei** Nemasys Vine Weevil predator

Sulphur Nature's Answer
Natural Fungus and Bug Killer

Tar oil Jeyes Fluid

Tetramethrin Doff
Flying Insect and Crawling Insect Killer (with d-phenothrin)

Thiacloprid Provado
Vine Weevil Killer 2

Typhlodromus pyri**
Typhlodromus

Yellow sticky traps*
For greenhouse pest control

Natural pest control

Pests, diseases and plant disorders can often be controlled with good growing techniques and garden hygiene. If you also encourage beneficial insects into your garden you should find that you need to resort to chemicals only rarely.

You must encourage the right mix of wildlife by providing conditions to suit them. If natural pest control is to be successful, you will have to tolerate a low level of pests to provide a food source for the predators so that they stick around.

Beating aphids Ladybirds are commonly known as the 'gardener's friend' because of their appetite for aphids, but many other insects – lacewings, parasitic wasps and hoverflies, for example – also eat vast quantities. Any nectar-producing and pollen-rich plants are useful for attracting predators; *Convolvulus tricolor* and the poached-egg plant (*Limnanthes douglasii*), for example, will lure hoverflies, which lay their eggs among aphid colonies.

Ground beetles feed at night on aphids, the eggs of carrot fly and cabbage root fly, as well as slugs. Encourage them by providing ground cover to hide in during the day. Use only short persistence products, like derris, and do not use slug pellets containing methiocarb, which is toxic to ground beetles.

Combating slugs Frogs and toads eat slugs and insects. To encourage them, build a pond with gently sloping sides surrounded by vegetation. Hedgehogs will also eat slugs. They are difficult to attract into a garden, but a logpile will provide a place where they can hibernate in winter, or you can buy a special hedgehog house. Before lighting a bonfire, it is important to look for sheltering hedgehogs.

Busy earthworms Perhaps the most beneficial creatures to the gardener are earthworms, which help to improve the soil by incorporating organic matter, without you digging it in, and opening it up with their tunnels. Chemicals were once used to clear lawns of wormcasts, but modern gardeners should just sweep off casts with a broom before mowing. Brandling worms are found in compost heaps, where they break down organic material.

New Zealand flatworms, which eat earthworms, have been found in the UK and could threaten soil fertility if they become established. They are around 15cm (6in) long, very flat, and are found under stones. Squash any you find.

Attracting birds Many garden birds eat pests. For example, blue tits eat caterpillars and aphids; starlings prey on grubs; sparrows, great tits and wrens consume insects; while song thrushes eat snails and slugs. If you have a cat, put a bell around its neck so the birds can hear it coming.

The best way to attract birds into the garden is to supply water, feed them in winter and put up nestboxes. You can also encourage them by growing plants with berries and seedheads. Feed birds in winter, when natural food is low, with a commercial wild-bird food or put out scraps of breakfast cereals, flaked oats, dried fruit, bacon rind, cheese, stale cake or cooked potato.

BENEFICIAL CREATURES

In the wild, all pests have natural enemies that keep them in check. Organic gardeners can call upon this army of allies by avoiding the use of chemical treatments that can cause these creatures harm and by providing the right sort of habitat. If you can encourage the insects and animals below into your garden, they will become your personal pest-control army.

Ground beetles
Scurrying, big black beetles that are more often seen at night. Both adults and their larvae are useful predators of slugs, caterpillars and aphids.

Hoverflies
A group of true flies that look like bees and wasps. Their greeny brown larvae, 12mm (½in) long, feed on aphids and can eat up to 100 a day.

Hedgehogs
They eat caterpillars, beetles and slugs at night. A logpile will provide shelter and a place to hibernate, but offer them dog food to eat, not milk.

Rove beetles
This group includes the distinctive devil's coach horse beetle (above). Both adults and larvae are predators of soil grubs, insects and slugs.

Ladybirds
A single larva can eat 500 aphids so they are worth encouraging. Two-spot and seven-spot ladybirds are the most common.

Wasps
Many solitary wasps are beneficial against aphids and caterpillars. Provide egg-laying sites by drilling 5–10mm (¼–½in) holes in posts.

Centipedes
These eat many small insects. Don't confuse them with millipedes, which feed on roots. Centipedes have one pair of legs per body segment.

Earthworms
Worms pull organic matter into the soil. They also open up the soil structure, aiding drainage and making it easier for plant roots to establish.

Bats
Night feeders of nocturnal flying insects. Encourage them with roosting boxes. They are threatened by the chemicals used in the treatment of roof timbers.

Frogs, toads and newts
These amphibians prey on slugs, flies and other insects. They need a pond in which to breed and will return to it year after year.

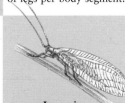
Lacewings
Adults and their larvae feed on aphids. You can buy chambers to protect them and lacewing eggs to introduce a colony into your garden.

Slow-worms
These legless lizards up to 30cm (12in) long eat the small greyish slugs that feed on the soft growth of young plants and vegetables.

Home
PRESERVING

Home preserving

Plants, like all living things, grow, die and decay. As soon as we pull up a carrot, harvest beans or pick fruit, the process of decay is set in motion. For this reason, all fruit and vegetables are best eaten fresh, but this is often not practical, especially when you have a glut of produce all ripe and ready for harvesting at the same time.

To cope with such inevitable surpluses there are ways of preserving your garden produce, and the following pages tell you all you need to know about freezing, bottling, pickling, making jams, jellies, chutneys and more.

The object of preserving is to arrest the process of decay when the fruit or vegetable is at its best. Fresh produce deteriorates as a result of chemicals within the plants and microscopic organisms that must be destroyed or inactivated to preserve the food.

Enzymes These are a group of complex chemicals essential for various biological processes. One example of enzymic action is the browning of cut fruit when exposed to the air.

This action is halted by freezing, and totally stopped by high temperatures. Therefore, blanch vegetables before you freeze them; this reduces the enzymic effect that takes place both after picking and when thawing begins.

Bacteria Apart from spoiling food in store, bacteria can in some cases cause food poisoning. Most are destroyed by temperatures around boiling point, but some produce spores that will survive up to 115°C (240°F). These temperatures are reached in a pressure cooker.

Freezing inhibits the growth of bacteria; but they are reactivated when the food is thawed. Acid, too, arrests bacterial growth and assists their destruction by heat. For this reason, foods low in acids require longer cooking at higher temperatures. High salt or sugar concentrations will also halt the growth of bacteria.

Yeasts These cause fermentation in sugar. They are destroyed by heat and inactivated by freezing, or where more than 60 per cent of a preserve consists of sugar.

Moulds These are fungal bodies. Most are destroyed by heat and, like yeasts and bacteria, are inhibited by freezing.

Sealing and storage

The correct sealing and storage of foods is as vital to successful preservation as careful processing. Inadequate sealing and inappropriate storage (leaving jars in a too-warm or light cupboard, or one in which they are constantly disturbed) can reactivate harmful bodies and spoil your preserves.

A word of caution If, when opened, the jars smell musty or the contents look slimy or mushy, it is likely that the contents have perished and it is best to throw them away without tasting.

RULES FOR SUCCESSFUL FOOD PRESERVING

- Ensure that all work surfaces are clean and use only clean, undamaged utensils.
- Prepare and preserve your produce as soon as possible after harvesting.
- When freezing or bottling, use only prime-quality produce; damaged, wind-fallen, or over-ripe fruits are suitable only for syrups and jellies.

- Where heat processes are recommended, follow the directions exactly.
- Label each jar or package with a description of the contents and the date of preserving.
- Store your preserves in a place that is cool, dry, dark and frost-free, where they will remain undisturbed until required for use.

Freezing

Freezing has two advantages over other methods of preserving fruits and vegetables at home. In the first place, it is simpler and quicker than heat preservation. Secondly, freezing makes it possible to store small quantities of food that it would be impractical to store by other means.

In most cases, too, more of the true flavour, colour and appearance of the food is retained by freezing than by other preservation methods.

However, the cost of running the freezer must be taken into consideration. Make sure it pays its way by filling it with frozen garden produce, so you can enjoy the fruits of your labour all year round: a full freezer will run more efficiently than one that is underused and kept half empty.

What to freeze

Most vegetables (see page 259) freeze well after blanching. The chief exceptions are salad vegetables, whose high water content makes them unsuitable and prone to turning to mush when thawed. Tomatoes can be frozen, though whole fruits will not retain their shape and texture when thawed.

Both soft fruits and tree fruits (see page 256) can be frozen either on their own, or in sugar or syrup. It is also possible to freeze several types of herbs (see page 260) in handy amounts to add directly to a dish when cooking.

Choosing a freezer

When buying a freezer, first decide what type and size will best suit your family's needs, whether you have sufficient space, and how much money you can allocate to keep the freezer stocked.

Domestic freezers and refrigerators are made in several sizes, whose capacity is measured in either litres or cubic feet. As a guide, 28 litres equals 1cu ft; so freezers whose stated capacities are either 280 litres or 10cu ft, will hold the same amount of food.

How much space do you need?

When deciding what size of freezer to buy, it helps to know that 28 litres (1cu ft) of freezer space will hold about 25lb (11kg) of frozen food. However, large quantities of stored joints of meat and poultry, which do not stack compactly, will reduce this figure.

The smallest available freezer is 57 litres (2cu ft), and the largest 775 litres (25cu ft), with food capacities, respectively, from 50lb (22kg) to 690lb (275kg).

As well as deciding how much total space you are likely to need, remember that only a certain amount of unfrozen food can be added to the freezer at any one time. Not more than a tenth of the total capacity of a freezer should be occupied by unfrozen food during a 24 hour period, so a 100 litre (3.5cu ft) freezer will take only 5kg (10lb) of unfrozen food in a day. This is sufficient for small batches of home-grown produce, but the total capacity of such a freezer is quite inadequate for most families.

A 400 litre (14cu ft) freezer, which can take up to 14kg (30lb) of unfrozen food a day, has the overall storage space to meet most families' needs.

Chest freezer or upright? The room you have is another factor to consider when choosing a freezer. There are two basic designs: the upright cupboard type, with outward-opening doors, and the chest cabinet with a lid cover.

Upright freezers occupy less floor space. They are fitted with shelves and baskets and often have additional shelves in the door. Combined fridge-freezer units like this are the most commonly found in homes today. Stacking food is easy, and the contents can be seen at a glance in their drawers or baskets. They are a little more expensive to run than chest freezers, because cold air escapes every time the door is opened, whereas in chest freezers the cold, heavy air sinks to the bottom.

The lid of a chest freezer makes an additional working surface. But they take up more floor space, and it is more difficult to stack and remove frozen foods than in the upright type.

For home freezing on a small scale, a single upright cabinet combining separate freezer and refrigerator sections may be sufficient.

However, such an arrangement is too small for most families, and would be inadequate for even the smallest household where the intention is to freeze regular batches of garden produce.

Where to put the freezer
The kitchen is not necessarily the best place for a freezer, since it will use more electricity to maintain its low temperature in these warm surroundings. The ideal place for a freezer is a cool, well-ventilated position. In a centrally heated house, the landing or the hall are often the coolest places, though remember that no freezer is completely silent. Other good situations include the garage, spare room or garden shed.

You can now buy freezers with locks, which are advisable if you have young children. You can also fit lights or bells in the house connected to the freezer outside to warn of failures or power cuts.

If you do decide to put the freezer in a garage or outhouse, make sure that the electric cables and fittings are sound, and adequate for the load. A freezer usually runs off a normal ring circuit. Follow the manufacturer's advice, and if in doubt consult a qualified electrician.

The building must also be absolutely dry, otherwise parts of the machine will corrode. A freezer situated in a garage may be prone to condensation, and this must be dried off when noticed so that the dampness does not affect the working parts of the freezer.

Wiring advice It is a good idea to have a permanently wired connection rather than a plug and socket, so that it cannot be turned off by mistake. If the freezer is connected to a socket, never use a multiple adaptor as this increases the risk of accidental disconnection.

If you have to use a switched socket, cover the switch with sticky tape as a safeguard. Whether or not there is a switch, stick tape over the plug, or pin a warning notice on the wall.

Check the location Finally, before choosing a freezer, check that narrow doors or awkward bends in the house will not prevent you putting it where you want it. Remember, too, that a freezer full of food is extremely heavy, so the floor must be strong enough to take the weight. If in doubt, ask a builder to check.

Getting the freezer ready
Before using a new freezer, wash out the inside with a solution of 4 teaspoons of bicarbonate of soda dissolved in 1 litre (2 pints) of

warm water. Dry the freezer thoroughly, switch it on and let it run for 12 hours to see that it is working before you stock it.

Study the manufacturer's leaflet to make sure that you use the machine correctly. Some freezers must be turned to a low temperature some time before freezing, and then turned up when the food is frozen. Others have a separate switch for the fast freezing of fresh food, and there are some with a separate compartment for freezing food before transferring it to the main body of the machine.

Do not add more than the permitted quantity of unfrozen food in any 24 hour period.

Unfrozen food will freeze more quickly if stacked loosely and packed in small quantities. Do not let it touch any frozen food already in the freezer, as this may lead to temperature variations which could spoil food that is already frozen.

Most foods freeze solid in 8 hours, after which they can be transferred to the storage section and stacked with the other contents of the freezer.

Defrosting your freezer
It is necessary to defrost a freezer only once or twice a year, provided that the loose frost that forms inside is removed regularly. Follow the manufacturer's guidelines as to when to defrost. Upright freezers need defrosting more often than chest-type freezers, but some of the latest models are designed to run 'frost-free'.

To defrost, remove the food and wrap it in layers of newspaper and a blanket. Put the papers and the blanket in the freezer for a few hours first to make them cold.

When the contents have been removed and wrapped, switch off the power and put bowls of hot water in the freezer to speed defrosting. Remove as much frost and ice as possible with a wooden or plastic scraper to reduce the amount of mopping up incurred as defrosting progresses. Never use a metal scraper, which could puncture the walls of the freezer.

Mop up the water as the frost and ice thaw, and finally wash the inside with a solution of 4 teaspoons of bicarbonate of soda, dissolved in 1 litre (2 pints) of warm water. If any smell lingers, wash the interior again with a solution of 3 tablespoons of vinegar to 1 litre (2 pints) of warm water.

Dry the cabinet thoroughly, switch on the current and close the freezer. After about an hour the freezer should be cold enough for the food to be replaced.

Work quickly, completing the defrosting and cleaning within a couple of hours. Finally, wipe down and polish the outside of the freezer before returning the contents.

Breakdowns and power cuts
When you buy a freezer, find out what service facilities are available in your area. In case of emergencies, note the telephone numbers of your local electricity board and the nearest freezer service centre. (Both may be found in local telephone directories.) Once the freezer is installed and working, check it from time to time to see that it is operating satisfactorily.

If it is fitted with an alarm, check it occasionally. Freezer alarms are battery-operated and need new batteries from time to time. If the red light – fitted to some freezers to show they are

---

THREE MAIN TYPES OF FREEZER

Combined refrigerator freezer Use the upper part of the freezer compartment for fast freezing. Sliding baskets give easy access to contents, which for convenience can be grouped into fruit, meat and other categories.

Upright freezer The upper shelves are for fast freezing, but can also be used for normal storage. Place often-used items as close as possible to eye level. Use door storage, if provided, for items in frequent use.

Chest freezer Fast-freezing compartment is at one end. Use the baskets for small, delicate packs, such as patés, bacon, cakes and flans. Place joints and chickens on the bottom. Stack soft-fruit containers at one end.

working – goes out, discover whether the bulb, rather than the freezer, has failed before calling in expert help. Use a thermometer to detect any rise in temperature and, if the freezer is definitely out of action, check the fuse in the plug.

Emergency repairs If you are unable to put things right yourself, get in touch at once with the nearest service organisation and, meanwhile, keep the freezer closed. Do not be tempted to check on the food, as every time you open the door you let warm air in and shorten the amount of time the food will stay frozen.

Frozen food will not suffer any damage for at least 12 hours following power failure – the exact period depends on the type of food, and the temperature outside the freezer. If expert help arrives within reasonable time, no further action need be taken.

If the freezer needs emptying to carry out repairs, remove the contents and wrap as for defrosting. In this case do not open the cabinet first to chill newspapers or blankets.

When you lose power When a power cut occurs, try to find out from your electricity supplier how long it is likely to last. If it is expected to last for more than 12 hours, or if service is not at hand in the event of a mechanical breakdown, you will need to act fast to save the contents of the freezer. The contents of a full freezer can be worth a considerable amount of money, but many home insurance policies will cover any loss.

If at all possible, contact friends living outside your immediate area

to see if you can transfer the food in your freezer into their for the duration of the power cut. Some service centres have facilities to store contents of domestic freezers in emergencies.

What to do if the food does thaw

If the food is beginning to defrost but there are still ice crystals in the centre, you can refreeze it. Vegetables that have not been thawed for too long, and still feel cold, can be thoroughly cooked and then refrozen in the cooked state. On no account should they be refrozen raw.

Cooked dishes, even if they still seem very cold, should never be re-frozen. They can, however, be eaten after a thorough reheating. If in doubt, destroy the food.

Holidays and house removals

Do not switch off the power when you go on holiday. Get a neighbour to come in and check your freezer once a day while you are away. Alternatively – and this would be impracticable in most households – use up the contents before you go away, and leave the freezer defrosted and clean. In this case, leave the lid or door open so that fresh air can circulate.

When moving house there is no need to run down frozen food stocks. As food will not be harmed by a power cut of about 12 hours, a freezer full of food can generally be moved without difficulty.

Switch off the freezer at the last minute, have it loaded on to the removal van just before setting off, and then have it unloaded and switched on at the next destination as soon as possible. Check before-

hand that the removal firm will be able to handle a freezer full of food.

Packaging materials

Frozen food must be packaged correctly to guard against various forms of deterioration. Packaging should be vapour-proof, so that the food will not dry out, and thick enough both to retain the aroma and flavour of each particular food and prevent them from tainting others. In practice, this means buying purpose-made bags and containers rather than using make-shift packaging that may be inadequate.

Oxygen can cause frozen food, especially meat and fruit, to deteriorate, so exclude as much air as possible from bags when packing food for freezing.

It is a good idea to pack items in portions, or in quantities you are likely to use, rather than in bulk. This makes it simple to take food out of the freezer as you need it, with minimum interference of the rest of the freezer contents.

Polythene bags These are widely used for packaging frozen foods, and are suitable for all foods except liquids. They are available in a variety of sizes and thicknesses, but the recommended gauge for freezer bags is 120–150.

Polythene bags are useful for odd-shaped, bulky objects such as poultry and joints of meat, since they can be wrapped tightly round the food to exclude air. They may also be used for loose items, such as sprouts or beans. However, these can freeze into awkward shapes that are difficult to pack. A way round the problem is to put the bag inside a carton and fill it with vegetables before freezing.

When the food has frozen solid the carton can be removed, and the resulting rectangular block will be easy to stack. Polythene bags also make useful liners for cartons or tubs made from cardboard or other absorbent materials.

Overwrapping Ideally, wrap large, bulky, or awkwardly shaped items – such as poultry with protruding joints, whole fish or cooked pies – in aluminium foil after being frozen in polythene bags. This minimises the danger of tears in the bags. Alternatively, put the frozen bags in cardboard boxes.

Plastic boxes Boxes with air-tight lids, sold in a variety of shapes and sizes, are ideal for frozen fruits, vegetables, sauces, liquids and cooked foods. If the lid is not airtight, apply freezer tape as

necessary to make a good seal. You can also recycle used takeaway cartons in this way – many are now reusable plastic, rather than foil.

Avoid using very large boxes, even for bulky items, as too much air is likely to be enclosed. Round plastic boxes are not a good idea as they waste space when stacked. When filling containers be sure to leave the recommended amount of space for the particular food between the contents and the top of the container.

Aluminium foil This material can be used to wrap such foods as sausages, bacon or cooked dishes that will not readily pack into polythene bags. It is particularly good for wrapping around awkwardly shaped items and since aluminium is a good conductor of heat, the package will freeze

---

PACKAGING MATERIALS

Polythene bags Generally made of 120–150 gauge polythene, these are excellent containers for non-liquid frozen foods. When freezing loose vegetables such as sprouts or beans put the bag into a rectangular plastic or cardboard box before packing. When freezing is complete, remove the box, leaving an easy-to-stack pack.

Overwrapping Bulky items, such as poultry, joints and pies, should be frozen in polythene bags before being given a protective overwrapping of aluminium foil.

Plastic boxes A wide variety of plastic containers, with fitted lids make ideal freezing packs, but remember to leave headspace above the food to allow for expansion as it freezes.

Aluminium foil Use this, as wrapping or as shaped containers, for freezing pies, puddings or pre-cooked meals. Heavy-gauge foil is more suitable than the thin kitchen type.

Waxed cartons Use yoghurt or margarine tubs as storage receptacles for gravies, purées and soups. If lined with polythene, they can be cleaned and reused.

quickly. Make sure you use special freezer foil as foil sold for general kitchen use is too thin.

Never allow foil to come into contact with acid foods, such as rhubarb and beetroot.

Trays and dishes made of aluminium foil come in a range of sizes and are useful for freezing cooked dishes, pies, patés, puddings and complete meals. Though such containers slow down the thawing process, they can afterwards be put straight in the oven for reheating, preferably on a baking tray. With careful use and cleaning they can be reused.

Waxed cartons Waxed boxes, cartons and tubs – many with fitted lids and some with polythene liners – are sold in a range of shapes and sizes. They are ideal for cooked dishes, gravies, fruits and vegetables, purées and soups. Seal any containers that are not airtight with freezer tape.

Line waxed containers with bags if the contents are liable to stain. Provided this is done, waxed containers can be used several times. Tubs and containers saved from yoghurt, soured cream and margarine can be used after thorough cleaning, provided they have an adequate wax lining or are lined with polythene.

Never pour hot foods into waxed containers, as the heat will melt the wax and make the tubs porous.

Glass Containers made of glass are not ideal for use in a freezer, as they become increasingly brittle at low temperatures. There is a danger of jars being crushed by the freezer lid if a chest has been overfilled, and it is necessary to thaw the contents before they can be removed. However, there are brands of glassware on the market that will cope with freezing temperatures as well as the high temperatures of an oven. In fact most can be used straight from freezer to oven.

Although convenient, the glass containers are expensive compared with other storage solutions.

Sealing containers

Polythene bags can be sealed with wire ties. If these are covered with paper or plastic they will not damage the bag, which can be reused. Some bags have a zip-lock closure, allowing them to be opened and closed many times. Make sure that polythene bags are sound before reusing. Wash the bags thoroughly after emptying and turn them inside out to dry.

When filling any bag or container, ensure as much air as possible is excluded before sealing. Freezer tape, which is made of polythene with an adhesive that has been formulated to last at low temperatures, is useful for sealing all bags and containers to ensure they are airtight. Tape is also useful for securing labels on packs.

Labelling frozen food

Every packet in the freezer should have a label, stating what it contains, including the amount or number of portions, the date on which it was frozen and the date by which it must be eaten.

It is time-wasting and possibly damaging to open sealed packages to find out if they contain for instance, peas or blueberries. Some polythene bags have a space for writing a label, but otherwise use special freezer labels that stick to packages or tie nonstick labels on firmly, or stick them on with freezer tape. Write on the labels with a pencil, felt-tip pen or freezer pen – a fountain pen or ball-point pen is likely to rub off.

Apart from the obvious information on contents, weight and date of freezing, it is also useful to note how much sugar, if any, the food contains if this will affect its subsequent cooking. These and similar details are sure to have been forgotten by the time the food is used.

Include any other information you may find useful when you come to use the food, such as the amount of cream or the time needed for thawing and reheating.

Colour coding can be a great help in identifying various types of food in the freezer. Use labels of one colour for fresh vegetables, another for cooked vegetables, a third for fruits, and so on. You may also want to group foods of similar types in baskets and trays.

Keeping freezer records Keep a record or logbook handy by the freezer, detailing every item that goes in and the date. Cross out food as you use it. In this way you can see at a glance how much is in the freezer and which items should be used by a given date.

A logbook will also tell you how much of each food you have used in the course of the year and enable you to adjust next year's stocks accordingly.

Packing the freezer

When food has been prepared, packaged, sealed and labelled, it is ready to go into the freezer. Remember that you should not put in an amount equalling more than a tenth of the freezer's total capacity for freezing at any one time. This will lower the temperature in the freezer too much for the food that is already frozen.

Foods for freezing must be quick-frozen before being stored in the main body of the freezer. Quick-freezing causes small ice crystals to form which can be retained within the cell structure, whereas slow freezing results in large crystals which damage the cell walls and reduce the food value, which is further lost in thawing.

For the initial freezing, follow the freezer manufacturer's recommendations. Set the gauge to the given temperature several hours in advance.

Some freezers have a special quick-freezing compartment or shelf. In others it is necessary to move some of the contents so that fresh foods can be quick-frozen against the base or sides of the freezer. Once the foods have frozen solid, return the freezer to its normal running temperature and stack the newly frozen food.

Arrange the frozen packages compactly to leave as little air space as possible between them, following whichever coding system you have adopted. Avoid stacking foods at the bottom or back of the freezer if you intend to use them within a short time.

RULES FOR SUCCESSFUL FREEZING

- Freeze only fresh food in perfect condition.
- Freeze fruits and vegetables as soon as possible after gathering and initial preparation.
- Pick only as much produce at one time as can be prepared and frozen without delay.
- Blanch vegetables prior to freezing.
- Cool hot foods quickly before freezing.
- Pack the prepared food into moisture-proof and vapour-proof bags or containers.
- Use meal-size packs whenever possible.
- Exclude as much air as possible from the packs.
- Label the packs and keep a freezer record.
- Freeze packs solid in the coldest part of the freezer.
- Follow the manufacturer's instructions on setting the temperature gauge.
- Thaw fruits slowly; cook most vegetables straight from the frozen state.
- Eat or cook food soon after removing from the freezer.
- Never refreeze food without cooking it first.
- Defrost the freezer when necessary.
- Have emergency contact numbers ready in the event of a breakdown or power cut.
- Keep the freezer fully stocked and, to save electricity, never open it for longer than necessary.

Freezing fruit

Most kinds of fruit will freeze well, though some varieties, because of their colour or size, are more suitable than others.

Methods of freezing, too, vary considerably with the type of fruit. Some soft fruits, for instance, may be frozen whole with no addition other than a little sugar; others, however, must be cooked or puréed before they are worth allocating valuable freezer space.

Similarly, a number of tree fruits – among them apricots, peaches and plums – require special treatment before freezing.

Whatever method is chosen, it is vital that as little time as possible is lost between harvesting and freezing. Pick the fruit in prime condition, rejecting any damaged produce.

Preparation

Select the fruit carefully, and prepare it as though for cooking – by hulling, removing stalks, peeling and slicing. Use only cold water when washing the fruit; drain and dry before freezing.

Methods of freezing fruits

Choose the freezing method best suited to the particular fruit, bearing in mind its final use. For example, a little loss in texture may be acceptable if the fruit is going to be used in a sauce or purée, while fruit to be used in fruit salads or fruit flans should retain as much texture as possible.

Dry-freezing This method is particularly suitable for berry fruits, such as blackberries, loganberries, raspberries and strawberries.

Sugar-freezing Like dry-freezing, this method is suitable for soft berry fruits including currants, and can also be used for blueberries, cherries and gooseberries.

Fruit frozen in this way is best used in cooked desserts, such as pies and puddings.

Syrup-freezing Though a little more trouble, freezing in syrup is an excellent way to bring out the flavour of such fruits as damsons, figs, grapes, melons and peaches, as well as fruits without much natural juice.

The syrup solution varies from light to heavy according to the type of fruit (see the chart on the following pages). Two pints of liquid syrup will cover around 1.5kg (3lb) of fruit.

Keep the fruit fully immersed in the syrup with a ball of crumpled greaseproof or waxed paper beneath the lid. Allow at least 1cm (½in) headspace between the fruit and the lid to allow for expansion during freezing.

Poaching The skins of such larger fruits as apricots, plums and peaches will harden during freezing unless the fruits are first poached. Do this by simmering them, stoned and halved, for a few minutes in a heavy syrup. Then allow them to cool and pack them into freezer-proof containers.

Purées Over-ripe but sound fruit of any kind may be frozen in this way. For fresh purées, rub the fruit through a fine sieve and sweeten with sugar before freezing.

For cooked purées, simmer the fruit in very little water, and rub through a sieve. Pack when cold.

Fresh fruit all year round Soft fruits, such as raspberries, freeze well, either dry, in sugar or in a syrup.

FIVE METHODS OF FREEZING FRUITS

Dry-freezing Spread the prepared, dry fruit in single layers on trays lined with waxed paper; open freeze for about 1 hour until firm, then pack into containers and stack in freezer.

Sugar-freezing Place the prepared, dry fruit in rigid containers, packed in alternate layers of sugar. Allow 100–175g caster sugar to 500g fruit (4–6oz of sugar to 1lb fruit). Stack in freezer.

Syrup-freezing Pack fruit in rigid containers and cover with a light syrup made with 500g sugar to 1 litre water (1lb sugar to 2 pints water). Double the sugar for a heavy syrup.

Poaching Simmer in a heavy syrup, made from 500g (1lb) sugar and 600ml (1pint) water, for a few minutes. Allow to cool, pack into rigid containers and freeze.

Purées Rub fruit – cooked or uncooked – through a sieve. Sweeten the purée during cooking or afterwards, pack and freeze. Alternatively, leave unsweetened.

Preventing discoloration

Apples and some other tree fruits turn brown when peeled and exposed to the air. While freezing inhibits this, some browning may still occur in frozen fruits such as apples and pears.

This can be prevented by adding lemon juice to the syrup solution. But as fruit treated in this way often absorbs too much lemon flavour, a solution of ascorbic acid, which does not affect the flavour, can be used instead. Dissolve crystals of ascorbic acid, available from chemists, in a little cold water and add to the syrup.

Packaging fruit for freezing

Small packs containing individual or only a few portions are generally the most convenient. This is because it is difficult to remove one or two portions from a six-portion pack without first thawing the whole contents.

Pack dry-frozen fruit in heavy polythene bags, and seal. Fruit frozen by any other method – dry sugar, syrup, poaching or purées – must be packed in rigid containers.

Leave headspace of about 1cm (½in) below the lid to allow for the expansion that occurs during freezing. Seal and label the containers, and freeze solid in the coldest part of the freezer before placing them in the storage compartment.

Freezing fruit for jam

If you are too busy to make jam at harvest time, there is no reason why you should not freeze the fruit until you have more time. The fruit can be frozen dry, or packed in sugar (not syrup). Sugar-freezing helps to retain the colour, an essential feature of well-made jam.

AT-AT-GLANCE GUIDE TO FREEZING FRUIT

Apples
Dry, With Or Without Sugar Peel, core and cut into thick slices. Blanch in boiling water for 1–2 minutes, and cool in chilled water. Alternatively, drop into water with ascorbic acid to prevent discoloration, then drain and dry. Pack in rigid containers, with or without sugar, leaving 1cm (½in) headspace, and freeze. Thaw in containers and use for pies and puddings.

In Syrup Cover prepared slices with light sugar syrup, adding 1½ tablespoons of lemon juice to every litre (2 pints) of syrup. Pack in rigid containers and keep the slices immersed. Allow 2.5cm (1in) headspace, and freeze. Use, thawed, in cooked desserts.

Puréed Cook slices to a pulp in very little water. Sieve, and pack when cold in rigid containers. Leave 1cm (½in) headspace, and freeze.

Apricots
In Sugar Wash, cut in half and remove stones. Scald in boiling water for 1–2 minutes to prevent them becoming tough during freezing, and drop into water with ascorbic acid. Drain and dry. Pack in dry sugar in rigid containers, leaving 1cm (½in) headspace, and freeze. Use as a pie filling.

In Syrup Pack either unpeeled halves, or peeled and sliced apricots, into rigid containers. Cover with a light sugar syrup, adding 1½ tablespoons of lemon juice to every litre (2 pints) of syrup. Keep the apricots immersed, with 2.5cm (1in) headspace, and freeze. Use in fresh or cooked desserts.

Puréed Use over-ripe apricots for puréeing. Peel, stone and slice the fruit before sieving. Sweeten to taste, and pack cold in containers, leaving 1cm (½in) headspace. Freeze.

Blackberries
Dry-Frozen As for blueberries.
In Sugar As for blueberries.

In Syrup Cover the fruit with heavy sugar syrup and pack in rigid containers, leaving 2.5cm (1in) headspace. Freeze. Use in cooked desserts.

Poached Simmer the cleaned fruit in very little syrup for a few minutes. When cold, pack into rigid containers with 1cm (½in) headspace. Freeze, and use as pie fillings, and for fools and mousses.

Blueberries
Dry-Frozen Pick over the fruit; wash and dry if necessary. Dry-freeze on trays, pack into heavy-duty polythene bags, seal and store in the freezer.

In Sugar Layer the prepared fruit with sugar in rigid containers, leaving 1cm (½in) headspace. Freeze. Best used in pies and puddings.

In Syrup Cover with light sugar syrup, pack with 2.5cm (1in) headspace, and freeze. Use in desserts.

Cherries
Dry-Frozen Use red rather than black varieties. Make them firm by leaving in chilled water for 1 hour, then drain, dry and remove the stones. Pack in rigid containers – preferably made of plastic – with 1cm (½in) headspace, and freeze. Use freshly thawed.

In Sugar Pack cleaned, stoned fruit in plastic containers, layered with sugar. Leave 1cm (½in) headspace, and freeze. Use as pie fillings.

In Syrup Freeze in light sugar syrup with the addition of 1½ tablespoons of lemon juice to every litre (2 pints). Freeze, and use for pies and puddings.

Currants (black, red, white)
Dry-Frozen Strip from the stalks, rinse and drain thoroughly. (A few sprigs of red currants may be frozen whole for use as garnishing.) Freeze in single layers on trays; when solid, pack in heavy-duty polythene bags. Use for fresh desserts, and in mousses and fools. Alternatively, pack in containers

without any sugar. Freeze, leaving 1cm (½in) headspace. Use for fresh desserts, fools, ices or in cooked puddings.

In Sugar Pack with dry sugar, leaving 1cm (½in) headspace. Freeze, and use in pies and puddings.

Puréed Cook blackcurrants to a pulp, and sweeten with caster sugar. Pack in rigid containers, with 1cm (½in) headspace, and freeze. Use for sweet sauces, in puddings and in ices.

Damsons
Dry-Frozen Wash in chilled water, cut into halves and remove the stones. The skins tend to toughen with freezing, so counteract this by using ascorbic acid in the chilling water. Dry, and pack in rigid containers with dry sugar. Leave 1cm (½in) headspace, freeze, and use for stewed desserts or pies.

In Syrup Pack the prepared fruit halves in rigid containers. Cover with cold, light sugar syrup, adding ½ teaspoon ascorbic acid to every litre (2 pints). Leave 2.5cm (1in) headspace, freeze, and use cooked.

Puréed Cook in a little water, rub through a sieve and sweeten. Pack the purée in containers, leaving 1cm (½in) headspace, and freeze. Use for pies and fools.

Figs
Dry-Frozen Wash carefully, cut off stalks and dip the figs in chilled water. Avoid bruising when drying. Freeze, unpeeled, on trays and pack in heavy-duty polythene bags. Thawed figs, peeled or unpeeled, may be served as a dessert.

In Syrup Peel, pack into rigid containers and cover with cold, light sugar syrup. Add 1½ tablespoons of lemon juice to every litre (2 pints). Leave 2.5cm (1in) headspace. Freeze, and serve as a dessert in syrup.

Continued on p258

AT-AT-GLANCE GUIDE TO FREEZING FRUIT

Gooseberries

Dry-Frozen Top and tail the berries, wash in chilled water and dry thoroughly. Place on trays and open freeze until solid then pack into polythene bags or containers, without sugar, and return to freezer. Use in pies.

In Sugar Pack the washed and dried fruit in rigid containers, layered with dry sugar and leaving 1cm (½in) headspace. Freeze, and use as pie fillings.

In Syrup Pack washed and dried fruit in rigid containers, cover with cold sugar syrup made from 500g (1lb) sugar to 600ml (1 pint) water. Leave 2.5cm (1in) headspace, and freeze. Use in cooked desserts.

Puréed Cook the gooseberries to a pulp in very little water; sieve and sweeten. Allow to cool and then pack in rigid containers with 1cm (½in) headspace, and freeze. Use for sauces, fools and mousses.

Grapes

Strip from the stalks, and freeze seedless varieties whole. Varieties with seeds, however, should be cut in half and the seeds removed. Pack in rigid containers and cover with cold, light sugar syrup, leaving 2.5cm (1in) headspace. Freeze, and use in fruit salads and jellies.

Greengages

As for damsons.

Loganberries

Dry-Frozen Rinse the fruit in chilled water, drain and dry. Freeze on trays, and pack in polythene bags. Use in fresh desserts.

In Sugar Pack the prepared fruit in rigid containers with dry sugar. Leave 1cm (½in) headspace. Freeze, and use as dessert fruits and in salads.

In Syrup Pack in rigid containers. Cover with heavy sugar syrup, leaving 2.5cm (1in) headspace, and freeze. Use in cooked desserts.

Puréed Rub the fruit through a fine sieve, and sweeten to taste. Pack in rigid containers with 2.5cm (1in) headspace and freeze. Use for fools and mousses.

Melons

Peel, cut in half and remove the seeds. Cut into cubes or scoop into balls, and pack in rigid containers. Cover with cold, light syrup, leaving 2.5cm (1in) headspace, and freeze. Use in fruit salads.

Mulberries

As for loganberries.

Peaches and Nectarines

In Sugar Prepare quickly, as the fruits discolour fast. To facilitate peeling, drop them into hot water for 1 minute, peel, cut into halves and remove the stones. Leave in halves or slice; brush with lemon juice or drop into water with ascorbic acid added. Drain, and dry on absorbent paper. Pack in layers of sugar in rigid containers, and freeze. Use, nearly thawed, in fresh or cream desserts.

In Syrup Pack halves or slices in rigid containers. Cover with cold, light sugar syrup, adding ½ teaspoon of ascorbic acid or 1½ tablespoons of lemon juice to every litre (2 pints) of syrup. Leave 2.5cm (1in) headspace in the containers, and freeze. Use in pies.

Puréed Simmer peeled halves in very little water, rub through a sieve and add 1 tablespoon of lemon juice to every 500g (1lb) of purée. Sweeten to taste, pack into rigid containers leaving 1cm (½in) headspace, and freeze. Use for sauces and soufflés.

Pear

Not recommended for freezing as they discolour badly and become squashy. If frozen at all, prepare and pack as for apples in syrup.

Plums

As for apricots.

Quinces

Peel, core and slice. Simmer until tender in water flavoured with orange and lemon juice. Lift out, drain and dry. When cool, pack in rigid containers and cover with cold, heavy sugar syrup made from the simmering liquid. Leave 2.5cm (1in) headspace, and freeze. Use with other fruits in pies and puddings.

Raspberries

Dry-Frozen Hull, rinse, drain and dry the fruit. Freeze on trays and pack in rigid containers or polythene bags. Use in fresh desserts.

In Sugar Pack the prepared fruit in containers with dry sugar, and freeze. This is the best method; thawed fruit can be used cooked or uncooked.

In Syrup Pack the prepared fruit in rigid containers. Cover with cold, light sugar syrup, leaving 2.5cm (1in) headspace. Freeze, and use for cream desserts.

Rhubarb

Dry-Frozen Wash, trim and cut stalks into 2.5cm (1in) lengths. Blanch in boiling water for 1–2 minutes. Drain, dry, pack in containers without sugar, and freeze. Use for stewed fruit and pies.

In Syrup Pack the fruit (prepared as above) in rigid containers and cover with cold, heavy sugar syrup. Leave 2.5cm (1in) headspace, and freeze. Use in pies, fools and crumbles.

Puréed Cook, pulp and sweeten if liked. Pack in containers, leaving 1cm (½in) headspace, and freeze when cold. Use for sauces.

Strawberries

As for raspberries. Ripe berries may also be made into uncooked purée and packed in rigid containers. Leave 1cm (½in) headspace. Use for mousses and ice creams.

Note the amount of sugar used with the fruit, so that this may be deducted when you come to make the jam. As a rough guide to quantity, pack the fruit in about a fifth its weight of sugar.

The pectin content of fruit decreases in frozen storage. To counteract this, freeze and use about a tenth more fruit than specified in the recipe, otherwise it may fail to set adequately.

To use the frozen fruit, place it, still frozen, in the preserving pan with very little water – or none at all for soft fruit. Heat gently until the juices run, and proceed as for fresh-fruit jams (page 271).

The temperature of a freezer should be maintained at –18°C (0°F). At this temperature, dry, frozen fruit will store satisfactorily for six to eight months, and fruit frozen in sugar or syrup for nine to twelve months. Purées have a storage life of some four to six months, and fruit juices can be stored for the same length of time.

Thawing frozen fruit

Whatever freezing method is used, all fruit should be thawed, unopened, in the package in which it was frozen. This is especially important for soft fruits.

Fruits to be served as a dessert should be thawed only to the chilled state. Leave them overnight in the refrigerator or leave them at room temperature for 3–4 hours (1 hour in cold water in an emergency).

Fruit that is likely to discolour should be kept submerged in its syrup while thawing.

Freezing garden vegetables

Most summer vegetables can be frozen. Pick them when young and in prime condition, and process them as soon as possible. Among the few exceptions are salad vegetables, whose high water content makes them unsuitable for freezing.

All vegetables should be prepared in the same way as for cooking, then blanched and dried before freezing.

Blanching

Blanching is essential, as it inhibits the action of enzymes which would otherwise affect the colour, flavour and nutritional value. Time it carefully so as not to destroy the texture of the vegetables (although over-blanching does less harm than too little), and blanch only 500g (1lb) of prepared vegetables at a time. Use boiling, lightly salted water and change it for every 3kg (6lb) of vegetables blanched.

Bring 3 litres (6 pints) of lightly salted water to the boil in a large pan. Put the prepared vegetables in a wire basket or muslin bag and plunge them into the pan. The heat should be high enough for the water to return to the boil in less than 1 minute. Cover the pan, and leave the vegetables in the boiling water for the recommended time.

Lift out immediately, and transfer to a large bowl of cold water until cool. Drain the vegetables thoroughly, and dry on kitchen paper or clean tea towels.

Pack the vegetables in rigid containers or polythene bags.

Remove as much air as possible from the bags, by squeezing them before sealing or by gathering them at the top and sucking the air out through a straw.

Allow an average of 100g (4oz) per portion and pack vegetables in two, four or six portions. Seal and label the packets and enter the details in the freezer logbook.

Storing and cooking

Most frozen vegetables will keep for 10–12 months and should be cooked from frozen. Put them in a small amount of boiling, lightly salted water, bring back to the boil and simmer until tender.

For steaming or baking, thaw them first, until they can be separated.

Freezing herbs

Home-grown herbs can be frozen, although they have a storage life of only six months. Also, since they become limp on thawing, they are

Text continued on p263

AT-AT-GLANCE GUIDE TO FREEZING VEGETABLES

VEGETABLE	PREPARATION AND PACKING	BLANCHING TIME	COOKING TIME
Artichokes, Globe	Cut off the coarse outer leaves and the stems; trim off the tops and remove the central hairy chokes (see page 76). Wash thoroughly, and blanch with a few drops of lemon juice in the water. Cool and drain upside down; pack in rigid containers.	7–9 minutes	Cook from frozen for about 10 minutes, or until the leaves pull out easily.
Artichokes, Jerusalem	Not recommended for freezing as vegetables. Make them into soup, freeze and store as other cooked dishes.		
Asparagus	Wash thoroughly, cut off woody parts, and grade according to thickness. Trim to even lengths. Blanch, cool and drain. Tie in bundles and pack in rigid containers, laying adjacent bundles tips to stalks. Separate the layers with waxed paper.	Thin stems: 2 minutes Thick stems: 4 minutes	Cook from frozen for 5–8 minutes, depending on thickness.
Aubergines	Peel and cut into slices about 2.5cm (1in) thick. Blanch, cool and dry thoroughly. Pack in rigid containers, separating the layers with waxed paper.	4 minutes	Thaw at room temperature until just beginning to soften. Dry well.
Beans, Broad	Remove from the pods, grading to size and discarding old and shrivelled beans. Blanch, cool and dry. Pack in bags or containers.	3 minutes	Cook from frozen for 7–8 minutes.
Beans, French	Top and tail, wash and blanch. Cool, drain and dry. Grade according to size, and cut large beans in half. Pack in bags.	2–3 minutes	Cook from frozen for 7–8 minutes if whole; for 5 minutes if cut.
Beans, Runner	Top, tail and string. Wash, and cut into 1cm (½in) pieces. Blanch, cool, drain thoroughly and dry. Pack in polythene bags.	2 minutes	Cook from frozen for 5 minutes.
Beetroot	Freeze only young, small beetroot about 7.5cm (3in) across. Wash carefully without breaking the skins and boil in water until tender. Cool under cold running water; rub off the skins. Slice or dice and pack in rigid, lined containers with 1cm (½in) headspace.		Store for no more than 8 months. Thaw at room temperature in containers and drain.

Continued on p260

AT-AT-GLANCE GUIDE TO FREEZING VEGETABLES

VEGETABLE	PREPARATION AND PACKING	BLANCHING TIME	COOKING TIME
Broccoli	Trim off the leaves and woody stems and wash thoroughly in salted water. Divide into sprigs. Blanch, cool, drain and dry. Pack in cartons, tops to tails, and separate the layers with waxed paper.	3–4 minutes	Cook from frozen for 5–8 minutes.
Brussels sprouts	Choose small, firm heads of uniform size. Remove the outer leaves, wash and blanch. Cool, drain and dry. Pack in polythene bags.	3–4 minutes, according to size	Cook from frozen for 8 minutes.
Cabbages (green and red)	Freeze only young, crisp cabbages. Trim off the outer leaves, wash and cut into rough shreds. Blanch, cool, drain and dry. Pack in polythene bags.	1 minute	Use within six months. Cook from frozen, for 8 minutes.
Carrots	Young carrots are best for freezing. Remove the tops, trim the roots, and wash. Peel if necessary. Blanch whole, cool, drain and dry. Pack the whole carrots in polythene bags; you can also slice or dice them. Place in rigid containers with 1cm (½in) headspace.	4 minutes	Cook from frozen for 8 minutes.
Cauliflowers	Freeze only firm, white cauliflowers. Break into small sprigs of uniform size, wash and blanch – add several drops of lemon juice to the water to preserve the colour. Cool, drain and dry thoroughly. Pack in rigid containers, separating the layers with waxed paper.	3 minutes	Use within six months of freezing. Cook from frozen for 8–10 minutes.
Celeriac	Trim off the roots and tops. Scrub and cook in water until almost tender. Peel, cut into slices or sticks; cool, drain and dry. Pack into rigid containers, with waxed paper between the layers, allowing 1cm (½in) headspace.		Cook from frozen for 8–10 minutes; or thaw in containers and use, dressed, as a salad.
Celery	May be frozen for cooking, but not for salads or eating raw. Cut off the roots and leaves; trim crisp stems, removing any strings. Scrub, and cut into 2.5cm (1in) pieces. Blanch, cool, drain and dry. Pack in small bags or place in rigid containers, leaving 1cm (½in) headspace.	3 minutes	Cook from frozen for 10 minutes or use frozen in stews, soups and casseroles. It can be thawed at room temperature for a couple of hours for use in stir-fries.
Chicory	Not suitable for freezing.		
Corn salad	Not suitable for freezing.		
Courgettes	Trim the ends from firm, young courgettes, wash and cut into 1cm (½in) thick slices. Blanch, cool, drain and dry. Alternatively, fry the slices in a little butter and cool quickly. Pack into rigid containers, separating the layers with waxed paper. Leave 1cm (½in) headspace.	1 minute	Thaw partially and fry in butter.
Cress	Not suitable for freezing.		
Cucumber	Not suitable for freezing.		

Continued on p261

AT-AT-GLANCE GUIDE TO FREEZING VEGETABLES

VEGETABLE	PREPARATION AND PACKING	BLANCHING TIME	COOKING TIME
Endive	Not suitable for freezing.		
Fennel, Florence	Trim off the roots, wash, and cut into 2.5–5cm (1–2in) lengths. Blanch, setting the liquid aside. Cool and drain, pack into rigid containers and cover with the blanching water. Leave 1cm (½in) headspace.	3 minutes	Use within six months of freezing. Cook from frozen in the blanching water for 30 minutes.
Kale	Not recommended for freezing.		
Kohlrabi	Freeze small roots, no more than 5–7.5cm (2–3in) across. Trim off the root ends and tops, peel, dice large roots but leave small roots whole. Blanch, cool, drain and dry. Pack whole kohlrabi in polythene bags; pack diced kohlrabi in rigid containers, leaving 1cm (½in) headspace.	Whole: 3 minutes Diced: 1½ minutes	Cook from frozen for 7–10 minutes, or until tender.
Leeks	Remove the outer leaves; cut off the root ends and most of the green tops. Wash thoroughly and cut into 2.5cm (1in) lengths. Blanch, drain, cool and dry. Pack in small quantities in polythene bags or rigid containers.	2 minutes	Use within six months. Use from frozen or thaw in the container and use in soups and stews.
Lettuce	Not suitable for freezing.		
Marrows (See also courgettees)	Not really suitable for freezing, unless quite young and tender. Peel, cut into 2cm (¾in) slices and blanch. Cool, drain and dry. Pack in rigid containers.	3 minutes	Partially thaw in the container and steam until tender, or fry in oil.
Mushrooms	Freeze only freshly picked mushrooms. Wipe them clean and trim the roots. Leave whole or cut into slices, and fry lightly in butter. Cool quickly and pack into small, rigid containers with 1cm (½in) headspace.		Use within three months. Partially thaw in the containers; fry in butter, or grill.
Onions	Although hardly worth freezing, they may be peeled, finely chopped or sliced and packed in small containers. Wrap the containers well to avoid the smell affecting other foods. Tiny onions may be peeled, blanched whole, cooked and dried. Pack in polythene bags.	Whole: 4 minutes	Use chopped raw onions, just thawed, in salads. Whole onions may be cooked from frozen. Serve with a sauce, or add to stews.
Parsnips	Trim the roots and tops of young parsnips. Peel and cut into slices, 1cm (½in) wide, or dice. Blanch, cool and drain. Pack in rigid containers with 1cm (½in) headspace.	2 minutes	Cook from frozen for 10 minutes.
Peas	Shell young, sweet-tasting peas and grade according to size. Blanch, cool quickly, drain and dry. Leave mangetout peas in pods, and blanch. Pack garden peas in polythene bags; pack mangetout peas in rigid containers with 1cm (½in) headspace.	1–2 minutes Mangetout: 2–4 minutes	Cook from frozen for 7 minutes.
Potatoes	Freeze small, new potatoes only, either raw or cooked. Scrape the potatoes, blanch (unless cooked), cool quickly, drain and dry. Pack in polythene bags. For chips, peel and wash firm potatoes, cut into uniform chips and part-fry in deep fat for about 3 minutes. Drain thoroughly and cool quickly. Pack in polythene bags.	3–4 minutes	Cook frozen (if blanched) for 15 minutes, or heat (if already cooked) in hot water. Partially thaw chips; fry for 3 minutes.

Continued on p262

AT-AT-GLANCE GUIDE TO FREEZING VEGETABLES

VEGETABLE	PREPARATION AND PACKING	BLANCHING TIME	COOKING TIME
Pumpkins and squashes	Wash, peel and cut in half. Scrape out seeds and strings and cut into cubes. Steam, bake or boil until tender. Drain and leave in chunks or mash to a purée. When cool pack in rigid contaners leaving 2.5cm (1in) headspace.		Cook from frozen, or thaw in containers at room temperature for about 2 hours.
Radishes	Not suitable for freezing.		
Salsify and scorzonera	Not recommended for freezing as they both discolour badly.		
Spinach	Trim stalks, wash thoroughly and drain. Blanch in small portions, cool quickly and squeeze out surplus moisture. Pack in rigid containers with 1cm (½in) headspace.	2 minutes	Cook from frozen, with butter for 7 minutes.
Swedes	Not recommended for freezing.		
Sweetcorn	Freeze only young cobs, with pale yellow kernels. Strip off the husks and tassels and trim the stalks close. Blanch a few at a time. Cool, drain and dry. Wrap each cob in foil or freezer paper, pack in bags or containers, and freeze. Alternatively, scrape the kernels from the blanched cobs, and pack in rigid containers with 1cm (½in) headspace.	Small: 4 minutes Medium: 6 minutes	Thaw completely, which takes 3–4 hours at room temperature, and boil for 5–10 minutes.
Sweet peppers	Keep green and red peppers separate. Wash, cut off stalk ends, deseed, and remove membranes. Cut in half lengthways, for stuffing, or into narrow slices. Blanch, cool, drain and dry. Pack in rigid containers, separating the sliced layers with waxed paper. Leave 1cm (½in) headspace.	Halves: 3 minutes Slices: 2 minutes	Thaw halved peppers to be stuffed. Use slices, unthawed, to flavour stews and casseroles.
Tomatoes	May be frozen whole, but only for cooking afterwards. Best frozen as a purée or juice. To freeze whole, wipe small, firm, ripe tomatoes and pack in polythene bags. To make into a purée, wash the tomatoes, quarter them, simmer for 5 minutes, and rub through a nylon sieve. Cool and pack in rigid containers with 1cm (½in) headspace. To prepare juice, wipe and core the tomatoes, cut in quarters and simmer for 10 minutes. Peel and put through a sieve, season with salt. Pack in rigid containers with 2.5cm (1in) headspace.		Thaw whole tomatoes in the containers, slip off the skins and use in cooked dishes. Use frozen purée in sauces, soups and casseroles, thaw the juice in the containers and serve chilled.
Turnips	May be frozen fresh or cooked. Trim the roots and tops from young turnips. Peel, dice and blanch. Alternatively, cook the peeled and quartered turnips until tender, then drain and mash. Cool, and pack in rigid containers with 1cm (½in) headspace.	2 minutes	Cook whole turnips without thawing for 8 minutes. Heat partially thawed, mashed turnips in a double boiler with butter.
Watercress	Not suitable for freezing.		

unsuitable for garnishing. Use them to flavour soups and stews by simply crumbling the frozen herbs into the dish to be cooked. There is no need to thaw them first.

Evergreen herbs are not worth freezing, as they are better used fresh. Some smaller herbs can be grown throughout winter in pots on the kitchen windowsill. In general, freeze only those herbs that are most often required for cooking, such as basil, chives, mint, parsley and tarragon. Pick the herbs fresh, and keep them separate to prevent them imparting their flavours to one another. Wash, drain and dry thoroughly.

It is unnecessary to blanch herbs. Instead, divide them into sprigs and pack in polythene bags. Herbs may also be frozen on trays, and packed in small portions to be used separately as required.

Yet another method is to chop the herbs finely and pack, with a little water, into ice-cube trays and freeze solid. Remove the frozen cubes and pack in bags in convenient portions. Use the cubes for flavouring while still frozen.

All herbs should be wrapped and sealed carefully to prevent other foods in the freezer taking up their scent or flavour. Store the packs of herbs in a container with a tight-fitting lid.

Storing cooked food

As well as storing fresh garden produce for later use, the freezer provides an ideal way to store cooked dishes, such as vegetable gratins and casseroles, fruit pies and fruit crumbles.

Leftovers can be made into purées by rubbing them through a sieve or blending them in the liquidiser. Use them later for making soups and sauces.

Cooked vegetables may be coated with a sauce, packed in rigid containers and frozen for later use. Leave 1cm (½in) headspace for expansion. If you are spending a whole day cooking, it is worthwhile making extra quantities so that you can store the surplus – when cold – in the freezer. Home-made bread, wrapped and frozen as soon as it is quite cool, will taste newly baked when thawed.

Since most frozen fruits are intended to be used as pie fillings, it is a good idea to freeze both fruit and pastry together. Line aluminium-foil plates with pastry, and sweeten the fruit to taste with sugar. Add a little cornflour to prevent the pastry from becoming soggy when thawed.

If you are using very soft, juicy fruit, brush the pastry base with a little melted butter before adding the fruit. Cover with the top crust, wrap in strong freezer foil, and freeze.

To cook the frozen pie, first leave it to thaw at room temperature for 2–4 hours before making a slit in the top crust and baking as you would a freshly made pie.

The following recipes are only a small selection of the many fruit and vegetable dishes that can be cooked in advance and frozen.

Straight to the pan Prepare beans before freezing – by topping and tailing, and cutting long beans in half – and they can be cooked from frozen.

Recipes for quick-frozen fruit or vegetable dishes

Fruit dishes

Apple cheese cake
2 large cooking apples
350g (12oz) shortcrust pastry
250g (½lb) caster sugar
125g (4oz) butter
2 eggs, beaten
Juice and grated rind of 2 lemons

Line two foil flan cases, 20cm (8in) in diameter, with the pastry. Cream the sugar and butter, and mix with the eggs. Chop and coarsely grate the peeled, cored apples and add, with the butter and egg mixture, to the lemon juice and rind.

Fill the flan cases. Bake at 200°C (400°F, gas mark 6) for 20 minutes, then lower the heat to 180°C (350°F, gas mark 4) until set, which will take about 30 minutes. Cool, wrap in foil or polythene, and freeze.

Blackberry flan
250g (½lb) rich shortcrust pastry
375g (¾lb) blackberries
175g (6oz) sugar
2 tablespoons cornflour

Roll out the prepared pastry. Fit it into a 20cm (8in) flan ring lined with foil. Prick the pastry base and bake blind at 200°C (400°F, gas mark 6) for 25 minutes. Remove from the oven and leave to cool. Wrap the flan, still in its foil case, in plastic film and foil, and freeze.

Hull and rinse the blackberries, put them in a pan with the sugar and 300ml (½ pint) of water. Bring to the boil and simmer for 10–15 minutes, or until the berries are soft but not broken up.

Stir the cornflour with a little of the juice, and blend it into the blackberries. Simmer gently until thickened.

Cool the berries quickly and pack them into a rigid container, leaving 1cm (½in) headspace. Wrap and freeze. Both the pastry case and filling will store in the freezer for up to six months. To use, thaw the flan case in its wrapping at room temperature; then fill with the blackberries, gently heated, and put in the oven for 15–20 minutes at 200°C (400°F, gas mark 6) to heat through. Serve with cream.

Cherry flan
150g (5oz) plain flour
75g (3oz) softened butter
1 egg yolk
250g (½lb) stoned black cherries
125g (4oz) ground almonds
125g (4oz) icing sugar
2 eggs

To make the pastry, put the flour in a bowl. Make a well in the centre, add the butter and egg yolk, and work together with your fingertips to a smooth paste.

Leave the pastry to relax for 15 minutes, then roll out and line a 20cm (8in) flan ring.

Prick the pastry case, and fill with the stoned cherries. Mix the ground almonds and sugar together. Beat the eggs, and add them to the almonds and sugar. Pour over the cherries.

Bake for 30 minutes at 200°C (400°F, gas mark 6). Cool, and freeze when cold.

Eve's pudding
750g (1½lb) cooking apples
Juice of 1 lemon
75g (3oz) demerara sugar
Almond essence
75g (3oz) caster sugar
75g (3oz) butter
2 eggs
75g (3oz) flour
Salt

Peel, core and thinly slice the apples, and brush with the lemon juice. Put the apple slices in a greased 1 litre (2 pint) pudding basin and sprinkle with demerara sugar, mixing it thoroughly with the apple slices. Add a few drops of almond essence.

Cream the caster sugar and butter until fluffy, then gradually beat in the lightly beaten eggs and fold in the flour, sifted with a pinch of salt. Spoon this mixture over the apples. Tie the pudding basin down with greaseproof paper, foil and string, allowing room for expansion. Freeze until solid and store for up to six months.

To use, steam the pudding from the frozen state for about 2 hours, turn out and serve.

Gooseberries, stoned apricots, damsons and plums can be prepared, frozen, and steamed in the same way, although traditionally Eve's pudding is always made with apples.

Raspberry cream
500g (1lb) raspberries
Juice of ½ lime
100–125g (4oz) sugar
300ml (½ pint) double cream
2 tablespoons icing sugar

Rub the raspberries through a sieve and mix in the lime juice and sugar, stirring until this has dissolved.

The raspberry purée may be mixed with cream before freezing, but this reduces the storage time. It is a better idea to freeze the purée in a rigid container, where it will keep for at least six months.

To use, thaw the purée at room temperature. Whip the cream with the icing sugar until fairly stiff. Blend in the raspberry purée, spoon into glasses and chill for 1 hour. Decorate with toasted hazelnuts.

Raspberry jam, uncooked
1kg (2lb) raspberries
2kg (4lb) caster sugar
1 bottle commercial pectin
4 tablespoons lemon juice

Crush the fruit and stir in the sugar. Leave for about 1 hour in a warm room, stirring the mixture until the sugar has dissolved. Add the pectin and lemon juice, and stir for 2 minutes. Pour into small pots and cover with lids or foil. Leave in a warm place for two days and then freeze.

Thaw for use as required, but once opened use within a few days.

Peach crème brulée
6 peeled peaches
Caster sugar
Whipped cream
Soft brown sugar

Slice the peeled peaches and sweeten to taste with caster sugar. Arrange in a foil dish and cover with whipped cream. Freeze and wrap in cling film or foil.

To serve, leave to thaw for about 4 hours at room temperature, or for 6 hours in the refrigerator. Sprinkle the cream thickly with brown sugar and place under a hot grill for a few minutes, until the sugar has melted.

Strawberry ice cream
500g (1lb) strawberries
125g (4oz) icing sugar
2 teaspoons lemon juice
Double cream

Stalk the strawberries, wash if necessary, and drain well. Rub them through a nylon sieve. Stir in the icing sugar and lemon juice. Whisk an equal quantity of double cream until floppy, and fold into the strawberry purée.

Freeze, stirring occasionally during the first 2 hours. Best stored in a rigid container.

Vegetable dishes

Artichokes à la Grècque
4–6 globe-artichoke fonds
125–150ml (5fl oz) olive oil
Juice of 1 small lemon
Bouquet garni
8 coriander seeds
8 peppercorns
Salt

Put a litre (2 pints) of water in a pan with the oil, lemon juice, bouquet garni, spices and salt. Bring to the boil and simmer for 5 minutes. Add the quartered artichoke fonds and cook for 20 minutes. Cool, and freeze in cartons with 1cm (½in) headspace.

Serve these pickled artichokes as a chilled hors d'oeuvre. Thaw in the containers, strain and arrange on small plates. Sprinkle with paprika.

Asparagus vol-au-vents

500g (1lb) prepared puff pastry
1 egg white
175g (6oz) cooked asparagus tips
300ml (½ pint) Béchamel sauce

Roll out the pastry until it's 1cm (½in) thick, cut into 7.5cm (3in) rounds and hollow out the centres. Set the cases on a moist baking sheet, brush with beaten egg white and bake for 20 minutes at 230°C (450°F, gas mark 8). Leave the pastry cases to cool, then pack in rigid containers, interlaced with waxed paper, and freeze. Fold the asparagus tips into the Béchamel sauce; cool and freeze separately.

Thaw the vol-au-vent cases at room temperature for about 4 hours, then heat through in the oven. Gently heat the asparagus filling and spoon into the cases. Snip a little parsley over the top.

Baked cucumber

2 cucumbers
Salt
Juice of 1 lemon
1 tablespoon sugar
1 tablespoon finely chopped mixed herbs such as parsley, chives or basil, preferably fresh
50g (2oz) butter

Peel the cucumbers, cut in half lengthways, scoop out the seeds and cut the flesh into cubes. Sprinkle with salt, lemon juice and sugar and leave for 1 hour. Drain, and place in an ovenproof dish. Sprinkle with the herbs, add knobs of butter and bake at 220°C (425°F, gas mark 7) for 30 minutes, turning from time to time. Cool, and freeze in cartons with 1cm (½in) headspace.

To serve, thaw before heating at 180°C (350°F, gas mark 4).

Bean and bacon pot

250g (8oz) broad beans, shelled
250g (8oz) potatoes
1 large parsnip
2 carrots
2 medium onions
250g (8oz) bacon
300ml (½ pint) tomato juice, freshly made or canned
Salt and pepper
2 tablespoons Worcestershire sauce – optional

Place the beans in a casserole, and add the peeled and diced potatoes, parsnip and carrots. Add the peeled and sliced onions. Dice the bacon and fry briskly for 1 or 2 minutes to seal. Add to the casserole with the tomato juice, and salt and pepper to taste. Cover and cook at 180°C (350°F, gas mark 4) for 1½ hours. Cool and freeze. When thawed and reheated, add the Worcestershire sauce.

Brussels sprouts au gratin

3kg (6lb) Brussels sprouts
1 litre (2 pints) white sauce

Cook the prepared sprouts and drain thoroughly. Arrange in foil dishes and cover with sauce, leaving 1cm (½in) headspace. Freeze when cool.

To serve, warm through in the oven, then brown under the grill after topping with grated cheese and knobs of butter.

Celery and leek casserole

2 large heads of celery
8 leeks
250g (½lb) chopped bacon
125g (4oz) butter
50g (2oz) flour
1 litre (2 pints) white stock
Salt and pepper

Prepare the celery and leeks and cut both into 2.5cm (1in) pieces.

Fry the leeks and bacon in the butter until golden, stir in the flour and cook for about 5–10 minutes. Gradually add the stock, bring to the boil and simmer until smooth.

Blend in the celery and season with salt and pepper. Cook in a foil-lined casserole for 45 minutes in the oven at 180°C (350°F, gas mark 4). Cool and freeze.

Thaw and reheat thoroughly.

Courgettes provençale

1.5kg (3kg) courgettes
Salt and pepper
Seasoned flour
6–7 tablespoons cooking oil
750g (1½lb) onions
1.25kg (2½lb) tinned tomatoes
Juice of 1 lemon
125g (4oz) grated Parmesan cheese

Cut the washed but unpeeled courgettes into 2.5cm (1in) slices, sprinkle with salt and leave for 5 minutes. Wipe dry, and coat with seasoned flour.

Fry in 4 tablespoons of the oil until golden, then drain. Fry the sliced onions in the rest of the oil.

Put layers of courgettes, onions and roughly chopped tomatoes in a foil-lined casserole, seasoning each layer and sprinkling with lemon juice; finish with a layer of tomatoes. Cover and freeze overnight; remove from the casserole, wrap and seal.

To cook, set the foil mould in the original casserole and bake in the oven at 190°C (375°F, gas mark 5) for 1¼ hours. Sprinkle with the cheese; brown under the grill.

Onions in white sauce

1kg (2lb) pickling onions
50g (2oz) butter
50g (2oz) cornflour
600ml (1 pint) white stock
300ml (½ pint) milk
Salt and pepper

Make a white sauce from the butter, cornflour, stock and milk. Season with salt and pepper.

Blanch the onions in boiling water for 2 minutes and refresh in cold water. Put them back in the pan with cold water to cover, bring to the boil and simmer until tender. Drain, and add to the white sauce. Cool, and freeze in waxed cartons or plastic boxes.

Thaw at room temperature in the containers and heat through gently before serving.

Pancakes stuffed with mushrooms

100–125g (4oz) plain or self-raising flour
Salt and pepper
1 egg
300ml (½ pint) milk
250g (8oz) mushrooms
25g (1oz) butter
1 tablespoon flour
225ml (8fl oz) single cream
1 tablespoon sherry
1 tablespoon chopped parsley

Make up a batter from the flour – sifted with a pinch of salt – the egg and the milk, and make eight pancakes. Leave the pancakes flat, to cool, separated by waxed paper.

Trim the mushrooms and slice thinly. Melt the butter and fry the mushrooms lightly, then stir in 1 tablespoon of flour and gradually blend in the cream. Bring to the boil and season lightly with salt and pepper. Remove from the heat and stir in the sherry and parsley. Spread the mushroom filling over the pancakes, roll them up and arrange in a rigid container or an ovenproof dish. Double wrap with foil, and freeze. They can be stored for up to two months.

To use, heat the pancakes from the frozen state for about 1¼ hours at 200°C (400°F, gas mark 6). After 1 hour, sprinkle the pancakes with finely grated cheese and return to the oven. Continue baking until golden-brown.

Pancakes can also be filled with creamed spinach, asparagus, cauliflower or broccoli in a rich white sauce.

Pasta sauce

500g (1lb) minced beef
1 large onion
2 tablespoons olive oil
6 large tomatoes
1 small green pepper
125g (4oz) mushrooms
300ml (½ pint) beef stock
150ml (5fl oz) red wine
2 tablespoons tomato paste
2 tablespoons oregano or basil
Salt and pepper

Fry the beef and finely chopped onion in the oil for 5 minutes, or until the meat has browned and separated into grains. Add the peeled and chopped tomatoes, the deseeded pepper and the chopped mushrooms, together with the stock and red wine. Bring to the boil over gentle heat, stir in the tomato paste and oregano or basil and season with salt and pepper.

Simmer for about 45 minutes, then cool and spoon into rigid containers. Wrap, and freeze solid, and store for up to three months. To use, cook slowly from the frozen state, adding a little more stock if necessary and, if you wish, seasoning with crushed garlic and more herbs. Use as a meat sauce with pasta dishes.

Piperade

500g (1lb) tomatoes
2 onions
4 peppers
3 tablespoons oil
Salt and pepper

Peel and slice the onions, deseed the peppers and cut them into strips, and skin the tomatoes. Heat the oil in a heavy pan, add the onions and fry them gently until golden. Add the peppers and cook for about 15 minutes, until soft.

Add the tomatoes, cover the pan and cook for a further 30 minutes, stirring often to prevent sticking. Leave to cool, then pour into rigid containers and freeze.

Piperade is delicious with pasta. Or, add 2 beaten eggs per person and cook in the same way as scrambled eggs.

Potato and cucumber pie

500g (1lb) potatoes
250g (8oz) cucumber
25g (1oz) butter or margarine
25g (1oz) flour
300ml (½ pint) milk
Salt
Large pinch cayenne pepper
2 or 3 eggs
125g (4oz) grated cheese

Thinly peel and dice the potatoes and cucumber. Cook in salted water for 5 minutes until just tender, and drain well.

Make a sauce with the butter, flour and milk, season to taste with salt and add the pepper. Hard boil the eggs, shell and chop roughly. Add the potatoes, cucumber and

chopped eggs to the sauce and simmer gently for 5 minutes. Turn out into a greased heat-proof dish and cool before freezing.

To serve, thaw, cover with the cheese. Heat through, then flash under the grill to brown the top.

Pumpkin soup

500g (1lb) pumpkin
2 large leeks
500g (1lb) tomatoes
50g (2oz) butter
2 tablespoons vegetable oil
1 litre (2 pints) chicken stock
Salt and pepper

Peel and dice the pumpkin. Wash the leeks thoroughly and slice thinly. Skin the tomatoes and slice. Melt the butter in a saucepan and add the oil. Add all the vegetables, and cook slowly for 10–15 minutes, stirring occasionally. Add the stock, and continue cooking until the vegetables are tender. Liquidise the soup, then cool and freeze.

Season to taste when reheating.

Ratatouille

1kg (1lb) tomatoes
Salt and pepper
1 large or 2 medium marrows
8 small aubergines
2 red or green peppers
4 chopped onions
2 or 3 garlic cloves
Bacon fat or vegetable oil

Skin the tomatoes, halve, sprinkle with salt and drain – cut side down. Cut the peeled marrow into large chunks, discarding the seeds. Cut the aubergines in half lengthways and slice across. Trim the bases off the peppers, remove the seeds, and slice.

Fry the onions with the crushed garlic in a little bacon fat or oil.

Add all the vegetables, season highly and simmer, covered, for about 30 minutes, until tender. Cool, pack in rigid containers with 1cm (½in) headspace, and freeze.

To serve hot, partially thaw and heat through gently. To serve cold, thaw in the fridge for 4 hours.

Savoury beetroot

50g (2oz) butter
1 large onion
500g (1lb) beetroot
1 large cooking apple
375g (¾lb) potatoes
Salt and pepper
3 tablespoons wine vinegar
1 heaped teaspoon sugar

Melt the butter in a frying pan, add the peeled, finely chopped onion. Cook gently until soft.

Peel the raw beetroot and grate into the pan. Peel the apple and grate into the pan. Stir around in the butter, then add the peeled and diced potatoes.

Season to taste, then add the vinegar and sugar. Stir, then cover the pan and cook slowly until the mixture is tender. Stir or shake the pan occasionally.

Cool before freezing.

Tomato provençale

1kg (2lb) tomatoes
Salt and pepper
½ tablespoon finely chopped basil or parsley
4 garlic cloves
4 finely chopped onions
4 heaped tablespoons bread-crumbs
2 tablespoons olive oil

Cut the tomatoes in half and sprinkle with salt and pepper. Mix the herbs, crushed garlic and onions with the breadcrumbs.

Cover each tomato half with the mixture and sprinkle with a little oil. Grill for 20 minutes. Wrap, pack in containers and freeze.

To serve, cook from frozen for 30 minutes in the oven at 190°C (375°F, gas mark 5).

Vegetable soup

2 leeks
2 carrots
½ celeriac
1 small cauliflower
50g (2oz) butter
25g (1oz) flour
600ml (1 pint) white stock or bouillon
Salt and pepper

Prepare the cleaned vegetables, cutting the leeks, carrots and celeriac into narrow slices and dividing the cauliflower into florets.

Melt the butter in a pan and sweat the vegetables until soft, then stir in the flour and cook to a roux. Gradually blend in the stock.

Simmer, covered, until the vegetables are tender, season lightly with salt and pepper and leave to cool. Blend the soup in the liquidiser until smooth and creamy, and leave to cool completely.

Pour the soup into rigid plastic containers, leaving 2.5cm (1in) headspace, and seal. Freeze solid and store for up to three months.

To use, heat the frozen soup gently, adding milk to the required consistency. Correct the seasoning.

Vegetable pie

1 onion
1 turnip
2–3 carrots
2 leeks
3 sticks of celery
50g (2oz) butter
450ml (¾ pint) parsley sauce

1 small can of butter beans
250g (8oz) shortcrust pastry

Chop the prepared vegetables. Melt the butter in a pan, add the vegetables and cook gently for 10 minutes; the vegetables should be soft, but not browned. Make the parsley sauce and season well. Stir in the vegetables, juices and add the butter beans.

Put the mixture into a 850ml (1½ pint) pie dish and top with pastry or mashed potato. Freeze until hard, place in a polythene bag, seal and label. Return to the freezer, use within 2 months.

Winter soup

3 to 4 heads of celery
250g (8oz) parsnips
250g (8oz) turnips
250g (8oz) onions
2 litres (4 pints) chicken stock
6 black peppercorns
1 bay leaf
125g (4oz) mushrooms – optional

Prepare the celery, and slice thinly. Peel the parsnips and turnips, and cut into dice. Peel and slice the onions. Put the stock and all the vegetables in a large saucepan and add peppercorns and bay leaf tied in muslin.

Bring to the boil, then simmer for 30 minutes. Add the cleaned and thinly sliced mushrooms, and simmer for a further 10 minutes.

Cool, and remove the muslin bag. Freeze in cartons, allowing 1cm (½in) headspace.

To use, heat the frozen soup gently, adding milk to the required consistency. Correct the seasoning.

Preserving by bottling

Apart from freezing, bottling is the only method of preserving food in which the natural taste and texture of the produce are retained almost intact. The process, which is not a difficult one, is basically that of packing fruit into bottling jars, covering the contents with water, syrup or brine, sterilising them at high temperatures, then sealing the jars while still hot to prevent the entry of bacteria.

For good results, you must stick carefully to the rules – especially those concerned with cleanliness – use the correct equipment and select only high-quality produce.

Equipment
You will not need a lot of specialist equipment, but make sure that you have the following essentials.

Bottles While good results can sometimes be achieved with improvised equipment, special preserving bottles with tops held on by screw caps or spring clips are a good idea. They are available in sizes from 0.5–2kg (1–4lb).

The tops of both types consist of metal or glass discs with rubber gaskets attached. When placed on top of the bottles the tops form an airtight seal. Once the air has been driven from the bottle by heating they create a germ-proof vacuum.

The slightest flaw in the rubber, or fault in a metal top, will destroy this effect, so spoiling the contents of the jar. Inspect the tops closely before use and never use them more than once. Additional tops may be purchased separately from the jars. Store them in airtight boxes, with a little talcum powder rubbed into the gaskets to keep them supple.

The modern jam jars which have twist-on tops with integral gaskets can also be used. These are useful for small quantities of fruit, and they have the advantage of fitting easily into an ordinary deep saucepan or pressure cooker.

Closures for ordinary rimmed jam jars, consisting of preserving caps with replaceable gaskets, are also available.

Sterilising pan You will need a large, deep pan for processing bottled fruit. Proprietary sterilisers, with false bottoms, thermometers and lids, can be bought, but they are expensive. Any deep vessel – such as a galvanised bucket or a large preserving pan – will serve equally well. Whatever vessel you use, it should be deep enough to incorporate a false bottom – a grid or a thick layer of newspaper – and at the same time contain sufficient water to reach the level of the liquid in the jars.

Taking the temperature If you use the slow water-bath method of sterilising, it is necessary to use a thermometer. The best, specially

Bottled plums Add some spice to plums at the bottling stage so that the flavours can infuse through the fruit while they are in storage. In a few months' time you will have a delicious ready-made dessert.

made for bottling and jam making, registers up to 110°C (230°F).

Packing Wooden bottling spoons, with small bowls and long handles, may be used to pack the produce into the containers. But smooth, clean, round-ended sticks will serve just as well.

Handling the bottles A large pair of bottling tongs – nonslip wooden or wire grips attached to a steel spring – are very useful when removing the heated bottles from the sterilising pan.

Checking and preparing the bottles
Before using either type of bottle, check the rim carefully for chips, as even the smallest will prevent an efficient seal. See that metal lids are not distorted or scratched, and

that the screw caps are not too loose or the spring clips weakened. Discard any rubber rings that show signs of drying or cracking. They will not make an efficient seal.

Test the jars and lids by filling the jars with water, putting on the lids and turning the jars upside down. If there is any sign of leakage after 10 minutes, the bottle or fittings are suspect.

Wash the jars thoroughly, and boil them for 5 minutes in a pan which has either a built-in false bottom or contains a grid or a thick pad of newspaper. Invert the jars to drain; but do not dry them, since it is easier to pack fruit into wet bottles.

Soak the rubber rings in warm water for 15 minutes, then dip them in boiling water immediately before putting them on. This will make the rings more supple.

TWO KINDS OF JARS FOR BOTTLING

Screw-top jars The metal lid, with rubber gasket attached, is held in place with a screw top. Jars are made in several sizes.

Clip on jars In this type, the glass top with detachable rubber ring is secured by a spring until the vacuum has been formed.

Bottling fruit

Generally it is easier to bottle fruit than vegetables and the end product is more attractive. For the best results and tastiest preserved fruits, be sure to follow these simple steps.

Step 1 Preparing the fruit

The fruit should be fresh and just ripe, and free from the slightest sign of disease or decay. The importance of inspecting the produce for bottling cannot be over stressed. All types of fruit are suitable for storing in this way, provided they are prepared correctly before being packed into the bottles.

Apples Peel, core and slice, and put straight into lightly salted water to prevent discoloration. Rinse before packing; or blanch for 2–3 minutes in boiling water until pliable, then pack.

Apricots Either bottle the fruits whole, or cut them into halves and remove the stones. Bottle quickly after preparing, and include a few kernels. These will help to bring out the flavour.

Cherries Bottle whole fruits, or stone them first, and add any juice to the syrup. As cherries are low in acid, add ¼ teaspoon citric acid to every 600ml (1 pint) of syrup.

Damsons and plums As a general rule, bottle these and other stone fruits whole after washing them. Very large plums may be halved and stoned, if preferred.

Figs These may be peeled or left with their skins on. Add ¼ teaspoon citric acid to every 600ml (1 pint) of syrup, and use equal amounts of syrup and fruit.

Gooseberries Only unripe gooseberries are suitable for bottling. Top and tail with scissors.

Peaches Halve and stone. Blanch, and peel off the skins. Pack into bottles without delay.

Pears Peel, halve and core dessert varieties, putting them straight into cold, lightly salted water with 1 teaspoon of citric acid. Rinse and pack quickly.

Treat cooking pears and quinces similarly, but simmer in syrup until soft before packing.

Rhubarb Cut trimmed rhubarb into 5cm (2in) pieces. This fruit will pack better if soaked overnight in hot syrup.

Soft fruits Fruits such as blackberries, currants and raspberries should be picked over, hulled or stripped from the stalks. Rinse if necessary, and drain well.

Enhance the flavour of strawberries by soaking them overnight in warm bottling syrup (see Step 2, below). A few drops of red food colouring added to the syrup improves the appearance.

Tomatoes Clean the ripe, firm tomatoes and bottle in a brine solution made from 15g (½oz) salt to 1 litre (1¾ pints) cold water.

Tomatoes may also be peeled and packed tight without liquid, but sprinkled with 1 teaspoon of salt and ½ teaspoon of sugar for every 500g (1lb) of fruit.

Step 2 Making the syrup

Water can be used for bottling, but syrup imparts a better flavour and colour. The strength of the syrup depends on the fruit, averaging about 200–250g (7–8oz) of sugar to every 600ml (1 pint) of water.

Add the sugar to half the water and boil for 1 minute before adding the rest of the water. Sometimes the syrup is poured cold over the fruit and sometimes it is used hot.

Step 3 Packing the fruit

Choose fruits of uniform size, and use a bottling spoon or wooden stick to pack them in tightly without damaging them. A 500g (1lb) bottle will hold up to 350g (12oz) of most types of fruit.

If syrup is to be added before processing it can be poured in when the bottle is full of fruit. It is easier, however, to pack the fruit and syrup in layers. Release any air bubbles by jerking the jar. Top up with syrup until the fruit is covered.

Step 4 Sterilising the fruit

There are four methods of sterilising bottled fruit.

Slow water-bath method

Slacken screw caps off a quarter of a turn to allow steam to escape during processing. Spring clips are designed to permit this to happen without being loosened.

Place the bottles on the false bottom of a large pan – a wire grid or thick layer of newspaper – and put folded cloth or newspaper between the bottles to prevent them touching as the water boils. Fill the pan with cold water until the bottles are completely submerged, cover with a lid and heat the pan slowly. After 1 hour the water should just be reaching

55°C (130°F). After a further 30 minutes the water should reach the recommended temperature (see chart below).

When the bottles have been kept at the correct temperature for the exact time, remove them from the pan with bottling tongs, or bale out sufficient water to enable you to pick them up with a cloth.

As each jar is removed, place it on a dry, wooden surface – it is liable to crack on a metal surface – and tighten the screw caps at once. As the bottles cool, screw down further if necessary.

The table of processing temperatures and times is for 1kg (2lb) bottles, which are the most practical. For 2kg (4lb) bottles add 5 minutes, and for bottles holding up to 3kg (6lb) add 10 minutes. Solid-packed tomatoes are a special case. Give 2kg (4lb) bottles

BOTTLING FRUIT BY WATER-BATH METHODS TIME CHART

The following times and temperatures are those recommended for 1kg (2lb) bottles. If 2kg (4lb) bottles are used, add 5 minutes. For 3kg (6lb) bottles, add 10 minutes. Double these times if tomatoes are being processed.

Whether by the slow or quick method, sterilising times are reckoned from the moment the water reaches simmering point.

FRUIT	TEMPERATURE °C (°F)	STERILISING SLOW	TIME (MINS) QUICK
Apples, packed solid	82 (180)	15	20
Apples, sliced	74 (165)	10	2
Apricots, whole and halved	82 (180)	15	10
Blackberries	74 (165)	10	2
Cherries, whole and stoned	82 (180)	15	10
Currants	74 (155)	10	2
Damsons, whole	82 (180)	15	10
Figs	88 (190)	30	40
Gages, whole	82 (180)	15	10
Gooseberries, dessert	82 (180)	15	10
Gooseberries, green	74 (165)	10	2
Loganberries	74 (165)	10	2
Mulberries	74 (165)	10	2
Nectarines, halved	82 (180)	15	20
Peaches, halved	82 (180)	15	20
Pears	88 (190)	30	40
Plums, halved and stoned	82 (180)	15	20
Plums, whole	82 (180)	15	10
Raspberries	74 (165)	10	2
Rhubarb	74 (165)	10	2
Strawberries	74 (165)	10	2
Strawberries, syrup-soaked	82 (180)	15	20
Tomatoes, solid pack	88 (190)	40	50
Tomatoes, whole	88 (190)	30	40

Stocking up for winter Produce harvested when it is at its best can be bottled and preserved for several months so that the taste of autumn plenty can be enjoyed throughout the cold winter months.

an extra 10 minutes, and 3kg (6lb) bottles an extra 20 minutes.

Quick water-bath method Fill the warm bottles with prepared fruit and pour in hot syrup up to the brim. Cover the bottles and place them in a pan in which a false bottom has been created, as described before. Pack further layers of newspaper or cloth between the bottles to prevent them banging together. Add warm water to cover the jars, and heat the water slowly so that it reaches simmering point after 30 minutes. Continue simmering for 2–50 minutes (see chart on left).

Remove the bottles using tongs and tighten screw tops.

Pressure-cooker method
A pressure cooker can be used for bottling fruit, provided it is deep enough to take the bottles together with the false bottom, as described above. The cooker must also be able to maintain a steady low pressure of 5psi – not all models can be set this low.

Pack the fruit into warm bottles and cover with boiling syrup to within 1cm (½in) of the top. Put on the tops, leaving the screw caps slightly loose. Pour about 2.5cm (1in) of boiling water into the

pressure cooker and add a little vinegar to prevent staining. Set the bottles on the false bottom, and separate them with cloth or newspaper.

Fasten the lid and heat gently with the vent open until steam jets out in a steady stream. Close the vent and bring up the pressure to 5psi (low). The time taken from the start of heating until pressure is reached should not be less than 5 minutes, nor more than 10 minutes.

For apples, rhubarb, all soft fruits, cherries, damsons, greengages and plums, hold the pressure for 1 minute. Extend this to 3–4 minutes in the case of apples if these are tightly packed, and also for halved apricots and whole or halved plums. Figs, pears and whole tomatoes need 5 minutes; solid-packed tomatoes, 15 minutes.

Remove the pressure cooker from the heat, but leave it to stand for 10 minutes before opening the vent. The sterilising process is still continuing during this time. Carefully lift the bottles out onto a dry wooden surface and tighten the screw caps.

Step 5 Testing the seal
Allow the bottles to cool completely, preferably overnight. Remove the screw caps or spring clips and test each bottle by picking it up with your fingertips, holding it by the lid only.

If the seal works, the vacuum inside the bottle will hold the lid securely. If the seal is faulty, the lid will come away.

Step 6 Storing bottled fruit
Wipe off any sticky marks and label the bottles to show the type of fruit, the date of bottling and the

covering liquid used. Store in a cool, dry, dark and well-ventilated place. To open bottled fruit, stand the jar in hot water for a few minutes and gently prise off the lid with the tip of a knife.

Bottling fruit purées
Misshapen but otherwise sound fruits can be preserved in pulp or puréed form for use as pie or pudding fillings. This is an economical way to store fruit for winter use, since large quantities can be reduced to a small bulk.

Pick over and prepare the fruit then simmer in a little water until thoroughly cooked. Pour into hot bottles while the fruit is still boiling hot; seal at once, using lids and gaskets dipped in boiling water immediately beforehand. Sterilise the bottles by the quick water-bath method, holding them at boiling point for 5 minutes.

Alternatively, you can make fruit purées by rubbing the cooked pulp through a nylon sieve and sweetening them to taste. Bottle and process in the same way.

Bottling fruit in brandy
The most popular fruits for this treatment are cherries, small plums, damsons, peaches and pears. Prepare them as for the water-bath method, and prick firm-skinned fruit with a stainless-steel fork so that the syrup is able to permeate the flesh.

Make a fairly heavy syrup from 500g (1lb) of sugar to 1 litre (2 pints) of water. Cook the syrup until it is thick, measure it, and when it is cool add an equal quantity of brandy.

Pack the fruit into bottles and fill them up with the cold brandy syrup, then process by the slow water-bath method.

THINGS THAT MAY GO WRONG

Fruit rises or sinks Overheating or too-rapid heating at the beginning of processing, may cause the fruit to rise or sink in the bottles. The same faults may occur if overripe fruit is used, or the contents of the bottles are packed too loosely. When fruit rises in the bottles, this may indicate that the syrup is too heavy.

Air bubbles These will appear in newly bottled fruit if they have not been released before processing. This is sometimes difficult to avoid, but the bubbles can be dislodged by knocking the jar several times against the palm of the hand.

Mould Insufficient or too-quick sterilising, or too a poor seal can allow mould to develop. Fermentation occurs in overripe fruit and may alsotake place in fruit that has not been sterilised sufficiently.

Spoiled fruit Deterioration in storage may also be due to insufficient heat, too short a heating period, or to a poor seal.

Bad flavour or colour These faults are usually due to processing unripe fruit, or to overcooking.

Bottling vegetables

Vegetables can be sterilised satisfactorily only in a pressure cooker capable of maintaining the required pressure very accurately. The older types of pressure cooker, with a spring-release pressure control, are unsuitable.

Check the manufacturer's instruction leaflet for any comments on vegetable preserving.

Step 1 Preparing the vegetables
Not all vegetables are recommended for bottling. The most suitable are summarised in the table, right. Wash the vegetables thoroughly and use only young, fresh produce of top quality.

Prepare the vegetables, and blanch them, as advised for freezing (see page 259).

Step 2 Packing the vegetables
Do not pack them too tightly, and leave a space of 2.5cm (1in) below the rim of the container.

Soup on the go Bottling in brine helps vegetables, such as carrots, turnips and celery, to retain their flavour. Preserved like this, they can be added to casseroles or soups whenever you need them.

Step 3 Adding the brine
Pack the vegetables into the bottles and cover with a boiling brine of 15g (½oz) cooking salt dissolved in 1 litre (2 pints) of water. For peas, add the same amount of sugar.

Put the lids on the bottles, and slacken screw caps by a quarter of a turn.

Step 4 Processing and sterilising
Pour about 600ml (1 pint) of cold water into the pressure cooker, with a little vinegar to prevent staining, and stand the bottles on folded newspaper or a cloth.

Make sure that the bottles do not touch each other or the sides of the pan.

Fasten the lid of the cooker, and turn on the heat with the valve or vent left open. When a steady stream of steam has been escaping for 10 minutes, set the control to a pressure of 10psi and maintain this for the required time.

At the end of the processing time, remove the cooker from the heat and allow to cool gradually.

When the cooker is cool and the gauge is showing zero, open the valve and remove the lid. Lift out the bottles carefully, as they will still be very hot. Stand them on a dry wooden surface, away from draughts, and tighten the screw caps immediately.

Step 5 Testing the seal
When the bottles have cooled completely, check the seal in the same way as for bottled fruit.

To use the vegetables, open the bottles and cook the contents in their brine. Discard the contents of any bottle if the vegetables are mushy, or if they have an odd smell.

BOTTLING VEGETABLES TIME CHART

The timing, in minutes, applies to 1kg (2lb) jars. Larger bottles are not recommended, but for smaller bottles the processing time can be reduced by 5 minutes.

VEGETABLE	PREPARATION	BLANCHING (IN MINUTES)	PROCESSING (IN MINUTES)
Asparagus	Wash, trim and pack upright in bundles.	2–3	40
Beans, Broad	Use young podded beans.	5	55
Beetroot	Blanch before peeling, and either dice or cut into slices.	15–20	40
Carrots	Wash and scrape. Leave young carrots whole; slice or dice older ones.	10	45
Cauliflower	Trim; wash well and break into florets about 2.5cm (1in) across.	3	50
Celery	Wash; trim to lengths to suit bottles.	6	40
Peas	Wash, pod and grade.	2–3	50
Potatoes, new	Wash and scrape. Grade according to size.	5	50
Sweetcorn	Strip kernels off cob with a stainless-steel knife.	2–3	50

Bottling tomatoes
Cherry tomatoes can be stored at their summer peak by bottling. 1kg (2lb 4oz) cherry tomatoes will be enough to fill a 1 litre (2 pints) bottling jar. This is an excellent way to preserve a glut of tomatoes that have all ripened together, and the finished result makes a delightful gift.

Wash the tomatoes and prick their skins with a cocktail stick. Pack the jar with the tomatoes, adding basil leaves, cloves of garlic and a light sprinkling of salt and sugar between the layers.

Line an oven tray with cardboard and stand the jar on it, with the lid closed, but not sealed. Sterilise in the oven at 120°C (250°F, gas mark ½) for 45 minutes, then seal and leave to cool.

Making jams from your garden fruits

Despite the widespread ownership of freezers, jam making is still far and away the most popular means of preserving fruit. Few occupations in the kitchen are more absorbing or satisfying, and there are fewer still in which the end product is so much better than any that can be bought from a shop.

Jam making is not difficult if you follow a few basic rules and doesn't require any special equipment. The most important tip is to choose the fruit carefully to achieve the best colour and flavour. Never use fruit that you would not be happy to eat.

Jams have so many uses and make such delightful gifts, that it is well worth making them in large quantities if you have enough fruit. As well as being the traditional accompaniment to bread and butter, home-made scones and pancakes, they also provide the fillings for sponge cakes, sweet omelettes, tartlets and biscuits. Baked and steamed puddings, trifles and ice-cream sauces are all given a lift by home-made jam.

Equipment
Most of the tools and utensils you will need can be found in the

The taste of summer A well-stocked cupboard of home-made jams will see you through the dark days of winter.

average kitchen. However, if you intend making large quantities, year after year, it may be worth investing in some new equipment. This can be used not only for jams, but all other kinds of preserves. Before you start, make sure you have the following essentials.

• **Preserving pan** The most useful piece of equipment is a preserving pan. A heavy-based saucepan can be used for small amounts of fruit, but a good-quality preserving pan will hold larger quantities and, once bought, will last for a lifetime.

Pans made of heavy aluminium or stainless steel are best. Tin-lined copper, unchipped enamel and Monel-metal (an alloy of several metals) may also be used, but not iron or zinc pans. Copper or brass pans are suitable for most jams and jellies, but as these metals are affected by acids, they cannot be used for pickles and chutneys, which require vinegar in their production.

The pan should have a heavy base to prevent burning the contents, a wide top for effective evaporation, and be deep enough to prevent the fruit boiling over.

• **Bowls and basins** You will need containers for the prepared fruit. Earthenware, enamel or plastic are all suitable.

• **Sieves and strainers** Nylon sieves are preferable to metal.

• **A measuring jug** Ideally made of heatproof glass, but enamel and stainless-steel jugs are also useful. Plastic jugs should be used only for cool and non-acid liquids. Look for a jug with fine gradations for accurate measuring.

• **Measuring cups and spoons** Cutlery spoons and cups vary in capacity, so a set of specially designed measuring cups and spoons are useful for accuracy.

• **Spoons** You will need a long-handled wooden spoon for stirring the cooking jam, and a slotted stainless-steel spoon for removing scum from the surface.

• **Knives and peelers** Stainless-steel blades will not discolour the flesh of the fruit. For preparing large quantities of fruit, special tools for coring apples and pears, removing the stones from cherries, and pulping fruit for purées can save a lot of time.

• **Scales** Next to a good-quality preserving pan, accurate scales are the most important tool in the jam-maker's kit of equipment.

Some preserving recipes specify very small amounts – of spices, for example. Scales for measuring minute quantities can be bought, but in most cases the exact amount is not critical. As a guide, a level standard teaspoon equals 5ml, or 2.5–3.5g, of most ground spices.

Always follow either the metric or imperial measurements in a recipe – never a combination of the two, as the conversions are approximate.

EQUIPMENT LIST

- Preserving pan
- Bowls or basins
- Sieves and strainers
- Measuring jug, cups and spoons
- Scales
- Long-handled wooden spoon
- Knives and peelers
- Slotted spoon
- Jam-jar filler or wide-necked funnel
- Thermometer
- Jam jars and covers

- **A wide-necked funnel** This makes it easy to fill jars without splashing. Special jam-jar fillers, made in metal or heatproof glass, are designed so that the jam can be scooped up without burning your fingers.
- **Thermometers** A sugar thermometer is useful for gauging the correct setting point. Warm the thermometer in hot water before placing it in the hot jam.
- **Jam jars and covers** Jars specially made for bottling can be

used for jam, but any empty honey, coffee or jam jars are suitable provided they are scrupulously cleaned – and, preferably, sterilised in boiling water – before use.

For covering the jars, you can buy packs containing waxed sealing discs, cellophane covers and rubber bands. But as the rubber bands may gradually become slack it is better to secure the cellophane covers with fine string.

Alternatively, use airtight, lined screw caps, Porosan preserving

skins, or greaseproof paper dipped in egg white.

Step 1 Preparing the fruit

Select fresh, firm and just-ripe fruit. You can use a mixture of underripe and ripe fruit, but avoid using overripe fruit since it will have lost much of its pectin content. This substance, which is found in the cell walls of fruit, forms a jelly when boiled with sugar and is what causes the jam to set. According to the type of fruit, the cells also contain varying amounts of acid, which help in releasing the pectin.

Wash and pick over the fruit, and discard any that are decayed, squashy or overripe.

Remove the stems and cores from soft berries such as strawberries and blackberries. Top and tail gooseberries. Strip currants and elderberries from the stalks, and peel, core and quarter apples and pears.

Cherries may be left whole, or the stones removed before or after cooking. Halve and stone plums, apricots and peaches.

Some people like the nutty taste of fruit kernels, and a few stones may be split, the kernels extracted and cooked with the fruit – allowing six per pound of jam.

Step 2 Softening the fruit

After this initial preparation, the next step is to pre-cook the fruits to soften their skins, evaporate some of the moisture and break down the cell walls.

You will probably need to add some water to the cooking pan, depending on the juiciness of the fruit, the type of pan and stove being used, and the amount of fruit being processed.

Deep purple, richly fruity A mature damson tree can yield a bountiful crop, perfect for making a batch of jam.

PREPARING FRUIT

Soft berries Remove stems and cores from soft fruits, such as strawberries.
Cherries Remove stones with either a sharp knife or with a patent stone remover.
Currants Use a table fork to strip currants and elderberries from their stalks.
Stone Fruits Cut apricots, peaches and plums into halves and remove stones.
Apples and pears For jam making, these fruits must be peeled, cored and quartered.
Hips Remove the seeds from halved rose hips with the handle of a teaspoon.

As a rough guide, you will not need to add water to juicy fruits such as strawberries, raspberries, blackberries, redcurrants and rhubarb. For fruits that do need water, weigh the fruit first. To plums and apples add half their weight of water. Pears and quinces need an equal weight. Evaporation is quicker in wide or shallow pans, so use more water and extra acid.

Bring the fruit to the boil and simmer gently until it has reduced to a pulp, and diminished by about a third. Do not stir the fruit during cooking.

Fruit in a deep pan or in a thick layer needs a slightly longer cooking time, as does fruit that is unripe or wet. If the stove gives a low heat intensity, this must also be allowed for during cooking.

Adding acid The acid contained in the fruit cells is released during the preliminary cooking, and this helps with the softening process.

But some fruits – sweet apples, bilberries, blackberries, cherries (except 'Morello' cherries), peaches, pears, quinces, raspberries and strawberries – are low in acid and you will need to add more during the initial cooking. To every 1kg (2lb) of fruit add 90ml (3fl oz) redcurrant or gooseberry juice, or 30ml (1fl oz) lemon juice (roughly 2 tablespoons), or citric acid.

Step 3 Adding pectin

Before you add any sugar you must determine the pectin content of the reduced pulp. You may have to add further pectin before achieving a perfect set in the finished jam. To test for pectin, take 1 teaspoon of fruit juice from the pan, and put it in a glass to cool. Add 3 teaspoons of methylated spirit and shake the mixture well.

After 1 minute, pour it gently into another glass.

If the jam juice has formed a single, large clot it contains a high amount of pectin; a few, smaller clots indicate a sufficient or fair pectin content, while a large number of small clots shows that the fruit needs added pectin.

After some experience, you will know in advance which fruits are naturally low and high in pectin, and you can amend the levels as necessary before you begin cooking the fruit. You can increase pectin levels by adding either lemon juice

TESTING FOR PECTIN

Low pectin levels are shown by a large number of very small clots. A few small clots show that it is adequate; a single large clot that the pectin level is high.

or a high-pectin fruit, to fruit in which pectin is scarce.

Cooking apples are high in pectin, and combine well with low-pectin fruits such as cherries and blackberries. Redcurrants also have a high pectin content and are often mixed with raspberries and strawberries, which are unlikely to set on their own.

Using pectin stock or pectin liquid or powder If it becomes obvious, after carrying out the pectin test, that the jam is low in pectin, you can add pectin stock or commercially prepared pectin – in liquid or powder form.

Pectin stock is made from apple, redcurrant or gooseberry juice. Place the prepared fruit in a pan with about 500ml (1 pint) of water to every 1kg (2lb) of fruit, and simmer until tender. Strain, and set the juice aside.

The following day, cook the pulp again with half the original amount of water. Simmer for about 1 hour and strain.

Mix the two batches of juice together. Bottle and sterilise the pectin stock if it is not needed for immediate use. To sterilise, fill heated preserving jars with boiling juice and immerse them in boiling water for 5 minutes.

Commercially prepared pectin should be added according to the manufacturer's instructions. Do not be tempted to add too much, or the flavour of the jam will be spoiled. As a general guide, use 125–250ml (4–8fl oz) of liquid pectin, or 15g (½oz) powdered pectin, to every 1kg (2lb) of fruit.

Step 4 Adding the sugar
Always use exactly the amount of sugar specified by the recipe. Too

little sugar will result in the jam setting poorly; too much will have the same effect, as well as ruining the flavour of the fruit.

The type of sugar used in jam making is not important, and there is little difference between results obtained with preserving, caster, lump or granulated sugar, although brown sugars impart their own flavour to the jam.

Lump and preserving sugar cause less scum than caster or granulated sugar. Preserving sugar also dissolves more quickly than granulated, but is more expensive.

How much sugar? The amount of sugar needed for setting depends on the amount of pectin present naturally in the fruit. For fruits with plenty of pectin, allow one-and-a-half times the amount of sugar to fruit. For example, with 1kg (2lb) blackcurrants (a high-pectin fruit), use 1.5kg (3lb) sugar.

If the pectin test shows that there is just enough pectin, use equal amounts of sugar and fruit. Add pectin to low-pectin fruits to raise the level and proceed as for fruits with sufficient pectin.

The best combination of flavour, setting and keeping qualities is obtained in a jam which contains around 60 per cent of added sugar. A finished quantity of 5kg (10lb) of jam should use up 3kg (6lb) of sugar. If you add 3kg (6lb) of sugar during production and the end result is more than 5kg (10lb) of jam, the preserve may begin to ferment during storage.

Before you add the sugar The sugar should be heated gently in the oven before you add it to the softened fruit, to avoid lowering the temperature of the jam.

Stir the jam constantly while gradually adding the sugar, and continue stirring until it has dissolved completely. Increase the heat, and bring the jam rapidly to boiling point. Keep the jam boiling quickly until setting point is reached – after 3–20 minutes, according to the type of fruit. Do not stir more than is necessary just to prevent the jam at the bottom of the pan from burning.

The heat should be high enough to keep the jam bubbling while being stirred. On the other hand, too much stirring will mix the rising scum into the jam. If this happens, adding a knob of butter or a few drops of glycerine to the jam will help to reduce the scum.

Boil only until setting point is reached. If boiled too little the jam

The cold-saucer setting test
If the slightly cooled jam wrinkles when you push your finger through it, then it is ready. In hot weather, put the saucer in the fridge for a minute or two first to speed up the process.

will not set; if boiled too much it will become sticky and dark and lose much of its flavour.

Step 5 Testing for setting point
To test for setting, remove the pan from the heat a few minutes after the jam reaches boiling point. There are several ways of testing for setting: the flake test, the cold-saucer test and the temperature test being the most practicable.

Flake test Stir the jam and scoop a little onto a wooden spoon. Allow a moment for the jam to cool, and then turn the spoon on its side to allow the jam to run off.

If the jam has been boiled enough to set, drops of jam will run together and fall off in large flakes. If several thin flakes run off the spoon in quick succession, the jam has not been boiled enough.

Cold-saucer test Spoon a little jam onto a cold saucer and leave to cool. If setting point has been reached, a skin will form over the surface and should wrinkle when pushed.

Temperature test Heat a sugar thermometer in hot water, then put it in the jam. Stir the jam gently with the thermometer for a moment or two to ensure an accurate reading.

If the temperature reads 105°C (220°F), the jam has probably reached setting point. But to be on the safe side, it is a good idea to carry out one of the other tests as well as a double check.

Step 6 Removing the scum
The jam is ready for potting when it has reached setting point. Take

These are the most successful ways to test whether your jam has reached setting point.

Flake test Scoop a little jam onto a spoon, allow it to cool, then turn the spoon on its side. If the jam is setting, it will run together and fall in large flakes.

Saucer test Allow a little jam to cool on a cold saucer. If setting point is reached, a skin will form on the jam's surface. This will wrinkle when pushed with the finger (see picture, below left).

Temperature test Heat a thermometer in hot water and dip it in the jam. Setting generally occurs at 105°C (220°F). Double-check with a different test.

the pan from the heat and leave the jam to settle for 10–15 minutes. Do not stir it.

When the resting time is up, remove the scum that has risen to the top of the jam using a perforated spoon. Drop in a walnut-size knob of butter to get rid of any traces of scum that still remain.

Step 7 Potting and storing
Give the hot jam a final stir, then pour it into clean, warm and dry jars, filling them right to the top. A wide-necked funnel is useful to minimise drips and spills.

Carefully wipe off any jam that has spilled on the outside of the jars – it will be hot – and cover the

Bottling the jam To help you to fill jars without spilling the hot jam, use a jug. If you have one, a wide-necked funnel is another useful aid.

surface immediately with a waxed disc – wax side down. Make sure that it lies flat on the surface.

Wipe the rims of the jars and cover them while the jam is still hot with cling film, greaseproof paper or parchment, folded down over the neck and tied securely. To ensure an airtight seal, it is crucial that the cover is put on while the jam is hot.

Label each jar with the name of the contents and the date of production and potting. If you make jam on a large scale, it is helpful to keep a logbook of each batch and to identify the batch on the labels. If something should go wrong in storage, you will then be able to check back on the amounts of sugar and fruit used in that particular batch.

When potting whole fruit, such as strawberries, the fruit should remain evenly distributed within the finished jam – neither floating to the top nor settling at the bottom of the jar. Achieving an even distribution is more likely if the jam is allowed to cool in the pan until a skin forms.

It is also important to store the jam correctly. The ideal storage conditions are in a dry, dark, cool and well-ventilated place that is protected from frost.

Low-sugar jams Jams with less than the usual amount of sugar can be made from fruits with good setting qualities. The proportions are 750g sugar to 1kg fruit (1½lb to 2lb). The jam will keep for only a few weeks unless stored in airtight jars, and once opened will remain in good condition for only ten days to a fortnight. The set will be less firm than usual.

Make the jam as already described, and test for setting by either the flake or the cold-saucer test. Pot at once in clean, hot jars and seal. If bottling jars are used, the keeping quality of the jam can be improved by sterilising the jars in boiling water for 5 minutes.

Making jams from preserved fruit

Bottled fruit (see pages 309–12) that has become misshapen or discoloured, or whose preserving fluid is losing its clarity, can be used for making jam, though you may not obtain so good a set as with fresh fruit. This, however, can be corrected by adding commercial pectin.

Pour the fruit and preserving liquid together into a pan and, by fast boiling, reduce the amount of

fluid by half. Add roughly half the amount of sugar specified in the recipe for making jam from fresh fruit, and continue boiling until the sugar is dissolved.

Test for setting after a few minutes. If there is no sign of the jam reaching setting point, add the commercial pectin according to the manufacturer's instructions, which will be given on the bottle.

Though excellent results can be obtained in this way, jams made from bottled fruits are unsuitable for storing; so always use them straight away.

Home-frozen fruit can also be made into jam, although the pectin content of soft-setting fruits, such as strawberries, may have diminished, making it essential to pay special attention to the pectin test.

Allow for any pectin deficiency by using ten per cent more fruit than specified, or use the same amount of fruit with ten per cent less sugar to give a lower yield. Alternatively, add pectin stock.

THINGS THAT MAY GO WRONG

However careful you are to pay close attention to every stage of jam making, the finished jam may sometimes be disappointing. By identifying the most likely cause, you can avoid making the same mistake next time you make jam.

Mould Possible causes are insufficient cooking at the preliminary stage, resulting in too little sugar in proportion to fruit. Alternatively, the jam may have been stored in a place that is damp or too warm.

Mould may also occur if the jam was sealed while only warm, not hot, or if the cover was loose.

Fermentation Tiny bubbles in the jam show that it is fermenting. This indicates that there is too little sugar; that the jam was stored in a warm place; or that the pots were loosely sealed.

Crystallisation This is generally a sign that the jam is lacking in acid, or contains too much sugar. Crystallisation is caused by cooking the jam too little or too much after adding the sugar; or by adding the acid after the sugar.

Poor setting Probably due either to insufficient pectin in the fruit or ineffective release of the pectin. This may happen if the fruit is not reduced sufficiently before the sugar is added, or if the jam is overcooked or undercooked afterwards.

Alternatively, the jam may contain too much sugar in relation to its acid and pectin content; or the vital acid may have been omitted.

Shrinkage This is due to evaporation caused by loose covering or storage in a warm place.

Recipes for home-made jams

Recipes containing 3kg (6lb) each of fruit and sugar yield about 5kg (10lb) of jam. Where smaller amounts of these ingredients are used, yields will be reduced in proportion.

Apple jam

3kg (6lb) sharp cooking apples
1 litre (2 pints) water
2 level tablespoons citric acid
12 cloves
3kg (6lb) sugar
Red colouring (optional)

Wash, dry and slice the apples, but do not peel or core. Simmer to a pulp, with the citric acid and cloves tied in a muslin bag.

Remove the cloves; sieve and weigh the pulp. Return to the pan, with 750g of sugar to every 1kg of pulp (1½lb to 2lb).

Stir until dissolved, and boil rapidly to setting point. Add a few drops of colour, if required; pot and cover.

Apple and date jam

To every 500g (1lb) of peeled, cored and sliced cooking apples, add 175–250g (6–8oz) of stoned dates, 500g (1lb) of sugar and the juice and grated rind of 1 lemon.

Place the apples in a pan with the rind and lemon juice, and cook gently until soft. Add the sugar and stir until dissolved. Add the chopped dates, simmer gently until thick, then pot in warmed jars and cover while hot.

Apple and ginger jam

3kg (6lb) apples
1 litre (2 pints) water
50g (2oz) ground ginger

Grated rind and juice of 4 lemons
500g (1lb) crystallised ginger
3kg (6lb) sugar

Peel, core and slice the apples. Put the peel and cores in a large muslin bag and place, with the apples, in the preserving pan, adding the ground ginger and the lemon rind and juice.

Simmer until tender, then remove the muslin bag. Add the finely chopped ginger and sugar. Stir until the sugar has dissolved, then boil rapidly to setting point.

Pot and cover.

Apricot jam

3kg (6lb) apricots
600ml (1 pint) water
3kg (6lb) sugar

Wash, halve and stone the apricots. Remove a few kernels and blanch in boiling water. Simmer the apricots with the water and kernels until the fruit is tender and the contents have reduced by about half. Add sugar, stir until dissolved and boil to setting point.

Using dried apricots To make jam from dried apricots, soak 1kg (2lb) of fruit in 3 litres (6 pints) of water for 24 hours. Simmer the apricots in the water in which they were soaked for about 30 minutes before adding 1 teaspoon of citric acid and 175g (6oz) of blanched almonds. Stir in 3kg (6lb) of sugar and boil to setting point.

Blackberry jam

3kg (6lb) blackberries
150ml (5fl oz) water
Juice of 2 lemons, or 1 teaspoon citric acid, or 300ml (½ pint) apple-pectin stock
3kg (6lb) sugar

Hull and pick over the berries; rinse and drain carefully. Put in a pan with the water, lemon juice or citric acid. If pectin stock is used, add it with the sugar after the preliminary cooking.

Simmer until the berries are soft, then add the sugar and stir until dissolved. Boil rapidly to setting point.

Blackberry and apple jam

2kg (4lb) blackberries
750g (1½lb) peeled and cored cooking apples
300ml (½ pint) water
3kg (6lb) sugar

Simmer the cleaned blackberries in half the water until soft, and simmer the chopped apples separately in the remaining water. Mash both to a pulp. Mix the two fruits, add the sugar and stir until dissolved. Boil rapidly to setting point.

For seedless jam, strain the blackberry pulp before mixing the juice and purée with the softened apples. Use 25 per cent less sugar than for whole-fruit jam.

Blackberry and elderberry jam

1.5kg (3lb) cultivated or wild blackberries
1.5kg (3lb) elderberries (prepared weight)
3kg (6lb) sugar
300–450ml (½ – ¾ pint) water

Simmer the stemmed and washed elderberries in the water until soft and pulpy; rub through a sieve to remove the seeds. Return the pulp to the pan, with the hulled and rinsed blackberries, and simmer for about 10 minutes or until soft.

Make the flavours your own Among the many benefits of making your own jam from home-grown produce is that you can make it in flavours, such as gooseberry, that are not easily available in the shops.

Add the warmed sugar, stir until dissolved, then boil rapidly until setting point is reached.

Blackcurrant jam

2kg (4lb) blackcurrants
1.5 litres (3 pints) water
3kg (6lb) sugar

Stem the currants, wash and drain carefully, put the fruit in a pan with the water and simmer until reduced by almost half. Stir frequently to avoid burning.

Add the sugar, stirring until dissolved; boil rapidly until setting point is reached.

Cherry jam

2.5kg (5lb) stoned, red cherries
Juice of 2–3 lemons, or
1 teaspoon citric acid
1.75kg (3½lb) sugar

Simmer the cherries for 30 minutes with the juice or citric acid, and with some stones tied in a muslin bag. Remove the stones, add the sugar and stir until dissolved. Boil rapidly until the jam reaches setting point.

Cherry and redcurrant jam

2kg (4lb) dark cherries (weight after stoning)
1kg (2lb) redcurrants
300ml (½ pint) water
3kg (6lb) sugar

Wash and stone the cherries, strip the currants from the stalks and rinse them. Simmer both with the water for 30 minutes, or until soft. Stir in the sugar; when dissolved, boil rapidly to setting point.

Damson jam

2.5kg (5lb) damsons
850ml–1 litre (1½–2 pints) water
3kg (6lb) sugar

Wash and dry the damsons; put in a pan with the water and simmer until pulpy. Remove the stones. Stir occasionally. Add the sugar, and when dissolved boil quickly until setting point is reached.

Gooseberry jam

2.25kg (4½lb) gooseberries
850ml (1½ pints) water
3kg (6lb) sugar

Top and tail the gooseberries, then wash and drain them thoroughly. Put in a pan with the water and simmer gently until the skins burst and the fruit has reduced to a pulp. Add the sugar, stirring until dissolved, then boil to setting point.

Variation Add a dozen elderflower heads, tied in a muslin bag, to the simmering fruit. Remove before adding the sugar.

Greengage jam

3kg (6lb) greengages
600ml (1 pint) water
3kg (6lb) sugar

Potted plums If you are lucky enough to have a mature plum tree in your garden, you may find yourself with more ripe fruit than you can eat; made into jam, it will see you through the year.

Wash, halve and stone the gages; crack a dozen stones and blanch the kernels. Simmer the fruit and kernels with the water for about 30 minutes, or until the gages are soft. Stir in the sugar until it has dissolved, then boil rapidly to setting point.

Alternatively, leave the gages whole and remove the stones as they float to the top while the fruit is simmering.

Loganberry jam

3kg (6lb) loganberries
3kg (6lb) sugar

Simmer the cleaned berries over a very low heat for 15–20 minutes or until reduced to a pulp, stirring constantly. Add the sugar, stirring until dissolved, then boil until setting point is reached.

Marrow and apricot jam

1kg (2lb) prepared marrow (peeled, seeded and cut into small chunks)

500g (1lb) fresh apricots or
250g (½lb) dried apricots
1.5kg (3lb) sugar
2 lemons
725ml (1¼ pints) water

If the apricots are dried, soak them overnight in 600ml (1 pint) of water, then simmer until tender. If the apricots are fresh, wash, halve and cook them gently in a little water until soft, removing the stones as they rise to the surface.

In another pan, cook the prepared marrow in a little water until tender, then mash to a pulp. Combine the marrow and apricots in one pan; add the lemon juice, grated rind and sugar.

Bring to the boil, stirring until the sugar has dissolved. Boil fast, stirring occasionally for 15 minutes, or until the jam has thickened.

Pot into warmed jars and cover while hot.

Marrow and ginger jam

3kg (6lb) marrow (prepared weight)
50g (2oz) root ginger
Juice and grated rind of 4 lemons
3kg (6lb) sugar

Peel the marrows and remove the seeds; cut the flesh into tiny cubes and steam until just tender.

Bruise the ginger, tie in a muslin bag and place in a pan with the steamed marrow and the juice, and rind of the lemons. Bring to the boil, stir in the sugar until it has dissolved, then boil rapidly to setting point.

For a pronounced ginger flavour, double the quantity of root ginger and leave the steamed marrow cubes, sprinkled with sugar, to stand for 24 hours. Put in the pan with the ginger, lemon juice and

rind, and heat carefully until the sugar has dissolved and the marrow cubes are transparent.

Test for setting with the saucer or flake test. Pot at once.

Peach jam

1.5kg (3lb) yellow peaches
300ml (½ pint) water
Juice and peel of 2 lemons
1kg (2lb) sugar

Cover the peaches with boiling water, leave for 1 minute, then peel; quarter the fruits and remove the stones. Put the peaches in a pan with the water, lemon juice and peel; simmer gently until reduced to a pulp. Remove the lemon peel. Stir in the sugar and boil rapidly until setting point is reached.

Variation Simmer 12 kernels for 1–2 minutes, then peel. Mix with the peach flesh, and simmer.

Peach and pear jam

1kg (2lb) peaches
1kg (2lb) pears (they must not be overripe)
2kg (4lb) sugar
4 lemons
125ml (5fl oz) water

Peel and stone the peaches; peel and core the pears. Chop both fruits roughly, place in a pan with the water and simmer gently until they are tender, but not mushy. Add the lemon juice, grated rind and sugar, and stir until the sugar has dissolved. Bring to the boil, then boil fast, stirring occasionally until set (about 20 minutes). Pot into warm jars and cover while hot.

Tea with a tasty tang Rhubarb may sound a tart alternative to the usual sweet flavours of soft summer fruits, but it makes a delicious jam, especially with an added hint of ginger (see recipe, right).

Plum jam
3kg (6lb) plums
850ml–1 litre (1½–2 pints) water
3kg (6lb) sugar
Wash and dry the plums; cut in half and remove the stones. Crack 12–24 stones, extract the kernels and blanch them. Put the plums, kernels and water in a pan and simmer until reduced by half.

Add the sugar, stirring until dissolved, then increase the heat and boil rapidly until setting point is reached.

Quince jam
2kg (4lb) quinces (prepared weight)
1–2 litres (2–4 pints) water
3kg (6lb) sugar
Juice of 2 lemons
Peel and core the fruit; cut the flesh into small cubes or grate on a coarse grater. Put in the pan with the water, cover and simmer for 30 minutes, or until tender.

Take off the lid and continue simmering until reduced. Add the sugar and lemon juice, stirring until the sugar has dissolved completely. Boil rapidly to setting point.

Raspberry jam
3kg (6lb) raspberries
3kg (6lb) sugar

Put the cleaned berries in a pan and cook gently until the juice begins to run, then simmer until soft. Stir in the sugar and boil rapidly to setting point.

A better-flavoured jam, but not of such good setting quality, can be obtained by using 2.5kg (5lb) of fruit to the same amount of sugar. Boil for 10 minutes, stir in the sugar and boil rapidly for 2 minutes.

Rhubarb and ginger jam
1.5kg (3lb) rhubarb (prepared weight)
1.5kg (3lb) sugar
Juice of 3 lemons
25g (1oz) root ginger

Wash and trim the rhubarb and cut into small chunks. Place in alternate layers with the sugar in a deep bowl, add the lemon juice and leave for about 8 hours. Put the contents of the bowl into a pan, with the bruised ginger tied in a muslin bag. Bring to boiling point, and boil rapidly to setting point.

Strawberry jam
3.5kg (1lb) strawberries
Juice of 2 lemons
3kg (6lb) sugar

Hull, wash and drain the strawberries thoroughly; put in a pan with the lemon juice and simmer until soft, stirring frequently to prevent burning. Add the sugar and stir while it dissolves. Boil rapidly to setting point. Remove the scum and leave the jam to cool until a skin has formed. Stir and pot.

Fruit jellies

Jelly and jam making are very similar, though the former requires rather more time and care. To make the perfect jelly, all traces of pulp, skin or pips must be completely eliminated, leaving only the richly coloured and flavoured juices.

This calls for considerably more fruit than is needed in making jam, and the choice of fruit is more limited. Only distinctively flavoured fruits such as redcurrants, quinces, blackcurrants, blackberries, elderberries, plums and greengages are really suitable, though these are often combined with apples to give a better set.

Equipment
The equipment and tools recommended for jam making are equally suitable for jellies.

• **Jelly bag** In addition to a good preserving pan, scales, measuring jugs and a thermometer, you will need a jelly bag for straining the fruit pulp. Thick flannel jelly bags, sold separately or attached to special drip stands, can be obtained from kitchen-equipment shops, but it is cheaper to make your own.

A home-made jelly bag can easily be improvised from a square of cotton or flannel, or from two or three layers of butter muslin or cheesecloth. But whether you use a bag or cloth, it should be thoroughly scalded before use.

Tie each corner of the cloth to

the legs of an upturned kitchen stool. Place a bowl or basin – earthenware, glass or plastic – beneath the jelly bag to catch the juice as it drips through.

• **Jars** Ordinary jam jars are suitable for jellies, provided they are clean and unchipped. Small glass jars, such as those which previously contained fish and meat paste, mustard, and other relishes, are ideal for jellies if first sterilised. Filled with glowing jelly, their attractive shapes permit them to be set directly on the table.

Step 1 Preparing the fruit
Fruits with distinctive flavours and colours are preferable, and they should contain enough pectin and acid to ensure a good set. Wild fruits or inexpensive varieties of cultivated fruits are ideal, since you will need quite a lot of them to make a worthwhile quantity. The yield of jelly from a given amount of fruit is considerably less than the yield of jam.

Suitable fruits, which must be fresh and just ripe, include crab and cooking apples, bilberries,

blackberries, blackcurrants, gooseberries, loganberries, quinces and redcurrants.

Used on their own, cooking apples tend to be insipid and so are usually mixed with other fruits. They are also used with wild berry fruits to improve the setting quality of the jellies.

Successful jelly cannot be made from cherries, pears, marrows or strawberries, because the additional pectin and acid needed would overpower the fruit flavour.

Before cooking, pick over the fruits and discard any that are overripe or of doubtful quality. Wash and drain thoroughly and chop large fruits into chunks, cutting out any bruised parts. There is no need to hull or stalk berries, or to peel and core apples, as the fruit pulp will be strained later on in the process.

Step 2 Softening the fruit
Simmer the fruit in the preserving pan with the correct amount of water. Very little water will be needed with juicy fruits such as loganberries and blackberries, but hard fruits such as apples and quinces need enough water to cover the fruit in the pan.

Testing for pectin. Carry out a pectin test at this stage (see page 272). If the pectin content is low, simmer the juice further to evaporate more of the water, or add previously prepared pectin-rich juice.

Step 3 Straining the pulp
As soon as the fruit has cooked to a pulp and the juices are running freely, strain the contents of the pan.

Tip them into a scalded jelly bag, having first placed a wide basin underneath to catch the juice as it strains through.

Leave the pulp to drain for several hours, or until there is no juice dripping through.

Do not squeeze the bag to extract the juice, since this will make the jelly cloudy.

If the fruit is rich in pectin, as is the case with apples, gooseberries and redcurrants, you can take two extracts of juice. For the initial softening of the fruit, use two-thirds of the recommended amount of water, then drain in the jelly bag for about 15 minutes. Return the pulp to the pan with the rest of the water and simmer for 30 minutes; drain the pulp again, this time for several hours.

Mix the two batches of juice, which will exceed the amount of juice you would have obtained from a single extraction, and process into jelly at once.

Step 4 Measuring the juice
When the pectin test gives a satisfactory result, measure the volume of juice obtained, return it to the pan and bring to the boil.

Step 5 Adding the sugar
A pectin-rich juice will need 1kg of sugar added for every litre of juice (1–1¼lb to 1 pint).

Do not add more than 750g sugar per litre (¾lb to 1 pint) of juice with a low pectin content.

Add the warmed sugar to the simmering juice, stirring constantly until fully dissolved.

Step 6 Test for setting
Continue boiling rapidly for about 10 minutes, when setting point is normally reached. Prolonged boiling at this stage results in a rubbery jelly.

Recipes for home-made jellies

Only the clear juices For making jellies, you must use a jelly bag to remove all the pulp, skin and pips from the fruit, but the pulp left in the bag can be used to create delicious fruit cheeses (see page 281) to make efficient use of the original fruit.

The flake test (see page 273) is the best way to determine the setting point of jelly.

When the boiling period is nearly finished, reduce the heat so that the boiling becomes less vigorous, though still steady, to avoid the risk of trapping air bubbles in the finished jelly.

Step 7 Removing the scum

As soon as setting point is reached, lift the pan away from the heat and quickly remove any scum. This can be done with a slotted spoon, dipped into boiling water and then shaken before use.

Alternatively, the jelly can be strained through a piece of scalded, fine linen.

Speed is important, as the jelly must be potted before it sets.

Step 8 Potting and storing

Pot the jelly in clean, warm jars, pouring it gently down the inside of the tilted jar to avoid creating air bubbles.

Cover the jelly surface at once with a disc, wax side down, and seal securely with cellophane covers and string. Avoid moving the jars until the jelly has set. Store jellies in a cool, dry, dark place.

Yields of jellies cannot be given, as these depend partly on the type of fruit used and on the amount of juice extracted. On average 5kg (10lb) of jelly can be expected for every 3kg (6lb) of sugar used.

Apple jelly
3kg (6lb) cooking apples
Ginger root or whole cloves
Juice of 1 lemon
Sugar

Wash the apples, cut them into chunks and put them in the preserving pan with water to cover. Apple jelly can be somewhat insipid unless the fruit has a distinctive flavour, but a bruised ginger root, or half a dozen whole cloves, can be added to the simmering fruit for extra flavour.

Strain the fruit pulp, measure, and return the juice to the clean pan. Bring to boiling point and add warm sugar at the rate of 750g for every litre (1lb to 1 pint). Boil to setting point.

Variation Essence of cloves or lemon, or strained lemon juice, may be used for flavouring instead of spices; add these just before setting point is reached. The colour of apple jelly can be improved by simmering a few blackberries, cranberries, loganberries, raspberries or redcurrants with the apples.

Bilberry jelly
2kg (4lb) bilberries
300ml (½ pint) water
1 teaspoon citric acid
Pectin stock
Sugar

Put the cleaned berries in a pan with the water and citric acid, and simmer gently. Strain the pulp for at least 1 hour, then test for pectin and add sufficient pectin (apple juice) for a satisfactory test result.

Measure the juice, bring to the boil in a clean pan and add 750g of sugar for every litre (¾lb to 1 pint). Boil until setting point is reached.

Blackberry jelly
2kg (4lb) blackberries
450ml (¾ pint) water
Juice of 2 lemons, or 1 teaspoon citric acid
Sugar

Rinse and drain the berries, put in a pan with the water and either lemon juice or citric acid. Simmer until soft, strain, and bring the extracted juice to boiling point. Stir in the sugar, allowing 750g of sugar to each litre of measured juice (1lb to 1 pint).

Blackberry and apple jelly
2kg (4lb) blackberries
1kg (2lb) cooking apples

1 litre (2 pints) water
Sugar

Rinse and drain the berries, wash and chop the apples and put both in a pan with the water. Simmer until soft, then strain the pulp and measure the juice.

Return to the pan, with 750g of sugar for every litre of juice (1lb to 1 pint). Boil until setting point is reached.

Blackcurrant jelly
2kg (4lb) blackcurrants
1 litre (2 pints) water
Sugar

Simmer the rinsed berries with two-thirds of the water until soft; strain for 15 minutes, then bring the pulp back to the boil with the remaining water. Strain again for 3–4 hours and mix the two batches of juice.

Measure the juice and bring to the boil, adding 1kg sugar for each litre (1–1¼lb to 1 pint). Boil to setting point.

THINGS THAT MAY GO WRONG

Faults in fruit jellies are basically the same as those that may occur with jams. But, in addition to the general rules, remember to simmer the fruit gently before straining, otherwise it may not have broken down completely to release the maximum amount of juice.

- Always bring the juice to boiling point before adding the sugar, and pot the jelly as quickly as possible after it has reached setting point.

- Avoid disturbing the jars until the jelly is completely set.

- Cloudy jelly may result from the pulp being squeezed during during straining.

- It is as well, too, not to leave the strained juice for more than 24 hours before adding the sugar to finish the jelly.

Crab-apple jelly

3kg (6lb) crab apples
Juice of 1 lemon
Sugar

Scrub the crab apples clean,
especially round the blossom ends,
and remove the stalks. Quarter the
fruits and put them in the pan with
the lemon juice and enough water
– about 2 litres (4 pints) – to cover
them.

Simmer over gentle heat until
completely tender, then strain and
measure the juice. Bring this to
boiling point, add 750g of sugar for
each litre (1lb to 1 pint) and boil
until set.

Gooseberry jelly

2kg (4lb) gooseberries
1 litre (2 pints) water
Sugar

There is no need to top and tail the
gooseberries. After washing them,
put the fruit in a pan with two-
thirds of the water, simmer until
quite soft, then strain for 15
minutes. Simmer the gooseberry
pulp for a further 30 minutes with
the remaining water; strain.

Mix and measure the two
batches of juice, boil, and stir in
1kg of sugar for each litre of juice
(1–1¼lb to 1 pint). Boil until setting
point is reached.

Loganberry jelly

2kg (4lb) loganberries
600ml (1 pint) water
Sugar

Simmer the berries in the water for
about 1 hour. Strain the pulp and
measure the juice. Bring to the boil,
adding 750g of sugar for every
litre of juice (1lb to 1 pint).

Quince jelly

2kg (4lb) quinces
Juice of 2 lemons, or 2 teaspoons
citric acid
3 litres (6 pints) water
Sugar

Scrub the quinces, cut into small
pieces and put in a pan with the
lemon juice, or citric acid, and
two-thirds of the water.

Simmer until quite tender, then
strain for 15 minutes. Return the
pulp to the pan with the remaining
water, and simmer for another
30 minutes. Strain and mix the two
batches of juice.

Measure the juice and bring to
the boil, stirring in 750g of sugar

to every litre of juice (1lb to 1 pint).
Boil until setting point is reached.

Redcurrant jelly

3kg (6lb) redcurrants
1 litre (2 pints) water
Sugar

Take two extracts from the pulp,
using just over half the water for
the first extract. Blend and
measure, bring to the boil and add
750g of sugar to each litre of juice
(1lb to 1 pint).

For a jelly with a stronger
flavour, simmer the fruit gently
without any water, strain and
measure the juice. Boil, and stir in
1kg of sugar for each litre (1¼lb to

A delicate touch for meaty dishes Herb jellies make versatile
accompaniments to roast meats, poultry and game, cold cuts and
pork or game pies.

1 pint). The yield will be smaller,
although tastier, than when two
batches of juice are extracted.

Rose-petal jelly

1kg (2lb) cooking apples
25g (1oz) dark red rose petals
600ml (1 pint) water
Juice of ½ lemon
Sugar

Wash and roughly chop the apples,
and put in a pan with the water
and lemon juice. Bring to the boil
and simmer gently until soft and
pulpy. Strain through a jelly bag

and discard the pulp. Remove the
pale bases from the rose petals; it
is best to choose old-fashioned,
scented varieties if you can, since
these will give a superior flavour to
more modern rose varieties. Rinse
the petals carefully and dry
thoroughly on absorbent kitchen
paper or in a soft towel.

Pound the dried petals with
2 teaspoons of sugar until well
broken up, put in a pan with
150ml (¼ pint) water and simmer,
covered, for about 15 minutes.
Strain through a fine sieve, muslin
or coffee filter.

Mix the apple and rose-petal juices, measure, and bring to the boil. Add 750g of sugar for each litre (1lb of sugar to 1 pint), stir until dissolved, then boil rapidly until setting point. A drop of red colouring may be added, although this should be unnecessary with dark red petals.

Sloe and apple jelly
1kg (2lb) sloes
2kg (4lb) cooking apples
Juice and peel of 1 lemon
Sugar

Wash and drain the sloes. Frost helps to break down the tough flesh, but if the sloes have been picked before the first autumn frosts, prick them with a silver fork. Put in a pan with the lemon juice and peel, and barely enough water to cover, and simmer until pulpy.

Wash and chop the apples, then simmer in a separate pan, with water to cover, until soft and pulpy. Strain the two fruit pulps and measure the juice.

Bring the juice to the boil, add the sugar at the rate of 750g to each litre of juice (1lb of sugar to 1 pint) and stir until dissolved. Boil to setting point.

Tomato jelly
1.5kg (3lb) ripe tomatoes
1.5kg (3lb) sugar
1 cup vinegar, preferably white
600ml (1 pint) water
About 6 cloves
½ stick cinnamon

Place the spices, enclosed in a muslin bag, in the water. Stew gently with the tomatoes, until soft. Remove the spice bag and rub the pulp through a sieve. Return to the pan, adding the vinegar and sugar, stir until the sugar has dissolved,

then boil rapidly until setting point is reached.

Making herb jellies
You can flavour jelly with most culinary herbs to create delicious condiments to serve with meat dishes, see opposite. Whatever the herb you choose, you must start with a basic stock of apple juice and white vinegar.

Apple stock
4.5kg (10lb) cooking apples
2.3 litres (4 pints) water
2.3 litres (4 pints) distilled malt vinegar

Wash and roughly chop the apples, including the peel and cores. Put them in a pan with the water and simmer for 45 minutes, or until the apples are soft and pulpy. Add the vinegar and cook for a further 5 minutes. Strain the mixture through a jelly bag for 2–3 hours or overnight.

Mint or sage jelly
15g (½oz) fresh mint or sage leaves
850ml (1½ pints) apple stock
675g (1½lb) sugar
Green colouring (optional)

Dip the mint or sage leaves in boiling water for 2–3 seconds, then rinse under cold water. Pat the leaves dry and chop them finely.

Pour the apple stock into a large pan, add the sugar and stir over a gentle heat until the sugar has dissolved. Boil rapidly for 5–10 minutes, or until setting point.

Remove from the heat, skim off any scum that has risen to the surface and stir in the herbs and a little food colouring, if you like.

Fruit cheeses and butters

Fruit cheeses and butters were as indispensable to teas on Victorian and Edwardian lawns as were cucumber sandwiches and gentleman's relish. They were used in place of dairy cheese, as accompaniments to bread and butter, and as fillings in cakes and trifles.

They have since lost something of their appeal, chiefly because they require a certain amount of trouble to make and have a relatively low yield in relation to the amount of fruit and sugar used. But as a treat for special occasions, or as a means of recapturing a bygone era, these preserves can hardly be bettered.

If you are making fruit jellies (see pages 277–81), you can often make use of the pulp that you would otherwise discard by turning it into a fruit cheese or butter. Start with Step 3, sieving the pulp.

Equipment
The basic equipment for making fruit cheeses and butters is the same as that for jam (see page 271); but, in addition, you will need a fine sieve. This should be made of nylon or plastic, but not of metal.

Step 1 Preparing the fruit
Almost any type of fruit is suitable for making these preserves – that is, both soft berries and tree fruits – and also some common vegetables.

Apples are often spiced with ginger, cinnamon, cloves or nutmeg; marrow or courgette can be flavoured with raspberries or strawberries; rhubarb with oranges or lemons; pears with ginger or cloves, and melon with ginger. Wash and pick over the fruits, discarding any that are diseased, and cutting out any bruised areas. Cut up large fruits, but do not waste time on stemming, coring, stoning or peeling.

Step 2 Softening the fruit
Place the fruit in a preserving pan with just enough water to cover it. Fruits that are low in acid, such as dessert apples, peaches and pears, will require the addition of 2 tablespoons of lemon juice or ½ teaspoon of citric acid to every 1kg (2lb) of fruit.

Simmer the fruit gently over a low, steady heat until it is thoroughly softened.

Step 3 Sieving the fruit
Once the fruit is soft, take it from the pan and rub it through a fine nylon or plastic sieve. Carefully weigh the sieved pulp and return it to a clean pan.

Step 4 Cooking the mixture
This method differs, depending on whether you are making a fruit cheese or a fruit butter.

Making fruit cheeses Allow equal amounts of sieved fruit pulp and sugar. If the pulp is runny, reduce it by fast boiling until thick – before adding the sugar.

Evaporation is an important part of the process, so do not cover the pan when reducing the fruit.

Stir the mixture until the sugar is completely dissolved, then

simmer it gently for about 1 hour. Stir constantly during cooking.

Making fruit butters In their finished state, these are less solid than cheeses and so should contain no more than half to three-quarters as much sugar as pulp. Stir the sugar into the pulp until dissolved, and add whatever spicy flavourings that are required at the same time.

Simmer the mixture, stirring frequently, until it becomes smooth and creamy.

Step 5 Testing for setting
Fruit cheeses are ready for potting when a wooden spoon, drawn over the base of the pan, leaves a clean-cut line. Remove butters from the heat when the last liquid evaporates and the surface is creamy.

Step 6 Potting and storing
Fruit cheeses were originally potted in moulds, but the cheeses can be turned out equally well from small glass jars or pots.

The containers should be warm, and brushed inside with a little glycerine. Seal the hot surface with a waxed disc, wax side down, and cover the container.

Fruit butters are potted in warm jars. They do not keep well, however, and should be airtight and, ideally, sterilised by boiling in water for 5 minutes.

Cheeses often improve with age, and should preferably mature for two months before using. Butters generally have a storage life of only a few weeks, and once opened should be eaten within a few days.

Recipes for fruit cheeses and butters

Fruit cheeses

Blackberry cheese
1kg (2lb) blackberries
500g (1lb) cooking apples
300ml (½ pint) water
Sugar

Wash and chop the apples; wash and drain the blackberries. Place the fruit in a pan with the water, and cook until soft and mushy. Rub through a sieve, then return the pulp to the pan, adding 500g (1lb) of sugar to every 600ml (1 pint) of pulp.

Stir until the sugar has dissolved, then bring to the boil and cook until thick, stirring occasionally.

The pulp from blackberry jelly can be used for this recipe. In this case, simmer the apples until tender, add the blackberry pulp and a little water, cook for a few minutes then sieve and proceed as described above.

Damson cheese
3kg (6lb) damsons
300ml (½ pint) water
Sugar

Wash the fruit and simmer with the water in a covered pan until soft; rub through a fine sieve and weigh the pulp. Reduce the pulp by simmering until thick, then add an equal amount of sugar to the sieved pulp, stirring until the sugar has dissolved completely. Boil until quite thick.

Medlar cheese
1kg (2lb) medlars
2 lemons
300ml (½ pint) water
½ teaspoon ground cinnamon
Sugar

Wash and quarter the medlars; wash the lemons, and slice or chop them. Place the prepared medlars and lemons, and 300ml (½ pint) of water, in a pan. Simmer gently until tender. Rub through a sieve then return the pulp to the pan, adding 350g (12oz) of sugar and ½ teaspoon of cinnamon to every 600ml (1 pint) of pulp.

Bring slowly to the boil, stirring until the sugar has dissolved, then simmer gently until thick.

Quince cheese
2kg (4lb) ripe quinces
Water
Sugar

Pick over the fruit, scrub and chop roughly. Put in a pan with enough water to just cover; put a lid on the pan and simmer until soft. Sieve and weigh the pulp, thicken the pulp by simmering to reduce its volume, then add the same weight of sugar as that of the sieved pulp. Stir until the sugar dissolves, then boil until the cheese is thick. Alternatively, peel and core the quinces and cook in water until soft. Pulp with a vegetable masher, and weigh before adding an equal weight of sugar.

Rhubarb cheese
1kg (2lb) rhubarb
Juice of 1 lemon
Sugar

Trim the rhubarb and cut into small chunks; simmer in a covered pan with the lemon juice until soft. Sieve and weigh the pulp. Reduce pulp until it has thickened, stir in an equal amount of sugar and boil until thick enough to leave a trail over the base of the saucepan.

It is advisable to carry out the pectin test (page 272) before sieving and, if necessary, to add some pectin stock or commercial pectin to the mixed pulp before reducing it.

Fruit butters

Apple butter
3kg (6lb) crab or windfall apples
1 litre (2 pints) water
1 litre (2 pints) cider
Sugar

Wash the apples, chop into large pieces and cook gently, in a covered pan, with the water and cider until soft. Rub through a fine sieve and weigh the pulp; allow 375g sugar for every 500g of pulp (¾lb sugar to 1lb pulp).

Simmer the pulp until it has reduced by about a third, and thickened. Stir in the sugar, and simmer until creamy.

Spiced apple butter To make this fragrant alternative, add 1 teaspoon ground cloves and 1 teaspoon ground ginger when you add the sugar.

Apricot butter
1.5kg (3lb) apricots
Sugar
Lemons
Cinnamon and cloves (optional)

Wash and halve the fruit, place in a pan with half a cup of water and simmer gently until really soft. Rub through a sieve, then return the pulp to the pan.

Allow 250g (8oz) of sugar, and the juice and grated rind of 1 lemon, to each pint of pulp. Add spices, if required, at the rate of

½ teaspoon each of ground cinnamon and cloves to every 600ml (1 pint) of pulp.

Bring to the boil, stirring until the sugar has dissolved, then simmer gently until thick.

Blackcurrant butter
2kg (4lb) blackcurrants
2 litres (4 pints) water
Sugar

Wash the fruit and simmer in the water until soft. Rub through a sieve and weigh the pulp. Allow 250–375g of sugar for each 500g pulp (½ –¾lb sugar for 1lb pulp). Boil the pulp until thick, add the sugar and stir until dissolved. Simmer to the desired consistency.

Gooseberry butter
2kg (4lb) ripe gooseberries
450ml (¾ pint) water
Sugar

Wash the gooseberries, then simmer the whole, ripe fruits in the water, rub through a sieve and weigh. Add 375g sugar to every 500g pulp (¾lb sugar for 1lb pulp). Stir to dissolve the sugar, and continue simmering until the pulp is thick and creamy.

Marrow butter
Marrow
Sugar

Wash and dry the marrow, cut into large pieces and simmer gently, without any water, to soften. Rub through a sieve and weigh the pulp; allow 250–375g sugar to every 500g pulp (½ –¾lb sugar for 1lb of pulp).

Boil until thickened, then add the sugar and stir until dissolved; flavour with the juice of 1 lemon

for each 500g (1lb) of pulp. Boil to the correct consistency.

Plum butter
1kg (2lb) plums
Sugar

Plums need not be stoned, but a few may be cracked open and the blanched kernels cooked with the fruit. Simmer gently, with a little added water if the plums are underripe, until soft. Rub through a fine sieve and weigh the pulp, allowing 250–375g of sugar to every 500g pulp (½ –¾lb sugar to 1lb of pulp).

Simmer the pulp until it has thickened, stir in the sugar and boil to the required consistency.

Tomato butter
1kg (2lb) ripe tomatoes
Juice of 2 lemons
Sugar

Quarter the tomatoes and simmer gently with the lemon juice. When soft, rub through a fine sieve and weigh the pulp, allowing 250–375g of sugar to every 500g pulp (½ –¾lb sugar to 1lb of pulp). Stir until dissolved.

Simmer the pulp until it has reduced and thickened, then add the sugar and boil to the required consistency.

Home-made syrups and juices

Summer weekends and school holidays offer the perfect opportunity to use surplus garden produce to make fruit juices and syrups. Syrups are especially versatile; diluted with water or milk they can be turned into delicious drinks, and they can be used to flavour jellies and puddings as well. Mixed with equal quantities of water, and frozen, they make superb iced lollies.

Syrups are a concentrated solution of fruit juice and sugar; while juices contain only a little added sugar. The same kinds of fruit can be used for both purposes, including black and red currants, blackberries, gooseberries, loganberries and strawberries.

Excellent syrups can also be made from gathered hedgerow fruits, such as rose hips and elderberries, while apple or pear

EQUIPMENT LIST

- Scales
- Large pan
- Jelly bag
- Measuring jug and ladle
- Funnel
- Bottles with screw tops or corks
- Brush
- Paraffin wax
- Earthenware bowl (hot method)
- Earthenware cask and square of cotton or muslin (cold method)

juice makes a refreshing summer drink. Elderflower cordial (right) is a delightful fragrant drink, made from the flowerheads of the plant.

Equipment

This varies considerably according to the method chosen. For the basic, hot-preparation method you will require a saucepan big enough to accommodate a large earthenware bowl.

If you are using the quick, hot method, you will need only a large pan. Cold methods require earthenware jars. Whichever method you choose, make sure that no iron, zinc or copper utensil comes into contact with the fruit.

Other essential items of equipment are a wooden spoon or pulper, and either a jelly bag or some muslin that can be attached to the upturned legs of a kitchen stool to act as a strainer.

The bottles you use should be cleaned and rinsed. They should be able to withstand moderate pressure, and be fitted either with screw tops, new corks or flip tops. You will also need a sugar thermometer, and a broad pan for sterilising the bottles. The pan must be deep enough to heat the bottles when placed on a grid (or trivet), or a wad of folded newspaper, to protect them from direct heat. The bottles should also be separated from each other by further wads of the same material.

Step 1 Preparing the fruit

Select ripe, juicy fruits and wash them gently in cold water. Fruits that are too ripe to use for making jam are ideal for syrups and juices, but discard any fruits that are unripe or overripe and beginning to go bad.

Step 2 Breaking down the fruit

Fruit juices are prepared only by hot methods. Though these are also the easiest ways of making syrups, cold methods give better flavours. Syrups are preserved by heating and sterilising, or by the addition of chemical preservatives.

Basic hot method Place the fruits in a large earthenware basin and mash them with a wooden spoon. Add 600ml of water to every 1kg (1 pint to every 2lb) of blackcurrants. For blackberries, add 100ml of water to every 1kg (4fl oz to every 2lb) fruit. There is no need to add water to other fruits, as they will yield their own juices as they are heated.

Fill a large pan with water, put the basin of fruit over it and heat until the juices start to flow, topping the pan up with water as necessary to prevent it from boiling dry and burning. Mash the fruit when the juice is flowing freely.

MAKING ELDERFLOWER CORDIAL

Prepare the flowers Gather about 30 flowering heads of elderflowers. Rinse in cold water and remove the stalks and leaves.

Make a syrup Dissolve 1kg (2lb) of sugar in 3 litres (6 pints) of boiling water and allow to cool. Add a sliced lemon and 2 teaspoons citric acid. Pour over flowers.

Steep, strain and bottle The elderflowers should be left to steep in the syrup for 24 hours. Finally strain the cordial through fine muslin and pour into clean bottles. Seal them immediately. Serve, diluted to taste, with a few slices of lemon and a sprig of mint.

Quick, hot method An alternative method is to put the fruits in a large pan, together with any water that is required, and bring rapidly to the boil. Continue boiling for 1 minute, crushing any whole fruits with a wooden spoon.

Although this is a faster method of breaking up the fruits than the basic hot method, there is a risk that the fruits may be overcooked in the process. If this does happen, it may easily spoil the flavour or the colour of the finished product.

Cold method (syrups only) Put the fruits in an earthenware jar and crush them thoroughly with a wooden spoon. Cover the jar with a thin cloth and leave it in either a warm room or a cupboard until you see tiny bubbles of gas forming on the surface, which shows that fermentation has begun. With most fruits, this happens within 24 hours, though blackcurrants may need as long as four or five days.

Step 3 Straining the pulp
Whatever the method of preparation, the pulp must now be strained to obtain the juice. The quickest and easiest way to do this is with a fruit press, but you can get equally good results by allowing the pulp to drain overnight through a jelly bag, or a few layers of muslin or cheesecloth attached to the upturned legs of a kitchen stool.

Next morning, thoroughly squeeze the bag of pulp to extract the last remaining drops of juice.

Step 4 Adding the sugar
When making syrup, add 375g of sugar to every 600ml of juice (¾lb to 1 pint). For fruit juices, add only 75g per 600ml (3oz per pint).

In each case, stir the mixture without heating until the sugar is dissolved.

Step 5 Straining the syrup
At this point, syrups should be strained again through a clean jelly bag or muslin. Fruit juices do not require straining a second time.

Step 6 Bottling
Pour the juice or strained syrup into bottles. Clean, unchipped sauce bottles with screw tops are ideal, but any sound, cork-stoppered bottle is suitable so long as new corks are provided. Boil both tops and corks for 15 minutes immediately before use.

Fill the bottles to within an inch or so of the tops, put the screw tops on or drive home the corks and secure them with wire to prevent them blowing out during sterilisation. Make a false bottom in the sterilising pan with a wire grid or a thick pad of newspaper.

Step 7 Sterilising the bottles
Stand the bottles on the false bottom and keep them separate with further pads of paper. Fill the pan with water up to the necks of the bottles, so that the contents are below the surface.

Slowly raise the temperature of the water to 77°C (170°F), and keep it there for 30 minutes. You can speed the process by raising it to 88°C (190°F) for 20 minutes. Do not exceed the times suggested, or you may spoil the flavour.

Step 8 Sealing the bottles
Grip the bottles with a thick cloth and remove them carefully from the pan. Seal the bottles by screwing the tops down hard or

driving the corks well in. You can give cork-stoppered bottles added protection with paraffin wax. When the bottles have cooled, brush melted wax over the cork and the top of the bottle.

Preserving syrups with chemicals
Many cooks prefer to avoid using additives in their recipes, particularly if their reason for growing and preparing their own food is to eliminate artificial additives from their diet. But if you do not want to sterilise your syrups, an alternative method of keeping them fresh is to add chemical preservatives.

Follow Steps 1 to 3 above, and to 600ml (1 pint) of extracted juice, add 500g (1lb) of sugar. Stir until the sugar is fully dissolved. At this point, too, correct the low acid content of strawberry syrups by adding 1 teaspoon of citric acid to each 600ml (1 pint) of juice. Clarify these and other syrups by straining them.

Using Campden tablets The best chemical preservative to use is sulphur dioxide, usually added in tablet form. Known as Campden tablets, they may be obtained from most chemists and wine-making supply shops.

Add one tablet, crushed and dissolved in 1 tablespoon of warm water, to each 600ml (1 pint) of juice. Since sulphur dioxide causes the colour of syrup to fade, a little artificial colouring may also be added at this stage, if you wish. Sterilise the stoppers and corks as described in Step 6. Just before filling, sterilise the bottles by boiling for a few minutes. Turn them upside down to drain.

Pour the syrup into the bottles, filling those with screw caps to within 1cm (½in) of the top and those with corks to within 2.5cm (1in). Having filled them, screw the caps on hard and push the corks home immediately.

Vegetable juices
Delicious and health-promoting drinks can be made from a wide range of vegetables. Carrots, celery, beetroot and cucumbers, for example, can all be used in this way, either singly or in combinations.

Though juices can be made by more old-fashioned methods, it is simpler to use a liquidiser or juicer. When using a liquidiser, scrub, peel and grate root vegetables, and chop the others before putting them raw into the machine.

With purpose-made juicers, you need only scrub clean the fruit and veg and cut it into small enough portions to feed into the machine.

Add a little orange juice to preserve the colour. Bottle the

vegetable juices without heating and put them in the refrigerator. Serve, chilled, within a few days.

Tomato juice Although tomatoes are, strictly speaking, a fruit, their savoury flavour means that tomato juice is generally thought of as a vegetable juice, and may be combined with other vegetables, such as carrots for a delicious healthy cocktail. To make tomato juice, wash the tomatoes, cut them into halves and cook gently until soft. Rub the tomatoes through a sieve and to each 600ml (1 pint) of sieved pulp, add 150ml (¼ pint) of water, 15g (½oz) of caster sugar, 1 teaspoon of salt and 1 teaspoon of freshly ground black pepper.

Reheat the juice, pour into bottles and sterilise.

For a tomato cocktail, mix equal quantities of tomato juice and apple juice, and add 1 teaspoon of honey to each 600ml (pint).

Storing
If you intend to keep fruit juices or syrups for any length of time, make sure that the seals are airtight and that the corks or stoppers are perfectly sterilised. When opened even those preserved by chemicals will last no more than a week or so. Store in a cool, dark place.

THINGS THAT MAY GO WRONG

Mould on the juice or cork This may be due to insufficient processing time, inadequate depth of water, ill-fitting corks, or corks that were insufficiently sterilised.

Cloudiness in the syrup A syrup that is not clear may have been caused by shaking the bottle before serving.

Stomach upsets Using iron, zinc or copper implements during processing can lead to upset stomachs when the syrup is consumed.

Recipes for syrups and juices

Most fruit syrups, especially those made from soft berry fruits, are prepared by the methods described in the preceding pages. But there are also a number of unusual and interesting variations, some of which are given below.

Blackberry syrup
3kg (6lb) ripe blackberries
Sugar
300ml (½ pint) water
Brandy

Wash and clean the fruit, and discard any berries that show signs of grub infestation. Put the water and berries together in a large earthenware bowl, and break up the fruits by the basic hot method described in Step 2.

Strain the pulp through muslin or a jelly bag and to each 600ml (1 pint) of juice, add 375g (¾lb) of sugar. Put the sweetened mixture into a pan and simmer for 10 minutes. Allow to cool slightly and add a wine glass of brandy.

Pour into clean, warmed bottles, then sterilise and seal as described in Steps 7 and 8.

Elderberry syrup
3kg (6lb) ripe elderberries
Sugar
300ml (½ pint) water
6 cloves and a piece of root ginger or 50g (2oz) cinnamon and 1 level teaspoon allspice

Strip the elderberries from the stalks, wash them and discard any that are shrivelled. Put the water and berries together in a large earthenware bowl and break up the fruits, using the basic hot method described in Step 2. Strain the pulp through muslin or a jelly bag and to each 600ml (1 pint) of juice, add 375g (¾lb) of sugar.

Put the sweetened mixture into a pan and simmer for 10 minutes, adding either the cloves and ginger or the cinnamon and allspice. Pour into clean, warmed bottles, sterilise and seal – using the methods described in Steps 7 and 8.

Nettle syrup
1kg (2lb) young nettle tops
White sugar
1.5 litres (3 pints) water

Gather the nettle tops only when they are young, tender and a delicate olive-green in colour. Wash and drain them, place them in a pan and simmer in the water for 1 hour. Strain through muslin and add 500g (1lb) of sugar to each 600ml (1 pint) of liquid.

Return to the pan and simmer for 5 minutes, stirring until the sugar is dissolved. Pour into bottles, sterilise and seal, following the methods described in Steps 7 and 8. This old country recipe for a blood-purifying drink is especially delicious when cooled and diluted with soda water.

Rose-hip syrup
1kg (2lb) ripe rose hips
3 litres (6 pints) water
500g (1lb) sugar

Wash the hips, remove the stalks and calyces, and put the hips through the coarse blade of a mincer or food processor. Add them to a pan containing 2 litres (4 pints) of boiling water, bring back to the boil, and remove the pan from the heat.

Allow to stand for 15 minutes, then strain through a jelly bag. Extract as much juice as possible.

Return the pulp to the pan with a further litre (2 pints) of boiling water. Bring back to the boil and remove from the heat. Leave for 10 minutes, then strain through a clean jelly bag.

Mix the two juice extracts, and boil in a clean pan until reduced to about 1 litre (2 pints). Add the sugar, stirring until dissolved. Bring to the boil and keep at boiling point for 5 minutes.

Pour into clean, warm bottles and seal at once with sterilised stoppers or corks. Use small bottles, if possible, for the syrup does not keep long once opened. Sterilise as described in Step 7.

Carrot juice
2kg (4lb) carrots
1 tablespoon orange juice

Scrub the carrots, but do not skin them. Grate to a pulp and sprinkle with orange juice before putting through the liquidiser. Strain, bottle and place in the refrigerator.

This weight of carrots will yield approximately 1.5 litres (3 pints) of juice, which should be drunk within a day or so.

Not only is carrot juice delicious by itself; it can also be blended with the juices of other vegetables – spinach, beetroot, lettuce or celery, for example – to provide a very nutritious breakfast drink, bursting with vitamins. A 50:50 mix of carrot juice and apple juice is another tasty combination.

Pickles through the year

No one witnessing the rush upon the produce stalls at village fêtes can fail to be impressed by the enormous popularity and range of home-made pickles. Onions, eggs, piccalilli and peaches glow invitingly in their jars, offering colours and flavours that no commercially produced pickle can imitate.

All four types of pickle – raw and cooked vegetable, sweet vegetable and fruit – are preserved by the action of the acetic acid in vinegar. The flavour is created by various combinations of spices. It is best to prepare the vinegars a month or so in advance so that the spices permeate them thoroughly.

Pickles are therefore prepared in three stages: making the vinegar; adding the vinegar to the produce; bottling, sealing and storing. Keep all pickles for at least a month before using.

Equipment
The most important rule when making either pickles or chutneys is that utensils made of copper or brass must never be used, since vinegar will react with them and spoil the preserve. Use only enamel, stainless-steel or aluminium pans, nylon sieves and wooden spoons.

In addition, you will need deep bowls or earthenware casseroles in which to salt the vegetables before bottling them, and some small squares of fine muslin, in which to wrap spices.

Bottling jars, either with clip-on lids or screw tops, are particularly recommended for pickles, though care must be taken to ensure that the metal tops do not come in contact with the corrosive vinegar. Fit discs of ceresin paper, obtainable from most chemists, within the metal lids, or use plastic-coated tops instead.

Ordinary jam jars are not really suitable, since even with Cellophane tops they cannot be made completely airtight. Lack of an airtight seal permits the vinegar to evaporate, and causes the pickle to dry out.

It is better to use large coffee or fruit-juice jars of the type with plastic lids. But if jam jars are the only type available, cover the tops with preserving skins to prevent evaporation.

Step 1 Preparing the vinegar
Most pickles are preserved in spiced vinegars, whose contents and flavours vary enormously

EQUIPMENT LIST
- Large jars or bottles
- Fine 'butter' muslin
- Large saucepan
- Large, deep bowls
- Jars with airtight lids
- Preserving skins or ceresin discs
- Wooden bottling spoon
- Bottling tongs
- Funnel
- Nylon sieve
- Scales

according to the recipe and to your individual taste. Follow the suggestions below for spicing your base vinegar; with experience, you will learn which flavours you like best and develop your own preferred combination of spices.

The vinegar itself must be of the best possible quality, as inferior vinegars will only lead to sharp or unpleasant-tasting pickles. The vinegars most suitable are the bottled malts (brown or white distilled). The more expensive white wine and cider vinegars can also be used, but their delicate flavours tend to be lost. A number of exceptions include a few fruit pickles, whose recipes require a more subtle base.

Allow the vinegar to mature
Spiced vinegars are at their best when they are allowed to mature for a month or two before being used. Use whole, rather than ground, spices, and adjust the amounts according to whether you want a hot or mild pickle.

Spices should not be placed directly in the vinegar. Tie them instead in a muslin bag and allow them to steep in a vinegar-filled, closed jar, shaking occasionally.

The following recipes for spice blends are intended for guidance only. Quantities may be increased or decreased, and other spices, such as crushed garlic, ginger and horseradish added. Ready-mixed pickling spices are also available.

For mild pickles
1 litre (2 pints) malt vinegar (brown or white distilled)
7g (¼oz) each of cinnamon bark, whole cloves, whole mace, allspice and white peppercorns

For hot pickles
1 litre (2 pints) malt vinegar (brown or white distilled)
25g (1oz) each of mustard seed and allspice
15g (½oz) each of cloves and black peppercorns
7g (¼oz) whole, crushed chillies

For fruit and sweet pickles
1 litre (2 pints) malt vinegar (brown or white distilled)
275g (10oz) brown sugar
Pinch of salt
½ teaspoon each of whole mixed spice and white peppercorns
4 whole cloves

Dissolve the brown sugar in the vinegar and add the pinch of salt before adding the spices.

To make all these spiced vinegars, tie the spices in a muslin bag and leave them to steep in the vinegar for one or two months, shaking the bottle occasionally to reinvigorate the spices.

Quick-spiced vinegar If you have not prepared the spiced vinegar in advance, you can make a sufficient supply for your batch of pickle by following the hot, quick method instead.

Put the vinegar and spices together into a bowl, cover with a lid or plate and stand the bowl over a pan of cold water. Bring the pan to the boil, then remove from the heat, but leave the bowl in the water for 2 hours.

Strain the vinegar before use in order to remove the spices.

Step 2 Preparing for pickling
Use only young, firm vegetables, and sound fruits that are only just ripe. Peel, wash and drain the

vegetables, rejecting any that are unsound. Chop, shred or leave them whole, as required by the recipe you are following.

Among the many fruits that are suitable for pickling are apples and crab apples, apricots, currants, damsons, gooseberries, cherries, grapes, peaches, pears and plums. Pick over the fruits, discarding any that are overripe or under-ripe or badly damaged.

If you intend to pickle whole fruits, prick them with a silver or stainless-steel fork or with a wooden cocktail stick to prevent shrinkage as they cook and to allow the vinegar to penetrate the skin and steep into the flesh.

Spice it up Add bite and colour to cold or cooked meats with a serving of home-made pickled vegetables.

Step 3 Salting vegetables
Vegetables – though not fruit – are greatly improved by being salted before they are pickled. Immerse the prepared vegetables in a brine solution of 125g (4oz) of coarse salt to 1 litre (2 pints) of water. Alternatively, place the vegetables in layers in a bowl, liberally sprinkling each layer with salt.

Whichever method you choose for salting, it is important to use coarse or block salt. Avoid using table salt, as this contains chemicals that may cloud the pickle and affect the taste.

Dry salting is recommended only for watery vegetables, such as marrows and cucumbers. Others are best saturated in brine.

When doing this, keep the vegetables submerged in the brine by pressing them down into the bowl with an upturned plate.

Step 4 Rinsing the vegetables
Leave the vegetables to salinate for about 24 hours. Drain off the brine or remove the vegetables from the dry salt, wash them thoroughly in cold water and drain.

Shrunken pickles May be caused by poor packing or sealing, or storing the bottles in a too-warm cupboard.

Cloudy vinegar Perhaps due to inadequate salting, stale spices or poor-quality vinegar.

Poor colour This may occur throughout the jar, or in the top layer only.

If evenly distributed, over-long cooking after adding the sugar may be the cause, or you may have used the wrong vinegar.

If only the top layer is affected, the pickle may have been undercooked, the storage place may be too warm or the cover of the jar may not be quite airtight.

Step 5 Bottling the pickles
Your choice of bottling method will depend on the type of vegetable or fruit you wish to preserve.

Cold pickling Pack raw, salted vegetables – such as onions, beans, cauliflowers, cucumbers or cabbages – into clean jars, leaving a headspace of about 2.5cm (1in). Drain off any water that collects in the bottom of the jar and fill up with spiced vinegar, covering the vegetables by at least 1cm (½in).

Make the jars completely airtight with screw-on plastic lids, or otherwise with metal tops protected from the vinegar by ceresin paper.

Hot pickling A few pickles (see recipes on the following pages) involve the use of cooked vegetables. Some are salted, some not; but almost all should be packed, immediately after cooking, into hot jars, covered with spiced vinegar and sealed.

Fruit pickles For each 2kg (4lb) of fruit, dissolve 1kg (2lb) sugar in 1 litre (2 pints) of vinegar – either malt or wine according to the recipe. Add the spices, tied in a muslin bag, cover the pan and bring to the boil. Simmer the fruit until tender, but not mushy.

Carefully strain off the spiced vinegar into a bowl or jug, remove the muslin bag, and pack the fruit into hot, clean jars, leaving about 2.5cm (1in) headspace.

Boil the vinegar rapidly in an uncovered saucepan until it is reduced to a thick syrup and pour it over the fruits, making sure they are covered by at least 1cm (½in) of liquid to allow for evaporation.

Cover the jars, seal them, and store in a dry, cool, dark place. They will be ready for use in six to eight weeks.

Step 6 Sealing and storing
As a general rule, all pickles should be covered and sealed immediately, whether using hot or cold vinegar.

Most uncooked pickles should be left to mature for about two months. An exception is pickled cabbage, which is ready for eating within a week.

Most cooked pickles are ready for the table after about a week. They generally store well, apart from pickled beetroot, which should be used within two months.

Once matured, your pickles can be put to many uses. Pickled onions need no introduction as the ideal companion of strong British cheese and bread, while pickled cucumbers, beetroot, red cabbage and piccalillis go well with cold meats and salads.

Some of the sweet and fruit pickles require a certain degree of enterprise when serving them. Try pickled peaches, apricots and pears with cream as the basis of a winter fruit salad. A small bowl of pickled blackcurrants or blackberries may be served with a board of British and Continental cheeses.

Topping up When adding vinegar to vegetables for pickling, make sure it comes right to the top of the preserving jar.

Recipes for pickles

Raw pickles

Pickled cabbage
1 large red or white cabbage
Spiced vinegar
Coarse salt

Choose firm, good-coloured cabbages. Remove the outer leaves, wash, cut into quarters, and discard the tough inner cores. Shred finely, layer with coarse salt, and leave to stand for 24 hours.

Drain and rinse thoroughly, pack into bottles and cover with cold vinegar. Seal at once.

Both red and white cabbage are ready for use after a week. Red cabbage will store for two or three months; white cabbage will store for up to two months.

Pickled cauliflower
4–6 cauliflowers
Spiced vinegar
Sugar (optional)
Coarse salt

Choose firm, close-knit heads and break into small florets. Steep in a brine solution of 500g (1lb) salt to 4 litres (1 gallon) of water for 24 hours. Rinse and drain thoroughly, and pack into jars. Cover with cold vinegar, and seal.

For a slightly sweeter pickle, add 2–3 teaspoons of sugar to every 600ml (1 pint) of spiced vinegar a few days before pickling.

Pickled cucumber
3 cucumbers, weighing about 1kg (2lb) in total
Coarse salt
Spiced vinegar

Wash the cucumbers, wipe them dry, but do not peel. Cut in half lengthways and chop into slices 1cm (½in) thick. Layer with salt in a deep dish and leave for 24 hours.

Drain off the liquid, rinse the cucumber in cold water and drain thoroughly again. Pack the cucumber into clean jars, cover with hot, spiced vinegar and seal at once. The pickle will be ready for eating after a week.

Pickled gherkins
1kg (2lb) gherkins
Coarse salt
Spiced vinegar
Sugar (optional)

Miniature cucumbers, also known as gherkins, are excellent for pickling and delicious used in salads or chopped in sandwiches. Prick each gherkin well with a silver or stainless-steel fork or a cocktail

Pickled gherkins The advantage of home pickling is that you can make the pickle as hot or as sweet as you like.

stick before soaking in brine for 72 hours. Drain, pot, and cover with hot vinegar.

Keep in a warm place for 24 hours, then drain off the vinegar and bring it to the boil. Pour the hot vinegar back over the gherkins, seal and keep it in a warm room for another 24 hours.

Repeat this process until the gherkins are an overall green. Top with more vinegar, if necessary, and seal at once. Pickled gherkins will be ready for eating in a month.

Pickled nasturtium seeds
Ripe nasturtium seeds
Coarse salt
Spiced vinegar

Nasturtium seeds can be used in many recipes instead of capers, but do not confuse them with the seeds of the caper spurge (*Euphorbia lathyrus*), which are poisonous. Pick the seeds on a dry day, wash, and steep in a brine solution of 50g (2oz) salt to 600ml (1 pint) water.

Drain, and pack into small jars to within 2.5cm (1in) of the top. Cover with cold, spiced vinegar and seal. Use in salads after about a month.

Pickled onions
3kg (6lb) pickling onions
Coarse salt
1 litre (2 pints) spiced vinegar

Steep the small, unpeeled onions in a brine solution for 12 hours. Drain, peel and soak in fresh brine for 24–36 hours.

Rinse and drain well, pack into jars and cover with cold vinegar. Leave for two or three months before using. Small shallots can be pickled in the same way as onions.

Pickled walnuts
1kg (2lb) green walnuts
Coarse salt
Spiced, or sweet, spiced vinegar

Use only immature, green walnuts, picked in June or July. Wear rubber gloves throughout the pickling process, since walnuts tend to stain the skin.

Prick the walnuts all over with a large needle. Discard the nut if there is any hardness at the end opposite the stalk, where the shell begins to develop.

Soak the walnuts in a brine solution of 175g (6oz) salt to 1 litre (2 pints) water for 48 hours. Drain, and steep in fresh brine for a further week.

Drain again, and leave exposed to the air for a day or two. The walnuts will turn black. Pack the nuts into clean jars and cover with cold, spiced vinegar. Seal at once.

For a sweet walnut pickle, use a sweet, spiced vinegar, as for fruit pickles. Pickled walnuts are ready for eating in about six weeks.

Onion and apple pickle
2kg (4lb) onions
1kg (2lb) cooking apples
Spiced vinegar

Peel the onions and cut into thin slices. Peel and core the apples and slice, or cut into cubes. Mix the two ingredients quickly or the apples will turn brown.

Pot at once in clean jars, cover with hot vinegar, and seal.

This pickle can be eaten the following day, as neither the onions nor the apples have been salted, but it improves with keeping.

Pickling mainstay Onions are a staple of pickles. They make tasty combinations with apples or cucumber, and smaller onions and shallots can be pickled on their own.

Onion, cauliflower and cucumber pickle
3kg (6lb) mix of pickling onions, cauliflowers and cucumbers
Coarse salt
Spiced vinegar
Dried red chillies

Peel the onions, break the washed cauliflowers into small florets and chop the washed cucumbers into 1cm (½in) pieces.

Mix thoroughly, layer with coarse salt and leave to stand for 24 hours.

Drain, rinse in cold water and drain again. Pack into jars, cover with cold, spiced vinegar and add one red chilli to each jar.

The pickle is ready for eating in about two months.

Onion, cauliflower, bean and marrow pickle
3kg (6lb) mix of pickling onions, cauliflowers, dwarf beans and marrow or courgette
Coarse salt
Spiced vinegar

Peel the onions, separate the cauliflowers into tiny florets and chop the beans into 2.5cm (1in) lengths. Peel the marrow or courgette, remove the seeds if using marrow and chop the flesh into 2.5cm (1in) cubes.

Steep the onions, cauliflowers and beans in brine, and layer the marrow with salt. Leave for 24 hours, drain, rinse and drain again. Pot in jars and cover with cold vinegar. Leave for about two weeks before eating.

Onion and cucumber pickle
1kg (2lb) onions
2–3 cucumbers
Coarse salt
Spiced vinegar

Peel and slice the onions; wash and dry the cucumbers and cut into 1cm (½in) slices. Mix thoroughly and place in layers with the salt in a deep bowl.

Leave for 24 hours, drain, and rinse in cold water. Drain well and pot in clean jars. Cover with spiced vinegar and seal at once. The pickle is ready in about two weeks.

Cooked vegetable pickles

Pickled beetroot
2kg (4lb) uncooked beetroot
Spiced vinegar

Wash the beetroot carefully without damaging the skin, then boil in lightly salted water for about 1½ hours, until tender. Leave to cool, rub off the skins and then cut into slices 5mm (¼in) thick.

Pack into jars and cover with cold vinegar. If you prefer a sweeter pickle, add a little sugar at this stage.

This pickle must be used within two months. However, you can make a beetroot pickle with a rather longer storage life by dicing the beetroot instead of slicing it, packing the pieces loosely into jars and covering with still boiling, spiced vinegar.

Pickled carrots

1kg (2lb) small carrots
725ml (1¼ pints) distilled white vinegar
250g (½lb) sugar
50g (2oz) pickling spice
150ml (¼ pint) water

Trim and scrape the carrots, simmer for 15–20 minutes in slightly salted water until just tender, then drain.

Boil the vinegar and water, together with the pickling spices in a muslin bag, for 10 minutes.

Remove the spices, add the sugar and the carrots, and boil until tender. Pack into hot jars and cover with the vinegar. Seal at once.

Pickled cauliflowers

1 large cauliflower
Spiced vinegar
2 teaspoons marjoram
A pinch each of salt and ground white pepper
1 red pepper, blanched and deseeded and finely chopped
Olive oil

Clean the cauliflower and break into florets. Boil in lightly salted water for 5 minutes, drain, and cover with boiling vinegar. Steep in vinegar for 24 hours, drain, and reserve the vinegar for use as the pickling liquid.

Pack the florets into jars – sprinkling each layer with marjoram, a pinch each of pepper and salt, and the red pepper.

Mix the cooled vinegar with olive oil in the proportion of 1 part vinegar to 2 parts oil; pour over the cauliflower and seal at once. The pickle can be used in three or four weeks.

Pickled eggs

12 new-laid eggs
1–1.25 litres (2–2½ pints) white wine or cider vinegar
12 cloves
25g (1oz) mixed pickling spice
2 blades of mace
Peel of ½ orange

Hard boil the fresh eggs and leave in cold water. Put the vinegar in a pan and add the cloves, spice, mace and orange peel, all tied in muslin. Cover with a lid, bring to the boil and simmer for 10 minutes. Leave to cool and remove the muslin bag.

Pour half the vinegar into a wide-necked jar with a tight-fitting top, and add the shelled eggs. Fill up with vinegar and seal.

The eggs will be ready for eating in about six weeks.

Pickled marrow

1kg (2lb) marrow
125g (4oz) coarse salt
1 teaspoon ground ginger
1 teaspoon curry powder
25g (1oz) mustard
6 peppercorns
125g (4oz) sugar
450ml (¾ pint) vinegar

Peel the marrow, remove the seeds and chop into small cubes. Sprinkle with the salt and leave overnight.

Add the ginger, curry powder, mustard, peppercorns and sugar to the vinegar, bring to the boil and boil for 5 minutes.

Add the rinsed and drained marrow cubes to the vinegar. Simmer until the marrow is tender, and pack into jars. Seal at once. The pickle can be used in three to four weeks.

Pickled mushrooms

500g (1lb) mushrooms
Malt or distilled vinegar
1 small onion
2 blades of mace
½ teaspoon each of ground ginger, salt and ground white pepper

Peel and trim the mushrooms. Put in a pan with enough vinegar to cover, and add the peeled, sliced onion, mace, ginger, salt and pepper. Cover with a lid and simmer until the mushrooms are tender and shrunken.

Pack into the jars and cover with strained vinegar. Seal at once. Leave for a month before eating.

Mustard pickle

375g (¾lb) peeled cucumber
375g (¾lb) peeled onions
500g (1lb) cauliflower florets
250g (½lb) green tomatoes
750g (1½lb) green peppers, *or*
500g (1lb) french or runner beans
500g (1lb) gherkins
250g (½lb) coarse salt
2.75 litres (5 pints) water
1.5 litres (3 pints) distilled vinegar
500g (1lb) sugar
40g (1½oz) mustard seeds
50g (2oz) plain flour
Pinch of turmeric
25g (1oz) dry mustard

Put the cucumber, onions, cauliflower, tomatoes and deseeded peppers (or beans) through the medium blade of a food processor. Slice the gherkins thickly. Mix the vegetables and soak overnight in the salt and water.

Put most of the vinegar in a pan with the sugar, mustard seeds and well-drained vegetables, and bring to the boil. Make a paste with the

remaining vinegar, flour, turmeric and dry mustard and add to the vegetable mixture.

Bring back to the boil, uncovered, and simmer for about 20 minutes, stirring occasionally, until tender. Pot in hot jars and seal at once.

Keep for about four to six weeks before eating.

Celery and cucumber pickle

2½ cucumbers
1 large onion
4 long sticks of celery
40g (1½oz) coarse salt
1 teaspoon of turmeric
75g (3oz) plain flour
50g (2oz) dry mustard
125g (4oz) sugar
300ml (½ pint) cider vinegar

Peel and cube the cucumbers, peel and finely chop the onion, and scrub and dice the celery. Mix well and add the salt, leave for 30 minutes, then drain.

Add the turmeric, flour, mustard and sugar to the vinegar and simmer for 2–3 minutes.

Add the vegetables and cook over a gentle heat for 30 minutes, stirring occasionally.

Pack in hot bottling jars, seal and sterilise (see Bottling, pages 267–70). The pickle can be used in three or four weeks.

Mixed pickle

3 cucumbers
40g (1½oz) coarse salt
600ml (1 pint) water
1 large carrot
1 green pepper, 2 red peppers, *or*
500g (1lb) french or runner beans
450ml (¾ pint) cider vinegar
750g (1½lb) sugar
25g (1oz) each of mustard seed, celery seed and turmeric

Wash the cucumbers and cut into pieces about 5cm (2in) long and 5mm (¼in) wide. Sprinkle with three-quarters of the salt, cover with the water and leave overnight. Rinse and drain.

Scrape or peel the carrot and cut into similar pieces. Boil for 5 minutes in lightly salted water, then drain.

Remove the stalk base and seeds from the green and red peppers, if using; chop finely. Put the vinegar in a pan with the sugar, and the spices tied in muslin. Add the vegetables and bring to boiling point.

Remove from the heat and pack in hot jars. Pour the strained vinegar over the vegetables and seal at once. Keep for six to eight weeks before eating.

Piccalilli

3kg (6lb) mixed vegetables (prepared weight)
500g (1lb) coarse salt
4 litres (8 pints) water
For a hot, sharp piccalilli:
3 teaspoons turmeric
8 teaspoons dry mustard
8 teaspoons ground ginger
175g (6oz) sugar
25g (1oz) cornflour
1 litre (2 pints) distilled vinegar
For a mild, sweet piccalilli:
3 teaspoons turmeric
4 teaspoons dry mustard
4 teaspoons ground ginger
275g (10oz) sugar
50g (2oz) cornflour
1.5 litres (3 pints) distilled vinegar

This popular pickle is made from fresh, crisp vegetables, such as beans (dwarf, broad or runner), red or white cabbage, cauliflowers, cucumbers, celery, gherkins, marrows, onions, shallots, peppers and green tomatoes.

Prepare the vegetables as for cooking, and cut into uniform small pieces. Keep the vegetables immersed in a brine solution of the salt and water, or spread them on a large dish and sprinkle with the dry salt. Leave overnight, then rinse and drain the vegetables thoroughly. Whether you choose to make a sharp or sweet piccalilli, proceed as follows:

Blend the turmeric, mustard, ginger and sugar with all but 2–3 tablespoons of the vinegar. Put in a large pan with the vegetables, bring to the boil and simmer for about 20 minutes, until the vegetables reach the degree of crispness or tenderness you prefer. Carefully lift out the vegetables with a slotted spoon and put at once into hot jars.

Blend the cornflour with the remaining vinegar and stir in the hot syrup. Boil for 2–3 minutes, stirring occasionally, then pour over the vegetables to cover.

Seal at once and store for four to six weeks before using.

Pimento pickle
18–24 pimentos
600ml (1 pint) spiced vinegar
50g (2oz) coarse salt
125g (4oz) sugar

Wash the pimentos, cut them into quarters and remove the seeds, membranes and stalks. Set these aside. Pour boiling water over the pimentos and leave for 20 minutes.

Put the pimento stalks and seeds in the vinegar with the sugar and salt, bring to the boil and simmer for 10 minutes. Drain the pimentos, and pack into jars, cover with the strained, hot vinegar and seal immediately. This pickle is ready after a couple of days, but do not keep for more than a month.

Green tomato pickle
3kg (6lb) green tomatoes
Coarse salt
Spiced vinegar
Sugar
1 large onion

Wash and dry the tomatoes, quarter or cut into slices. Layer with the salt and leave overnight.

Drain off the liquid, put the tomatoes in a pan and cover with vinegar in which sugar has been dissolved at the rate of 50g to each litre (1oz per pint).

Add the thinly sliced onion, bring to the boil and simmer for about 30 minutes, until tender. Pour into warm jars and seal. Keep for a month before using.

Red tomato pickle
3kg (6lb) small tomatoes
Spiced vinegar

Choose small barely ripe tomatoes. Cover with boiling water for 1–2 minutes, then peel off the skins.

Put the tomatoes in an ovenproof dish, and pour over enough vinegar to cover. Put foil or a lid over the dish and cook in the oven at a temperature of 180°C (350°F, gas mark 4), for 30 minutes. Pack the whole tomatoes carefully into hot jars, cover with hot vinegar and seal. Keep for a month before using.

Sweet pickle
1kg (2lb) mixed vegetables
25g (1oz) pickling spice
600ml (1 pint) malt or distilled vinegar
50g (2oz) plain flour, or 25g (1oz) cornflour
175g (6oz) sugar
150g (5oz) sultanas
Coarse salt

Cut the prepared vegetables – such as cauliflowers, marrows, onions, cucumbers, small green tomatoes and beans – into small pieces. Soak overnight in brine. Rinse well in cold water and drain.

Tie the spices in a muslin bag, place in the vinegar and boil, reserving 2 tablespoons of vinegar to make a paste with the flour and sugar. Stir this into the hot vinegar, and remove the spices.

Simmer until the mixture begins to thicken, then add the vegetables and sultanas and boil for 5 minutes. Pot in hot jars and seal at once.

Keep for four to six weeks before using.

Ploughman's delight With a selection of delicious homemade pickles in your storecupboard, you will never be stuck for a tasty accompaniment to a simple plate of bread and cheese.

Sweet apple and cucumber pickle

1kg (2lb) dessert apples
(prepared weight)
2 cucumbers
4 onions
300ml (½ pint) vinegar (unspiced)
250g (½lb) granulated sugar
1 teaspoon celery seeds
½ teaspoon each of ground ginger
and turmeric
¼ teaspoon ground white pepper

Peel and core the apples and chop finely. Peel and dice the cucumbers; peel the onions and chop finely. Put the vinegar in a pan with the sugar, celery seeds and spices. Bring to the boil, stirring until the sugar has dissolved, then add the apples, cucumbers and onions. Bring back to the boil and simmer for 20–30 minutes. Pot the pickle in hot jars, and seal. Keep for at least a month before using.

Fruit pickles

Apple pickle

1kg (2lb) cooking apples
1kg (2lb) sugar
600ml (1 pint) sweet, spiced
vinegar

Dissolve the sugar in the hot vinegar in a large pan.

Peel, core and slice the apples and add at once to the vinegar in the pan. Bring to the boil and simmer gently until tender. Lift out and pack the apples into hot jars. Increase the heat and boil the syrup rapidly until it has reduced by half. Pour over the apples and seal. The pickle can be used in two or three weeks.

Apricot pickle

1kg (2lb) apricots
1–1.5kg (2–3lb) sugar
450ml (¾ pint) sweet, spiced,
white wine vinegar

Cut the apricots into halves and remove the stones. Put the apricots in an ovenproof dish and cook, covered, in the oven at a temperature of 180°C (350°F, gas mark 4), for 15–20 minutes, or until the skins are peeling off.

Remove from the oven, take off the skins and pack the apricots in hot jars. Dissolve the sugar in the hot, spiced vinegar and pour over the apricots. Seal at once, and leave for a month before eating.

Blackberry pickle

1kg (2lb) blackberries
500g (1lb) sugar
300ml (½ pint) white vinegar
(wine or malt)
1½ teaspoons each of whole
cloves, allspice and cinnamon

Dissolve the sugar in the vinegar, and add the spices tied in a muslin bag. Bring to the boil and add the cleaned and hulled blackberries. Cover, and simmer until tender.

Remove the spices, pour off the vinegar and pack the blackberries into hot jars. Reduce the syrupy vinegar by half through fast boiling, and pour it over the blackberries. Seal at once, and leave for a month before eating.

Blackcurrants may be pickled in exactly the same way.

Pickled cherries

1kg (2lb) stoned Morello cherries
300ml (½ pint) distilled vinegar
500g (1lb) sugar
2 cloves
1½ teaspoons cinnamon bark
1–2 pieces bruised root ginger

Heat the vinegar and dissolve the sugar, add the spices in a muslin bag and bring to the boil. Add the stoned cherries and cover the pan. Cook until soft.

Remove the spices, lift out the cherries with a slotted spoon and pack into hot jars. Boil the vinegar rapidly until it has reduced by half, then pour over the cherries.

Seal at once, and leave for a month before eating.

Crab apple pickle

1.5kg (3lb) crab apples
¼ lemon
600ml (1 pint) malt vinegar
1kg (2lb) sugar
2 cloves
2 pieces bruised root ginger
1 cinnamon stick

Choose small, unblemished fruits, remove the stalks, wash them thoroughly and dry. Put the crab apples and lemon in a pan with enough water to cover the fruit. Bring to the boil and simmer, covered, until the crab apples are almost tender. Carefully lift out the apples and leave to drain.

Measure 300ml (½ pint) of the apple cooking liquid and put in a pan with the vinegar. Add the sugar and stir until dissolved, then add the spices tied in muslin.

Bring to the boil, return the apples to the pan and simmer, covered, until tender but still whole. Lift out the apples and pack them into hot jars.

Reduce the syrup by half and pour over the whole apples. Seal at once, and leave for a month before using.

Damson pickle

2kg (4lb) damsons
1kg (2lb) sugar
600ml (1 pint) sweet, spiced,
white vinegar (malt or wine)
½ lemon

Wash and dry the damsons. Prick them thoroughly all over with a stainless-steel or silver fork.

Dissolve the sugar in the vinegar, stirring all the time, then add the damsons and sliced lemon.

Cover the pan and simmer gently until just tender. Lift out the damsons and pack into warm jars. Boil the syrup rapidly until reduced by half, pour it over the damsons and seal at once.

This pickle is best left for two months before using.

Gooseberry pickle

2.5kg (5lb) green gooseberries
1.5kg (3lb) sugar
1 litre (2 pints) sweet, spiced,
white wine vinegar

Top and tail the gooseberries, rinse and drain. Dissolve the sugar in the vinegar, add the gooseberries and simmer, covered, over a very gentle heat until just soft. Lift out the gooseberries and leave to drain.

Reduce the syrup until thick. Pack the gooseberries into warm jars, pour the syrup over them and seal at once.

Store for two or three months before using.

Peach pickle

1kg (2lb) peaches
1–1.5kg (2–3lb) sugar
450ml (¾ pint) sweet, spiced,
white vinegar

Follow the method for apricot pickle.

Pickled pears

2kg (4lb) pears
1kg (2lb) sugar
600ml (1 pint) sweet, spiced,
white vinegar

Choose cooking pears or firm, barely ripe dessert pears. Peel, quarter and core unless the pears are quite small, in which case they may be left whole. Dissolve the sugar in the vinegar and bring to the boil. Add the pears and cover the pan with a lid.

Simmer gently until the pears are soft, lift out and drain, then pack into hot jars. Boil the syrup until it has reduced to a thick consistency, pour over the pears and seal at once. The pears can be eaten after a month.

Pickled plums

1kg (2lb) plums
1kg (2lb) sugar
600ml (1 pint) sweet, spiced,
white vinegar
Juice and rind of ½ lemon

For this pickle, select firm, medium-sized plums. Wash and dry the plums, and prick them thoroughly.

Boil the sugar and vinegar to a syrup. Add the plums and simmer, covered, until tender. Remove and drain the plums, put in warm jars, and reduce the syrup by boiling until thick. Pour over the plums. Cover at once, and store for two or three months before using.

Rich and spicy chutneys

The character of a good chutney depends on the careful blending of the ingredients, so that they balance and complement each other. This can be achieved only by long, slow cooking, followed by a lengthy period of maturation in the jar.

In pickling, one of the main objectives is to preserve the colour, shape and texture of the original fruit or vegetables. In chutneys, however, the vegetables and fruit are chopped, cooked, mixed with spices and other ingredients, and reduced to a smooth pulp in which only the flavour of the produce is recognisable. Both fruit and vegetable chutneys improve with keeping. Properly stored, they will remain in good condition for years.

Equipment
Use the same equipment for chutney making as for pickles. It is

BRUISING SPICES

If preferred, or if ground spices are unavailable, whole spices may be used. Bruise, or half crush them with the back of a spoon, before tying them in muslin.

important that cooking should be done in a heavy-based pan of stainless steel or well-scoured aluminium. Sieves should be of fine nylon or stainless steel.

Step 1 Preparing the ingredients
Wash and prepare the ingredients by peeling, coring, topping and tailing, as appropriate. Ensure the smooth texture of the chutney by finely chopping or mincing the fruit and vegetables, especially in the case of onions.

Step 2 Softening tough vegetables
If tough fruit or vegetables – such as beetroot – are included in the recipe, you will find it quicker and more economical on fuel to soften them first. Do this by placing them in a pan with a little of the vinegar and cooking them gently, covered by a lid, until soft. Then add the remaining ingredients, including the rest of the vinegar.

Step 3 Cooking
Use ground spices, rather than whole, if available. If this is not possible, use whole spices, bruised and tied in a muslin bag. Remove the bag from the pan when you have finished cooking.

Many recipes specify the use of ginger – ground, whole root or crystallised. These options are

interchangeable: 1 unit of ground ginger is equivalent to 1½ units of root ginger or 4 units of crystallised ginger.

Dark-coloured chutneys are made by cooking the sugar with the other ingredients over a long period, or by using brown sugar. For light-coloured chutneys, add the sugar when the other ingredients are well softened, and use white sugar rather than brown.

Good-quality malt vinegar is recommended for most chutneys. Savings can be made on the amounts of vinegar needed by using just enough to cover the fruit or vegetables at the beginning of cooking, and adding the rest towards the end.

Green tomato chutney Chutneys are a great way of coping with a glut of garden produce. There are many types that can be made from garden fruit and vegetables and you can make up your own variations.

With the exceptions of sugar and vinegar, cook all the ingredients for the same length of time, otherwise the texture will be rougher and the flavour of late-added ingredients will dominate. If sugar and vinegar are added late in the cooking, first dissolve the sugar in the vinegar.

Simmer chutneys for an average of 1–2 hours, until they reach a jam-like consistency. Evaporation is an important part of the process, so always cook them uncovered.

Certain ingredients, such as blackberries, require sieving. Do this after the chutney has been simmering in an open pan for

1 hour. Remove the pan from the heat, rub the contents through a sieve and return them to the pan. Continue simmering until the chutney thickens.

If the mixture becomes too thick, add a little more vinegar. Chutneys thicken as they cool.

Step 4 Potting and storing
Pot chutney at once, while still hot, in clean, warm jars. Screw-cap jars are the best for giving an airtight seal, but metal lids must be provided with vinegar-proof linings of ceresin paper, plastic or cork. Preserving skin can be used, but

Recipes for fruit and vegetable chutneys

The most common failing of stored chutneys is that they dry out and shrink. They may also darken, perhaps because brown sugar or vinegar was used instead of white.

A poor seal Drying and shrinking is usually due to inadequate covering and the lack of an airtight seal.

Contamination Poorly sealed jars may also lead to contamination, noticeable as a dark layer at the top of the jar, or the darkening of the entire contents.

Bad storage Darkening may also arise from over-long storage or from storage in too warm a place.

should be tied down tight or the chutney will tend to shrink and harden during storage.

If screw-capped jars are not available, use ordinary jam jars and lay greaseproof-paper discs on the chutney, covering the jars with a clean cloth dipped in melted paraffin wax.

Once the chutney has cooled completely, store the jars in a dry, cool, dark cupboard or larder until they are eaten.

Leave chutneys for two or three months before serving. They generally improve as they mature and, provided they are properly potted and stored, they should remain in good condition for up to three years.

Unless you are certain of your family's preference for mild or hot chutneys, make a small trial batch before beginning large-scale chutney making.

Chutneys taste spicy when freshly made, but usually mellow in storage. The amount of spices may be reduced or increased to taste, but always follow the recommended quantities of sugar and vinegar.

Apple chutney I
Makes 4kg (8lb) of chutney
3kg (6lb) cooking apples
1kg (2lb) onions
300ml (½ pint) water
40g (1½oz) salt
40g (1½oz) ground ginger
2 tablespoons ground cinnamon
¼ teaspoon cayenne
1 litre (2 pints) vinegar
1kg (2lb) sugar (brown or white)
500g (1lb) golden syrup

Simmer the peeled and finely chopped apples, and the peeled, chopped onions, for 20 minutes in the water before adding the salt, spices and half the vinegar.

Cook until soft, then add the sugar, syrup and the rest of the vinegar. Simmer until smooth and thick. Pot and cover.

Apple chutney II
Makes 4kg (8lb) of chutney
3.5kg (7lb) cooking apples
2–3 garlic cloves
1 litre (2 pints) vinegar
1.5kg (3lb) brown or white sugar
500g (1lb) sultanas
250g (½lb) crystallised ginger

1 teaspoon each of mixed spice, cayenne and salt

Simmer the peeled and finely chopped apples with the crushed garlic in almost a quarter of the vinegar until soft. Add the sugar, sultanas, ginger and spices, and cook for a further 20 minutes.

Stir in the remaining vinegar and simmer until thick. Pot in hot jars and seal.

Apple and red pepper chutney
Makes 1kg (2lb) of chutney
2 large cooking apples
4 red peppers
2 aubergines
250g (½lb) onions
2 garlic cloves
175g (6oz) stoned raisins
1–2 teaspoons curry powder
Pinch of saffron powder (optional)
6 chillies
1 piece of root ginger
50g (2oz) brown sugar
600ml (1 pint) spiced vinegar

Peel and core the apples, cut the base from the peppers and remove the seeds and membranes. Peel the aubergines, onions and garlic. Thinly slice the apples, peppers, aubergines and onions. Chop the raisins and put all the ingredients in a pan with the crushed garlic.

Mix the curry powder and saffron (if used) with a little vinegar, and add to the pan with the bruised chillies and ginger, tied in muslin, and half the vinegar. Simmer until soft, then add the sugar and remaining vinegar and continue cooking until the chutney is smooth and thick. Pot at once.

Apple and tomato chutney
Makes 2.5kg (5lb) of chutney
1kg (2lb) apples
1kg (2lb) red tomatoes
500g (1lb) onions
1 garlic clove
250g (½lb) sultanas
1 tablespoon mustard seeds
500g (1lb) demerara sugar
25g (1oz) salt
2–3 teaspoons curry powder
Pinch cayenne
1 litre (2 pints) malt vinegar

Peel and core the apples, slice thinly and cook in a little water until tender. Peel and slice the tomatoes; peel the onions and chop finely. Add these ingredients to the pan with the crushed garlic, the chopped dried fruit, and the mustard seeds tied in a muslin bag.

Stir in the salt, curry powder, cayenne and half the vinegar.

Bring to the boil and simmer until soft, then add the sugar and the remaining vinegar and cook until smooth and thick. Remove the muslin bag; pot at once.

Apricot chutney
Makes 1kg (2lb) of chutney
250g (½lb) dried apricots
125g (4oz) stoned raisins
125g (4oz) sultanas
2 crushed garlic cloves
Juice and grated rind of 1 lemon
2 teaspoons pickling spice
1 teaspoon salt
600ml (1 pint) white vinegar
500g (1lb) brown sugar
500g (1lb) apples

Wash the apricots and cut into small pieces. Soak for 3 hours, drain, and put in a pan with the chopped raisins, sultanas, garlic, lemon juice and rind, the pickling spice tied in a muslin bag, the salt

and half the vinegar. Bring to the boil and simmer for 30 minutes.

Stir in the sugar, the grated apples and the remaining vinegar. Simmer to a jam-like consistency. Remove the muslin bag before potting and sealing.

Beetroot chutney
Makes 2kg (4lb) of chutney
1kg (2lb) uncooked beetroot
500g (1lb) onions
750g (1½lb) cooking apples
500g (1lb) seedless raisins
3 tablespoons ground ginger
1kg (2lb) granulated sugar
1 litre (2 pints) malt vinegar

Peel and grate the beetroot; peel the onions and chop finely; peel, core and chop the apples. Put in a pan with the raisins, ginger, sugar and vinegar. Bring to the boil. Simmer until thick, then pot.

Blackberry and apple chutney
Makes 4kg (8lb) of chutney
3kg (6lb) blackberries
1kg (2lb) cooking apples
1kg (2lb) onions
25g (1oz) salt
50g (2oz) dry mustard
50g (2oz) ground ginger
2 teaspoons ground mace
1 teaspoon cayenne
1 litre (2 pints) malt vinegar
1kg (2lb) brown sugar

Wash and drain the hulled blackberries and simmer for 20 minutes, then rub through a sieve. Peel, core and chop the apples, and peel and chop the onions. Put all the ingredients, except the sugar, in a pan.

Simmer for 1 hour then add the sugar and cook until thick. Pot the chutney at once.

Cranberry and apple chutney

Makes 2–2.5kg (4–5lb) of chutney
1kg (2lb) cranberries
1kg (2lb) cooking apples
500g (1lb) onions
750g–1kg (1½–2lb) brown sugar
1½–2 teaspoons ground ginger
2 teaspoons allspice
Pinch each of ground cloves, nutmeg, dry mustard, cayenne
25g (1oz) salt
Juice and grated peel of 2 oranges
1 litre (2 pints) malt vinegar

Place the cranberries in a pan with the peeled, cored and chopped apples and the peeled and chopped onions.

Add all the other ingredients and bring to the boil, then simmer the chutney until all the liquid has evaporated. Pot at once.

Damson chutney

Makes 3.5–4kg (7–8lb) of chutney
3.5kg (7lb) damsons
4 onions
500g (1lb) stoned raisins
250g (½lb) stoned dates
2 garlic cloves
50g (2oz) ground ginger
Pinch of ground allspice
25g (2oz) salt
1.5kg (3lb) brown sugar
2.75 litres (5¼ pints) malt vinegar

Wash, rinse and dry the damsons; chop the peeled onions, the raisins and the dates, and crush the garlic.

Place the fruits, onions, garlic, spices and salt in a pan with the sugar and vinegar. Simmer until quite soft and thick. Remove the damson stones before potting.

Gooseberry chutney

Makes 2kg (4lb) of chutney
1.5kg (3lb) gooseberries
250g (½lb) onions
175g (6oz) stoned raisins
350g (12oz) granulated sugar
½ teaspoon mixed spice
1 teaspoon crushed mustard seeds
25g (1oz) salt
600ml (1 pint) white vinegar

Chop the peeled onions and cook in a little water until tender. Drain. Put the washed, topped and tailed gooseberries into a pan with the onions, raisins and remaining ingredients.

Simmer gently for about 1 hour until the chutney has thickened, then pot at once.

Indian chutney

Makes 2.5–3kg (5–6lb) of chutney
1kg (2lb) cooking apples
500g (1lb) onions
8 garlic cloves
2.5 litres (4½ pints) malt vinegar
1kg (2lb) soft brown sugar
50g (2oz) salt
500g (1lb) stoned raisins
125g (4oz) dry mustard
150g (5oz) ground ginger
4 teaspoons cayenne

Peel, core and slice the apples, peel and chop the onions, and crush the garlic cloves.

Simmer the apples in the vinegar with the onions, garlic, sugar and salt until soft.

Rub through a fine sieve and return to a clean pan. Add the chopped raisins and stir in the mustard, ginger and cayenne pepper. Leave the mixture overnight, covered with a cloth, in a warm room or airing cupboard before potting.

Marrow and apple chutney

Makes 3kg (6lb) of chutney
2kg (4lb) marrow
75g (3oz) coarse salt
1kg (2lb) cooking apples
500g (1lb) shallots
500g (1lb) granulated sugar
Mixed bruised ginger, chillies and black peppercorns
1 litre (2 pints) white vinegar

Peel the marrow, remove the seeds and cut the flesh into small chunks. Place in a bowl, sprinkling each layer with salt, and leave overnight. Wash and drain thoroughly.

Put in a pan with a little vinegar, the finely chopped, peeled and cored apples, the peeled, chopped shallots and the spices tied in a muslin bag. When soft, add the remaining vinegar and sugar, and simmer until thick. Remove the spices before potting.

Mixed-fruit chutney

Makes 1.5–2kg (3–4lb) of chutney
1.5kg (3lb) mixed apples, pears, damsons and ripe tomatoes
125g (4oz) stoned dates
500g (1kg) onions
2 garlic cloves
250g (½lb) brown sugar
Salt
25g (1oz) mustard seeds
1 teaspoon each of ground pepper, allspice, cloves and ginger
600ml (1 pint) malt vinegar

Peel and core the apples and pears, stone the damsons and skin the tomatoes. Put through a mincer or chop finely in a food processor with the dates, the peeled, chopped onions and the garlic. Mix thoroughly and blend in the sugar and a pinch of salt.

Cook the spices in the vinegar, together with the mustard seeds

tied in muslin, for 15 minutes, then add the fruit mix. Simmer gently to the required consistency, stirring occasionally. Remove the muslin bag and pot the chutney.

Mixed-fruit chutney, Chinese style

Makes 3kg (6lb) of chutney
1kg (2lb) plums
1kg (2lb) fresh, ripe apricots
1 large or 2 small pineapples
1kg (2lb) brown sugar
600ml (1 pint) white wine vinegar

Skin and halve the plums and apricots, remove the stones and chop the flesh finely. Peel the pineapple, discard the hard central core, and cut the flesh into small chunks.

Put the fruit in a pan with the sugar and about half of the vinegar. When the sugar has dissolved, taste the chutney to determine whether it needs more sugar or vinegar. Simmer until quite soft and thick, stirring frequently. Pot at once.

Peach chutney

Makes 1.5kg (3lb) of chutney
1.5kg (3lb) small ripe peaches
1 lemon
2 garlic cloves
250g (8oz) seedless raisins
25g (1oz) stem ginger
1 green pepper
500g (1lb) brown sugar
1 teaspoon cayenne
1 litre (2 pints) cider vinegar
Salt

Peel and stone the peaches and cut into chunks. Place in a pan with the minced lemon, crushed garlic, chopped raisins, ginger and pepper, having first removed the seeds

from the pepper. Add the sugar, cayenne and vinegar, and simmer until soft and thick. Season to taste with salt before potting.

Pear and ginger chutney

Makes 2kg (4lb) of chutney
1.5kg (3lb) pears
500g (1lb) onions
1 orange
1 lemon
125g (4oz) seedless raisins
250g (½lb) granulated sugar
Large pinch ground cloves
1 tablespoon ground ginger
¼ teaspoon salt
3 black peppercorns
300ml (½ pint) malt vinegar

Chop the peeled and cored pears and the peeled onions. Grate the peel from the orange and lemon and extract the juice. Place these ingredients in a pan with the raisins, sugar, spices and salt, and the peppercorns tied in muslin.

Add the vinegar and simmer until the consistency is soft and thick. Remove the peppercorns before potting.

Pear and lemon chutney

Makes 2kg (4lb) of chutney
1.5kg (3lb) pears
5 shallots
3 garlic cloves
1 large lemon
125g (4oz) stem ginger
125g (4oz) sultanas
125g (4oz) seedless raisins
500g (1lb) brown sugar
600ml (1 pint) white wine vinegar
1 teaspoon each of salt, pepper, cinnamon, coriander and turmeric.

Dice the peeled and cored pears, chop the peeled shallots and crush the garlic. Cut the lemon into thin

slices, discarding the pips, and chop the stem ginger. Put these ingredients in a pan with the sultanas, raisins (whole), sugar, spices and vinegar.

Simmer gently until all the ingredients are soft and the chutney has a firm consistency. Pot at once.

Pepper chutney
Makes 1.5kg (3lb) of chutney
3 red peppers
3 green peppers
500g (1lb) ripe tomatoes
350g (12oz) onions
500g (1lb) cooking apples
1 teaspoon each of ground allspice and mustard seeds
2 teaspoons peppercorns
250g (½lb) demerara sugar
475ml (16fl oz) malt vinegar

Cut the base from the peppers and remove the seeds; mince or chop finely. Peel and quarter the tomatoes, peel and chop the onions, and peel, core and chop the apples.

Simmer these ingredients for about 1½ hours with the vinegar and sugar, together with the allspice, peppercorns and mustard seeds tied in a muslin bag.

Pot as soon as the required consistency is obtained.

Plum chutney
Makes 2.25g (4½lb) of chutney
1kg (2lb) stoned plums
500g (1lb) apples
500g (1lb) shallots or onions
500g (1lb) stoned raisins
175g (6oz) brown sugar
25g (1oz) salt
1 teaspoon each of ground ginger and allspice, dry mustard and nutmeg
600ml (1 pint) vinegar

Chop the stoned plums, the peeled and cored apples, the peeled shallots and the raisins. Place in a pan with the sugar, salt, spices and vinegar. Bring to the boil; simmer until soft and thick. Pot at once.

Pumpkin chutney
Makes 2kg (4lb) of chutney
1.25g (2½lb) pumpkin flesh
500g (1lb) red tomatoes
250g (½lb) onions
50g (2oz) sultanas
750g (1½lb) soft brown sugar *or* 350g (12oz) each of caster sugar and soft brown sugar
2 garlic cloves
2 teaspoons each of ground ginger, black pepper and ground allspice
2½ tablespoons salt
600ml (1 pint) tarragon vinegar

Cut the peeled pumpkin flesh into small pieces; slice the peeled tomatoes and peeled onions. Put these ingredients in a pan with the sultanas, sugar, crushed garlic, spices, salt and vinegar.

Bring to the boil and simmer gently until soft, and the chutney is of the consistency of jam. Pot the hot chutney at once.

Rhubarb chutney
Makes 3kg (6lb) of chutney
2.5kg (5lb) rhubarb
1kg (2lb) onions
1 litre (2 pints) white vinegar
1kg (2lb) granulated sugar
½ teaspoon salt
2 tablespoons ground ginger
3 teaspoons mixed spice

Cut the washed and dried rhubarb into small chunks; mince the peeled onions. Place in a pan with a third of the vinegar, the sugar, salt, ginger and spice, and simmer

gently until the rhubarb is soft. Add the remaining vinegar and simmer to the required consistency, stirring frequently.

For a hot chutney, use 3 teaspoons of curry powder instead of the mixed spice. Pot at once.

Tomato chutney
Makes 2.5–3kg (5–6lb) of chutney
3kg (6lb) ripe tomatoes
500g (1lb) onions
300ml (½ pint) spiced vinegar
25g (1oz) salt
1½ teaspoons paprika
Large pinch of cayenne
350g (12oz) granulated sugar

Peel and chop the tomatoes and put in a pan with the peeled, minced onions. Simmer until reduced to a thick pulp. Pour in half the vinegar, the salt and the spices and continue cooking until thick.

Add the remaining vinegar, after dissolving the sugar in it. Cook until the chutney is the required consistency, then pot and cover.

Softening up Tough vegetables like beetroot need to be cooked in some of the vinegar before adding the rest of the ingredients.

Sauces and relishes

Sauces, ketchups and relishes – so rich and diverse in flavour and texture – can quite easily be made from the produce of your garden. They can be used as accompaniments to hot curries, as side dishes with a cheeseboard or as flavourings in soups or stews.

Ketchups are usually made from the juice of not more than two kinds of vegetables or fruits. They are concentrated, with one dominating flavour. The flavours of sauces tend to be more subtle, as the result of blending a larger number of ingredients.

Relishes differ from both of these in that they consist of coarsely chopped vegetables or fruit, which are seasoned with spices and pickled in vinegar. Some are cooked, others are not; and some are made with hot vinegar while in others it is added cold.

Equipment
Since relishes, sauces and ketchups are made with vinegar, which is a mild acid, use only heavy-based pans of aluminium or stainless steel, never iron or copper. For the same reason, use only sieves made from stainless steel or nylon. Other equipment needed is listed right.

Sterilising and storing
Some of these preserves tend to ferment in storage – especially those made with mushrooms and ripe tomatoes, which have a low acid content. This can be overcome by sterilising immediately after bottling, as for fruit syrups (see page 284).

> **EQUIPMENT LIST**
> - Small knife and peeler
> - Mincer
> - Muslin for wrapping whole spices
> - Wooden spoon
> - Funnel
> - Ladle
> - Measuring jug and scales
> - Jars with screw tops, or corks
> - Large preserving pan
> - Newspaper
> - Ceresin papers and paraffin wax

Tie down corks to prevent them blowing out during sterilising. Secure screw caps loosely. Set the bottles on a false bottom or trivet in a pan deep enough to hold them upright, and do not allow them to touch each other or the sides of the pan.

Pour in warm water to cover the contents of the bottles, heat to a temperature of 77°C (170°F) and maintain this temperature for 30 minutes; or heat to 88°C (190°F) and maintain this for 20 minutes. After sterilising, tighten screw caps, or seal corks with melted paraffin wax.

The seals must be completely airtight or the contents will spoil. Once opened, sauces must be used up quickly. But most ketchups and relishes can be opened and re-covered as the need arises, and will keep for several months.

Recipes for sauces and ketchups

Apple sauce
1kg (2lb) apples
1 tablespoon sugar
300ml (½ pint) water
25g (1oz) butter
6 cloves
1 teaspoon ginger

Chop the washed, unpeeled apples finely. Put in a pan with the sugar, spices, water and butter. Simmer, uncovered, over a low heat until soft and pulpy.

Rub through a sieve, pour into clean, warm bottles and cover with screw caps or corks. Sterilise in a hot water-bath.

Blackberry ketchup
2.5kg (5lb) blackberries
Spiced white vinegar
Sugar

Wash the fruit and simmer, uncovered, without any extra water over gentle heat until soft. Rub through a sieve and measure the resultant purée.

For every 600ml (1 pint) of blackberry purée allow 300ml (½ pint) of vinegar and 50g (2oz) of sugar. Simmer the sauce to the consistency of thick cream. Pour into hot bottles, sterilise and seal.

Damson sauce
2kg (4lb) damsons
250g (½lb) onions
¼ teaspoon each of ground ginger, allspice, mace and dry mustard
125g (4oz) stoned raisins
1–2 chillies
12 peppercorns
250g (½lb) sugar
40g (1½oz) salt
1 litre (2 pints) white vinegar

Wash the damsons. Peel and slice the onions. Put in a pan with the spices, chillies, peppercorns, half the vinegar and the raisins.

Simmer, uncovered, over a gentle heat until tender. Sieve, and add the sugar, salt and the remaining vinegar.

Return to a clean pan and cook very gently until the sauce has the consistency of thick cream. Bottle while hot, and cover at once.

You can make plum sauce in the same way, but use currants instead of raisins.

Grape ketchup
Follow the recipe for blackberry ketchup, using grapes instead of blackberries and doubling the amount of sugar.

Mushroom ketchup
1.5kg (3lb) mushrooms
75g (3oz) salt
600ml (1 pint) vinegar
1 teaspoon each of peppercorns and allspice
½ teaspoon each of ground mace and ginger
¼ teaspoon each of ground cloves and cinnamon

Trim the mushrooms and break into pieces. Sprinkle with the salt and leave overnight. Rinse them well and mash with a wooden spoon.

Simmer in the vinegar, with the spices, for 30 minutes in a covered pan. Sieve, pour into hot bottles and seal. Sterilise in a hot water-bath for 30 minutes.

Rhubarb sauce
2.5kg (5lb) rhubarb
2.5kg (5lb) onions
25g (1oz) salt
20 peppercorns
1 chilli

1–2 teaspoons each of dry mustard and curry powder
25g (1oz) bruised root ginger
1.5 litres (3 pints) malt vinegar
1.5kg (3lb) brown sugar

Wash and trim the rhubarb, but do not peel. Cut into chunks. Peel and chop the onions. Put in a heavy-based pan with the salt, peppercorns, chilli, spices and vinegar. Simmer, uncovered, stirring frequently, for 2 hours.

Rub through a sieve and return to the pan with the sugar. Boil until the sauce is like thick cream. Bottle and seal at once.

Green tomato sauce
1.5kg (3lb) green tomatoes
750g (1½lb) cooking apples
2 small shallots or onions
250g (½lb) sugar
½ teaspoon each of ground pepper and dry mustard
1 tablespoon salt
300ml (½ pint) malt vinegar
1 teaspoon ground pickling spice
Gravy browning (optional)

Wash the tomatoes, peel and core the apples and peel the shallots or onions. Cut into small pieces and put in a pan with all the other ingredients. Simmer, uncovered, for about 1 hour, or until soft.

Add a few drops of browning, if necessary, to improve the colour. Sieve and bottle while still hot.

Red tomato sauce
3kg (6lb) ripe tomatoes
250g (½lb) sugar
300ml (½ pint) spiced white vinegar (see page 299)
2 tablespoons tarragon vinegar
1 tablespoon salt
Pinch of cayenne pepper
½ teaspoon paprika

Slice the washed tomatoes and cook, uncovered, over a low heat until soft and the skins are coming off. Rub the pulp through a fine sieve and put in a clean pan with the other ingredients. Simmer to the consistency of thick cream.

Bottle immediately and sterilise in a hot water-bath. Screw the caps tight or seal the corks.

Tomato and apple sauce

1kg (2lb) ripe tomatoes
1kg (2lb) cooking apples
4 onions
300ml (½ pint) vinegar
4 chillies
250g (½lb) sugar
24 peppercorns
16 cloves
25g (1oz) bruised root ginger
25g (1oz) salt

WHAT MAY GO WRONG

If the preserves shrink after a few months in store, this is almost certainly due to evaporation caused by a faulty seal. This can also lead to the contamination of the contents of the bottle.

A dark layer at the top of the bottle, which should be removed before serving, is probably due to the storage place being too warm.

Mould on the preserve or cork may be due to insufficient processing time; to the water in the preserving pan not being deep enough; or to corks that were not sufficiently sterilised.

STERILISING KETCHUPS

To prevent fermentation in storage, place the filled bottles in a pan of water and heat them for 20–30 minutes.

Wash and cut up the tomatoes, peel, core and chop the apples and peel and chop the onions. Cook these together in a covered pan over low heat until soft.

Add the vinegar, chillies, sugar, spices and salt; simmer, covered, for 30 minutes. Sieve, and cook until it resembles thick cream. Pour into hot bottles and seal.

Tomato and green pepper ketchup

3.5kg (7lb) ripe tomatoes
8 large onions
50g (2oz) bruised root ginger
2 level tablespoons whole cloves
8 green peppers
2 litres (4 pints) distilled vinegar
5 teaspoons salt
250g (½lb) demerara sugar
2 tablespoons whole allspice
10cm (4in) stick of cinnamon

Skin and chop the tomatoes and onions. Cut the base off the peppers, remove the seeds and membranes and chop the flesh. Put in a pan with the vinegar, salt and sugar, and the spices tied in a muslin bag.

Bring to the boil and simmer, uncovered, for 1 hour, stirring frequently. Remove the spices and rub the pulp through a sieve. Simmer again until the ketchup has a creamy consistency, then pour into hot bottles, seal and sterilise.

MAKING TOMATO KETCHUP

Makes 1.2 litres (2 pints)
4 bay leaves
6 black peppercorns
1 teaspoon each of mustard seeds and caraway seeds
250ml (9fl oz) cider vinegar
4.5kg (10lb) tomatoes
500g (1lb 2oz) onions
500g (1lb 2oz) sugar
150g (5½oz) salt
200ml (7fl oz) sunflower oil
200ml (7fl oz) vinegar

Nothing artificial Home-made tomato ketchup is tastier than the shop-bought variety and you know exactly what's in it.

Spice the vinegar Put the spices in a pan with the cider vinegar. Heat to simmering point then strain.

Prepare the ingredients Chop the tomatoes, cook for 2–3 minutes then press through a sieve. Chop the onions and cook in a little water until soft, then purée. Simmer the sugar, salt, sunflower oil and vinegar in a pan until the sugar has dissolved.

Combine and bottle Pour the tomatoes and onion purée into a pan and bring to the boil, stirring constantly. Stir in the flavoured vinegar and simmer for 30 minutes, until pulpy. Pour into sterilised glass jars and seal.

Recipes for vegetable relishes

Beetroot relish
500g (1lb) beetroot
500g (1lb) white cabbage
250g (½lb) sugar
600ml (½ pint) white vinegar
1 tablespoon fresh or dried grated horseradish
1 teaspoon salt
1 teaspoon pepper

Chop the beetroot roughly, and the cabbage very finely. Place in a pan with the other ingredients, and stir until the sugar has dissolved.

Cook gently for 20 minutes. Pot into warm jars and cover.

If you like your relishes with a little more bite, try the alternative version below.

Beetroot and horseradish relish
500g (1lb) beetroot
115g (4oz) fresh horseradish
½ teaspoon salt
115g (4oz) sugar
300ml (½ pint) white wine vinegar

Cook the beetroot, then peel and grate coarsely. Trim, peel and grate the horseradish, and place all the ingredients in a large bowl. Stir until the sugar has dissolved.

Pack the relish into clean, dry jars. It will store in the refrigerator for up to a month.

Celery relish
2 green peppers
2 red peppers
500g (1lb) onions
3 tablespoons salt
625g (1¼lb) sugar
4 tablespoons mustard seeds
Large pinch turmeric
300ml (½ pint) distilled vinegar
5 tablespoons water
5 celery sticks

Remove the base, seeds and membranes from the peppers and peel the onions. Finely chop the peppers and onions. Mix the dry ingredients and blend into the vinegar and water.

Bring to the boil and add the diced celery with the peppers and onion. Simmer in a covered pan for 3 minutes and pot in hot jars, covering the vegetables with the hot liquid. Seal to make it airtight.

Corn relish
6 corn cobs
½ small white cabbage
2 onions
2 small red peppers
2 teaspoons salt
2 teaspoons flour
½ teaspoon turmeric
175g (6oz) sugar
2 teaspoons dry mustard
600ml (1 pint) distilled vinegar

Boil the corn for 3 minutes and strip from the cobs. Prepare and mince the cabbage, onions and peppers, and put in a pan with the corn. Bring to the boil.

Mix the dry ingredients thoroughly and gradually blend in the vinegar. Add to the vegetables and simmer for 30 minutes, stirring occasionally. Pot in hot jars, and seal immediately.

Pepper relish
1 small cucumber
2 large onions
2 cooking apples
10 chillies
1 tablespoon salt
200g (7oz) sugar
300ml (½ pint) white vinegar

Peel the cucumber and onions, and peel and core the apples. Mince them, drain if necessary, and mix in a bowl. Add the crushed chillies.

Mix together the salt, sugar and vinegar and stir into the contents of the bowl until the sugar has dissolved. Pot, without cooking, in sterilised jars and seal.

Mustard relish
1.5kg (3lb) apples
500g (1lb) onions
1 tablespoon mustard seeds
1 litre (2 pints) vinegar
250g (½lb) sultanas
500g (1lb) sugar
2 teaspoons dry mustard
1 tablespoon salt

Core the peeled apples and chop the peeled onions. Simmer, until soft, with half the vinegar and the mustard seeds in a muslin bag.

Add the other ingredients, blending the remaining vinegar with the mustard.

Stir to dissolve the sugar and boil to the required thickness, stirring occasionally. Remove the mustard seeds, pot and seal.

Tomato relish
2kg (4lb) ripe tomatoes
3 large onions
25g (1oz) salt
3 large celery sticks
1 red pepper
500g (1lb) sugar
1 tablespoon mustard seeds
450ml (¾ pint) vinegar

Skin and finely chop the tomatoes and onions. Mix in a bowl, sprinkle with the salt and leave overnight. Leave to drain through a colander for 5–6 hours.

Finely chop the cleaned celery and deseeded pepper, and mix in a bowl with the sugar, mustard seeds and vinegar. Stir in the tomatoes and onions and mix well. Pot in sterilised jars and seal.

Tomato and horseradish relish
2kg (4lb) ripe tomatoes
1 large onion
2 large apples
450ml (¾ pint) vinegar
2 teaspoons pickling spices
2 teaspoons salt
½ teaspoon cayenne pepper or paprika
500g (1lb) sugar
3 tablespoons grated horseradish

Skin the tomatoes; peel and finely chop the onion; peel, core and chop the apples.

Cook to a thick pulp, stirring at first to prevent burning. Meanwhile, boil the vinegar and pickling spices together for 10 minutes, strain and add the vinegar, salt and cayenne to the tomatoes.

Boil to reduce the mixture to a thick, creamy texture, then stir in the sugar and horseradish. Cook for 10 minutes. Pour into hot bottles, seal and sterilise.

A relish with bite Grated horseradish added to beetroot turns an otherwise sweetish pickle into a tangy, lively relish.

Flavoured vinegars

Flavoured vinegars are not as widely used as they were 100 years ago, in the golden era of Mrs Beeton. Then, no salad was complete without its accompanying bottles of celery, cucumber or tarragon vinegar. Cold meats were dressed with horseradish vinegar, while chilli vinegars made a spirited addition to soups, stews and curries.

Fruit vinegars, too, were used – as flavourings for steamed puddings, soothing cures for sore throats or simply – diluted with water – as cooling summer drinks.

Apart from being simplicity itself to make, flavoured vinegars are an inexpensive way of using up small quantities of surplus garden produce. The only expense is the vinegar itself.

Wine vinegar is the best base for most of the recipes given here, since its flavour, which tends to be less harsh than that of malt vinegar, will not obliterate the delicate flavours imparted by the additional ingredients.

Among the exceptions are condiments containing such strong-tasting ingredients as chillies and horseradish. For these, the cheaper malt vinegars will suffice and will carry the stronger flavours beautifully.

Equipment
Apart from bottles, only standard items of kitchenware are needed, see list in panel.

Fruit vinegars
These are made from soft fruits such as raspberries, blackberries and blackcurrants. Put the fruits in a bowl, bruise them with a wooden spoon and to each 1kg (2lb), add 1 litre (2 pints) of good-quality wine vinegar.

Cover the bowl with a cloth and leave it to stand for three or four days, stirring twice a day.

Strain the juice through clean muslin, put it into a pan and boil for 10 minutes.

Pour the fruit vinegar into warmed bottles, and either screw on the tops or drive home the corks and seal them with paraffin wax.

For a sweet vinegar, add 1kg (2lb) of granulated sugar to each litre (2 pints) of strained liquid, just before boiling. Some older recipes also recommend the addition of a glass of brandy to each bottle of fruit vinegar.

Use the vinegars, diluted, as a summer drink or, undiluted, as a flavouring for puddings.

Vegetable vinegars
These are made from delicately flavoured vegetables such as cucumbers and celery, or strong-tasting roots and fruits like horseradish, peppers and chillies. The former can be used to flavour

fish and salads, while the latter make a fiery accompaniment to grills and barbecues.

Chop, grate or split the vegetables, according to the recipe. Place them in a large jar and cover with good-quality vinegar.

Cover the jar and leave it to stand for the specified period, stirring or shaking occasionally. Strain the vinegar through muslin, and bottle.

Herb vinegars
Made with garden herbs such as tarragon, thyme, mint, basil or marjoram – singly or in combination – they can be used to flavour dressings and sauces. Pick the herbs just before they flower and put the leaves and tender parts of the stalks into a large jar.

Bruise the herbs with a wooden spoon, cover them with wine vinegar and leave to stand for six to eight weeks. If a clear glass jar is used, stand it in a dark cupboard to prevent loss of colour.

After this period, strain the vinegar through muslin and bottle it, first placing a sprig or two of the particular herb in each bottle.

Recipes for vinegars

MAKING APPLE VINEGAR

Prepare the apples Wash, core and chop apples. Place in a large clean bowl, bucket or jar. Bruise the fruit with a wooden spoon.

Steep in vinegar Add white vinegar. Cover and leave to stand for four days, stirring occasionally.

Strain and bottle Strain the pulp into a clean pan and add sugar. Boil for 10 minutes and pour into warm, sterilised bottles and seal.

Celery vinegar
Finely chop a large head of washed celery – leaves and all – and place in a jar. Pour over white wine vinegar and leave, covered, for two weeks. Strain and bottle. Use to dress cold chicken.

Chilli vinegar
Use about 50g (2oz) of red chillies, split in half and steeped in 1 litre (2 pints) of wine or malt vinegar. Steep, covered, for four to six weeks. Strain and bottle.

Cucumber vinegar
Peel and finely chop 8 small cucumbers and 3 onions. Steep for a week in 1 litre (2 pints) of white wine vinegar, shaking occasionally. Bottle the strained vinegar, and use in dressings for summer salads and cold fish dishes.

Fruit vinegars
Cover 500g (1lb) of soft fruit, such as currants or raspberries, with 600ml (1 pint) of white vinegar. Leave to stand for 4 days, stirring occasionally, then strain.

Place the liquid in a pan with 250g (½lb) of sugar to each pint of liquid, bring to the boil, and boil for 10 minutes. Bottle and seal.

Garlic vinegar
Peel 50g (2oz) of garlic and chop thinly. Add it to 600ml (1 pint) of vinegar and leave for two weeks. Strain into a clean bottle.

Horseradish vinegar
Steep 75g (3oz) of grated horseradish and 25g (1oz) of finely chopped shallot, in 1 litre (2 pints) of malt or white vinegar for about a week. Shake frequently, strain and bottle the vinegar. It is best used in dressings.

Drying – the economical way to preserve

Lavender vinegar
Method as for tarragon vinegar. The lavender makes a pleasant change in salad dressings, and the vinegar can also be used on a cloth pad to relieve headaches. Use white vinegar.

Mint vinegar
Pick fresh, healthy mint leaves, strip the leaves from the stalks, wash and dry. Pack 100–175g (4–6oz) of mint into a jar, pour 1 litre (2 pints) of wine vinegar over it, cover and steep for three weeks. Strain, and use in salad dressings and mint sauce.

Onion vinegar
Add 125g (4oz) of finely chopped onions to 1 litre (2 pints) of white wine vinegar. Steep for two weeks, shaking often. Strain and bottle. Use in dressings for beetroot and green salads.

Rose-petal vinegar
Fill a 1 litre (2 pints) jar half full with clean, dark, rose petals, preferably from old-fashioned, scented roses. Press the petals well down and top up with white wine vinegar. Leave, covered, for two or three weeks, then strain and bottle. This delicately flavoured, pink vinegar is ideal with summer salads.

Tarragon vinegar
Half fill a 1 litre (2 pints) jar with fresh young tarragon leaves. Top up with good white wine vinegar and leave, covered, for four weeks. Strain and bottle, adding a sprig of tarragon to each bottle. Use in salad dressings and white sauces.

Other herbs, such as dill, thyme and marjoram, may be treated in the same way.

For thousands of years, drying was the only known method – apart from salting – of preserving food. To this day, in tropical climates, fruits such as figs, dates and grapes are still dried in the sun, while in northern Europe, drying fish by sun, wind or smoke remains a thriving industry.

In Britain's more variable climate, surplus garden produce is better dried indoors where a steady temperature can be guaranteed. The process is simple, if lengthy, and the expense negligible. There are two principal requirements: the correct temperature and adequate ventilation.

Food to be dried should be laid out on trays or racks, which can be made by stretching muslin over a wooden frame and fixing it in place with tacks. When drying small quantities, use a wire cake tray covered with muslin.

Methods of drying
Drying by artificial heat can be carried out in a single operation in a cool oven over a period of several hours. The correct temperature is 50–65°C (120–150°F, gas mark ¼). Alternatively, it can be spread over several days by using the residual heat of the oven after cooking another dish. An oven thermometer is useful for gauging the low temperatures needed.

A rack positioned over the boiler or in the airing cupboard can also be used for drying, provided the food is protected from dust and there is adequate ventilation.

Fruits and vegetables that have been dried correctly will keep for many months. The flavour and texture are restored by soaking before cooking.

Drying fruit
Stone fruits, such as apricots, peaches and plums, are excellent for drying. So, too, are apples, grapes and pears. The fruits should be sound and just ripe.

Wash the fruits, then halve, slice, or leave them whole – according to type. Lay them on muslin-covered trays and dry at a temperature of 50–65°C (120–150°F, gas mark ¼). The temperature must not rise above 50°C (120°F) for the first hour, or the fruit will harden and the skins may burst.

The temperature may then be allowed to rise gradually to 65°C (150°F) for a further 3–6 hours, depending on the fruit.

Dried fruits should feel springy and soft, not brittle, and should not

exude moisture when pressed. Leave them to cool at room temperature for 12 hours; cover them with a cloth to exclude light, which may affect the colour. Pack the dried fruit in boxes lined with greaseproof or waxed paper.

The cover need not be completely airtight, but the boxes must be stored in a dry place.

Apples In the 16th century, whole apples, peeled and cored, used to be dried in the chimney. Today, they are more usually dried as rings, which take up less storage space.

Choose firm, crisp, juicy apples. Peel, core and cut them crossways into even rings about 5mm (¼in) thick. Drop the slices into a bowl of lightly salted water – 1 teaspoon of salt to 1 litre (2 pints) of water – to prevent them from going brown.

Pat the rings dry and thread them onto bamboo canes cut to fit the oven width. Hang the canes in the oven, set to the correct cool temperature, and leave the oven door slightly ajar.

Drying should be complete in 4–6 hours, when the apple rings will look like chamois leather. Cool for 12 hours before packing.

STEPS IN DRYING FRUIT

Step 1 Lay pepared fruit on a muslin-covered rack or tray, spacing the pieces evenly.

Step 2 Dry in the oven at 50–65°C (120–150°F) until the juices have evaporated.

Step 3 Remove tray from the oven, cover fruit with a cloth and leave to cool for 12 hours.

Step 4 When cool, pack fruit in boxes lined with greaseproof paper and store in a dry place.

Apricots, peaches and plums
As stone fruits shrink during drying, use large, firm, ripe fruits. Use dark-coloured varieties of plums; these may be left whole, but apricots and peaches should be halved and stoned.

Place the fruit in single layers on covered trays, cut surfaces uppermost to prevent the juices from dripping down.

Dry slowly at a temperature of 50°C (120°F, gas mark ¼), in an oven or airing cupboard, with the door left open. Maintain this temperature until the skins begin to shrivel, then raise the temperature to 65°C (150°F).

Whole fruit may take up to two days to dry; halved stoned fruit about a day. Drying is complete if no juice flows, and the skin remains unbroken, when the fruit is gently squeezed. Leave the fruits to cool for 12 hours before storing.

Grapes Home-grown grapes, preferably the seedless varieties, may be dried and used as a substitute for sultanas in cakes and puddings. Pick ripe grapes, separate them into single berries and wash them, discarding any that have withered. Remove excess moisture with a towel, and spread the grapes on covered trays.

Dry them in an airing cupboard, with the door left open, or in a cool oven, at a temperature gradually rising to 65°C (150°F), for about 8 hours. Cool overnight at room temperature, then pack and store.

Pears Peel, core and quarter the fruits and drop them into lightly salted water – 1 teaspoon of salt to 1 litre (2 pints) of water – to prevent discoloration during preparation. Dry the pears on muslin trays for 4–6 hours, with the cut surfaces uppermost.

Cooking with dried fruit

Failures with dried fruits are usually due to insufficient soaking before use, or to adding sugar at too early a stage.

Soak all dried fruits in cold water to plump them up before cooking. Soak stone fruits for at least 24 hours; apples and pears for about 12 hours. Cook them in the water in which they were soaked, and use as fillings for pies and puddings.

Bring to the boil very slowly and simmer gently until tender. Do not add sugar until the fruits have almost finished cooking, then sweeten to taste.

Drying vegetables

Root vegetables can be stored in boxes of peat or sand, so drying is unnecessary. Most other vegetables are better preserved by freezing or bottling, but young peas, french and runner beans, mushrooms and onions can be dried.

Prepare peas and beans for drying as for cooking, then blanch them in boiling water for about

5 minutes before rinsing them in cold water. Soak up surplus moisture with a paper towel or clean tea cloth, then dry them on trays in a cool oven or airing cupboard until quite hard.

Allow to cool completely, before packing in airtight containers. Store in a cool, dry place.

To cook, soak the dried beans or peas for 12 hours in cold water mixed with 1 teaspoon of bicarbonate of soda to improve the colour. Strain and rinse, then cook in salted water until tender.

Mushrooms Flat cap or field mushrooms are the most suitable for drying. Pick them fresh, trim any ragged edges, and peel them if dirty; otherwise wipe them clean with a soft, damp cloth.

Remove the stalks – which can be used in soups, sauces or for vegetable stock – and cut large mushrooms into halves or quarters. Thread them on string, using a poultry or packing needle to push through the centre.

Tie a thick knot between each mushroom, allowing 5cm (2in) between them so that they do not touch when hung up. Thread about a dozen mushrooms on each string.

Hang the strings up to dry in a warm, airy place, such as over the boiler or in the airing cupboard with the door ajar. They take a couple of days to dry and will then have a leathery colour and texture.

Store dried mushrooms in jars in a dry cupboard; or leave the strings hanging in the kitchen, away from dust and steam.

Dried mushrooms can be used to flavour soups, stews, casseroles and sauces, and need no soaking beforehand. Simply break them off the string and add to the pan.

To fry or grill dried mushrooms, soak them first for about an hour in cold water or milk. Dry carefully before cooking.

Onions Whole onions are usually stored in nets or tied in strings, but it is useful to have a supply of dried onion rings. These can be left until the supply of whole onions is finished, or until the bulbs start to deteriorate in late winter or spring.

Peel and cut medium-sized onions into 5mm (¼in) slices. Separate these into single rings and discard the centre circles, using these the same day in salads, cheese sandwiches or for cooking.

Blanch the rings chosen for drying in boiling water for 30 seconds, strain through a colander and rinse in cold running water. Drain, and spread them out on kitchen paper or a cloth to absorb the excess moisture.

As an alternative to blanching, mix the onion rings with salt and sugar – 1 tablespoon of cooking salt and 1 teaspoon of sugar to 1kg (2lb) onions. Heat slowly in a heavy-based pan, stirring carefully until the rings have softened; this will crisp the rings as they dry.

Spread the blanched and dried, or softened, rings in single layers on muslin-covered trays, and dry in a cool oven with a maximum temperature of 65°C (150°F, gas mark ¼), with the door left ajar until the rings are crisp and dry. This will take about 3 hours. Those softened with sugar and salt will dry more quickly.

Leave the rings to cool completely before packing them into jars and storing in a cool, dry place. To use the onions, soak them in warm water for 30 minutes and add them to stews and casseroles.

Drying herbs

Herbs, like any other garden produce, are at their best when freshly picked. But, since most are annuals or deciduous perennials, it is not always possible to have fresh herbs to hand. Drying is the best method to preserve them.

Picking the herbs

It is important to harvest herbs at the right time. In most cases, it is the leaves that are used for flavouring, and these should be picked while still young, in early to midsummer. They should be picked before the flowers develop as the leaves then become tough.

Choose warm, dry days for harvesting. Mornings are the best times for picking herbs, after the dew has evaporated and before the

sun scorches the leaves. It is best to pick one variety of herb at a time and prepare it for drying. The process is quite lengthy, and some patience is needed in dealing with the smaller herbs. It becomes easier with practice.

Examine each branch or shoot carefully, and pull off and discard any damaged or diseased leaves. Strip large-leaved herbs, such as sage and mint, from their stalks, but leave small and feathery herbs, such as chervil and fennel, on the stalks until drying is complete.

Drying methods

Drying depends on abundant dry, fresh air rather than on heat, so artificial warmth is not essential. An airing cupboard, a well-ventilated larder or a garden shed are suitable, even if it takes longer to dry them there than in an oven or over a radiator.

Save the flavour for another season Pick only the healthiest, young leaves for drying and you will preserve the very best of their flavour.

Tie the herbs in small bunches and dip them in boiling water for a few seconds. In addition to cleaning them, this also helps to preserve their colours. Shake off excess moisture and leave to dry on absorbent kitchen paper.

Air drying Hang the bunches up to dry, leaves downwards, wrapped loosely in muslin or thin paper bags to keep the dust out and to catch any falling leaves or seeds. Do not use plastic bags, which may cause moulds to develop.

The time needed to dry fresh herbs depends on the size of the branches and the humidity of the place where they are hung. On average, allow between seven and ten days.

Drying on a rack Drying can be speeded by placing the blanched herbs, well spaced out, on a tray.

Place the tray in an airing cupboard, over a radiator, or in the warming drawer of a cooker, and turn the leaves or stalks frequently to ensure even drying. They should be dry in two or three days.

Oven drying Herbs can also be dried in an oven. Leaves of sage, mint, rosemary, thyme and parsley, stripped from their stalks, are particularly suitable for this.

Place blanched leaves, well spaced, on a muslin-covered tray in an oven set to the lowest possible temperature.

Leave the door ajar to allow the moisture to escape.

Turn the leaves over after 30 minutes to ensure even drying; they will be quite dry after about an hour. Leave in the oven until they are cool.

Storing herbs

The process of packing and storing is identical, whichever method of drying is chosen. Crumble the dried herbs through your fingers, and discard the hard leafstalks and midribs. Store in small, airtight containers, preferably made of pottery or opaque glass.

If you use glass containers, store them in a dark place so that the herbs do not lose their colour.

Using dried herbs

Use fresh herbs for flavouring, garnishing and in cold drinks. Dried herbs are suitable only for use in cooked foods, and even then need to be treated with care. As the flavours are concentrated, a smaller amount is needed than with fresh herbs. For instance, where a recipe requires 1 teaspoon of fresh herbs, substitute half the amount of dried herbs.

Do not shake dried herbs from their containers into foods that are cooking. The rising heat and steam may result in moulds growing in the herb jar. Remove the required amount with a spoon, and close the jar immediately.

SMALL-LEAVED HERBS

Tie freshly picked herbs into bunches, and dip them briefly into boiling water.

Shake excess moisture off the herbs, then leave them to drain on absorbent paper.

Hang the bunches, leaves down, and stored in paper bags in an airy place.

Discard twigs and leaf ribs, and crumble the dried leaves into airtight jars or pots for storage.

Oven dried Woody herbs, such as rosemary and thyme, can be dried quickly in the oven.

Drying herbs for a bouquet garni

This traditional flavouring bundle consists of a sprig of parsley, another of thyme and a bay leaf, tied in a small muslin bag. It is used to flavour stocks, soups, sauces and casseroles.

If you are drying these herbs, it is a good idea to prepare a number of bouquets garnis and store them in an airtight, screw-top jar, ready for use as required.

Infused oils

Another delicious way of preserving the flavours of herbs and spices is by infusing them in oils, which will absorb the flavour and which you can then use in your cooking. Garlic and chilli oil are perhaps the most commonly seen, but most culinary herbs can also be used.

Use only high-quality and neutral oils, such as mild olive oil, sunflower oil or soya oil. They will absorb the flavours and aromas of the added ingredients without overpowering them with their own flavours. Extra virgin olive oil has too strong a flavour for many aromatic herbs, so if you use olive oil, choose a lighter refined oil or one that is a blend of refined and virgin oils.

Remove the herbs from the oil once it has infused, so that they do not start to turn mouldy and taint the oil. If you leave the herbs in for decoration, use the oil within 1 month.

Basil oil

150g (5½oz) fresh basil leaves
1 litre (1¾ pints) olive oil

Wash and dry the basil. Place in a 1 litre (1¾ pint) glass bottle and push down with the handle of a wooden spoon. Pour the oil into a pan and heat to 40°C (75°F). Pour the hot oil over the basil, seal the bottle with a cork and leave to infuse for three to four weeks. Use the oil within a few weeks or strain through a fine sieve to remove the basil leaves and transfer to a clean bottle for longer storage.

Garlic oil

2 cloves garlic
1 sprig each of fresh thyme and rosemary
1 small dried red chilli
500ml (1 pint) olive oil

Peel the garlic and bruise it with the blade of a knife. Place it in a glass bottle with the herbs and chilli. Pour over the oil, seal with a cork and leave to infuse for a week.

Thyme oil

200g (7oz) sprigs fresh thyme
1 litre (1¾ pints) olive oil *or* sunflower oil

Wash and pat dry the thyme. Strip the leaves from the stalks, place on a wooden board and bruise them with a rolling pin. Place the leaves and oil in a bowl and cover with a cloth or plate. Leave to infuse for two weeks, then strain and pour into bottles.

This oil is delicious as a salad dressing or as a bathoil to help to relieve a cold.

Making your own wine

The ancient tradition of country wine making in Britain has never died out. This is not surprising, since home-made wine has much to offer. Apart from allowing you to entertain friends at a fraction of the cost of buying commercial wines, there is the pleasure of acquiring a creative and satisfying hobby and of finding additional uses for garden produce.

The principles of wine making are very simple and you do not need to buy a great deal of expensive equipment. Many of the items you need can be found in a well-equipped kitchen, and the remainder bought from a chemist or from one of the ever-growing number of shops specialising in home brewing.

The results of your efforts should be at least as drinkable as the less expensive commercial wines, and will certainly offer much more variety. After a little practice, you could soon be producing a range of beverages with a distinctive flavour and character.

In spite of the many concentrates and kits sold for home wine making, it is still cheaper and more satisfying to use produce grown in your garden or gathered in the countryside. There is no great skill required to achieve a pleasant-tasting wine, and with a little care, good results are assured.

Main ingredients
Almost all garden fruits and vegetables, many wild hedgerow plants and even the petals of scented flowers can provide the basis for delicious wines. Apart from the plants themselves, the principal ingredients are yeast, sugar and water.

All 'country' wines, made from these homely ingredients, are improved by the addition of grapes. Raisins, sultanas or concentrated grape juice may be used instead of fresh grapes for this purpose.

Yeast The key process in wine making is the conversion of sugar in the fruit or vegetable juice to alcohol and carbon dioxide. The process, known as fermentation, is carried out by the enzymes secreted by yeast cells. These tiny cells, invisible to the naked eye, grow on most fruit skins, especially those of grapes. However, the wild strains produced on fruits in Britain are unsuitable for making wine of good quality, so you will need to add extra yeast to the must.

Bakers' or brewers' yeasts are unsuitable and so you must buy special wine yeasts, which provide both a stronger wine and a firmer sediment. Wine yeasts are available in tablet, granular or liquid forms. Sachets of 'super yeast' are particularly useful for the beginner,

Wine from the vine Grapes are the best fruit for wine making. Their ideal balance of acids, mineral salts, tannin and vitamins assists fermentation.

since they also contain the correct balance of nutrient salts that will encourage the yeast to grow. This type of yeast starts fermenting extremely quickly, falls cleanly to the bottom of the jar and produces a good-flavoured wine.

For those who like to experiment, there are special yeasts produced in the great wine-growing districts – Sauternes, Burgundy, Bordeaux and so on. When added to the must of a wine, they help to impart their characteristic flavour.

Whatever type is chosen, it is always better to add activated, rather than dormant, yeast to the must. This ensures prompt fermentation and helps to avoid infection by microorganisms. As the sachets contain dormant yeast, it is necessary to activate it before adding it to the must.

Starter bottles
To activate yeast, place it in a sterilised bottle containing a little boiled and cooled fruit juice that has been slightly sweetened. Grape juice is ideal, but the juice of any sharp-tasting fruit, such as oranges, will do.

Leave plenty of air space in the bottle, plug the neck lightly with cotton wool, and leave it in a warm place for several hours or over-night. A stream of bubbles indicates that the yeast is active and ready to be added to the must. In the case of 'super yeast', this may occur within 4 or 5 hours. Other types, however, take up to two days.

Some of the remarkable qualities of yeast are reflected in the fact that if you wish to make several batches of wine within a short time, you need use only three-quarters of the contents of the bottle and replace the amount taken out with fresh fruit juice, cold boiled water and sugar. Within two days, you will have another large colony of yeast cells.

Water Use tap water – hard or soft – or water from a spring or well. Rainwater is unsuitable, unless first filtered and boiled.

Sugar The alcohol in wine is produced exclusively from sugar, either from that contained in the basic fruit or vegetable juice or from the extra sugar added to the must. Grapes and honey apart, all musts require some additional sugar.

Ordinary white granulated sugar is the most suitable – except when making Madeira-type wines, when brown sugar should be used. Chemicals such as saccharin are suitable only for sweetening finished wine.

Wine makers often ask whether a particular fruit will produce dry or sweet wine. The answer is that any wine will be as dry or sweet as you make it, for this depends on the amount of sugar you use – not the type of fruit. Generally, the more sugar you use, the longer the wine will take to ferment and the stronger it will be.

Bear in mind that the natural sugar content of fruit and vegetables may vary from year to year, so the quantities of sugar recommended in the recipes are only an approximate guide.

Though you can produce good wines simply by following the recipes, perfectionists should measure the natural sugar content of the must with a hydrometer and add only enough sugar to produce the amount of alcohol required.

UNDERSTANDING TERMS USED IN WINE MAKING

Airlock A device that excludes airborne bacteria and other sources of infection from the must during fermentation, but allows gas to escape. It works in much the same way as the U-trap under a sink.

Body A word used to describe the density of a wine. Some wines taste thin and watery, while others are 'full bodied'.

Carbon dioxide A gas formed during fermentation, which escapes through the airlock.

Decant To pour wine from a bottle into a glass container suitable for table use, leaving any sediment behind in the bottle. Hold the bottle against the light, and decant the wine slowly, so that you can stop pouring as soon as the sediment reaches the neck of the bottle.

Dry The term used to describe a wine with no trace of sweetness.

Fermentation The process whereby sugar is converted by yeast into alcohol and carbon dioxide.

Finings Substances such as isinglass and bentonite that are sometimes stirred into wine to help it to clear.

Hydrometer An instrument for measuring the specific gravity in a liquid. It is used in wine making to measure the sugar content.

Lees A sediment, composed of dead yeast and pulp tissue, that collects in the bottom of the jar while the wine is fermenting.

Maturation The mellowing of a new wine by storage to the point when it is ready to drink.

Must The term used to describe the mixture of ingredients before they have been fermented.

Racking The removal of clear wine from a vessel containing lees. Each wine needs at least two rackings to get rid of all sediment.

Siphon A plastic or rubber tube used for racking and bottling wine.

Specific gravity In wine-making terms, the amount of sugar contained in a must or wine.

Locked out The water trapped within the airlock (dyed red here for clarity) acts as a barrier to microbes but allows gas to bubble through it and escape from the fermenting must.

Secondary ingredients

In addition to the basic materials used for wine making, various additives are needed to ensure reliable fermentation and a good-tasting wine.

Nutrient Like all living things, yeast requires feeding in order to function properly. All the elements it needs are present in pure grape juice and also in some other fruits, but are lacking in vegetables, herbs, flowers and honey.

Therefore, to ensure good fermentation in wines made from fruits and vegetables, it may be necessary to add nutrient to the yeast. This is sold as crystals containing ammonium phosphate and other vitamins, added at the rate of half a level teaspoon for every 4 litres (1 gallon).

Acid Yeast can flourish only in an acid solution, and wine, too, requires acid to assist in the development of a good bouquet and flavour. Citric-acid crystals are best, but tartaric or malic acid may also be used, or a combination of all three. The acids may be bought as crystals from a chemist's or home-brewing shop.

Almost every must will require some acid; the amount depends on the natural acidity of the basic material. Some musts – made from honey, flowers, herbs or vegetables, for instance – will require the full dose of 5g per litre (¾oz per gallon) while others, such as rhubarb and redcurrants, need considerably less.

Tannin Tannin gives red wine its bite and character and is also beneficial in white wines, though to a lesser extent. Half a level

teaspoon of grape tannin – a brown powder – is sufficient for around six bottles of wine.

Some wine makers prefer to use cold tea instead. Half a cup is usually enough, depending on the strength of the tea.

Campden tablets These are the winemaker's cure-all. One, dissolved in 600ml (1 pint) of cold water, is the perfect sterilising agent for wine-making equipment. Every item must first be washed in this solution. One tablet dissolved in a gallon of must, or of finished wine, will prevent oxidation and the

growth of spoilage organisms. Add two tablets to sweet wines after racking, to stabilise them and prevent further fermentation.

Pectin-destroying enzyme
Added to all fruit wines, the enzyme improves both juice extraction and flavour by breaking down the pectin in the fruits. It also reduces the risk of haziness in the finished wine.

Add the enzyme at an early stage, before sugar is added to the must. A rounded teaspoon to every 4 litres (1 gallon) should be enough for most types of fruit.

EQUIPMENT

As you get more keen you may buy additional items, such as a press, juice extractor and corking tool, but the basic equipment you'll need is both inexpensive and long-lasting.

• **Bottle brush** For cleaning fermentation jars as well as bottles.

• **Bottles** Use only orthodox wine bottles – dark for red wine, clear for white. Champagne bottles are essential for sparkling wines.

• **Corks** Always use undamaged corks. Pierced corks are unsuitable. Sterilise all corks before use.

• **Fermentation and storage jars** One-gallon glass jars are generally used to contain the wine during fermentation and storage. Start with two jars.

• **Fermentation lock or airlock** This essential item of equipment prevents the admission of air and spoilage organisms during ermentation. A bored cork or rubber bung is needed to fit each lock onto a jar.

• **Hydrometer and testing jar** Not absolutely essential, but the best means of controlling the sugar and alcohol content of your wine.

• **Large saucepan** For preference, use one made of stainless steel or unchipped enamel.

• **Long-handled wooden spoon** For macerating flowers or fruit, and for stirring all types of must.

• **Nylon straining bag and sieve** The bag is an additional aid when straining pulp.

• **Polythene funnel** Useful when pouring the must into a fermentation jar.

• **Polythene mashing bin** A white polythene bin with a tight-fitting lid is best. Coloured plastic buckets may contaminate the wine.

• **Polythene tubing** You will need about 1.4m (4½ft) for siphoning the wine from one container to another.

Wine making, step-by-step

Making your own wine can be as simple or as complicated as you wish: a pleasant pastime for a wet afternoon, or a deeply absorbing hobby. You will make adjustments as you gain experience. But as nothing is more encouraging to the beginner than early success, here is a step-by-step guide to making your first half-dozen bottles – about 4 litres (1 gallon) of wine.

Step 1 Preparing the must

As a rough guide, use 1.5–2kg (3–4lb) of vegetables or fruit for each gallon of wine, depending on the strength of the material's flavour. Methods of extracting the juice such as pressing, soaking or using a domestic extractor, depend on the fruits or vegetables used.

Using vegetables Clean and prepare vegetables as for cooking (coarse, end-of-season vegetables may be used), cut them into small pieces to reduce cooking time and simmer in boiling water until tender.

When cool, strain the liquor into a bin, using a nylon sieve to catch the pulp. Stir in the concentrated grape juice if included in the recipe, and add the sugar, acid, tannin, nutrient and yeast.

Pour the must into a fermentation jar, top up with cold, boiled water and fit an airlock.

Using flowers Carefully comb the petals or blossoms from the stalks with a fork or pick them off

Keep it clean If you want to be successful in your wine making, you need to ensure that all bottles, airlocks and siphon tubes are sterilised before use.

by hand. Place the petals in a plastic bin – making sure that all stems and leaves are excluded – pour boiled hot water over them, and macerate to a soft consistency with the back of a wooden or plastic spoon.

Stir in one teaspoon of citric acid and one crushed Campden tablet, cover the bin and leave it to stand in a temperature of about 21°C (70°F).

Macerate the petals again on each of the following three days. Strain and press them to extract the liquor. Stir in the concentrated grape juice, together with the sugar, tannin, nutrient and yeast. Pour into a fermentation jar and top up with cold boiled water, and fit an airlock to prevent possible infection from airborne spores.

Using fruit Wash the fruits and remove any damaged portions. (Windfalls and bruised fruits are quite suitable for wine making.) Then either pass them through a

juice extractor or macerate to a pulp using a wooden rolling pin. You can also buy special macerating attachments for drills.

If you extract the juice, dilute it and make it into wine in the same way as vegetable and flower liquors. If you ferment the fruit on the pulp, first crush it and then drop it into a bin containing water in which a Campden tablet, some pectin-destroying enzyme and a little citric acid have been dissolved. Cover the bin and leave it in a warm room.

After 24 hours add raisins, sultanas or concentrated grape juice, together with activated yeast. Re-cover the bin and return it to its warm position for a further four or five days. Keep the floating pulp moist by pushing it beneath the surface of the liquid twice a day.

Strain and press the pulp, add the sugar to the liquid and stir until it is dissolved. Pour the must into a fermentation jar, top up with cold boiled water, and fit an airlock.

Mead Though mead takes 1.5kg (3lb) of honey to make six bottles of dry table mead, so can be rather expensive, it is easy to make and can be ready for drinking in just three months.

Simply dissolve the honey in warm water and pour it into a fermentation jar. When cool, add the acid, tannin, nutrient and yeast and top up with cold boiled water.

Step 2 Fermentation

Whatever the basic ingredients, the yeast will now be working in the must and an airlock must be fitted to the fermentation jar. Make sure that the pierced cork is of the right size, insert the tube of the airlock in the cork, put a few drops of

Using a press A small press will enable you to get more juice out of your fruit than mashing by hand allows. The macerated fruit is packed into a nylon-mesh bag which is placed inside the press.

water in the airlock and seal the jar with the cork.

The end of the tube should only just protrude through the cork and must be above the liquid. As an extra precaution against unwanted microbes, you can place a little tuft of cotton wool in the top of the airlock.

Tie a label on the jar stating its contents, the quantities used and the date when it was made.

Stand the jar in a warm place. An average living room, with a temperature of 21°C (70°F), is ideal. Avoid excessive heat as this may kill the yeast and, in consequence, halt fermentation.

Too low a temperature may prevent or slow down fermentation but will not harm the yeast.

Waste not After pressing, the fibrous remains of the fruit (in this case grapes) can be added to the compost bin.

THINGS THAT MAY GO WRONG

Stuck fermentation The commonest problem in wine making is that fermentation stops too soon. There are a number of causes:

1 The yeast has converted as much sugar as it can and has reached the limit of its alcohol tolerance. The remaining sugar sweetens the wine. If it is too sweet, try blending it with a dry wine.

2 The yeast is lacking acid or nutrient. Add some and stir the wine.

3 The must is too hot or too cold and the yeast is inhibited. Move the jar to a different position; overheating, however, may have killed the yeast.

4 The must needs to 'breathe'. Splash it into another jar to release the carbon dioxide, but don't expect any immediate results. It may be a day or two before the bubbles start rising again.

5 The yeast colony has died and needs replacing. Start fresh yeast in a large jar and add the stuck must in stages, making sure that the previous batch is fermenting before adding more.

Using the hydrometer before fermentation has started, and after it has stopped, will indicate the amount of sugar converted and therefore the amount of alcohol produced. This information will help you to identify why the fermentation has stuck.

Excessive dryness If, when fully fermented, the wine has too dry a taste, sweeten it with saccharin. Don't use sugar as fermentation may start up again.

Clearing If a wine fails to clear naturally, use wine finings – consisting of isinglass, gelatin or bentonite – following the manufacturer's instructions given on the packet. Filtering is very rarely necessary and is recommended only as a last resort.

Vinegary taste A wine or must imperfectly corked or left open to the air is likely to develop a vinegary smell. There is no cure for this, and any wine so infected should be thrown away.

to decompose and this imparts an unpleasant flavour to the wine.

It is also important to leave as much of the sediment behind in the original jar as you can. The best way to rack a wine is to siphon the clearing wine into another jar.

First sterilise a storage jar and place it on the floor. Set the jar of wine on a table above the storage jar and remove the airlock. Place one end of a polythene or rubber siphoning tube into the wine just above the level of the sediment and gently suck the other end of the tube until it is filled with wine.

Squeeze this end to prevent the wine escaping until you have placed it in the storage jar, then release the pressure. Gravity will pull the wine from the jar above to the one beneath.

Carefully tilt the upper jar so that the end of the siphon remains clear of the sediment until the last of the wine has been removed. Discard the sediment, wash and sterilise the jar and airlock, dry them and put them away. Top up the jar of wine with cool, boiled water or some weak, cold tea. Add one Campden tablet, fit a bung, or a clean airlock, tie on a descriptive label and store the jar in a cool place.

Maturing

After six or eight weeks a further sediment will be seen and by this time the wine may be quite bright. It now needs to be racked again in the same manner as before.

Bottling

You need to store light and medium wines for up to eight months in the jar before bottling. Heavy and strong wines may need two years, or even longer.

The beginner's commonest mistake is impatience to see the wine in the bottle. If wine is bottled too soon, fermentation may start again, especially in hot weather. The wine will then become hazy and fizzy. The bottle might blow its cork, or even explode.

Corking Sterilise the bottles thoroughly and use new corks. Soak the corks in hot water to make them supple and to get rid of the 'corky' flavour they might impart to the wine. Give them a final rinse in a solution made up with a Campden tablet. You can also use sterilised flip-top bottles.

Siphon the wine from the jar into the bottles and drive the corks well home. Softened cylindrical corks can be thrust home by hand, or, more efficiently, with a corker.

If T-shaped stoppers are used, fasten them on with string or wire before laying the bottles down. Do not overfill the bottles or the air will be so compressed when the corks are fitted that it will push them out a little, leaving them unsightly and the wine at risk.

Store the bottles on their sides so that the corks, or rubber bungs in the case of flip-top bottles, remain wet and keep the seal. Leave the bottles in store for at least a month, and preferably much longer. Traditionally last year's vintage is drunk after the current year's harvest.

White wines should be put in the refrigerator for at least an hour before drinking. Red wines, however, should be drunk at room temperature. They also benefit by removing the cork half an hour or so before drinking, to allow them to 'breathe'. Even better, pour them into a decanter or carafe.

Fermentation will start again if the jar is moved to a warmer place.

Do not expect any sudden and spectacular change, as signs of fermentation may not appear for a day or two. By then, and probably sooner, you should see bubbles of carbon dioxide rising in the must and forcing their way through the water in the airlock.

For a week or so, fermentation will be extremely vigorous, before settling down to a steady rhythm. Keep an eye on it as vigorous fermentation can blast through the airlock, forcing the water out. If this happens, simply wash out the airlock, add a little water to it and replace in the jar. Once fermentation settles down, the

particles of pulp and dead yeast cells will begin to form a sediment in the bottom of the jar.

Prolonged fermentation When making strong dessert wines that are about 16 per cent alcohol, it is advisable to begin with only about half the sugar needed, and to add the rest gradually as fermentation proceeds. In this way the alcoholic tolerance of the yeast can be built up to a really strong wine.

If you add all the sugar at the outset, it may be too much for the yeast and fermentation may stop prematurely. This results in a sweet, low-alcohol wine.

Dissolve the sugar in a little wine before adding it to the

fermentation jar. Dry sugar will simply lie on the bottom of the jar and impede the action of the yeast.

Racking

When bubbles cease to rise in the jar, and there is no movement of gas through the water in the airlock, it is time to rack the wine from its sediment even though it is not perfectly clear. The time it takes for the wine to clear varies considerably, depending on the sugar content and temperature, but even with a light, dry wine it may take a month.

It is important to remove the wine from the sediment as soon as fermentation has finished because the pulp and dead yeast soon start

Recipes for country wine

Inquiring how to make a certain kind of wine is like asking the best way to cook an egg. Elderberry wine, for example, may be made in 20 different ways and each of them equally successful. For this reason the following recipes are simply suggestions. All are based on the basic methods described in the preceding pages.

The amount of sugar used when making wine is critical. Though it is unnecessary to adhere slavishly to the recipe, bear in mind that low sugar gives quick results, a dry wine and low alcohol content; high sugar means slow results, and a sweet, strong wine.

Apple wine
3.5kg (7½lb) mixed apples (windfalls will do)
250g (½lb) sultanas
875g (1¾lb) sugar
3 litres (5½ pints) water
1 teaspoon citric acid
1 Campden tablet
1 teaspoon pectin-destroying enzyme
Hock yeast and nutrient

Pour the water into a bin and add the citric acid, the pectin-destroying enzyme and a crushed Campden tablet.
 Wash the apples, crush them into a mash or cut them up and drop them into the bin. Cover the bin and leave it in a warm place for 24 hours. Activate the yeast in a starter bottle (see page 305). Add the sultanas, nutrient and yeast to the mash, re-cover the bin and place it in the warm for 4 or 5 days.

Press and strain the pulp and add the sugar, dissolving this first in warm water. Pour the strained must into a clean fermentation jar, top up with cold water and fit an airlock to the jar.
 Label and store the jar at room temperature until fermentation is complete.

Beetroot wine
2.25kg (4½lb) scrubbed, diced beetroot
250g (½lb) concentrated red grape juice
1kg (2lb) sugar
15g (½oz) citric acid
½ teaspoon grape tannin
4 litres (7 pints) water
Bordeaux yeast and nutrient

Simmer the diced beetroot until tender. When cool, strain the liquor into a bin.
 Activate the yeast and add it to the liquor, together with the concentrated grape juice, the acid, tannin, nutrient and sugar dissolved in warm water. Pour the must into a fermentation jar and proceed as for apple wine.

Bilberry wine
1kg (2lb) bilberries
250g (½lb) concentrated red grape juice
1kg (2lb) sugar
1 teaspoon tartaric acid
1 Campden tablet
1 teaspoon pectin-destroying enzyme
½ teaspoon grape tannin
3 litres (5½ pints) water
Burgundy yeast and nutrient

Pour the water into a bin and add the tartaric acid, the pectin-destroying enzyme and a crushed Campden tablet.

Crush the bilberries (if you are not using a juicer) and drop them into the bin. Cover the bin and leave it in a warm place for 24 hours.
 Proceed as for beetroot wine.

Blackberry 'port'
1.75kg (3½lb) wild blackberries
250g (½lb) blackcurrants
525g (1lb 2oz) raisins
1.3kg (2¾lb) sugar
1 Campden tablet
1 teaspoon pectin-destroying enzyme
3½ litres (6 pints) water
Port yeast and nutrient

Pour the water into a bin and add the pectin-destroying enzyme and a crushed Campden tablet.

Wash and crush the blackberries and blackcurrants and proceed as for apple wine. But, since this is a high-alcohol wine, add the sugar in small doses each time fermentation slows down.
 Best results are obtained by using a hydrometer, but there is also a good rule-of-thumb method. Put in half the total amount of sugar at first, half the remainder about ten days later and the rest about eight days after that.
 When adding the extra sugar, extract a little of the wine and dissolve the sugar in it. Pour the solution back gently.

Blackcurrant wine
1kg (2lb) blackcurrants
250g (½lb) raisins
1kg (2lb) sugar
1 Campden tablet
1 teaspoon pectin-destroying enzyme
4 litres (7 pints) water
Burgundy yeast and nutrient
Saccharin
Proceed as for apple wine, but as this is a sweet wine add saccharin to taste when fermentation is finished and the wine has been siphoned into a storage jar.

Laid down to rest Just as with commercial wine making, bottles should be stored on their sides so that the contents keep the corks damp, retaining a good seal.

Carrot wine

2.25kg (4½lb) diced carrot
250g (½lb) concentrated white grape juice
1kg (2lb) sugar
20g (¾oz) citric acid
4 litres (7 pints) water
Sauternes yeast and nutrient
Saccharin

Simmer the diced carrot until tender. When cool, strain the liquor into a bin.

Proceed as for beetroot wine, but since this is a sweet wine add saccharin to taste as soon as fermentation is finished.

Celery wine

2.25kg (4½lb) chopped celery
250g (½lb) concentrated white grape juice
1kg (2lb) sugar
15g (½oz) citric acid
5 teaspoons grape tannin
4 litres (7 pints) water
Chablis yeast and nutrient
Simmer the chopped celery until tender. When cool, strain the liquor into the bin and proceed as for beetroot wine.

Cherry wine

2.25kg (4½lb) assorted cherries
250g (½lb) sultanas
875g (1¾lb) sugar
1 teaspoon citric acid
½ teaspoon grape tannin
1 teaspoon pectin-destroying enzyme
1 Campden tablet
3½ litres (6 pints) water
Bordeaux yeast and nutrient
Saccharin

Pour the water into a bin and add the citric acid, pectin-destroying enzyme and a crushed Campden tablet. Wash the cherries, remove

Try something different Don't restrict yourself to only fruity flavours: carrots make a delicious sweet wine. Beetroot is another excellent vegetable to use.

the stalks, put them into the bin and proceed as for apple wine. Add saccharin to taste as soon as fermentation is finished.

Crab-apple wine

2.25kg (4½lb) crab apples
250g (½lb) sultanas
1.3kg (2¾lb) sugar
1 teaspoon citric acid
1 teaspoon pectin-destroying enzyme
1 Campden tablet
3½ litres (6 pints) water
Sauternes yeast and nutrient

Follow the recipe given for apple wine.

Damson wine

2.25kg (4½lb) damsons
250g (½lb) raisins
1kg (2lb) sugar
1 teaspoon tartaric acid
1 teaspoon grape tannin
1 Campden tablet
1 teaspoon pectin-destroying enzyme
3½ litres (6 pints) water
Bordeaux yeast and nutrient

Use tartaric acid and add grape tannin using apple wine method.

Elderberry 'port'

1kg (2lb) elderberries
250g (½lb) blackcurrants
525g (1lb 2oz) blackberries
525g (1lb 2oz) raisins
1.3kg (2¾lb) sugar
1 teaspoon pectin-destroying enzyme
1 teaspoon tartaric acid
1 Campden tablet
3½ litres (6 pints) water
Port yeast and nutrient

Pour the water into a bin and add the tartaric acid, the pectin-

destroying enzyme and a crushed Campden tablet.

Wash the elderberries, blackcurrants and blackberries, mash them into a pulp and proceed as for apple wine. But since this is a high-alcohol wine, add the sugar in small doses as in blackberry 'port'.

Elderflower wine

1 litre (2 pints) elderflower florets
525g (1lb 2oz) concentrated white grape juice
800g (1¾lb) sugar
2 teaspoons citric acid
1 Campden tablet
4 litres (7 pints) water
Sauternes yeast and nutrient

Carefully remove the stalks, leaves and stems of the elderflowers and discard them. Place the florets in a bin, pour hot water over them and macerate with the back of a wooden spoon. Add 2 teaspoons of citric acid and a crushed Campden tablet, cover the bin and leave it in a warm place. Macerate the florets again on each of the following three days, then press them and strain off the liquor.

Finally pour the liquor into a fermentation jar and proceed as for apple wine.

Gooseberry wine

1.75g (3½lb) gooseberries
250g (½lb) sultanas
1kg (2lb) sugar
1 Campden tablet
1 teaspoon pectin-destroying enzyme
3½ litres (6 pints) water
Hock yeast and nutrient

Pour the water into a bin and add the tartaric acid, the pectin-destroying enzyme and a crushed Campden tablet.

Wash the gooseberries, crush them into a mash and proceed as for apple wine.

Grape wine (red)

8kg (18lb) black grapes
1 teaspoon pectin-destroying enzyme
1 Campden tablet
Pommard yeast
(No water required. With English grapes you may need to add some sugar to bring the specific gravity up to 1.090.)

Rich and fruity Elderberries gathered from hedgerows produce a dark, full-bodied wine with a high alcohol content.

Wash the grapes, drop them into a bin with the pectin-destroying enzyme and a crushed Campden tablet, and mash them into a pulp. Cover, and leave it in a warm place for 24 hours.

Activate the yeast, add it to the pulp, re-cover the bin and return it to a warm place for eight or ten days.

Press and strain the pulp and add the sugar if necessary.

To extract the gallon of grape juice required in this recipe, a wine press is essential. Pour the must into a fermentation jar and proceed as for apple wine.

Grape wine (white)

8kg (18lb) white grapes
1 teaspoon pectin-destroying enzyme
1 Campden tablet
Hock yeast
(No water or sugar required)

Put the grapes through a juice extractor or press them to extract the juice. Pour the juice into a jar, add the pectin-destroying enzyme and a crushed Campden tablet, fit an airlock and leave it in a warm place for 24 hours.

Activate the yeast, add it to the juice, re-fit the airlock and place the jar in an even temperature until fermentation is complete. Rack, and add one Campden tablet.

Honey wine (mead)

1.5kg (3lb) honey
20g (¾oz) citric acid
1 level teaspoon grape tannin
4 litres (7 pints) water
Maury yeast and nutrient

Dissolve the honey in warm water, pour it into a fermentation jar and, when cool, add the acid, tannin, nutrient and yeast.

Top up with cold boiled water, fit an airlock to the jar and store it in a warm place until fermentation is complete.

Mulberry wine

1kg (2lb) mulberries
525g (1lb 2oz) sultanas
1.3kg (2¾lb) sugar
1 teaspoon tartaric acid
1 teaspoon grape tannin
1 teaspoon pectin-destroying enzyme
1 Campden tablet
3½ litres (6 pints) water
Port yeast and nutrient

Pour the water into a bin and add the tartaric acid, pectin-destroying enzyme, tannin and a crushed Campden tablet.

Wash the mulberries, mash into a pulp and proceed as for apple wine. Since this is a high-alcohol wine, add the sugar in small doses as described for blackberry 'port'.

Plum wine

2.25kg (4½lb) Victoria plums
525g (1lb 2oz) raisins
1.3kg (2¾lb) sugar
1 teaspoon citric acid
1 Campden tablet
1 teaspoon pectin-destroying enzyme
½ teaspoon grape tannin
3½ litres (6 pints) water
Sherry yeast and nutrient

Pour the water into a bin, add the tannin, the citric acid, the pectin-destroying enzyme and a crushed Campden tablet, and proceed as for apple wine.

Because this is a high-alcohol wine, add the sugar in small doses, following the method as described for blackberry 'port'.

Raspberry wine

1kg (2lb) raspberries
525g (1lb 2oz) sultanas
1kg (2lb) sugar
1 teaspoon pectin-destroying enzyme
1 Campden tablet
3½ litres (6 pints) water
Port yeast and nutrient
Saccharin

Pour the water into a bin and add the pectin-destroying enzyme and a crushed Campden tablet.

Wash the raspberries, crush them into a mash and proceed as for apple wine.

This is a sweet wine, so when fermentation is complete add saccharin to taste.

Rhubarb wine

2.25kg (4½lb) chopped rhubarb
Thinly pared rind of 1 lemon
250g (½lb) sultanas
1.3kg (2¾lb) sugar
1 Campden tablet
1 teaspoon pectin-destroying enzyme
3½ litres (6 pints) water
Graves yeast and nutrient

This wine should be made in May or early June. Pour the water into a bin and add the pectin-destroying enzyme and a crushed Campden tablet.

Discard the leaves and feet of the rhubarb, wipe and chop the stems, drop them into the bin with the lemon rind, and proceed as for apple wine.

Index

Page numbers displayed in bold type
indicate main entries.
Numbers in italic refer to illustrations
and their captions.

Picture credits

Photographs are from the sources credited in the following list. Where there is more than one photograph on a page, each is distinguished by its position, using the following key:
L = left, R = right, T = top, C = centre, B = bottom, BL = bottom left, CR = centre right and so on.

Spine Mark Winwood
Front cover T Punchstock/Digital Vision, **BL (frieze #1)** Mark Winwood, **CL (frieze #2)** Photolibrary.com/Sheila Jolley, **CR (frieze #3)** Getty Images Ltd/Johner Images, **BR (frieze #4)** Getty Images Ltd/Anthony-Masterson
Back cover Photolibrary.com/Sheila Jolley

2–3 ShutterStock, Inc/Andrew Cribb
5–7 Mark Winwood
10 © Reader's Digest/Sarah Cuttle
11 Mark Winwood
12 © Reader's Digest/Sarah Cuttle
13 TL, TC © Reader's Digest/Mark Winwood
13 BR © Reader's Digest/Sarah Cuttle
14 © Reader's Digest/Sarah Cuttle
15–16 © Reader's Digest
17 Cranfield University Soil Survey and Land Research Centre
18 © Reader's Digest/Mark Winwood
22 T © Reader's Digest/Sarah Cuttle
22 R © Reader's Digest/Mark Winwood
23–26 © Reader's Digest/Mark Winwood
27 C, R © Reader's Digest/Sarah Cuttle
27 BL © Reader's Digest/Mark Winwood
28 © Reader's Digest/Sarah Cuttle
29–34 Mark Winwood
36 © Reader's Digest
37 © Reader's Digest/Sarah Cuttle
38 TL, C, BL © Reader's Digest
38 TR © Reader's Digest/Sarah Cuttle
39–40 © Reader's Digest/Mark Winwood

41 TL © Reader's Digest/Sarah Cuttle
41 TC, BC © Reader's Digest/Mark Winwood
41 R Helen Spence
41 BL Mark Winwood
42 Mark Winwood
46 © Reader's Digest/Mark Winwood
48 © Reader's Digest
49 TL, CL, BL © Reader's Digest
49 BR © Reader's Digest/Sarah Cuttle
51 Wolfgang Redeleit
53 © Reader's Digest
55 L The Garden Collection/Jonathan Buckley/Design Bunny Guinness
55 TL, TR © Reader's Digest/Sarah Cuttle
55 TC © Reader's Digest/Mark Winwood
56 L © Reader's Digest/Mark Winwood
56 R © Reader's Digest/Sarah Cuttle
57 L © Reader's Digest/Sarah Cuttle
57 R Mark Winwood
59 © Reader's Digest/Sarah Cuttle
60–61 ShutterStock, Inc/Peter Brett Charlton
62 iStockphoto.com/Brett Charlton
64–65 Mark Winwood
68 © Reader's Digest/Sarah Cuttle
70–71 © Reader's Digest/Mark Winwood
75 ShutterStock, Inc/Matka Wariatka
77 © Reader's Digest
79 Mark Winwood
80–84 © Reader's Digest/Mark Winwood
85 ShutterStock, Inc/Juriah Mosin
88–90 © Reader's Digest/Mark Winwood
96 © Reader's Digest/Maddie Thornhill
97 T © Reader's Digest/Sarah Cuttle
97 B © Reader's Digest/Maddie Thornhill
99 ShutterStock, Inc/Liz Van Steenburgh
100 Mark Winwood
102 L ShutterStock, Inc/Robert Taylor
102 R © Reader's Digest/Sarah Cuttle
104 Photolibrary.com/J Wade
108 © Reader's Digest/Mark Winwood
109 ShutterStock, Inc/Nathalie Dulex

110 ShutterStock, Inc/Heather M Hood
112 Mark Winwood
116 © Reader's Digest/Sarah Cuttle
119 T iStockphoto.com/Stephen Blose
119 B ShutterStock, Inc/Ekaterina Shlikhunora
120 ShutterStock, Inc/Vasilev Ivan Mihaylovich
123 Mark Winwood
124 © Reader's Digest/Mark Winwood
128 TL, BL © Reader's Digest/Mark Winwood
128 BR © Reader's Digest/David Murray
130–2 Mark Winwood
134 ShutterStock, Inc/AnneKitzman
137 © Reader's Digest/Julie Bennett
138 ShutterStock, Inc/jean-Louis Vosgien
140 TL © Reader's Digest/Sarah Cuttle
140 TC, CR, R © Reader's Digest/Mark Winwood
140 BL © Reader's Digest/Sarah Cuttle
141 © Reader's Digest/Mark Winwood
144 ShutterStock, Inc/Olga Vasi Kova
151 © Reader's Digest/Sarah Cuttle
152 Mark Winwood
154 ShutterStock, Inc/C. Rene Ammundsen
156 ShutterStock, Inc/Robyn Makenzie
160 © Reader's Digest/Mark Winwood
162 www.gournmetmushrooms.co.uk
163 ShutterStock, Inc/Mark William Penny
164 ShutterStock, Inc/Stefen Redel
165 T ShutterStock, Inc/Paul Maguire
165 B ShutterStock, Inc/Peter Baxter
167 L ShutterStock, Inc/Gordon
167 TR ShutterStock, Inc/Sergei Didyk
168 © Reader's Digest/Mark Winwood
171 Mark Winwood
175 ShutterStock, Inc/Sharon D
177 ShutterStock, Inc/Gordana Sermek
182 © Reader's Digest/Mark Winwood
183–5 Mark Winwood
189–90 © Reader's Digest/Mark Winwood

192 Mark Winwood
195 © Reader's Digest/Sarah Cuttle
196 Mark Winwood
201 L © Reader's Digest/Sarah Cuttle
201 R ShutterStock, Inc/Elana Elisseeva
202 © Reader's Digest
207 ShutterStock, Inc/Neil Roy Johnson
211–12 © Reader's Digest/Mark Winwood
218 ShutterStock, Inc/Carolyn Brule
221 L, C © Reader's Digest/Mark Winwood
221 R Mark Winwood
222 © Reader's Digest
223 © Reader's Digest/Martin Brigdale
226–7 Mark Winwood
228 © Reader's Digest/Mark Winwood
229 ShutterStock, Inc/Truyen Vu
230 © Reader's Digest/Mark Winwood
231 ShutterStock, Inc/Ewa Brozet
232 © Reader's Digest/Mark Winwood
233 ShutterStock, Inc/Lagui
234 © Reader's Digest/Mark Winwood
235 ShutterStock, Inc/Vasilev Ivan Mihaylovich
236–7 naturepl.com/Georgette Douwma
250 © Reader's Digest/Martin Brigdale
256 iStockphoto.com/Dori O'Connell
263 ShutterStock, Inc/Spauln
267 L iStockphoto.com
267 R © Reader's Digest
269 © Reader's Digest/Laurie Evans
270 L © Reader's Digest/Udo Loster
270 R © Reader's Digest/Ulrich Kopp
271 © Reader's Digest/Pia Tryde
272 Mark Winwood
273–4 © Reader's Digest
275 Mark Winwood
276 © Reader's Digest
277 © Reader's Digest/Pia Tryde
278 © Reader's Digest
279 © Reader's Digest/Martin Brigdale
280 © Reader's Digest/Laurie Evans

281–6 © Reader's Digest
287 L © Reader's Digest
287 R ShutterStock, Inc/Andrey Armyagov
288 © Reader's Digest/Udo Loster
290 © Reader's Digest/Peter Williams
292 © Reader's Digest
295 © Reader's Digest/Martin Brigdale
297 © Reader's Digest/Ulrich Kopp
298 © Reader's Digest
299 © Reader's Digest/Ulrich Kopp
300 ShutterStock, Inc/Elena Schweitzer
301 ShutterStock, Inc/Elena Elisseeva
302 T © Reader's Digest/Sarah Cuttle
303 © Reader's Digest/Pia Tryde
304 Mark Winwood
305 ShutterStock, Inc/Adam Gryko
306 ShutterStock, Inc/Miroslav Tolimir
307 Celia Coyne
309 ShutterStock, Inc/Melaie de Fazio
310 ShutterStock, Inc/Dizeloid
311 iStockphoto.com/Maria Brzostowska

Food From Your Garden & Allotment
was published by The Reader's Digest Association Limited, London.

First edition copyright © 2008
The Reader's Digest Association Limited
11 Westferry Circus, Canary Wharf
London E14 4HE

We are committed both to the quality of our products and the service we provide to our customers. We value your comments, so please do contact us on **08705 113366** or via our website at **www.readersdigest.co.uk**

If you have any comments or suggestions about the content of our books, email us at **gbeditorial@readersdigest.co.uk**

Book Code 400-363 UP0000-1
ISBN 978 0 276 44263 6
Oracle Code 250011666S.00.24

Food From Your Garden & Allotment
is based on material previously published in Reader's Digest *Food From Your Garden* (1977 and 1994).

Editorial consultant
Daphne Ledward

Assistant editors
Celia Coyne and Helen Spence

New illustrations
Richard Bonson

Designer
Martin Bennett

Proofreader
Barry Gage

Indexer
Marie Lorimer

For Reader's Digest

Project editor
Alison Candlin

Art editor
Julie Bennett

Editorial director
Julian Browne

Art director
Anne-Marie Bulat

Head of book development
Sarah Bloxham

Managing editor
Nina Hathway

Picture resource manager
Sarah Stewart-Richardson

Pre-press account manager
Dean Russell

Product production manager
Claudette Bramble

Senior production controller
Sandra Fuller

Origination
Colour Systems Limited, London

Printing and binding
Printed in China